Technical, Social, and Legal Issues in Virtual Communities:

Emerging Environments

Subhasish Dasgupta
George Washington University, USA

Managing Director:	Lindsay Johnston
Senior Editorial Director:	Heather A. Probst
Book Production Manager:	Sean Woznicki
Development Manager:	Joel Gamon
Acquisitions Editor:	Erika Gallagher
Typesetter:	Jennifer Romanchak
Cover Design:	Nick Newcomer, Lisandro Gonzalez

Published in the United States of America by
Information Science Reference (an imprint of IGI Global)
701 E. Chocolate Avenue
Hershey PA 17033
Tel: 717-533-8845
Fax: 717-533-8661
E-mail: cust@igi-global.com
Web site: http://www.igi-global.com

Library of Congress Cataloging-in-Publication Data

Technical, social, and legal issues in virtual communities: emerging environments / Subhasish Dasgupta, editor.
    p. cm.
  Includes bibliographical references and index.
  Summary: "This book examines a variety of issues related to virtual communities and social networking, addressing issues related to team identification, leader-member issues, social networking for education, participation in social networks, and more"--Provided by publisher.
    ISBN 978-1-4666-1553-3 (hbk.) -- ISBN 978-1-4666-1554-0 (ebook) -- ISBN 978-1-4666-1555-7 (print & perpetual access) 1. Electronic villages (Computer networks) 2. Online social networks. 3. Virtual reality. I. Dasgupta, Subhasish, 1966-
  TK5105.83.T43 2012
  302.30285--dc23
                    2012002098

British Cataloguing in Publication Data
A Cataloguing in Publication record for this book is available from the British Library.

The views expressed in this book are those of the authors, but not necessarily of the publisher.

Table of Contents

Section 2
Business Applications of Social Networks

Section 3
Cross Cultural and International Studies

Detailed Table of Contents

Section 1
Social Aspects of Virtual Communities and Social Networks

Managers are increasingly interested in the social web, as it provides numerous opportunities for strengthening and expanding relationships with customers, but the network processes that lead to these user-based assets are poorly understood. In this paper, the authors explore factors influencing use and participation in virtual social networks. They also discuss unusual drivers and inhibitors present with virtual social networks—highlighted by the presence of positive network externalities and fears that the content will be misused. The authors offer hypotheses stemming from a model of how these factors work together, test the model with a dataset collected from two different virtual social networks, and discuss the implications of this work. The findings offer managers insights on how to nurture Web 2.0 processes.

Chapter 2

Online Social Networking (OSN) systems such as Ning, MySpace, Facebook and Friendster have achieved tremendous popularity. However, little research has been conducted to determine factors motivating users with varying capabilities to use and adopt OSN systems addressing target tasks, with varying system capabilities and characteristics. The relationships between user characteristics and use/performance have not been adequately addressed. This study used a cross-sectional survey of 262 graduate and undergraduate students to examine how end user Computer Self-Efficacy (CSE) affects performance and use of OSN systems and how "fit" determines whether there are user, task and/or systems characteristics associated with the best performance and usage levels. Significant direct and indirect relationships were found between CSE, task and system characteristics as measured by performance and use, and these relationships were further significantly strengthened when there was good "fit" between the variables. Results indicate that users having high self-efficacy "fit" with task or systems characteristics produce higher performance and use.

Chapter 3
Daniel M. Eveleth, University of Idaho, USA
Alex B. Eveleth, Western Washington University, USA

While previous research has identified group identification as an important factor in affecting relevant outcomes (e.g., satisfaction, turnover, commitment) in face-to face environments, this paper provides initial evidence to support the proposition that group identification also matters in virtual environments. In particular, the authors found that team members' perceptions of the leader-member exchange relationship and the team's past performance are related to individuals' identification with the virtual team and that identification affects satisfaction and behavioral intentions. Individuals who perceive leader-member exchange as high (e.g., the leader displays a willingness to help the team member solve problems and the leader recognizes the member's potential) and who report that their teams perform well had stronger identification with the team. Individuals who reported strong identification with their team were more satisfied with the team and had greater intentions to perform positive behaviors in the future.

Chapter 4
Mark H. Palmer, University of Missouri-Columbia, USA
Jack Hanney, University of Missouri-Columbia, USA

This article describes advantages and disadvantages of federal government centralized geographic information networks and decentralized peer-to-peer geographic information networks as they pertain to North American Indian tribal governments and communities. Geographic information systems (GIS) are used by indigenous groups for natural resource management, land claims, water rights, and cultural revitalization activities on a global-scale. North American groups use GIS for the same reasons, but questions regarding culturally appropriate GIS, cross-cultural understandings of geographic knowledge, and cultural assimilation through Western digital technologies have been raised by scholars. Two network models are germane to American Indian government operations and community organizations. The first is a prescriptive top-down network emanating from federal government agencies. Federal agencies are responsible for the diffusion of nationwide GIS programs throughout indigenous communities in the United States. A second, potentially more inclusive model is a decentralized peer-to-peer network in which all nodes are responsible for the success of the network.

Chapter 5
John Warmbrodt, Consultant, USA
Hong Sheng, Missouri University of Science and Technology, USA
Richard Hall, Missouri University of Science and Technology, USA
Jinwei Cao, University of Delaware, USA

Video blogs (or vlogs) are a new form of blogs where each post is a video. This study explores a community of video bloggers (or vloggers) by studying the community's structure as well as the motivations and interactions of vloggers in the community. A social network analysis of a list of personal vloggers identifies the community's structure. Open-ended interviews with core vloggers in the sample provide in-depth understanding on the motivations and interactions of the vloggers. Overall, the results indicate that the vloggers' community exhibits a core/periphery structure. Such a community is formed based on shared interest and active interactions. In addition, the rich communication provided in video blogs allows for a more personal and intimate interaction, making vlogs a potentially powerful tool for business applications.

With advances in communication technology and online pedagogy, virtual learning communities have become rich learning environments in which individuals construct knowledge and learn from others. Typically, individuals in virtual learning communities interact by exchanging information and sharing knowledge and experiences with others as communities. The team at the Virtual Learning Community Research Laboratory has employed an array of methods, including social network analysis (SNA), to examine and describe different virtual learning communities. The goal of the study was to employ mixed methods to explore whether the content of students' interaction reflected the fundamental elements of community. SNA techniques were used to analyse ties and relationships among individuals in a network with the goal of understanding patterns of interactions among individuals and their activities, and interviews were conducted to explore features and student perceptions of their learning community.

Chapter 7

Social identity is a key construct to understand online community life. While existing online identity studies present a relatively static conception of identity, grounded in user profiles and other personal information, in this paper the authors investigate more dynamic aspects of identity, grounded in patterns of social interaction in Facebook community life, drawing on social science research on identity theory and social identity theory. The authors examine the tensions experienced by people between assimilation and differentiation with respect to group identities and role identities. The study provides a framework for understanding how users construct self-presentations in different online social interactions, actively managing identity, rather than merely declaring it in a relatively static profile. The authors speculate on how social computing environments could more effectively support identity presentation.

Section 2
Business Applications of Social Networks

Chapter 8

Virtual communities are groups of people with similar interests who meet online and together act as a learning environment, place for social support, or as bodies for influencing public opinion. In this paper, the authors identify characteristics of a virtual community that influence its members to customize e-services provided to or received by the virtual community. The authors propose a theoretical framework of factors influencing service customization in a virtual community that has been validated with two case studies conducted in health-focused virtual communities. The findings confirm that the quality of the learning environment, social support, and the virtual community's ability to influence public opinion, positively contribute to the perceived usefulness and active participation in the community by its members. In turn, these factors were found to have a positive influence on customization of e-services by the members, based on the community's suggestion. The research also suggests several areas of focus to enhance e-service customization through virtual communities.

Norazah Mohd Suki, Universiti Malaysia Sabah, Malaysia

T. Ramayah, Universiti Sains Malaysia (USM), Malaysia

Michelle Kow Pei Ming, Universiti Sains Malaysia (USM), Malaysia

This paper examines job searching among employed job seekers through the social networking sites. One hundred ninety survey questionnaires were distributed to employed job seekers who have used online social networking sites via the snowball sampling approach. The collected data were analysed using Structural Equation Modeling (SEM) technique via the Analysis of Moment Structure (AMOS 16) computer program. The results showed that perceived usefulness and perceived enjoyment are positively and significantly related to the behavioural intention to use online social networking sites as a job search tool, whereas perceived ease of use is not positively and significantly related. The study implies that the developers of online social networking sites must provide additional useful functionalities or tools to help users with their job searches. These sites must also assure that they do not disclose individuals' private and confidential information without the consent. The paper provides insight for employed jobseekers by using online social networking sites as a job search tool.

Katherine Karl, University of Tennessee, Chattanooga, USA

Joy Peluchette, University of Southern Indiana, USA

Christopher Schlaegel, Otto-von-Guericke-University, Magdeburg, Germany

This study examines gender and cultural differences in reactions and responses to a Facebook 'friend' request from the boss. The auhtors found respondents were more likely to have positive (e.g., pleased, honored) reactions followed by questionable reactions (e.g., worried, suspicious) and least likely to have negative reactions (e.g., disgusted, offended). Although most respondents would accept the request, many would have reservations about doing so. Contrary to expectations, no gender differences were found. Significant cultural differences were found such that U.S. respondents were more likely than German respondents to have negative and questionable reactions and German respondents were more likely than U.S. respondents to have positive reactions. Implications and suggestions for future research are then discussed.

Omer Rana, Cardiff University, UK

Simon Caton, Karlsruhe Institute of Technology, Germany

With the increasingly ubiquitous nature of social networks and Cloud computing, users are starting to explore new ways to interact with and exploit these developing paradigms. Social networks reflect real world relationships that allow users to share information and form connections, essentially creating dynamic virtual communities. By leveraging the pre-established trust formed through friend relationships within a social network "Social Clouds" can be realized, which enable friends to share resources within the context of a social network. The creation of Social Clouds gives rise to new business models through collaboration within social networks. In this paper, the authors describe such business models and discuss their impact.

Chapter 12

Katerina Voutsina, London School of Economics and Political Science, UK

The impact of virtual networks on economic activity and organizational affairs has long occupied the Information Systems (IS) academic community. Yet what has been paid less attention is the impact of networks on the way contemporary workers perceive themselves at work. Taking into account this gap in the literature, the paper aspires to bring forward issues referring to the implication of virtual networks in the construction of occupational identity of highly-skilled Information Technology (IT) contractors. Drawing upon data from interviews with thirty highly-skilled IT contractors, the paper suggests that the virtual networks among IT contractors and individuals who share the same occupational interests become for the contractors the locus of social interaction, the hub of knowledge generation, the source of occupational control and thus the primary object of professional identification.

Section 3
Cross Cultural and International Studies

Chapter 13

Demosthenes Akoumianakis, Technological Education Institution of Crete, Greece

Recent scholarship has demonstrated that virtual communities can be traced in the online 'tells' retained by popular virtual settlements like Facebook and Twitter. In this article, the authors push this line of research toward an analysis of pre-requisites and constrains of virtual settlements that determine the understanding of community life across settlements. The approach followed is grounded on a 'practice lens' that views virtual communities as enacted cyber-structures revealed through cultural artifacts facilitated by affordances inscribed into virtual settlements. The presence or absence of key affordances determines not only what is retained as online 'tells' in a virtual settlement but also the type and range of cultural artifacts, as well as how these artifacts are used across virtual settlements.

Chapter 14

Sunitha Kuppuswamy, Anna University Chennai, Chennai, India
P. B. Shankar Narayan, Pondicherry University, Puducherry, India

Social networking websites like Orkut, Facebook, Myspace and Youtube are becoming more and more popular and has become part of daily life for an increasing number of people. Because of their features, young people are attracted to social networking sites. In this paper, the authors explore the impact of social networking sites on the education of youth. The study argues that these social networking websites distract students from their studies, but these websites can be useful for education based on sound pedagogical principles and proper supervision by the teachers. Moreover, the research concludes that social networking websites have both positive as well as negative impact on the education of youth, depending on one's interest to use it in a positive manner for his or her education and vice versa.

Chapter 15

Katherine Karl, University of Tennessee Chattanooga, USA

Joy Peluchette, University of Southern Indiana, USA

Christopher Schlagel, Otto-von-Guericke-University Magdeburg, Germany

This paper examines cultural and gender differences in student reports of the likelihood that they would post various types of information on their Facebook profiles and their attitudes regarding non-students accessing their profiles. Significant gender and country differences were found. In general, U.S. students were more likely than German students to report they would post extreme information. Males in both countries (U.S. and Germany) were more likely than females to self-promote and be extreme in the information they would post and less concerned if employers viewed their profiles. Both U.S. and German students reported several items they would likely post on their profiles, but did not want employers to see. Implications of these results and recommendations for future research are also discussed.

Chapter 16

Lhoussain Simour, Sidi Mohamed Ben Abdellah University, Morocco

Electronic connections allow the individual to be at various global sites while sitting in front of his or her computer. By being electronically connected, one's participation in virtual worlds raises important questions about the nature of our communities and problematizes our identities. This paper examines how experiences in virtual interactions affect people's real lives and what impact computer mediated communication has on the formation of a virtual community and its relation to individuals' identities. Virtual communities stimulate experiences that redefine the basic concepts and contexts that have characterized the essence of human societies. They offer new contexts for rethinking the concept of identity and provide a new space for exploring the extent to which participation in computer mediated interaction modifies the subject in terms of identity, leading to a reconstruction and a reconstitution of self.

Chapter 17

Kiyana Zolfaghar, K.N.Toosi University of Technology, Iran

Abdollah Aghaie, K.N.Toosi University of Technology, Iran

Trust as a major part of human interactions plays an important role in addressing information overload and helping users collect reliable information in SocialWeb applications. This paper examines the current situation and future trends of computational trust for these systems. Achieving this, the authors present an overview of existing social trust mechanisms and identify their strengths and weaknesses through discussion and analysis. In this paper, the authors also provide a comprehensive framework of social trust-inducing factors that contribute to the trust formation process and discuss key research issues and challenges to find future research trends in computing trust in the SocialWeb context.

Chapter 18

Rajalakshmi Kanagavel, Anna University, India

Chandrasekharan Velayutham, Anna University, India

In today's world where Internet has experienced tremendous growth, social networking sites have become highly significant in peoples' lives. This comparative study between India and the Netherlands will concentrate on youngsters more precisely college going students in Chennai and Maastricht. The research explores how college students create identity for themselves in the virtual world and how they relate to others online. It will analyze the cultural differences from the youth perspective in both the countries and discuss whether social networking sites isolate youngsters from the society or help them to build relationships; the participation in these sites is also explored. Survey technique, interview, and online observation were the research methods used. Findings show that Indian students spend more time in these sites than Dutch students and Dutch students participate more actively than Indian students. It was also found that virtual interaction taking place in these sites is just a supplement to real life interaction.

Chapter 19

Dimitrina Dimitrova, York University, Canada
Emmanuel Koku, Drexel University, USA

This paper explores how management practices shape the way dispersed communities of practice (CoPs) function. The analysis is a case study of a dispersed community engaged in conducting and managing collaborative research. The analysis uses data from a social network survey and semi-structured interviews to capture the management practices in the community and demonstrate how they are linked to the patterns of information flows and communication. This analysis is a test case for the broader issue of how distributed communities function. It shows that even highly distributed CoPs may have a dual life: they exist both online and offline, in both face-to-face meetings and email exchanges of their participants. The study examines a dispersed community engaged in conducting and managing collaborative research. The analysis uses data from a social network survey and interviews to examine its managerial practices, information exchanges and communication practices.

Chapter 20

Chris Kimble, Euromed Management, Université Montpellier II, France

This article reports on a study of learning and the coordination of activities in a geographically distributed community (a research consortium) using survey / Social Network Analysis methods combined with interviews. This article comments on and expands some of the important issues that were raised. After outlining the wider context, it highlights two broad themes related to research in the area of Virtual Communities: the nature of the communities themselves and the way in which they are studied. Following this, four areas for future research are outlined: the continuing role of face-to-face communication in Virtual Communities; the significance of the dual nature of such groups; the importance (or otherwise) of the structure of such communities; and the role played by exogenous factors. The article concludes with some comments on where this field relates to the debate among social theorists about the role of agency and structure in human activities.

Preface

INTRODUCTION

Virtual communities have changed the way we work and live. Social networks have provided an environment in which people can meet to create virtual communities of family members, professionals, and business contacts. Changes in the environment in which virtual communities operate have led to an increased need for research in the area. There are many aspects of virtual communities that have to be studied. As technologies change, so does the environment for virtual communities, thereby increasing the need for better understanding of the community and group dynamics. This book, Technical, Social and Legal Issues in Virtual Communities: Emerging Environments is a collection of research papers that investigate a number of issues identified above.

This book consists of 20 chapters and is divided into three sections. Section 1 examines social aspects of virtual communities and social networking. Section 2 is a collection of chapters on business applications of social networks, and Section 3 examines cross-cultural and international studies in the field. The following paragraphs I summarize the essential findings of the chapters in each section.

Section 1: Social Aspects of Virtual Communities and Social Networking

This section includes chapters that report on research on social issues in the area of virtual communities and social networking. In the first chapter, Pagani and Hofacker, identify drivers and inhibitors of use and participation in social networks, and propose a theoretical model regarding use and participation in virtual social networks. According to the model, network size influences perceived usefulness of a social networking site. Perceived usefulness affects simple site use and active participation in the site. Site use and active participation in turn impact fear and risk. The conceptual model was empirically tested using data from a sample of users on Facebook and StudiVZ, a European social networking site. Results show that perception of network size positively influences perceived usefulness of a social network site. Perceived usefulness affects propensity to visit the site and actively participate. Any fears that users may have do not reduce their chances of visiting the site, but reduce the likelihood of users to contribute to the content.

In the second chapter, Mew and Money examine the effects of Computer Self Efficacy (CSE) on use and adoption of social networking. They argue that relationships between user characteristics and use/performance have not been adequately addressed. Therefore, they examine how a user's CSE can influence perception of system usefulness, how increased CSE helps users to perform better in and engage in complex tasks, and whether there is a synergistic relationship between CSE and task or system complexity that leads to better performance. The theoretical model was empirically tested using data from 262 undergraduate and graduate students who use online social networking software. The study found significant relationships between CSE, task and system characteristics. It also found that greater the "fit" between CSE with task or system characteristics, higher the performance and use of the system.

In Chapter 3, *Team Identification, Team Performance, and Leader-Member Exchange Relationships in Virtual Groups*, authors Eveleth and Eveleth provide evidence to support the proposition that group identification matters in virtual environments. A leader-member exchange relationship can be influenced by the leader's willingness to help and mentor other team members. Members in groups where leader-member exchange relationship is high, and groups perform well, report stronger identification with the team.

Chapter 4, *Geographic Information Networks in American Indian Governments and Communities* by Palmer and Hannery examines the advantages and disadvantages of centralized and decentralized federal government geographic information networks. There are two types of models considered in this paper. One is a top-down federal government mandated system. Here the federal government agencies are responsible for the use and diffusion of the network. The other is a decentralized peer-to-peer network in which all nodes are responsible for the success of the system. These two models are discussed in detail and examples are provided.

The next chapter, *Understanding the Video Bloggers' Community*, examines the structure and workings of a video bloggers' community. The authors, Warmbrodt, Sheng, Hall and Cao performed a social network analysis to provide an insight into the structure of the community. Interviews with core bloggers provided information about the activities of bloggers. Results show that the community followed a core/periphery network structure. A core/periphery network structure has some form of centralization as a core, but also has a less centralized periphery. The network structure has an impact on the communication effectiveness of networks.

In Chapter 6, Daniel and Schwier analyze students' engagement and activities in a virtual learning community. In most virtual learning communities participants learn by exchanging information with others. In this research the authors used Social Network Analysis to examine structure of the community, and analyze relationships between participants. Interviews were used to gather information about user perceptions regarding their learning community.

In the final chapter of this section, authors Zhang, Jiang and Carroll draw upon social science research in identity theory and social identity theory to discuss social identity in Facebook community life. The study provides a framework for understanding how users actively manage their identity and identity presentations in a online community, and this identity is constantly changing and is dynamic compared to the static social identity they display in real-life, non-electronic environments. The researchers discuss how the environment of social computing allows users to actively manage their identity presentations.

In this section consisting of seven chapters, we discuss a number of social issues related to virtual communities and social networking. These research papers use different theories from the social sciences to explain social phenomena in the social computing environment. They employ a variety of research methods including social network analysis, survey questionnaires, and interviews. Overall, these chapters provide us with a valuable insight into the social issues that are important and changing in this new environment.

Section 2: Business Applications of Social Networks

In this section we have a collection of chapters that explore the utilization of social networks in business. Chapter 8 of the book entitled, *The Role of Virtual Communities in the Customization of E-Services*, Karakostas, Kardaras, and Zichova present a theoretical framework of factors influencing customization of e-services in a virtual community. They validate the model using case studies from two health focused health communities. Survey questionnaires were used to collect data to empirically validate the model. According to their findings, factors such as quality of the learning environment, social support, and the community's ability to influence public opinion, positively influence perceived usefulness and active participation in the community. These factors were also found to have a positive impact on customization of e-services by members of the community.

In Chapter 9, authors Suki, Ramayah and Ming discuss job search using social networking sites. The Technology Acceptance Model (TAM) was used as the conceptual model to explain use of social networking sites. According to TAM external variables influence perceived ease of use and perceived usefulness of a social networking site, and these in turn influence use attitude toward using the site. Attitude affects behavioral intention to use, and actual use. An additional variable, perceived enjoyment was also used in the study. Data was collected from job seekers and analyzed using Structural Equation Modeling. Results showed that intention to use is significantly affected by perceived usefulness and is not influenced by perceived ease of use. Also, perceived usefulness has a positive effect on ease of use, and perceived enjoyment has a positive effect on intention to use online social networking sites as a job search tool. The results collectively confirm that the TAM, with modifications, can explain the use of social networking sites for job search.

The next chapter poses an interesting question: Should employees accept their boss's Facebook "friend" request? Here authors, Karl, Peluchette, and Schlaegel examine gender and cultural differences related to this question. Data was collected from respondents in the US and Germany. The results of the study show that initial reaction of an individual after receiving such a "friend" request from their boss is a positive one; this reaction is followed by an intention to question it. Most people are likely to accept such a request, but they do have reservations about doing so. No gender differences were found. Significant cultural differences were found though – US respondents were found to have more negative and questionable reaction to the "friend" request than their German counterparts.

In Chapter 11 business models for online social networks are presented. According to the authors, Rana and Caton, social networks reflect real-world relationships. These relationships in the social networking environment serve as "social clouds" according to the authors, and these clouds help participants share resources. The creation of Social Clouds can give rise to new business models. In this paper the business models are presented and discussed.

In Occupational Networking as a Form of Professional Identification: The Case of Highly Skilled IT Contractors (Chapter 12), Voutsina examines he role of occupational identity of information technology contractors. In this study data was collected using interviews. Results show that virtual communities among IT contractors become the center of social interaction and their primary object of professional identification.

Section 3: Cross Cultural and International Studies

Third and final section of the chapters include cross cultural and international studies. In the chapter, Tracing Community Life Across Virtual Settlements, Akoumainakis uses concepts from the theory of virtual settlements and practice-based analysis to provide a practice lens for analyzing cross-settlement community life in virtual communities. The result is a conceptual model that frames boundary spanning virtual communities based on the principles of virtual settlements.

In Chapter 14, The Impact of Social Networking Websites on the Education of Youth, Kuppuswamy and Narayan, claim that some of the existing features and capabilities of social networking sites can be used to provide a better educational experience for the younger generation. Although a lot has been said of websites serving as a distraction for students, the authors argue that social networking sites can be useful for education based on sound pedagogical principles and proper supervision by teachers. Data was collected using questionnaires and in-depth interviews. Based on evaluation of the data, the authors present information about student use of social networking websites, and how they can be used in education.

The next chapter provides a cross-cultural examination of student attitudes and gender differences in Facebook profile content. In this study the authors Karl, Peluchette and Schlagel do a comparative study of students in the US and Germany. They found that males in both countries would be most likely to self-promote themselves. Students from both countries identified items that they would like to post on their profiles but did not want employers to see them.

In Chapter 16, Networking identities: Geographies of interaction and computer mediated communication; Simour discusses the social computing environment from a computer-mediated communication perspective. This paper examines how virtual communities affect people's lives and the role computer-mediated communication plays in the creation of virtual communities and shaping individuals' identities. The paper utilizes virtual participation on the net and face-to-face interviews for data collection.

Computational Trust in SocialWeb is the next chapter (chapter 17). In this chapter, Zolfaghar and Aghale review existing research in the area of computations trust in SocialWeb. They argue that success of the SocialWeb is dependent on the perceived trust placed on technologies by users. The chapter presents an overview of existing trust mechanisms available in SocialWebs and discusses the strengths and weaknesses of each. The authors also present key research issues in the area of computational trust.

In the next chapter (chapter 18), Kanagavel and Velayutham investigate the impact of social networking on college students in India and the Netherlands. They conducted a cross-cultural empirical study of the use of social networking sites by Indian and Dutch students that involved online observation and survey questionnaires. They found that Dutch students participate more actively than Indian students, and for most students, in both countries, online interaction is only a supplement to face-to-face social interaction.

In Managing Collaborative Research Networks (Chapter 19), Dimitrova and Koku examine how communities of practice work. Using survey questionnaires and follow-up semi-structured interviews they capture the management practices in the community. They found that communities of practice have both an online and a face-to-face component.

In the last article of this section and the book, Kimble identifies some research challenges for studies of virtual communities using online tells. The author used social network analysis and a survey to collect data from members of a geographically distributed research consortium. Based on analysis, he identified four areas for future research: the continuing role of face-to-face communication in virtual communities, the significance of the dual nature of such groups, the importance of the structure of such communities, and the role played by exogenous factors.

In summary, this collection of papers in the area of virtual communities and social networking discusses a wide variety of issues that are relevant to both research as well as practitioner communities. I believe the book makes a valuable contribution to the research in this area.

Subhasish Dasgupta
George Washington University, USA

Section 1
Social Aspects of Virtual Communities and Social Networks

Chapter 1
Use and Participation in Virtual Social Networks:
A Theoretical Model

Margherita Pagani
Bocconi University, Italy

Charles Hofacker
Florida State University, USA

ABSTRACT

Managers are increasingly interested in the social web, as it provides numerous opportunities for strengthening and expanding relationships with customers, but the network processes that lead to these user-based assets are poorly understood. In this paper, the authors explore factors influencing use and participation in virtual social networks. They also discuss unusual drivers and inhibitors present with virtual social networks—highlighted by the presence of positive network externalities and fears that the content will be misused. The authors offer hypotheses stemming from a model of how these factors work together, test the model with a dataset collected from two different virtual social networks, and discuss the implications of this work. The findings offer managers insights on how to nurture Web 2.0 processes.

INTRODUCTION

Many of the most innovative new services that are appearing in the modern economy represent attempts to aid and harness human social processes. Virtual Social Networks such as Second Life, Facebook, LinkedIn, MySpace and many others do not specifically offer content created by the sponsoring firm. Rather, these websites function as a platform for a virtual community, allowing members to create the content that attracts new members. For example, a blogging site offers a variety of content generation tools but it is the users that write the blogs, not the firm. This user-generated content in turn attracts readers, some of whom will in turn create even more content. Similarly, the site del.icio.us allows community members to produce content in the form of tagged

DOI: 10.4018/978-1-4666-1553-3.ch001

bookmarks. These bookmarks can be useful to other visitors who are seeking interesting articles and who can use the tools provided by the site to find other users' bookmarks.

All the above services exhibit some unusual properties that are of significant importance but have not been examined to date.

First, the value of the service to any one user depends in a generally positive way on the number of other users who are using the service. This is in sharp contrast to most offline services. Typically, competition from other users, crowding and simple logistical issues will often produce a reduction in total advantages to any one user as the number of other users increases. In contrast to the offline world, social network websites exhibit positive consumption externalities: the more users who also consume the product, the greater the potential value as the site becomes more useful in satisfying user social needs. The size of the group that "contributes" makes the site more useful for users (for instance a forum with many lurkers will be valuable only if there are also contributors). We also believe that the size of the total virtual group (and not just only the active contributors) matters to the individual user because it influences how many people can be reached by the message and will be potentially able to read the post or interact. While there are numerous macroeconomic models for how externalities function, previous research has not looked closely at these positive consumption externalities from the point of view of the individual user.

A second unusual aspect of social networking websites is the risks that users run in availing themselves of the service. Often when a user posts some content, he or she incurs some risk in revealing more information about himself or herself. Among other things, users may fear that this information might be subject to misuse by the site owners, by hackers, or by other participants (Walker & Johnson, 2006).

A third unusual aspect about these electronic services is that they offer two logical steps or levels of involvement. The user can simply use this Social Network by signing up and browsing the content already present on the site. In a second step or level of involvement, the user can actively participate by expressing his or her own identity and creating his or her own content to be browsed by others. Previous research has not drawn a clear distinction between these two levels of electronic service "use".

The explosive growth of the social web has changed the manager's role from a broadcaster pushing out messages and materials to an aggregator who brings together content, enables collaboration, and builds and participates in communities (Weber, 2007). Content includes new ideas, research, and opinions. Collaboration creates an open environment in which people can, and do, share knowledge. Managers are increasingly interested in creating social webs as they provide opportunities for strengthening and expanding relationships with customers (Weber, 2007) or benefit from new marketing tools such as special interest discussion groups related to products or product categories (Boyd et al., 2007).

To summarize the development so far, this research effort is in response to the need for an expanded, yet still parsimonious, analysis of user behavior in virtual social networks (VSNs), a topic growing in importance as "social media" grow in importance.

Few empirical studies in marketing have tackled this issue. These studies focus on proving the presence of network effects (Nair et al., 2004), investigating the nature of network effects (Shankar & Bayus 2003), or analyzing the role of network effects in diffusion (Gupta, Jain, & Sawhney 1999). However, no study has explicitly examined the impact of network effect on active and passive use. This issue is important for several reasons. First social networks are being adopted by companies as marketing tool with increasing frequency. Second, what influences perceived usefulness and the influence of network effects has important implications for managerial strategies.

Could there be an interaction effect, such that network effects *enhance* the effect of usefulness? What does the empirical evidence show?

The primary goal of this article is to answer these questions through empirical analyses.

In what follows, we draw on recent theoretical work to guide executives and scholars in identifying factors influencing use and participation in virtual social networks. We will proceed in this paper by reviewing theories of use in the study of virtual social networks followed by a look at the theoretical underpinnings of how users accept new technology, a category that presumably includes social media. In the section that follows that one, we go beyond simple adoption of virtual social networks, and talk about active participation in these networks, behavior that we think constitutes a discrete, second step. Finally, we will offer hypotheses stemming from a model of these factors, test the model with a dataset collected from two different social networks, and discuss the implications of our work.

THEORETICAL BACKGROUND

Virtual Social Network

A virtual network is defined by a set of actors and the relationships (ties) among them. Virtual networks can be classified into six main types (Stephenson, 2002): (1) Work network: With whom do you exchange information as part of your daily work routines (2) Social network: With whom do you "check in," inside and outside the office, to find out what is going on (3) Innovation network: With whom do you collaborate or kick around new ideas (4) Expert knowledge network: To whom do you turn for expertise or advice (5) Career network: Whom do you go to for advice about the future (6) Learning network: Whom do you work with to improve existing processes or methods.

Social networking sites are web based services that allow individuals to construct a public or semi-public profile within a bounded system, articulate a list of other users with whom they share a connection, and view and traverse their list of connections and those made by others within the system (Boyd & Ellison, 2007). A social networking site can be seen as a group in which individuals come together around a shared purpose, interest, or goal (Rothaermel & Sugiyama, 2001). Most depend on electronic communications to support interaction among members who are not physically collocated (Andrews, 2002). In this study we focus on virtual social network defined as a group of people interacting predominantly in cyberspace for their own common interests, relationship building, transactions, and fantasies (Hagel & Amstrong, 1997; Koh et al., 2007). A virtual social network is a social structure made of nodes (i.e. individuals) that are tied by one or more specific types of interdependency, such as values, visions, ideas, financial exchange, friendship, etc. The resulting structures are often very complex.

Analyses of human social networks have a long history in both the sociological and anthropological literature (Milardo, 1988). However, relatively few studies have attempted to investigate complete social networks in humans (McCarty et al., 1997) and previous research has tended to focus on determining total network size (Hill & Dunbar, 2003; Johnson et al., 1995; Killworth et al., 1990, 1998; McCarty et al., 2001; Pool & Kochen, 1978), with relatively little attention paid to user behavior within these networks.

Most activity in a virtual social network takes the form of posting or viewing opinions, questions, information, and knowledge within the community's message boards. Consequently, posting (active usage) and viewing (passive usage) are fundamental elements in the ongoing life of any virtual social network. For example, on Facebook active usage might involve creating your profile, sending messages to friends who are also on Facebook, updating your current status, activities or profile, or uploading pictures. On YouTube it might involve uploading your own movies or contents, or uploading recordings you have saved on your VCR from your favorite television programs.

On the other hand passive usage might involve "subscribing" to Facebook, i. e. acquiring a login, browsing other peoples' profiles, and reading their status updates without uploading contents or commenting, likewise on YouTube it might involve viewing other peoples' content.

Adoption of a New Technology

Information Systems (IS) researchers have made significant efforts in leveraging theories to examine and predict the determinant factors of Information Technology (IT) adoption. Such theories include innovation diffusion theory (Agarwal & Prasad, 1998; Moore & Benbasat, 1991; Rogers, 1995), Theory of Reasoned Action (TRA) (Fishbein and Ajzen, 1975), Theory of Planned Behavior (TPB) (Ajzen, 1991; Mathieson, 1991), Decomposed Theory of Planned Behavior (Taylor & Todd, 1995) and the Technology Acceptance Model (TAM) (Davis, 1989; Davis et al., 1989).

Although there are numerous studies in the field of adoption and diffusion of marketing-enabling technology (Daghfous et al., 1999; Holak & Lehman, 1990; Labay & Kinnear, 1981; Rogers, 1995), previous work has focused mainly on the adoption of devices and technology (Au & Enderwick, 2000; Davis, 1989; Verhoef & Langerak, 2001). In contrast, the adoption of social networking services and enabling technologies, analyzed in this study, is considerably less pronounced in the literature. This research effort is in response to the need for more substantive, theory-based research, creating a more in-depth understanding of user behavior with respect to virtual social networks.

The speed with which a new technology is adopted is thought to be driven by a variety of individual difference factors (e.g. age, income, lifestyle etc.), as well as factors pertaining to the innovation itself (Meuter et al., 2005). In this paper, we will be focusing on the latter set of factors. Meuter et al. (2005) cite a number of such factors pertaining to electronic service innovations, but featured prominently among these are the relative advantage the innovation offers the adopter, and the risks it poses to those same adopters. In the case of social network technology, the advantages of virtual social networks pertain to their ability to enable social contacts of various sorts, and this enabling drives adoption. Such advantages are created from the presence of other adopters. Conversely, the risks imposed by social network technologies come from the site itself, as well as the data generated by these social contacts.

Likewise, the Technology Acceptance Model, or TAM, posits that a technological innovation will be adopted to the extent that it proves useful, and is not overly difficult to use (Davis, 1989). Here again we see an implicit cost and benefit assessment applied as users ponder whether to adopt a technology of some sort. In the case of virtual social networks, benefits arise to the user to the extent that the site is useful in allowing social interaction, and the extent to which such interaction is possible due to the presence of other potential social actors. Such drivers lead to adoption while a difficult interface can act as an inhibitor to adoption.

Use and Participation in Virtual Social Networks: Drivers and Inhibitors

In a virtual social network (VSN) activity can take the form of posting or viewing opinions, questions, information, knowledge and other content within the community's message structure (Koh et al., 2007). Posting and viewing are fundamental elements in the ongoing life of any virtual social network. Recent literature (Huang et al., 2007) analyzes participation in social network websites and the effects of word of mouse on user behavior.

Prior studies (Godwin, 1994; Kim, 2000; Koh et al., 2007; Williams & Cothrel, 2000) propose a set of stimulation drivers encouraging participation in VSNs such as the level of leadership involvement, the presence of offline interaction, usefulness, and IT infrastructure quality. Current research in this area is looking at different factors explaining the adoption and participation in VSN. There is network effects, critical mass theory, form of the production function, role of social referral, and last but not least simply the ease of use of 2.0-like applications that lower the adoption barrier and that just was not there in former software generations.

One of the contributions of this work is that we specifically measure both simple use and active participation in the social network platform, where active participation requires a higher level of involvement. Participation in virtual social networks is in effect a question of self-expression and identity (Schau & Gilly, 2003). Expression of any sort cries out for an audience, and the audience helps drive the benefits, but it can also create certain risks to he or she who is doing the expressing. We describe now the main benefits and risks influencing user behavior in social networks.

Usefulness

Virtual social networks are sustainable only when they provide benefits that surpass the costs of membership (Butler, 2001). An important element of a viable community is the ongoing provision of content that members perceive as valuable or useful (Hagel, 1997). This was supported also by recent research in the gratifications of Internet use (Papacharissi & Rubin, 2000; Ko et al., 2005).

In addition to the content itself, the platform being used to create and view that content is im-

portant as well. That a software platform needs to be useful in executing user tasks, whatever those might be, has been a compelling notion in the IS literature since at least the introduction of the Technology Acceptance Model (Davis, 1989). Davis (1989) popularized the variable Perceived Usefulness and also provided a valid scale for its measurement based on such items as speed, performance, productivity, effectiveness, and so forth. Since that time, Perceived Usefulness has been shown to play a prominent role in the use of self-service technologies (Weijters et al., 2007), in loyalty in electronic retailing (Balabanis et al., 2006) and in mobile commerce adoption (Wu & Wang, 2005), among other areas. Consistent with this principle we expect that the perception of usefulness will trigger more frequent activity by community members.

Network Size

One of the unusual properties of social networks – alluded to above - is that they exhibit positive externalities (Srinivasan et al., 2004) and that value is proportional to the number of its users as stated by Metcalfe's Law (Reed, 2001; McAfee and Oliveau, 2002). The more users that communicate on a network, the more value it has. Network effects are a primarily reason that the Web is such a vibrant and exciting place today. A network effect causes a good or service to have a value to a potential customer dependent on the number of customers already owning that good or using that service. Recent examples on the Web include everything from Wikipedia itself, to eBay's auction network, Google AdSense, and even the burgeoning market of Web 2.0 mash-ups like HousingMaps.

While economists have studied the basic phenomenon of externalities for many years, almost nothing is known about how the phenomenon works at the level of the individual participant in social networks (Hofacker et al., 2006). We presume that the user is capable of detecting, reacting to, and assessing the benefits that can be derived from other participants. One contribution of this work is to explicitly look at how the number of other participants is perceived at the individual level, and how this perception drives a benefit of a service.

Fear and Risk

There is an extensive literature on user online privacy and its importance and that literature directly bears on the fear and risks that might inhibit active behavior in social networks. For our purposes, we note that privacy shows up as a key factor in numerous electronic service quality scales (Collier & Bienstock, 2006; Parasuraman et al., 2005; Santos, 2003; Wolfinbarger & Gilly, 2003; Yang & Jun, 2002; Yoo & Donthu, 2001). Privacy pertains to the beliefs that a service might not be sufficiently safe, secure and reliable to use (Walker & Johnson, 2006). Research has in fact shown (Evans et al., 2001; Hoffman et al., 1999; Liebermann & Stashevsky, 2002; Xie et al., 2004) that privacy concerns have a strong impact on behavior.

Privacy is also implicated in users' ability to control impressions and manage social contexts. Preibusch, Hoser, Gürses, and Berendt (2007) argued that the privacy options offered by Social Networking Sites (SNSs) do not provide users with the flexibility they need to handle conflicts with friends who have different conceptions of privacy.

Based on Westin's (1967) definition of privacy, Smith et al. (1996) identified four factors of online privacy: unauthorized secondary use of personal information, improper access of digitally stored personal information, collection of personal information, and errors in collected personal information. Other researchers (Atkinson et al., 2007; Hersberger et al., 2007) discuss issues to do with risks to personal information online. Metzger and Docter (2003) considered

online privacy concerns to include anonymity, intrusion (e.g., spam, data mining), surveillance and autonomy. Regan (2002) argued that personal information flows can be thought of as a common pool of resources and that overuse or misuse, such as through privacy violations, may have a strong impact on online behavior.

All previous studies have shown that security and privacy represent a critical factor with which the user decides on the quality of an electronic service. This in turn drives satisfaction and other important marketing indicators.

HYPOTHESES

Based on the theoretical review described above, we now formulate a set of hypotheses.

Previous studies demonstrate that the value of a network is positively related to the number of its users as made famous by Metcalfe's Law (McAfee & Oliveau, 2002; Metcalfe, 1980; Reed 2001; Sohn et al., 2002; Wyner, 1999). While the exact functional form of the law is not exactly what Metcalfe described, Brooks (2008) and Weber (2007) have showed that the size of the online social network population is one of the most important benefits of using social networking websites to gather sources. A similar result was claimed also by Kiesler and his colleagues (2002) who found that Internet usage is positively influence by social network size.

Conceptually, network effects occur when the size of the network, or the number of users, makes the product more valuable for subsequent users (Reibstein, 2009).

The two key characteristics of most network effect technologies are: 1) they create a productivity-bonus tied to the social behavior of groups of people (i.e., the network users); and 2) they create a new expectation for the amount and quality of data available to the network users.

We therefore hypothesize that:

H1: Members who perceive the community as being larger, perceive the community as being more useful.

Perceived usefulness has been identified consistently in the literature as being significant in determining usage intention (Agarwal & Prasad, 1999; Davis, 1989; Dishaw & Strong, 1999; Gefen & Keil, 1998; Igbaria et al., 1996; Moon & Kim, 2001; Taylor & Todd, 1995; Venkatesh, 2000; Venkatesh & Davis 1996). While most of these studies have analyzed the influence of usefulness on the adoption of technology in general without specifically looking at virtual social networks, one exception is the empirical study into sustaining virtual social networks done by Lin (2007), who also considers the influence of perceived usefulness.

We would then expect that higher perceived usefulness of a social network will lead to more use and more content consumption or simple use of the site. What's more, usefulness, in this context, refers to the usefulness of the site as a platform for a social network and it therefore stands to reason that an increment in usefulness provides a relative advantage in the ability of that platform to encourage active participation, where users send out relational ties, modify or add to their profiles, or otherwise produce content. So, these ties might be in the simple use of the platform, for example consuming content produced by other users, or actively creating content that functions as an outreach to other users. We then propose that:

H2a: Higher perceptions of usefulness will lead to higher levels of site use by community members, and

H2b: Higher perceptions of usefulness will lead to higher levels of participation by community members.

There are certainly inhibitors to social network use that balance the positive effects of perceived network size and usefulness. These inhibitors come in the form of various security and reliability fears (Atkinson et al., 2007; Hersberger et al., 2007). These fears are likely to be heightened as users seek to actively participate in the community, adding information to their profiles, chatting, or otherwise making their own presence more obvious to the rest of the community. Conversely, such fears should not be a strong factor as users merely browse the content created by other community members, and simply use the platform without active participation. We therefore propose:

H3a: Fears, concerns and other costs of membership will not act to reduce simple use of the social network platform.

H3b: Fears, concerns and other costs of membership will act, however to reduce active participation.

The overall theoretical framework, including these hypotheses, is pictured in Figure 1.

METHODOLOGY

Research Sample for Analysis

To test the model we conducted a field survey on a sample of users of two social networks, Facebook and StudiLN. Facebook is a social network with more than 62 million active users worldwide. From September 2006 to September 2007 the site's traffic ranking increased from 60th to 7th and it is the most popular website for uploading photos, with 14 million uploaded daily (Alexa, n.d.). StudiVZ is a social networking platform for students (in particular, college and university students in Europe) based in Berlin. StudiVZ claims to be one of the biggest social networks

Figure 1. The Conceptual model with hypotheses

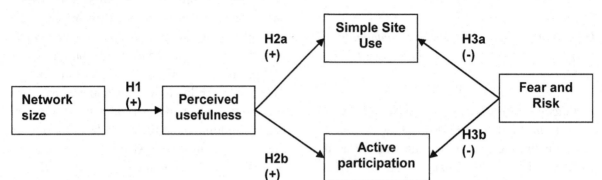

in Europe, with about four million members as of August 2007 mostly in German-speaking countries Germany, Switzerland and Austria.

We focus our analysis on the Italian version called StudiLN. This social network allows users to create or participate in discussion groups, send personal messages, upload, share and comment on photos. It is smaller but roughly comparable to Facebook. In both communities, when a user is online, their presence is signaled by a status tag next to the user's name, highlighting the possibility of an immediate, live interaction with the user.

The survey, conducted in the period January – April 2008, was offered to 1,680 users of the above networks. We adopted a snowball sampling method which relies on referrals from initial subjects to generate additional subjects (Goldenberg et al. 2009).

The survey resulted in 336 total respondents (response rate 20%). Valid completed questionnaires were 326. Of the respondents, 175 (52%) were from StudioLN and 161 (48%) from Facebook. The total sample was composed by male (42%) and female (58%). All respondents were students aged 19 - 26 years old. The two social networks were also compared in terms of pictures uploaded, discussion groups frequented, number of friends in the community and in the real world, number of meetings with friends during a week, use of the community during the week, time spent in the community for each session. All the items

are similar in the two social networks except for the number of picture uploaded and active participation in discussion groups. These two items are rated higher by Facebook users.

We administered the survey through Web-based questionnaire systems available through Facebook and StudioLN, the two relationship social networks studied. The questionnaire was pre-tested asking to 20 online social network users if they had problem to understand the meaning of the questions and if so how to improve them. We adopted a participating pretest (Babbie, 1973) involving an interview setting where respondents were asked to explain reactions to question form, wording and order.

Invitation to complete the questionnaire was sent as a text message through the private message function offered by the two social networks. This method was chosen because it guaranteed that all the respondents not only had some familiarity with the service, but also were members of the community. Furthermore it was presumed to be more effective since, using the community message system, there is no request of personal email addresses and thus no privacy related concern on the part of potential respondents.

Measures

The questionnaire consisted of a series of five point Likert scale items pertaining to online behavior.

The wording and literature sources for the items are summarized in Table 1.

We utilized two different items to measure the perception of the number of other users, asking about the user population, as well as the respondent's sense of the number of users online at any one time.

We also included six items to measure the perceived usefulness of the social network, adopting items appearing in Davis (1989).

The items were adapted (see Table 1) so as to describe the specific context of a social network where the task of the social network is to manage friendship relationships and to incorporate recent research in the gratifications of Internet use (Pa-pacharissi & Rubin, 2000; Ko et al., 2005). The new scale considers the "social" aspects while Davis 1989's scale is related to job performance. This "redeveloped" scale has not been validated before.

The item "work more quickly" was modified to "keep friends even if I have little time", "job performance" was adapted with "get over my shyness", "increase productivity" was adapted with "know more people", "effectiveness" with "meet people with the same interest as mine", "makes job easier" with "hide my personal defects", the final item "useful" was not changed.

We also included five items to measure fears pertaining to social networks. These fears represent

Table 1. Source of survey items

	Scale for measuring Network Size	Adapted from
NS1	The community has many users	Metcalfe, 1980; Wyner, 1999; Reed 2001; McAfee and Oliveau, 2002; Sohn et al. 2002
NS2	The community has many users online at the same moment	Brooks, 2008
Scale for measuring Usefulness		
US1	The VSN allows me to keep friends even if I have little time	(work more quickly) Davis, 1989
US2	The VSN me to get over my shyness	(job performance) Davis, 1989
US3	The VSN allows me to know more people than I could know without it	(increase productivity) Davis, 1989
US4	The VSN allows me to meet people with the same interests as mine	(effectiveness) Davis, 1989; Papacharissi & Rubin, 2000; Ko, Cho & Roberts, 2005
US5	The VSN allows me to hide my personal defects	(makes job easier) Davis, 1989
US6	I find the VSN very useful	(useful) Davis, 1989
Scale for measuring perceived Fear and Risk		
CO1	I fear that the social network is not sufficiently safe, secure and reliable to use	Walker and Johnson, 2006; Xie et al. 2004
CO2	I fear that my data could be used for commercial purposes	Smith, Milberg, & Burke, 1996; Evans et al., 2001; Liebermann et al., 2002; Xie et al., 2004
CO3	I fear that other users could abuse (misuse) my data	Fried, 1970; Westin, 1967
CO4	I fear that my data are exposed to hacker's attacks	Hoffman, Novak, and Peralta 1999
CO5	I fear that The Website might not work properly	Walker and Johnson, 2006
Scale for measuring Simple Site Use		
US1	I regularly use The Website	
Scale for measuring Active Participation		
PA1	I actively participate in VSNs (discussion groups, send personal messages, upload, share and comment on photos)	

Respondents were asked to rate from 1 (totally disagree) to 5 (totally agree) their level of agreement or disagreement with the following statements in relation to the specific social network they are using.

a cost or risk associated with the community. As can be seen from Table 1, risks can include the notion that the service is not sufficiently safe, secure or reliable to use (Walker & Johnson, 2006). Additional fears focus on the possibility that companies might seek to obtain and use personal information for marketing purposes (Evans et al., 2001; Liebermann & Stashevsky, 2002; Smith et al., 1996; Xie et al., 2004), that other users could misuse the focal user's data in some way (Fried, 1970; Westin, 1967), that third parties such as spammers or hackers could expose the user's data to misuse (Hoffman et al., 1999), or that in general, the virtual social network might not work properly (Walker & Johnson, 2006). These five items were taken from different sources as in the literature as there is not an extant validated scale. All items are included in Table 1.

Finally, content consumption and creation were measured asking users to evaluate their viewing activity (simple use) and their active posting activity (i.e. create or participate in discussion groups, send personal messages, upload, share and comment on photos).

EMPIRICAL RESULTS

Principal Components and Reliability

Following the first step of the Gerbing and Anderson (1988) two-step procedure, we carefully assessed the measurement model. We began with a principle component analysis on all variables, followed by Varimax rotation. In all cases we utilized the criteria that factor loadings should be .5 and above and that cross-loadings should fall below .2 (Hair et al., 1998). The internal consistency of the instruments was further tested via reliability analyses, utilizing Cronbach's alpha.

High communality values were observed for the factors related to network size, usefulness and total costs/risks of membership indicating that the total amount of variance that the observed variables

share with all other variables on the same factor is high. Figure 2 shows the summaries of the principle components and their item loadings. Reliability analysis revealed a Cronbach Alpha of .754 for the usefulness, .721 for the fears of membership component and .760 for network size. For these three constructs the reliability test results show values well exceeding the .6 recommended by Hair et al. (1998) as the lower limit of acceptability. The other two items, Virtual Social Network Use and Participation were not expected to load on any components, but were included as a check for discriminant validity. In fact, these items did not form an internally consistent dimension, with an Alpha value of .166, nor did they load on any of the other dimensions.

The discriminant validity—the extent to which different constructs diverge from one another—was assessed across the scales by respecifying the initial measurement model in a series of constrained models in which each intertrait correlation was constrained to unity. In every instance the difference in χ^2 value between each of the constrained models with the baseline measurement model was found to be significant, thus providing evidence of discriminability (Gerbing & Anderson, 1988).

Confirmatory Factor Analysis

A second confirmatory factor analysis step was performed using Lisrel 8.80 (Bentler, 1989) to provide further insight on the measurement properties of the items (Figure 3). The covariance matrix for the network size, usefulness and fear items was used as input in the analysis. A three-dimensional factor model fit these items very well, with a χ^2 of 244.45 on 62 degrees of freedom (p = 0) and goodness of fit measures all above .80 (Bentler-Bonett Normed Fit Index was 0.88, the Non-Normed Fit Index (NNFI) was 0.88, the Comparative Fit Index was .91, the Goodness of Fit Index was 0.90 and the Adjusted Goodness of Fit Index was 0.85). Finally, the Root Mean

Figure 2. Factor analysis: Rotated component matrix

	Component			
	Usefulness	Fear and Risk	Network size	4
Keep friends with little time	.695			
Useful Website	.664			
Know more people	.660			
Defeat shyness	.603			
Know people with same interests	.589			
Hide personal defects	.500			
Privacy issues		.860		
Hacker's attacks		.854		
Data can used for commercial purposes		.852		
Virtual Social Network doesn't work		.715		
Website is not sufficiently safe, secure and reliable		.601		
Total registered users			.645	
Online network people			.629	
Active Participation				.670
Virtual Social Network use				.506
Cronbach Alpha	**.754**	**.721**	**.760**	.166

Extraction Method: Principal Component Analysis.
Rotation Method: Varimax with Kaiser Normalization.
a Rotation converged in 4 iterations.

Square Residual for the covariance matrix, based on five point Likert items, was 0.11 and the root mean square error of approximation (RMSEA) was 0.094.

Test of Hypotheses and Structural Equation Modeling

We now proceed to test the other hypotheses, using the path parameters of the structural equation model, a model fit as the second part of the two-step Gerbing and Anderson (1988) procedure.

Figure 4 provides a summary of model results. The model yielded a χ^2 of 52.64 on 18 degrees of freedom, with a Bentler-Bonett Normed Fit Index of .95. The Non-Normed Index was .95, the Goodness of Fit Index was .96 and a Comparative Fit Index was .97 all within the accepted thresholds. The fit was therefore quite good (Hu & Bentler, 1999).

Our hypothesis H1 posited a significant relationship from network size, to the usefulness of the network. In our sample, network size did significantly influence usefulness (ß=.211, p < 0.001). This hypothesis is confirmed.

We next hypothesized that Usefulness would influence Virtual Social Network use (H2a) and community participation (H2b). As far as Virtual Social Network use was concerned, we observed ß=.56, with p<.0001, thus confirming the hypothesis. For participation, the value of the path, ß=.21, is reliably different from zero at p < .0001. Thus both H2a and H2b were confirmed.

Findings emerging from the structural equation model show that fears act like costs that work against active participation (H3b) (ß= - .141, p = 0.009), rather than against simple use (H3a) of the Virtual Social Network (ß = -.003, p=.953). These findings therefore support both H3a and H3b.

Figure 3. Confirmatory factor analysis

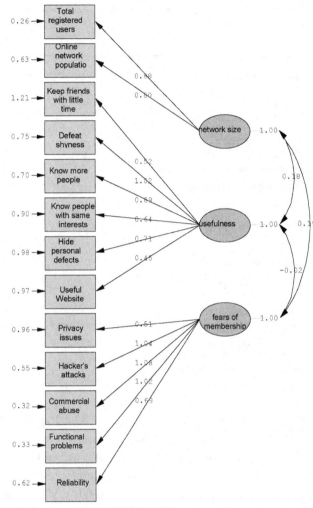

Chi-Square=244.45, df=62, P-value=0.00000, RMSEA=0.094

In summary, the overall fit of the conceptual model was good and the results supported all hypotheses.

DISCUSSION AND IMPLICATIONS

The purpose of the present study was to explore factors influencing use and participation in virtual social networks. Based on previous empirical findings and theoretical considerations our results show that perceptions of network size enhance the perceived usefulness of a social network site (H1). This usefulness in turn influences the users' propensity both to visit the site and to actively participate on it (H2a, H2b). The fears that users have in terms of social network websites do not reduce their likelihood to use or visit the site, but these fears do indeed reduce the tendency to actively participate by creating content (H3).

Understanding the drivers influencing active use in this arena is not merely important to social networking sites such as Facebook, but also to many commercial sites that are attempting to

Figure 4. Structural equation model

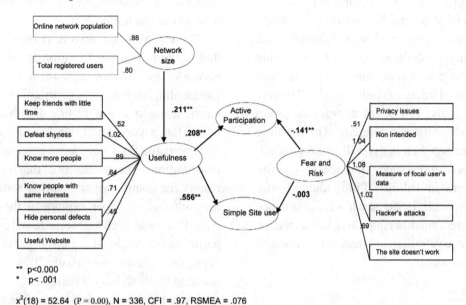

** p<0.000
* p< .001

x^2(18) = 52.64 (P = 0.00), N = 336, CFI = .97, RSMEA = .076

harness the energy created in the content generation and consumption cycle. We now discuss how management can use these results to nurture Web 2.0 processes. We start off by talking about enhancing the benefits of network size.

Enhancing the Benefits of Network Size

Given the importance of signaling the number of other participants (**H1**), we emphasize that conveying social presence (Koh et al., 2007) is critical to jump-starting a virtual community. In terms of contributions from the community, Williams and Cothrel (2000) argue that encouraging content production requires a clear vision, the presence of opinion leaders, and dissemination of basic guidelines, among other things. Other authors (Hennig-Thurau et al., 2004) emphasize the presence of skilled guides or moderators. All of these tactics are likely to make the site more useful, which will then generate additional users (H2a) and additional content (H2b). To this list we would add the concepts of contribution task modularity and transparency (Benkler, 2002). In

other words, the process of contributing needs to be available in small obvious chunks, allowing participants to accurately assess their ability to perform the contribution, and the platform needs to allow contribution at low levels of contributor effort. This would make the platform more useful for those who would contribute but cannot commit a high degree of time to their contributions. Our results suggest further that community management can encourage contributions by communicating the presence of other users and participants.

Mitigating the Costs and Risks of Membership

Our results suggest that much of the costs of memberships are costs that act against contribution, rather than against joining. That is, fears may reduce participation but not initial joining behavior (H3). There are then two general approaches to managing the negative impacts of fears of membership on members' post-joining activities: development of internal social structure or use of communication technologies. Internal structure addresses the negative consequences of size by constraining or channeling interaction within a social structure. For example, organizations or teams may establish norms, formal roles, structures, and procedures in order to reduce the costs associated with spamming, free-riding and other anti-social behavior (Galbraith, 1973; Haveman, 1993; Indik, 1965). The appropriate group culture can also offer encouragement to first-time posters to get over their fears (Williams & Cothrel, 2000). Other features, such as member anonymity and the general invisibility of individual identity (Finholt & Sproull, 1990) may lower the salience of a structure's membership, and hence reduce the negative psychological effects of creating or consuming content.

LIMITATIONS AND FUTURE RESEARCH

To create a general framework, the current study focuses on developing the constructs of network size, usefulness and fears of membership and analyzing their impact on posting and viewing activity. This approach furthers our understanding of drivers and inhibitors of user participation in virtual social networks in several ways. First, by articulating the elementary constructs that are both simplified and grounded in prior empirical and theoretical studies, this work can serve as the foundation for computational and analytical models that consider other aspects of the dynamics of online behavior in virtual social networks.

The results from this study, taken as a whole, suggest that future research on virtual social networks issues should consider the influence of perceived network size and how the perception of network externalities works as a function of actual network size and perceived network size. Granovetter (1978) assumes that there is a critical group size threshold for the adoption of a social network where the utility of that network exceeds the users perceived adoption costs. Thirty years after Granovetter's work, there are numerous data

sources and communities available that could be used to test the notion.

There is also recent work (Ebel et al., 2002) that suggests that participation in virtual social networks might follow a power law. In a Power Law, scaling the frequency distribution in a log-log metric leads to a straight-line distribution function. Thus a very small number of participants is responsible for a very large percentage of the contributions. The generality of that result and its results for companies sponsoring virtual social networks have not been explored in the literature. A modeling approach to group size and community participation might also take a game theoretic approach (Blume & Durlauf, 2003), or system thinking methodology (Gharajedaghi, 2006).

Likewise, the empirical work presented here is based on a sample of online social structures that make use of one type of social network (based on relationships), have minimal internal structures, and exist in a public network (the Internet). The sample size is not representative of active and passive users. Although this sample represents a common and popular type of online social structure, future work that considers other types of technology (i.e. digital IPTV) and different contexts would increase the validity of the general model. Assessment of the impact of internal structures, such as moderation and member screening on a structure's ability to attract and retain members would also be useful when developing the social and managerial infrastructure to support online communication.

The results of this study suggest that size has a positive effect on the sustainability of online social structures. Larger networks are better able to attract members, but privacy issues reduce the posting activity, which in turn influences the total attraction of the social network.

It is clear then, as it is with traditional social structures, that developing and maintaining sustainable online social structures requires that the fundamental problem of balancing the positive and negative impacts of network size and communication activity be solved in order to maintain a resource pool for the future while providing benefits for the members in the present. This suggests that rather than focusing on computer mediated communication technologies as revolutionary forces that fundamentally change the problem of social organization, researchers and practitioners would be better served by theories that characterize them as additional tools in the organizers' repertoire for dealing with certain fundamental problems. While the model presented in this work provides an initial step, there is much work that remains to be done in the development of a practical understanding of the challenges of organizing and the true opportunities provided by new technologies in the realm of developing and maintaining sustainable social structures.

ACKNOWLEDGMENT

The authors acknowledge Customer & Service Science Lab (Bocconi University) for the support provided

REFERENCES

Alexa. (n.d.). Retrieved March 8, 2008, from http://www.Alexa.com

Andrews, D. (2002). Audience-specific online community design. *Communications of the ACM*, *45*(4), 64–68. doi:10.1145/505248.505275

Atkinson, J., Johnson, C., & Phippen, A. D. (2007). Improving protection mechanisms by understanding online risk. *Information Management & Computer Security*, *15*(5), 382–393. doi:10.1108/09685220710831125

Babbie, E. R. (1973). *Survey research methods*. Belmont, CA: Wadsworth.

Balabanis, G., Reynolds, N., & Simintiras, A. (2006). Bases of E-Store Loyalty: Perceived Switching Barriers and Satisfaction. *Journal of Business Research*, *59*(2), 214–224. doi:10.1016/j.jbusres.2005.06.001

Benkler, Y. (2002). Coase's Penguin, or, Linux and the Nature of the Firm. *The Yale Law Journal*, *112*(3), 369–436. doi:10.2307/1562247

Bentler, P. M. (1989). *EQS Structural Equations Program Manual*. Los Angeles, CA: BMDP Statistical Software.

Bhattacherjee, A. (2001). Understanding Information Systems Continuance: An Exptectation-Confirmation Model. *Management Information Systems Quarterly*, *25*(3), 351–370. doi:10.2307/3250921

Blume, L., & Durlauf, S. N. (2003). Equilibrium Concepts for Social Interaction Models. *International Game Theory Review*, *5*(3), 193–209. doi:10.1142/S021919890300101X

Boyd, J. T., Peters, C. O., & Tolson, H. (2007). An exploratory investigation of the virtual community MySpace.com. *Journal of Fashion Marketing and Management*, *11*(4), 587–603. doi:10.1108/13612020710824625

Brooks, K. (2008). Networking the pros and cons of trolling the internet for sources sites. *Quill*, *January/February*, 25-26.

Butler, B. (2001). Membership size, communication activity, and sustainability: The internal dynamics of networked social structures. *Information Systems Research*, *12*(4), 346–362. doi:10.1287/isre.12.4.346.9703

Collier, J. E., & Bienstock, C. C. (2006). Measuring Service Quality in E-Retailing. *Journal of Service Research*, *8*(3), 260–275. doi:10.1177/1094670505278867

Davis, F. D. (1989). Perceived Usefulness, Perceived Ease of Use and User Acceptance of Information Technology. *Management Information Systems Quarterly, 13*(2), 319–339. doi:10.2307/249008

Ebel, H., Lutz-Ingo Mielsch, & Bornholdt, S. (2002). Scale Free Topology of E-Mail Networks. *Physical Review E: Statistical, Nonlinear, and Soft Matter Physics, 66*(3), 1–4. doi:10.1103/PhysRevE.66.035103

Evans, M., O'Malley, L., & Patterson, M. (2001). Bridging the Direct Marketing-Direct Consumer Gap: Some Solutions from Qualitative Research. *Qualitative Market Research: An International Journal, 4*(1), 17–24. doi:10.1108/13522750110364532

Finholt, T., & Sproull, L. (1990). Electronic groups at work. *Organization Science, 1,* 41–64. doi:10.1287/orsc.1.1.41

Fried, C. (1970). *An anatomy of values: Problems of personal and social choice.* Cambridge, MA: Harvard University Press.

Galbraith, J. (1973). *Designing Complex Organizations.* Reading, MA: Addison-Wesley Publishing Co.

Gerbing, D. W., & Anderson, J. C. (1988). An Updated Paradigm for Scale Developent Incorporating Unidimensionality and its Assessment. *JMR, Journal of Marketing Research, XXV,* 186–192. doi:10.2307/3172650

Gharajedaghi, J. (2006). *Systems Thinking: Managing Chaos and Complexity: a platform for designing business architecture.* Burlington, MA: Elsevier.

Godwin, M. (1994). Nine principles for making virtual communities work. *Wired 2.06,* 72-73.

Granovetter, M. (1978). Threshold Models of Collective Behavior. *American Journal of Sociology, 83*(6), 1420–1443. doi:10.1086/226707

Hagel, J., & Armstrong, A. (1997). *Net Gain: Expanding Markets through Virtual Communities.* Boston: Harvard Business School Press.

Hair, J. F. Jr, Anderson, R. E., Tatham, R. L., & Black, W. C. (1998). *Multivariate data analysis* (5th ed.). Upper Saddle River, NJ: Prentice Hall.

Haveman, H. A. (1993). Organizational size and change: Diversification in the savings and loan industry after deregulation. *Administrative Science Quarterly, 38,* 20–50. doi:10.2307/2393253

Hennig-Thurau, T., Gwinner, K. P., Walsh, G., & Gremler, D. D. (2004). Electronic Word-of-Mouth Via Consumer-Opinion Platforms: What Motivates Consumers to Articulate Themselves on the Internet? *Journal of Interactive Marketing, 18*(1), 38–52. doi:10.1002/dir.10073

Hersberger, J. A., Murray, A. L., & Rioux, K. S. (2007). Examining information exchange and virtual communities: an emergent framework. *Online Information Review, 31,* 2. doi:10.1108/14684520710747194

Hill, R. A., & Dunbar, R. I. M. (2003). Social Network Size in Humans. *Human Nature (Hawthorne, N.Y.), 14*(1), 53–72. doi:10.1007/s12110-003-1016-y

Hofacker, C. F., Goldsmith, R. E., Bridges, E., & Swilley, E. (2006). E-Services: A Synthesis and Research Agenda. *Journal of Value Chain Management, 1*(1), 13–44.

Hoffman, D. L., Novak, T. P., & Peralta, M. A. (1999). Building Consumer Trust Online. *Communications of the ACM, 42*(4), 80–85. doi:10.1145/299157.299175

Hu, L. T., & Bentler, P. M. (1999). Cut-off criteria for fit indexes in covariance structure analysis: conventional criteria versus new alternatives. *Structural Equation Modeling, 6,* 1–55. doi:10.1080/10705519909540118

Huang, C. Y., Shen, Y. Z., Lin, H. X., & Chang, S. S. (2007). Bloggers' Motivations and Behaviors: A Model. *Journal of Advertising Research, 47*(4), 472–484. doi:10.2501/S0021849907070493

Indik, B. P. (1965). Organization size and member participation. *Human Relations, 18*, 339–350. doi:10.1177/001872676501800403

Kim, A. (2000). *Community Building on the Web*. Berkeley, CA: Peachpit Press.

Ko, H., Cho, C., & Roberts, M. S. (2005). Internet Uses and Gratifications: A Structural Equation Model of Interactive Advertising. *Journal of Advertising, 34*(2), 57–71.

Koh, J., Kim, Y. G., Butler, B., & Bock, G. W. (2007). Encouraging Participation in Virtual Communities. *Communications of the ACM, 50*(2), 69–73. doi:10.1145/1216016.1216023

Liebermann, Y., & Stashevsky, S. (2002). Perceived risks as barriers to Internet and ecommerce usage. *Qualitative Market Research: An International Journal, 5*(4), 291–300. doi:10.1108/13522750210443245

Lin, H.-F. (2007). The role of online and offline features in sustaining virtual communities: an empirical study. *Internet Research, 17*(2). doi:10.1108/10662240710736997

McAfee, A., & Oliveau, F.X. (2002). Confronting the limits of networks. *MIT Sloan Management Review, Summer*, 85-87.

Metzger, M. J., & Docter, S. (2003). Public opinion and policy initiatives for online privacy protection. *Journal of Broadcasting & Electronic Media, 47*(3), 350–374. doi:10.1207/s15506878jobem4703_3

Meuter, M. L., Bitner, M. J., Ostrom, A. L., & Brown, S. W. (2005). Choosing among Alternative Service Delivery Modes: An Investigation of Customer Trial of Self-Service Technologies. *Journal of Marketing, 69*(2), 61–83. doi:10.1509/jmkg.69.2.61.60759

Papacharissi, Z., & Rubin, A. (2000). Predictors of internet use. *Journal of Broadcasting & Electronic Media, 44*(2), 175–196. doi:10.1207/s15506878jobem4402_2

Parasuraman, A., Zeithaml, V. A., & Malhotra, A. (2005). E-S-Qual: A Multiple-Item Scale for Assessing Electronic Service Quality. *Journal of Service Research, 7*(3), 213–233. doi:10.1177/1094670504271156

Payne, A., & Frow, P. (2005). A Strategic Framework for Customer Relationship Management. *Journal of Marketing, 69*(4), 167–176. doi:10.1509/jmkg.2005.69.4.167

Reed, D. P. (2001). The Law of the Pack. *Harvard Business Review*, (February): 23–24.

Regan, P. M. (2002). Privacy as a common good in the digital world. *Information Communication and Society, 7*(1), 92–114.

Reibstein, D. J. (2008). A Broader Perspective of Network Effects. *JMR, Journal of Marketing Research, XLVI*, 154–156.

Rothaermel, F., & Sugiyama, S. (2001). Virtual Internet communities and commercial success: Individual and community-level theory grounded in the atypical case of TimeZone.com. *Journal of Management, 27*(3), 297–312. doi:10.1016/S0149-2063(01)00093-9

Santos, J. (2003). E-Service Quality: A Model of Virtual Service Quality Dimensions. *Managing Service Quality, 13*(3), 233–246. doi:10.1108/09604520310476490

Schau, H. J., & Gilly, M. C. (2003). We Are What We Post? Self-Presentation in Personal Web Space. *The Journal of Consumer Research, 30*(3), 385–405. doi:10.1086/378616

Smith, H. J., Milberg, S. J., & Burke, S. J. (1996). Information Privacy: Measuring Individuals' Concerns About Organizational Practices. *Management Information Systems Quarterly, 20*(2), 167–196. doi:10.2307/249477

Srinivasan, R., Lilien, G. L., & Rangaswamy, A. (2004). First in, First Out? The Effects of Network Externalities on Pioneer Survival. *Journal of Marketing, 68*(1), 41–58. doi:10.1509/jmkg.68.1.41.24026

Walker, R. H., & Johnson, L. W. (2006). Why consumers use and do not use technology-enabled services. *Journal of Services Marketing, 20*(2), 125–135. doi:10.1108/08876040610657057

Weber, L. (2007). *Marketing to the Social Web.* Hoboken, NJ: John Wiley & Sons.

Weijters, B., Devarajan Rangarajan, D., Falk, T., & Schillewaert, N. (2007). Determinants and Outcomes of Customers' Use of Self-Service Technolog in a Retail Setting. *Journal of Service Research, 10*(1), 3–21. doi:10.1177/1094670507302990

Westin, A. F. (1967). *Privacy and Freedom.* New York: Atheneum.

Williams, R. L., & Cothrel, J. (2000). Four Smart Ways to Run Online Communities. *Sloan Management Review, 41*(4), 81–91.

Wolfinbarger, M., & Gilly, M. C. (2003). Etailq: Dimensionalizing, Measuring and Predicting Etail Quality. *Journal of Retailing, 79*(3), 183–198. doi:10.1016/S0022-4359(03)00034-4

Wu, J. H., & Wang, S. C. (2005). What Drives Mobile Commerce? An Empirical Evaluation of the Revised Technology Acceptance Model. *Information & Management, 42*, 719–729. doi:10.1016/j.im.2004.07.001

Xie, E., Teo, H., & Wan, W. (2004). Volunteering Personal Information on the Internet: Effects of Reputation, Privacy Notices, and Rewards on Online Consumer Behaviour. *Research, 18*(4), 336–355.

Yang, Z., & Jun, M. (2002). Consumer Perception of E-Service Quality: From Internet Purchaser and Non-Purchaser Perspectives. *The Journal of Business Strategy, 19*(1), 19–41.

Yoo, B., & Donthu, N. (2001). Developing a Scale to Measure the Perceived Quality of an Internet Shopping Site (Sitequal). *Quarterly Journal of Electronic Commerce, 2*(1), 31–46.

This work was previously published in the International Journal of Virtual Communities and Social Networking, Volume 2, Issue 1, edited by Subhasish Dasgupta, pp. 1-17, copyright 2010 by IGI Publishing (an imprint of IGI Global).

Chapter 2
Effects of Computer Self Efficacy on the Use and Adoption of Online Social Networking

Lionel Mew
George Washington University; American University, USA

William H. Money
George Washington University, USA

ABSTRACT

Online Social Networking (OSN) systems such as Ning, MySpace, Facebook and Friendster have achieved tremendous popularity. However, little research has been conducted to determine factors motivating users with varying capabilities to use and adopt OSN systems addressing target tasks, with varying system capabilities and characteristics. The relationships between user characteristics and use/performance have not been adequately addressed. This study used a cross-sectional survey of 262 graduate and undergraduate students to examine how end user Computer Self-Efficacy (CSE) affects performance and use of OSN systems and how "fit" determines whether there are user, task and/or systems characteristics associated with the best performance and usage levels. Significant direct and indirect relationships were found between CSE, task and system characteristics as measured by performance and use, and these relationships were further significantly strengthened when there was good "fit" between the variables. Results indicate that users having high self-efficacy "fit" with task or systems characteristics produce higher performance and use.

INTRODUCTION

OSN Websites are internet sites that facilitate building of personal social networks online. People throughout the United States and around the world are increasingly using these applications,

and venture capitalists are funding online social networking companies at rates not often seen in today's economy (Wildbit, 2005; Kopytoff, 2004; Rosenheck, 2003). It is generally accepted that social networking software is a strongly emerging trend in information technology that impacts

DOI: 10.4018/978-1-4666-1553-3.ch002

lifestyles and work. Leonard (2004) notes that, "like e-mail, like using a search engine, social networking is a part of the Internet way of life. And [sic] it's barely getting started."

Friendster was the first social networking application to hit the market. Founded in 2002 by Jonathan Abrams, Friendster went online in March, 2003. By August, 2003, Friendster had over a million users and was growing by 15% per week (Rosenheck, 2003). In early 2004, Friendster claimed to have more than 5 million registered users (Kopytoff, 2004). By December, 2004, Friendster claimed to have more than 13 million registered users (Friendster, personal communication, December 15, 2004). As of late 2006, Friendster claimed to have over 20 million users for which there were over 19 million personal profiles (Wikipedia, 2006b). However, during the past few years, Facebook and MySpace have far outpaced Friendster which, as of 2006, only has 0.24% of the market (Auchard, 2006). Also in 2006, Facebook experienced users boycotting the system after making changes that creators considered upgrades. In 2009, Facebook finally and expectedly exceeded MySpace in U.S. traffic. The rapidity with which Friendster lost market share, the quick domination of MySpace and Facebook, the strong reaction against new Facebook features, and the (relatively) quick dominance of Facebook over MySpace are examples of enormous unpredicted changes in usage. Social networking is quickly becoming more relevant. It is part of the emerging Enterprise 2.0 paradigm. Newman and Thomas (2009) note that Enterprise 2.0 helps organizations by, "finding and retaining better employees, using employee time more effectively, communicating with the customer better, and receiving feedback faster. If only to prevent your organization from becoming obsolete, you will need to get on board with these new ideas and strategies" (p. 18). More adults are using social networking software, according to Solis (2009). As more people use social software and it becomes

a larger part of peoples' lives, both for work and for recreation, it becomes increasingly important to fully understand the factors influencing acceptance, usability and use of these systems; and to incorporate user characteristics in their design.

These rapid changes in use and acceptance of OSN systems involving millions of users raise three important question addressed in this research. Does user computer self-efficacy cause end users to adopt and use OSN systems? How does the interplay of user, task and system characteristics affect utilization and end user performance? What factors affect the ability or desire of users to use more complex systems and perform more complex tasks?

Scope of the Study

This study conducted cross-sectional research to measure the patterns of OSN usage across 262 graduate and undergraduate students in the metropolitan DC area. The study examined user-reported usage and performance of OSN applications used by study participants. Major dimensions of the study included user characteristics, task characteristics and software characteristics constructs. Dependent variables included OSN performance and use.

Research Questions

The study focused on the following research questions: 1. How does a user's CSE affect individual perception of OSN system usefulness? 2. To what extent does increased CSE cause OSN users to perform better, use increasingly complex systems and engage in more challenging tasks? 3. Is there a synergistic effect between CSE and task or system complexity that yields increased performance or utilization among OSN users? 4. Are there fits among CSE task and system characteristics associated with the best performance and utilization among OSN users?

Literature Review

Researchers increasingly began investigating explanations for variables governing individual use of computer systems during the mid 1970's. One of the first of these was Ajzen & Fishbein's (1977, 1980) Theory of Reasoned Action, first developed in 1967 and revised and expanded during the 1970s. It was developed following attitude research from Expectancy Value models, at a time when social psychologists were unable to explain disconnects between attitude and behavior. The theory has three main parts, and suggests that an individual's intent plays the greatest part in predicting and influencing actions and behavior. When individuals intend to do something, they will probably do it. The two factors affecting intent are attitude and subjective norms.

The theory has been shown to have demonstrated validity and strong predictive utility in wide ranges of scenarios and behaviors (Budd, 1986; Prestholdt, Lane & Mathews, 1987). In a 1988 meta-analysis Sheppard, Hartwick and Warshaw found strong support for the overall predictive utility of the model based on 87 separate studies. Critics of the theory point to two limitations: 1) it is often difficult to differentiate between attitudes and norms, since either can be contextualized as the other, and 2) there is no mechanism for control of intentions, so intent to perform behavior is tantamount to action (Wikipedia, 2006a).

An extension of TRA, Izek Azjens' Theory of Planned Behavior (TPB) was designed to address one of the major shortcomings of TRA, which does not consider constraints on individuals' ability to act on their intentions. TPB Shares with TRA the constructs of behavioral beliefs (attitudes) and normative beliefs, but also considers beliefs about factors affecting performance of the behavior, and perceived power of those factors, or control beliefs (Ajzen, 1991).

By adding control beliefs, and perceived and actual behavioral control constructs, it largely addresses the limitation of TRA with regard to control issues. This extension has also been found to have demonstrated validity and strong predictive validity in numerous empirical studies. In a 2001 meta-analysis of 185 independent studies, Armitage and Conner found that TPB "accounted for 27% and 39% of the variance in behavior and intention, respectively" (p. 471).

When applied to information systems, TRA/TPB suggests that if a user believes using a computer (a behavior) associates with a positive outcome, they will use or intend to use the computer (perform the behavior). The user's attitude about a behavior is formed by their belief that the behavior results in a particular outcome, and an evaluation of the outcome. If the outcome is perceived as positive, the user may perform or intend to perform the behavior. The subjective norm also influences the user's attitude toward the behavior. The subjective norm is the user's perception of what their peers feel they should do. Fishbein and Ajzen (1980) assert that people are strongly influenced by the subjective norm.

Although TRA has been found to have some shortcomings (often difficult to differentiate between attitudes and norms, intention to perform behavior is tantamount to action), Compeau and Higgins (1995) note that the Theory of Reasoned Action is still widely used today in IS literature. TRA/TPB also exert a significant effect on development of IS research and theory.

Davis' (1986, 1989) Technology Acceptance Model (TAM), based on the TRA/TPB, is often applied in IT settings. This theory considers two factors, Perceived Usefulness (PU) and Perceived Ease of Use (PEoU). The factors ease of use and usefulness have been shown over numerous studies to be strong measures of intent to use the applications. TAM is still widely considered the preeminent model for technology acceptance (Goodhue, 1995).

One of the major criticisms of TAM is that it does not consider task or user characteristics. However, Davis (1989) suggests that researchers explore other variables that may affect PU,

PEoU and use. Wixom and Todd (2005) note that attempts to extend TAM have used three primary approaches: by introducing factors from related models, by introducing additional or alternative belief factors, and by examining external variables which are antecedents or moderators of PU and PEoU.

There are several studies (Dishaw, Strong & Bandy, 2002; Al-Gahtani & King, 1999; Venkatesh, Morris, Davis, & Davis, 2003) that attempt with varying degrees of success to extend TAM to user and task characteristics. In a 1999 study, Dishaw and Strong extend the TAM model with TTF constructs, and other studies have made theoretical extensions to add fidelity to the model. Studies in other fields such as education, medicine and law enforcement have also added theoretical extensions to improve on the TAM model in specific situations (Malhotra & Galletta, 1999; Lin, Hu & Chen, 2004). Since Wixom and Todd (2005) note that TAM extensions have usually been attempted using working portions of other theoretical models, adding new belief factors, and by considering moderators of PU and PEoU, it would be appropriate to attempt to extend TAM by adding task or user characteristics. However, there may be more appropriate models to extend, such as TTF, since its use of task and technology characteristics is widely used, and have been validated and accepted.

Goodhue and Thompson (1995) focused on developing measures for individual performance, and constructed the Task Technology Fit (TTF) model, which combines task characteristics and technology characteristics in an attempt to develop a comprehensive model. They assert that, "for an information technology to have a positive impact on individual performance, the technology: (1) must be utilized and (2) must be a good fit with the tasks it supports" (1995, p.213). In other words, for a technology to have a positive effect on individual performance it must be used and it must be a good fit for the task at hand. The TTF model is significant in introducing task characteristics and the concept of fit as considerations.

It focuses on the fit between technology and user tasks in achieving individual performance. Goodhue and Thompson anticipated the model would address the link between information systems and performance.

Seminal articles include Goodhue's 1995 paper introducing the TTF concept, Goodhue and Thompson's 1995 paper on individual performance conducting initial validation of the instrument, and Zigurs and Buckland (1998), which applied TTF to the group environment of group support systems. Many studies in the IS field have refined and explored that impacts of TTF application. Goodhue and Thompson's (1995) study initially validating the instrument was followed by Goodhue's (1998) work which found their instrument to have excellent reliability and discriminant validity, and strong predictive validity. Others have found the theory and instrument to have strong predictive utility.

In a study on information systems for project management, Bani Ali (2004) developed a model combining fit among CSE, task and system characteristics to examine relationships on how those factors affected performance and system utilization. Bani Ali's (2004, p. 12) study examines "whether computer skills empower individuals to present higher performance, use more sophisticated systems and engage in more challenging tasks." He developed a new model called the task-person-technology-fit model, which combines CSE and TTF in the project management software domain. According to Bani Ali, in the TPTF model, "computer self-efficacy is extended by examining how computer skills might empower individuals to handle more complex tasks and motivate them to use more sophisticated systems or more advanced features for the same system. The TTF model is extended by examining how the interactions among systems, tasks and skills might affect system utilization and individual performance" (Bani Ali, 2004, p. 20). Bani Ali's work on project management software is extended in the present study to the realm of OSN applications.

Research Propositions

This study examines the direct relationships between CSE, task and systems characteristics and performance and utilization. Then, the concepts of fit as moderation and fit as gestalts are examined. Propositions for the direct relationships include:

P1: CSE is positively related to individual OSN utilization.

P2: CSE is positively related to individual performance in OSN systems.

The first two propositions address the expectation that a high level of CSE leads to higher performance and increased use of OSN systems. Propositions 3 and 4 address whether High levels of CSE relate to use of more complex tasks and more complex systems.

P3: CSE is positively related to task characteristics.

P4: CSE is positively related to system characteristics.

The following propositions address the concept of fit and its effect on performance and utilization of OSN systems.

P5: Task characteristics and CSE cooperatively impact performance and utilization of OSN systems.

P6: System characteristics and CSE cooperatively impact performance and utilization of OSN systems.

P7: The congruence of CSE, task and system characteristics is related to performance and utilization of OSN systems.

Propositions 5 and 6 address whether task or system characteristics moderate the relationship between CSE and performance or utilization of OSN systems. Proposition 7 addresses whether a holistic view of the internal congruence of CSE, task and system characteristics leads to an enhanced understanding of factors increasing performance or utilization. These propositions are summarized in Figure 1.

Methodology and Sample

A survey of college students was conducted using an online survey tool. There were a total of 262 participants consisting of graduate and undergraduate students from DC metro area colleges. Eighty-four percent of participants fully completed the survey. To achieve conceptual clarity, constructs, variables and operationaliza-

Figure 1. High level research model

Factor	Relationship	Dependent Variable	Proposed Relationship
CSE	Direct	Performance	Positive
CSE	Direct	Use	Positive
CSE	Direct	Task Characteristics	Positive
CSE	Direct	System Characteristics	Positive
CSE	Moderated by Task Characteristics	Performance	Positive
CSE	Moderated by System Characteristics	Performance	Positive
CSE	Moderated by Task Characteristics	Use	Positive
CSE	Moderated by System Characteristics	Use	Positive
CSE	"Fit" among Task and System Characteristics	Performance	Positive
CSE	"Fit" among Task and System Characteristics	Use	Positive

tion were carefully defined at the theoretical level. The measurement items contained in the survey instrument for the most part had not been previously used. They were either new, modified from previous studies and instruments, or were not been used in the same context as the current work. Consequently, the items underwent an instrument validation process to make certain of their construct validity and reliability.

The validation process involved review of the instrument by subject matter experts to ensure face and content validity, readability testing and statistical validity and reliability testing for discriminant validity and consistency. Reliability in test-retest was not considered, as it was anticipated that participants would only be administered the instrument once. Measurement domains were verified by subjecting responses to a principle components factor analysis with varimax rotation. The factor analysis and internal consistency checks were performed to verify construct validity and scale reliability. In conducting the factor analysis, all α values were found to be over the 0.70 threshold selected for the study.

Once the constructs were validated and simplified via the factor analysis, three separate analyses were conducted to determine direct relationships, and the effects of fit as moderation, and gestalt effects of fit. Direct relationships were tested using a simple regression analysis. The moderation effects of fit were tested using multiple regression analysis, and the gestalt effects of fit were tested using a cluster analysis.

Factor Analysis

A factor analysis was conducted to examine the internal consistency and reliability of constructs. Reliability analysis of measurement items proposed to measure the performance impact of OSN software yielded 3 factors with eigen values greater than one, with a resulting high $\alpha = 0.930$, well above the .070 level selected for the study. Factor loadings are all above the 0.50 threshold, and the

loading of the items is dispersed between the three factors. The first factor explains 28 percent of the variance, the second explains 25 percent and the third explains 20 percent, each well above the 5 percent minimum for retention, and explaining 73 percent of the total variance. Chronbach Alpha statistics were computed for each factor to assess scale reliability, and each coefficient is well over the minimum of 0.70, exhibiting high values of 0.909, 0.901 and 0.826, respectively, indicating an adequate level of internal consistency. All of the factors are retained, and OSN performance was therefore represented by 3 factors consisting of 15 items.

Factor analysis of items designed to measure use yielded 3 factors with eigenvalues greater than 1. The loadings were all above the .050 threshold established for the study, and the loading of the items is dispersed between the three factors, explaining 63 percent of the total variance. The first factor explains 25 percent of the variance, the second explains 23 percent and the third explains 15 percent, each well above the 5 percent minimum for retention. Chronbach Alpha statistics were computed for each factor to assess scale reliability, and each coefficient is over the minimum of 0.70, at 0.907, 0.886 and 0.722, respectively, indicating an adequate level of internal consistency. All of the factors were retained; OSN use was represented by 3 factors consisting of 19 items.

Reliability analysis of the 10 items proposed to measure task characteristics yielded 2 factors with eigen values greater than one. Factor loadings were all above the 0.50 threshold, and loading of the items was dispersed between the 2 factors, explaining 60 percent of the total variance. The first factor explained 33 percent of the variance and the second explained 27 percent, each well above the 5 percent minimum. Chronbach Alpha statistics were computed for each factor to assess scale reliability, and each coefficient was over the minimum of 0.70, at 0.841 and 0.777, respectively, indicating an adequate level of internal consistency. All factors were retained, and OSN

Task Characteristics was represented by 2 factors consisting of 10 items.

Reliability analysis of the 30 items initially proposed to measure CSE resulted in a high α = 0.961, well above the 0.070 threshold. There was no significant increase in Chronbach Alpha if any items were deleted, so all were retained. Factor analysis yields 4 factors with eigen values greater than one. Factor loadings were all above the 0.50 threshold, and loading of the items was roughly dispersed between the factors. The first factor explains 26 percent of the variance, the second explains 18 percent, the third also explains 18 percent, and the fourth explains 14 percent, each well above the 5 percent minimum for retention, and contributing to the cumulative 77 percent of variance explained. Chronbach Alpha statistics were computed for each factor to assess scale reliability, and each coefficient was well over the minimum of 0.70, exhibiting high values of 0.969, 0.948, 0.973 and 0.892, respectively, indicating an adequate level of internal consistency. All of the factors were retained, and OSN performance was represented by 4 factors consisting of 30 items.

Reliability analysis of the 11 items proposed to measure CSE yielded one factor with eigen value greater than one, explaining 67 percent of the variance, above the minimum 60 percent total and 5 percent per factor required for retention. Factor loadings were all above the 0.50 threshold. Chronbach Alpha statistics indicated an adequate level of internal consistency. The factor was re-

tained, and OSN CSE was represented by 1 factor consisting of 11 items.

Figure 2 summarizes the factors, percent of variance explained, and compares the rotated factors with Bani Ali's (2004) factor analysis.

Previous research [prior to Bani Ali's (2004) application of the TPTF model to the project management domain] noted that CSE loaded on one factor in the factor analysis. Bani Ali (2004) found in his study on project management software, that there were two CSE factors that loaded during his factor analysis, which he labeled "CSE with support" and "CSE without support." CSE loads on one factor in the present work, as in research previous to Bani Ali. This is explained by the fact that there is little or no live technical support for typical OSN applications. In the project management domain examined by Bani Ali, end users typically have extensive technical support available. That Bani Ali's results differ from the present work as well as previous research underscores the uniqueness and complexity of the project management domain. Although this does not affect the significance of the CSE construct in either study, it demonstrates the differences between domains, and that there may be differences in the effects of CSE among supported and unsupported applications.

Regarding the software characteristics construct, Bani Ali found in his 2004 study that previous research demonstrated items loading one factor for software integration, i.e. how well the

Figure 2. Factor analysis summary and comparison with Bani Ali (2004)

Construct	Factors	% Variance Explained	Bani Ali (2004) Factors
Performance	3	73.65	3
Use	3	67.42	3
Task Characteristics	2	72.70	2
System Characteristics	4	87.57	5
CSE	1	73.86	2

software works with other hardware and software. In his study, however, items load on two factors which he terms internal and external integration. Internal integration measures how the software works with other applications on the user's computer. External integration is a measure of how well the software works with other computers and Internet applications. The integration items load on one in the current work.

ANALYSIS

Direct Relationships

The first tests conducted were simple regression analyses to determine whether direct relationships existed between CSE and performance, and CSE and use; and between CSE, task and system characteristics. It was found that there were strong, positive and direct relationships between CSE and performance (β=.574, ρ=.003, R^2=.330) and CSE and use (β =.503, ρ=.012, R^2=.253). Positive direct relationships between CSE and task characteristics (β=.407, ρ=.048, R^2=.166) and CSE and system characteristics (β=.426, ρ=.038, R^2=.181) were also found. In terms of the research propositions, the results show that all were supported, as depicted in Figure 3.

Effects of Fit as Moderation

Moderation effects were investigated to determine whether the effects of CSE on performance or use

were moderated by a third variable, either task or system characteristics. Nine multiple regression analyses were conducted to evaluate whether task characteristics moderated the relationship between CSE and performance. The predictor factors were the 3 derived task characteristics factors and CSE, and the criterion variables were the three performance factors also derived through factor analysis. There was a significant relationship between the first criterion variable and the entire set of predictor variables, $\square$ = 5.201 to 6.336, ρ = 0.007 to 0.015. The sample multiple correlation coefficients are from 0.576 to 0.613. From 33 to 38 percent of the variance of the performance in the sample could be accounted for by CSE and task characteristics. Both variables are important for better predictive modeling. The second and third performance factors could not be demonstrated to have a relationship with the predictor factors. However, it should be noted that the first criterion factor explains more of the variance in the factor analysis than any of the other components.

Another set of multiple regression analyses were conducted to evaluate whether task characteristics moderates the relationship between CSE and use. The predictor variables were the three derived task characteristics factors and CSE, and the criterion variable was use. There was a significant linear relationship between the criterion variable and the second predictor variable and CSE, $\square$ = 3.942, ρ = 0.035. The sample multiple correlation coefficient was 0.522, indicating a strong correlation. About 27% of the variance of

Figure 3. Summary of direct relationships

Research Proposition (Generalized)	Result
P1: CSE is positively related to individual OSN utilization.	Supported
P2: CSE is positively related to individual performance in OSN systems.	Supported
P3: CSE is positively related to task characteristics.	Supported
P4: CSE is positively related to system characteristics.	Supported

the performance in the sample could be accounted for by this relationship.

Fifteen multiple regression analyses were conducted to evaluate whether system characteristics moderated the relationship between CSE and performance. The predictor factors were the 5 factor analysis derived systems characteristics factors and CSE, and the criterion variables were the three derived performance factors. There was a significant relationship between the first criterion variable and the entire set of predictor variables, $\square = 5.205$ to 5.322, $\rho = 0.013$ to 0.015. The sample multiple correlation coefficients ranged from 0.576 to 0.613, indicating a strong correlation. From 33 to 34 percent of the variance of the performance in the sample could be accounted for by CSE and system characteristics. There was also a significant relationship between the third criterion variable and the third predictor variable and CSE, $\square = 3.500$, $\rho = 0.049$. The sample multiple correlation coefficient was 0.500, again indicating a strong correlation. About 25% of the variance of the performance in the sample could be accounted for by this relationship. Based on the analysis, there is a moderating influence of system characteristics on CSE regarding both performance and use.

Both task and system characteristics have a moderating effect on CSE with regard to performance and use. A summary of supported interactions is provided in Figure 4.

Effects of Fit as Gestalts

A cluster analysis was used to provide insight into fit propositions (P5, P6 and P7) using cluster analysis instead of the fit as moderation/interaction analysis used in the previous section. The analysis verifies the moderating perspective of fit (Propositions 5 and 6) independently of the previously conducted interaction analysis, and investigates whether congruence of the clustering dimensions affects performance and use. The sample was divided into subgroups (clusters) using CSE, task characteristics and software characteristics as clustering dimensions. An analysis of variance was then used to determine the relationship of the clusters to the dependent variables, performance or use.

The selection of variables was based on the research propositions; to test P5, all possible combinations of CSE and task characteristics were tested. Fourteen possible dimensions were examined, which yielded six clusters. Eighty-four combinations of clusters and dependent variables were examined, which yielded 19 clusters having significant relationships with performance and system utilization, $\square = 3.184$ to 16.414, $\rho < 0.001$ to 0.044. The critical F-Value F $(2,160) = 3.06$. This analysis provides support for Proposition 5, with relationships between each aspect of the cluster and the dependent variables. Although each individual variable was not shown to have a relationship, there are significant relationships addressing all clustering dimensions and all dependent measures.

Figure 4. Summary of effects of fit as moderation

Research Proposition	Number of Supported Interactions
P5: Task characteristics and CSE cooperatively impact performance and utilization of OSN systems.	5
P6: System characteristics and CSE cooperatively impact performance and utilization of OSN systems.	17

Additional cluster analyses were conducted to determine whether CSE moderates the effects of system characteristics on performance and use. The selection of variables was again based on the research propositions, to test P6, all possible combinations of CSE and system characteristics were tested. Twenty-eight possible dimensions were examined, which yielded 13 clusters. Ninety-one combinations of clusters and dependent variables were found, of which 49 had significant relationships with performance and system utilization, $\square$ = 3.045 to 7.557, ρ < 0.001 to 0.049. The critical F-Value F (2,160) = 3.06. This analysis provides support for Proposition 6, with relationships between each aspect of the cluster and the dependent variables. Although each individual variable was not shown to have a relationship, there are significant relationships addressing all clustering dimensions and all dependent measures (Figure 5).

Finally, cluster analyses were conducted to determine whether the congruence of CSE, task and systems characteristics were related to performance and use. The selection of variables was based on the research propositions, to test P7, all possible combinations of CSE, task and system characteristics were tested. Eight possible dimensions were examined, which yielded 28 clusters. There were 46 cluster analysis results showing significant, homogeneous and well-defined clusters. The cluster analysis provides support for Proposition 7 and the gestalt perspective of fit, with relationships between each aspect of the cluster and the dependent variables. Although each individual variable was not shown to have a relationship, there are significant relationships addressing all clustering dimensions and all de-

pendent measures. Examination of dimension means plots shows nicely the differences between clusters in all cases. The *F* values and significance are reasonable even when not considering the exploratory nature of the cluster analysis method.

The analysis shows that congruence between CSE and task characteristics and CSE and software characteristics has a significant influence on performance and use. The analysis also supports the effects of congruence between CSE, software characteristics and analyzability as measured by performance and use, and the effects of CSE, software characteristics and equivocality, with performance and use as dependent variables. Support is found for congruence between CSE, software characteristics and task complexity having an effect on performance or use (Figure 6).

DISCUSSION OF RESULTS

The results of this study demonstrate that direct and fit relationships between task and technology characteristics and computer self efficacy have a significant impact on end-user performance and OSN system use. The authors proposed that individual performance and OSN system use would increase in the presence of increased fit between CSE, task and OSN system characteristics. This premise was investigated first by examining the direct effects of CSE task and OSN system characteristics as predictor variables on the criterion variables performance and use, then by examining fits of the factors on performance and use using moderation and gestalts perspectives of fit. The

Figure 5. Summary of cluster analyses

Factors	Dependent Variables	Number of Significant Clusters
CSE, Task Characteristics, System Characteristics	Performance, Use	46

results of the study provide support for both direct and fit effects of CSE on performance and use.

Four direct tests of the effects of CSE on performance and use were conducted, and all were supported. OSN users with high CSE perform better than those with lower CSE, and it was established that they use their OSN systems more. Users with high CSE engage in more complex tasks and use more sophisticated OSN systems than users with low CSE. Better fit between CSE, task and OSN system characteristics yields increased individual performance and increased usage. CSE is moderated by OSN system characteristics as measured by usage. Finally, when CSE, task and OSN system characteristics are congruent, performance and use are both increased.

When the direct effects of CSE were tested, results show that CSE is positively related to individual performance. CSE is positively related to task and OSN system characteristics. Users with high levels of CSE engage in more complex tasks and use more sophisticated OSN systems. Consistent with Bani Ali's (2004) findings, CSE is found to be positively related to task characteristics. Users with high levels of CSE involve themselves in tasks that require a high level of complexity. There is also a significant relationship with ease of use. An implication of this is that users who have higher CSE involve themselves with using and understanding OSN systems that are more complex, perform better and use the OSN systems more extensively, leading them to find that the OSN systems are easy to use.

In testing for the interactions task characteristics and CSE on individual performance, it was found that task characteristics has significant moderating effects on CSE with regard to performance and use. The interaction of OSN system characteristics has a moderating effect on CSE and the relationship between CSE and performance and use.

The analysis shows that congruence between CSE and task or software characteristics has a significant influence on performance and use. The analysis also supports the effects of congruence between CSE, software characteristics and task characteristics as measured by performance and use, and the effects of CSE, software characteristics and task characteristics, with performance and use as dependent variables. Support is found for congruence between CSE, software characteristics and task characteristics having an effect on performance and use. There are many combinations of CSE, software characteristics and task complexity that have significant effects on performance.

Figure 6. Summary of research propositions

Research Proposition	Result
P1: CSE is positively related to individual OSN utilization.	Supported
P2: CSE is positively related to individual performance in OSN systems.	Supported
P3: CSE is positively related to task characteristics.	Supported
P4: CSE is positively related to system characteristics.	Supported
P5: Task characteristics and CSE cooperatively impact performance and utilization of OSN systems.	Supported
P6: System characteristics and CSE cooperatively impact performance and utilization of OSN systems.	Supported
P7: The congruence of CSE, task and system characteristics is related to performance and utilization of OSN systems.	Supported
CSE is positively related to social support	Supported

Comparison with Previous Research

Figure 7 shows a comparison of the results of this study and Bani Ali's (2004) study in terms of generalized propositions. It can be seen that there is little difference between the studies in terms of proposition support. There are, however, significant differences in the way variables rotated into factors, as previously discussed. It is also interesting to note that the results from this study were substantially similar to research prior to Bani Ali, while the results from Bani Ali's project management domain varied. These results support Bani Ali's contention that the project management domain is complex and unique.

IMPLICATIONS

This study finds that there is a direct relationship between CSE and use and CSE and performance. The implication of this positive effect of CSE in the current work is that Bandura's model of self-efficacy holds true for the user characteristics construct in the OSN domain. The self-efficacy construct, the concept that level of belief in an individual's ability to complete a task has a significant effect on ultimate success, is widely accepted in the social domain, but has been little researched in the information systems domain. The self-efficacy concept suggests that users

with high self-efficacy are more likely to attempt complex tasks, and these tasks will seem simpler and easier to them. The validation of this concept in the OSN domain is significant in developing an understanding of what motivates OSN users to adopt and use these systems. However, there is not a good understanding of what moves specific groups of individuals to adopt and use one particular system. In other words, we have developed a better grasp of what users do, but not of the initiating forces or motivation.

This work also extends the Task-Person-Technology-Fit (TPTF) model synthesized by Bani Ali (2004), whose work on project management software is extended in the present study to the realm of OSN applications and voluntary use systems. The findings imply that the model is applicable and appropriate for OSN systems, and for use in developing models measuring use and performance in OSN and other voluntary use systems. This is significant because it interjects a person, or user, construct into the fit model to understand information system performance and use. Previous fit research relied largely on task and technology fitments.

The extension of the TPTF theory into the realm of voluntary use systems is significant, because an emerging picture tells us that there are very different dynamics in user behavior between user behaviors in voluntary versus non-voluntary use systems. Additional research must be conducted

Figure 7. Proposition comparison with Bani Ali (2004)

Research Proposition (Generalized)	Result	Bani Ali (2004)
P1: CSE is positively related to individual utilization.	Supported	Supported
P2: CSE is positively related to individual performance.	Supported	Supported
P3: CSE is positively related to task characteristics.	Supported	Moderately Supported
P4: CSE is positively related to system characteristics.	Supported	Supported
P5: Task characteristics and CSE cooperatively impact performance and utilization.	Supported	Supported
P6: System characteristics and CSE cooperatively impact performance and utilization.	Supported	Supported
P7: The congruence of CSE, task and system characteristics is related to performance and utilization.	Supported	Supported

to begin to understand the differences between the two scenarios. The authors suggest there are two components to achieving this understanding. First, the implication of the extension into OSN and voluntary use systems is that this model may be considered for use when developing, managing, researching and using these systems types (voluntary usage). Based on the findings herein, successful developers must take user characteristics, in the form of CSE, into consideration as they build systems. The strength of the relationships between use, performance and CSE indicate that developers and managers of such systems can adapt this model to measure use and performance. Researchers can use the CSE construct in developing assessments and perhaps predictions of the strength of future performance and use models for OSN and voluntary use systems.

The second issue is what domain is being addressed by the OSN system? The empirical evidence clearly indicates that many systems have been initiated, served some purpose (for users) in a domain, and in some cases been successful, while in others floundered or disappeared. This has happened with curious rapidity. Explaining user initial appeal and enthusiasm;" why" this OSN was successful, and not that similar one is of great interest to marketers, mangers (who may seek to employ this new technology in a organizational setting), users (who will not want to miss out in the networked world), and researchers seeking to simply understand the behavior. One suggestive, but as yet un-assessed theory argues that the network effects of efficiency and effectiveness may play a role both in the creation of new OSNs and their apparent rapid adoption growth. Simply stated, structural holes exist between two (or more) networks where individuals (nodes) in two or more different networks do not share redundant relationships, but may in fact have information that would be of value to the members of the networks (if the networks were to be strongly connected). The theory postulates that it would be inefficient for the networks to continue to grow beyond

some point because the members of a network will share extensive redundant information and become inefficient. To deal with his efficiency problem, a network may obtain value from a non redundant contact between two contacts, one from each network. (Burt, 1992) A simple example of the inefficiency was described as a partial factor in the demise of Friendster in 2003. The Friendster system's engineering success eventually became a problem. The system's network "…calculated a single user's connection to other users within four degrees of separation, which could mean hundreds of thousands of individuals" (Chafkin, 2007) every time a page loaded. A new user required that new calculations be completed (creating performance problems), and gave "… users a vivid sense of how they fit into their social groups as well as into the larger world." (Chafkin, 2007)

Burt's Structural Holes theory argues that individuals observe advantages in an "opportunity" when they control the information and benefits as a gatekeeper of a structural hole (for one of the networks). The strategist who sees this entrepreneurial opportunity will withdraw, expand, or embed the new information within the present network boundaries. The authors postulate that a further option in the OSN environment is for the strategist (user or entrepreneur) to develop a new network around the new information domain (content, task, interest, etc.). This leads to the observed and ongoing potential for the expansion of OSN systems (with somewhat similar features and functions as limited by legal mechanisms) in some domains, and the creation of new networks that users may join in other differentiated domains. While Bani Ali (2004) examined the largely mandatory use of project management systems in a relatively functionally constrained project management domain, the present work investigates the completely voluntary use of many OSN systems, and performance measurement issues in non-mandatory systems across domains. In voluntary use systems, utilization is a strong predictor of performance. Applications are used based on their merits, rather than by mandate. The current work examines interactions between CSE, task and OSN system characteristics and their effects on performance and utilization, both individually and holistically. The significance of this approach is evidenced by the difference in results achieved by this study versus Bani Ali (2004). The results of this study are more closely aligned with research published previous to Bani Ali. The inference is that there are differences between mandatory and voluntary use systems which have been captured by the current study. The current work validates that there is a strong relationship between CSE and performance, and that utilization is a strong predictor of performance in voluntary use systems.

This study finds that CSE is positively related to both task and systems characteristics. This implies that users with higher levels of CSE will use more complex OSN systems to perform more difficult tasks, a significant implication of itself, and adding further support to extension of the TPTF theory to the OSN domain. This finding supports Bandura's assertions regarding the effects of CSE. Developers and managers of OSN systems can leverage the CSE factor of users to ensure that systems are geared towards enabling users to perform complex and difficult tasks. Researchers can incorporate the CSE factor to better model future systems.

An implication of the results is that OSN developers must understand the effects of CSE fit and its effect on individual performance and use. To develop OSN systems where members perform well and exhibit high OSN system use, the relationships between CSE, task and OSN system characteristics must be considered during development. The better the fit between these factors, the more likely users will perform well and use the OSN systems. The congruence of these dimensions should also be considered.

OSN providers must also consider steps they may take to increase the CSE of users. Online, virtual or real training courses, improved manuals, help applications and similar items may help to

increase user CSE, which in turn leads to increased performance and use. If users are knowledgeable and confident in abilities to use the applications, they will perform better and use the OSN systems more. Measures to increase social support among users may also increase CSE, performance and use.

This study finds that system characteristics and CSE cooperatively impact performance and utilization of OSN systems, and that the congruence of CSE, task and system characteristics is related to performance and utilization of OSN systems. The implication is that combinations of CSE, task and system characteristics do two things: 1) they moderate the effects of each other with regards to performance and use, and 2) they affect each other in previously unknown ways, as measured by performance and use. There are non-linear combinations of CSE, task and system characteristics that synergistically affect performance and use. OSN system developers and managers can use this knowledge to investigate and find serendipitous combinations of CSE, task and system characteristics that maximize individual performance and use.

For developers and academics, all tenets of the study provide additional options for measuring IS effectiveness, performance and use. Measures of IS effectiveness are becoming increasingly important as OSN systems become more sophisticated, and user expectations increase. The current work adds a user characteristics construct to OSN and IS performance measurement. IS effectiveness can be measured by using the performance and use constructs in this study.

The authors pondered three questions at the start of this research: 1. does user computer self-efficacy affect end users' adoption and use of OSN systems, 2. how does the interplay of user, task and system characteristics affect utilization and end user performance?, and 3. what factors affect the ability or desire of users to use more complex systems and perform more complex tasks? The short answer is that the rapid changes in use and acceptance of OSN systems by millions of users are at least partially related to end user characteristics in the form of CSE. User, task and system characteristics directly affect utilization and end user performance. Task and system characteristics moderate the effects of CSE on performance and use. Finally, certain "fits" among user, task and systems characteristics have a synergistic effect yielding high performance and use. In general, users with higher CSE tend to use more complex systems and perform more complex tasks. It is not surprising that this study found that relationships existed between CSE and performance and use. However, the authors were certainly surprised by the strength and extent of the relationships. The fact that a significant relationship was found to exist for each research proposition portends that it may be possible to build an instrument to predict performance and use based on CSE. It is obvious that user characteristics play a large role in individual performance and use of OSN systems. It is anticipated that future research will yield more detailed models incorporating user characteristics to better explain why end users adopt and use OSN systems.

The authors believe that this work adds to the body of knowledge in several ways: 1) it extends Bandura's self-efficacy construct to the OSN voluntary use domain, 2) it extends Bani Ali's TPTF model to the OSN voluntary use domain, 3) it adds a new user characteristics construct to OSN and IS performance measurement, and 4) it relates CSE to both task and systems characteristics. The work provides significant insight for both developers and academicians in helping refine models of performance and usage of online systems. Finally, the work suggests that there are still some important unexplored questions regarding the proliferation of OSNs. Specifically, what is it that has prompted so many of the OSNs to be rapidly developed? The authors suggest that additional theories of networks and social structure will be important in furthering our understanding of this complex question. At present we are developing a more robust picture of the

motivation for usage, but researchers may need to expand the theoretical domains of networking to develop a more complete picture of the overall OSN phenomena.

REFERENCES

Ajzen, I. (1991). The Theory of Planned Behavior. *Organizational Behavior and Human Decision Processes*, *50*, 179–211. doi:10.1016/0749-5978(91)90020-T

Ajzen, I., & Fishbein, M. (1977). Attitude-Behavior Relations: A Theoretical Analysis and Review of Empirical Research. *Psychological Bulletin*, *84*(5), 888–918. doi:10.1037/0033-2909.84.5.888

Ajzen, I., & Fishbein, M. (1980). *Understanding attitudes and predicting social behavior*. Englewood Cliffs, NJ: Prentice-Hall.

Al-Gahtani, S. S., & King, M. (1999). Attitudes, satisfaction and usage: factors contributing to each in the acceptance of information technology. *Behaviour & Information Technology*, *18*(4), 277–297. doi:10.1080/014492999119020

Armitage, C. J., & Conner, M. (2001). Efficacy of the Theory of Planned Behaviour: A meta-analytic review. *The British Journal of Social Psychology*, *40*, 471–499. doi:10.1348/014466601164939

Auchard, E. (2006, August 22). *Friendster looks to recover lost glory*. Retrieved August 22, 2006, from http://news.yahoo.com/s/nm/20060822/tc_nm/friendster_dc_4&printer=1

Bani Ali, A. (2004). *Project Management Software Effectiveness Study*. Unpublished doctoral dissertation, George Washington University, Washington, DC.

Budd, R. J. (1986). Predicting cigarette use: The need to incorporate measures of salience in the theory of reasoned action. *Journal of Applied Social Psychology*, *16*, 663–685. doi:10.1111/j.1559-1816.1986.tb01752.x

Burt, R. S. (1992). *Structural Holes.* Cambridge, MA: Harvard University Press.

Chafkin, M. (2007, June 1). How to kill a-Great idea! *Inc.com,* Retrieved March 2, 2010, from http://www.inc.com/magazine/20070601/features-how-tokill-a-great-idea.html

Compeau, D. R., & Higgins, C. A. (1995, June). Computer self-efficacy: Development of a measure and initial test. *Management Information Systems Quarterly, 19*(2), 189–211. doi:10.2307/249688

Davis, F. D. (1986). *A Technology Acceptance Model for Empirically Testing New End-User Information: Theory and Results, Doctoral Dissertation.* Unpublished doctoral dissertation, MIT Sloan School of Management, Cambridge, MA.

Davis, F. D. (1989). Perceived Usefulness, Perceived Ease of Use, and User Acceptance of Information Technology. *Management Information Systems Quarterly, 13*(3), 319–340. doi:10.2307/249008

Dishaw, M. T., & Strong, D. M. (1999). Extending the technology acceptance model with task-technology fit constructs. *Information & Management, 36*(1), 9–21. doi:10.1016/S0378-7206(98)00101-3

Dishaw, M. T., Strong, D. M., & Bandy, D. B. (2002, August 9-12). Extending the Task-Technology Fit Model with Self-Efficacy Constructs. In *Proceedings of the Eighth Americas Conference on Information Systems,* Dallas, TX.

Goodhue, D. L. (1995, December). Understanding User Evaluations of Information Systems. *Management Science, 41*(12), 1827–1844. doi:10.1287/mnsc.41.12.1827

Goodhue, D. L. (1998). Development and measurement validity of a task-technology fit instrument for user evaluations of information systems. *Decision Sciences, 29*(1), 105–138. doi:10.1111/j.1540-5915.1998.tb01346.x

Goodhue, D. L., & Thompson, T. L. (1995, June). Task-technology fit and individual performance. *Management Information Systems Quarterly, 19*(2), 213–236. doi:10.2307/249689

Kopytoff, V. (2004, February 9). Clicking for Connections. *San Francisco Chronicle,* E-1. Retrieved October 13, 2004, from http://sfgate.com/cgi-bin/article.cgi?file=/c/a/2004/02/09/BUGMD4RAMALDTL

Leonard, A. (2004, June 15). You are who you know. *Salon.com Technology.* Retrieved October 13, 2004, from http://www.salon.com/tech/feature/2004/06/15/social_soctware_one/

Lin, C., Hu, P. J., & Chen, H. (2004). Technology Implementation Management in Law Enforcement. *Social Science Computer Review, 22*(1), 24–36. doi:10.1177/0894439303259881

Malhotra, Y., & Galletta, D. F. (1999, January 4-7). Extending the Technology Acceptance Model to Account for Social Influence: Theoretical Bases and Empirical Validation. In *Proceedings of the 32nd Hawaii International Conference on System Sciences (HICSS-32).* Washington, DC: IEEE Computer Society.

McCarthy, C. (2009, February 10). Whee! New numbers on social network usage. *CNET News, The Social.* Retrieved February 25, 2009, from http://news.cnet.com/8301-13577_3-10160850-36.html

Newman, A. C., & Thomas, J. G. (2009). *Enterprise 2.0 Implementation.* New York: McGraw-Hill.

Prestholdt, P. H., Lane, I. M., & Mathews, R. C. (1987). Nurse turnover as reasoned action: Development of a process model. *The Journal of Applied Psychology, 72,* 221–227. doi:10.1037/0021-9010.72.2.221

Rosenheck, D. (2003, August 4). Will you be my Friendster? *New Statesman*. Retrieved October 13, 2004, from http://www.newstatesman.com/200308040005

Sheppard, B. H., Hardwick, J., & Warshaw, P. R. (1988, December). The Theory of Reasoned Action: A Meta-Analysis of Past Research with Recommendations for Modifications and Future Research. *The Journal of Consumer Research*, *15*(3), 325–343. doi:10.1086/209170

Solis, B. (2009, January 19). Social Networks Grow Up: More Adults Connecting Online. *PR 2.0*. Retrieved March 4, 2009, from http://www.briansolis.com/2009/01/social-networks-grow-up-more-adults.html/

Venkatesh, V., Morris, M. G., Davis, G. B., & Davis, F. D. (2003, September). User Acceptance of Information Technology: Toward a Unified View. *Management Information Systems Quarterly*, *27*(3), 325–478.

Wikipedia. (2006a). *Theory of reasoned action*. Retrieved October 25, 2006, from http://en.wikipedia.org/wiki/Theory_of_reasoned_action

Wikipedia. (2006b). *Friendster*. Retrieved October 25, 2006, from http://en.wikipedia.org/wiki/Friendster

Wildbit. (2005). *Social Networks Research Report*. Retrieved February 8, 2006, from http://tidbit.wildbit.com

Wixom, B. H., & Todd, P. A. (2005, March). A Theoretical Integration of User Satisfaction and Technology Acceptance. *Information Systems Research*, *16*(1), 85–102. doi:10.1287/isre.1050.0042

Zigurs, I., & Buckland, B. K. (1998, September). A Theory of Task/Technology Fit and Group Support Systems Effectiveness. *Management Information Systems Quarterly*, *22*(3), 313–334. doi:10.2307/249668

This work was previously published in the International Journal of Virtual Communities and Social Networking, Volume 2, Issue 1, edited by Subhasish Dasgupta, pp. 18-34, copyright 2010 by IGI Publishing(an imprint of IGI Global).

Chapter 3

Team Identification, Team Performance and Leader–Member Exchange Relationships in Virtual Groups:
Findings from Massive Multi–Player Online Role Play Games

Daniel M. Eveleth
University of Idaho, USA

Alex B. Eveleth
Western Washington University, USA

ABSTRACT

While previous research has identified group identification as an important factor in affecting relevant outcomes (e.g., satisfaction, turnover, commitment) in face-to face environments, this paper provides initial evidence to support the proposition that group identification also matters in virtual environments. In particular, the authors found that team members' perceptions of the leader-member exchange relationship and the team's past performance are related to individuals' identification with the virtual team and that identification affects satisfaction and behavioral intentions. Individuals who perceive leader-member exchange as high (e.g., the leader displays a willingness to help the team member solve problems and the leader recognizes the member's potential) and who report that their teams perform well had stronger identification with the team. Individuals who reported strong identification with their team were more satisfied with the team and had greater intentions to perform positive behaviors in the future.

INTRODUCTION

As communication and collaboration technologies continue to evolve the number and variety of

DOI: 10.4018/978-1-4666-1553-3.ch003

geographically- and temporally-dispersed groups have also increased. Virtual teams, for example, have grown in popularity among organizations for such tasks as project management and problem solving (Kirkman, Rosen, Tesluk, & Gibson, 2004), and formal and informal communities of practice have capitalized on the functionality of telecommunication and information technologies to bring together individuals for the purposes of knowledge sharing and learning (e.g., Lesser & Storck, 2001). In addition, many computer-game developers have purposefully made virtual groups part of their games, requiring players to collaborate in 'guilds' in order to succeed in the games, and social networking sites such as Facebook most often serve as a virtual space where individuals can strengthen their relationships with individuals from their place-based community (Lampe, Ellison & Steinfield, 2006). The success or failure of these virtual groups in the variety of settings may be in large part a function of the extent to which individuals in the groups come to identify with the group. However, little is known about identification in virtual groups (Yu & Young, 2008).

Social identification has long been an important construct in the study of individual behavior in groups. First introduced by Tajfel (1982) and developed in collaboration with Turner (1982), Social Identity Theory suggests that individuals categorize themselves (and others) according to characteristics of groups to which they belong. For example, an individual may identify with a religious organization, an age group, a political party, or a work group. When individuals "define

themselves with attributes that overlap with the attributes they use to define the (group), they are strongly identified with the group" (Dutton, Dukerich, & Harquail, 1994, p. 256), and they will perform behaviors in support of the group (Ashforth & Mael, 1989; van Knippenberg & van Schie, 2000).

The goal of this study is to extend our understanding of the identification concept by looking at specific antecedents and consequences of group identification in a virtual environment. We propose and test a model of group identification in virtual teams that suggests that the team's past performance and an individual's relationship with his or her team leader impact the individual's identification with the group, and an individual's level of identification with the group will impact his or her intentions about future behavior and the individual's level of satisfaction with the group (see Figures 1 and 2).

Identification. Social Identity Theory states that individuals seek to define themselves within the context of a social environment (Ashforth & Mael, 1989; van Knippenberg & Schie, 2000; Mael & Tetrick, 1992), forming a self-concept that includes personal attributes (e.g., physical traits, interests, skills) and social attributes (e.g., the goals, values, processes of a specific group).

Figure 1. Proposed model

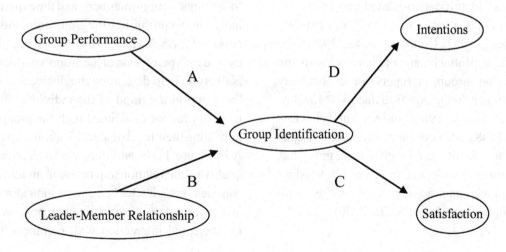

Figure 2. Revised model

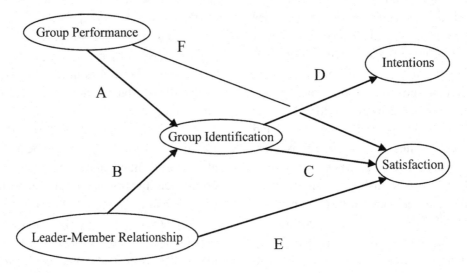

When the attributes of an individual's self-concept are consistent with the attributes of a social group the strength of the individual's identification with the group is high. Individuals who identify with a group are more likely to exhibit attitudes and behaviors consistent with and beneficial to the group (van Knippenberg & Schie, 2000). For example, the extent to which a consumer identifies with a company, brand, or product will affect such things as loyalty (Chaudhuri & Holbrook, 2001), positive word of mouth (Harrison-Walker, 2001), and intentions to purchase (Madrigal, 2001). Undesirable employee-oriented outcomes such as absenteeism and turnover are negatively related to an identification-related construct, i.e., commitment to a supervisor, group, or organization (Clegg, 1983; Cotton & Tuttle, 1986); the psychological attachment of employees to the organization, group, or supervisor is positively related to such things as job satisfaction (Mowday, Porter, & Steers, 1982), citizenship behaviors (Organ, 1988), and attendance (Mathieu & Zajac, 1990); and identification with a work group has been correlated with such things as job satisfaction, turnover intentions, and job involvement (van Knippenberg & van Schie, 2000).

The effort individuals give to social identification processes is thought to be driven by a need for a positive self-esteem and a desire to reduce uncertainty about how to behave or what to expect in a social environment (Hogg & Terry, 2000). Identifying with a group or set of groups helps improve an individual's self-esteem, and by reducing uncertainty an individual increases his or her level of confidence or self-efficacy about the performance of social-oriented tasks. Factors that affect individuals' tendencies to identify with specific groups over others include the distinctiveness of the group relative to other groups, the prestige of the group, the awareness or presence of 'outgroups' or non-members, and the experiences individuals gain through the group-formation process (Ashforth & Mael, 1989). We suspect that an individual's perception of the group's performance is likely to help determine the distinctiveness of the group in the mind of the individual and the level of prestige associated with the group, thus impacting their level of identification (See Arrow A in Figure 1). In addition, we suspect that the quality of the relationship between an individual and the team's leader is a strong indicator of the group formation or socialization process (e.g., interpersonal interaction with members, nature of group's goals, perceived similarity with others in the group), and therefore, a good predictor of group identification (see Arrow B in Figure 1). Further, we believe that individuals' levels of identification with a virtual group will impact their levels of satisfaction with the group (see Arrow C in Figure 1) and their intentions with respect to future behavior relevant to the group (see Arrow D in Figure 1).

Team performance and identification (Arrow A, Figure 1). While teams can be created to serve a variety of objectives, they are often used for knowledge-related tasks (e.g., problem solving). In such instances, team performance can be conceptualized along the lines of productivity (e.g., goal accomplishment) and with respect to learning (e.g., displaying a willingness to learn through taking risks, trying new things, and seeking feedback). As stated earlier, Ashforth and Mael (1989) suggested that two factors that impact an individual's level of identification with a group are the distinctiveness of the group and the prestige of the group. Team performance is a salient indicator of how unique one team is over another and is an easy measure of the status associated with identifying "with a winner" (Ashforth & Mael, 1989, p. 25). Thus, team performance should affect individuals' levels of identification with the team.

Leader-member relationship and identification (Arrow B, Figure 1). Previous research has considered the effects of leader-member relationships and individuals' perceptions of transactional/transformational leadership on a number of significant organization outcomes. For example, in a meta-analysis study Gerstner and Day (1997) found significant correlations between the leader-member relationship and job performance, satisfaction, commitment, turnover intentions, and other important organization outcomes. Recently, Epitropaki and Martin (2005) found that organization members' perceptions of transformational and transactional leadership (a concept related to leader-member exchange) affect identification with the organization.

Leader-member exchange relationships refer to a group member's perception of the relationship between the leader and the member. A high quality relationship is one where the individual rates his or her leader positively on such behaviors as the leader's willingness to help the individual solve problems and whether or not the leader recognizes the individual's potential. Phillips, Douthitt and Hyland (2001) found that the extent to which a leader exhibited consideration behaviors (e.g., showing concern and respect for followers) impacted individuals' levels of attachment to the team. This link between a leader's behavior and identification with the group is likely to be an example of one factor mentioned by Ashforth and Mael (1989) that strengthens an individual's level of group identification; specifically, the nature of the experiences an individual gains through the group formation or development process. A leader plays a central role in stating, clarifying and rewarding team goals and organizing and facilitating interaction patterns among team members during the team development process. While Social Identity Theory states that successful group development is not a necessary requirement for an individual to identify with a group, the process of group development, facilitated by the behaviors of the leader, likely "cue(s) the psychological grouping of individuals since they can be used as bases for categorization" (Ashforth & Mael, 1989, p. 25). Therefore, it is likely that the quality of the leader-member relationship affects individuals' tendencies to identify with a team or not.

Identification and satisfaction (Arrow C, Figure 1). Satisfaction with jobs, goods or services is a central construct in management and marketing research because of many links between satisfaction with a target (e.g., job) and meaningful organization outcomes. For example, customer satisfaction is often linked to firm profitability (e.g., Anderson, Fornell & Rust, 1997; Rust, Ambler, Carpenter, Kumar & Srivastava, 2004) and job satisfaction is often correlated with such things as intentions to stay, citizenship behaviors, and organization commitment. Previous studies of face-to-face and computer-mediated teams have identified team processes (Flanagin, Park, & Seibold, 2004) as significant predictors of an individual's satisfaction with the group. Chatman and Flynn (2001) found that team norms were correlated with satisfaction with the team; van Knippenberg and van Schie (2000) found that identification with a group was related to job satisfaction; and Kleinman, Palmon, and Lee (2003) found that the group's conflict style (e.g., collaboration) was related to satisfaction with a team's solution. Further, Chidambaram (1996) found that satisfaction with the group's output is related to team members' attitudes toward each other. Taken together, this evidence suggests that individuals who strongly identify with the team (thus, fulfilling a need for self-esteem and uncertainty reduction) will report higher levels of satisfaction with the team than will those who report lower levels of identification.

Identification and intentions (Arrow D, Figure 1). When individuals have some degree of volitional control over a behavior the individuals form specific intentions about the behavior, and these intentions are a good predictor of subsequent behavioral outcomes (Ajzen & Fishbein, 1980; Fishbein & Ajzen, 1975; Doran, Stone, Brief & George, 1991). In attitude literature the construct is often called "behavioral intention" (Ajzen & Fishbein, 1973). In the motivation literature it has been called personal goals (Locke & Latham, 1990; Earley & Lituchy, 1991), and it is closely related to goal commitment (Hollenbeck & Klein, 1987), and effort (Vroom, 1964; Porter & Lawler, 1968). Regardless of its label the construct is generally conceptualized as the consequence of cognitive judgments about one's expectancies and valences of the potential outcome associated with performing the behavior; one set of expectancies and valences comes from judgments about a normative group's views about the behavior (Jian & Jeffres, 2006). According to Ajzen and Fishbein (1973) prior to determining his or her intentions

an individual forms beliefs about whether a specific referent group or individual would think the individual should or should not perform the behavior. The individual would then combine this belief with his or her level of motivation to comply with the referent to form subjective norms about the behavior and then intentions about future behavior (Ajzen & Fishbein, 1980). When individuals identify with a specific group the group's beliefs are salient and the motivation to comply with the group is high (e.g., Jian & Jeffres, 2006; Shamir, 1990; Terry & Hogg, 1996). Thus, we suspect that in virtual teams, individuals who strongly identify with the team will report strong intentions to perform behaviors in support of or consistent with the well being of the group.

METHODS

Respondents and Setting

In 2005 Edward Castronova published a book (i.e., *Synthetic Worlds*) that looked at the economics behind "worlds" created in the online environment (Castronova, 2005). In particular, he focused much of his discussions on massive multi-player online role playing games (MMORPG), the setting for the study presented here. MMORPGs require individuals to select a role and a character, and then collaborate with others to accomplish tasks. A character (i.e., avatar) and the virtual world are persistent (i.e., the story and the events continue even if a specific player is not playing). By design the games require players to participate in cross-functional teams, perform specialized tasks, take on leader or follower roles, and exhibit many other 'real-world' traits and behaviors; albeit in the context of fighting dragons, retrieving treasure, and the like. This type of game design places a heavy reliance on the performance of virtual teams. For an individual to succeed in the game he or she must be able and willing to work in a team environment; and we can assume that to be satisfied with the game individuals must also be satisfied with the experiences they have in the virtual team, including their perceptions of the team-leader's behavior, motivation and ability.

Because this study was designed to investigate antecedents and consequences of an individual's identification to a virtual team the MMORPG setting seemed to be an excellent environment for exploring these relationships in a virtual environment. Participation on a team is necessary; teams are cross-functional; team leaders "hire" team members and manage the team processes toward the accomplishment of specific tasks and goals; and team members can "quit" the team and either join another team or quit the game if they are not satisfied. Recently, Castronova (2008) replicated a finding in a MMORPG setting that is common in face-to-face settings and then convincingly argued that empirical work in virtual worlds provide promise for understanding social science concepts and relationships. Given the strong similarity between team conditions in a MMORPG setting and other 'real-world' virtual-group settings, the environment seems to be an excellent place to investigate the antecedents and consequences of virtual-team identification.

Subjects for our study were recruited through messages posted on online discussion threads for three popular MMORPGs (World of Warcraft, Everquest, and Vanguard) over a two-week period. As part of a larger survey the questionnaire contained measures of identification with the team, leader-member-relationship ratings, team performance, satisfaction, and intentions. We received a total of 169 usable responses (i.e., individuals who reported playing follower roles rather than leader roles). Respondents ranged in age from 16 to 74 with a mean of 28 years; 42 percent of the respondents were female. With respect to education, 3.2 percent had some high school education; 7.1 percent received a high school diploma; 45.2 percent had some undergraduate education (i.e., 1 to 3 years). Undergraduate degrees were received

by 19.8 percent of respondents, and 15.8 percent had graduate-level training.

Measures

Group identification. The measure for identification to the team (also known as a 'guild' in the games) was adapted from items reported by Mael and Tetrick (1992). The four items (e.g., when I talk about the guild, I usually say "we" rather than "it" or "they.") were anchored by: (1) *strongly agree* and (7) *strongly disagree*. In previous studies the measure has exhibited internal consistency and concurrent validity (e.g., van Knippenberg & Schie, 2000).

Leader-member relationship. To assess the quality of the leader-member relationship (LMX) each respondent rated his or her leader on a set of items adapted from the LMX-7 scale (Graen & Uhl-Bien, 1995). The nine items (e.g., my guild leader is willing to use his or her authority to help me solve my specific problems, my guild leader recognizes the potential of my character.) were anchored by: (1) *rarely* and (5) *very often*; thus, a higher score indicates a high-quality relationship from the perspective of the respondent. The LMX-7 scale has been widely used in the past, exhibiting internal consistency and concurrent validity (e.g., Graen, Novak & Sommerkamp, 1982; Scadura & Schriesheim, 1994).

Team performance. The measure for team performance was adapted from descriptive terms used in a previous team-oriented study (Kirkman, Rosen, Tesluk, & Gibson, 2004) that utilized process improvement as an indicator of team performance. Because virtual teams are often relied upon for knowledge development and management, teams that exhibit process improvement (i.e., learning) behaviors are said to perform at the highest levels. In MMORPG settings teams must adapt and learn as tasks and goals increase in difficulty and challenge as the game progresses. The six items (e.g., my guild adapts and improves; my guild seeks feedback; my guild looks for novel or creative solutions) were anchored by: (1) *strongly agree* and (7) *strongly disagree*.

Intentions. The measure for intentions was adapted from the work of Fishbein and Ajzen (1975) and focused on the individual's intentions relevant to the game (i.e., future purchase behavior and word-of-mouth statements). The four items (i.e., In the future I intend to: say positive things about the game to others, do more business with the company who created the game, recommend this game to someone who asks for advice, encourage friends and family to play the game) were anchored by: (1) *strongly disagree* and (7) *strongly agree*.

Satisfaction with the team. The measure for satisfaction was adapted from the work of Edwin Locke (1969). The four items (i.e., my decision to join this guild was a wise one; I am always delighted with the guild; overall, I am satisfied with the guild; I think I did the right thing when I decided to join this guild) were anchored by: (1) *strongly agree* and (7) *strongly disagree*.

Control variables. Age, gender, game type (i.e., Everquest, World of Warcraft, and Vanguard), and tenure in the team were measured to serve as control variables in the regression analyses.

RESULTS

Prior to performing the analysis study variables were re-coded so that the sign of the variables were consistent (i.e., a higher number reflects stronger team identification, higher quality leader-member relationship, higher team performance, higher satisfaction, and positive intentions). Descriptive statistics, Pearson correlations, and reliability estimates for each variable are shown in Table 1. Measures of identification, team performance, leader-member relationship, satisfaction, and intentions were reliable (Cronbach's alpha equal to .90. 94, .93, .91 and .90, respectively). In addition, the correlations between team performance and team identification (r =.64), between LMX and team identification (r =.58), between team

identification and satisfaction (r =.69), and between team identification and intentions (r =.38) were positive and significant (p <.01), offering preliminary support for the relationships outlined in Figure 1 (i.e., A, B, C, D, respectively).

To analyze the model (one that includes mediated relationships) we followed a commonly accepted method (Baron & Kenny, 1986), a method that has also been used in a previous study that looked at satisfaction, leadership and attachment relationships in a face-to-face team environment (Phillips, Douthitt & Hyland, 2001). The method involves three steps: 1) Regress the mediator (i.e., identification) on the independent variables (i.e., LMX and team performance) to see that the independent variables' regression weights are statistically significant, 2) Regress the dependent variables (i.e., intentions and satisfaction) on the independent variables (i.e., LMX and team performance) to see that the independent variables' regression weights are statistically significant; and 3) Regress the dependent variables (i.e., intentions and satisfaction) on the mediator (i.e., identification) and the independent variables (i.e., LMX and team performance) to see that the mediator variable's regression weight is statistically significant while the regression weights for the independent variables are not. If this is the result then the mediator is said to completely mediate the relationship between the independent variables and the dependent variables. Otherwise, partial mediation is the case.

Identification. When identification was regressed on LMX and team performance (Step 1) the relationships between LMX and identification and between team performance and identification were statistically significant and positive (i.e., ß =.31, p <.001; ß =.44, p <.001, respectively) (see Table 2). Leader-member relationship ratings and team performance accounted for variance in identification with the team above and beyond age, gender, game, and tenure in the team. These results provide strong support for the relationships depicted by *Arrow A* and *Arrow B* in Figure 1.

Table 1. Correlations and descriptive statistics for study variables

	Variables	Mean	s.d.	1	2	3	4	5	6	7	8	9	10
1	Age	28.02	9.46										
2	Gender	.42	.50	-.24*									
3	Game Type 2	.43	.50	-.36**	.53**								
4	Game Type 3	0.06	.24	.02	-.06	-.22**							
5	Tenure	10.18	16.46	.18*	-.06	-.08	.21**						
6	Leader-Member Relationship	2.88	.77	-.18*	.10	.11	-.04	.20*	(.93)				
7	Team Performance	5.67	1.18	-.10	.04	.13	-.23**	.03	.61**	(.94)			
8	Team Identification	5.22	1.01	-.01	.00	.09	-.16*	.15	.58**	.64**	(.90)		
9	Satisfaction	5.75	1.16	-.10	.09	.12	-.24**	.06	.72**	.74**	.69**	(.91)	
10	Intentions	5.41	1.33	-.18*	.17*	.27**	-.07	-.20*	.20*	.26**	.38**	.32*	(.90)

***p<.001; **p<.01; *p<.05

Note: The Cronbach's Alpha for each of the five scales is reported in parentheses. *Tenure* refers to the number of months a respondent reported being in the guild. Gender is a dummy-coded variable that represents maleness (1 = male, 0 = female); *Game Type 2* and *Game Type 3* are dummy-coded variables that represent respondents who participate in *World of Warcraft* and *Everquest*, respectively. The left-out group represents respondents who participate in *Vanguard*.

Satisfaction with the team model. When satisfaction with the team was regressed on LMX and team performance (i.e., Step 2) the relationships between LMX and satisfaction and between team performance and satisfaction were statistically significant and positive (i.e., ß =.45, p <.001; ß =.44, p <.001, respectively) (see Table 3). Leader-member relationship ratings and team performance accounted for variance in satisfaction with the team above and beyond age, gender, game, and tenure in the team.

When satisfaction with the team was regressed on identification, LMX and team performance (i.e., Step 3) the relationships between identification, between LMX and satisfaction, and between team performance and satisfaction were significant and positive (i.e., ß =.26, p <.001, ß =.37, p <.001; ß =.33, p <.001, respectively) (see Table 4). This indicates that the effects of LMX and team performance on satisfaction with the team were not completely mediated by identification. These results provide strong support for the relationship

depicted by *Arrow C* in Figure 1, and suggest that the leader-member relationship and team performance also impact satisfaction with the team directly.

Intentions. When intentions was regressed on LMX and team performance (i.e., Step 2) the relationships between LMX and intentions was not statistically significant (i.e., ß =.31, p =.35), and the relationship between team performance and intentions was marginally significant and positive (i.e., ß =.19, p <.10) (see Table 3). Only team performance accounted for variance in intentions above and beyond age, gender, game, and tenure in the team.

When intentions was regressed on identification, LMX and team performance (i.e., Step 3) the relationships between identification and intentions were significant and positive (i.e., ß =.43, p <.001) and the relationships between LMX and intentions and between team performance and intentions were not statistically significant (i.e., ß = -.04, p >.05; ß =.00, p >.05, respectively) (see Table 4).

Table 2. Step 1 of the Analysis: Hierarchical regression analyses of identification on the independent variables

Variables	b (s.e.)	ΔR^2
Step 1		
Age	-.00 (.01)	
Gender	-.02 (.01)	
Game Type 2	.12 (.22)	
Game Type 3	-.82 (.39)*	
Tenure	.01 (.01)*	
(Constant)	5.16 (.33)***	
Step 2		.417***
Age	.01 (.01)	
Gender	-.09 (.16)	
Game Type 2	.09 (.17)	
Game Type 3	-.24 (.30)^t	
Tenure	.01 (.01)	
LMX	.40 (.11)***	
Team Performance	.38 (.07)***	
(Constant)	1.65 (.42)***	
Total R^2	.483***	

n = 137 ***p<.001; **p<.01; *p<.05; ^{t} p<.10

Note: *Tenure* refers to the number of months a respondent reported being in the guild. *Game Type 2* and *Game Type 3* are dummy-coded variables that represent respondents who participate in *World of Warcraft* and *Everquest*, respectively. The left-out group represents respondents who participate in *Vanguard*.

This indicates that the effects of team performance on intentions determined in Step 2 of the analysis were completely mediated by identification, providing some support for the proposed model. In addition, the results offer strong support for the relationship depicted by *Arrow D* in Figure 1.

DISCUSSION

One interesting and important finding from this study is that team identification in a virtual environment matters. The extent to which individuals identified with their virtual team explained unique variance in their levels of satisfaction with the team and their intentions to stay and intentions to make positive word of mouth statements about the game to others. Given the context of

this study was for-profit computer games, game developers at the minimum should be interested in these results. According to these results, current game customers are more satisfied, more likely to continue purchasing the game (the games have a monthly subscription fee) and more likely to tell potential customers about the game if they have a strong identification with their virtual team. More generally, managers of virtual teams in organizations, facilitators of communities of practice, and developers of social networks could conclude from these results that it is important to consider the relationship between individuals' levels of identification with a group and the long term-longevity and goals of the group. In a company that uses a knowledge-management system, for example, the quality of the shared information relies heavily on the contributions of the members, and thus,

Table 3. Step 2 of the Analysis: Hierarchical regression analyses of satisfaction and intentions on the independent variables

Variables	Satisfaction		Intentions	
	b (s.e.)	ΔR^2	b (s.e.)	ΔR^2
Step 1				
Age	-.01 (.01)		-.01 (.01)	
Gender	.26 (.24)		.08 (.27)	
Game Type 2	-.07 (.25)		.58 (.28)*	
Game Type 3	-1.36 (.44)**		.06 (.50)	
Tenure	.01 (.01)		-.01 (.01)*	
(Constant)	6.00 (.37)***		5.50 (.42)***	
Step 2		.590***		.064**
Age	.00 (.01)		.00 (.01)	
Gender	.16 (.14)		.05 (.26)	
Game Type 2	-.10 (.15)		.56 (.28)*	
Game Type 3	-.61 (.27)*		.38 (.50)	
Tenure	.00 (.01)		-.02 (.01)*	
LMX	.69 (.10)***		.17 (.18)	
Team Performance	.43 (.06)***		.21 (.12)ᵗ	
(Constant)	1.24 (.38)**		3.69 (.70)***	
Overall				
Total R^2		.680***		.170***

n = 137 ***p<.001; **p<.01; *p<.05; ᵗ p<.10

Note: *Tenure* refers to the number of months a respondent reported being in the guild. *Game Type 2* and *Game Type 3* are dummy-coded variables that represent respondents who participate in *World of Warcraft* and *Everquest*, respectively. The left-out group represents respondents who participate in *Vanguard*.

the willingness of members to participate (Jian & Jeffres, 2006). If the extent to which an individual identifies with the group (i.e., the virtual community or the company) impacts satisfaction and intentions to stay and to tell others about the group, understanding how to increase members' identification with the group is a significant issue.

We can also assume that the quality of the information generated, 'stored' and shared in a community is affected by members' identification with the community. The community of practice literature (e.g., Wenger, 1998) suggests that identification develops in communities of practice concurrently with a sense of belonging, increasing levels of involvement and feelings of meaningfulness; and the result is a social-learning

environment that supports the development and sharing of knowledge within the community. Specifically, as individuals' personal identities become more in line with the community, members also feel a greater attachment or sense of belonging to the community that reinforces the value or importance of participation in the community. Further, individuals develop a belief that participation in the community has lead to meaningful changes in their abilities, and they become more involved in the community. The resulting environment is one where knowledge is created, codified, and stored in a decentralized manner, shared through such behaviors as telling war stories, and applied to practice (Baker-Eveleth, Sarker & Eveleth, 2005).

Table 4. Step 3 of the Analysis: Hierarchical regression analyses of satisfaction and intentions on the mediator and independent variables

Variables	Satisfaction		Intentions	
	b (s.e.)	R^2	b (s.e.)	R^2
Age	.00 (.01)		-.01 (.01)	
Gender	.18 (.13)		.10 (.24)	
Game Type 2	-.13 (.14)		.51 (.26)*	
Game Type 3	-.54 (.26)*		.51 (.47)	
Tenure	.00 (.01)		-.02 (.01)**	
LMX	.57 (.10)***		-.06 (.18)	
Team Performance	.32 (.07)***		.00 (.12)	
Identification	.30 (.08)***		.57 (.14)***	
(Constant)	.74 (.38)^t		2.74 (.70)***	
		.715***		.267***

n = 137 ***p<.001; **p<.01; *p<.05; ^{t} p<.10

Note: *Tenure* refers to the number of months a respondent reported being in the guild. *Game Type 2* and *Game Type 3* are dummy-coded variables that represent respondents who participate in *World of Warcraft* and *Everquest*, respectively. The left-out group represents respondents who participate in *Vanguard*.

Further, results of this study offer evidence about two factors that affect the level of an individual's group identification. Team performance and the quality of the leader-member relationship each explained unique variance in identification with the team. These findings support the theoretical evidence that a team's performance helps lead to stronger identification through its ability to make a team appear more distinct than other teams and through the ability of performance to be one indicator of the prestige associated with a team. In addition, these findings support the Social Identity Theory literature that suggests that team-development processes, in which the team leader plays a critical role, also play a role in affecting the level of identification individuals have with a group. Leaders who exhibit positive leader behaviors are more likely to have team members who identify with the team, and thus, more likely to be satisfied with the team and to stay. Recent research in face-to-face environments also highlights the critical role of leadership on the development of communities of practice (Baker-Eveleth, Eveleth & O'Neill, 2010). Specifically, leader support had a positive effect on the formation or development of attachments with the community (i.e., identification and belongingness). And interaction with the leader played a central role in the extent to which members took action as a result of their membership (i.e., involvement) or saw the value of taking action in the future (i.e., meaningfulness).

Further, the importance of team performance and leader-member relationships is apparently more important than we had expected prior to this study. We theorized that the impact of these two variables on satisfaction and intentions was mediated by identification; however, both variables affected satisfaction with the team through identification and directly; identification, performance and leader-member relationships each explained unique variance in satisfaction. Only in the case of intentions did identification completely mediate the relationship between team performance and intentions.

CONCLUSION

While the tools are available for enabling the creation of virtual teams, and the opportunities exist to capitalize on the skills and insights of dispersed individuals, much still remains to be learned about the factors that affect virtual-team behaviors, processes and outcomes. Much of what we know about teams is the result of research on co-located, face-to-face groups; though the number of virtual team studies is growing. Identifying the extent to which phenomena we see in face-to-face teams transfer to the virtual-team environment is one way to highlight the challenges and opportunities faced by managers of virtual teams, promoters of communities of practices, and facilitators of other forms of virtual communities and groups. In each of these instances, the form of communication is a central factor in how team members interact and in the nature of the relationships that develop. The term *media richness* (Daft & Lengel, 1986) is often used to highlight the lean nature of computer-mediated communication, and thus, the ability (or lack of ability) to utilize verbal and non-verbal cues beyond those of printed text. If virtual environments limit the amount and type of social information available, it is possible that members will rely more heavily on objective or salient indicators (e.g., team performance) to determine the distinctiveness of the group, and thus, their level of identification with the group.

In addition, if social cues are more limited in these 'lean' virtual environments then leaders must take some care to think about how to develop a positive relationship with team members with the communication technologies and behaviors that are available. In addition to the results presented here that leader-member relationships matter, there is other evidence that such things as trust (Jarvenpa & Leidner, 1999) and liking (Weisband & Atwater, 1999) develop in virtual environments, albeit more slowly (Wilson, Straus, & McEvily,

2006). The same may be true of leader-member relationships.

These results suggest that leaders of virtual teams and those who select and mentor the leaders of virtual teams must think about how to exhibit behaviors that affect the leader-member relationship. We know that in face-to-face settings such things as setting positive expectations and frequent communications between leader and follower are variables that impact perceptions of the exchange favorably (e.g., Kacmer, Witt, Zivnuska, & Gully, 2003; Wayne, Shore, & Liden, 1997). Identifying individuals who display these behaviors may be helpful for selecting virtual-team leaders, and understanding how to perform these behaviors in a virtual environment may be helpful for training leaders how to perform. In MMORPG settings in particular, game developers may want to consider creating mechanisms that help followers match with leaders, or screening mechanisms that help quantify and describe leadership styles or potential team leaders so that customers who wish to be followers are more likely to end up on a team where the relationship with the leader is positive.

Another interesting insight from this study is the rich team-oriented environment that exists in online role playing games. Collaborating teams in MMORPGs seem to be more than analogies to virtual teams. They are virtual teams. Yee (2006) and others have researched this emerging environment; one that is experienced by millions of players around the globe. It is easy to think about MMORPGs as 'breaks' from the real world; however, given the evolution of the web environment from a source of information (Web 1.0), to a space for interaction (Web 2.0), to a space to be immersed (Web 3.0), understanding the phenomena present in MMORPGs may help lead the way in how organizations evolve the practice of virtual teams. We suspect that the use of avatar technology (e.g., Gerhard, Moore, & Hobbs, 2004), the immersive nature of MMORPG video environments (Takatalo, Hakkinen, Komulainen,

Sarkela, & Nyman, 2006) and the ability to create a feeling of being present in a gaming environment (Gerhard, Moore, & Hobbs, 2004) may offer significant insights in how organizations develop and manage virtual teams in the future.

REFERENCES

Ajzen, I., & Fishbein, M. (1973). Attitudinal and normative variables as predictors of specific behaviors. *Journal of Personality and Social Psychology*, *27*, 41–57. doi:10.1037/h0034440

Ajzen, I., & Fishbein, M. (1980). *Understanding attitudes and predicting social behavior*. Englewood Cliffs, NJ: Prentice-Hall.

Anderson, E. W., Fornell, C., & Rust, R. T. (1997). Customer satisfaction, productivity, and profitability: Differences between goods and services. *Marketing Science*, *16*(2), 129–145. doi:10.1287/mksc.16.2.129

Ashforth, B. E., & Mael, E. (1989). Social identity theory and the organization. *Academy of Management Review*, *14*, 20–39. doi:10.2307/258189

Baker-Eveleth, L. J., Eveleth, D. M., & O'Neill, M. (2010). Developing a community of practice through classroom climate, leader support and leader interaction. In *Proceedings of the American Society of Business and Behavioral Sciences Conference*, Las Vegas, NV.

Baker-Eveleth, L. J., Sarker, S., & Eveleth, D. M. (2005). Formation of an online community of practice: An inductive study unearthing key elements. In *Proceedings of the Hawaii International Conference on System Sciences*, Big Island, Hawaii.

Baron, R. M., & Kenny, D. A. (1986). The moderator-mediator variable distinction in social psychological research: Conceptual, strategic, and statistical considerations. *Journal of Personality and Social Psychology*, *51*(6), 1173–1182. doi:10.1037/0022-3514.51.6.1173

Castronova, E. (2005). *Synthetic Worlds: The Business and Culture of Online Games*. Chicago: The University of Chicago Press.

Castronova, E. (2008). *A test of the law of demand in a virtual world: Exploring the petri dish approach to social science* (CESifo Working Paper Series No. 2355). Retrieved May 1, 2009, from http://ssrn.com/abstract=1173642

Chatman, J. A., & Flynn, F. J. (2001). The influence of demographic heterogeneity on the emergence and consequences of cooperative norms in work teams. *Academy of Management Journal*, *44*(5), 956–974. doi:10.2307/3069440

Chaudhuri, A., & Holbrook, M. B. (2001). The chain of effects from brand trust and brand affect to brand performance: The role of brand loyalty. *Journal of Marketing*, *65*(2), 81–93. doi:10.1509/jmkg.65.2.81.18255

Chidambaram, L. (1996). Relational development in computer-supported groups. *Management Information Systems Quarterly*, *20*(2), 143–163. doi:10.2307/249476

Clegg, C. W. (1983). Psychology of employee lateness, absence, and turnover: A methodological critique and an empirical study. *The Journal of Applied Psychology*, *68*, 88–101. doi:10.1037/0021-9010.68.1.88

Cotton, J. L., & Tuttle, J. M. (1986). Employee turnover: A meta-analysis and review with implications for research. *Academy of Management Review*, *11*, 55–70. doi:10.2307/258331

Daft, R. L., & Lengel, R. H. (1986). Organizational information requirements, media richness and structural design. *Management Science, 32*(5), 554–571. doi:10.1287/mnsc.32.5.554

Doran, L. I., Stone, V. K., Brief, A. P., & George, J. M. (1991). Behavioral intentions as predictors of job attitudes: The role of economic choice. *The Journal of Applied Psychology, 76*, 40–45. doi:10.1037/0021-9010.76.1.40

Dutton, J. E., Dukerich, J. M., & Harquil, V. V. (1994). Organisational images and member identification. *Administrative Science Quarterly, 39*(2), 239–263. doi:10.2307/2393235

Earley, P. C., & Lituchy, T. R. (1991). Delineating goal and efficacy effects: A test of three models. *The Journal of Applied Psychology, 76*, 81–98. doi:10.1037/0021-9010.76.1.81

Epitropaki, O., & Martin, R. (2005). From ideal to real: A longitudinal study of implicit leadership theories, leader-member exchanges and employee outcomes. *The Journal of Applied Psychology, 90*, 659–676. doi:10.1037/0021-9010.90.4.659

Fishbein, M., & Ajzen, I. (1975). *Belief, attitudes, intentions, and behavior: An introduction to theory and research*. Reading, MA: Addison-Wesley.

Flanagin, A. J., Park, H. S., & Seibold, D. R. (2004). Group performance and collaborative technology: A longitudinal and multilevel analysis of information quality, contribution equity, and members' satisfaction in computer-mediated groups. *Communication Monographs, 71*(3), 352–372. doi:10.1080/0363452042000299902

Gerhard, M., Moore, D., & Hobbs, D. (2004). Embodiment and copresence in collaborative interfaces. *International Journal of Human-Computer Studies, 61*(4), 453–480. doi:10.1016/j.ijhcs.2003.12.014

Gerstner, C. R., & Day, D. V. (1997). Meta-analytic review of leader-member exchange theory: Correlates and construct issues. *The Journal of Applied Psychology, 82*, 827–844. doi:10.1037/0021-9010.82.6.827

Graen, G., Novak, M., & Sommerkamp, P. (1982). The effects of leader-member exchange and job design on productivity and job satisfaction: Testing a dual attachment model. *Organizational Behavior and Human Performance, 30*, 109–131. doi:10.1016/0030-5073(82)90236-7

Graen, G. B., & Uhl-Bien, M. (1995). Relationship-based approach to leadership: Development of leader-member exchange LMX theory. *The Leadership Quarterly, 6*, 219–247. doi:10.1016/1048-9843(95)90036-5

Harrison-Walker, L. J. (2001). The measurement of word-of-mouth communication and an investigation of service quality and customer commitment as potential antecedents. *Journal of Service Research, 4*, 60–75. doi:10.1177/109467050141006

Hogg, M. A., & Terry, D. J. (2000). Social identity and self-categorization processes in organizational contexts. *Academy of Management Review, 25*(1), 121–140. doi:10.2307/259266

Hollenbeck, J. R., & Klein, H. J. (1987). Goal commitment and the goal-setting process: Problems, prospects, and proposals for future research. *The Journal of Applied Psychology, 72*, 212–220. doi:10.1037/0021-9010.72.2.212

Jarvenpa, L., & Leidner, D. E. (1999). Communication and trust in global virtual teams. *Organization Science, 10*, 791–815. doi:10.1287/orsc.10.6.791

Jian, G., & Jeffres, L. W. (2006). Understanding employees' willingness to contribute to shared electronic databases: A three-dimensional framework. *Communication Research, 33*, 242–261. doi:10.1177/0093650206289149

Kacmar, K. M., Witt, L. A., Zivnuska, S., & Gully, S. M. (2003). The interactive effect of leader-member exchange and communication frequency on performance ratings. *The Journal of Applied Psychology*, *88*, 764–772. doi:10.1037/0021-9010.88.4.764

Kirkman, B., Rosen, B., Tesluk, P. E., & Gibson, C. B. (2004). The impact of team empowerment on virtual team performance: The moderating role of face-to-face interaction. *Academy of Management Journal*, *47*, 175–192.

Kleinman, G., Palmon, D., & Lee, P. (2003). The effects of personal and group level factors on the outcomes of simulated auditor and client teams. *Group Decision and Negotiation*, *12*, 57–84. doi:10.1023/A:1022256730300

Lampe, C., Ellison, N., & Steinfield, C. (2006). A Face(book) in the crowd: Social searching vs. social browsing. In *Proceedings of the 2006 20th Anniversary Conference on Computer Supported Cooperative Work* (pp. 167-170). New York: ACM Press.

Lesser, E. L., & Storck, J. (2001). Communities of practice and organisational performance. *IBM Systems Journal*, *40*(4), 831–841.

Locke, E. A. (1969). What is job satisfaction? *Organizational Behavior and Human Performance*, *4*(4), 309–336. doi:10.1016/0030-5073(69)90013-0

Locke, E. A., & Latham, G. P. (1990). *A theory of goal setting and task performance*. Englewood Cliffs, NJ: Prentice-Hall.

Madrigal, R. (2001). Social identity effects in a belief-attitude-intentions hierarchy: Implications for corporate sponsorship. *Psychology and Marketing*, *18*, 145–165. doi:10.1002/1520-6793(200102)18:2<145::AID-MAR1003>3.0.CO;2-T

Mael, F., & Tetrick, L. (1992). Identifying organizational identification. *Educational and Psychological Measurement*, *54*, 813–824. doi:10.1177/0013164492052004002

Mathieu, J. E., & Zajac, D. M. (1990). A review and meta-analysis of the antecedents, correlates, and consequences of organizational commitment. *Psychological Bulletin*, *108*, 171–194. doi:10.1037/0033-2909.108.2.171

Mowday, R. T., Porter, L. W., & Steers, R. M. (1982). *Employee-organization linkages: The psychology of commitment, absenteeism, and turnover*. New York: Academic Press.

Organ, D. W. (1988). *Organizational Behavior*. Lexington, MA: Lexington Books.

Phillips, J. M., Douthitt, E., & Hyland, M. A. M. (2001). The role of justice in team member satisfaction with the leader and attachment to the team. *The Journal of Applied Psychology*, *86*(2), 316–325. doi:10.1037/0021-9010.86.2.316

Porter, L. W., & Lawler, E. E. (1968). *Managerial attitudes and performance*. Homewood, IL: Irwin.

Rust, R. T., Ambler, T., Carpenter, G. S., Kumar, V., & Srivastava, R. K. (2004). Measuring marketing productivity: Current knowledge and future directions. *Journal of Marketing*, *68*(4), 76–89. doi:10.1509/jmkg.68.4.76.42721

Scandura, T. A., & Schriesheim, C. A. (1994). Leader-member exchange and supervisor career mentoring as complementary constructs in leadership research. *Academy of Management Journal*, *37*(6), 1588–1602. doi:10.2307/256800

Shamir, B. (1990). Calculations, values, and identities: The sources of collectivistic work motivation. *Human Relations*, *43*, 313–332. doi:10.1177/001872679004300402

Tajfel, H. (1982). *Social identity and intergroup relations*. Cambridge, UK: Cambridge University Press.

Takatalo, J., Hakkinen, J., Komulainen, J., Sarkela, H., & Nyman, G. (2006). Involvement and presence in digital gaming. In *Proceedings of the 4th Nordic Conference on Human-Computer Interaction* (Vol. 189, pp. 393-396).

Terry, D. J., & Hogg, M. A. (1996). Group norms and the attitude-behavior relationship: A role for group identification. *Personality and Social Psychology Bulletin, 22*(8), 776–793. doi:10.1177/0146167296228002

Turner, J. C. (1982). Towards a cognitive redefinition of the social group. In Tajfel, H. (Ed.), *Social identity and intergroup relations* (pp. 66–101). Cambridge, UK: Cambridge University Press.

van Knippenberg, D., & van Schie, E. C. M. (2000). Foci and correlates of organizational identification. *Journal of Occupational and Organizational Psychology, 73*(2), 137–147. doi:10.1348/096317900166949

Vroom, V. H. (1964). *Work and motivation*. New York: Wiley.

Wayne, S. J., Shore, L. M., & Liden, R. C. (1997). Perceived organizational support and leader-member exchange: A social exchange perspective. *Academy of Management Journal, 40*, 82–111. doi:10.2307/257021

Weisband, S., & Atwater, L. (1999). Evaluating self and others in electronic and face-to-face groups. *The Journal of Applied Psychology, 84*, 632–639. doi:10.1037/0021-9010.84.4.632

Wilson, J. M., Straus, S. G., & McEvily, B. (2006). All in due time: The development of trust in computer-mediated and face-to-face teams. *Organizational Behavior and Human Decision Processes, 99*, 16–33. doi:10.1016/j.obhdp.2005.08.001

Yee, N. (2006). Motivations for play in online games. *Cyberpsychology & Behavior, 9*(6), 772–775. doi:10.1089/cpb.2006.9.772

Yu, C., & Young, M. (2008). The virtual group identification process: A virtual educational community case. *Cyberpsychology & Behavior, 11*(1), 87–90. doi:10.1089/cpb.2007.9929

This work was previously published in the International Journal of Virtual Communities and Social Networking, Volume 2, Issue 1, edited by Subhasish Dasgupta, pp. 52-66, copyright 2010 by IGI Publishing(an imprint of IGI Global).

Chapter 4
Geographic Information Networks in American Indian Governments and Communities

Mark H. Palmer
University of Missouri-Columbia, USA

Jack Hanney
University of Missouri-Columbia, USA

ABSTRACT

This article describes advantages and disadvantages of federal government centralized geographic information networks and decentralized peer-to-peer geographic information networks as they pertain to North American Indian tribal governments and communities. Geographic information systems (GIS) are used by indigenous groups for natural resource management, land claims, water rights, and cultural revitalization activities on a global-scale. North American groups use GIS for the same reasons, but questions regarding culturally appropriate GIS, cross-cultural understandings of geographic knowledge, and cultural assimilation through Western digital technologies have been raised by scholars. Two network models are germane to American Indian government operations and community organizations. The first is a prescriptive top-down network emanating from federal government agencies. Federal agencies are responsible for the diffusion of nationwide GIS programs throughout indigenous communities in the United States. A second, potentially more inclusive model is a decentralized peer-to-peer network in which all nodes are responsible for the success of the network.

INTRODUCTION

Geographic information systems (GIS) are digital software packages that incorporate spatially referenced database information that can be analyzed statistically or through the creation of maps and cartographic models. As with other database systems, information is collected, stored in computers, and can be manipulated. Information and communication technologies (ICT) like GIS can transform cultural concepts like community, privacy, space, time and reality which can funda-

DOI: 10.4018/978-1-4666-1553-3.ch004

mentally change cultural practices (Brey, 2003). GIS are now important resource management tools for indigenous people on a global-scale, including North American Indian tribal governments (Chapin et al., 2005; Smith, 2008). Many American Indian tribal governments make every effort to retain control over proprietary geographic information and GIS applications. Some scholars raised concerns about the security of proprietary knowledge and information held within digital systems like GIS (Marchand & Winchell, 1992; Palmer, 2007; Rundstrom, 1995). Other concerns involved development of a new model for providing technical assistance and training to members of American Indian tribal governments and communities which emphasizes peer-to-peer networks over the expert instructor/student experience (Palmer, 2009). This article describes some of the advantages and disadvantages of federal government centralized GIS networks and decentralized peer-to-peer geographic information networks as they pertain to North American Indian tribal governments and communities.

Issues regarding the centralization of geographic information held in large, nationwide repositories were among the many topics that emerged in the GIS and society debate during the 1990s. Important contributions regarding the social implications of GIS include a book entitled *Ground Truth* by John Pickles (1995); a 1995 special issue of *Cartography and Geographic Information Systems (CaGIS)* on GIS and society; a special issue of *CaGIS* on public participation GIS in 1998; and the book *Digital Places* by Michael Curry (1998). In a very broad sense, the debate informed scholars and practitioners that GIS simultaneously shape and are shaped by the institutions that construct, implement, and transfer the technology to other locations and organizations (Harvey & Chrisman, 1998; Sheppard, 1995). This includes government agencies.

The United States Bureau of Indian Affairs (BIA) serves as an example of a top-down GIS model that emanated from the agency's center and diffused throughout Indian Country. As with most state developed, nationwide mapping and GIS programs, the BIA constructed a standardized system that could be implemented within interdepartmental offices. Some scholars argue that GIS standardization can have adverse affects upon epistemological diversity within American Indian communities and represent yet another method of assimilating all American Indians into the fabric of American society (Palmer, 2007; Rundstrom, 1995). On the other hand, North American Indian groups and communities adopt scientifically constructed maps, geographic information, and computer software to revitalize their communities (Duernden & Kahn, 1996; Smith, 2008; Sparke, 1998).

Digital technologies can simultaneously empower and marginalize indigenous communities (Dyson et al., 2007; Palmer, 2009). In recent years, indigenous groups have adopted digital forms of media—especially audio and video recording—to represent inter-related concepts of place and identity. The capacity of emerging technologies to foster humanistic cultural expression has been noted by Dyson:

The multimedia capabilities, storage capacity and communication tools offered by information technology provide new opportunities to revitalize indigenous cultures and languages, and to repatriate material back to communities from national cultural institutions. In particular the graphical, video and audio facilities of multimedia speak directly to cultures which are principally rooted in spoken language, music, dance, ceremony and visual forms of artistic expression. (2007)

New digital technologies have the capacity to mediate not only indigenous cultural practices, but also the socio-spatial characteristics of indigenous communities. How can the adoption of audio-visual media *and* geographic information systems facilitate sovereignty for indigenous peoples?

Other research on information technologies and indigenous people explores the positive and negative impacts or the transformative capabilities of information technologies (IT) on indigenous communities and their culture (Miller, 1998). Some scholars view indigenous cultural knowledge as threatened. The close relationship between indigenous identities, language, and land has been unsettled by the movement of many indigenous peoples away from their traditional lands, and by the decrease of native speakers of indigenous languages (Dyson et al., 2007). An alternative approach focuses on the ways in which indigenous cultural practices shape IT (Salazar, 2007). A new wave of research concerned with IT and indigenous people addresses issues like cultural preservation and revitalization (Auld, 2007; Holton et al., 2007; Keegan et al., 2007; Leavy, 2007) IT and GIS transformation of communities (Eglash, 2007; Palmer, 2007; Turk, 2007), access to IT (Betts, 2007; Daly, 2007), indigenous media, cultural politics and social movements (Ginsburg, 1997; Smith, 2005, 2006; Wilson & Stewart, 2008), and educational uses of IT (Donovan, 2007; Goodwin-Gomez, 2007), and indigenous knowledge (Dyson, 2007; Leclair & Warren, 2007; Salazar, 2007). Lacking in this rich body of literature is research on indigenous peoples, virtual communities, social networks, and GIS.

PRESCRIPTIVE AND PEER-TO-PEER NETWORKS

Networks are a series of interconnected hubs and nodes that may be hierarchical, but lack any kind of discernable center (Castells, 1999).

Relationships between nodes are asymmetrical, but they are all necessary for the functioning of the network - for the circulation of money, information, technology, images, goods, services, or people throughout the network. The most critical distinction in this organizational logic is to be or not to be - in the network. Be in the network, and you can share and, over time, increase your chances. Be out of the network, or become switched off, and your chances vanish since everything that

counts is organized around a worldwide web of interacting networks (Castells, 1999, p. 6).

However, there may be a tendency to centralize authority, information, or knowledge in what Bruno Latour calls centers of calculation. It is within centers of calculation that information on people or places is accumulated. Scientists and technicians convert information into inscriptions like maps, statistical tables, or digital databases (Latour, 1987). Spatially, centers of calculation take on a star-like shape (Latour, 2005) and are major hubs within prescriptive networks. The star-like networks resemble a core and periphery geography in that there are unequal relationships between those individuals and materials in the core and those individuals on the periphery who are dependent upon the core for materials, technical assistance, software, and education. Prescriptive networks are: (1) tightly ordered normalized spaces; (2) restrictive; (3) predictable and standardized; (4) regulatory; (5) paternal and formalized (Murdoch, 2006). From this, we might assume that the networks refer to systems of almost panoptic power in which centers succeed in exercising effective control over all aligned entities and spaces. However, hubs and nodes can work together. Reciprocity is integral to the success of networks and "the interaction between networks gives rise to a multiplicity, various orderings of similar objects (digital computers, GIS software, data), do not always reinforce the same simplicities or impose the same silences. Instead they may work-and relate – in different ways" (Law & Mol, 2002, p. 7).

There are multiple definitions of peer-to-peer systems (Androutsellis-Theotokis & Spinellis, 2004). Peer-to-peer networks are file-sharing systems that combine techniques for data mining among communities of decentralized computers, and that allow individual users to download files between one another (Golle et al., 2001). Scholars have noted that, "In a P2P system, users submit queries and receive results (such as actual data, or pointers to data) in return. Data shared in a P2P system can be of any type; in most cases users share files. Queries can also take any appropriate form given the type of data shared. For example, in a file-sharing system, queries might be unique identifiers, or keywords with regular expressions. Each node has a collection of files or data to share" (Yang et al., 2003, p. 4).

Characteristics of peer-to-peer GIS networks include shared distribution of resources and services like data, software, applications, technical assistance, and education opportunities. On the other hand, a peer-to-peer network may also include nodes having their own specialty and/or expertise. For instance, one node may specialize in forest or range management mapping and relational database development, another may focus on educational module development, and yet others might concentrate on the integration of indigenous knowledge and GIS. The key spatial arrangement of peer-to-peer networks is decentralization in which all nodes share partial responsibility for the success of the network and there is no centralized driving force. Each network node maintains its own autonomy. This spatial arrangement should be present in a network in which all nodes are created equal. Peer-to-peer networks typically can be thought of as a three tier hierarchy that includes infrastructures, applications, and communities (Schoder & Fischbach, 2005). The remainder of this article will focus on communities. Some characteristics of peer-to-peer network communities include community interests, trust, and network responsibilities. For instance, members of a P2P network may share common goals, objectives, and interests, but not a common geographic location. When a member decides to join a network, they will be sharing information and opening up their systems to potential strangers. Thus, a great deal of trust is needed. Once information is accessible to the network, participants or participating nodes are responsible for the network's information and success of the virtual community (Schoder & Fischbach, 2005).

PRESCRIPTIVE GOVERNMENT GIS NETWORKS

GIS data, hardware, and software emanate in large government agency offices, and diffuse out to North American Indian tribal governments. This has been the pattern of GIS development within tribal governments in the United States (Chapin et al., 2005; Smith 2008). Some would argue that this connection embeds GIS and multiple actors within colonial networks connecting states, institutions, corporations, and indigenous peoples throughout the United States (Palmer, 2007; Rundstrom, 1995). GIScientist Renee Sieber argued that in some cases the success of GIS ultimately rests upon the group's ability to conform to the rules and procedures of GIS adoption, meaning that a great deal of time, money, and effort are placed into the development of standardized and general datasets such as county boundaries, census data, hydrology, roads, and school districts; so instead of reinventing the wheel, grassroots organizations and indigenous groups should take advantage of accessible data at little or no cost (Sieber, 2000).

Government agencies standardize data to meet their everyday needs like managing municipal facilities, natural resources, property, and cadastral maps. Governments have specific tasks they perform within the realm of public space. These activities are conducted and performed for the good of the general public overall, and not just one or two specific groups within the total population. According to Scott, the lack of context and particularities is not an oversight; it is the necessary first premise of any large-scale planning exercise and that modern institutions "[do] not successfully represent the actual activity of the society they depicted, nor were they intended to; they represented only that slice of it that interested the official observer" (Scott, 1998, p. 3).

Standardization including the classification of ecosystems, hydrological systems, and even indigenous knowledge systems can be achieved through the development of GIS databases located within a central location. A centralized, nationwide GIS development project began at the Bureau of Indian Affairs (BIA) Geographic Data Service Center (GDSC) in mid-1980s (Palmer, 2009). The Nationwide GIS Database at the BIA was known as the BIA Nationwide Database (BND); a standardized data structure that was implemented across several reservations (U.S. BIA, 1988). According to geographer Mark Monmonier, "nothing better reflects the government cartographer's bureaucratic mentality than the standards and specifications of a nationwide series of topographic maps...The national mapping organization willingly sacrifices political, ethnic, and physical boundaries to the convenience of uniformly spaced medians and parallels/a divide and conquer strategy that makes complete coverage seem both doable and essential" (Monmonier, 1996, pp. 123-124). Through processes of standardization, government agencies can:

1. Enter, store, edit, and manipulating geographic information
2. Enter and store relevant text and symbology
3. Make maps
4. Link text and attribute data to maps
5. Automate measurements of direction, distance, area and shape (Duerden, 1992).

Uniformity is one of the advantages of a centralized top-down system. This supports Sieber's argument that readily available digital data sources should be exploited by local community groups, including indigenous communities (Sieber, 2000). The availability of software for free or reduced cost is another advantage of working closely with a federal agency like the BIA. In addition to software, the agency also offers a number of GIS training workshops and technical assistance via the Internet or by phone.

It can also be disadvantageous to connect with and some cases become dependent upon centralized networks like the one at the BIA. In the past, American Indian tribal governments did not participate in the development of geographic information systems technology and data at the BIA (Palmer, 2009). This goes against the trend of public participation policy that was initiated in the late 1960s and early 1970s, allowing the citizens of a democracy to participate in government, and decision-making at the local, state, and federal government levels. In fact, the BIA could have focused on developing GIS within individual tribal governments. But, the BIA decided that the centralized, prescriptive model was the most cost-efficient way to implement GIS throughout Indian country during the 1980s and 1990s (U.S. BIA, 1988).

Top-down GIS may have a negative impact upon social relationships within tribal communities, including the marginalization of elders and the knowledge kept within oral traditions (Palmer, 2007, 2009). Standardize GIS data may not accurately represent indigenous ontologies and epistemologies. For instance, a mountain may be represented in GIS as a point or polygon area, assigned a set of attributes, and quantified in some manner. However, in many American Indian communities mountains may have more significance, there may be deeper meaning embedded within the landscape. As Keith Basso showed in his book *Wisdom Sits in Places* Western Apache teachings and knowledge are embedded within the mountains and landscape. Apaches are constantly reminded of the stories and teachings each time they pass through the landscape, it keeps them living right (Basso, 1997). Indigenous knowledge is kept among different groups and/or elders. Various landforms and rivers hold knowledge. Knowledge is not centralized, but rather decentralized. Might there be a more appropriate model for GIS development within indigenous communities?

DECENTRALIZED GIS NETWORKS

Decentralized GIS network development in American Indian tribal governments may be difficult to achieve. Unlike the First Nations of Canada, tribal government GIS development in the United States followed the same trajectory as their lead federal agencies including the BIA GDSC, the United States Bureau of Land Management (BLM), the United States Geological Survey (USGS), the United States Environmental Protection Agency (EPA), and the National Aeronautics and Space Administration (NASA) (Chapin et al., 2005). Will tribal GIS users create decentralized peer-to-peer networks in the future? Decentralization may not occur at the tribal government-level, but may emerge at the community-level. Indigenous knowledge is not held in centralized repositories or held by one all knowing being. Rather, indigenous knowledge networks are decentralized with individuals keeping specialized knowledge pertaining to geography or tribal history or medicinal plants just to name a few.

Communities of GIS users have interests. Such interests include natural resource management, water rights, land-use, protection of sacred sites, or cultural sustainability. Interests lead to the making of maps and GIS databases, serving the interests of individuals or groups (Wood, 1992). What would motivate American Indian tribal groups to construct and maintain a peer-to-peer GIS network? Trust is another issue associated with communities of GIS users. According to geographer Francis Harvey, "One of the most pervasive concepts in human society is trust. Trust can be rational or irrational, but in either case expresses underlying confidence…A user's trust in GIS is perhaps most closely related to their knowledge and understanding of the technology" (Harvey, 2002, p. 31). Considering the colonial experiences of American Indians within North American, how important is trust in the development of peer-to-peer networks? What about the responsibilities of individuals within peer-to-peer networks? Mak-

ing maps, GIS data, and sharing these products are all big responsibilities (Wood, 1992). Who is responsible for data, representations, codes, or extensions that float between users within a peer-to-peer network? Geographer Michael Curry posed similar questions: "If I purchase data, I am in a position to claim that those data come with a claim of accuracy and that any errors or omissions within those data are not my responsibility" (Curry, 1995, p. 64). It is becoming more difficult to determine who is responsible for GIS products: the software engineers, scientists, technicians, or the provider of the tools and data?

Thinking about network communities, trust, and responsibilities, we will describe two examples of IT communities: Data Basin and The Indigenous Mapping Network (IMN). The IMN is a more grassroots, public participation GIS website, while Data Basin represents a data-sharing network. Data Basin is a virtual GIS community that connects conservationists, data sets, tools, and expertise. The primary hub of the Data Basin network is the Conservation Biology Institute in Corvallis, Oregon. The IMN emerged from the Intertribal GIS Council as a virtual GIS community with a mission to provide tools to indigenous groups for the protection, preservation, and enhancement of culture and resources. The two communities have advantages and disadvantages.

Data Basin has several advantages that might fit within a peer-to-peer network model. The structure of data sharing and access allows for flow. By having personal profiles for data contributors, Data Basin allows users to check the qualifications of other users. This operates as a quality control and data reliability system. The "Snapshot" feature allows each user to modify and combine data to visualize their ideas and theories and display them for other users. Managed by the Conservation Biology Institute and Rhiza Labs, Data Basin provides the datasets and tools for users to build their snapshots or download for use in desktop GIS software. Most of the data contained in the website is related to physical geography and conservation, which may limit the usefulness of the site.

The IMN has few similarities to Data Basin. GIS data provided on the site is oriented more towards cartography, GIS and indigenous issues. Also, instead of being managed by a corporation or conservation organization, the IMN is facilitated by a board of volunteers who represent indigenous communities. The information on the website is less about the hard datasets and more about community knowledge and news distribution, and the IMN lacks some of the technological benefits of a top-down system. There are no datasets or software tools to download, no heavily detailed GIS maps to overlay or interact with, and no overarching system of quality control.

More specifically, the two community websites are very different when considering community, trust, and responsibility. The IMN seems to serve American Indian interests more immediately than Data Basin. Community activist news and information offered up front by the IMN may assist American Indian communities more directly than the sheer data sharing of Data Basin. However, much of the datasets provided in Data Basin could be very beneficial to American Indian projects and research. The average user must have access to GIS software and have the appropriate knowledge to analyze the datasets. A similar conclusion could be drawn about trust issues. It may be easier for American Indian communities to trust a website maintained by a group of volunteers from similar communities instead of a website ran by a non-governmental organization (NGO). This represents another problem when considering responsibility. While intentions may be good, a group of volunteers may have less accountability than a well-funded NGO. If questions were raised about data or information provided by the website, then Data Basin may have a quicker response or be able to troubleshoot data with less difficulty. When all the factors are considered equally, the two websites appear to represent the difference between a top-down system and a bottom-up system.

CONCLUSION

Map and GIS development, within American Indian tribal governments, is strongly shaped by historical relations with the United States federal government and its adjoining agencies like the BIA. The relationships are unique in that indigenous tribal governments, with a degree of sovereignty, are very connected to technological developments within other federal agencies. This arrangement has led to a top-down implementation of GIS within American Indian tribal governments. Top-down networks have advantages including access to data, technical assistance, and education. There are disadvantages as well. For example, centralized federal government GIS urgently needs to increase American Indian participation in the development GIS and other natural resource management plans. Although efforts like integrated resource management have attempted to cooperate with tribal entities, the program has not achieved great success to date. Because few American Indian tribal governments have experience developing their own decentralized GIS networks, the processes may be difficult to achieve, especially if tribes continue to rely on the federal government expertise. However, tribal governments do have interests in how GIS can and will be used in their communities. Yet, issues of trust and responsibility will have to be addressed before frail peer-to-peer GIS networks can gel. There are attempts to decentralize through the Indigenous Mapping Network and Data Basin. Perhaps they can become templates for future GIS development within tribal governments.

There is a great need for scholars to conceptualize and theorize geographic information systems beyond software packages and now think about 'GIS' as an interconnected network of virtual communities and social networks; a geoweb of humans, computer hardware, software, internet connections, geographic information and local knowledge with a global reach. Future research initiatives will not have to reinvent the wheel. The study of indigenous geographic information networks may employ theoretical perspectives associated with science and technology studies (STS) including the social construction of technology, the social-shaping thesis, technological-shaping thesis, and actor-network theory (ANT) (Brey, 2003). Of particular interest here is ANT, combined with insights found in the critical GIS literature, can describe and explain the centering processes associated with network hubs and nodes and the kinds of human and non-human materials that flow through networks. Finally, additional research on information technologies, GIS, and indigenous people needs to be carried out, utilizing the vast number of case studies available in the literature. The book *Information technology and indigenous people* edited by Dyson, et al. (2007) is a good starting point for those scholars interested in developing and constructing a more theoretically-based research agenda. In fact, successful peer-to-peer geographic information network models have the potential to put declining indigenous languages back into practice; leading to the formation of a virtual communities and social networks of native speakers, connected across space by information and communication technologies.

REFERENCES

Androutsellis-Theotokis, S., & Spinellis, D. (2004). A survey of peer-to-peer content distribution technologies. *ACM Computing Surveys, 36*(4), 335–371. doi:10.1145/1041680.1041681

Auld, G. (2007). Ndjebbana talking books: A technological transformation to fit Kunibidji social practice. In Dyson, L. E., Hendriks, M., & Grant, S. (Eds.), *Information technology and indigenous people* (pp. 197–199). Hershey, PA: Idea Group Publishing.

Basso, K. (1997). *Wisdom sits in places*. Albuquerque, NM: University of New Mexico Press.

Betts, J. D. (2007). Community computing and literacy in Pascua Yaqui Pueblo. In Dyson, L. E., Hendriks, M., & Grant, S. (Eds.), *Information technology and indigenous people* (pp. 305–309). Hershey, PA: Idea Group Publishing.

Brey, P. (2003). Theorizing modernity and technology. In Misa, T. J., Brey, P., & Feenberg, A. (Eds.), *Modernity and Technology*. Cambridge, MA: MIT Press.

Castells, M. (1999). *Information technology, globalization and social development* (UNRISD Discussion Paper No. 114). Geneva, Switzerland: United Nations Research Institute for Social Development.

Chapin, M., Lamb, Z., & Threlkeld, B. (2005). Mapping indigenous lands. *Annual Review of Anthropology, 34*, 619–638. doi:10.1146/annurev.anthro.34.081804.120429

Curry, M. (1995). Rethinking rights and responsibilities in geographic information systems. *Cartography and Geographic Information Systems, 22*, 58–69. doi:10.1559/152304095782540573

Curry, M. (1998). *Digital place: Living with geographic information technologies*. New York: Routledge Press.

Daly, A. (2007). The diffusion of new technologies: Community online access centres in indigenous communities in Australia. In Dyson, L. E., Hendriks, M., & Grant, S. (Eds.), *Information technology and indigenous people* (pp. 272–285). Hershey, PA: Idea Group Publishing.

Donovan, M. (2007). Can information communication technology tools be used to suit Aboriginal learning pedagogies? In Dyson, L. E., Hendriks, M., & Grant, S. (Eds.), *Information technology and indigenous people* (pp. 93–104). Hershey, PA: Idea Group Publishing.

Duerden, F. (1992). GIS and land selection for native claims. *The Operational Geographer, 10*(4), 11–14.

Duerden, F., & Kuhn, R. G. (1996). The application of geographic information systems by First Nations and government in northern Canada. *Cartographica, 33*(2), 49–62.

Dyson, L. E., Hendriks, M., & Grant, S. (2007). *Information technology and indigenous people.* Hershey, PA: Idea Group Publishing.

Eglash, R. (2007). Ethnocomputing with Native American design. In Dyson, L. E., Hendriks, M., & Grant, S. (Eds.), *Information technology and indigenous people* (pp. 210–219). Hershey, PA: Idea Group Publishing.

Ginsburg, F. (1997). 'From little things, big things grow': Indigenous media and cultural activism. In Fox, R. G., & Starn, O. (Eds.), *Between Resistance and Revolution: Cultural Politics and Social Protest* (pp. 118–144). New Brunswick, NJ: Rutgers University Press.

Golle, P., Leyton-Brown, K., Mironov, I., & Lillibridge, M. (2001). Incentives for Sharing in Peer-to-Peer Networks. In *Electronic Commerce* (LNCS 2232, pp. 75-87).

Goodwin-Gomez, G. (2007). Computer technology and native literacy in the Amazon rain forest. In Dyson, L. E., Hendriks, M., & Grant, S. (Eds.), *Information technology and indigenous people* (pp. 117–119). Hershey, PA: Idea Group Publishing.

Harvey, F. (2002). Developing GI infrastructure for local government: The role of trust. In D. Turlloch, E. Epstein, D. Moyer, S. Ventura, B. Niemann, & R. Chenoweth (Eds.) *Proceedings of the Geographic information science & technology in a changing society: A research definition workshop*, Columbus, Ohio.

Harvey, F., & Chrisman, N. R. (1998). Boundary objects and the social construction of GIS technology. *Environment & Planning A, 30*, 1683–1694. doi:10.1068/a301683

Holton, G., Berez, A., & Williams, S. (2007). Building the Dena'ina language Alaska archive. In Dyson, L. E., Hendriks, M., & Grant, S. (Eds.), *Information technology and indigenous people* (pp. 205–208). Hershey, PA: Idea Group Publishing.

Keegan, T. T., Cunningham, S. J., & Apperley, M. (2007). Indigenous language usage in a bilingual interface: Transaction log analysis of the Niupepa web site. In Dyson, L. E., Hendriks, M., & Grant, S. (Eds.), *Information technology and indigenous people* (pp. 175–188). Hershey, PA: Idea Group Publishing.

Latour, B. (1987). *Science in action: How to follow scientists and engineers through society.* Cambridge, MA: Harvard University Press.

Latour, B. (2005). *Reassembling the social: An introduction to actor-network-theory.* Oxford, UK: Oxford University Press.

Law, J., & Mol, A. (2002). *Complexities: Social Studies of Knowledge Practices.* Durham, NC: Duke University Press.

Leavy, B. (2007). Digital songlines: Digitising the arts, culture and heritage landscape of aboriginal Australia. In Dyson, L. E., Hendriks, M., & Grant, S. (Eds.), *Information technology and indigenous people* (pp. 159–169). Hershey, PA: Idea Group Publishing.

Leclair, C., & Warren, S. (2007). Portals and potlatch. In Dyson, L. E., Hendriks, M., & Grant, S. (Eds.), *Information technology and indigenous people* (pp. 1–13). Hershey, PA: Idea Group Publishing.

Marchand, M. E., & Winchell, R. (1992). Tribal implementation of GIS: a case study of planning applications with the Colville Confederated Tribes. *American Indian Culture and Research Journal, 16*(4), 175–183.

Miller, C. J. (1998). The social impacts of televised media among the Yucatec Maya. *Human Organization, 57*(3), 307–314.

Monmonier, M. (1996). *How to Lie with Maps*. Chicago: University of Chicago Press.

Murdoch, J. (2006). *Post-structuralist geography: A guide to relational space*. London: Sage.

Palmer, M. (2007). Cut from the same cloth: The United States Bureau of Indian Affairs, geographic information systems, and cultural assimilation. In Dyson, L. E., Hendriks, M., & Grant, S. (Eds.), *Information technology and indigenous people* (pp. 220–231). Hershey, PA: Idea Group Publishing.

Palmer, M. (2009). Engaging with Indigital geographic information networks. *Futures, 41*, 33–40. doi:10.1016/j.futures.2008.07.006

Pickles, J. (1995). *Ground truth: The social implications of geographic information systems*. New York: Guilford Press.

Rundstrom, R. A. (1995). GIS, Indigenous peoples, and epistemological diversity. *Cartography and Geographic Information Systems, 22*, 45–57. doi:10.1559/152304095782540564

Salazar, J. F. (2007). Indigenous peoples and the cultural construction of information and communication technology (ICT) in Latin America. In Dyson, L. E., Hendriks, M., & Grant, S. (Eds.), *Information technology and indigenous people* (pp. 14–26). Hershey, PA: Idea Group Publishing.

Schoder, D., & Fischbach, K. (2005). Core Concepts in Peer-to-Peer (P2P) Networking. In R. Subramanian & B. Goodman (Eds.), *P2P Computing: The Evolution of a Disruptive Technology*. Hershey, PA: Idea Group Inc.

Scott, J. C. (1998). *Seeing like a State: How Certain Schemes to Improve the Human Condition have Failed*. New Haven, CT: Yale University Press.

Sheppard, E. (1995). GIS and society: towards a research agenda. *Cartography and Geographic Information Systems, 22*(1), 5–16. doi:10.1559/152304095782540555

Sieber, R. E. (2000). Conforming (to) the opposition: the social construction of geographic information in social movements. *International Journal of Geographical Information Science, 14*(8), 775–793. doi:10.1080/136588100750022787

Smith, L. (2008). Indigenous geography, GIS, and land-use planning on the Bois Forte Reservation. *American Indian Culture and Research Journal, 32*(3), 139–151.

Smith, L. C. (2005). *Meditating Indigenous Identity: Video, Advocacy, and Knowledge in Oaxaca, Mexico*. Unpublished doctoral dissertation, University of Kentucky.

Smith, L. C. (2006). Mobilizing indigenous video: The Mexican Case. *The Journal of Latin American Geography, 5*(1), 113–128. doi:10.1353/lag.2006.0012

Sparke, M. (1998). A Map that Roared and an Original Atlas: Canada, Cartography, and the Narration of a Nation. *Annals of the Association of American Geographers. Association of American Geographers, 88*(3), 463–495. doi:10.1111/0004-5608.00109

Turk, A. (2007). Representations of tribal boundaries of Australian Indigenous peoples and the implications of geographic information systems. In Dyson, L. E., Hendriks, M., & Grant, S. (Eds.), *Information technology and indigenous people* (pp. 232–244). Hershey, PA: Idea Group Publishing.

U.S. Bureau of Indian Affairs (U.S. BIA). (1988). *Issue paper: Indian integrated resource information program*. Lakewood, CO: Department of the Interior.

Wilson, P., & Stewart, M. (2008). *Global Indigenous Media: Cultures, Practices, and Politics*. Durham, NC: Duke University Press.

Wood, D. (1992). *The power of maps*. New York: Guildford Press.

Yang, B., & Garcia-Molina, H. (2002). *Designing a super-peer network*. Palo Alto, CA: Stanford University. Retrieved from http://dbpubs.stanford.edu/pub/2002-13

This work was previously published in the International Journal of Virtual Communities and Social Networking, Volume 2, Issue 2, edited by Subhasish Dasgupta, pp. 1-10, copyright 2010 by IGI Publishing(an imprint of IGI Global).

Chapter 5
Understanding the Video Bloggers' Community

John Warmbrodt
Consultant, USA

Hong Sheng
Missouri University of Science and Technology, USA

Richard Hall
Missouri University of Science and Technology, USA

Jinwei Cao
University of Delaware, USA

ABSTRACT

Video blogs (or vlogs) are a new form of blogs where each post is a video. This study explores a community of video bloggers (or vloggers) by studying the community's structure as well as the motivations and interactions of vloggers in the community. A social network analysis of a list of personal vloggers identifies the community's structure. Open-ended interviews with core vloggers in the sample provide in-depth understanding on the motivations and interactions of the vloggers. Overall, the results indicate that the vloggers' community exhibits a core/periphery structure. Such a community is formed based on shared interest and active interactions. In addition, the rich communication provided in video blogs allows for a more personal and intimate interaction, making vlogs a potentially powerful tool for business applications.

INTRODUCTION

Blogs are journal based web sites that typically use content management tools to allow the authors to post contents on the websites (Gordon, 2006). Video blogs (or vlogs) are blogs where each post is a video. Although a post may also include text to provide context for the video, the focus of the post is a video. The use of videos provides more freedom for video bloggers (vloggers) to express their opinions/views and interact with their viewers more directly and interactively (Miles, 2003). Vlogging also fulfills a few social needs such as being connected, finding validation for one's

DOI: 10.4018/978-1-4666-1553-3.ch005

experience and ideas, and being a producer as well as a consumer (Luers, 2007). Each vlogger interacts with other vloggers and together they form vloggers' communities.

Just as the number of blogs has increased significantly in the last few years, vlogging has become increasingly popular as well. In January of 2005, Mefeedia, an online directory of vloggers, listed just 617 vlogs. As of August 2009, this number had increased to 27,782 (Mefeedia.com, 2009). As a relatively new but popular form of blogs, vlogs use rich media and allow for more direct interactions, therefore, have great potential for business applications. For example, traditional media outlet ABC News in January 2007, signed Amanda Congdon, who became popular as the host of the highly popular video blog Rocketboom, to host a video blog on ABC News (Holahan, 2006). This example illustrates that vlogs can not only serve as web based journals for everyday users, but can also be used by businesses to directly communicate with their customers or promote new products.

Despite the increasing popularity and importance of vlogs, little academic research has been done to study the vloggers' community, or the interactions among vloggers. As the main motivation for vlogging is to socially interact with other vloggers (Luers, 2007; Miles, 2003), it is important to study the interaction in this new type of virtual community. Specifically, this paper seeks to identify and understand the structure of the vloggers' community, the motivation and characteristics of vloggers forming the community, and the interactions within the community.

LITERATURE REVIEW

Blogs and Vlogs

Blogs are typically based upon similar content management software tools. These software tools allow their authors to quickly post new content to their blogs in what has been described as "pushbutton publishing for the people."(Schiano, Nardi, Gumbrecht, & Swartz, 2004, p. 1). Bloggers usually have common goals and interests. Based on Armstrong and Hagel's (1996) categorization, blogs can be viewed as communities of interests. Compared to physical communities, virtual communities such as blogs provide a way for people to socialize with others but also maintain a distance from others, and can usually break down societal and organizational barriers (Kiesler, 1986).

While blogs are traditionally text based, the same tools can be used to post videos. A vlog, as mentioned before, is a type of blog that consists of videos posted to a blog. Videos posted on the blogs are typically no longer than five or ten minutes in length (Luers, 2007). Vlogging became popular due to the decreasing barriers of entry to Internet video publishing. Much of the initial success of vlogs comes from video hosting websites such as blip.tv (http://blip.tv) and Youtube (http://www.youtube.com) which offer free hosting. These video hosting sites allowed vloggers to combine current blogging technology with hosted videos to create vlogs. The videos posted to the vlog typically start with a brief intro that lets the viewers know what they are watching. Some vlogs use a format very similar to television shows. Since vlogs use existing blog technology, they typically allow the viewers to leave text comments, creating a more intimate and interactive experience than traditional media.

There are three main types of vlogs: personal vlogs, news shows, and entertainment orientated vlogs (Luers, 2007). Personal vloggers talk about or even share their life experiences captured by a video camera and are thus more of a personal media than a television show. News shows are informal newscasts on a wide variety of topics. An example of a news show is Rocketboom (http://www.rocketboom.com). These shows are somewhat similar to a newscast found on TV, but more interactive, focused on web culture, and informal. Also there are vlogs that exist for purely entertainment reasons such as AskANinja (http://www.askaninja.com), or a sitcom format such as the Carol and Steve show (http://www.stevegarfield.blogs.com/videoblog/carol_and_steve_show/index.html) (Clayfield, 2007).

Among the few existing research studies about vlogs, some examined vlogging technologies. For example, Parker and Pfeiffer (2005) investigated ways to make vlogs more interactive than just having videos posted on a blog site. Miles (2006) identified current limitations of vlogs and how these limitations could be addressed with future technologies.

Other researchers investigated the difference between vlogging and traditional media (e.g., television and independent films) (Clayfield, 2007; Luers, 2007; Miles, 2007), and found that unlike traditional media such as broadcast television, the major motivation for vlogging is to receive feedback and support from other vloggers and find friendships in the vloggers' community, thus fulfilling some social needs of the vloggers (Luers, 2007). Therefore, vloggers' interactions with one another are foundations of the vloggers' community. To study such interactions, we use social network analysis, a powerful tool for investigating the interactions between social entities such as people, corporations, or other organizations (Wasserman & Faust, 1994).

Social Network Analysis

A social network consists of nodes and links, where nodes are the social entities and links are the relationships between nodes. Social network analysis allows researchers to visualize and conduct mathematical analysis on a network of social entities, and therefore understand the structure of the relationships among the actors (Wasserman & Faust, 1994).

Centrality

Social network analysis uses certain measurements to identify the important actors in a network (Wasserman & Faust, 1994). The most common measurement of importance is centrality. Individuals with high centrality have higher influence in the network. There are three widely used measures of centrality: degree centrality, closeness centrality, and betweenness centrality (Freeman, 1977).

Degree centrality measures the number of ties an actor has to other actors within the network (Wasserman & Faust, 1994). Illustrated in Figure 1, node C has the highest degree centrality and is thus the most central node because it is connected to three other nodes. Node D is peripheral and has a low degree centrality because it is connected to only one other node.

Figure 1. Example of degree centrality

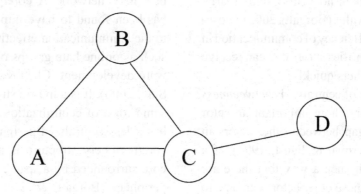

Another way of looking at degree centrality is the degree to which an individual can communicate with others directly or quickly (Borgatti, 2005). According to social network theory, a large amount of interaction by an individual will not only change that individual's relative position in the network, but will also affect others positions. Degree centrality identifies those with a high number of connections with others, and these individuals are likely leaders or hubs in the network.

The major limitation of the degree centrality is that it could only be used to compare centrality scores within a single network. However, this limitation can be overcome by using scores standardized for network size.

The next centrality measure is *closeness centrality*. It is based upon distance between one actor and all other actors in a network. Closeness measures how easy it is for one actor to be able to communicate with others in the network (Wasserman & Faust, 1994). The fewer actors an actor has to go through to get to any other actors, the closer the actor is (Wasserman & Faust, 1994).

Borgatti (2005) noted that nodes with low closeness scores have short distances from others, and so tend to receive information sooner, assuming that what flows originates from all other nodes with equal probability, and whatever is flowing manages to travel along the shortest paths. In the case of information traveling through a network, normally nodes with low closeness scores are well-positioned to obtain novel information early, when it has the most value (Borgatti, 2005). Closeness measures the efficiency of communication in the network and identifies actors that can receive information from others quickly.

The last measure of centrality is *betweenness centrality*. It measures how important an actor is at bridging the gap between other actors in the network (Wasserman & Faust, 1994). If a network is set up in such a way that there are no other paths that these other actors can take to communicate with each other, this actor in the middle has high betweenness (Wasserman & Faust, 1994). Removing a node with high betweenness can disrupt the flow of information through the network and introduce fragmentation (Borgatti & Everett, 2006).

Therefore, betweenness measures the amount of network flow that a given node "controls" (Borgatti, 2005). It shows whether an individual plays the role of a broker or gatekeeper (Wang & Chen, 2004). A broker exchanges information between two other nodes and a gatekeeper withholds information from passing between nodes. Notice in Figure 2, the "G" node has high betweenness centrality and is connecting the ABCDEF and HIJKL networks together into one big network.

Network Centralization and a Core/Periphery Structure

Network Centralization looks at the centrality measures at a network wide level and determines the extent to which the network exhibits a star structure. Centrality refers to the importance of an individual actor; while centralization refers to the network as a whole. For each of Freeman's centrality measures, a network centralization score can be calculated which indicates how centralized the network is. Network centralization is important to this research because it shows overall how centralized or decentralized the network of vloggers may be.

A common social network structure is a core/periphery network. A core/periphery structure has been found to have important implications to the communication effectiveness of networks such as online hate groups or open source software development (Chau & Xu, 2007; Long & Siau, 2006). It is a hybrid structure that exhibits some form of centralization as a core, but also has a less centralized periphery. The prototype core/periphery structure is a dense, connected core surrounded by a sparse, loosely connected periphery (Borgatti & Everett, 1999; Long & Siau, 2006) (Figure 3 shows an example where

Figure 2. Example of betweenness: a node bridging two clusters of nodes

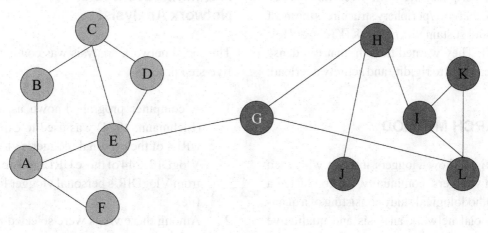

the dark nodes are the core and the lighter nodes are the periphery). This structure is somewhere in between a highly central star network and a fully decentralized network (Borgatti & Everett, 2006). The presence of core/periphery structure is determined by fitting a social network to a mathematical model. A fit of.5 (50%) or greater is considered a good fit (Long & Siau, 2006).

One unique feature of this structure is that it cannot be subdivided into exclusive cohesive subgroups, although some actors are connected more than others (Borgatti & Everett, 1999). Also, nodes in the core are very close to each other, but are also close to the periphery. However, nodes in the periphery are relatively close to only the core. Krebs and Holley (2004) noted that this arrangement allows information to move the fastest through the network. In addition, the network becomes more robust and stable. They also noted that organizations move from a scattered structure

Figure 3. A core/periphery network

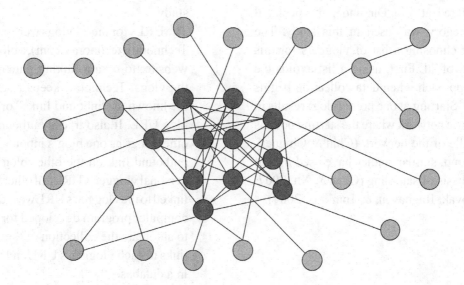

to a core/periphery network over time. They concluded that core/periphery structure is the most efficient and sustainable network (Krebs & Holley, 2004). They warned though, that too dense of a core can lead to rigidity and activity overload.

RESEARCH METHOD

To investigate how vloggers interact with each other in a vloggers' community, we conducted a multi-methodological study consisting of a quantitative social network analysis and qualitative interviews. The social network analysis identified the overall structure of the vloggers' community as well as the relationships among all the vloggers in the community. The qualitative interviews of the vloggers in the core of the community, on the other hand, provided an in-depth understanding of the interactions of the vloggers. The data was collected in the spring of 2007.

This study used a sample of vloggers who identified themselves as personal vloggers from VlogDIR, a well-known vlogger directory site (vlogdir.com) that was a primary video blog directory at the time this study was conducted, where vloggers voluntarily opt-in to a certain category of the directory. A list of personal vloggers who have registered at VlogDir under the personal vlogger category was used in this study. The reasons for choosing a list of vloggers for this study are twofold. First, using a list avoids the snowball approach when data collection begins at one blog. Starting at one point (vlog) results in an ego-centric network where the starting point is in the middle of the network (Chin & Chignell, 2006). Second, similar studies have used lists of blogs as a basis of sampling (Chau & Xu, 2007; Kumar, Novak, Raghaven, & Tomkins, 2004).

A Quantitative Social Network Analysis

The social network analysis was conducted in a five-step process.

1. A computer program known as a spider (Eichmann, 1994) was used to capture the URLs of the personal vlogger's vlogs from VlogDIR. 244 of these URLs were collected from VlogDIR's personal vlogger list into a file.

2. Among these vlogs were selected that met the following criteria: 1) The URL had to be a personal vlog. This means that the vlog clearly indicates that it is about someone's life or describes its contents as personal. A content analysis of a video easily determined the subject matter of the vlog as personal or not. 2) If a URL was found to be a personal vlog, it had to have three video postings within the last three months of the time of this study. This second criteria was chosen to ensure that the personal vloggers in this study were representative of currently active vloggers that had a history of video postings. This resulted in a total of 74, of the original 244 vlogs selected for the remainder of the study.

3. The URLs for the 74 vlogs were entered into Technorati (technorati.com), a blog tracking website, to obtain linking patterns among the vlogs. Technorati keeps track of what are known as "inbound links" or links to a blog URL. It also tracks outbound links to other blogs as one blog's inbound link is an outbound link on the other blog. For each personal vlogger's URL, all other URLs that linked to the vlogger's URL were captured. A computer program developed for this study to automate the collection of these inbound links to each vlogger's URL and store them in a database.

4. A socialmatrix was built based on the links among the vlogs that were collected. A sociomatrix is a mathematical representation of a social network that uses data placed in rows and columns to signify relationships between individuals in the network. Table 1 is a theoretical example of a sociomatrix that represents linking relationships for four individuals.

In this example, a link exists between A&B, B&D, A&C, and D&A. Notice that self relationships, known as reflexive ties, are usually ignored and result in a blank diagonal line in the sociomatrix (Wasserman & Faust, 1994).

The links gathered from Technorati were examined to see if any personal vloggers from the sample (the cleaned URL list from VlogDir) had linked to other personal vloggers from the sample. If so, an indication of the link was placed into a sociomatrix. Another computer program was developed to automate the generation of the sociomatrix. This sociomatrix was 74 rows by 74 columns. Links between vlogs were represented by placing 1s in the respective rows and columns of both vlogs. A social network formed this way is known as an undirected network since the direction of the link was not considered. Since we were only interested in the interactions of personal vloggers, this type of social network is appropriate for this study.

5. The sociomatrix was then used as the dataset for UCINET, a social network analysis software package. UCINET is commonly used for social network research. In this study, UCINET created the visualization of the network as well as calculated the social network measures of centrality and core/periphery fitness.

Table 1. A Sociomatrix

0	A	B	C	D
A	0	1	1	1
B	1	0	0	1
C	1	0	0	0
D	1	1	0	0

Results

Figure 4 shows the social network of the vloggers' community. The dots are the nodes that represent the vloggers and the arrows are the links between the nodes. Nodes with no links were removed from the graph. This resulted in a final network of thirty four active nodes.

Results of the centrality measures are presented in Table 2.

At the individual level, nodes 12, 34, 35, 27, 17, and 7 had the highest degree centrality. These nodes had a degree of 9 or higher. All of these nodes were part of the core. The core's density is rather low, resulting in a loose core. Nodes 35, 7, 34, 12, 27, and 37 had the highest betweenness centrality. These nodes had a normalized between of 13 or higher. These nodes served as bridges and connected most of the loose core together. Nodes 12, 34, 7, 17, 35, and 27 had the highest closeness centrality. These nodes had a normalize closeness of 48 or higher. These nodes were also in the core.

The network centralization scores are presented in Table 3.

According to Long and Siau (2006), the network centralization scores were relatively low. All of the centralization scores were less than 50% which is the midpoint between a centralized and decentralized network. The highest level of centralization was exhibited when calculated using closeness. This means that overall nodes had a higher level of closeness than degree or betweenness.

Figure 4. Social network of vloggers' community

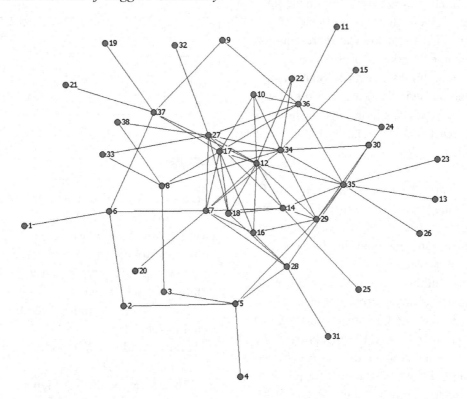

Results of core/periphery analysis are shown in Table 4.

Nodes 7,12,14,16,17,18,27,28,29,34,35, and 36 were in the core. The rest of the nodes were in the periphery. These determinations were derived by shifting the nodes between the core and periphery until the maximum Pearson's correlation between the observed data and an ideal core/periphery network was achieved. Overall, this network exhibits a core/periphery structure since a fitness score over .50 indicates a good fit of the core/periphery model.

Qualitative Interviews

Although the results of social network analysis indicate the network structure to be core/periphery, it did not provide in-depth information on the underlying reasons for the core/periphery structure of the community. To better understand why and how the vloggers interacted in the community,

we interviewed thirteen vloggers who had the highest degree centrality scores in the network. These vloggers were selected for interviews as they were most active in the network. The interviews were open-ended phone interviews following the purposive sampling technique (Cooper & Emory, 1995). In addition to general demographic information such as age, gender, and occupation, each interviewee provided answers to the following questions.

- When did you start vlogging?
- How much time do you spend watching vlogs?
- How often do you post vlogs?
- How do you see your role in the vlogger's community?
- What types of vlogs do you like to watch?
- Why do you vlog?
- Do you think it's important for people to watch and comment on other people's

Table 2. Individual centrality measures

Node	Degree	Normalized Degree	Normalized Closeness	Normalized Betweenness
1	1	2.703	28.030	0.0
2	2	5.405	32.456	1.491
3	2	5.405	33.636	1.294
4	1	2.703	28.244	0.0
5	5	13.514	38.947	10.259
6	4	10.811	38.542	8.747
7	9	24.324	49.333	15.883
8	5	13.514	41.111	5.709
9	2	5.405	35.238	0.824
10	4	10.811	40.217	0.403
11	1	2.703	31.092	0.0
12	11	29.730	52.857	15.051
13	1	2.703	33.036	0.0
14	7	18.919	47.436	7.433
15	1	2.703	33.945	0.0
16	5	13.514	43.023	1.077
17	9	24.324	48.684	10.077
18	5	13.514	43.023	1.718
19	1	2.703	30.081	0.0
20	1	2.703	33.333	0.0
21	1	2.703	30.081	0.0
22	2	5.405	37.374	0.043
23	1	2.703	33.036	0.0
24	2	5.405	35.922	0.503
25	1	2.703	32.456	0.0
26	1	2.703	33.036	0.0
27	9	24.324	48.052	14.698
28	6	16.216	43.529	9.942
29	7	18.919	46.835	9.798
30	2	5.405	38.144	0.0
31	1	2.703	30.579	0.0
32	1	2.703	32.743	0.0
33	2	5.405	34.906	0.234
34	1	27.027	50.685	15.099
35	1	27.027	48.684	21.681
36	7	18.919	44.578	11.737
37	6	16.216	42.529	13.993
38	2	5.405	34.906	0.234

Table 3. Network centralization scores

Network Degree	Normalized Network Degree	Network Betweenness	Network Closeness
20.27%	1.80%	17.46%	30.05%

vlogs in the vlogger's community? Please explain.

• Is it important to you that others watch and comment on your vlog? Please explain.

The interviews were recorded and subsequently transcribed. The data was then coded into themes following guidelines on open coding suggested by Strauss & Corbin (1998). In this study, open coding was performed by first breaking the data into concepts about vlogging. Then, categories were formed by logically grouping the concepts together.

Qualitative Results

The results of open coding were a list of concepts, which were then categorized into four themes. Each theme was created by logically grouping the specific concepts together into a broader category. The first theme identified from this study was interactions in the community, which revealed interaction patterns in the community and provided an in-depth understanding for the core/periphery structure of the community. The other three themes included characteristics of vloggers, motivations for vlogging, and reasons to choose video as a medium for blogging. These themes provided descriptive information about vloggers

and the vlog community, which also helps us better understand the community.

Interactions in the Community

Vloggers watch and create vlogs based upon their interests. This creates a community based upon the interactions of those with the same interests. Unlike television, bloggers can pick and choose what vlogs they would like to watch. Vloggers typically watch vlogs that they enjoy and those of their friends or people they know. A vlogger noted that "we can be very specific and subjective which allows us to choose what we want to watch and not watch." and another said "I watch people that I like."

In addition, vlogging is a highly interactive medium, which allows for conversations and connections with other vloggers. Unlike television, vlogs allow for conversation between the vlog author and the viewers. Viewers can comment on vlogs and vloggers can comment on each others' vlogs which leads to conversations. The exchange of feedback is a social norm in the vlogger community. Vloggers even go as far as integrating other vloggers into their videos. One vlogger explained that "there is a whole conversation and it's [vlogging] more of an interactive medium than just television. You watch something you like and you comment on it and maybe if you can, make

Table 4. Core/periphery analysis results

Nodes in Core	Nodes in Periphery
7 12 14 16 17 18 27 28 29 34 35 36	*1 2 3 4 5 6 8 9 10 11 13 15 19 20 21 22 23 24 25 26 30 31 32 33 37 38*

Final Core/Periphery Fitness: 0.544

a video about it or mesh it up or do something like that. I love it when people take other [vlogger's] videos and then put them together to make something interesting."

Overall vloggers were found to be supportive of each other and offered help or advice when they could. Leaving positive feedback on a vlog was interpreted by vloggers as someone who watched and enjoyed their vlog enough to leave a comment that acknowledged that they enjoyed it. All vloggers had statements similar to "the comments kind of spur me on and get me excited and keeps me going", "when someone comments on my vlog it can be like "wow, somebody watched me and acknowledged my existence in the universe", and "gives us some satisfaction knowing that, hey some people are watching and they enjoyed it enough." Vloggers even encouraged each other to post more vlogs, especially the newer ones that were still finding their voice. One vlogger had an insightful comment: "A lot of people have trouble finding their voice. So many people say that I don't have anything to say and who would want to listen to me. That's a big myth that the entertainment industry has perpetrated on all of us is that they are the only ones who have something to say and we're supposed to listen. We all have something to say." Sometimes this support came in the form of constructive criticism for their show. These comments served as useful ways to increase the production quality of vlogs they were written for. They also served as a feedback mechanism to determine which topics or vlogs styles the audience enjoys so that they may be incorporated into future vlogs. Comments such as "I get some constructive criticism and things like that. It makes your videos better and ups the quality of your video" and "If I don't have comments, I'm thinking people didn't like it. So, yeah, it's a gauge that helps me know if people like that type of video and I should make something similar to that kind next time" clearly indicate that a portion of the comments are directly related to the video content.

It was also found that those with similar interests would typically be the ones to comment on a vlogger's vlog. Most vloggers gave statements similar to "I'll get comments from many people who share similar interests." Therefore, one interesting note about the vloggers' community is that; since it consists of vloggers creating, watching, and commenting on vlogs based upon interests, it is a somewhat decentralized community. There is no one is in direct control of the community. Instead, the culmination of all of the individual vlogger interactions is what creates a loosely bounded and decentralized community. A vlogger notes that "other than reading vlog posts and watching each others' videos, no one was directly telephoning anyone, directing anyone, there has been no one single mastermind behind the movement."

Comments left on vlogs almost always led to other forms of online interactions such as instant messaging, e-mail, and other means. Some vloggers also used social networking sites such as Facebook (facebook.com) or Myspace (myspace.com). Vloggers often did not comment on the comments left on their vlogs but instead used personal e-mail to respond as evident in statements such as "I've instant messaged them, we e-mail" and "I have people contact me through either e-mail or maybe a social networking site. They say, hey, I enjoyed this particular video or whatever and send a request on Facebook or Myspace or something like that."

Frequently online friendships turned into real life interactions such as group events or local meet-ups. Although the vloggers' community is somewhat a decentralized community, the most active vloggers who share common interests formed a core group and organized larger group events like VloggerCon (a conference created specifically for vloggers; vloggercon.com). Another indication of the existence of the core group was that most of the vloggers interviewed (those in the core group based on the social network analysis) had attended VloggerCon. One of the organizers of VloggerCon said that "There are not many real-life opportunities for people to interact, which is one of the reasons why I did VloggerCon". Most vloggers in this study who attended VloggerCon gave statements similar to "I've been to VloggerCon last year… it was cool to meet a bunch of people I could not have met otherwise. I met a lot of people that I am a fan of. It was a really needed experience." Also a vlogger mentioned that they have met their online vlogger friends in person with the statement "After getting more comfortable we might go to lunch or something."

Characteristics of Vloggers

Vloggers reported that they primarily vlogged during their free time. Jobs and family responsibilities often took precedence over vlogging. Some vloggers spend up to two to three hours a day watching vlogs and post up to every day, especially during special weeks such as videoblogging week (videobloggingweek2007.blogspot. com). A vlogger explained that she "used to spend a huge amount of time watching video blogs. It was basically 2-3 hours a day. More recently I haven't had much time because I graduated from school and I work." Another said that "I have over 250 videos on my site at the moment. There have been weeks where I posted 3 or 4 videos a week. However I recently got married and for a lack of a better expression, marriage stuff has been taking up a lot of my time."

Another characteristic is that vloggers usually had experience with blogs and/or video production before they started vlogging. Many were using video long before they started putting their videos online and some of them even knew how to edit their videos and burn them to compact disc. Vloggers made statements such as "I knew how to shoot a video", "I was kind of playing around making movies probably for a couple of years before I put it online", about prior video experience. As for previous experience with text blogging, five out of the thirteen vloggers reported that they had previous blogs.

Most vloggers interviewed also had standards for production quality, both in terms of the audio/video quality and original/creative content. Vloggers had expectations of audio quality in the vlogs that they watched and also expected for the content of the video to be creative/original. Supporting statements were: "I like shows that have good enough production quality. If the sound level is going up and down really bad where I have to keep adjusting my audio controls, even if it's really funny or everyone is talking about it, for me I won't go back to those shows" "They are doing something original or presenting it in an original way. Not just talking about the same stuff that everyone else is talking about."

Motivations for Vlogging

Vlogs are a new form of consumer created media beyond text blogs or public access television. Vloggers make videos and post them on the internet for anyone to watch, which allows them to have a voice and engage in intelligent conversations. Statements such as "I just like the fact that people have to do something intelligent and communicate and have a voice and not have to go through like studios or TV stations" and "It's so awesome to make media and that your media consumption is made by people you know" give some indication as to why vlogs are becoming such a popular form of consumer created media.

Another prominent motivation for vlogging was to post and watch vlogs about peoples' personal lives. One vlogger summed it up with "I'm really most interested in peoples' stories about their personal lives". Others said that they "like a lot of personal video blogs where you get to know people and they create out of their own lives" and "tend to go more towards a personal-like real life video blog." This involved sharing personal stories, expressions, opinions, environments, and creativity with their family, friends, or other vloggers. A few supporting statements are "I want to do something creative/artistic" and "I do it sometimes to tell a story to communicate with people." and "I put them [videos] online and have them available for my family to see and those who live close by." Part of the reasons for sharing with other vloggers beyond family and friends was to gain attention from others. One vlogger reported "Ever since I was a little kid I liked attention. I get attention and I like being in the center. I like being kind of the center of the attention." Another said "I love to be on camera and like for other people to watch."

Often time vloggers also saw their videos as a way to entertain others, as one vlogger said "It's partly to entertain people." Some vloggers found that vlogging was fun to do and even considered it a personal hobby. One stated "I'm just doing it for fun really and I do it more for myself than for anybody who's watching really", and "It's just fun to do and is an interesting hobby for me."

Vloggers also found that vlogging is a great way to make friends with people around the world based upon similar interests. One vlogger stated "I have made friends all across the world, especially folks that have a genuine interest in Japan often keep coming back to my site, as do other videobloggers."

Reasons to Choose Video as a Medium for Blogging

Vloggers chose video mainly for its advantages over other media, such as text and audio. First and foremost, video is a rich medium consisting of a combination of audio and moving images. Vloggers found that video created a more personal experience than text or photos as they could see facial expressions and hear tones of voice. For example, one vlogger stated that "When you meet them [other vloggers] it's like you know them because you have seen their facial expression and you've heard their tone of voice." Another vlogger explained that the visual aspect of video provided more intimate and personal information when he stated "You get to see people's spaces.

You see their environment and even if you don't get to see that person, you get to see something visual that they created. I think you get a lot more kind of rich personal information than you would get from a text blog and so you create a situation where you tend to know the person, you feel closer to them than you would with just written or even audio kinds of blogs."

Vloggers also stated that they had greater flexibility with video than with text or photo blogs and it was much easier than public access TV. With a video camera it was as easy as recording a show and uploading it online. For example a vlogger cited that he "loves being able to just turn on the camera and make something" with vlogs.

Vloggers were also able to express themselves more with video than with other forms of media such as writing. Another vlogger stated "I'm able to do more with videos than I can with writing."

Discussion and Implications

The results of social network analysis on personal vloggers in VlogDIR suggest that the vloggers' community is a decentralized community and exhibits a core/periphery structure. Core/periphery is a hybrid structure that exhibits some form of centralization as a core, but also has a less centralized periphery. According to Krebs and Holley (2004), core/periphery structure is the most efficient and sustainable network (Krebs & Holley, 2004), as this arrangement allows information to move the fastest through the network.

The qualitative interview results confirm this finding and indicate that a possible reason for such a structure is that vloggers watch and create vlogs mostly based upon interests. Vloggers that share similar interests, views, or opinions are usually inter-connected and this forms the bases of the community. Since vloggers in a community could have various interests, the network formed based on these different interests will naturally be less centralized. Vloggers with similar interests are likely to form a core group with some people more actively involved in the core and others in the periphery.

The qualitative interview results also show that vlogs are a highly interactive medium and are filled with conversations. Interactions in the form of feedback occur quite frequently and are a social norm of the vlogger's community. Feedbacks provided by other vloggers often supportive and considered a source of satisfaction. This exchange of feedback is what creates the vlogger's community. However, vloggers also have other forms of online communication and sometimes even move their interactions offline in the form of groups or one-on-one meetings, which further facilitate the formation of the core of the community. Such interactions in the vlogger's community are somewhat similar to interactions in other forms of blog communities (Boyd, 2006; Herring & Scheidt, 2004; Nardi, Schiano, Gumbrecht, & Swartz, 2004; Wang, Deng, & Chiu, 2005).

In addition, according to the qualitative interviews, the major motivations for vlogging include sharing personal stories and opinions with others, gaining attention from others, entertaining others, and making friends with others based upon similar interests. Many of these motivations were also found to be motivations for text and photo blogging (Boyd, 2006; Herring & Scheidt, 2004; Rosenbloom, 2004; Wang, Deng, & Chiu, 2005).

The differences between vlogs and other forms of blogs generally have to do with the richness of the media added by video. Based on the qualitative interview results, it appears that video tends to make vlogs more personal and emotionally intimate than text blogs. As one vlogger reported when watching vlogs, he is able to sense their emotions as they are conveyed through tone of voice or facial expressions in the video. Also the use of video creates new opportunities and vloggers found that they could do more with videos than writing alone.

Vlogs are a new form of consumer created media. Traditionally, sharing video with a large audience was only possible through television stations or movie theaters. While there are programs that television studios offer to everyday individuals such as public access, they are subject to many stipulations such as a full production schedule of half hour episodes which make them inaccessible to most people. Blogging was seen as a new wave of consumer journalism when it became popular. Vlogs are now enjoying that same status as another form of consumer created media. This is most apparent in one vlogger's enthusiastic statement of "It's so awesome to make media and that your media consumption is made by people you know."

Overall, the results of this research help us to better understand the vloggers' community and how vloggers interact with each other in the community. The results offer many implications for both individuals and businesses. Since vlogs allow communication at a more personal, realistic level, individuals can use vlogs to raise awareness about themselves or other issues. They may be able to make more friends and maintain active interactions with friends using vlogs. They may also be able to use vlogs to gain a cross-cultural understanding and thus be more empathetic to other cultures. Businesses could also use vlogs to communicate with consumers, promote products or services, and improve customer service. Using vlogs, they can make their messages more personal and interactive, and thus raise customers' awareness to their products or services. For example, companies can communicate to their customers more directly than television advertisements and even respond to comments left on their vlogs.

Another implication lies in the structure of the vlogger community. Since the vlogger community is a core/periphery structure, one can utilize this structure by identifying and reaching the core group of vloggers. This should generate network wide awareness much faster than reaching someone in the periphery. For example, companies can use social network analysis to identify vloggers in the core group and collaborate with them to quickly disseminate promotional messages.

Limitations and Future Research

This research is one of the first to investigate the nature of the vloggers' community, and therefore, it has a few limitations. However, these limitations also create opportunities for future research. For example, this study only focuses on linkages between vloggers - in the form of hyperlinks to each other's vlogs - in studying the social network in the vloggers' community. As the results of the qualitative study suggest, vloggers communicate and connect in other ways beyond the hyperlinks formed on their vlogs. Therefore, a study of a more complete social network of vloggers that includes other forms of online interactions such as vlog comments, e-mails, instant messages, as well as offline interactions, would likely provide additional insights into the vlogging community.

Another limitation of this study is the relatively small sample size, because the current study was limited to only active personal vloggers. Although focusing on just one type of vlog allows for better control of the study and is a common approach in the initial stage of a research, in the future, it will be interesting to increase the sample size by including other types of vlogs and explore the differences and similarities between personal vlogs and other types of vlogs.

Finally, the current study is not a longitudinal study, therefore, the social network derived from the study is only a snapshot of the vloggers' community at its early stage. As many social communities, the vloggers' community is constantly changing over time. It will be interesting and necessary to conduct a longitudinal study to investigate how the vlogger network changes over time.

CONCLUSION

This multi-methodological research was designed to explore a vloggers' community, an emerging social community that has received little attention in academic research. A quantitative social network analysis revealed that the vloggers' community was largely decentralized, in which no individuals had significant sway over the community. The vlogger's community also exhibits core-peripheral structure, with some actively connected vloggers in the core group and loosely connected vloggers in the peripheral group. A qualitative, open-ended interview study confirmed this finding and provided additional insights into the vloggers' community. The qualitative results indicated that: a) interaction is at the core of the vloggers' community; b) many vloggers had previous experience with video, text blogging, or both; c) vloggers were strongly motivated by the opportunity to share their life stories, experiences, and cultures with others; and d) video was chosen for blogging because it allows for more intimate and emotional interaction than other online communication medias.

REFERENCES

Armstrong, A., & Hagel, J. (1996). The Real Value of On-Line Communities. *Harvard Business Review, 74*(3), 134–141.

Borgatti, S. P. (2005). Centrality and network flow. *Social Networks, 27*(1), 55–71. doi:10.1016/j.socnet.2004.11.008

Borgatti, S. P., & Everett, M. G. (1999). Models of Core/Periphery Structures. *Social Networks, 21*, 375–395. doi:10.1016/S0378-8733(99)00019-2

Borgatti, S. P., & Everett, M. G. (2006). A Graph-Theoretic Perspective on Centrality. *Social Networks, 28*(4), 466–484. doi:10.1016/j.socnet.2005.11.005

Boyd, D. (2006). A Blogger's Blog: Exploring the Definition of a Medium. *Reconstruction: Studies in Contemporary Culture, 6*(4). Retrieved from http://reconstruction.eserver.org/064/boyd.shtml

Chau, M., & Xu, J. (2007). Mining Communities and Their Relationships in Blogs: A Study of Online Hate Groups. *International Journal of Human-Computer Studies, 65*(1), 57–70. doi:10.1016/j.ijhcs.2006.08.009

Chin, A., & Chignell, M. (2006). *A Social Hypertext Model for Finding Community in Blogs*. Paper presented at the ACM Conference on Hypertext and Hypermedia, New York.

Clayfield, M. (2007). A Certain Tendency in Videoblogging and Rethinking the Rebirth of the Author. *Post Identity, 5*(1). Retrieved from http://hdl.handle.net/2027/spo.pid9999.0005.2106.

Cooper, D. R., & Emory, C. W. (1995). *Business Research Methods* (5th ed.). Scarborough, ON, Canada: Thomson Nelson.

Eichmann, D. (1994). The RBSE Spider: Balancing Effective Search against Web Load. In *Proceedings of the First World Wide Web Conference*, Geneva, Switzerland.

Freeman, L. C. (1977). A Set of Measures of Centrality Based on Betweenness. *Sociometry, 40*, 35–41. doi:10.2307/3033543

Gordon, S. (2006). Rise of the Blog (Journal-Based Website). *IEE Review, 52*(3), 32–35. doi:10.1049/ir:20060301

Herring, S., & Scheidt, L. (2004). Bridging the Gap: A Genre Analysis of Weblogs. In *Proceedings of the Hawaii International Conference on System Science*, Waikoloa, HI.

Holahan, C. (2006). Q&A with Amanda Congdon. *BusinessWeek*. Retrieved from http://www.businessweek.com/technology/content/nov2006/tc20061114_907330.htm

Kiesler, S. (1986). The Hidden Messages in Computer Networks. *Harvard Business Review, 64*, 46–60.

Krebs, V., & Holley, J. (2002). *Building Smart Communities Through Network Weaving*. Retrieved from http://www.orgnet.com/Building-Networks.pdf

Kumar, R., Novak, J., Raghaven, P., & Tomkins, A. (2004). Structure and Evolution of Blogspace. *Communications of the ACM, 47*(12), 35–39. doi:10.1145/1035134.1035162

Long, Y., & Siau, K. (2006). Social Network Dynamics for Open Source Software Projects. In *Proceedings of the Americas Conference on Information Systems*, Acapulco, Mexico.

Luers, W. (2007). Cinema Without Show Business: A Poetics of Vlogging. *Post Identity, 5*(1). Retrieved from http://hdl.handle.net/2027/spo.pid9999.0005.2105.

Miles, A. (2003). Softvideography. In Eskelinen, M., & Koskimaa, R. (Eds.), *Cybertext Yearbook 2002-2003* (pp. 218–236). Saarijarvi, Finland: University of Jyvaskyla.

Miles, A. (2006). A Vision for Genuine Rich Media Blogging. In Bruns, A., & Jacobs, J. (Eds.), *Uses of Blogs* (pp. 213–222). New York: Peter Lang.

Miles, A. (2007). New Media Studies and the New Internet Cinema. *Post Identity, 5*(1). Retrieved from http://hdl.handle.net/2027/spo.pid9999.0005.2102

Nardi, B. A., Schiano, D. J., Gumbrecht, M., & Swartz, L. (2004). Why We Blog. *Communications of the ACM, 47*(12), 41–46. doi:10.1145/1035134.1035163

Parker, C., & Pfeiffer, S. (2005). Video Blogging: Content to the Max. *IEEE MultiMedia, 12*(2), 4–8. doi:10.1109/MMUL.2005.41

Rosenbloom, A. (2004). Into the Blogosphere: Introduction. *Communications of the ACM, 47*(12), 30–33. doi:10.1145/1035134.1035161

Schiano, D. J., Nardi, B. A., Gumbrecht, M., & Swartz, L. (2004). Blogging by the Rest of Us. In *Proceedings of the ACM Conference on Computer Human Interaction*, Vienna, Austria.

Strauss, A., & Corbin, J. (1998). *Basics of Qualitative Research: Techniques and Procedures for Developing Grounded Theory*. London: Sage.

Wang, H., Deng, Y., & Chiu, S. (2005). Beyond Photoblogging: New Directions of Mobile Communication. In *Proceedings of the Conference on Human Computer Interaction with Mobile Devices and Services*, Salzburg, Austria.

Wang, J., & Chen, C. (2004). An Automated Tool for Managing Interactions in Virtual Communities - Using Social Netwrok Analysis Approach. *Journal of Organizational Computing and Electronic Commerce, 14*(1), 1–26. doi:10.1207/s15327744joce1401_1

Wasserman, S., & Faust, K. (1994). *Social Network Analysis: Method and Applications*. Cambridge, UK: Cambridge University Press.

This work was previously published in the International Journal of Virtual Communities and Social Networking, Volume 2, Issue 2, edited by Subhasish Dasgupta, pp. 43-59, copyright 2010 by IGI Publishing(an imprint of IGI Global).

Chapter 6
Analysis of Students' Engagement and Activities in a Virtual Learning Community:
A Social Network Methodology

Ben K. Daniel
University of Saskatchewan, Canada

Richard A. Schwier
University of Saskatchewan, Canada

ABSTRACT

With advances in communication technology and online pedagogy, virtual learning communities have become rich learning environments in which individuals construct knowledge and learn from others. Typically, individuals in virtual learning communities interact by exchanging information and sharing knowledge and experiences with others as communities. The team at the Virtual Learning Community Research Laboratory has employed an array of methods, including social network analysis (SNA), to examine and describe different virtual learning communities. The goal of the study was to employ mixed methods to explore whether the content of students' interaction reflected the fundamental elements of community. SNA techniques were used to analyse ties and relationships among individuals in a network with the goal of understanding patterns of interactions among individuals and their activities, and interviews were conducted to explore features and student perceptions of their learning community.

INTRODUCTION

Traditional classrooms offer interesting contrasts to e-learning classroom environments when considering the types of communities that can evolve within these environments. In traditional classroom, learning communities are visible to the instructor and students can easily make connections with peers due to availability of rich visible social cues. As such, research suggested that instructors can actively nurture the sense of a community among students (Daniel, Schwier, & Ross, 2005). In virtual learning communities, however, where learners are often isolated from

DOI: 10.4018/978-1-4666-1553-3.ch006

each other and the instructor, developing a sense of a community, though critical, can be difficult. The sense of isolation among learners in online environments can be minimized if forethought is given to the development of the online milieu that can foster a sense of a community among learners. As McDonald, Noakes, Stuckey and Nyrop (2005) observed that in many online contexts learners report feeling disconnected, and experience an isolation or social exclusion that impacts on their levels of participation, satisfaction and learning.

This study employed social network analysis (SNA) techniques to visualise and understand structural patterns of interactions in a formal virtual learning community. The structural pattern of the network was corroborated by data drawn from participants through interviews and focus groups in which participants openly discussed their experiences about sense of a community online and factors that they considered critical to maintain it.

In recent years, many methods have been employed to study the flow of information among individuals and communities, ranging from empirical to theoretical. The defining feature of SNA is its focus on the structure of relationships, ranging from casual acquaintance to close bonds. SNA assumes that relationships are important. It maps and measures formal and informal relationships to understand what facilitates or impedes the knowledge flows that bind interacting units, who knows whom, and who shares what information and knowledge with whom by what communication media (e.g., data and information, voice, or video communications). SNA is a method with increasing application in the Social Sciences and has been applied in areas as diverse as psychology, health, business organization, and electronic communications. More recently, interest has grown in the analysis of leadership networks to sustain and strengthen their relationships within and across groups, organizations, and related systems.

A social network is a set of individuals who are connected to one another through socially meaningful relationships (Hanneman & Mark, 2005). According to social network theory, social relationships are viewed in terms of nodes and ties. Nodes are individual actors within the network, and ties represent the flow of relationships between actors. In its most simple form, a network graph represents a map of all of the relevant ties between the nodes in the community. De Laat (2002) used social SNA to understand interactions patterns in virtual communities.

Several measures have been employed to understand the structure of a social network. These measures include "betweenness" which refer to the degree an actor lies between other individuals in the network. For example it describes the extent to which an actor is directly connected only to those other individuals that are not directly connected to each other. Betweenness is sometimes described as an intermediary; liaisons; bridges. Betweenness also connotes the number of actors in which a node is connected to indirectly through their direct links.

SNA can also describe a broad suite of techniques that incorporate a variety of methods and applications, yielding a rich research tradition that is beyond the scope of this study to summarize fully. Important threads have included the development of methodologies to characterize networks, including mathematical tools such as graph theory, which incorporate rich statistical tools to handle interdependency among represented nodes and edges in a given graph. These relations defined by linkages among nodes are a fundamental component of SNA and are increasingly used to understand and describe various social networks (Freeman, 2004; Scott, 2000).

There is significant potential for employing SNA techniques to understand virtual communities. Wellman (1999) proposed mapping the virtual community activities onto social networks, taking into consideration among others features such as density (how people in the network are connected to each other), boundedness (how closed the community is), range (how wide is the range of relationships), or strength of ties (how wide and strong are connections between people). The notion of connection between people in the virtual community implies social interaction (Garton, Haythornthwaite, & Wellman, 1999). Rafaeli, Ravid and Soroka (2004) explored the activities of spectators (lurkers) in virtual learning communities, and using SNA they included activity measures such a as reading a posting to determine the level of the social interaction. Further, Daniel and Poon (2006) used SNA to build models of social interactions in video-mediated virtual communities, and employed several sources of data to describe the structural and relational features of the network.

DESCRIPTION OF STUDY

The team at Virtual Learning Community employed an array of methods including Thurstone scaling, content analysis and Bayesian belief networks to examine and described different kinds of virtual learning communities (Schwier & Daniel, 2008). This study focused on the analysis of interactions patterns using social network analysis (SNA) to examine the structural patterns of an emergent community and sought to learn more about it by exploring students' experiences in relations to their sense of a community online. SNA network data was followed by focus group data and individual interview data to explore the students' and instructor's experiences. The questions addressed in the study included:

1. Can the patterns or distribution of ties in a network help us understand the level of intellectual discourse in a virtual learning community?
2. What are students experiences regarding sense of a community in a virtual learning environment?

Participants

The study was composed of 14 student volunteers and the instructor of the class, recruited from a group of 16 potential participants. All 14 of the participants were graduate students enrolled in a year-long course in educational communications and technology at the graduate level who had completed the course within the previous two years.

Eight participants were interviewed individually (including the instructor), and one focus group was held with 7 participants. The leading questions in interviews and the focus group probed whether participants experienced a feeling of a community in that class, and if so, whether the type of community was social, technological, and academic. Additional survey questions gathered participants' experiences on the fundamental elements of a VLC identified in earlier studies (Schwier, 2002). Interviews and focus group were recorded using a digital audio recorder and were transcribed verbatim. Thematic analysis was applied in the analysis of the data. Content analysis was applied to the analysis of the online transcripts. All data were entered into Atlas.ti and thematic analysis was performed.

The typical pattern the class followed was to post an introduction, assigned readings and questions for a topic and require an initial posting from each student. Then each student was required to respond to at least two postings from other students, but all students were encouraged to use the discussion board to communicate regularly with each other. All activities around a particular topic were completed within one calendar week. A significant characteristic of the group was that they were comprised almost exclusively of Western, English-speaking graduate students, with the exception of one student from China. Additionally, twelve of the participants were female, and two were male. All of the students exhibited facility with writing, and there was ample evidence that students were willing to engage in academic discourse with each other and with the instructor.

Methods and Data Analysis

In order to visualise the patterns of interaction among participants, interactions were codified into a four dimensional matrix. A matrix of a network of size n is a square matrix (n x n) whose elements represent ties (links) among individuals or agents in a given network. The network is presented as graph with a number of nodes representing individuals and ties representing relationships among them based on relational data model. The relational dimension between nodes A and B is recorded as 1 in the cells (A, B) and (B, A) if a tie is present between them; and as 0 if there is no tie. In other words, if the relation is directional, an arc (flow) from source A to sink B and vice versa is recorded as 1 in cell (A, B), and a 0 in cell (B, A), this is also referred to as adjacency. *Adjacency* is the graph theoretic expression of the fact that two agents, represented by nodes, are directly related, tied, or connected with one another (Robinson & Foulds, 1980). Formally it is presented as:

Let n_i, $n_j \in$ N denote agents i and j in a set of N agents. Let a_{ij} denote the existence of a relation (arc) from agent i to agent j. Agents i and j are adjacent if there exist either of the two arcs, a_{ij} or a_{ji}. Given a graph $D = (N, A)$, its adjacency matrix A(D) is defined by A(D) = (a_{ij}), where a_{ij} = 1 if either a_{ij} or a_{ji}, and 0 otherwise.

The number of arcs (links) beginning at a node is called the *outdegree* of the node.

And they suggest connections, and in our case initiation of engagement or discourse. Outdegree is measured as the row sum for the node in a dichotomous matrix:

$$\text{outdegree of actor i} = \sum_j a_{ij} \qquad (1)$$

The number of arcs ending at a node is called the *indegree* of the node, indicating the reception of engagement. The column sum (for a node) in a dichotomous matrix measures the indegree of the node:

$$\text{indegree of actor j} = \sum_i a_{i.} \qquad (2)$$

The initiation and reception of engagement can all sum up to the level of participation in the community. Other measures such as intensity of the engagement can also be measured using certain statistical index. An actor can be a *transmitter* (the arc is away from the node), a *receiver* (the arc is toward the node), a *carrier* (there are at least two arcs, one toward and one away) or *isolated* (when there is no arc that relates the actor with any actor in the network. Wasserman and Faust (1994) suggested that a node is a transmitter if its indegree is zero and its outdegree is non-zero. A node is a receiver if its indegree is non-zero and its outdegree is zero, and it is *isolated* if both indegree and outdegree are zero.

These measures can be made comparable across communities of different sizes (different numbers of entities) by normalizing (dividing by the total number of possible non-reflexive arcs or ties, which is N-1. A *reflexive tie* is a tie with oneself.).An entity is *connected* when there is at least one arc or set of arcs that relate the actor with another actor (Wasserman & Faust, 1994). Entities may be directly related (*adjacent*, with a one-step arc between them) or indirectly related (more than one one-step apart). The second set of data was drawn from interviews and focus groups and was analyzed through a process of inductive reasoning. Inductive analysis suggests that "the patterns, themes, and categories of analysis come from the data; they emerge out of the data rather than being imposed on them prior to data collection and analysis" (Patton, 2002). Trustworthiness was done through triangulation and evaluative criteria to ensure the validity of the study and how well the realities of the participants were presented in the results.

Sense of Community

The researchers were also interested in exploring the sense of a community among the students.

Sense of community has traditionally been associated with groupings of people from geographical locations (e.g., villages, suburbs, towns, and cities). McMillan and Chavis (1986) defined a sense of a community as a feeling that members have of belonging, a feeling that members matter to one another and to the group, and a shared understanding among the members and that their needs will be met through their commitment to be together. A sense of a community is a result of interaction and deliberation among members of a community brought together by similar interests and common goals (Westheimer & Kahne, 1993). A sense of a community emerges when people interact in a cohesive manner, continually reflecting upon the work of the group while always respecting the differences individual members bring to the group (Graves, 1992). Preece (2000) provided a useful definition of online community, stating that an online community should consist of people who interact as they strive to satisfy their own needs or perform special roles, a shared purpose such as an interest, need, information exchange, or service that provides a reason for the community, policies that guide people's interactions, and computer systems which support and mediate social interaction and facilitate a sense of togetherness. This definition, it seems reflects the presence of a strong sense of community online.

Rovai (2002) extended the notion of the sense of a community to online learning environments. He suggested that virtual classrooms have the potential of building and sustaining the sense of a community. A review of the literature suggests that there is no consensus for a definition of "sense of a community." This is perhaps because a sense of community is context dependent and unique to each community examined (Sarason, 1986). Consequently, a way to describe the sense of community in any particular community requires an understanding of the fundamental social aspects of the community.

RESULTS

McCalla (2000) noted that any virtual community is essentially a learning community. To fully understand the process of learning inherent in virtual learning communities, it is necessary to understand the nature of intellectual and non-intellectual discourse taking place in the community (Daniel, McCalla & Schwier, 2005) and to examine the flow of information and knowledge among members of the community.

Further, it is suggested in this article that a virtual learning community's potential for enhancing learning depends on its ability to strengthen relationships among its members and to maintain relevant thematic discourse and greater autonomy during discourse, while encouraging a greater sense of a community among participants. The learning process in virtual learning communities is not necessarily similar to the learning process in traditional classrooms, although there are inevitable similarities. In addition, learning in virtual learning communities requires that community goals be strategically aligned with members' goals and interests. Further, in order to sustain participation there should be a periodic check-and-balance on changes in participants' goals and interests.

Visualization of Interactions

Using UCINET 6 (Borgatti & Freeman, 2002) software, a network (see Figure 1), composed of 15 actors/nodes (N=15) with connections indicating the flow of interactions, which subsequently determined community structure as well as patterns of discourse was generated. In order to examine, understand and visualize the patterns of interaction among participants, interactions were codified into a two dimensional matrix. A matrix of a network of size *n* is a square matrix (**n x n**) whose elements represent ties (links) among individuals or agents in a given network (see Figure 1).

Figure 1. Binary matrix showing engagement

Internal_ID	ID	Rk	MD	Bn	Da	De	Di	Dk	Dna	Hr	Jf	Jn	La	Rg	Ra	Rn
1	Rk		0	1	1	1	1	1	0	0	1	0	1	0	1	1
2	MD	1		1	0	0	1	1	1	1	0	1	0	1	0	0
3	Bn	1	1		1	1	1	1	0	1	1	1	1	1	1	0
4	Da	1	1	1		1	1	0	1	1	1	1	1	0	1	0
5	De	1	1	1	1		1	1	1	1	1	1	1	1	1	1
6	Di	1	1	1	1	1		1	0	1	1	1	1	0	1	1
7	Dk	1	1	1	1	1	0		1	1	1	1	1	0	1	1
8	Dna	1	1	1	1	1	0	1		1	1	1	0	1	1	0
9	Hr	1	1	1	1	1	1	1	1		1	1	1	1	1	0
10	Jf	1	1	1	1	1	1	1	1	1		1	0	1	0	1
11	Jn	1	1	1	1	1	1	1	1	1	1		1	1	1	0
12	La	1	0	1	0	1	0	1	1	1	1	1		0	1	0
13	Rg	1	0	1	1	1	1	1	0	1	1	1	1		1	1
14	Ra	1	1	1	0	1	1	1	1	1	1	1	0	1		1
15	Rn	1	1	1	0	1	1	1	1	1	1	1	0	0	1	

The network is presented as a graph with nodes representing individuals and ties representing relationships among them based on a relational data model. The relational dimension between nodes *A* and *B* is recorded as 1 in the cells (*A, B*) and (*B, A*) if a tie is present between them; and as 0 if there is no tie. In other words, if the relation is directional, an arc (flow) from source **A** to link **B** and vice versa is recorded as 1 in cell (*A, B*), and a **0** in cell (*B, A*), this is also referred to as adjacency. *Adjacency* is the graph theoretic expression of the fact that two agents, represented by nodes, are directly related, tied, or connected with one another (Robinson & Foulds, 1980).

Figure 2 is a graphic representation of information flow with lines indicating engagement between nodes (individuals) in the community. The dashed lines indicate one-way communication while the solid lines suggest two-way communications. In other words, if *x* sends *t* number of messages to *y*, and *y* sent back *q* number of messages to *x*, then it is assumed that there is a certain reciprocal relationship between *x* and *y*. In Figure 2, this is indicated by solid line. The criterion used for constructing the graph is based on graph theoretic expression (Robinson & Foulds, 1980) described in the methods and data analysis

section earlier. Further, if x send messages to y and y does not send back any messages, then there is no reciprocal relationship. This is indicated by dashed lines. Interestingly, when viewed graphically, there are similarities in the patterns of one-way and two-way communication. The visual suggests that reciprocity is uneven in this group. There were more reciprocal connections in the group than one-way connections, but both structures appear substantial and similar. On close examination, parsing one-way and two-way connections, and then combining them, reveals several reciprocal relationships that mask a mirror image distribution of unidirectional communication in the group.

Social network researchers often measure network activity for a node by using the concept of degrees—the number of direct connections a node has. In SNA the notion of degree suggests the number of connections an individual has in the network. Freeman outdegree and indegree measures are some of the most commonly used degree of centrality used for various reasons. In this study we employed Freeman's indegree and outdegree measures to determine the number of connections among individuals in the community. In this study an indegree reveals the number

Figure 2. Graphical view of the flow of information and interaction patterns among individuals in the community

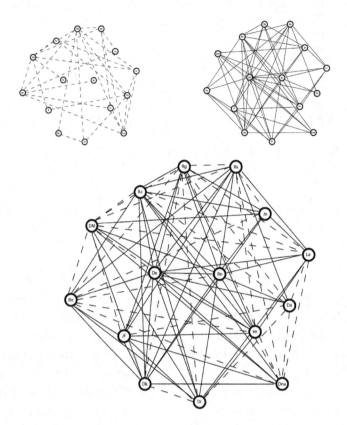

of individuals who have read messages in the community (read is implied in that when *x* sends *n* messages to *y*. It is assumed by default that *y* has read the *n* messages sent by *x)*. While outdegree measures the number of messages an individual sent to all other individuals in the community. Table 1 summarises the results of the in-degree and out-degree measures.

The degree of centrality in social network theory is the most intuitive network conceptualization of centrality, and it has a simple theoretical relationship with accuracy. The centrality of an individual is simply the number of people that person is directly tied to. A node with a high degree of centrality suggests a high proportion of connectivity with other nodes in the network. In this case this was measured by either the number of messages an individual sent to others or received

from other members of the community. The total number of messages a person sent to members of the community shows their outdegree centrality. For example, in Table 1 in the table RN has the lowest outdegree of centrality, meaning that s/he sent out only seven messages compared to RK who has a high proportion of outdegree centrality (109).

Indegree, on the other hand, shows the number of message a person has received from other members of the community. In Table 1, Bn has the highest indegree of centrality (79), compared to DM who has only 12 (which implies, she has only received a total of 12 messages from others in the community). In Figure 3 the proportions of the distribution of indegree and outdegree measures among all the members of the network are shown.

Table 1. The degrees of connectivity among individuals in the network

Actor	Outdegree	Averages	Indegree	Averages
Rk	109	0.9	18	0.03
Dm	24	0.04	12	0.02
Bn	67	0.11	79	0.13
Dna	25	0.04	39	0.06
De	54	0.09	56	0.09
Di	24	0.04	35	0.05
Dk	54	0.09	51	0.08
Dn	11	0.01	29	0.04
Hr	57	0.09	43	0.07
Jf	41	0.07	38	0.06
Jn	59	0.1	74	0.12
La	13	0.02	31	0.05
Rg	16	0.02	26	0.04
Ra	21	0.03	29	0.04
Rn	7	0.01	33	0.06

In Figure 3, Rk has a high outdegree of centrality. Theoretically, a high outdegree of centrality in the network implies that an actor can gain access to more information or knowledge but it might not be known what the content of interaction might entail, unless content analysis of messages is carried. In this case, the highest outdegree associated with RK relates to the fact that most of the community members turn to that individual for help. It can mean that an actor has the possibility of influencing other actors in the network through multiple channels of communication. For example, RK's position is regarded as the most influential in the network. In contrast, peripheral actors maintain few or no connections with others and thus are located at the margins of the network. For instance, Rn has a relatively low proportion of outdegree centrality and can be considered a spectator or "lurker". However, spectators in social network terms are not necessarily unimportant. In fact they can maintain an important location measured in "prestige". In a social network, a prestige location suggests that

an individual is a recipient of many directed ties, but initiates few relationships. In other words, they do not reciprocate.

Participants' Perceptions and Experiences

In order to understand the sense of community that formed among students and the factors that sustained it, the students' experiences and perceptions were explored in an interview or focus group. Personal features that might contribute to an increased sense of community in online learning environments were also explored with participants.

Sense of Community

The sense of a community was explore with the purpose of gaining understanding of learners' prior training, experience and their professional affiliations along four dimensions: common identity; shared understanding among individuals; boundaries, participation and guiding social protocols; and peer-support and reciprocity. Findings suggested evidence of a strong sense of community among the participants defined around intellectual discourse and academic professionalism. However, there was no attempt to pre-test whether sense of community pre-existed or not in the group studied.

The group studied described itself as "academic" community more than "social," as participants commented:

It was definitely based around academic. As much as you got to know little things about each other it is not necessarily a social community. Because there was always a purpose and most of the discussion, even though you could tell little bit about peoples' personalities, they were all based around the fundamental issues that we were studying, I thought.

Figure 3. Distribution of indegree and outdegree measures of centrality in the sample

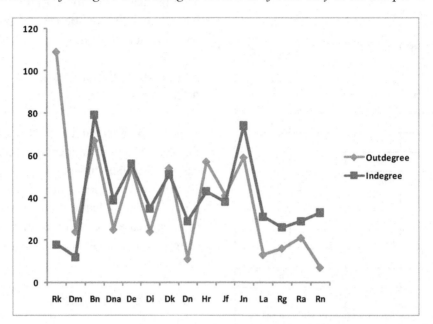

Yes. I would say it's a community in every sense... you know... we weren't just on that one hour we had to post out things on. You check in and got to know each other's personalities, and I think got to know a little bit about each other.

Participants mentioned a strong feeling of togetherness as an academic community during their interactions with each other. They pointed out a feeling of togetherness is another indicator of a sense of community. The feeling of togetherness denotes recognition of membership in a community and the feeling of friendship among peers, cohesion and bonding among participants as they work, collaborate and learn together as a community, and regularly participate in community social rituals (such as lunch together). The feeling of togetherness in the community enables participants to personally connect to each other, and to openly and respectfully challenge each other's ideas without fear of negative sanctions and exclusion from the community. The feeling of togetherness in the group can be treated as a casual but important indicator of community, and it is also an important element of a community identity.

Identity in the Community

In virtual learning communities, identity plays an important role in defining members' participation in a community and it can affect how people socially network with each other (i.e., whom they choose to exchange information and share knowledge with in a community). A community's identity is largely formed by the community's history or heritage; including members' shared goals, shared values, and shared interests (Barb & Duff, 1998; Preece, 2000). A group identity can influence the way individuals contribute to their community. For example, effective communication can be enhanced if one knows the identities of those with whom one is communicating, and there is some evidence that individuals connect with others in multiple online environments, but also often connect with each other in person (Baym, 2009), suggesting that the identity within communities are influenced by multimodal connections.

One study revealed that a stronger group identity can lead into a greater attribution of similarity when members are physically at a distance (Blanchard & Horan, 2000). Consistent with this research, key results from this study suggest that the group identity played a key role in shaping and fostering a sense of a community. Furthermore, 64% of the participants mentioned that they felt a strong sense of community because they shared common goals and had a common identity, while 38% reported neutral feeling of a common identity. Participants also reported that their group identity was primarily socially constructed around shared professional and learning goals rather than social aspects. As one participant indicated:

I think we have a common identity. I think we were all focusing on the same identified or recognized goals, that is to say we all had a common focus in educational technology. We had common interests too, I suppose. We were all just working towards that. For me, there was a feeling of interdependency in the community too.

Our observation suggest that when an individual identifies with a certain group, whether virtual or not, it suggests interdependence and positive attachment to that particular group. Group identity also creates a feeling of togetherness. Such a feeling can also be influenced by what people share in common, whether in the past or in the present. It is not uncommon for people who interact or grow up with certain groups of people to experience a strong feeling of togetherness to an extent they identify with the group.

Such is the strong identity present in family ties, kinship, religious groups, war veterans, and other bounded groups. However, in professional life, people are more inclined to identify with those with whom they share the same experiences or are trained in the same profession. In other words, professionals seem to associate more with those they easily identify with professionally. Within such groups they can readily build trust and shared understanding.

Shared Understanding

Participants indicated that they join communities when they share goals and values with others in the community. Similarity in backgrounds, interests and goals among participants enable them to share common experiences, swap stories and learn from each other as they interact as a community. Previous research revealed that sharing experiences in virtual learning communities is an expression of mutual interdependence, which can ultimately influence the process of learning in communities (Daniel, Schwier, & Ross, 2006).

Participants were asked whether they believed most people in the community shared common goals and values. Nearly 80% of the participants (11 of 14) stated they had common goals and shared values. Although there were shared goals and values within the group, participants exhibited diversity and multiple perspectives during discourse on issues critical to their community, and they were willing to collaborate with other members of the community to achieve common goals. Participants demonstrated multiple perspectives by sharing personal experiences.

There was certainly a common goal in among the group. While we were in that community, we did diverge from the common goal and that was nice. We did so, but in an academic way, whether it was philosophy or a different epistemology or whatever it happened to be. There would be strands in the discussion that would take off into another academic area. I didn't... there wasn't a lot of chitchat and when it was there I have to admit that I did not take part in it that much. So I guess from my point of view, it's... I was trying to establish... "We're here for a reason. Let's just get this done." But at the same time, I did go off on the tangents as well... the academic tangent.

Further, in order to harness the value of diversity, participants demonstrated respect toward each other and to the ideas expressed in the community. When people demonstrate a certain level of respect toward each other and exhibit a sense of belonging to a community, they can individually contribute useful knowledge, which can benefit others in the community. It is also likely that when people share common goals and shared values, they develop a sense of trust, which is critical to the process of learning in virtual learning communities. Further, shared goals and values can enhance shared understanding. As Schwier and Daniel (2008) suggested, the process of establishing shared understanding often draws upon a set of shared beliefs, experiences and knowledge.

Even though sharing experiences is critical to generating tacit knowledge, it is informal, and typically voluntary. Individuals typically need to be highly motivated to share their personal life experiences and participate socially with others in the community.

Boundaries, Participation, and Social Protocols

In virtual learning communities, effective participation requires the presence of either explicit or implicit social control mechanisms (social protocols of interaction). First is the presence of implied boundaries, which in turn suggests membership and promotes a sense of belonging (Baym, 1995, 2009; Herring, 1996; Kollock & Smith, 1999). Boundaries are increasingly difficult to prescribe, as networked relationships cut across modes of communication and shared interests (Baym, 2007, 2009). In the case of formal virtual learning communities, boundaries and protocols can be initially set by the moderator/instructor of the class, and over time, vibrant learning communities can shape social engagement protocols to meet the context and preferences of the participants. Preece (2006) noted that a virtual community with good

sociability has social policies that can support the community's purpose and are understandable and socially acceptable within the context of the community.

Participants were asked whether there were social protocols in the community and whether or not these were linked to any expectations. Approximately 67% of the participants indicated the presence of social protocols while 33% reported that they were not aware of any social protocols. Participants also mentioned that there were clear expectations from the instructor about the content of the course (78%), while 22% felt there were either no clear expectations connected to participation or they were not sure.

When inquiring about the presence of social protocols in the community, we were aware that people can respond differently to any set of social protocols or rules of engagement in a formal learning environment. Such reaction could possible influence the way in which people participate and respond to the question. Participants were asked to what extent the presence of social protocols influenced participants' engagement during discourse and their contribution to the community. Approximately 45% reported that social protocols had influenced their participation and contribution to the community to a great extent, while 55% mentioned social protocols had little or no influence on their participation in the community.

In almost any community, virtual or otherwise, there can be deviant behaviours in the community that breach social protocols. In some communities a breach of social protocols can draw sanctions from the moderator or group. Sanctions in virtual communities can negatively reflect on an individual contribution to the community. When asked whether there were explicit sanctions attached to any violation of social protocols in the community, 68% indicated responded that it was unlikely that violation of social protocols could lead to sanctions, 22% of participants however mentioned violations of social protocols would cause sanctions to be imposed and 11% were not sure whether breaching social protocols in the community would be sanctioned.

Peer-Support and Reciprocity

One of the most important binding factors in a virtual community appears to be reciprocity. As illustrated in Figure 2, the group in this study demonstrated a significant amount of reciprocity in the SNA, but from that figure alone we know little about the meaning of that reciprocity to participants. Reciprocity connotes a mutual and shared interchange of favours or privileges, especially the exchange of information, knowledge and experiences among individuals. Rheingold (1993, 2003) noted that in virtual communities, information is the primarily commodity that is exchanged. Participants request information or ask questions and other members provide answers or information either directly to the group or in private correspondence. This is one of the factors that encourage individuals to join virtual communities. But he and others also emphasized the importance of shared support and emotional connections as well (Baym, 1997, 2009; Preece, 1999, 2000; Rheingold, 1993).

In this study the frequency of sharing class-related resources among participants suggested reciprocity. Approximately 56% indicated that they frequently shared resources with others in the community, while 44% mentioned they less frequently shared resources with their peers. The researchers were also interested in finding how participants sought information and support when faced with problems related to the course. Approximately 78% mentioned the instructor of the class as the main source of help and support. While 11% sought help from their friends in the class and 11% sought help from outside sources, including people who had previously taken the course. These results describe the nature of information and help seeking behaviours among the group, which also suggest their reciprocal

relationships and peer-support. The act of peer-support in a virtual community can be treated as a reinforcement of members' sense of a belonging to a community and their duty to reciprocate in relationships with others. A community with high rates of reciprocity among its members suggests a high level of social networking, which is also an element of social capital (Putnam, 1993). Since participation in communities is primarily voluntarily, it is expected that reciprocal relationships are not obligatory, as participants in this study suggest:

If <name> helps me with something, he's not doing it because he wants something back, but the expectation is that if he's going to need help in the future, me or somebody else in the community is going to provide it.

Well, participation in a community shouldn't have to force being in contact with people. It should just come naturally. It shouldn't be, "Oh, you know I haven't written to them in a few weeks. If this community is going to make it I have to write to people.

The kinds of reciprocal relationships described in this community are similar to generalized reciprocity, which is responsible for generating social capital (Putnam, 2000). Putnam (2000) describes generalized reciprocity as: "I'll do this for you now, without expecting anything immediately in return and perhaps without even knowing you, confident that down the road you or someone else will return the favour". In virtual learning communities, reciprocal relationships similar to the one described above, transactions of information take place between individuals who are symmetrically placed (i.e., they exchange among peers).

Autonomy and Social Resilience

When participation in a community is voluntary and people are free to participate whenever they can, there is a greater sense of autonomy within the community. Schwier (2001) defined autonomy as the ability of individual to have the capacity and authority to conduct discourse freely, or withdraw from discourse without penalty. An individual's autonomy is a critical value that influences participation in a community.

My main value in this community is autonomy in learning - I am in control of what I choose to learn. Others, even the instructor, have little control over that autonomy. On the other hand, it is important for me to show respect and caring towards everyone else in the community. This means valuing difference.

Autonomy implies that people can engage in discourse more freely and meaningfully. But it is also important to note that in formal virtual learning communities, where there are clear sets of expectations and goals to reach, social protocols, whether explicit or not, can guide individuals toward achieving goals and provide a context for amicable discourse. In some situations, high autonomy can encourage lurking. Lurking without proper social protocols presents an interesting but often unresolved social problem. Lurking without social protocols occurs when members of a virtual community read messages but seldom engage in any reciprocal relationships or directly participate and contribute to the community. Some members do not consider themselves to be lurkers even though they grossly violate the social protocols or expectations of reciprocity in the community. The results revealed instances where individuals proudly labelled themselves lurkers, and announced to the group that they would not participate regularly. They treated their reluctance to participate actively as a personality characteristic, similar to being shy in large groups. But reticence in a virtual community creates an even stronger opportunity for the individual to become isolated. If members fail to participate in a virtual group, they essentially disappear from the community,

but they sometimes leave a residue of concern or resentment about their silence.

In some virtual learning communities individuals' interests are not easily aligned with community interests, and it can be complicated if there is a considerable diversity among members of the community. An effective way to promote a sense of community in the face of diversity is to inculcate in the community a sense of social resilience. In this study, social resilience in a virtual learning community defined as an individual's ability to adapt and readily adjust to changes brought about by being a member of a diverse group.

Results also showed that diversity in knowledge and skills among participants in the community was viewed as a positive contribution to the knowledge base of the community and a potential conduit for high quality discourse and social networking. Participants in the study mentioned that the quality of discourse was enhanced because of the diverse range of issues that were addressed in the community. In most cases the issues seemed to have covered individuals' interests and were all attributed to the diversity in members views.

In addition, participants stated that everybody was knowledgeable in specific knowledge domains. Others felt that some people had more technical skills than others. There were also personal attributes that participants indicated were important in fostering a greater sense of a community and greater individuals' autonomy and success. These included:

- Motivation to learn course material;
- Demonstration of maturity and motive;
- Openness to diverse views and expression of courtesy to peers;
- Mutual respect and shared understanding;
- Shared experiences and new observations and insights;
- Freedom of discourse;
- Deep reflection about content and views learned from others;

- Expression of personal views without fear of negative feedback from peers and instructor;
- Intellectual curiosity and firm goal orientation;
- Diversity in individuals' backgrounds;
- Willingness to collaborate with peers;
- Positive work ethic;
- Willingness to freely engage in intellectual discourse with peers and openness to diversity;
- Treating negative feedback as a reflective view for personal check-and-balance but not as personal failures or attacks;
- Establishment of relaxed community rituals (e.g. common lunch) where each individual is treated as equal, one and a colleague;
- Frequent face-to-face community meetings so that members can establish new rapport and maintain old one with others in the community;
- Humour, organization, attentiveness and rigour in open discourse in the community.

Trust and Awareness

Trust implies a feeling that community members can be trusted, and represents a willingness to rely on other members of one's community in whom one has confidence (Moorman, Zaltman, & Deshpande, 1993). There are fundamentally two aspects of trust: credibility and benevolence (Doney & Cannon, 1997). Credibility suggests that one can rely on the words of others in a community and benevolence is the extent to which a learners are interested in the welfare of others in the community and are willing to offer peer-support when needed (Rovai, 2002). Trust includes the confidence and expectation that people will act in consistent, honest and appropriate ways, which they will be reliable and trustworthy. Closely linked to the norms of reciprocity and networks

of civic engagement (Putnam, 1993; Coleman, 1988), trust allows people to collaborate and to work together as a community.

Trust is a dynamic phenomenon, one that evolves, mutates and regenerates. Under favourable conditions, people can develop trusting relationships with others and such relationships can be maintained or destroyed. In a situation where individuals are strangers, it often takes a longer period of time and positive interactions to develop trust. At the same time continuous and negative interactions can destroy the potential for trust to develop.

In virtual communities, trust is mainly dependent on different forms of awareness Daniel, Schwier, and McCalla (2003). For example, awareness about the presence of individuals in the community, awareness of individuals' demographic backgrounds, awareness of individuals' capabilities and skills in performing specific tasks and awareness of personal or professional affiliations can all promote trust.

Participants were asked about their levels of awareness of other group members before joining the course. Results indicated that they had little prior awareness (56% suggested they knew nobody while 44% knew few of the people in the class). In asking about prior awareness, we were aware of the fact that awareness takes a long time to develop. Awareness can develop as participants get to know each other by working and learning together and interacting socially. Results from the focus group also confirmed this line of thinking as one member commented:

I think that's natural that in any environment in the beginning—you don't know who you're talking to or not quite sure what they're talking about. I think you just feel more comfortable as the year went on. I certainly did; anyway, especially in a different... you know people would try to include me. The welcome video that everybody shot, that was really helpful.

In virtual communities, awareness can be linked to trust. However, as indicated earlier there are several kinds of awareness, which can differently influence trust (Daniel, Schwier, & Ross, 2005). In our previous work we concentrated on different kinds of knowledge and demographic awareness. We direct the reader to Daniel, McCalla, and Schwier (2005) for a comprehensive discussion of different forms of knowledge and demographic awareness in virtual communities. We found that levels of trust and different kinds of awareness were correlated. Depending on the nature of awareness the relationship can be positively or negatively correlated. For instance, when people become aware that they share certain goals with certain individuals, it might cultivate trusting relationships. Similarly, getting to know that others do not share the same goals or lack of knowledge thereof, might negatively deflate the level of trust.

Knowledge Awareness

Knowledge awareness is information about other learners' activities and knowledge—what individuals know (competence awareness) and what they can do (capability awareness). Knowledge awareness allows a better understanding of shared knowledge, since it provides information about the knowledge of the community.

Knowledge awareness can also breed trust in a community. Knowledge awareness is an important component of social capital in virtual communities (Daniel, McCalla, & Schiwer, 2005) and it plays a major part in how the learning environment creates collaborative opportunities naturally and efficiently (Ogata & Yano, 2000). We asked the extent to which participants were willing to trust others based on what they know.

Most of the participants reported that they can trust their peers when it comes to capabilities and the quality of intellectual discourse. Others based their level of trust in others on similarity of prior training and their knowledge of a domain.

Studies show that when people meet each other for the first time they develop mental models of each other and the content of their discussion (Norman, 1986). Their opinions are influenced partly by such things as age, gender, physical appearance and the context of the meeting. Mental models tend to be developed very quickly but can be remarkably powerful and resistant to change, even when evidence suggests they are not completely correct (Wallace, 1999). So another feature of reduced social presence, particularly in low bandwidth environments, is that the ways people form impressions of each other is different, and this can have positive or negative effects depending on the context.

Conversely, there are times when not being able to see the person with whom you converse and knowing you may never meet them can be a positive feature of these environments because people are encouraged to disclose more about themselves online (Lea, O'Shea, Fung, & Spears, 1992; Walther, 1996). Furthermore, when people discover they have similar problems, opinions or experiences they may feel closer, more trusting and be prepared to reveal even more. We asked how likely individuals were willing to trust others based on their awareness of others' demographic backgrounds. Little or no difference in their levels of trust was reported by participants. In an attempt to understand whether trust in others can be based on similarity in profession, we asked to what extent individuals' trust in others was based on their professional affiliation. The majority of participants indicated that their trust level based upon professional affiliation of others was neither great nor small.

The findings presented above showed different forms of knowledge awareness and the extent to which each kind of awareness can influence the amount of trust that builds among participants. Some participants indicated they were more likely to trust their peers to a greater extent (33%) if they are knowledgeable about the content of the course while 67% reported that they trusted in peers as members of the community regardless of what they know.

A learning community affords connections among learners by participating in a classroom where students are valued and respected and a climate of trust and acceptance is recognized (Ritter & Polnick, 2008). The overall level of trust in a community indicates the amount of social cohesion and sense of a community among its members. In general, in virtual communities where individuals are strangers and interact anonymously with each other, the notion of trust is even more important and difficult to achieve. It can be slow to develop, due to the absence of social cues in virtual environments. Since trust is a fundamental determinant of a sense of a community and social capital, we asked participants about their overall perception of the level of trust in the community at the end of the class, and whether they felt the level of trust among people in the class had grown stronger, weaker, or stayed about the same over time. The majority of the respondents (68%) indicated that they observed no changes in the overall level of trust in the community over time.

Understanding and measuring trust in virtual communities can be a difficult process Daniel, McCalla, and Schwier (2002); however, there are at least two ways to discern and measure trust in virtual learning communities. One way is to treat trust as an attribute of an individual's beliefs or perceptions in what others can do for them. Another approach is to consider the community a social unit and study how activities in the community are organized, conducted and guided. In other words, people trust others in a community because they believe they share common identity, common goals and norms. When people trust in each other, it is likely that they develop norms or protocols to sustain that level of trust.

In addition, regardless of the kinds of awareness present in a community, individuals' choices can to some extent influence the strength and the extent of relationship they have with others and the nature of trust they build among each other.

In other words individuals can choose the kinds of information they are willing to make public in the community or even choose who to relate to in the community. For instance, certain individuals might choose to relate to others solely based on their demographic knowledge, while others might base their connections with others on their professional affiliations and common identity.

Though research commonly treats awareness as a positive aspect that can promote effective interaction among groups and individuals in communities, high levels of awareness can threaten the privacy of individuals who will be exposed.

CONCLUSION

Learning communities can exist in both traditional classrooms and e-learning environments. Traditional classrooms offer some interesting contrasts to the online environment when considering the types of communities that can evolve. In traditional classrooms, learning communities are easily visible to the instructor and students can easily make connections with peers due to availability of rich visible social cues. Instructors can also nurture the sense of a community among students with little difficulty. In other words, the conditions for communities to emerge are convenient. In virtual learning communities, where learners are typically isolated from each other and the instructor, developing a sense of a community can be a more challenging process.

The sense of isolation among learners in online environments can be minimized if forethought is given to the development of the online milieu that can foster a sense of a community among learners. Our research suggests that students can experience a sense of community online if the environment is intentionally structured and nurtured and when certain fundamental issues are addressed, including trust, awareness of personal and community issues, social protocols and reciprocal relationships (Schwier & Daniel, 2008).

The social network analysis (SNA) techniques presented here helped us map and visualise the flow of information and engagement among individuals in the community. The high number of reciprocal relationships and engagement among students measured by out-degree and indegree indices implied a strong sense of community. The SNA, while valuable, did not provide understanding of the motivations for engagement, and whether the interactions actually indicated a sense of learning community. By corroborating the SNA observations with interview and focus group data, the sense and depth of perceived community emerged. The study does not discuss whether sense of community pre-existed or not in the group studied. It does not explore what sustains, strengthens or limits sense of community in distributed settings. At this point, it is it is unknown what brings about the sense of community in the group. This might be attributed the structure of the learning course, and the role of the instructor or the technology used.

Overall, the results of the study presented here led suggest that the nature of social networking within a particular community is of fundamental importance when making judgments about the community and the extent to which people can engage in productive interactions. In a virtual learning environment, individuals and their information seeking behaviours are often thought of in terms of different kinds of physical information structures such as books, documents, web sites, databases, knowledge repositories and formal course content. However, it is argued in this article that a significant component of learners' information and knowledge needs are drawn from the relationships with peers, instructors and others outside the community. Improving the ways in which people can connect to each other to acquire useful information and knowledge is central to learning in virtual communities.

Since, virtual learning communities are built on connections. Better connections usually provide better information exchange, knowledge sharing and better learning opportunities. In addition, bet-ter connections lead to more effective interaction and productive discourse. It is also likely that better connections can foster better relationships among members in the community and can encourage members to develop and share experiences to learn from each other.

However, in a more general sense, it is argued in this article that having many connections in a virtual learning community does not say much about the additional knowledge actually contributed. Connectivity does not provide insight into the content or meaning of the messages sent and received. In addition, some individuals in the same virtual learning community may have few connections in the formal online environment, yet they might be socially connected through other media.

This is based on the notion that people tend to use a specific communication medium when there is a need for it. For example **RN** may not necessarily virtually communicate with **DM**, especially when it is possible to convey the same message in face-to-face interactions. Similarly, other individuals might have failed to send messages to **RK** because there was no immediate need. In essence, the convenience of the medium and the necessity to interact with others can determine individuals' degrees of centrality in a network.

In addition, people occupying a central position technically in a network are not necessarily advantaged socially compared to people on the periphery. Being in a central position with a number of one-way connections to others, such as **BN** exhibited, may not indicate an advantaged position. It may be that removing peripheral connections that act as hubs for people who communicate unidirectional will fragment the network or cause unproductive cliques to form.

In order for individuals to connect with each other, build a better sense of community and learn together, they should have common interests, shared history, shared values and goals. In virtual learning communities participants must maintain a level of shared understanding and trust to sustain the community. Awareness is one of the fundamental factors needed to enhance shared understanding and trust.

Awareness is one of the critical aspects of a virtual learning community (Schwier & Daniel, 2008). The ability of individuals to have better connections and productive relationships can depend on different forms of awareness. In other words, the extent to which individuals can develop relationships depends on who they know (awareness), what others in the community know (knowledge awareness), and what others are able to offer (competence awareness) to the community. It is also possible that individuals' personal backgrounds (demographic awareness) and professional affiliation (professional awareness) can influence their level of participation in a community, which can then influence the overall social capital of that community.

Another important factor in enhancing the sense of community is the instructor of the course. Findings in this study suggested that an instructor needs to explicitly nurture the sense of community among students and diversify activities to suit individuals' interests, while at the same time play the role of a peer and helper in the community. The findings about the role of the instructor as a peer and helper corresponds to studies which suggest that online space levels the traditional power relationship between the instructor and the students, generating equitable participation where the instructor does not dominate the discussion (Bump, 1990; Heuer & King, 2004; Hiltz, 1986).

Within the social dimensions of the online space, patterns such as the role of the instructor, establishing relationships, and developing identity all exist and can influence community-building and the learning process. These patterns emerge because of the nature of the virtual learning environment when participants are previously unknown to each other and are communicating at a distance. However, the social dimension of community building leads to "the opportunity to interact with other learners in sharing, construct-

ing, and negotiating meaning," which in turn leads to knowledge construction (Lock, 2002).

Results drawn from SNA research can contribute to our understanding of various reasons and motivations underlying individuals' participation in discourse in virtual learning communities. In addition, once SNA techniques are employed, and patterns of interactions within a community are clearly understood, one can leverage this knowledge to improve the flow of information and knowledge in the community.

It is also suggested that results drawn from this work can help inform researchers and educators about the shape and vitality of particular virtual learning communities in order to devise ways of nurturing and supporting these communities. We also feel that much can be learned about the nature and the process of learning in virtual learning communities from students' experiences and perceptions. By employing multiple methods of analysis, both structural and functional variables of learning in virtual learning communities can be understood and appropriate strategies can be devised to support them. Overall, the results of this study suggest a need to conduct more research to understand the nature of engagement in virtual communities and the types and processes of learning embedded in these social systems.

REFERENCES

Baym, N. K. (1995). The emergence of community in computer-mediated communication. In Jones, S. (Ed.), *CyberSociety* (pp. 138–163). Newbury Park, CA: Sage.

Baym, N. K. (2007). The new shape of online community: The example of Swedish independent music fandom. *First Monday*, *12*(8). Retrieved from http://firstmonday.org/issues/issue12_8/baym/index.html.

Baym, N. K. (2009). A call for grounding in the face of blurred boundaries. *Journal of Computer-Mediated Communication*, *14*(3), 720–723. doi:10.1111/j.1083-6101.2009.01461.x

Blanchard, A., & Horan, T. (2000). Virtual communities and social capital. In Lesser, E. (Ed.), *Knowledge and social capital* (pp. 159–178). Boston, MA: Butterworth Heinemann. doi:10.1016/B978-0-7506-7222-1.50010-6

Borgatti, E., & Freeman, L. C. (2002). *UCINet 6 Network analysis software. Analytic technologies*. Retrieved from http://www.analytictech.com/downloaduc6.htm

Bump, J. (1990). Radical changes in class discussion using networked computers. *Computers and the Humanities*, *24*, 44–65. doi:10.1007/BF00115028

Coleman, J. S. (1988). Social capital in the creation of human capital. *American Journal of Sociology*, *94*, 95–120. doi:10.1086/228943

Collison, G., Elbaum, B., Haavind, S., & Tinker, R. (2000). *Facilitating online learning: Effective strategies for moderators*. Madison, WI: Atwood.

Daniel, B. K., McCalla, G., & Schwier, R. (2003). Social Capital in Virtual Learning Communities and Distributed Communities of Practice. *The Canadian Journal of Learning Technology, 29*(3), 113–139.

Daniel, B. K., & Poon, N. (2006, July). Social Network Techniques and Content Analysis of Interactions in a Video-Mediated Virtual Community. In *Proceedings of the 6th IEEE International Conference on Advanced Learning Technologies*, Kerkrade, The Netherlands.

Daniel, B. K., Schwier, R. A., & Ross, H. (2005, October 24-28). Intentional and Incidental Discourse Variables in a Virtual Learning Community. In *Proceedings of E-Learn 2005: World Conference on E-Learning in Corporate, Government, Healthcare, and Higher Education*, Vancouver, BC, Canada. De Laat, M. F. (2002, March). *Network and content analysis in an online community discourse*. Paper presented at the Networked Learning Conference, Sheffield, UK.

Doney, P. M., & Cannon, J. P. (1997). An examination of the nature of trust in buyer-seller relationships. *Journal of Marketing, 61*(2), 35–51. doi:10.2307/1251829

Freeman, L. C. (2004). *The development of social network analysis: A study in the sociology of science*. Vancouver, BC, Canada: Empirical Press.

Garton, L., Haythornthwaite, C., & Wellman, B. (1999). Studying online social networks. In Jones, S. (Ed.), *Doing internet research* (pp. 75–105). Thousand Oaks, CA: Sage.

Graves, L. N. (1992). Cooperative learning communities: Context for a new vision of education and society. *Journal of Education, 174*(2), 57–79.

Hanneman, R. A., & Riddle, M. (2005). *Introduction to social network methods*. Riverside, CA: University of California, Riverside. Retrieved from http://faculty.ucr.edu/~hanneman/

Heuer, B. P., & King, K. P. (2004). Leading the band: The role of the instructor in online learning for educators. *The Journal of Interactive Online Learning, 3*(1), 1–11.

Hiltz, S. R. (1984). *Online communities: A case study of the office of the future*. Norwood, NJ: Ablex.

Kollock, P., & Smith, M. (1999). *Communities in cyberspace*. London, UK: Routledge.

Lea, M., O'Shea, T., Fung, P., & Spears, R. (1992). 'Flaming☐ in computer-mediated communication: Observations, explanations, implications. In Lea, M. (Ed.), *Contexts of computer-mediated communication* (pp. 89–112). London, UK: Harvester-Wheatsheaf.

Lock, J. V. (2002). Laying the groundwork for the development of learning communities with online courses. *Quarterly Review of Distance Education, 3*, 395–408.

McCalla, G. (2000). The fragmentation of culture, learning, teaching and technology: Implications for artificial intelligence in education research. *International Journal of Artificial Intelligence, 11*(2), 177–196.

McDonald, B., Noakes, N., Stuckey, B., & Nyrop, S. (2005). *Breaking down learner isolation: How social network analysis informs design and facilitation for online learning.* Retrieved February 4, 2011, from http://cpsquare.org/wp-content/uploads/2008/07/stuckey-etal-aera-sna.pdf

McMillan, D. W., & Chavis, D. M. (1986). Sense of community: A definition and theory. *American Journal of Community Psychology, 14*(1), 6–23. doi:10.1002/1520-6629(198601)14:1<6::AID-JCOP2290140103>3.0.CO;2-I

Moorman, C., Deshpande, R., & Zaltman, G. (1993). Factors affecting trust in market research relationships. *Journal of Marketing, 57*, 81–102. doi:10.2307/1252059

Norman, D. A. (1996). Cognitive engineering. In Norman, D. A., & Draper, S. W. (Eds.), *User centered systems design-new persepectives on human-computer interaction* (pp. 31–61). Hillsdal, NJ: Lawrence Erlbaum.

Ogata, H., & Yano, Y. (2000). Combining knowledge awareness and information filtering in an open-ended collaborative learning environment. *International Journal of Artificial Intelligence in Education, 11*, 33–46.

Patton, M. Q. (2002). *Qualitative research and evaluation methods* (3rd ed.). Thousand Oaks, CA: Sage.

Preece, J. (1999). Empathetic communities: Balancing emotional and factual communication. *Interacting with Computers, 12*(1), 63–77. doi:10.1016/S0953-5438(98)00056-3

Preece, J. (2000). *Online communities: Designing usability and supporting sociability.* Hoboken, NJ: Wiley.

Putnam, R. D. (1993). *Making democracy work: Civic traditions in modern Italy.* Princeton, NJ: Princeton University Press.

Rafaeli, S., Ravid, G., & Soroka, V. (2004, January). *De-lurking in virtual communities: A social communication network approach to measuring the effects of social capital.* Paper presented at the Hawaii International Conference on System Sciences.

Rheingold, H. (1993). *The virtual community: Homesteading on the virtual frontier.* New York, NY: Addison-Wesley.

Rheingold, H. (2003). *Smart mobs.* New York, NY: Basic Books.

Ritter, C., & Polnick, B. (2008). Connections: An essential element of online learning communities. *International Journal of Educational Leadership Preparation, 3*(3). Retrieved from http://ijelp.expressacademic.org.

Robinson, D. F., & Foulds, L. R. (1980). *Digraphs: Theory and techniques.* New York, NY: Gordon and Breach.

Rovai, A. P. (2002). *Building sense of community at a distance*. Retrieved from http://www.whateverproductions.net/Rovai-2.pdf

Sarason, S. B. (1986). Commentary: The emergence of a conceptual center. *Journal of Community Psychology, 14,* 405–407. doi:10.1002/1520-6629(198610)14:4<405::AID-JCOP2290140409>3.0.CO;2-8

Schwier, R. A. (2001). Catalysts, emphases, and elements of virtual learning communities. Implication for research. *The Quarterly Review of Distance Education, 2*(1), 5–18.

Schwier, R. A., & Daniel, B. K. (2008). Implications of Virtual Learning Communities for Designing Online Communities of Practice in Higher Education. In Kimbel, C., & Hildreth, P. (Eds.), *Communities of Practice: Creating Learning Environments for Educators*. Greenwich, CT: Information Age Publishing.

Scott, J. (2000). *Social network analysis: A handbook* (2nd ed.). London, UK: Sage.

Wallace, A. R., & Boylan, C. R. (2001, December). *Interaction patterns in the extended classroom via satellite technology in the Australian outback*. Paper presented at the Annual Meeting of the New Zealand Association for Educational Research, Christchurch, NZ.

Walther, J. B. (1996). Computer-mediated communication: Impersonal, inter-personal and hyperpersonal interaction. *Human Communication Research, 23*(1), 3–43.

Wasserman, S., & Faust, K. (1994). *Social network analysis: Methods and applications*. Cambridge, UK: Cambridge University Press.

Wellman, B. (1999). The network community: An introduction. In Wellman, B. (Ed.), *Networks in the global village* (pp. 1–48). Boulder, CO: Westview Press.

Westheimer, J., & Kahne, J. (1993). Building school communities: An experience-based model. *Phi Delta Kappan, 75*(4), 324–328.

This work was previously published in the International Journal of Virtual Communities and Social Networking, Volume 2, Issue 4, edited by Subhasish Dasgupta, pp. 31-50, copyright 2010 by IGI Publishing (an imprint of IGI Global).

Chapter 7
Social Identity in Facebook Community Life

Shaoke Zhang
Pennsylvania State University, USA

Hao Jiang
Pennsylvania State University, USA

John M. Carroll
Pennsylvania State University, USA

ABSTRACT

Social identity is a key construct to understand online community life. While existing online identity studies present a relatively static conception of identity, grounded in user profiles and other personal information, in this paper the authors investigate more dynamic aspects of identity, grounded in patterns of social interaction in Facebook community life, drawing on social science research on identity theory and social identity theory. The authors examine the tensions experienced by people between assimilation and differentiation with respect to group identities and role identities. The study provides a framework for understanding how users construct self-presentations in different online social interactions, actively managing identity, rather than merely declaring it in a relatively static profile. The authors speculate on how social computing environments could more effectively support identity presentation.

INTRODUCTION

Online community life has increasingly become a significant part of our social life, and become an arena of research in domains such as sociology, information science and organizational studies. Studies in community informatics recently have been directed to social network websites (e.g., Facebook, MySpace, etc.), an Internet phenomenon that grounds on a simple idea that social actors being connected to one another benefits. In this paper, we investigate social identity, a key construct in traditional community life, in an online community based on a social network website, Facebook.

Nowadays, no term has been so pervasive and abused like "community". Now any group of people who are physically or virtually related

DOI: 10.4018/978-1-4666-1553-3.ch007

can be named a community. For example, there are university community, corporate community, district community, academic community (e.g., CHI community, ACM community), sports community, customer community, and even user community (e.g., Facebook community). Such a circumstance implies that the "community" is significant to our social life while its definition and boundary are pretty vague.

Community is important in that it provides a mediating social mechanism that relates the individual to the larger society, helping to satisfy the need of each. As Sanders (1958) pointed out, the institutional concreteness endues community critical significance in our social life. While society is usually understood primarily in terms of abstract concepts, in community, people confront the tangible manifestations of society's major institutional complexes. People are social in the way they engage in activities in schools, companies, golf course, pubs, homes, or even virtual groups that are of communities. On the other hand, the definition of "community" is rather vague, especially in the era of information age. Are those so-called "online community" really communities? Are social network sites such as Facebook a community? Or are the social groups that are constituted in Facebook communities?

Identity theories provide us a perspective to understand these issues. Social identities, as self reflected answers to the question "who I am" or "who we are" drawn from experience of previous social interactions, help people define themselves and give them guidelines for proper social intercourse with others in social life. According identity theories, a community can be viewed as a set of people who share certain distinctive identities (i.e., community identities). By providing relative stable, consistent and enduring answers to the question "who we are", community identities serves as a coherent bonding for all community members, which also helps discriminate themselves from other people outside the community.

In sociology and social psychology, identities have been of interest for decades (Stryker, 1968; Stryker & Burke, 2000; Turner, 1985). Advanced information technologies help create new forms of social life, from technology-mediated communities to even entirely virtual communities whose operations are mainly carried out over the Internet. Recently, researchers in information science began to give attention to identities, and a few studies are emerging (DiMicco & Millen, 2007; Hewitt & Forte, 2006; Zhao, Grasmuch, & Martin, 2008). However, scrutinizing current studies, we found most of them only touched the surface of the subject matter by grounding identity only in user profiles, and ignored social interactions in which social identities are constructed and enacted. Appealing to us is the issue of how identities are embedded and enacted in social interactions in online community life.

In this paper, we report our qualitative study on Facebook, the most popular social network website, with regard to social identities embedded in Facebook activities. We discuss people's tension between assimilation and differentiation as implied by social identity theory and self-categorization theory (Turner 1985). We argue that people are trying to be different not just in inter-group level as suggested in self-categorization theory. They are also trying to be different inside the group. We also discuss how Facebook can uphold community life by supporting social identities.

IDENTITY: A KEY CONSTRUCT

Identity has been a key construct in studies of various social units ranging from individuals, neighborhood, social groups, organizations, communities, to societies (Stryker, 1968; Tajfel & Turner, 1979), affecting both the satisfaction of the individuals and the effectiveness of the social units. Identity deals with the question "Who am I", which usually refers to further questions of belongings and of locating oneself in social contexts. A relatively stable, consistent and enduring answer to them invoke coherence and continuity of self fundamental to mental health, which also ensures the coherence and distinctiveness of social units.

Identity Theory and Social Identity Theory

There have been two main theories of identity: identity theory (Stryker, 1968) and social identity theory (Tajfel & Turner, 1979). Identity theory takes a symbolic interactionist view that society affects social behavior through its influence on self (Hogg, Terry, & White, 1995). According to identity theory, the symbol of role, as the relative stable, morphological components of social structure, is constructed and perceived by individuals through social interactions. People come to know who they are and what they should do based on such social roles and positions, for example, as a father, an environmentalist, a Republican. A similar idea was in Goffman's (1959) notion of "face", which asserted that individuals were attempting to influence the social situation by expressing and presenting themselves in a more flexible way to give favorable impression.

Social identity theory, on the other side, is more relevant to individual's perception of their membership, rather than role, in different social units. According to social identity theory (Tajfel & Turner, 1979), and later social categorization theory (Turner, 1985), people tend to classify themselves and others into various social categories, for example, gender, occupation, city, interests. Each category has prototypical characteristics abstracted from the members. By social categorization and social comparison, individuals gain a definition of who they are in terms of the defining characteristics of the category, as well as self-enhancement as being distinct or better than outside persons.

These two theories are compatible in that both theories address the structure and function of the socially constructed self as a dynamic construct that mediates the relationship between social structure and individual behaviors (Hogg, Terry, & White, 1995). While identity theory is primarily a sociological theory that sets out to explain individual's role-related behaviors inside certain social group, social identity theory is a social-psychological theory that focuses on membership in a social unit and intergroup relationships.

Social identity is important according to both theories. First, social identities encompassing salient roles or group classifications enable individuals to define and locate themselves in social environments, as well as motivate and regulate their social behaviors. Second, social identities provide individuals with a systematic means of defining others by cognitively segmenting and ordering the social environment. Understanding others' roles and classifications helps people understand the world, and sets a basis for further interaction. Third, shared social identities endue social groups' coherence that is critical for the viability and prosperity of the group.

Needs for Similarity and Distinctiveness

In social identity theory and self-categorization theory, the key idea is that a social category (e.g., a sport team) into which one falls, and to which one feels one belongs, provides a definition of "who I am" in terms of the defining characteristics of the category. For example, saying "I am a psychologist" indicates the acknowledgement of being in a group of people who study psychology. This categorical information also conveys rich information of what we do and what are proper way of our activities. According to Turner (1985), this categorization is accompanied by inter-group social comparisons with in-group favoring evaluation over out-groups in the service of positive self-esteem. Being a psychologist makes the individual distinguished from other people who are not expert or who are experts in other areas. The social comparison process accentuates both perceived similarity among members inside the categories and perceived differences from people outside the categories.

Therefore, just as Brewer (1991) claimed, social identity can be viewed as a reconciliation of opposing needs for assimilation and differentiation from others. Individuals avoid self-concepts that are either too narrowly personalized or too broadly inclusive, but instead define themselves in terms of distinctive category memberships. Compared with inter-group level differentiation in Turner (1987), we argue that the differentiation can exist in different levels. According to identity theory, people apply identities to themselves as a consequence of the structural role positions they occupy (Stryker, 2000), which implies that people can have distinct roles inside the group (i.e., intra-group comparison).

SOCIAL IDENTITY IN COMMUNITIES

A community to which individuals belong provides individuals certain aspects of identity. Community identity, in turn, helps individuals define who they are and give them guidelines for proper social intercourse in community life. Ever since when "Gemeinschaft", the precursor of the concept "community", was discussed, Tönnies (1887) claimed that the bonds of Gemeinschaft derive from personal identification based on the common place where people lived and worked.

In the era of the Internet, the common place where people live and work has been dramatically extended and transformed. It is no longer physically bounded in time and location. This transformation can give rise to new features of identity in terms of how it is formed, developed, and enacted. While the Tönnies' notion of identity is "embodied" based on soil, in contemporary com-

munity identity should be understood in a more symbolic way with regard to things like sacred structure, emotional connection, and identification (Carroll, 2011). The soil itself is less important than the situated events and human interactions that transpire on it. Identity is constituted through the social or symbolic interchange, through shared values and visions, through shared heritage, and the soil becomes essentially a vivid prop for this.

One critical conception for the retention of community identity is "boundary maintenance" (Sanders, 1958). As the term implies, any social system to persist must keep a boundary between itself and other systems, large or small, so that it does not merge with another system to the point that it no longer exists as a separate entity. Compared to Gemeinschaft, contemporary communities are much less confined by physical boundaries but more by social boundaries as defined by things like shared value, shared activity, or common fate, as well as its frame of reference. For example, when it comes to the NBA, the fans of Lakers and the fans of Clippers can be considered as two different communities even if these fans are all in the same city (i.e., Los Angeles), because they just go to watch different games and share different or even competing enthusiasm. However, they can also be viewed as one community as NBA fans in contrast with fans of other kinds of sports or leagues.

The boundaries of community are shifting and much more dynamic in contemporary communities with the meditation of information and communication technologies. First, people may experience more identities with the facilitation of technologies, considering that people have more opportunity to get access to resources, activities, and people who share interests, and more social groups and events can be constituted and supported. Second, people may experience richer identities in different levels. They can involve in many different social groups and take diverse roles. Finally, the increasing overlaps and interactions between the communities or social groups are making their boundaries even more blurred.

CURRENT STUDIES OF ONLINE IDENTITY

There have been several studies on the issue of "identity" online. Most studies of "online identity" or "virtual identity" in community networks refer to the "digital profile" that "enables individuals to express their interests outside contexts" that can be "established at logon" (Jordan, Hauser, & Foster, 2003; Chewar, McCrickard, & Carroll, 2003), or just "personal information" as purely static data to be managed (Madden, Fox, & Smith, 2007). Some other studies deem identity as "personal private information" to be protected and related to privacy and information security in terms of "identity deception" and "identity theft" (Donath, 1995; Lu & Ali, 2004). We can see identity is considered as static data that are not related to social interactions or community life.

Other studies were studying online "identity" in the sense of being "part of individual's self concept" (Tajfel, 1981). A famous and influential example is Turkle's work (Turkle, 1995). These work, however, focused on virtual spaces such as MUDs, where people are anonymous and identities are arbitrary. This is different from social networks (e.g., Facebook), where almost everyone uses their real name, and cannot escape their embodied selves and behavioral norms in their daily life.

When it comes to identity in social network websites, Facebook specifically, online identities are explored corresponding to their self concept in real life. Zhao, Grasmuch, and Martin (2008) conducted content analysis of profiles of 63 Facebook accounts, and divided users into three categories: visual (having wall posts and pictures) enumerative (having interests and hobbies), and narrative (having "about me"), according to a continuum of implicit and explicit identity claims. Similarly, DiMicco and Millen (2007) investigated characteristics in Facebook user profiles including age, number of friends, number of company friends, job title, job description, job start date, number of groups joined, job-related groups joined etc.,

and divided users into three categories: reliving the college days, dressed to impress, and living in the business world. Hewitt and Forte (2006) investigated students' perception of their instructor based on whether they have seen the instructor's profile and whether they are connected to the instructor.

A closer scrutinize of these social network studies reveals that they presented a static conception of identity, grounded only in user profiles and other characteristics. We would like to view identity as a more dynamic conception of constructing self-presentations in social contexts: while identities are consequences of social interactions, they are also underlying motives of social interactions, and thus is presented in social interactions (Simon, 2004). In this paper, we will investigate identities as presented in the context of online social interactions.

Facebook is a good platform for this investigation because it supports user activities ranging from individual (e.g., status updates), dyadic (e.g., comments in wall), to group (e.g., small Facebook Groups) and large community (e.g., large events) level. We would like to explore 1) whether and how social identities are embedded in online social interaction; 2) how social identities are related to the tension between assimilation and differentiation; 3) how Facebook features can support social identities in community life.

METHOD: SCENARIO-BASED INTERVIEWS

We conducted a scenario-based interview. In the interview, participants were asked to reveal and explain their recent Facebook activities in details (i.e., scenarios) to understand how their identities are enacted, constructed, and embodied in these social interactions. Each participant was interviewed by two interviewers, and each interview lasted for about 40 minutes. Participants also completed questionnaires on identity in each scenario.

We recruited the participants with advertisement post in Facebook Page of the University, asking for participants who use Facebook daily. They participated in this study voluntarily without compensation. Finally we conducted 10 interviews. All of the participants were college students in a large eastern university, 5 undergraduates, 1 master student, and 4 PhD students. Half of the participants were females and half of them were males. Four of them are from United States, five from Asia, and one from Africa. Their ages range from 19 to 29, with the average of 23.4 (SD=3.13). All participants used Facebook daily. Five of them used it less than half an hour per day; three of them used Facebook between half an hour to one hour per day; the other two used Facebook between one and two hours per day. The number of their friends ranges from 59 to 684, with the average of 372.3 (SD=207.9).

In the interview, we first asked the participants to show their Facebook pages, and briefly explain how they usually use the Facebook daily, who do they usually communicate in Facebook, and the relationships between online (especially Facebook) and offline interactions. Interestingly, although the background of our participants was pretty diverse, their reports were very similar. They use Facebook primarily to communicate with current friends in the campus; secondly they communicate with friends from previous schools. The activities they showed were mostly status updates (with comments), post in wall (with replies), tagged photos, Facebook Events, Facebook Groups, Facebook Pages, chats, as well as message inbox. A large part of the activities are related to offline activities, for example, talking about where to have lunch, photos of football games. Another large part was sharing interesting information such as videos. It is understandable their Facebook usage was similar: one the one hand, the usage is largely confined by the affordance that Facebook features currently provides; on the other hand, they are all basically college students with similar campus life despite their other different characteristics.

Then participants were asked to select five recent activities as scenarios to discuss with us (e.g., status update, posts in wall, tagged photos, Facebook Events, Facebook Groups). In a story telling way, participants were asked to explain social interactions and social contexts to us. To increase the diversity and diminish the bias of selection of scenarios, participants were encouraged to select scenarios with different Facebook features. However, it totally depended on participants on which scenarios were chosen.

We called the interview "scenario based" because most of discussions were focused on these selected scenarios. In each scenario, the participants were asked to describe the activity contexts, people involved, their motivation or goals, people's relationships, their roles, activity processes, conversation contents, related artifacts (e.g., updated photos) if there is any. In this way, we not only observed their online activity traces, but we collected more contextual information and their explanations of why and how these activities had happened and what the consequences were.

They were then asked to rate in seven-point Likert scales on questions including how similar they are (group similarity), how distinguished they are from other people (group distinctiveness), how unique the participant's role in these people is (role distinctiveness). For each question, the participants were asked to explain "how". Participants also answered 4-item questionnaire of group identification adapted from Mael and Tetrick (1992), which measures member identification with the selected social category, and an 1-item questionnaire of role verification adapted from Ma and Agarwal (2007), which measures perceived confirmation from other members of the participant's belief about his or her role identities inside the category, in 7-point Likert scales.

RESULTS

We collected 50 scenarios from the 10 participants. Two of the authors collaborated to clean the data and discuss the main purposes, activities, and identities embodied in each scenario. In the data analysis process, we paid specific attention to how their identities were enacted, constructed, and embodied in these online social interactions.

The Dynamic Construction of Identities

In the study, we confirmed that identity is more like a dynamic conception of constructing self-presentations, which is multifaceted and adjustable in social contexts. Social identities are enacted in social interactions with different levels and salience.

Identities are Modulated by Social Contexts

While many existing studies tried to understand identities through user's static profiles, we found participants were experiencing much richer and more concrete identities in social interactions supported by Facebook. We found that different aspects of identity were activated in different social contexts.

For example, when participant 1 showed us a thread of comments in a "wall", he described the people involved as a soccer team (with high score of group identification: 5.75 out of 7) talking about a member's farewell match. In a photo of fireworks, he describe himself as one of the Penn Staters (with score of group identification of 4) because it is an important annual event at Independence Day in the university, as well as photographers (with score of group identification of 1.75) when people were discussing photographic techniques in the comments of the photo. He also described himself as a Chinese student and one of a group of travelers (with score of group identification of 2.15) when discussing his profile photo of horse riding in China. Congruent with social identity theory (Turner, 1985), we confirmed the responsiveness of social identity to immediate social contexts, which has been ignored in existing studies on Facebook identity.

It is very interesting how these multiple aspects of social identities could be integrated into individual's self-concepts. There were both hierarchical and intersection representations in this case. Since the soccer team was from Penn State, the identity as a member of the soccer team could be viewed as a subgroup identity of the identity of Penn Stater, which was triggered in the firework event photo. These two identities were hierarchical (Gaertner et al., 1993), and the subgroup identity (i.e., soccer team) not only included all features of superordinate identity (i.e., Penn Stater), but also entailed more specific features. Therefore, the subgroup identity was much more salient than the general superordinate identity.

Furthermore, there were also intersection representations as mentioned by Roccas and Brewer (2002). On the one hand, this participant possessed a set of Penn Stater-related identities (i.e., studying, living, and playing at an American university); on the other hand, he demonstrated his ethic identity (i.e., Chinese student). The combination of them reduced these multiple and diverse social identities to a single and more exclusive social identity (i.e., Chinese student in an American university), which made the individual more distinct.

Coexistence of Different Levels of Identity

While most of existing empirical studies either took the perspective of social identity theory or identity theory, few studies investigated group identity and role identity at the same time. In this study, we found the coexistence of both. For example, participant 1 would emphasis his role of the vice captain when talking about his soccer team. Participant 3 described herself as a rookie and catcher in a softball team. Participant 8 described himself as a drummer of a rock band, which included a group identity of the rock band and a role identity of drummer.

We found even different levels of group identity could be activated concurrently. For example, participant 10 discuss a photo of social gathering in her birthday party, she said all the five friends were from the same continent (Africa), and she also specified one friend was from the same country (Cameroon). This finding confirms Gaertner et al.'s (1993) model of hierarchical nature of social identity, and implies that online identity is also a conceptual structure with different levels with different salience.

Hornsey and Hogg (2000) claimed that including inclusive superordinate identify (i.e., Africa) was a good strategy for intergroup harmony, which was applied in this case by enacting the continent level of identity. Emphasizing the similarity of these people helped constructing the identities.

The distinctiveness also helped constructing the identities. The superordinate identity (i.e., Africa) was enacted and reported in the social comparison also because people from this continent are minority group in the United States. The subgroup identity (i.e., Cameroon) was even stressed because it was even more distinct, thought there is only one such person.

Similarity, Distinctiveness, and Group Identity

We categorized participants' ratings on group similarity and group distinctiveness into low (with scores between 1 and 4) and high (with scores between 5 and 7) groups, and investigated how group identification will be influenced by group similarity and distinctiveness. Accordingly, we got four types of social groups, and we call them cliques, close-by friends, associates, and acquaintances. As demonstrated in Figure 1, social groups with both high similarity and high distinctiveness have the strongest group identity; social groups

with both low similarity and low distinctiveness have the weakest group identity.

Cliques: High Similarity with High Distinctiveness

The 21 social groups both high on similarity and high on distinctiveness are usually small groups having intensive activities such as bands, sport teams, and close friends who usually hand out in bars together. We call them cliques. Their group identity was the highest (mean= 4.90, SD=1.48)

Participant 3 reported that her softball team members are similar (score of 5) because they were all "passionate, energetic, healthy, and love softball". She also reported this team as distinctive (score of 5) because "only single-minded people are willing to spend so much time to play it every Saturday", and thus were different from general people. The score of her group identification of this team was also 5.

Participant 4 showed us a Facebook Group, which is her high school band. They have been together for seven years. She did not play in the band but every time the band was playing, she went to watch and bring food to them. She rated both the group similarity and distinctiveness as high (score of 7), and the group identification is also high (6.75), just as she said, "birds of the same feathers flock together".

Close-By Friends: High Similarity with Low Distinctiveness

The 8 social groups rated as high on similarity and low on distinctiveness are usually close-by friends who have much intercourse but are not specifically bound by specific activities or groups. Their group identity is not high (mean=3.59, SD=1.54).

For example, Participant 1 reported a friend who talked with him on his wall as similar (score of 5): "we attended the same high school; we both play soccer a lot; we are both admitted to the top universities in China; both of our majors

Figure 1. Group identification is influenced by group similarity and distinctiveness

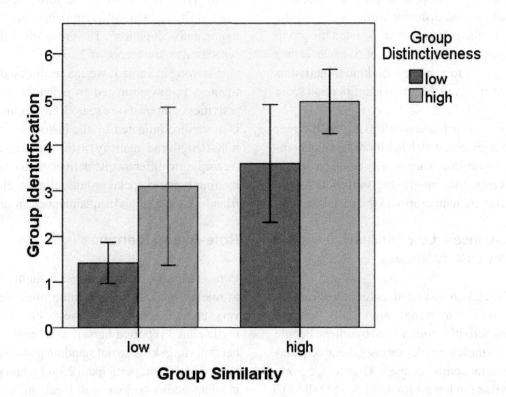

are computer science; both of us came to United States for PhD". However, he rated their distinctiveness from others just 3, because "I have a lot of similar friends who play soccer, who are PhD's in Computer Science". The group identification was rated 2.25.

Participant 6 commented on a funny picture of him, his sister, and his girl friend together, saying that "we have a lot of similarities, and we play together a lot" (similarity of 6), however, he rated the distinctiveness as low (score of 3) because "we are just at the same level of peers, like other students". The score of group identification was 4.25.

In these social groups, people seem do not have strong group identity, but they have strong bonds to each other. In seems that, social ties, rather than social identity, may apply better to such circumstances.

Associate: Low Similarity with High Distinctiveness

The 8 social groups rated low on similarity and high on distinctiveness are usually people who temporarily involved in low-demand activities with a minimal requirement to participate. They participate in certain events together but don't have much communication besides that. Their average group identity was not high (mean=3.09, SD=2.07).

For example, in the annual firework, participant 1 rated group similarity as low (score of 2) because "all people attending the event are different" while rated group distinctiveness as 5 because "we are participants in the event". And the score of group identification was 4.

Participant 9 was tagged in a photo of an event called "LGBT Pride" in New York with other four friends. He rated group similarity as low (score of 2) because "we have different life styles, education levels, and different attitudes toward the life/work balance". However, he rated the group distinctiveness as high (score of 6) because "we usually go out to explore such kind of activities in New York". And the group identification score was 4.5.

The size of such social groups is usually larger than other groups, which has more sense of community. These groups are usually based on certain social events. The shared event itself endued them distinctiveness temporarily in the social context.

Acquaintances: Low Similarity with Low Distinctiveness

The 13 social groups rated as low on similarity and low on distinctiveness are usually personal status and activities commented by others. People involves in these activities are just general acquaintances who randomly comment. The average group identity was the lowest (mean=1.85, SD=0.98).

For example, participant 2 added his new roommate as friend on Facebook, with another friend commenting "funny you two know each other". He rated group similarity and distinctiveness as low (both as 2) because "we just know each other" and "we are just common friends". The group identification was very low (score of 1).

Four friends commented on participant 7's status update "caught in the rain shower on my way back on a bike....but I am still alive...." Participant 7 rated both the group similarity and

distinctiveness as low as 2 because "we are just general friends with different personality, tastes, major, and occupation". The group identification score is also low (score of 2.25).

Showing in Table 1, we can see group distinctiveness is discriminated by whether common activities or interests are shared. Group similarity is more discriminated by the history of interactions (length and intensity) in the social assembly. According to different distinctiveness and similarity, four types of social groups, cliques, close-by friends, associates, and acquaintances, are defined.

Role-Based Identities

Intra-group role distinctiveness is highly related to role verification. While some roles were not very unique, some others were. For example, participant 3 reported herself as a "rookie", and her "sporting skills do not standout personally" in the softball team; participant 2 said while people in a Facebook event were all local musicians, he was the drummer; participant 6 thought himself pretty unique because he is "boy friend" of one and "elder brother" of the other in a photo of three.

Individuals can have several roles in the same group, probably because role in more related to structural position in the whole group as well as various inside relationship. Just as participant 1 reported that he was the vice captain of the soccer team, "that was because I am the best friend of the captain, and we built the team together". Here both "vice captain" and "best friend" are

Table 1. Examples of social groups with different levels of similarity and distinctiveness

		Distinctiveness	
		low	high
Similarity	low	**Acquaintances** e.g., connecting to new roommate, general comments on personal status updates	**Associates** e.g., World Cup comments, a TV show fans, large event gathering, high school get together
	high	**Close-by Friends** e.g., old friends greeting on walls, close friends sharing funny videos	**Cliques** e.g., rock band, softball team, soccer team, honor scholar program

role identities. The former refers to the structure position in the whole team, and the latter refers to the structures position in the network of social relationships (i.e., social ties).

There are implications that role distinctiveness will also influence group identification. For example, when participant 1 was talking about his soccer team, he emphasized that he was the vice captain. A more evident example comes from participant 2, who initiated a Facebook Group on active minds with dozens of members. Although he rated the group similarity as low (score of 3) because "we don't know each other very well", and the score of group distinctiveness as relatively high (5) because "we are all interested in mental health issue", the group identification score was 7, because "I am the founder and leader of this group".

How Facebook Supports Social Identities

While we categorized the activities into status updates (with comments), posting on walls (with replies), tagged in photos, Facebook Events, and Facebook Groups, according to Facebook features. We did not find significant evidence that the type of technical features is influencing users' identities.

Instead, we found their identities depended more on the social gatherings or groups where the identities were situated. For example, general friends can comment on your wall while very close friend can also comment. There can be Facebook Groups of small bands with high group identification; meanwhile some Facebook Groups are large communities with thousands of people (e.g., The World Cup 2010) with lower group identification. Facebook serves as a platform to facilitate social interactions from dyadic level to large communities of various kinds of social groups.

Moreover, Facebook as an online platform greatly facilitates student's community life by providing more convenient ways for these social groups to communicate and collaborate. It also provides more opportunities for students to find interested resources and people with shared interests. Just as participant 6 said, from his friends Facebook activities he was usually surprised to find some of friends share some interest that he had never known, which sometimes starts new conversations or even further social activities. This suggests that online technologies such as Facebook facilitate richer community experience not only by making community identities more concrete in tangible social interactions, but also by extending new opportunities to new identities.

CONCLUSION AND DISCUSSION

Social identity is a key construct to understand online communities. Existing studies of online identity ignored social interactions and community life where social identities are constructed and embodied. In this paper, we explored the modality of social identities in the ecology of Facebook-mediated community life. We demonstrated that identity is more of a dynamic concept of constructing self-presentations, as moderated by and adjusted in social contexts, in online environment. Through the interview we investigated users' tension between being similar and different at the same time. We found that group similarity and distinctiveness together influence group identifications, which confirms social identity theory. Furthermore, we proposed that intra-group level role distinctiveness can be another source of differentiation, and we found it can influence both role identity and group identity.

This paper first calls attention to social interactions in studying identity in online social network. While most of existing studies on online identity focus on relatively stable characteristics such as user profile, we demonstrate the feasibility of understanding identity embodied in social interactions. We argue that social identities could be and should be understood in tangible social contexts. Social identities are more concretely enacted and function in tangible social contexts than in abstracted statements such as profiles and questionnaires.

Second, social identity is a rather complex social mechanism as it shows in the study. While we investigated inter-group level social comparison as implied by social identity theory, we extended the differentiation level to include intra-group role distinctiveness. Even in the same social group, different levels of social categories can be activated, with different identity salience. Identity salience depends on the factors such as context for social comparison (e.g., people from Africa as minority group), current social activity (e.g., the sport team vs. the whole university), and individual affiliations (e.g., the country vs. the continent).

How these multiple aspects of social identities can be integrated into self concept is a very interesting topic. In this paper, we demonstrated different combinations such as hierarchical and intersection identities as well as inter-group level combining intra-group level identities. Further investigations should be made on the enactment, appropriation, and integration of these multiple social identities.

Third, we explored the relationship among similarity, distinctiveness, and social identities. Social identities on one hand maintain the coherence of social groups, which usually require conformity of its members; on the other hand, social identities help keep the boundaries of different social groups. Our exploratory categorization of the four types of social groups demonstrates that social identity can be an effective construct to investigate online community life.

Furthermore, we found social tie as an inevitable conception to investigate community life. Some social groups are primarily common-identity based; some others are more common-bond based. Close-by friends in our study are one example. Furthermore, social ties inside social groups influence both role identities and group identity. Therefore, we would argue that social

identity and social tie are two complementary constructs to understand community life. Just as Ren, Kraut, and Kiesler (2007) claimed, they are two different mechanisms of people's attachment to the community.

Our study gives design implications from the perspective of social identity. First, the notion that identity is mainly supported by static features such as users' profiles may constrain our community design. Understanding identities as enacted, constructed, and embodied in social interactions calls for more sensemaking features of identities in supporting online interactions. Understanding identities as a complex and dynamic social mechanism calls for collaborative sensemaking of different identities. Our categorization of group identities based on similarities and distinctiveness suggests that online community design (e.g., Facebook Group) should take different kinds of social groups into account.

As an exploratory study, this paper sets the first step for further studies. Important issues we would like to explore are that 1) for individuals, how different aspects of identities are related and integrated to construct a unified "self", that upholds their community life; 2) for social groups, whether different members perceive different group identity or hold different identity salience; how this relationship is modulated by their role identity; how people with different role identities can be integrated as an successful online group; 3) for a whole community (e.g., the university campus), how different social groups are overlapping and inter-related; whether social group identities (e.g., a university volleyball team) comprise community identity (e.g., the university), or whether they are just identities in different levels.

REFERENCES

Brewer, M. B. (1991). The Social Self: On Being the Same and Different at the Same Time. *Personality and Social Psychology Bulletin, 17*(5), 475–482. doi:10.1177/0146167291175001

Carroll, J. M. (2011). *The Neighborhood and the Internet: Design Research Projects in Community Informatics*. London, UK: Routledge.

Chewar, C., McCrickard, D. S., & Carroll, J. M. (2005). Analyzing the social capital value chain in community network interfaces. *Internet Research, 15*(3), 262–280.

DiMicco, J. M., & Millen, D. (2007). Identity management: Multiple presentations of Self in Facebook. In *Proceedings of the GROUP 2007 Conference* (pp. 383-386). New York, NY: ACM Press.

Donath, J. S. (1998). Identity and Deception in the Virtual Community. In Kollock, P., & Smith, M. (Eds.), *Communities in Cyberspace* (pp. 29–59). London, UK: Routledge.

Gaertner, S. L., Dovidio, J. F., Bachman, B. A., & Rust, M. C. (1993). The common ingroup identity model: Recategorization and the reduction of intergroup bias. *European Review of Social Psychology, 4*, 1–26. doi:10.1080/14792779343000004

Goffman, E. (1956). *The Presentation of Self in Everyday Life*. New York, NY: Anchor Doubleday.

Hewitt, A., & Forte, A. (2006). Crossing Boundaries: Identity Management and Student/Faculty Relationships on the Facebook. In *Proceedings of the CSCW 2006 Conference*. New York, NY: ACM Press.

Hogg, M., Terry, D., & White, K. (1995). A tale of two theories: A critical comparison of identity theory with social identity theory. *Social Psychology Quarterly, 58*, 255–269. doi:10.2307/2787127

Hornsey, M. J., & Hogg, M. A. (2000). Assimilation and diversity: An integrative model of subgroup relations. *Personality and Social Psychology Review, 4*, 143–156. doi:10.1207/S15327957PSPR0402_03

Jordan, K., Hauser, J., & Foster, S. (2003). The Augmented Social Network: Building identity and trust into the next-generation Internet. *First Monday, 8*(8).

Lu, H., & Ali, A. (2004). Prevent Online Identity Theft – Using Network Smart Cards for Secure Online Transactions. In *Information Security* (LNCS 3225, pp. 342-353).

Ma, M., & Agarwal, R. (2007). Through a Glass Darkly: Information Technology Design, Identity Verification, and Knowledge Contribution in Online Communities. *Information Systems Research, 18*(1), 42–67. doi:10.1287/isre.1070.0113

Madden, M., Fox, S., & Smith, A. (2007). *Digital footprints: Online identity management and search in the age of transparency*. Washington, DC: Pew Internet and American Life Project. Retrieved October 31, 2010, from http://www.pewinternet.org/PPF/r/229/report_display.asp

Mael, F., & Tetrick, L. (1992). Identifying organizational identification. *Educational and Psychological Measurement, 52*(4), 813–825. doi:10.1177/0013164492052004002

Ren, Y., Kraut, R., & Kiesler, S. (2007). Applying Common Identity and Bond Theory to Design of Online Communities. *Organization Studies, 28*(3), 377–408. doi:10.1177/0170840607076007

Roccas, S., & Brewer, M. B. (2002). Social identity complexity. *Personality and Social Psychology Review, 6*, 88–106. doi:10.1207/S15327957PSPR0602_01

Sanders, I. T. (1958). *The Community: An Introduction to a Social System*. New York, NY: Ronald Press Company.

Simon, B. (2004). *Identity in Modern Society: A Social Psychological Perspective*. London, UK: Blackwell.

Stryker, S. (1968). Identity Salience and Role Performance: The Relevance of Symbolic Interaction Theory for Family Research. *Journal of Marriage and the Family, 30*(4), 558–564. doi:10.2307/349494

Stryker, S., & Burke, P. J. (2000). The Past, Present, and Future of an Identity Theory. *Social Psychology Quarterly*, *63*(4), 284–297. doi:10.2307/2695840

Tajfel, H. (1981). Social stereotypes and social groups. In Turner, J. C., & Giles, H. (Eds.), *Intergroup Behavior* (pp. 144–167). Oxford, UK: Basil Blackwell.

Tajfel, H., & Turner, J. C. (1979). An Integrative Theory of Intergroup Conflict. In Austin, W. G., & Worchel, S. (Eds.), *The Social Psychology of Intergroup Relations* (pp. 33–47).

Tönnies, F. (1887). *Community and Civil Society*. Cambridge, MA: Cambridge University Press.

Turkle, S. (1995). *Life on the Screen*. New York, NY: Simon & Schuster.

Turner, J. C. (1985). Social categorization and the self-concept: A social cognitive theory of group behavior. In Lawler, E. J. (Ed.), *Advances in group processes: Theory and research* (*Vol. 2*, pp. 77–122).

Zhao, S., Grasmuch, S., & Martin, J. (2008). Identity Construction on Facebook: Digital empowerment in Anchored relationships. *Computers in Human Behavior*, *24*(5), 1816–1836. doi:10.1016/j.chb.2008.02.012

This work was previously published in the International Journal of Virtual Communities and Social Networking, Volume 2, Issue 4, edited by Subhasish Dasgupta, pp. 64-76, copyright 2010 by IGI Publishing (an imprint of IGI Global).

Section 2
Business Applications of Social Networks

Chapter 8
The Role of Virtual Communities in the Customization of E-Services

Bill Karakostas
City University London, UK

Dimitris Kardaras
Athens University of Economics and Business, Greece

Adéla Zichová
City University London, UK

ABSTRACT

Virtual communities are groups of people with similar interests who meet online and together act as a learning environment, place for social support, or as bodies for influencing public opinion. In this paper, the authors identify characteristics of a virtual community that influence its members to customize e-services provided to or received by the virtual community. The authors propose a theoretical framework of factors influencing service customization in a virtual community that has been validated with two case studies conducted in health-focused virtual communities. The findings confirm that the quality of the learning environment, social support, and the virtual community's ability to influence public opinion, positively contribute to the perceived usefulness and active participation in the community by its members. In turn, these factors were found to have a positive influence on customization of e-services by the members, based on the community's suggestion. The research also suggests several areas of focus to enhance e-service customization through virtual communities.

INTRODUCTION

Rheingold (2000) defines virtual communities as social aggregations that emerge from the Internet where a sufficiently large number of people carry on public discussions long enough, with sufficient human feeling, to form webs of personal relationships. As the Internet and Web has evolved, so have the virtual communities, from simply "meeting places" to discuss topics of interest, to places where e-services are provided, enhanced and consumed. In business environments, virtual communities such as customer groups can evaluate products and services offered by a company,

DOI: 10.4018/978-1-4666-1553-3.ch008

and can provide valuable feedback to both their members and to the service providers themselves. Hagel and Armstrong (1997) emphasize the need to recognize the business potential of virtual communities by arguing that commercial success online will belong to those who organize virtual communities that meet multiple social and commercial needs.

Today, there is a demand for products and services that are flexible enough to match exactly the requirements of different individuals or groups. Mass customization is the process of applying technology and management methods to provide product variety and customization through quick responsiveness and flexibility (Kotha, 1995). In services, mass customization is an enabler in order to meet the needs and wants of customers (Rust & Kannan, 2002). Customization is a process that can be applied by the providers of the product/services, by the recipients (customers) of the products/services, or by both. Virtual communities are often formulated around the provision of a service electronically (e-service). For example, virtual communities are created around the provision of e-health services, allowing their members to obtain better information about the provided e-services, offer mutual support, and, in general, maximize the benefits obtaining from such e-services. To make the most of the offered services, virtual community members may seek to customize them, following experience, suggestions and advice from other community members.

The research question posed in thus paper, therefore is: can a virtual community act as the enabler or the motivator of e-service customization for its members? If so, what are the essential functions and features that are required from the community in order to support or enhance the service customization activities of its members?

In the rest of the paper, first we survey research in the areas of virtual communities, e-services and e-service customization. Then, we introduce a causal model and hypothesis for e-service cus-

tomization enabling factors in virtual communities, and describe the research methodology we employed in order to prove the research hypothesis made. Next, we discuss the findings from applying the e-service customization factors causal model to two case studies on health related virtual communities. Finally, we discuss the implications from the findings on e-service customization and virtual communities more generally.

LITERATURE SURVEY

The definition of virtual communities varies, depending on the perspective from which they are considered. From a business perspective, Hagel and Armstrong (1997) define virtual communities as online groups of people with common interests and needs. Preece (2000) looks at virtual communities from the e-commerce perspective and argues that, according to e-commerce entrepreneurs, any communication software such as a bulletin board can be regarded as a virtual community. Balasubramanian and Mahajan (2001) consider the virtual community from an economical perspective, and they define them as any entity that exhibits the following characteristics:

- It is made up of an aggregation of people.
- Members are rational utility-maximizers.
- Members interact with one another without physical collaboration; however, not every member must necessarily interact with every other member.
- Members are engaged in a social-exchange process which includes mutual production and consumption. Each member is engaged in the consumption process; however, not everyone is involved in the production.
- Social interactions between members revolve around a well-understood focus that encompasses a shared objective, shared property, or shared interest.

In addition to their contribution to the spread of virtual communities, Internet and the Web have also been responsible for transforming services into e-services. E-service examples include customized travel packages, insurance policies, software-support agreements, training plans, legal contracts, financial investments plans, healthcare and health treatments (Kratochvil & Carson, 2005). However, the term e-services does not imply purely IT, Web or infrastructure services; the e-service business model also includes service product, service environment and service delivery (Rust & Kannan, 2002). The technology therefore, is an enabler in e-service in order to meet the needs and wants of customers, and thus enable the growth of the market and revenue (Rust & Kannan, 2002). Kratochvil and Carson (2005) add that competition among companies lies in the ability to give the customers exactly what they want, when they want it, but still profitably and at a price acceptable to the customers. This is where the flexibility of customization comes to play. E-service customization refers to the ability to adapt and/or manipulate services and e-services in such a way that preferences, expectations and requirements of individual consumers are met (Kardaras & Karakostas, in press).

A study conducted by Papathanassiou et al (2004) reported that in the service sector, the dynamically changing customer needs, high heterogeneity of markets and quite fast technological changes create an environment where mass customization should be considered as a high priority competitive strategy. Customization of services thus becomes a business strategy (Cao et al., 2006). Service providers must differentiate their offerings from others to sustain their market share and profitability, and they need to introduce new options and choices that give customers some customization and control of the service content and its availability (Kratochvil & Carson, 2005).

Customizing e-services is not a one-way process (Kardaras & Karakostas, in press). The process is an iterative loop, relying on inputs from both the service provider and the customer, who provide feedback to each other. Both the providers and customers need to have processes in place so as to implement service customization. This view is supported by Cao et al. (2006) who propose that service customization should not only be applied to the content of an activity, but also to the structure of the service that is built dynamically according to the requirements of the customers. Kardaras and Karakostas (in press) also argue that customization can take place at different points: In *provider-driven* approaches, customization takes place at the point where the service is created. The service provider controls the resources and processes, however, customizing e-services is more complex than customizing physical products, and thus the provider likely needs sufficient feedback from the customer. *Customer-driven customization* is more appropriate for e-services and takes place at the point where the service is consumed. Here, customers are in control of the processes and resources, and the providers learn and perhaps adapt their services based on the feedback they receive from the customers.

In terms of how e-services can be customized, a study by Ansari and Mela (2002) suggests that service providers consider the following approaches:

- **Onsite:** Companies either customize their websites themselves, or they allow the users to customize the content on their own. The company-initiated customization often appears in a form of a recommender system, where the customization is based on the implicitly revealed preferences of the users, such as previous purchases. The user-initiated customization elicits user preferences and gives them control in defining their needs and wants.
- **External:** The focus is on bringing customers to the website in the first place. For this, customized emails, banner advertisements, affiliate sites or content in other media that may be relevant to the site users are employed.

Kratochvil and Carson (2005) suggest that several aspects need to be considered in service customization:

- **What:** What the services offer to the customer – functions, quality, security or availability?
- **Where:** Are the services easy to access?
- **When:** Are the available resources aligned with the customer's access habits?
- **How:** Are the processes customized for the customer, and is the service deployed via a number of media?

Ongoing services are therefore likely to be modified through the learning relationship formed between the customer and the company, thus this collaborative customization and service regeneration can result in an expanding scope of services offered (Peters & Saidin, 2000). In this paper we argue that virtual communities foster such collaborative customization, and we try to identify the specific factors that contribute toward it.

RESEARCH HYPOTHESES

We have based our research hypotheses on the Technology Acceptance Model, and in particular on its perceived usefulness and perceived ease of use criteria. The perceived usefulness is defined by Davis (1989) as the subjective probability that by using a specific application system the user will increase his or her job performance. From the virtual community perspective, perceived usefulness indicates the level to which a community member believes in his/her ability to obtain services and information, share experiences with other members and enhance his or her performance when exchanging information while using the community (Lin, 2007). The perceived ease of use is described by Davis (1989) as the degree to which a person believes that the use of a particular system will be effortless This signifies the effort

that an individual member will have to expend when using the community (van der Heijden, 2000) and whether or not the members will find the community easy to manage (Lin, 2007). For example, web sites with high ease of use encourage higher user involvement and sense of belonging with the community (Teo et al. 2003).

Analysis of the literature has also shown that members join communities because of the social identification with the community (Pentina et al., 2008), which can influence the member's consumption choices. It is therefore proposed that the degree to which an individual member will be open to the community's influence is determined by the member's perception of the community's ease of use and usefulness. Subsequently, we form the following research hypotheses H1, H2:

H1: Perceived usefulness of the virtual community positively affects the member's intention to customize services as suggested by the community.

H2: Perceived ease of use of the virtual community positively affects the member's intention to customize services as suggested by the community.

In addition, it has been argued that ease of use can strongly predict the behavior of online customers, primarily through its effect on perceived usefulness (Moon & Kim, 2001). It is thus hypothesized that the more easy to use a community is perceived to be by its members, the more useful it will also be considered by them to be. Thus, an additional hypothesis H3 is formulated.

H3: Perceived ease of use positively affects the perceived usefulness of the virtual community.

Aside from perceived ease of use and perceived usefulness of the virtual community, it is suggested that the degree of participation alone contributes to how open a member is to influences by the community. A member's participation depends on his/her satisfaction with the services provided, both core services and supporting ones (van Riel et al. 2001). In turn, satisfaction was found to have a positive effect on trust (Bauer & Grether, 2005). The literature also suggests that participation depends on the usefulness of the service provided (Koh et al., 2007), as well as on how experienced users become in using the service and how frequently they use it (Sousa et al., 2008). In addition, participating members could also be subject to

interpersonal influence, as they try to establish their identity in relation to those of other members (Bearden et al., 1989). Because of their high degree of expertise, some virtual communities can exert pressure on the individual members by controlling the transfer of information, and thus influencing their decisions about how to use a service (Pentina et al., 2008).

Other research has also shown that members join communities because of the social identification with the community (Pentina et al., 2008), which can influence the member's consumption choices, regardless of whether they participate in the community actively (i.e. by contributing to the discussions) or passively (e.g. by reading the posts made by other members) (Koh et al., 2007). It is thus hypothesized that participation itself has an effect on how susceptible a member is to the community's influence, and the level of participation is affected by the community's perceived usefulness. Thus, the following hypotheses H4, H5 were made:

H4: *Participation in the virtual community positively affects the member's intention to customize services as suggested by the community.*

H5: *Perceived usefulness positively affects participation in the virtual community.*

Existing research depicts virtual communities as holding three major roles: serving as a learning environment, providing social support, and influencing public opinion (Josefsson & Ranerup,

2003; Schlager & Fusco, 2003; Cothrel & Williams, 1999; Lin & Lee, 2006). The quality of the learning environment, affecting how members can become their own experts in the field of the community (Josefsson & Ranerup, 2003), comprises three factors: information quality, system quality and service quality (Lin, 2007). Information quality includes aspects such as information currency, accuracy or completeness (Nelson et al., 2005). According to Perkowitz and Etzioni (1999), information is considered useful only when the user considers the information to be informative, accurate and up-to-date. System quality comprises reliability, response time, flexibility or convenience of access (Nelson et al., 2005). Van der Heijden (2000) adds that presentation attractiveness is also positively related to the attitude toward the system, simply because users prefer to visit systems that are more attractive. Yoo et al. (2002) argue that in case of virtual communities, members are reluctant to participate when they experience difficulty in navigating the community website, delays in response, lack of access and disconnections.

Service quality dimensions consist of 11 criteria identified by Zeithaml et al. (2000). The most likely quality aspects were identified as the user interface quality, responsiveness, need fulfilment and security (Gummerus et al., 2004), as well as personalization (Keating at al. 2003). In information-sensitive communities, such as e-health, trust has been showed as a highly important parameter of the service quality (Gummerus et al., 2004; Leimeister et al., 2005). Effective communities deliver relevant information and services (Wilkins et al., 2002), and in such trouble-free systems, members create, share and manage the user-generated content (Lechner & Hummel, 2002), which builds trust, brand awareness and adds value (Macaulay et al. 2007). Therefore, it is proposed that the quality of the learning environment has an effect on the factors influencing the decision-making process of the individual community members, which leads to hypotheses H6a, H6b, H6c.

H6a: *The quality of the learning environment positively affects the degree of participation in the virtual community.*

H6b: *The quality of the learning environment positively affects the perceived usefulness of the virtual community.*

H6c: *The quality of the learning environment positively affects the perceived ease of use of the virtual community.*

While the potential access to knowledge is said to be of greater interest than the opportunity to meet new people or help others through the virtual community (Hall & Graham, 2004), the quality of the social support provided by the human participants is valued just as that of the information and service presented. Personal gain, such as help with solving particular problems and receiving help and support from others, seems to be more important than the communal goals, such as sharing knowledge and working collaboratively (Hall & Graham, 2004). Although social bonding among members depend on the local culture and on the user's gratification of the community (Ishii & Morihiro, 2007), successful communities were found to provide space for both receiving and providing social support (Josefsson, 2005). Moreover,

Jawecki et al. (2008) recommend that the community's social environment needs to be full of encouragement, challenge and support, especially in creative communities. It is thus argued that the quality of the social support has an effect on the factors influencing the decision-making process of the individual, leading to the following hypotheses

H7a: *The quality of the social support positively affects the degree of participation in the virtual community.*

H7b: *The quality of the social support positively affects the perceived usefulness of the virtual community.*

H7c: *The quality of the social support positively affects the perceived ease of use of the virtual community.*

The final hypothesis of the research model relates to the virtual communities' ability to influence public opinions. The purpose of the communities is to encourage knowledge-sharing and create an environment where all questions and answers are shared by all participants (Yager, 2002). A learning cycle exists in a community, with knowledge and capacity generated in individuals finding their way back to the community through new values, new artifacts and new tools, all of which become a part of the community's knowledge base (Schlager & Fusco, 2003). The knowledge base can be expanded by e-portfolios, modeling examples or simulations (Schlager & Fusco, 2003), as well as by information presented in forms of statistics and reports (Josefsson & Ranerup, 2003). Consequently, the expanded knowledge base reduces the member's uncertainty about the area of expertise of the virtual community and enhances the uncertainty reduction when dealing with complex products (Adjei et al., 2007). It is therefore proposed that this enhanced knowledge base acts as a means to influencing the public opinion, which has an effect on the perceived usefulness of the community, leading to hypothesis H8.

H8: *The ability to influence public opinion positively affects the perceived usefulness of the virtual community.*

As a result of the decision to focus the case studies on e-health related communities, the above research model was adjusted appropriately. After reviewing several health communities, it was found that the community discussions touch both the physical health services, such as hospitals and medication, as well as online e-health tools, such as electronic health records. Therefore, the initial hypotheses H1, H2 and H4 were each refined to two sub-hypotheses, covering both health and e-health. The final research model is depicted in Figure 1.

H1a: *Perceived usefulness of the virtual community positively affects the member's intention to customize e-health services as suggested by the community.*

H1b: *Perceived usefulness of the virtual community positively affects the member's intention to customize physical health services as suggested by the community.*

H2a: *Perceived ease of use of the virtual community positively affects the member's intention to customize e-health services as suggested by the community.*

H2b: *Perceived ease of use of the virtual community positively affects the member's intention to customize physical health services as suggested by the community.*

H4a: *Participation in the virtual community positively affects the member's intention to customize e-health services as suggested by the community.*

H4b: *Participation in the virtual community positively affects the member's intention to customize physical health services as suggested by the community.*

RESEARCH METHOD

The causal factors model of Figure 1 was validated using data from two online surveys conducted in two health-focused virtual communities– a general health community in the US, and a cancer-focused community in Britain. The original

Figure 1. Research model for virtual community influence on service customization

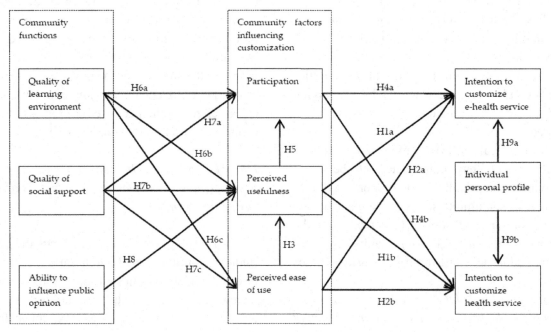

research model was adjusted for a better fit to these two communities, and an online survey was developed to test it. The validity of the research hypotheses was tested by computing variances and statistical correlations. Subsequently, the empirical data was analyzed both together and separately for each community, as well as in light of additional demographic data collected from the two communities. Additional feedback was solicited from representatives of the communities' providers in order to obtain an opinion of health care professionals.

Two almost identical online questionnaires were used in this research. Each questionnaire consisted of a brief explanation of why the research was conducted and with the researcher's contact details. The actual questionnaire began with four demographic questions, asking the respondents to indicate their age group, gender, length of their membership in the particular community, and the frequency of their usage of the community. The subsequent questions were statements, relating to the criteria of the research hypotheses defined above. Seven of the nine criteria contained three statements each, while the last two contained four. The statements were developed based on the research model presented in the previous section, the particulars of the case studies, and questionnaires used in previous related case studies. As an example, the following statements were used for the Quality of Learning Environment criterion:

- The information provided by the virtual community is accurate (Nelson et al., 2005)
- The virtual community provides me with a complete set of information (Nelson et al., 2005)
- Information provided by the other members is always correct (Leimeister et al., 2005)

The respondents were asked to indicate the level of their agreement or disagreement with each statement using a 5-point Likert scale from "strongly disagree" to "strongly agree". The following topics were covered by the questionnaire whose details are included in Appendix A:

- Demographics (age, gender)
- Duration of membership in the community
- Frequency of usage of the community's web site
- Quality of learning environment
- Quality of social support
- Ability to influence public opinion
- Participation
- Perceived usefulness
- Perceived ease of use
- Individual profile
- Intention to customize health services.

ANALYSIS OF THE SURVEY RESULTS

In total 31 valid questionnaires were received and analyzed. Due to space considerations the remaining of this section only discusses the analysis of questions directly pertaining to service customization aspects.

Customization influences

As members may be influenced by communities differently, the following questions were used to determine the member's inclination to customize following suggestions by the community:

ppa: *When it comes to customizing products and services to match my preferences I prefer to follow my own feelings and opinions, rather than what I find in the online community's discussions.*

ppb: *When it comes to customizing products and services to match my preferences I prefer to follow suggestions of my family and friends, rather than what I find in the online community's discussions.*

ppc: *When it comes to customizing products and services to match my preferences I prefer to follow suggestions of a professional in a given field (e.g., a physician/GP in the healthcare field), rather than what I find in the online community's discussions.*

The responses summarized in Figure 2 indicate that the virtual community members are most likely to trust either themselves or a healthcare professional, rather than the community. However, when choosing between the community and the family members or friends, 49% of respondents indicate that they would prefer the community, while only 19% are certain that they would choose the advice of their friends or family.

Intention to Customize Online Services

These statements were used to determine whether the members would customize online e-health services based on the community suggestions:

c1a: *I am very likely to follow community suggestions on using web based electronic health records to communicate with my healthcare providers.*

c1b: *I am very likely to follow community suggestions on customizing online health tools.*

c1c: *I am very likely to follow community suggestions on self-diagnosing over the internet.*

c1d: *I am very likely to follow community suggestions on online monitoring of chronic health conditions.*

Figure 2. Customization influences

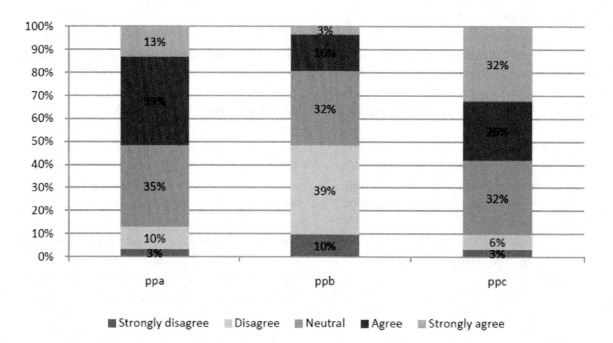

The results (Figure 3) indicate that the strongest inclination to customize e-health services is in case of web based electronic health records, and even more in case of online health tools, with 29% and 45% agreements respectively. However, there are strong disagreements in terms of accepting community suggestions about self-diagnosing and monitoring health conditions online, with 51% (32+19) disagreement in the first case and 41% (35+6) in the second.

Intention to Follow Community Health Advice

These statements were used to determine whether the members would be prepared to follow community health recommendations and advice, rather than creating their own, customized solutions.

c2a: I am very likely to follow community suggestions on choosing a healthcare facility to treat my condition.

c2b: I am very likely to follow community suggestions on changing my lifestyle.

c2c: I am very likely to follow community suggestions on participating in clinical trials.

c2d: I am very likely to follow community suggestions on choosing health/medical insurance plans.

Responses (Figure 4) about willingness to go with the community health advice indicate agreement with using suggestions of the online community for choosing healthcare facilities (45%) and lifestyle changes (42%). Disagreements prevail in using the community suggestions for clinical trials and health insurance, with 42% of undecided respondents in each category.

DISCUSSION AND CONCLUSION

The research revealed that in the case of healthcare, the learning environment and social support that the community provides, together with its ability to influence public opinion, are significant contributors to how useful the community is perceived and how much participation in the community is valued. The importance of the social

Figure 3. Intention to customize e-services

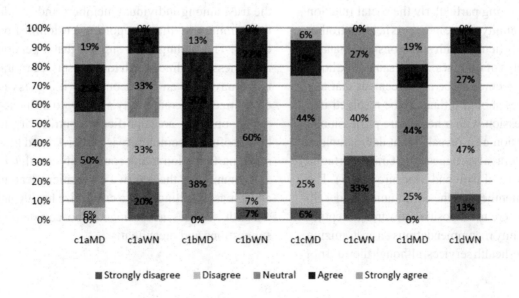

Figure 4. Intention to follow community health advice

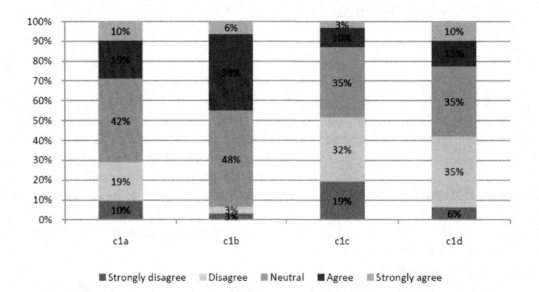

support factor was consistent with other studies, such as (Hall & Graham, 2004), (Lin, 2007) and (Roffe & Foster, 2008). In turn, the perceived usefulness of the community was found to have a positive effect on the willingness of individual members to customize health services following the suggestions of the community.

The qualitative feedback from the community members as well as healthcare providers supported this, highlighting particularly the social function of the community where members help each other cope with difficult health situations and manage the symptoms of illnesses. At the same time however, there seemed to be an agreement that any health issues should ultimately be resolved in a personal session with a healthcare professional. The discussion also revealed that demographics played a role, as also suggested in Grace-Farfaglia et al. (2006) and Ishii and Morihiro (2007). The youngest members of the community (under 30 years old) were most positive towards accepting the community recommendations on customizing health and e-health services, although they did not

display such a strong affinity to the community as the older members. Also, those who visited the community web site several times a week or more, as well as those who were members for more than six months, displayed stronger inclinations towards accepting the customization suggestions from the community. This possibly indicates that, particularly in the healthcare field, active and long-time membership helps increase the trust among individual members and within the community, thus supporting customization efforts. The findings also suggest that a general awareness of online health tools or service rating tools may have an effect on the willingness to customize. The community's ability to influence public opinion, are significant contributors to how useful the community is perceived and how much participation in the community is valued.

In summary, the positive correlations lead to an increased willingness to customize health and e-health services according to the community suggestions and mean that:

- The more the community is regarded as a quality learning environment, the more the member values his/her participation in it.
- The more the community is regarded as a quality learning environment, the more useful it is perceived by the member.
- The more the community is regarded as a quality social support space, the more the member values his/her participation in it.
- The more the community is regarded as a quality social support space, the more useful it is perceived by the member.
- The more the community is accepted as a shaper of the public opinion, the more useful it is perceived by the member.
- The easier the community is to use, the more useful it is perceived by the member.
- The more useful the community is perceived, the more the member values his/her participation in the community.
- The more useful the community is perceived, the higher intention to customize health services according to the community suggestions the member displays.

In conclusion, this paper presented research of virtual communities and their influence on service customization. Evidence from the literature suggests that the role of virtual communities in service customization has not yet been studied. The findings highlight the importance of the community functions which determine how useful the community is perceived and how being a member of the community is valued. The perceived usefulness of the community was the major factor that determined the member's acceptance of customization suggestions from the community. Moreover, the paper discussed demographical characteristics that contribute to the willingness to customize services. The virtual communities were found to be a strong decision-making factor for individual members, as almost half of the respondents (15 out of 31, or 49%) would prefer to follow suggestions on customization from the community instead of those made by other family members or friends. This indicates that the virtual communities have a considerable importance when choices are to be made, and they should be considered as a significant resource of information.

As the survey was limited to health related virtual communities it would be useful to extend it to different types of communities such as, for example, communities for e-government, financial services etc. Also a larger number of respondents would allow more rigorous statistical analyses of the responses (for example, factors analysis) to be made.

REFERENCES

Adjei, M., Noble, S., & Noble, C. (2007). Online Customer-to-Customer Communications as Drivers of Relationship Quality and Purchase Behavior. In *Proceedings of the AMA Winter Educators' Conference* (Vol. 16, pp. 166).

Ansari, A., & Mela, C. (2002). E-Customization. *JMR, Journal of Marketing Research, 40*(2), 131–145. doi:10.1509/jmkr.40.2.131.19224

Balasubramanian, S., & Mahajan, V. (2001). The Economic Leverage of the Virtual Community. *International Journal of Electronic Commerce, 5*(3), 103–138.

Bauer, H., & Grether, M. (2005). Virtual Community Its Contribution to Customer Relationships by Providing Social Capital. *Journal of Relationship Marketing, 4*(1-2), 91–109. doi:10.1300/J366v04n01_07

Cao, J., Wang, J., Law, K., Zhang, S., & Li, M. (2006). An Interactive Service Customization Model. *Information and Software Technology, 48*(4), 280–296. doi:10.1016/j.infsof.2005.04.007

Cothrel, J., & Williams, R. (1999). On-Line Communities. *Knowledge Management Review, 1*(6), 20–25.

Davis, F. (1989). Perceived Usefulness, Perceived Ease of Use, and User Acceptance of Information Technology. *Management Information Systems Quarterly*, *13*(3), 319–340. doi:10.2307/249008

DeLone, W. H., & McLean, E. R. (2003). The DeLone and McLean Model of Information Systems Success: A ten-Year Update. *Journal of Management Information Systems*, *19*(4), 9–30.

Grace-Farfaglia, P., Dekkers, A., Sundararajan, B., Peters, L., & Park, S. (2006). Multinational Web Uses and Gratifications: Measuring the Social Impact of Online Community Participation across National Boundaries. *Electronic Commerce Research*, *6*(1), 75–101. doi:10.1007/s10660-006-5989-6

Gummerus, J., Liljander, V., Pura, M., & van Riel, A. (2004). Customer Loyalty to Content-Based Web Sites: The Case of an Online Health-Care Service. *Journal of Services Marketing*, *18*(3), 175. doi:10.1108/08876040410536486

Hagel, J. III, & Armstrong, A. (1997). *Net Gain: Expanding Markets through Virtual Communities*. Boston: Harvard Business School Press.

Hall, H., & Graham, D. (2004). Creation and Recreation: Motivating Collaboration to Generate Knowledge Capital in Online Communities. *International Journal of Information Management*, *24*(3), 235–246. doi:10.1016/j.ijinfomgt.2004.02.004

Ishii, K., & Morihiro, O. (2007). Links between Real and Virtual Networks: A Comparative Study of Online Communities in Japan and Korea. *Cyberpsychology & Behavior*, *10*(2), 252–257. doi:10.1089/cpb.2006.9961

Jawecki, G., Fueller, J., & Verona, G. (2008). Innovative Consumer Behavior in Online Communities. In *Advances in Consumer Research - European Conference Proceedings* (Vol. 8, pp: 513-518).

Josefsson, U. (2005). Coping with Illness Online: The Case of Patients Online Communities. *The Information Society*, *21*(2), 143–153. doi:10.1080/01972240590925357

Josefsson, U., & Ranerup, A. (2003). Consumerism Revisited: The Emergent Roles of New Electronic Intermediaries between Citizens and the Public Sector. *Information Polity: The International Journal of Government & Democracy in the Information Age*, *8*(3/4), 167–180.

Kardaras, D., & Karakostas, B. (in press). *Services Customization Using Web Technologies*. Hershey, PA: IGI Global.

Keating, B., Rugimband, R., & Quzai, A. (2003). Differentiating between Service Quality and Relationship Quality in Cyberspace. *Managing Service Quality*, *13*(3), 217–232. doi:10.1108/09604520310476481

Koh, J., Kim, Y., Butler, B., & Bock, G. (2007). Encouraging Participation in Virtual Communities. *Communications of the ACM*, *50*(2), 69–73. doi:10.1145/1216016.1216023

Kotha, S. (1995). Mass Customization: Implementing the Emerging Paradigm for Competitive Advantage. *Strategic Management Journal*, *16*, 21–42. doi:10.1002/smj.4250160916

Kratochvil, M., & Carson, C. (2005). *Growing Modular: Mass Customization of Complex Products, Services and Software*. Berlin: Springer.

Lanseng, E., & Andreassen, T. (2007). Electronic Healthcare: A Study of People's Readiness and Aattitude toward Performing Self-Diagnosis. *International Journal of Service Industry Management*, *18*(4), 394–417. doi:10.1108/09564230710778155

Lechner, U., & Hummel, J. (2002). Business Models and System Architectures of Virtual Communities: From a Sociological Phenomenon to Peer-to-Peer Architectures. *International Journal of Electronic Commerce*, *6*(3), 41–53.

Leimeister, J., Ebner, W., & Krcmar, H. (2005). Design, Implementation, and Evaluation of Trust-Supporting Components in Virtual Communities for Patients. *Journal of Management Information Systems, 21*(4), 101–135.

Lin, H. (2007). The Role of Online and Offline Features in Sustaining Virtual Communities: An Empirical Study. *Internet Research, 17*(2), 119–138. doi:10.1108/10662240710736997

Lin, H., & Lee, G. (2006). Determinants of Success for Online Communities: An Empirical Study. *Behaviour & Information Technology, 25*(6), 479–488. doi:10.1080/01449290500330422

Macaulay, L., Keeling, K., McGoldrick, P., Dafoulas, G., Kalaitzakis, E., & Keeling, D. (2007). Coevolving E-tail and On-Line Communities: Conceptual Framework. *International Journal of Electronic Commerce, 11*(4), 53–77. doi:10.2753/JEC1086-4415110402

Moon, J., & Kim, Y. (2001). Extending the TAM for a World-Wide-Web Context. *Information & Management, 38*(4), 217–230. doi:10.1016/S0378-7206(00)00061-6

Nelson, R., Todd, P., & Wixom, B. (2005). Antecedents of Information and System Quality: An Empirical Examination within the Context of Data Warehousing. *Journal of Management Information Systems, 21*(4), 199–235.

Papathanassiou, E. (2004). Mass Customisation: Management Approaches and Internet Opportunities in the Financial Sector in the UK. *International Journal of Information Management, 24*(5), 387–399. doi:10.1016/j.ijinfomgt.2004.06.003

Pentina, I., Prybutok, V., & Zhang, X. (2008). The Role of Virtual Communities as Shopping Reference Groups. *Journal of Electronic Commerce Research, 9*(2).

Perkowitz, M., & Etzioni, O. (1999). Towards Adaptive Web Sites: Conceptual Framework and Effectiveness. *Computer Networks, 3*(11), 1245–1258. doi:10.1016/S1389-1286(99)00017-1

Peters, L., & Saidin, H. (2000). IT and the Mass Customization of Services: The Challenge of Implementation. *International Journal of Information Management, 4*(2), 103–119. doi:10.1016/S0268-4012(99)00059-6

Preece, J. (2000). *Online Communities: Designing Usability, Supporting Sociability*. Chichester, UK: John Wiley & Sons.

Rheingold, H. (1993). *The Virtual Community: Homesteading on the Electronic Frontier*. London: MIT Press.

Roffe, L., & Foster, C. (2008). *Macmillan Online Discussion Study: Exploring Macmillan's Share Discussion Forum*. Southampton, UK: Macmillan Cancer Support and University of Southampton School of Nursing and Midwifery.

Rust, R., & Kannan, P. (2002). *E-Service: New Directions in Theory and Practice*. Armonk, NY: M.E. Sharpe.

Rust, R., & Kannan, P. (2003). E-Service: A New Paradigm for Business in the Electronic Environment. *Communications of the ACM, 46*(6), 36–42. doi:10.1145/777313.777336

Schlager, M., & Fusco, J. (2003). Teacher Professional Development, Technology, and Communities of Practice: Are We Putting the Cart Before the Horse? *The Information Society, 19*(3), 203–220. doi:10.1080/01972240309464

Skinner, R. (2003). The Value of Information Technology in Healthcare. *Frontiers of Health Services Management, 19*(3), 3–15.

Sousa, R., Yeung, A., & Cheng, T. (2008). Customer Heterogeneity in Operational E-Service Design Attributes: An Empirical Investigation of Service Quality. *International Journal of Operations & Production Management, 28*(7), 592–614. doi:10.1108/01443570810881776

Teo, H., Chan, H., Wei, K., & Zhang, Z. (2003). Evaluating Information Accessibility and Community Adaptivity Features for Sustaining Virtual Learning Communities. *International Journal of Human-Computer Studies, 59*(5), 671–697. doi:10.1016/S1071-5819(03)00087-9

Van der Heijden, H. (2000). *Using the Technology Acceptance Model to Predict Website Usage: Extensions and Empirical Test*. Amsterdam, The Netherlands: Vrije Universiteit.

Wilkins, L., Swatman, P., & Castleman, T. (2002). Mustering Consent: Government-Sponsored Virtual Communities and the Incentives for Buy-in. *International Journal of Electronic Commerce, 7*(1), 121–134.

Wilson, E. V. (2006). *The Case for E-Health in the Information Systems Curriculum*. Madison, WI: University of Wisconsin.

Yager, T. (2002). Sense of Community. *InfoWorld, 24*(38), 32.

Yoo, W., Suh, K., & Lee, M. (2002). Exploring the Factors Enhancing Member Participation in Online Communities. *Journal of Global Information Management, 10*(3), 55–71.

Zeithaml, V., Parasuraman, A., & Malhotra, A. (2000). *A Conceptual Framework for Understanding e-Service Quality: Implications for Future Research and Managerial Practice*. Marketing Science Institute.

APPENDIX A

Detailed Questionnaire Description

Part A

- Demographics (age, gender)
- Duration of membership in the community
- Frequency of usage (daily, several times per week, once a week, less – see Leimeister et al., 2005)

Part B

The following questions use a 5-point Likert scale from "strongly disagree" to "strongly agree".

Quality of learning environment:
- The information provided by the virtual community is accurate (Nelson et al. 2005)
- The virtual community provides me with a complete set of information (Nelson et al. 2005)
- Information provided by the other members is always correct (Leimeister et al. 2005)

Quality of social support:
- The virtual community shows a sincere interest in solving member problems (DeLone & McLean, 2003)
- The experiences of the other members help me to cope with my own problems (Leimeister et al. 2005)
- The other members would never consciously give me wrong information (Leimeister et al. 2005)

Ability to influence public opinion:
- The virtual community is trustworthy (DeLone & McLean, 2003)
- I depend on the recommendations of the community members for health service information (Ridings et al. 2006)
- If I need information about health services, I prefer to find it through the community discussion boards (Ridings et al. 2006)

Participation:
- I enjoy being a member of the virtual community (Teo et al. 2003)
- I believe that it is worthwhile for me to use the online community (Lin & Lee, 2006)
- I will recommend that other people use the online community (Lin & Lee, 2006)

Perceived usefulness:
- Using the virtual community enhances my ability to get information from community members (Lin, 2007; Davis, 1989)
- Using the virtual community helps satisfy my social needs (Lin, 2007; Davis, 1989)
- Using the virtual community enables me to share knowledge with community members (Lin, 2007; Davis, 1989)

Perceived ease of use:

- It would be easy for me to become skilful at using the virtual community (Lin, 2007; Davis, 1989)
- My interaction with the virtual community is clear and understandable (Lin, 2007; Davis, 1989)
- Learning to operate the virtual community is easy for me (Lin, 2007; Davis, 1989)

Individual profile:

- When it comes to customizing products and services to match my preferences, I prefer to follow my own feelings and opinions, rather than what I find in virtual community's discussions.
- When it comes to customizing products and services to match my preferences, I prefer to follow suggestions of my family and friends, rather than what I find in virtual community's discussions.
- When it comes to customizing products and services to match my preferences, I prefer to follow suggestions of a professional in a given field (e.g., a physician/GP in the healthcare field), rather than what I find in virtual community's discussions.

Intention to customize e-health services:

- I am very likely to follow community suggestions on using web based electronic health records to communicate with my healthcare providers
- I am very likely to follow community suggestions on customizing online health tools (e.g., WebMD's Health Manager)
- I am very likely to follow community suggestions on self-diagnosing over the internet (Lanseng & Andreassen, 2007)
- I am very likely to follow community suggestions on online monitoring of chronic health conditions (Wilson, 2006)

Intention to customize health services:

- I am very likely to follow community suggestions on choosing a healthcare facility to treat my condition
- I am very likely to follow community suggestions on changing my lifestyle (e.g., weight loss, healthy living)
- I am very likely to follow community suggestions on participating in clinical trials (e.g., for new drug treatments)
- I am very likely to follow community suggestions on choosing a health/medical insurance plan (Skinner, 2003)

This work was previously published in the International Journal of Virtual Communities and Social Networking, Volume 2, Issue 1, edited by Subhasish Dasgupta, pp. 35-51, copyright 2010 by IGI Publishing (an imprint of IGI Global).

Chapter 9
Explaining Job Searching Through Social Networking Sites:
A Structural Equation Model Approach

Norazah Mohd Suki
Universiti Malaysia Sabah, Malaysia

T. Ramayah
Universiti Sains Malaysia (USM), Malaysia

Michelle Kow Pei Ming
Universiti Sains Malaysia (USM), Malaysia

ABSTRACT

This paper examines job searching among employed job seekers through the social networking sites. One hundred ninety survey questionnaires were distributed to employed job seekers who have used online social networking sites via the snowball sampling approach. The collected data were analysed using Structural Equation Modeling (SEM) technique via the Analysis of Moment Structure (AMOS 16) computer program. The results showed that perceived usefulness and perceived enjoyment are positively and significantly related to the behavioural intention to use online social networking sites as a job search tool, whereas perceived ease of use is not positively and significantly related. The study implies that the developers of online social networking sites must provide additional useful functionalities or tools to help users with their job searches. These sites must also assure that they do not disclose individuals' private and confidential information without the consent. The paper provides insight for employed jobseekers by using online social networking sites as a job search tool.

1. INTRODUCTION

Online social networking sites are a type of virtual community (Murray & Waller, 2007). Users of online social networking sites will create their own profile with their personal information and will usually add their friends, friends of friends or new friends. Online social networking sites are usually used to keep in touch with friends and families by posting their updates, photos, blogs, and chatting, apart from enjoyment and relaxation. There are many consumer-networking sites

DOI: 10.4018/978-1-4666-1553-3.ch009

available such as Facebook, MySpace, Friendster, Hi5, Bebo and Multiply. Facebook claims that it has 200 million active users who have returned to the site in the last 30 days (as of April 2009) (Facebook, 2009). According to Warr (2008) as of March 2008, Facebook claimed that there were 66 million active users. Within a year, from 2008 to 2009, Facebook's active users increased by 134 million.

A study was conducted on passive job seekers (employed job seekers) adoption of e-recruitment technology in Malaysia by Tong (2009). The online social networking sites used for sourcing of candidates are LinkedIn and Facebook. According to Kow (2009), the author's employer uses LinkedIn to source for candidates in the U.S. The author's employer with headquarters located in the U.S. had successfully hired some key positions via LinkedIn, which attracted a sizable pool of applicants. From the research conducted, the author recommended to the HR management team that LinkedIn and Facebook should be used as one of the sourcing methods. The recruiters of the author's company with plants and offices in Asia (Thailand, Singapore, China, and Malaysia), U.S. and Europe have been using Facebook and LinkedIn to source for candidates since November 2008. However, the author did not conduct a research on the employed job seekers'

acceptance of the online social networking sites as a job search tool. This research will cover this gap since the author will obtain the employed job seekers' view on their intentions to use of online social networking sites for job searching. Since most of the researches were conducted on the third party e-recruitment web sites and corporate career web sites, the author seeks to examine this alternative recruitment source that is social networking sites.

2. LITERATURE REVIEW

2.1 Conceptual Model and Hypotheses

The Technology Acceptance Model is a highly validated model and was tested by many researchers in their study (refer to Figure 1). This research also bases its model on the extended TAM model by Tong (2009) but introduces an intrinsic motivation variable which is perceived enjoyment (refer to Figure 2).

2.2 Perceived Ease of Use (PEOU)

Perceived ease of use is defined as "the degree to which a person believes that using a particular

Figure 1. Technology Acceptance Model (TAM)

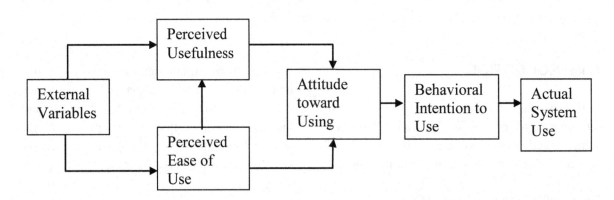

system would be free from effort" (Davis, 1989). All else being equal, an application perceived to be easier to use is more likely to be accepted by the users (Davis, 1989). In majority of the research conducted using the TAM model, perceived ease of use was found to have positively influenced the behavioural intention to use a system (Fagan, Wooldridge, & Neill, 2008; Guriting & Ndubisi, 2006; Hsu, Wang, & Chiu, 2009; Huang, 2008; Ramayah, Chin, Norazah, & Amlus, 2005). However, it is also found in other research that perceived ease of use is found to have not directly influenced the behavioural intention to use a system (Ruiz-Mafé, Sanz-Blas, & Aldas-Manzano, 2009). Generally, when a system is found to be easy to use, users will have the intention to use the system. In this research, the author will examine the relationship between perceived ease of use and the behavioural intention to use online social networking sites as a job search tool. The first hypothesis is therefore constructed as follows:

H1: There is a positive influence of perceived ease of use on the behavioural intention to use online social networking sites for job search.

Perceived ease of use has also been found to influence behavioural intention to use indirectly through perceived usefulness (Davis, 1989; Ha & Stoel, 2009; Norazah, Ramayah & Norbayah, 2008; Oh, Ahn & Kim, 2003; Ruiz-Mafé et al., 2009). According to Venkatesh and Davis (2000), the less effort a system is to use, the more using it can increase job performance. This means that when a system is easy to use, users will perceive that the system is more useful. Systems that are difficult to use are less likely to be perceived as useful and thus lead to decreased usage. In general, if a system is easy to use, less effort is required by the users, therefore increasing the likelihood of usage.

Particularly in e-recruitment, Tong (2009) discovered that perceived ease of use is not positively

Figure 2. Proposed research framework

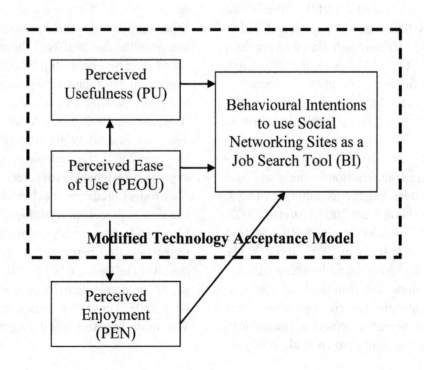

related to perceive usefulness in e-recruitment adoption. This indicates that even though the system is easy to use, it is not necessary that it is perceived as useful by the users. However, in this research, the author would like to re-examine the relationship between perceived ease of use and perceived usefulness. Thus it is hypothesized that:

H2: There is a positive influence of perceived ease of use on perceived usefulness of online social networking sites for job search.

2.3 Perceived Usefulness (PU)

Perceived usefulness is defined as "the degree to which a person believes that using a particular system would enhance his or her job performance" (Davis, 1989). Within the organisational context, a system that is high in perceived usefulness is one that the user believes will have a positive use-performance relationship. Previous researches have shown that perceived usefulness influences computer usage directly. In general, when the users found that the system is useful for them, then they will have the intention to use it and lead to the actual usage of the system. Based on previous research using the TAM model, it is found that perceived usefulness is the primary antecedent that determines the behavioural intention to use a computer system (Davis, 1989; Venkatesh & Davis, 2000).

Perceived usefulness was found to have positively influenced the behavioural intention to use a computer system (Fagan et al., 2008; Guriting & Ndubisi, 2006; Ha & Stoel, 2009; Hsu et al., 2009; Huang, 2008; Norazah et al., 2008; Ruiz-Mafé et al., 2009; Seyal & Rahman, 2007; Tong, 2009). However, in some other research conducted based on the TAM model in a mandated environment. Instead, it is found that perceived usefulness does not directly influence the behavioural intention to use a computer system (Brown et al., 2002). In

e-recruitment context, Tong (2009) discovered that perceived usefulness is positively related to behavioural intention to use e-recruitment for job search. In this research, the author seeks to re-examine this relationship. The third hypothesis therefore states:

H3: There is a positive influence of perceived usefulness on the behavioural intention to use online social networking sites for job search.

2.4 Perceived Enjoyment (PENJOY)

Perceived enjoyment is a type of intrinsic psychological motivation (Davis et al., 1989). Perceived enjoyment is defined as "the extent to which the activity of using the computer is perceived to be enjoyable in its own right, apart from any performance consequences that may be anticipated" (Davis et al., 1992). Social networking site is a new method for people to socialise with one another. Through this method, people will feel that they are having fun while enjoying the rich features provided in the social networking sites. When they perceive these social networking sites as enjoyable, they will use it more frequently and spend more time on it (Rouibah, 2008). Perceived enjoyment was found to be positively influenced by behavioural intention to use a computer system (Davis et al., 1992; Lee, Cheung & Chen, 2007; Teo, Lim & Lai, 1999). According to Van der Heijden (2004) "for hedonic systems, perceived enjoyment (a dimension of perceived playfulness) is a stronger predictor of behavioural intention to use than is perceived usefulness" (Van der Heijden, 2004). However, there are other researches suggesting that perceived enjoyment does not positively influenced the behavioural intention to use a computer system (Fagan et al., 2008; Shin & Kim, 2008; Venkatesh, Speier, & Morris, 2002). The fourth hypothesis is thus created:

H4: There is a positive influence of perceived enjoyment on the behavioural intention to use online social networking sites for job search.

Perceived enjoyment was found to be related to perceived ease of use. Some studies have shown that the perceived enjoyment influence the perceived ease of use of a computer system or application (Fagan et al., 2008; Kim, Oh, & Park, 2008; Yi & Hwang, 2003) whereas some studies have shown that the perceived ease of use influenced the perceive enjoyment of the computer system or application (Igbaria et al., 1996; Liao, Tsou, & Huang, 2007; Rouibah, 2008). Common sense predicts that when a computer system or technology is perceived to be easy to use, it will lead to perceived enjoyment. However, this may not always be true. For example, for the case of wired voice telephony, it is very easy to use, however it is not perceived as enjoyable as compared to short message service (SMS), where Korean users find it very enjoyable to send short messages to friends (Kim et al., 2008).

For this research, the relationship used is the perceived ease of use influences the perceived enjoyment of social networking sites. This relationship is chosen because when users perceive that the online social networking sites are easy to use and user friendly, they will then be able to enjoy using the social networking sites. If the online social networking sites are found to be not user friendly or difficult to use then the users will not enjoy using the social networking sites. The next hypothesis states therefore:

H5: There is a positive influence of perceived ease of use on perceived enjoyment of online social networking sites.

2.5 Behavioral Intention (BI)

According to Warshaw and Davis (1985), behavioural intention is defined as "the degree to which a person has formulated conscious plans to perform or not to perform some specified future behaviour". This is in line with the Theory of Reasoned Action (Fishbein & Ajzen, 1975) and its successor the Theory of Planned Behaviour (Ajzen, 1985), where it is stated that behavioural intention is a strong predictor of actual behaviour. Intention is defined as "the cognitive representation of a person's readiness to perform a given behaviour, and it is considered to be the immediate antecedent of behaviour" in Theory of Planned Behaviour (Ajzen, 1991).

Studies on intention to use a computer system is mostly for the new technologies and studies on the actual usage is usually conducted on the computer systems that have already been used for long (Ramayah & Ignatius, 2005). Since online social networking sites as a job search tool is a new technology, this study investigates the factors that influence the behavioural intention to use the online social networking sites as a job search tool.

3. METHODOLOGY

190 survey questionnaires were distributed to employed job seekers who have used online social networking sites via the snowball sampling approach. This sampling method is useful when researchers are trying to reach populations that are inaccessible or hard to find (Trochim, 2002). The collected data were analysed using Structural Equation Modeling (SEM) via the Analysis of Moment Structure (AMOS 16) computer program, a second-generation multivariate technique. It is used in confirmatory modeling to evaluate whether the data collected fit the proposed theoretical model. The variables used were adapted as follows: Behavioural Intention to Use (Warshaw &

Davis, 1985), Perceived Usefulness, Perceived Ease of Use, and Perceived Enjoyment (Davis et al., 1989).

4. FINDINGS AND DISCUSSION

4.1 Descriptive of Samples

A total of two hundred and fifty questionnaires were distributed to employed job seekers in Malaysia and 190 completed questionnaires were used with 82.6% response rate. Table 1 describes personal profile of the respondents. There were 64.7% female respondents and 35.3% were male respondents. The average ages of the respondents were 31 years old with the youngest respondent aged 22 years old and oldest respondent aged 49 years old. As for the ethnic distribution, 117 respondents were Chinese (61.6%). Majority of the respondents hold a Bachelors Degree (66.3%) as the highest level of education, earns an annual income of RM30,001 to RM60,000.

The majority of the respondents' nature of the current job is from Information Technology (19.5%) with average number of years of working experience in the current company of 3.98 years. The average number of years using online social networking sites is 3.09 year with average number of years using the Internet of 10.55 years. As stated in Table 2, Facebook is the most popular online social networking sites (91.6%), followed by Friendster (52.1%), and LinkedIn (15.3%). Thirty five respondents (18.4%) used online social networking sites for job search. This result shows that using online social networking sites as a job search tool is not a common trend in Malaysia. Many users of the online social networking sites do not use these online social networking sites as a job search tool yet. Over the past one month, the majority of the respondents used online social networking sites a few times a week (25.8%). They spent 10 to 20 minutes (28.4%) each time using social networking sites.

4.2 Reliability and Validity

Convergent validity, discriminant validity, and reliability of all the multiple-item scales were performed following the guidelines from previous literatures (e.g., Fornell & Larcker, 1981; Gefen & Straub, 2005). The measurement properties are reported in Tables 3 and 4. Reliability was assessed in terms of composite reliability (CR), which measured the degree to which items are free from random error and therefore yield consistent results. Composite reliabilities in the measurement model ranged from 0.874 to 0.973 (see Table 4), above the recommended cutoff of 0.70 (Fornell and Larcker, 1981). Convergent validity was assessed in terms of factor loadings and average variance extracted (AVE). It requires a factor loading greater than 0.50 and an average variance extracted no less than 0.50.

All items had significant factor loadings higher than 0.50 (Table 3). AVE ranged from 0.683 to 0.868, suggesting adequate convergent validity. Thus, all factors in the measurement model had adequate reliability and convergent validity. To examine discriminate validity, we compared the shared variances between factors with the average variance extracted of the individual factors. Table 4 shows the inter-construct correlations off the diagonal of the matrix. This showed that the shared variance between factors were lower than the average variance extracted of the individual factors, confirming discriminate validity (Fornell & Larcker, 1981). In summary, the measurement model demonstrated discriminate validity.

4.3 Structural Model

The research model was tested using Structural Equation Modeling (SEM) techniques via the AMOS 16 computer software. SEM is a model analysis technique encompassing methods such as covariance structure analysis, latent variable analysis, confirmatory factor analysis, path analy-

Table 1. Profile of respondents

Variable	Frequency	Percentage
Gender		
Female	123	64.7
Male	67	35.3
Race		
Malay	32	16.8
Indian	37	19.5
Chinese	117	61.6
Others	4	2.1
Marital Status		
Single	108	56.8
Married	77	40.5
Divorced	5	2.6
Education Level		
High School and below	1	.5
Certificate/Diploma	32	16.8
Bachelors Degree	126	66.3
Masters Degree	29	15.3
Others	2	1.1
Annual Income		
RM30K and below	45	23.7
RM30,001 to RM60,000	99	52.1
RM60,001 to RM90,000	26	13.7
RM90,001 to RM120,000	8	4.2
Over RM120,000	12	6.3
Job Level		
Top Management	10	5.3
Middle Management	34	17.9
Professional Staff/Leader/Supervisor/Engineer	106	55.8
Support Staff/Non-Executive Staff/Administrative	33	17.4
Others	7	3.7
Nature of Current Job		
Engineering	23	12.1
Production	10	5.3
Information Technology	37	19.5
Finance/Accounting	15	7.9
Sales/Marketing	17	8.9
Human Resource	27	14.2
Education	19	10.0
Consultancy	12	6.3
Customer Service/Administration/Business	17	8.9
Support	13	6.8
Others		

sis and linear structural relation analysis (Hair, Black, Babin, Anderson, & Tatham, 2006). SEM is also particularly useful in this paper because it can estimate "a series of separate, but interdependent, multiple regression equations simultaneously" in a specified structural model (Hair et al., 2006). Therefore, SEM is the most suitable analysis to estimate the strength of casual relationship of these constructs. As suggested in the literatures (Bollen & Curran, 2006; Joreskog & Sorbom, 1996; Kline, 1998) the model fit was assessed using several indices (refer to Table 5).

The accepted thresholds for the indices χ^2/df ratio should be less than 3; the values of GFI, NFI, CFI, and IFI should be greater than 0.9; and RMSEA is recommended to be up to 0.05, and is

Table 2. Online social networking sites usage

Variable	Frequency	Percentage
Access Internet		
Home/Private Room	168	88.4
Office	91	47.9
Internet Cafe	16	8.4
Libraries/Community Centres	4	2.1
Others	6	3.2
Used Social Networking Sites		
Facebook	174	91.6
Friendster	99	52.1
LinkedIn	29	15.3
MySpace	15	7.9
Others	12	6.3
Used Online Social Networking Sites for Job Search		
Yes	35	18.4
No	155	81.6
Frequency Using Online Social Networking Sites over the Past One Month		
Less than once a week	29	15.3
Once a week	27	14.2
2 or 3 times a week	27	14.2
A few times a week	49	25.8
About once a day	33	17.4
Several times a day	25	13.2
Time Spent Each Time Using Online Social Networking Sites over the Past One Month		
Less than 10 minutes	27	14.2
10 - 20 minutes	54	28.4
20 - 30 minutes	28	14.7
30 minutes - 1 hr	35	18.4
1 - 1.5 hrs	14	7.4
1.5 - 2 hrs	19	10.0
2 hrs or more	13	6.8

acceptable up to 0.08 (Gefen & Straub, 2005). RMSEA should be below 0.10 (Browne & Cudeck, 1993). As shown in Table 5, degrees of freedom for the research model is 145 with number of distinct sample moments is 190 and number of distinct parameters to be estimated is 45. Moreover, all of the model-fit indices exceed the respective common acceptance levels suggested by previous research, demonstrating that the model exhibited a good fit with the data collected. Thus, we could proceed to examine the path coefficients of the structural model.

4.4 Analysis of Paths

The results of the model imply that all the variables in the model were statistically significant as well. These parameters provide evidence of strong support for overall stability of the model. Furthermore, the squared multiple correlations for the structural equations index, which indicate the relative amount of variance of the dependent variable explained by the explanatory variables (see Joreskog & Sorbom, 1996), was 30%. The R^2 value of 0.30 suggests that 30% of the variance

Table 3. Reliability and factor loadings

Constructs /Measurement Items	Standardized Loadings	CR	AVE
Perceived Usefulness		0.973	0.868
PU1	0.884		
PU2	0.937		
PU3	0.931		
PU4	0.972		
PU5	0.933		
Perceived Ease of Use		0.953	0.734
PEOU1	0.893		
PEOU2	0.875		
PEOU3	0.801		
PEOU4	0.829		
PEOU5	0.883		
Perceived Enjoyment		0.955	0.716
PENJOY1	0.807		
PENJOY2	0.927		
PENJOY3	0.719		
PENJOY4	0.935		
PENJOY5	0.825		
Intention		0.874	0.683
IU1	0.819		
IU2	0.981		
IU3	0.883		
IU4	0.565		

in behavioural intention to use online social networking sites as a job search tool is explained by the independent variables (perceived usefulness, perceived ease of use and perceived enjoyment).

Having established the adequacy of the model's fit, it is appropriate to examine individual path coefficients. This analysis is presented in Table 6. Structural model is illustrated in Figure 3.

Table 4. Correlation analysis

Variables	1	2	3	4
(1) Perceived Ease of Use	0.734			
(2) Perceived Usefulness	0.13*	0.868		
(3) Perceived Enjoyment	0.54**	0.13*	0.716	
(4) Behavioural Intention	0.12*	0.58**	0.19**	0.683
Mean	3.83	2.55	3.88	2.69
Standard Deviation	0.72	0.90	0.66	0.96

** $p<0.01$, * $p<0.05$

Table 5. Model fit summary for research model

Fit Indices	Benchmark	Value
Absolute Fit Measures		
CMIN (χ^2)		243.933
DF		145
CMIN (χ^2)/DF	3	1.682
GFI (Goodness of Fit Index)	0.9	.883
RMSEA (Root Mean Square Error of Approximation)	0.10	.060
Incremental Fit Measures		
AGFI (Adjusted Goodness of Fit Index)	0.80	.847
NFI (Normed Fit Index)	0.90	.933
CFI (Comparative Fit Index)	0.90	.972
IFI (Incremental Fit Index)	0.90	.972
RFI (Relative Fit Index)	0.90	.921
Parsimony Fit Measures		
PCFI (Parsimony Comparative of Fit Index)	0.50	.824
PNFI (Parsimony Normed Fit Index)	0.50	.791

Table 6 enumerated that the perceived ease of use is not significantly affected by intention to use online social networking sites as a job search tool ($\beta = 0.013$; $p > 0.05$), which rejects *H1*, but perceived ease of use has a significant positive effect on perceived usefulness ($\beta = 0.125$; $p < 0.10$), thus *H2* is confirmed. Perceived usefulness has a positive effect on the intention to use online social networking sites as a job search tool ($\beta = 0.508$; $p < 0.05$), which supports *H3*. Perceived enjoyment has a positive effect on intention to use online social networking sites as a job search tool ($\beta = 0.176$; $p < 0.05$), confirming *H4*. The perceived

ease of use is significantly affected by Perceived enjoyment ($\beta = 0.578$; $p < 0.05$), which corroborates *H5*. Figure 3 describes the structural model of the study.

Perceived ease of use is not significantly related to the behavioural intention to use online social networking sites as a job search tool. This finding is consistent with the findings of other studies where perceived ease of use is not positively related to the behavioural intention to use a computer system or application (Ramayah & Bushra, 2004; Ruiz-Mafé et al., 2009). Perceived ease of use was found to be directly related to perceived usefulness but not

Table 6. Path coefficients and hypothesis testing

Path			Estimate	S.E.	C.R.	P	Support
Intention	<---	Perceived ease of use	.013	.108	.154	.877	No
Perceived usefulness	<---	Perceived ease of use	.125	.099	1.648	.099	Yes
Intention	<---	Perceived usefulness	.508	.071	7.210	.000	Yes
Intention	<---	Perceived enjoyment	.176	.117	2.105	.035	Yes
Perceived enjoyment	<---	Perceived ease of use	.578	.068	7.931	.000	Yes

Figure 3. Structural model

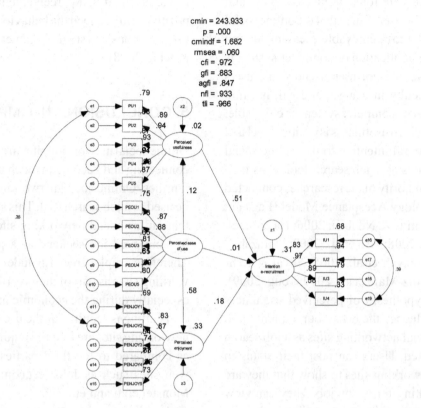

so much of the direct influence of perceived ease of use on behavioural intention to use or actual usage. This finding is not consistent with majority of the research conducted using the TAM model, where perceived ease of use was found to have positively influenced the behavioural intention to use a system (Fagan et al., 2008; Guriting & Ndubisi, 2006; Huang, 2008; Hsu et al., 2009; Norazah et al., 2008). It is found that users who have familiarised with the computer system and have used it for long time, their perceived ease of use of the computer system has a lower effect on behavioural intention to use the computer system (Venkatesh, Morris, Davis, & Davis, 2003). However, if an application is easy to use, it may not necessarily lead to the intention to use the application. Although the online social networking sites are easy to use and user friendly, this does not influence the users' intention to use online social networking sites as a job search tool.

It is worth noting that perceived ease of use is positively related to perceived usefulness of online social networking sites as a job search tool. This relationship has been proven by many studies (Davis, 1989; Ha & Stoel, 2009; Liao et al., 2007; Oh et al., 2003; Ramayah et al., 2005; Ruiz-Mafé et al., 2009; Seyal & Rahman, 2007). When the application is perceived to be easy to use and user friendly, it will lead to the users perceiving that the application is useful. Therefore, in the case of online social networking sites as a job search tool, users perceive the application to be easy to use and will continue to use the application and eventually find that the application is useful as a job search tool.

Perceived ease of use is also found to be positively related to perceived enjoyment. Other studies which have also found this similar relationship includes Igbaria et al. (1996); Liao et al. (2007); Rouibah (2008). Since the online social networking sites are found to be easy to use and user friendly, the users found that the online social networking sites to be enjoyable, pleasant, fun and positive. If an application or computer system is difficult to use and not user friendly, the users will find difficulty in using it and will not find the application or computer system as enjoyable.

Next, Perceived usefulness is positively related to the behavioural intention to use online social networking sites as a job search tool. This is in line with the majority of the researches conducted on the Technology Acceptance Model (Fagan et al., 2008; Guriting & Ndubisi, 2006; Ha & Stoel, 2009; Huang, 2008; Hsu et al., 2009; Norazah et al., 2008; Ramayah et al., 2005; Seyal & Rahman, 2007; Ruiz-Mafé et al., 2009; Tong, 2009). Hence, the hypotheses of perceived usefulness positively influence the behavioural intention to use online social networking sites as a job search tool is accepted. Users can post their status in the social networking sites to show that they are currently looking for a new job. They can view the listings of the jobs posted online and apply directly. Besides, they can contact the recruiters directly as well as contact their friends who are in their list of connections to enquire regarding the job openings posted in the social networking sites.

Similarly, perceived enjoyment is also positively related to the behavioural intention to use online social networking sites as a job search tool. This finding is consistent with the findings of many other studies (Liao et al., 2007; Ramayah and Ignatius, 2005; Ramayah et al., 2005; Rouibah, 2008). Users of online social networking sites find online social networking sites as fun, enjoyable, pleasant, positive and exciting. Online social networking sites are easy to use and they provide many enjoyable features and applications where users can play games, quizzes, hug a friend virtually, write on the friend's wall, send messages, and many more. These enjoyable features and applications, makes the users addicted to the online social networking sites and they will go into the application frequently. Nevertheless, preceding

research found that perceived enjoyment do not positively influenced the behavioural intention to use a computer system (Fagan et al., 2008; Shin & Kim, 2008).

5. CONCLUSION AND IMPLICATIONS

Online social networking sites are mostly used for connecting and keeping in touch with friends and families. Online social networking sites can also be used as a job search tool. This study concluded that online social networking sites are accepted by employed job seekers' as a job search tool. Therefore, employers can include online social networking sites as part of their recruitment strategy especially during the economic meltdown where cost cutting is required as the use of online social networking sites are free and require minimal cost as compared to the third parties' e-recruitment web sites such as Jobstreet.com, JobsDB.com, Monster.com and etc.

Employers who intend to use online social networking sites as a recruitment tool should design their recruitment strategy in the online social networking sites to be easy to use and user friendly. Employers can create their own Facebook page or LinkedIn group. They can post the jobs listing in these pages or have an automated feed of the jobs listing in these pages. The links to the company's corporate recruitment application should also be provided so that the user can immediately submit their application into the company's corporate recruitment websites. Recruiters can also use the chat feature available to chat with the potential candidates and build their networks. In case there are any job vacancies available and suitable for this particular candidate, the recruiter can contact the candidate immediately. Developers of online social networking sites should develop the online social networking sites to be as user friendly as possible.

Recruiters who use the online social networking sites as a recruitment tool should try to include the element of fun in the recruitment strategy. Recruiters can make the pages or groups in the online social networking sites more interesting by adding videos that show the work life balance of the employees, the nice working environment in the company, or employees' video or photo competition. Recruiters can also make the pages or the groups in the online social networking sites to be more interactive, where employed job seekers' can post discussions, and have real-time chat.

It is recommended to future researches to conduct a study on the active job seekers such as fresh graduates' and final year students' acceptance of online social networking sites as a job search tool and expand this research to other countries as currently this study is limited to employed job seekers in Malaysia. Other social media technologies such as blogs, podcasts, and video sharing web sites such as YouTube.com should also be studied as they can also be used for recruitment and job search purposes. Future researchers should also increase the sample size and to have a more balanced demographic of the respondents. A longitudinal approach can be taken to study the effect of increased experience in using online social networking sites that could influence the intention to use online social networking sites as a job search tool.

REFERENCES

Ajzen, I. (1985). From intentions to actions: A theory of planned behaviour. In Kuhi, J., & Beckman, J. (Eds.), *Action-control: From Cognition to Behavior* (pp. 11–39). Berlin: Springer.

Ajzen, I. (1991). The theory of planned behavior. *Organizational Behavior and Human Decision Processes*, *50*(2), 179–211. doi:10.1016/0749-5978(91)90020-T

Brown, S. A., Massey, A. P., Montoya-Weiss, M. M., & Burkman, J. R. (2002). *European Journal of Information Systems*, *11*, 283–295. doi:10.1057/palgrave.ejis.3000438

Browne, M. W., & Cudeck, R. (1993). Alternative ways of assessing model fit. In Bollen, K. A., & Long, J. S. (Eds.), *Testing structural equation models* (pp. 136–162). Mewbury Park, CA: Sage.

Davis, F. D. (1989). Perceived usefulness, perceived ease of use, and user acceptance of information technology. *Management Information Systems Quarterly*, *13*(3), 319–340. doi:10.2307/249008

Davis, F. D., Bagozzi, R. P., & Warshaw, P. R. (1989). User acceptance of computer technology: a comparison of two theoretical models. *Management Science*, *35*(8), 982–1003. doi:10.1287/mnsc.35.8.982

Davis, F. D., Bagozzi, R. P., & Warshaw, P. R. (1992). Extrinsic and intrinsic motivation to use computers in the workplace. *Journal of Applied Social Psychology*, *24*(14), 1111–1132. doi:10.1111/j.1559-1816.1992.tb00945.x

Facebook. (2009). *Home*. Retrieved from http://www.facebook.com

Fagan, M. H., Wooldridge, B. R., & Neill, S. (2008). Exploring the intention to use computers: An empirical investigation of the role of intrinsic motivation, extrinsic motivation, and perceived ease of use. *Journal of Computer Information Systems*, 31–37.

Fishbein, M., & Ajzen, I. (1975). *Belief, attitude, intention and behavior: An introduction to theory and research*. Reading, MA: Addison-Wesley.

Fornell, C., & Larcker, D. F. (1981). Evaluating structural equation models with unobservable and measurement error. *Journal of Marketing Research*, *18*, 39–50. doi:10.2307/3151312

Gefen, D., & Straub, D. W. (2005). A practical guide to factorial validity using PLS-graph: Tutorial and annotated example. *Communications of the AIS, 16*(5), 91–109.

Guriting, P., & Ndubisi, N. O. (2006). Borneo online banking: evaluating customer perceptions and behavioural intention. *Management Research News, 29*(1-2), 6–15. doi:10.1108/01409170610645402

Ha, S., & Stoel, L. (2009). Consumer e-shopping acceptance: Antecedents in a technology acceptance model. *Journal of Business Research, 62,* 565–571. doi:10.1016/j.jbusres.2008.06.016

Hair, J. F. Jr, Black, W. C., Babin, B. J., Anderson, R. E., & Tatham, R. L. (2006). *Multivariate data analysis* (6th ed.). Upper Saddle River, NJ: Pearson Prentice Hall.

Hsu, M. K., Wang, S. W., & Chiu, K. K. (2009). Computer attitude, statistics anxiety and self-efficacy on statistical software adoption behavior: An empirical study of online MBA learners. *Computers in Human Behavior, 25,* 412–420. doi:10.1016/j.chb.2008.10.003

Huang, E. (2008). Use and gratification in e-consumers. *Internet Research, 18*(4), 405–426. doi:10.1108/10662240810897817

Igbaria, M., Parasuraman, S., & Baroudi, J. (1996). A motivational model of microcomputer usage. *Journal of Management Information Systems, 13*(1), 127–143.

Kim, G. S., Oh, J., & Park, S. B. (2008). An examination of factors influencing consumer adoption of short message service (SMS). *Psychology and Marketing, 25*(8), 769–786. doi:10.1002/mar.20238

Kow, M.P.M. (2009). *Feasibility study on sourcing of passive candidates via social networking sites.*

Lee, M. K. O., Cheung, C. M. K., & Chen, Z. H. (2007). Understanding user acceptance of multimedia messaging services: An empirical study. *Journal of the American Society for Information Science and Technology, 58*(13), 2066–2077. doi:10.1002/asi.20670

Liao, C. H., Tsou, C. W., & Huang, M. F. (2007). Factors influencing the usage of 3G mobile services in Taiwan. *Online Information Review, 31*(6), 759–774. doi:10.1108/14684520710841757

Murray, K. E., & Waller, R. (2007). Social networking goes abroad. *International Educator, 16*(3), 56–59.

Norazah, M. S., Ramayah, T., & Norbayah, M. S. (2008). Internet shopping acceptance: examining the influence of intrinsic versus extrinsic motivations. *Direct Marketing: An International Journal, 2*(2), 97–110. doi:10.1108/17505930810881752

Oh, S., Ahn, J., & Kim, B. (2003). Adoption of broadband Internet in Korea: The role of experience in building attitudes. *Journal of Information Technology, 18,* 267–280. doi:10.1080/0268396032000150807

Ramayah, T., & Bushra, A. (2004). Role of self-efficacy in e-library usage among students of a public university in Malaysia. *Malaysian Journal of Library & Information Science, 9*(1), 39–57.

Ramayah, T., Chin, Y. L., Norazah, M. S., & Amlus, I. (2005). Determinants of intention to use an online bill payment system among MBA students. *E-Business, 9,* 80–91.

Ramayah, T., & Ignatius, J. (2005). Impact of perceived usefulness, perceived ease of use and perceived enjoyment on intention to shop online. *ICFAI Journal of Systems Management, 3*(3), 36–51.

Ramayah, T., Ignatius, J., & Aafaqi, B. (2004). PC usage among students in a private institution of higher learning: The moderating role of prior experience. *Journal of Business Strategy*.

Ramayah, T., Muhamad, J., & Noraini, I. (2003, May 13-15). *Impact of intrinsic and extrinsic motivation on Internet usage in Malaysia*. Paper presented at the 12th International Conference on Management of Technology, Nancy, France.

Rouibah, K. (2008). Social usage of instant messaging by individuals outside the workplace in Kuwait. *Information Technology & People*, *21*(1), 34–68. doi:10.1108/09593840810860324

Ruiz-Mafé, C., Sanz-Blas, S., & Aldas-Manzano, J. (2009). Drivers and barriers to online airline ticket purchasing. *Journal of Air Transport Management*.

Seyal, A. H., & Rahman, N. A. (2007). The influence of external variables on the executives' use of the Internet. *Business Process Management Journal*, *13*(2), 263–278. doi:10.1108/14637150710740491

Shin, D.-H., & Kim, W. Y. (2008). Applying the Technology Acceptance Model and Flow. *Cyberpsychology & Behavior*, *11*(3), 378–382. doi:10.1089/cpb.2007.0117

Teo, T. S. H., Lim, V. K. G., & Lai, R. Y. C. (1999). Intrinsic and extrinsic motivation in Internet usage. *Omega*, *27*(32), 25–37. doi:10.1016/S0305-0483(98)00028-0

Tong, D. Y. K. (2009). A study of e–recruitment technology adoption in Malaysia. *Industrial Management & Data Systems*, *109*(2), 281–300. doi:10.1108/02635570910930145

Trochim, W. M. K. (2005). *Probability and non-probability sampling*. Retrieved from http://socialresearchmethods.net/kb/sampprob.htm

Van der Heijden, H. (2004). User acceptance of hedonic information systems. *Management Information Systems Quarterly*, *28*(4), 695–704.

Venkatesh, V., & Davis, F. D. (2000). A theoretical extension of the technology acceptance model: four longitudinal field studies. *Management Science*, *46*(2), 186–204. doi:10.1287/mnsc.46.2.186.11926

Venkatesh, V., Morris, M. G., Davis, G. B., & Davis, F. D. (2003). User acceptance of information technology: toward a unified view. *Management Information Systems Quarterly*, *27*(3), 425–478.

Venkatesh, V., Speier, C., & Morris, M. G. (2002). User acceptance enablers in individual decision making about technology: Toward an integrated model. *Decision Sciences*, *33*(2), 297–316. doi:10.1111/j.1540-5915.2002.tb01646.x

Warr, W. A. (2008). Social software: fun and games, or business tools? *Journal of Information Science*, *34*(4), 591–604. doi:10.1177/0165551508092259

Warshaw, P. R., & Davis, F. D. (1985). Disentangling behavioral intention and behavioral expectation. *Journal of Experimental Social Psychology*, *21*, 213–228. doi:10.1016/0022-1031(85)90017-4

Yi, M., & Hwang, Y. (2003). System self-efficacy, enjoyment, learning goal orientation, and the technology acceptance model. *International Journal of Human-Computer Studies*, *59*, 439–449. doi:10.1016/S1071-5819(03)00114-9

This work was previously published in the International Journal of Virtual Communities and Social Networking, Volume 2, Issue 3, edited by Subhasish Dasgupta, pp. 1-15, copyright 2010 by IGI Publishing (an imprint of IGI Global).

Chapter 10
Should Employees Accept Their Boss's Facebook 'Friend' Request?
Examining Gender and Cultural Differences

Katherine Karl
University of Tennessee, Chattanooga, USA

Joy Peluchette
University of Southern Indiana, USA

Christopher Schlaegel
Otto-von-Guericke-University, Magdeburg, Germany

ABSTRACT

This study examines gender and cultural differences in reactions and responses to a Facebook 'friend' request from the boss. The auhtors found respondents were more likely to have positive (e.g., pleased, honored) reactions followed by questionable reactions (e.g., worried, suspicious) and least likely to have negative reactions (e.g., disgusted, offended). Although most respondents would accept the request, many would have reservations about doing so. Contrary to expectations, no gender differences were found. Significant cultural differences were found such that U.S. respondents were more likely than German respondents to have negative and questionable reactions and German respondents were more likely than U.S. respondents to have positive reactions. Implications and suggestions for future research are then discussed.

INTRODUCTION

"Help! My boss wants to be my 'friend' on Facebook, what do I do? Should I "ignore" the request and if so, how might that affect our relationship on the job? Or, should I accept the request but only allow him or her limited access to my profile?" As the popularity of Facebook has exploded around the globe, more and more users are facing this online social networking dilemma. As of January 2010, Facebook had 400 million active users with over 150 million new members added in

DOI: 10.4018/978-1-4666-1553-3.ch010

2009 alone, making it the world's largest social networking site ("Facebook Press Room," 2010). Membership gains have been particularly strong in Europe, increasing by 10 million in 2009 and comprising about one third of Facebook's active monthly users (Eldon, 2009). The college student age group that the site originally aimed to serve (18 to 24 year-olds) is arguably having the hardest time getting used to sharing what used to be their exclusive virtual domain. Due to the widespread use of Facebook, the original younger users are finding that they are sharing the same virtual space with their elders (e.g., their parents, grandparents, other relatives) or other individuals whom they are typically more conscious about how they present themselves (e.g., their boss, professor, some co-workers).

The situation becomes even more complex when individuals may be confronted with a 'friend' request from one of these sources. For example, Kimberley Swann, a teenager in the U.K., indicated on her Facebook page that she thought her job was boring and was subsequently sent a termination notice from her boss via Facebook (Morgan, 2009). Another U.K. woman regrets that she added her boss as a 'friend' after posting a complaint about him on her Facebook page. The boss responded with "Hi... I guess you forgot about adding me on here?... Don't bother coming in tomorrow" (Kelly, 2009). An additional example is a bank intern who emailed his boss late in the day of Halloween, informing him he could not be at work because of a family emergency. The next day, his boss found a photo of him at a Halloween party dressed in a fairy costume holding a wand and a can of beer. His boss then e-mailed the intern with the message "nice wand" and blind copied the entire office. Within hours, the embarrassing photo and email messages were all over the internet (Waller, 2007).

The scenarios mentioned above are all examples of uncomfortable or difficult situations that employees have experienced as a result of having their boss as part of their Facebook 'friend' network. As noted earlier, the receipt of a 'friend' request from one's boss may present a particularly challenging dilemma for Facebook users since the employment relationship may be at stake. If a subordinate accepts the boss's 'friend' request, the boss can have access to personal information which the subordinate may not want the boss to see. If the subordinate ignores the request, the boss may feel snubbed and retaliate in some way that is harmful or damaging to the "real-life" relationship that the subordinate has with the boss. The purpose of this study is to examine how individuals indicate that they would react and respond to 'friend' requests from their boss and how gender and culture impact these reactions and responses. Drawing from the self-presentation literature, we provide a rationale for possible reactions and responses, as well as provide recommendations for Facebook use in the workplace.

Theoretical Framework

According to Goffman's (1959) theory of self-presentation, we are all actors who stage daily performances in an attempt to manage the impressions of our audience. Although we have the ability to choose our stage, props, and costume to suit the situation, our main goal is to maintain coherence from one situation to another. When in a public or professional setting, individuals are typically "onstage" and actively engaged in managing the impressions of their audience. In contrast, "backstage" is a place where actors tend to be themselves, loosening some of their self-imposed restrictions. Access to backstage is usually limited to a very select and small group of people. This separation helps actors maintain their onstage personas or facades. For many individuals, co-workers are different and separate from non-work friends; both of those groups are different and separate from family members.

In the physical world, we use time and space to separate the incompatible aspects of our lives and may even organize our activities to prevent overlap (Donath & Boyd, 2004). However, in the virtual world, all one's social network 'friends' are in one virtual space. Even though users can now classify people into specific groups such as friends, co-workers, or relatives, and grant each category a different level of access to various items, Facebook's default setting is "share"; according to Facebook's chief privacy officer, only about 20% of users change their privacy settings (Stross, 2009). Thus, for most Facebook members (80%), everyone accepted as a 'friend' has the same access, thus there is no separation between the backstage and the front stage. Lampinen, Taminen, and Oulasvirta (2009) refer to this as the co-presence of multiple groups or having "all my people right here, right now". They define co-presence as a "situation in which many groups important to an individual are simultaneously present in one context and their presence is salient for the individual" (p. 1).

This lack of boundaries or separation between the multiple groups to which one belongs may present a potential dilemma for Facebook users. For example, someone who has been accustomed to using Facebook to keep in touch with college friends might be reluctant to accept a 'friend' request from a work colleague or a church friend. The tension caused by mixing personal and professional personas was evident in a recent study by Skeels and Grudin (2009) who surveyed 430 Microsoft employees on their perceptions regarding the usefulness of social network sites in the workplace. They analyzed 211 free text responses, as well as comments recorded in 30 semi-structured interviews. One participant said, "The thing that's difficult with Facebook is that you've got social and you've got people from work too and they're completely different, you know, audiences, and they probably shouldn't be seeing the same things." Another said, "My main concern is my ability to keep my personal and professional networks separate except where they genuinely overlap." (p. 6) Likewise, Donath and Boyd (2004) noted that encountering people from

different aspects of someone's life can be quite revealing and the discomfort can be felt both by the performer caught in two roles and the observer. This can even be more disconcerting when there are hierarchical or authority differences between the two parties (Skeels & Grudin, 2009).

'Friend' Requests from One's Boss

Before opening its doors to everyone, Facebook initially extended membership rights to a limited number of corporations with select email addresses including Accenture, Amazon, Apple, Gap, Intel, Intuit, Microsoft, Pricewaterhouse Coopers, Electronic Arts, Pepsi, and Teach for America (Arrington, 2006). Today, the corporate view of social networking in the workplace appears to be somewhat mixed. Some companies see employees' use of social networking as a concern because of its potentially negative impact on productivity. In fact, one report suggests that Facebook use in the workplace leads to lost productivity and is costing the U.S. $3.4 billion a year (Perrier, 2007). In response, employers have installed monitoring devices to control employee Internet usage (Arnold, 2009; Roberts, 2008). For example, a 2007 Electronic Monitoring and Surveillance Survey by the American Management Association and the ePolicy Institute found that 65% of employers use software to block connections to inappropriate websites. Yet, computer monitoring devices can not completely eliminate productivity losses due to Facebook use because users can now post messages and check their site via their cell phones (Yuan & Buckman, 2006).

A survey of 800 companies in Germany revealed that while about 50% of employees are participating in online social networks, only 15% of the companies surveyed had specific guidelines regarding employee use of online social networks ("Facebook, Twitter, LinkedIn and Compliance", 2009). The results of the survey also showed that most companies fear that employee activities in online social networks may affect the company's reputation but only 4% indicated they regularly monitor what employees are saying about the company on social networking sites. However, 24% of the companies surveyed reported that they had to use regulatory measures because of their employees' social network activities.

Other organizations have taken a more positive view of social networking and are using sites like Facebook for a variety of purposes including networking, sharing recruitment information, and advertising. For example, CEO Jeremy Burton of Serena Software Inc., recently encouraged his 800 employees to join Facebook saying "Social networking tools like Facebook can bring us back together, help us get to know each other as people, help us understand our business and our products, and help us better serve our customers" (Roberts, 2008). These companies see social networking as a means of building social capital, resulting in a greater number of interactions between employees across all levels of the organization. While these companies might view social networking as a benefit for the organization, not all employees may be eager to have such close interactions with those they work with, especially their boss.

Anecdotal evidence suggests most people agree it is acceptable for a boss to accept a 'friend' request from a subordinate, but it is not appropriate for a boss to initiate such a request to a subordinate (Horowitz, 2008). For example, Diaz (2008) interviewed supervisors who voiced concerns such as, "whenever you are in a power position, you have to be careful." Thus, similar to Goffman's (1959) concept of backstage, the issue of unequal power appears to be a concern for many with regard to workplace relationships. Some individuals felt that personal life should be kept separate from professional life. For instance, some writers have warned students not to 'friend' the boss because they are likely to expose more personal information than they would ever share at the office (Horowitz, 2008). Likewise Ruetti-

mann (2009) recommends that students decline an invitation from the boss and pretend like it never arrived in their inbox. He explains "your supervisor isn't your friend, you have no idea what he will do with your personal information, and he does not need that kind of access into your life." In contrast, Rutledge (2008) claims there may be advantages to 'friending' the boss. For example, Facebook can be an opportunity for more personalized networking and "these personal connections can become a major asset when you're looking to move forward in your career or find a new job."

We identified four studies examining virtual 'friend' relationships in the workplace. DiMicco and Millon (2007) examined 48 Facebook profiles of IBM employees to see how users managed their personal identity within a social network originally designed for college years. They then conducted follow up interviews with eight employees. They found that employees seemed relatively unconcerned that coworkers or managers might be viewing their profiles. Some were unconcerned because they felt that Facebook was outside of work and was therefore irrelevant. For example, one of their respondents reported that Facebook was "for fun" and he hoped that if his manager ever saw his profile, he would understand that it has "nothing to do with his professional life" (p. 385). Other respondents were unconcerned because they had intentionally "cleansed" their profiles before starting their jobs. Likewise, Lampinen et al. (2009) interviewed five medical students and five employees of a large IT company and concluded that individuals deal with the co-presence of multiple groups in one virtual space by self-censorship and relying on the goodwill and discretion of other users.

In their study of Microsoft employees, Skeels and Grudin (2009) found that several participants experienced uneasiness when 'friended' by a senior manager. For example, one said, "It led to a dilemma because what do you do when your VP invites you to be his friend?" and another said "If a senior manager invites you, what's the protocol for turning that down?" (p. 7). The authors noted that most respondents said they dealt with this tension of crossing hierarchy, status or power boundaries by restricting what they posted; however, they were still concerned about their friends' postings as exhibited by the following comment: "Can I rely on my friends to not put something incredibly embarrassing on my profile?" An even more awkward situation might be accepting the boss' 'friend' request and then realizing that one may have friends that one would rather the boss not know about. Additionally, what are the consequences of deleting the boss as a 'friend'?

Managers have also expressed concern about how workplace hierarchy can impact the use of social networking (Skeels & Grudin, 2009). One manager wrote, "Anyone can find you on these sites, so you cannot be entirely honest, or yourself, without concerns that the wrong person will see your silly photo or hear about your bad day. Especially as a manager, it is dangerous to have too much personal information available on the internet." (p. 7). A survey of 100 Canadian senior executives conducted by staffing firm OfficeTeam, found that 72% of senior executives would be uncomfortable about being 'friended' on Facebook by people they manage, and 69% reported they would be uncomfortable being social network 'friends' with their boss ("Your Boss Doesn't Want to be Your Facebook friend," 2009). Similar numbers reported discomfort regarding 'friending' co-workers (69%), vendors (85%) or clients (76%). Likewise, a survey of 1,203 social network users in the UK conducted by people search engine yasni.co.uk found that 86% did not want to be 'friends' with their boss and 69% did not want to be 'friends' with their colleagues. Seventy eight percent reported their social networking pages contained potentially embarrassing material, but 94% reported the material would not be a problem if their parents, grandparents or bosses did not want to add them as 'friends'. Nearly 80% said they had received

a 'friend' request from someone they didn't want to accept, but felt they had no choice ("Bosses Unpopular as Facebook friends," 2009).

Gender Differences in Reactions to 'Friend' Requests from the Boss

Earlier, we provided anecdotal evidence that many individuals feel uncomfortable or powerless to refuse a 'friend' request from their boss given their concerns about workplace hierarchy. Additional research suggests this discomfort is likely to be more so for female employees. For example, research has shown that power or status differentials are associated with both generalized harassment or bullying and sexual harassment (Browne, 2006). Women have historically been more likely than men to be victims of abuse due to power differentials in the workplace (Browne, 2006). It has also been reported that women perceive a broader range of social-sexual behaviors as harassing and the difference between males and females was larger for behaviors that involve hostile work environment harassment, derogatory attitudes toward women, dating pressure, or physical sexual contact than it is for sexual propositions or sexual coercion (Rotundo, Nguyen, & Sackett, 2001). Additional research has shown that most women would be offended by sexual overtures at work, while a substantial majority of men would be flattered (Gutek, 1985). Additionally, women report they would be more upset if someone of high status in their organization persisted in asking them out on a date despite their repeated refusals than if the requests came from someone with lower status (Bourgeois & Perkins, 2003). While a 'friend' request from one's boss does not rise to the level of a date request, it is possible that it may be perceived by some women as a precursor to a date request. Therefore, we believe that 'friend' requests from one's boss will be perceived most negatively by females who have male bosses.

CULTURAL DIFFERENCES IN REACTIONS TO 'FRIEND' REQUESTS FROM ONE'S BOSS

While there has been some examination of cross-cultural differences in web usage and on-line communication (e.g., Cakir & Cagiltay, 2002; Pfeil, Zaphiris, & Ang, 2006), how these differences may impact interactions via social networking has received limited attention to date (Lewis & George, 2008). Moreover, existing research findings are mixed, making it difficult to make predictions. For instance, one of the most popular frameworks for studying international culture has been that of Geerte Hofstede who identified the following dimensions of culture: individualism, uncertainty avoidance, masculinity, power distance and long-term orientation (Hofstede, 1980). Of most relevance to this study is the dimension of power distance, which is the extent to which less powerful members of institutions or organizations within a country expect and accept that power and authority are distributed unequally (Hofstede, 1991). Of the fifty-three countries in Hofstede's (1980) original data, the United States and Germany had similar scores for power distance (with raw scores of 40 and 35, respectively). These findings suggest there may be a high degree of similarity between German and U.S. respondents in their response to 'friend' requests from authority figures. Because the scores are mid-range, they also indicate that individuals in both countries would demonstrate some level of deference to those in authority positions and may, therefore, be uncomfortable receiving 'friend' requests from these sources. At the same time, because of their tendency to defer to authority figures, they may feel they have no choice but to accept their boss's 'friend' request.

Hypotheses

A consistent theme running through the literature reviewed above, which is also consistent with Goffman's (1959) self-presentation theory, is the notion of boundaries or separation. It appears that most people believe it is appropriate to change one's role, costume, and props to fit the situation, and that it is not appropriate to let everyone into one's backstage area. In addition, the issue of unequal power distribution appears to be important for boss/subordinate relationships. Respondents may have negative reactions receiving 'friend' requests from their boss but, at the same time, they may feel powerless to refuse such requests. Therefore, we predict:

Hypothesis 1: Both German and U.S. respondents will be more likely to have negative or questionable reactions than positive reactions to a 'friend' request from their boss.

Hypothesis 2: Both German and U.S. respondents will be most likely to accept their boss's 'friend' requests, but will have reservations about doing so.

Hypothesis 3: Female respondents with male bosses will have the most negative reactions to a 'friend' request from their boss.

METHOD

Sample

Because undergraduate students are the primary users of social networking sites, we intentionally recruited these students to complete our survey. The U.S. sample included undergraduate students enrolled in management and business communications courses at a medium-sized university located in the Midwestern part of the United States. Participation was voluntary although minimal course credit was given. Of the 300 surveys distributed, 208 were returned for a response rate of 69%. Twenty five individuals were eliminated because they were not members of Facebook, leaving 183 U.S. respondents. The German sample included undergraduate students enrolled in management and economics courses. Participation was voluntary and the response rate was approximately 95%. Three individuals were eliminated because they were not members of Facebook, leaving 172 German respondents. The total combined sample consisted of 172 males (46.2%) and 200 females (53.8%). The average age was 21.74 (SD = 2.03) and the average hours worked per week was 15.14, although there was considerable variation (SD = 13.91). A comparison of respondents from the two samples revealed that the average hours worked per week was significantly higher [F (1, 371) = 54.28, p <.000] in the U.S. sample (M=20.19, SD=13.06) than it was in the German sample (M=10.25, SD = 13.06).

Survey Instrument

The survey instrument consisted of four measures: (1) demographic items including gender, age, academic major, and hours worked per week, and social network usage; (2) reaction to a 'friend' request from one's boss; (3) response to a 'friend' request from one's boss; and (4) opinion of one's boss.

- **Reaction to boss 'friend' request:** This measure included the following statement: Assume you received the following email message from Facebook: "*Mr./Ms. X (who is your boss), added you as a friend on Facebook. We need you to confirm that you are, in fact, friends with Mr./Mrs. X. To confirm this friend request, follow the link below.*" Respondents were then asked to indicate how they would feel if they received that email from their boss using a 16 item list and a 5-point rating scale (1=strongly disagree, 5=strongly agree). The 16 items were grouped into three subscales as follows: *Positive* = delighted, excited, good, flattered, honored, pleased; *Questionable* = worried, nervous, concerned, suspicious; and *Negative* = sickened, repulsed, disgusted, offended, bad, and displeased.

- **Response to boss 'friend' request:** Respondents were asked to indicate how they would respond to the 'friend' request from their boss. This measure included four options: (1) respond that you do not know the person, (2) ignore, not respond, (3) accept as a 'friend', but with reservations, and (4) accept as 'friend'. For the second option, respondents were asked to explain why they chose to ignore the 'friend' request.

- **One's opinion of boss:** In an attempt to examine possible explanations as to why respondents might have negative reactions to a 'friend' request from their boss, we also asked them to describe their boss using a 7-item scale. Respondents were asked the following: "For each of the following items, please use the same scale as above to indicate the extent to which you agree or disagree that each is an accurate description of your boss." Sample items included: competent, fair, trustworthy, and approachable. Coefficient alpha for this scale was.88. Respondents were also asked to provide demographic information on their boss, such as gender, age, race, and marital status.

RESULTS

Before testing our hypotheses, we conducted a principal components analysis with a varimax rotation on the 16 items measuring respondent reactions to a 'friend' request from their boss. Three factors emerged including *Positive*, *Negative*, and *Questionable* reaction factors. Coefficient alphas for these scales were.89,.90, and.89, respectively.

Means, standard deviations and correlations among main variables are shown in Table 1. These results show that our respondents generally had positive opinions about their boss (M = 3.75, SD =.79) and were somewhat neutral in their responses to the *positive* and *questionable* reaction items (M = 2.97, SD = 74; and M = 2.57,

SD = 1.07; respectively) and generally disagreed with the *negative* reaction items (M = 1.88, SD =.77). The more positive our respondents opinions of their boss, the more likely they were to react positively to a 'friend' request from their boss (r =.11, p <.05) and accept the boss's request (r =.29, p <.001). We also found a significant relationship between country and opinion of one's boss. An examination of the means revealed that U.S. respondents rated their boss higher than German respondents [M = 3.97, SD =.81 and M = 3.53, SD =.70, respectively; F (1, 368) = 31.31, p <.001]. Additionally, U.S. respondents were more likely to have *negative* reactions to their boss's 'friend' request (r =.12, p <.05). The means for the U.S. and German respondents were 1.97 (SD =.64) and 1.79 (SD =.87), respectively [F (1, 370) = 5.1, p <.05]. Surprisingly, an examination of the frequencies indicated that 61% of male respondents had male bosses and 71% of female respondents had female bosses.

To test hypothesis 1, we conducted an ANOVA with repeated measures in which type of reaction (*positive, questionable, negative*) was entered as the within subjects variable and opinion of boss was entered as a covariate. A significant effect for type of reaction was found. To test for significant differences between means, we selected the pairwise comparison option which compares

differences between the estimated marginal means and adjusts for multiple comparisons using the Bonferroni test. These results showed significant differences among all three means such that respondents were most likely to have *positive* reactions (M = 2.96, SE =.04), followed by *questionable* reactions (M = 2.58, SE =.06), and least likely to have *negative* reactions (M=1.88, SE =.04). Thus, hypothesis 1 was not supported.

In hypothesis 2, we predicted that most respondents would accept their boss' 'friend' request but would have reservations about doing so. An examination of the frequencies shows that most respondents (46.1%) would accept the request from their boss. The second most frequent response was that they would accept with reservations (38.5%). Thus, hypothesis 2 was only partially supported. We also examined the impact of respondent's gender and boss's gender on responses to a 'friend' request from one's boss using a cross tab analysis and Pearson's Chi Square statistic. We found no significant differences based on boss's gender or respondent's gender.

To examine the impact of gender and culture on respondents' reactions to a 'friend' request from their boss, we conducted three ANOVAs using country, respondent's gender and boss's gender as the between subjects variables, and opinion of boss as a covariate. Means and standard devia-

Table 1. Means, standard deviations and correlations among all variables

	Variable	M	SD	1	2	3	4	5	6	7
1	Country	.49	.50							
2	Employee Gender	1.54	.50	-.10						
3	Boss' Gender	1.46	.50	.01	.31***					
4	Opinion of Boss	3.75	.79	.28***	.01	-.02				
5	Positive Reaction	2.97	.74	-.10	-.04	.03	.11*			
6	Questionable Reaction	2.57	1.07	.07	.04	.07	-.10	-.35***		
7	Negative Reaction	1.88	.77	.12*	-.03	.01	-.11	-.32***	.55***	
8	Response to Boss' Friend Request	3.28	.78	.11*	-.07	.00	.29***	.47***	-.41***	-.36***

Note: Country was coded Germany = 0 and U.S. = 1; Gender was coded 1 = male and 2 = female; Response to Boss' Friend Request was coded 4 = accept, 3 = accept with reservations, 2 = ignore, and 1 = respond that you do not know; *p <.05, **p <.01, *** p <.001.

tions for each of the reaction measures by country, respondent's gender and boss's gender are shown in Table 2. Although we predicted an interaction between respondent's gender and boss's gender such that the females with a male boss would have the most negative reactions, the interaction was not significant nor were there any significant main effects for gender. Thus, hypothesis 3 was not supported.

With regard to cultural differences, a significant main effect for country was found for all three reaction variables such that U.S. respondents were more likely than German respondents to have *negative* and *questionable* reactions [F (1, 357) = 10.14, p <.01; and F (1, 385) = 4.20, p <.05; respectively] and German respondents were more likely than U.S. respondents to have *positive* reactions [F (1, 385) = 7.77, p <.01]. We also found a significant interaction between gender and country for the *positive* reaction measure such that German males and females had similar reactions; however, U.S. females were more likely than U.S. males to have *positive* reactions [F (1, 385) = 6.53, p <.05]. See Figure 1. We also examined the impact of country on responses to a 'friend' request from one's boss using a cross tab analysis and Pearson's Chi Square statistic. We found U.S. respondents were more likely than German respondents to accept their boss's 'friend' request, whereas German respondents were more likely than U.S. respondents to accept with reservations (X^2 = 13.36, p <.01). See Figure 2.

Qualitative Analysis

Of the 24 U.S. respondents who provided an explanation as to why they would ignore their boss's 'friend' request, 38% did so because they believed their professional life should be kept separate from their personal life. For example, one wrote "I like to keep my personal life separated from work life. I do not share online profiles with coworkers at all." Twenty-one percent chose to ignore their boss for privacy reasons. The remaining 36% indicated a variety of reasons including that ignoring would be the easiest thing to do as opposed to refusing the request, that they would feel uncomfortable, or they disliked their boss. Of the 14 German respondents who provided an explanation as to why they would ignore a 'friend' request from their boss, 53% mentioned that they wanted to separate their private life from their work life, 14% mentioned that their boss is not their friend, and 14% said they would ask their boss why he/she wants to do this. Thus, in both

Table 2. Means and standard deviations for respondent reactions to a "friend" request from their boss by country, respondent's gender, and boss's gender

Type of Reaction		Germany	U.S.	Males	Females	Male Boss	Female Boss
Positive	**M**	**3.03**[a]	**2.90**[b]	**2.93**	**3.00**	**3.05**	**3.03**
	SD	*.69*	*.78*	*.71*	*.76*	*.65*	*.70*
Questionable	**M**	**2.50**[a]	**2.64**[b]	**2.50**	**2.65**	**2.50**	**2.64**
	SD	*.99*	*1.15*	*1.09*	*1.04*	*1.09*	*1.04*
Negative	**M**	**1.79**[a]	**1.96**[b]	**1.87**	**1.88**	**1.78**	**1.80**
	SD	*.63*	*.87*	*.80*	*.72*	*.62*	*.65*

Note: means with different superscripts are significantly different from one another at p <.05.

Figure 1. Interaction between gender and country on positive reactions to a "friend" request from one's boss

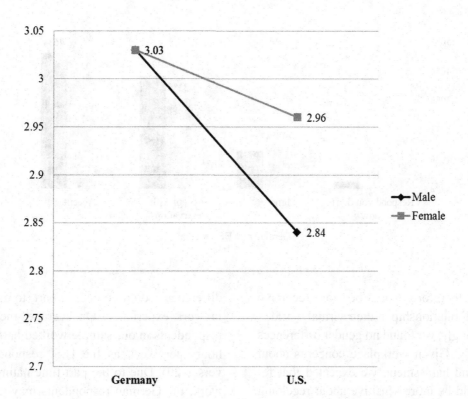

countries, privacy and separation appear to be the key concerns.

DISCUSSION

The results of this study suggest that young employees are more likely to have positive (e.g., pleased, honored) or questionable reactions (e.g., worried, suspicious) than negative reactions (e.g., disgusted, irritated, offended) to a Facebook 'friend' request from their boss. However, the generally neutral responses provided by many respondents may indicate that they possibly have never considered the likelihood of such a request and were unsure as to how they would react. Despite providing neutral responses, the vast majority of our respondents indicated that they would accept their boss's 'friend' request, although many said

they would have reservations about doing so. Only 15% of our respondents indicated that they would reject their boss' 'friend' request. We believe this may be due to our respondents being relatively young and inexperienced in the workplace. It is likely that they have never considered the possible negative consequences of sharing their Facebook profile with their boss. There is also research indicating that today's younger generation is much less concerned about privacy than previous generations (e.g., Robinson, 2006). On the other hand, it is possible that many of our respondents carefully monitored the content of their sites so they were unconcerned about their boss having access to their site. It is also important to note that our respondents had relatively high opinions of their boss. Thus, it is likely they had positive or friendly relationships with their boss in the real

Figure 2. Percentage of response types to a "friend" request from one's boss

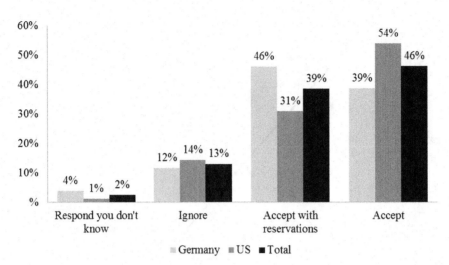

world and, therefore, would be more receptive of a 'friend' relationship in their virtual world.

Surprisingly, we found no gender differences in our study. Given workplace concerns about romance and harassment, we expected that females would be more sensitive about receiving such a request from their boss, particularly of the opposite gender. One possibility is that our female respondents had such high opinions of their boss that such risks were of little concern. Another possibility is that requests for virtual "friendships" are not taken too seriously and are perceived as less awkward or threatening than real world relationships. It is also possible that, since a majority of our female respondents also had female bosses, a larger sample would produce different results.

Significant differences based on culture were found. U.S. respondents were more likely than German respondents to have negative or questionable reactions whereas German respondents were more likely than U.S. respondents to have positive reactions. Further examination revealed a significant interaction such that there was no difference between German males and females in their responses to the positive reaction measure; however, U.S. females were more likely than U.S. males to have positive reactions. These cultural differences could be due, in part, to differences in work experience. On average, the German respondents in our sample worked half as many hours per week as the U.S. respondents (10 versus 20). Due to the part time nature of their work, the German respondents may have been less concerned than the U.S. respondents about possible negative consequences of 'friending' their boss. Their profile content could be more professional and free of problematic comments or photos as was found in a recent study. When comparing U.S. and German student reports of profile content, researchers found that U.S. students were significantly more likely than German respondents to post controversial or problematic content (e.g., comments or photos related to substance abuse or sexual content) (Karl, Peluchette, & Schlaegel, 2010).

Implications

Our findings have some important implications for both employees and managers. As previously mentioned, some organizations are using Facebook to build relationships within the firm. Using social media may be a powerful business tool but evidence suggests that organizations need to "tread lightly" in this arena due to potential legal concerns. The legal system has lagged behind technology growth, putting companies at potential risk for litigation if they are without policies for appropriate technology use (Smith, 2009). Typically, this does not require the establishment of new policies, just a modification of existing policies to include social media. As part of this process, it is recommended that companies outline their philosophy on social media, make reference to specific social networking sites, and to be clear about expectations for online behavior (Arnold, 2009; Gray, 2009). Because technology changes, policies need regular updating and it is important to provide training for both managers and employees.

Since managers set the tone for the workplace, their use of social media is of particular concern in terms of how it impacts the work environment. Because activity with social media like Facebook typically occurs outside working hours and on personal computers, companies may be hesitant to restrict their managers from 'friending' their employees online for fear of violating state privacy laws or laws which prevent regulation of off-premises conduct (Arnold, 2009). However, managers need to be aware that, while sending a 'friend' request to an employee might seem rather fun and friendly, it could have unintended consequences. Even if the manager is comfortable initiating the request, the employee may not feel the same way, creating a potentially negative undertone to their working relationship. Furthermore, once 'friends' on Facebook, the boss has access to personal information about the employee which could end up being argued as the basis for any adverse employment actions (Smith, 2009). Thus, managers should be prudent in using Facebook to connect with their employees, recognizing the potential risks to the employment relationship. For companies that have developed policies about social media, managers play a key role in championing the policy and communicating it to employees (Gray, 2009).

Employees also need to practice prudence in their use of Facebook to minimize the potential risks to their employment relationship. Some may work at firms that have embraced the use of Facebook as part of their workplace culture and feel that, politically, they do not have much choice but to accept a 'friend' request received from their boss. In doing so, it would be important for the employee to make some quick decisions about information accessibility on their profile. Even if the boss does not initiate a 'friend' request, he or she could still be a Facebook user and be able to view the employees' profile pictures, as well as those of their friends. Thus, employees need to determine how they wish to present themselves on Facebook, understanding that more than just their real friends may be looking.

Limitations and Future Research

This study is also not without some limitations of note. Since the boss's 'friend' request in this study was fictitious, there could be a discrepancy between how respondents reported they would act and their actual reactions if they were to receive such a request. Future researchers should examine employee reactions to actual Facebook 'friend' requests from their supervisors. Another limitation is that respondents in this study were relatively young and many worked only part time. Future studies should continue to explore employee perceptions of a boss's 'friend' request among older, more experienced employees. We also recognize that that some of the nonsignificant results from this study may be due to the age of our respondents and would not occur when sampling Generation X or Baby Boomers. For example, it is possible that millennial females are less modest about their on-stage social networking presentation of self and, therefore, feel less threatened by male 'friend' requests. On the other hand, females from earlier generations, who grew up around different norms and conflicts, might have a different reaction. Future research should extend this study with the addition of a generational variable.

As noted earlier, it is also possible that the individuals in our sample did not foresee any negative consequences of accepting 'friend' requests from their boss either because they have kept their profile "clean" or because they would use Facebook's privacy settings to severely limit what information their boss might have access to (Raynes-Goldie, 2010). More qualitative research exploring employee reactions is needed to clarify why they tended to give neutral responses. Employee reactions to 'friend' requests may depend on their boss's characteristics, for example, his or her social capital (Steinfield, DiMicco, Ellison, & Lampe, 2009). In the present study, we only surveyed employees and not their boss. Recent research (Wang, Moon, Kwon, Evans, & Stefanone, 2010) shows that gender and appearance moderate an individual's willingness to make friends with others on Facebook. Therefore, future research should survey both the employees and their respective supervisors and use a multi-level research design to examine the factors that moderate and/ or mediate the relationship between supervisors and subordinates in the use of online social networks in the organizational context. Finally, even though some organizations are promoting the use of Facebook and other social networking sites as a means to improve communication, teamwork, and employee development (Arnold, 2009), the results of this study show that many subordinates would rather not connect with their bosses through Facebook. In the future, researchers should examine organizational policies and practices that may lessen negative reactions.

REFERENCES

Arnold, J. (2009, December). Twittering and Facebooking while they work. *HR Magazine*, 53–55.

Arrington, M. (2006). Facebook goes beyond college, high school markets. *TechCrunch*. Retrieved March 29, 2009, from http://www.techcrunch.com/2006/04/26/facebook-goes-beyond-college-high-school-markets/

Bosses Unpopular as Facebook friends. (2009, April 29). *The Globe and Mail*, B20.

Bourgeois, M. J., & Perkins, J. (2003). A test of evolutionary and sociocultural explanations of reactions to sexual harassment. *Sex Roles*, *49*(7/8), 343–351. doi:10.1023/A:1025160120455

Browne, K. R. (2006). Sex, power, and dominance: The evolutionary psychology of sexual harassment. *Managerial and Decision Economics*, *27*, 145–158. doi:10.1002/mde.1289

Cakir, H., & Cagiltay, K. (2002). Effects of cultural differences on e-mail communication in multicultural environments. In F. Sudweeks & C. Ess (Eds.), *Proceedings of the Third International Conference on Cultural Attitudes towards Technology and Communication* (pp. 29-50). Montreal, Canada: School of Information Technology, Murdoch University.

Diaz, J. (2008). Facebook's squirmy chapter. Site's evolution blurs line between boss and employee. *The Boston Globe*. Retrieved March 29, 2009, from http://www.boston.com/lifestyle/articles/2008/04/16/facebooks_squirmy_chapter/

DiMicco, J. M., & Millen, D. R. (2007). Identity management: multiple presentations of self in facebook. In *Proceedings of GROUP*, *2007*, 383–386.

Donath, J., & Boyd, D. (2004). Public displays of connection. *BT Technology Journal*, *22*(4), 71–82. doi:10.1023/B:BTTJ.0000047585.06264.cc

Eldon, E. (2009). *Europe grew by 10 million new Facebook users last month, Here's the top 20 gainers*. Retrieved January, 6, 2010, from http://www.insidefacebook.com/2009/11/06/europe-grew-by-10-million-new-facebook-users-last-month-heres-the-top-20-gainers/

Facebook, T. LinkedIn and Compliance: What are companies doing? (2009). *Society of Corporate Compliance and Ethics*. Retrieved June 22, 2010, from http://www.corporatecompliance.org/AM/Template.cfm?Section=Surveys&CONTENTID=4741&TEMPLATE=/CM/ContentDisplay.cfm

Facebook, Press Room. (2010). *Company Statistics*. Retrieved January 6, 2010, from http://www.facebook.com/press/info.php?statistics

Goffman, E. (1959). *The presentation of self in everyday life*. Garden City, NY: Double Day Anchor.

Gray, K. (2009). *Social networking policies vary by job, company*. Retrieved September 2, 2009, from http://moss07.shrm.org/hrdisciplines/employeerelations/articles/Pages/SocialNetworkingPolicies.aspx

Gutek, B. A. (1985). *Sex and the Workplace: The Impact of Sexual Behaviour and Harassment on Women, Men and the Organization*. San Francisco, CA: Jossey-Bass.

Hofstede, G. (1980). *Culture's Consequences: International Differences in Work-Related Values*. Thousand Oaks, CA: Sage.

Hofstede, G. (1991). *Cultures and Organizations—Software of the Mind*. London: McGraw-Hill.

Horowitz, E. (2008). Befriending your boss on Facebook. *The Age*. Retrieved March 28, 2009, from http://thebigchair.com.au/news/career-couch/befriending-your-boss-on-facebook

Karl, K., Peluchette, J., & Schlaegel, C. (2010). A cross-cultural examination of student attitudes and gender differences in Facebook profile content. *International Journal of Virtual Communities and Social Networking, 2*(2), 11–31.

Kelly, C. (2009, August 15). Fired on Facebook: Don't rip boss when he's your 'friend'; Woman let go after rant: 'I guess you forgot about adding me on here?' *The Toronto Star*, A03.

Lampinen, A., Tamminen, S., & Oulasvirta, A. (2009). "All my people right here, right now": Management of group co-presence on a social networking site. In *Proceedings of GROUP, 2009*, 81–290.

Lewis, C., & George, J. (2008). Cross-cultural deception in social networking sites and face-to-face communication. *Computers in Human Behavior, 24*(6), 2945–2964. doi:10.1016/j.chb.2008.05.002

Morgan, T. (2009, February 27). Fired for saying my job was boring on Facebook. *The Express*, 43.

Perrier, F. (2007). *Facebook cost US $ 3.4 billion to the corporate world in lost productivity*. Retrieved December 27, 2008, from http://www.franckperrier.com/2007/11/14/facebooks-productivity-cost-to-the-corporate-world-us-34-billion/

Pfeil, U., Zaphiris, P., & Ang, C. S. (2006). Cultural differences in collaborative authoring of Wikipedia. *Journal of Computer-Mediated Communication, 12*(1), 88–113. doi:10.1111/j.1083-6101.2006.00316.x

Raynes-Goldie, K. (2010). Aliases, creeping, and wall cleaning: Understanding privacy in the age of Facebook. *First Monday, 15*(1-4).

Roberts, B. (2008). Social networking at the office. *HRMagazine, 53*(3), 81–83.

Robinson, T. G. (2006). Not so private lives. *CED, 32*(9), 45–46.

Rotundo, N., Nguyen, D., & Sackett, P. R. (2001). A meta-analytic review of gender differences in perceptions of sexual harassment. *The Journal of Applied Psychology, 86*(5), 914–922. doi:10.1037/0021-9010.86.5.914

Ruettimann, L. (2009). *How to avoid your boss on Facebook*. Retrieved March 29, 2009, from http://www.lemondrop.com/2009/02/12/facebook-friend-your-boss/

Rutledge, P. (2008). *The truth about profiting from social networking.* Upper Saddle River, NJ: Pearson Education, FT Press.

Skeels, M. M., & Grudin, J. (2009). When social networks cross boundaries: A case study of workplace use of Facebook and LinkedIn. In *Proceedings of the GROUP, 2009,* 95–104.

Smith, J. (2009). Number of US Facebook users over 35 nearly doubles in last 60 days. *Inside Facebook.* Retrieved January 6, 2010, from http://www.insidefacebook.com/2009/03/25/number-of-us-facebook-users-over-35-nearly-doubles-in-last-60-days/

Social networking explodes worldwide as sites increase their focus on cultural relevance. (2008, August 12). Retrieved December 30, 2008, from http://www.comscore.com/press/release.asp?press=2396

Steinfield, C., DiMicco, J. M., Ellison, N. B., & Lampe, C. (2009). Bowling online: Social networking and social capital within the organization. In *Proceedings of the fourth international conference on communities and technologies 2009* (pp. 245-254).

Stross, R. (2009). When everyone's a friend, is anything private? *The New York Times.* Retrieved March 29, 2009, from http://www.nytimes.com/2009/03/08/business/08digi.html?_r=2&pagewanted=print

Waller, M. (2007). Bank's fairy demonstrates magic of the net. *Times (London, England),* 56.

Wang, S. S., Moon, S.-I., Kwon, K. H., Evans, C. A., & Stefanone, M. A. (2010). Face off: Implications of visual cues on initiating friendship on Facebook. *Computers in Human Behavior, 26*(2), 226–234. doi:10.1016/j.chb.2009.10.001

Your Boss Doesn't Want to be Your Facebook friend. (2009, August 21). *The Globe and Mail,* B12.

Yuan, L., & Buckman, R. (2006). Social networking goes mobile; MySpace, Facebook strike deals with cell companies; A new set of safety concerns. *Wall Street Journal,* D1.

This work was previously published in the International Journal of Virtual Communities and Social Networking, Volume 2, Issue 3, edited by Subhasish Dasgupta, pp. 16-30, copyright 2010 by IGI Publishing (an imprint of IGI Global).

Chapter 11
Business Models for On–Line Social Networks:
Challenges and Opportunities

Omer Rana
Cardiff University, UK

Simon Caton
Karlsruhe Institute of Technology, Germany

ABSTRACT

With the increasingly ubiquitous nature of social networks and Cloud computing, users are starting to explore new ways to interact with and exploit these developing paradigms. Social networks reflect real world relationships that allow users to share information and form connections, essentially creating dynamic virtual communities. By leveraging the pre-established trust formed through friend relationships within a social network "Social Clouds" can be realized, which enable friends to share resources within the context of a social network. The creation of Social Clouds gives rise to new business models through collaboration within social networks. In this paper, the authors describe such business models and discuss their impact.

1 INTRODUCTION

The Internet and the World Wide Web has profoundly changed society and business – in education, healthcare, research, defense and economy. The underlying computing and communication infrastructure which has enabled these changes is now being used to support a "service-oriented" computing economy. The resulting markets that we envision will enable both owners of home

computers and established business to trade their excess capacity for a variety of incentives (such as monetary rewards, service credits, software maintenance contracts, advertising revenue etc) and enable the creation of capability by aggregating software services from multiple providers. In the same way, economic models associated with social media on the Internet have been driven by user numbers; hence the greater the number of individuals that can be attracted to visit a Web site,

DOI: 10.4018/978-1-4666-1553-3.ch011

the greater the *likelihood* that an advertiser will be able to attract them to their own Web portal. Whereas search engines have primarily focused on associating advertisements with responses returned from user queries, social networking sites are able to take advantage of interconnectedness between users and the various information that users selectively reveal about their interests to the social network site.

According to a report by the Office of Communications (Ofcom) in the UK (Ofcom, 2008), adult social networkers use a variety of sites, with the main ones being Bebo, Facebook and MySpace. The report indicates that it is common for adults to have a profile on more than one site – with each adult having a profile on 1.6 sites on average. Of the social networking sites surveyed in the report, it was found that 39% of adults have profiles on two or more sites. Half of all current adult social networkers say that they access their profiles at least every other day. The site people choose to use varies depending on the user. Children are more likely to use Bebo (63% of those who have a social networking site profile), and the most popular site for adults is Facebook. There is also a difference between socio-economic groups: ABC1s with a social networking profile were more likely to use Facebook than C2DEs, who were more likely to have a profile on MySpace. According to Alexa. com the top social networking sites are Facebook, QQ (from China) and Twitter.

Major software vendors such as Microsoft and Google are adopting the "social" model of interaction within their software. For instance, Microsoft Office 2010 integrates "social connections" with on-line services. Integrating enterprise computing software with mobile devices (such as Google's Android phones) also facilitates social collaboration between users in a way that was not previously possible with enterprise management systems, and provides a useful model of feedback and interaction between employees of an organisation. In the same context (Black & Jacobs, 2010; Black et al., 2010) provide case

studies to demonstrate how social media may be used to improve software quality – where "quality" can be measured in a number of ways – and includes: fitness for purpose, on time and budget delivery, user interaction experience, delivery in accordance with project management process, and new understanding gained from engagement with the project. They demonstrate how user interaction design (during software development and beta testing) can be used to generate better customer satisfaction, and in particular how social media enables an organization to build a distributed knowledge base and increase employees' sense of connection to the company's initiatives and each other.

2 EMERGENCE OF SOCIAL NETWORKS AND CLOUD COMPUTING

Social networking has become an everyday part of many peoples' lives as evidenced by the huge user communities that are part of such networks. Facebook, for instance, was launched in February 2004 by Harvard undergraduate students as an alternative to the traditional student directory. Intended to cover interaction between students at Universities – Facebook enables individuals to encourage others to join the network through personalised invitations, friend suggestions and creation of specialist groups. Today Facebook has a much wider take up than just students at Universities. Facebook now facilitates interaction between people by enabling sharing of common interests, videos, photos, etc. Some social network populations exceed that of large countries, for example Facebook has over 350 million active users. Social networks provide a platform to facilitate communication and sharing between users, in an attempt to model real world relationships. Social networking has now also extended beyond communication between friends; for instance, there are a multitude of integrated applications that are now made available by companies, and some organizations use such applications, such as Facebook Connect to authenticate users, i.e. they utilize a user's Facebook credentials rather than requiring their own credentials (for example the Calgary Airport authority in Canada uses Facebook Connect to grant access to their WiFi network). This ability to combine a third party application (including its local data) to authenticate users demonstrates the service-oriented approach to application development. By tapping into an already established community around a particular social networking platform, it becomes unnecessary to require users to register with another system.

The structure of a Social Network is essentially the formation of a dynamic virtual community with inherent trust relationships between friends. (Szmigin et al., 2006) identify how "relationship marketing" (identified as referring to all marketing activities directed towards establishing, developing and maintaining successful relational exchanges) can be facilitated through the creation of on-line communities. They discuss how on-line communities can be used to facilitate interaction and bonding between consumer and suppliers, intermediate parties and specific brands. Similarly, (Shang et al., 2006) discuss how brand loyalty can be achieved through various types of participation within an on-line community (focusing specifically on the www.frostyplace.com – a virtual community of Apple users in Taiwan). They discuss the motivation for individuals to promote certain products during on-line discussions (active participants) and for others to remain as *lurkers* (passive participants). The study particularly focuses on the incentives for participants to contribute to an on-line community, based on the perception of a user about the degree of relevance towards an object that is being discussed – focusing on both cognitive (based on utilitarian motive – concerning an individual's concern with the cost and benefit of the product or service) and affective (a value-expressive motive, referring to an individual's interest in enhancing

self-esteem or self-conception, and in projecting his/her desired self-image to the outside world through the product or service).

It is also useful to understand, for instance, how such trust relationships could be used as a foundation for resource (information, hardware, services) sharing. Cloud environments are typically focused on providing low level abstractions of computation or storage. Using this approach, a user is able to access (on a short term/rental basis) capacity that is owned by another person or business (generally over a computer network). In this way, a user is able to outsource their computing requirements to an external provider – limiting their exposure to cost associated with systems management and energy use. Computation and Storage Clouds are complementary and act as building blocks from which applications can be constructed – using a technique referred to as "mash-ups". Storage Clouds are gaining popularity as a way to extend the capabilities of storage-limited devices such as phones and other mobile devices. There are also a multitude of commercial Cloud providers such as Amazon EC2/S3, Google App Engine, Microsoft Azure and also many smaller scale open clouds like Nimbus (Keahey et al., 2005) and Eucalyptus (Nurmi et al., 2009). A Social Cloud (Chard et al., 2010), on the other hand, is a scalable computing model in which virtualized resources contributed by users are dynamically provisioned amongst a group of friends. Compensation for use is optional as users may wish to share resources without payment, and rather utilize a reciprocal credit (or barter) based model (Andrade et al., 2010). In both cases guarantees are offered through customized Service Level Agreements (SLAs). In a sense, this model is similar to a Volunteer computing approach, in that friends share resources amongst each other for little to no gain. However, unlike Volunteer models there is inherent accountability through existing friend relationships. There are a number of advantages gained by leveraging social networking platforms, in particular one can gain access to huge user communities, can exploit existing user management functionality, and rely on pre-established trust formed through existing user relationships.

3 BUSINESS MODELS

There is a considerable literature on what constitutes a "business model", with definitions that range from very broad ones (Afuah & Tucci, 2001) to those that are very specific (Osterwalder, 2004). According to (Taylor & McKee, 2010), this term gained significant popularity during the Internet bubble when every successful business needed a good business model, but was somewhat discredited when the bubble burst. Perhaps, the most commonly used minimal description of the term is simply that the business model articulates how the business makes money (Taylor & McKee, 2010). An alternative, perhaps more useful definition from (Afuah & Tucci, 2001), is that a business model defines *the method* of doing business by which a company can sustain itself and generate revenue. (Timmers, 1998) focuses on business models for electronic commerce and provides a framework for the classification of such business models. Timmers describes a business model as:

- An architecture for the product, service and information flows, including a description of the various business actors and their roles; and
- A description of the potential benefits for the various business actors; and
- A description of the sources of revenues.

Using this definition, (Stanoevska-Slabeva et al., 2008) propose the MCM-Business Models Framework – enhancing Timmers' work. The MCM-Business Models Framework consists of the following:

- **The Social Environment (an aspect not considered by Timmers):** reflects external influences on the business models, such as legal and ethical aspects. It refers to the social and regulatory context in which a business model is development and implemented.
- **Features of the medium:** expresses the possibilities for electronic transactions over a specific medium – e.g. using a centralized or decentralized IT infrastructure.
- **Potential Customer:** covers all aspects of target groups and customers – which vary depending on the product or service being considered.
- **The component Value Chain:** reflects participants involved in the delivery of the offered product or service and their interrelationships. In the case of Facebook (discussed in section 3.1), this would be the application developers, the advertisers, the advertising network etc. In the context of electronic services, this would be the content/service owner, content aggregators, content providers, portal owners and the user.
- **Features of the product:** captures the overall experience of the user when interacting with the product.
- **Financial flow:** explains the earning logic of the business model and makes it clear which elements of the value chain contribute from a financial perspective.
- **Flow of goods and services:** identifies all the processes within the company and the value chain necessary for the creation of the product or service.

3.1 Business Models for Social Networks

Business models in social networking are often closely aligned with the capability being offered to facilitate better interaction between users. Therefore, in addition to supporting site advertising – which has seen limited benefit for many social network sites – many of these sites also use connectivity between people to identify possible product placement opportunities. This has been widely adopted in, for example Second Life, where companies typically launch new virtual products in order to perform market research or to better understand acceptance and impact of a product within the virtual markets of Second Life. The business models within Facebook and other social networking sites include:

• **Advertising:** This is one of the major source of revenue for many on-line portals and social networking sites. Advertising revenue is often dependent on the number of people visiting a Web site. Advertising can be based on a "Cost per Click" (or a variant "Pay per Click") or a "Cost per Acquisition" (Ghosh & Yang, 2009). In Cost per Click, an advertiser pays the social networking site when their advertisement is clicked on. The simplest of these is a flat rate, where the advertiser and publisher agree a fixed amount that will be paid for each click, based on the particular areas of their Web site or network where the advert is hosted. The alternative is an auction-based approach (Google Adwords for example), in which an advertiser and host sign a contract that allows them to compete against other advertisers in a private auction hosted by a publisher or an advertising network. Each advertiser informs the host of the maximum amount they are willing to pay for a given advertising spot (often based on a keyword), usually using online tools. The auction plays out in an automated fashion every time a visitor triggers the advert. The Cost per Thousand Impressions (CPT) is a variant, where the advertiser is charged for every thousand displays of the advertisement. This approach does not provide any measure of "effectiveness" of the advertising campaign, and hence more or less similar to the conventional mass marketing approach.

The alternative is a Cost per Acquisition or Action, where the advertiser pays for each specified action (a purchase, a form submission, and so on) linked to the advertisement. In such a scenario, an advertiser only pays for the advert when the desired action has occurred. An action can be a product being purchased, a form being filled, etc. The desired action to be performed is determined by the advertiser.

The fee paid by the advertiser (to the advertising agent or network) as identified above may be fixed for each click (as in CPC) or action (as in CPA) or for every thousand displays (as in CPT), or vary. The fee may be dynamically calculated if based on an auctioning or automated bidding approach, where an advertising network or advertiser may bid for particular keywords or categories or for a particular space on a site. Bidding is automatically carried out and based on attributes such as a bid amount, CPC, a maximum value for a daily spend amount, etc. The bidding process may also include quality factors for the advertisement such as the Click Through Rate (CTR), which measures the effectiveness of the advertisement, and is calculated by the number of clicks or actions that lead to the advertisement.

Facebook also now enables the development of a specialist Quiz or questionnaire – encouraging individuals to participate by comparing their score on such a Quiz to their friends. In doing so, a user is often required to fill in an email address and a telephone number. A Quiz can also be created by an advertising network and distributed to users. The outcome of such a Quiz can be used to identify lifestyle trends and common interests across a group of users. All useful data for targeted advertising.

- **"Freemium"** (or Subscription): This approach involves developing multiple versions of an application. One version is released to the user community for free, whereas a "pro" version is then provided for a fee. The fee can be a one-off payment, or may involve a time limited access to the application via an on-line system. In this model, it is necessary for the developer to continue to innovate and support new functionality within their application, to encourage users to continue to use their site. Delivery of the application is generally over the network and based on a code generated when a user registers for the "pro" version. This approach is commonplace in many applications/games that are provided over social networks. Here, a user who is willing to "invest" in the application can progress faster in the game than their peers.

- **Branding and Cost Per Share**: This approach relies on promoting a particular brand through a social network platform. The approach relies on "viral marketing" (Leskovec et al., 2007), where a user interacts with a brand message or campaign, resulting in his/her friends being notified of the user's activity with the brand. This type of brand enforcement enables greater awareness of a particular type of product brand and is much more effective than an email campaign, where only a single receiver may be involved. This is achieved in systems such as Facebook by a user becoming a "fan" of something, this results in a broadcast to all their friends announcing their support for a particular product, idea, event etc. Yubo and Jinhong also identify

how word-of-mouth endorsements can be better exercised in the context of a virtual social network (Yubo & Jinhong, 2008). Even-dar and Shapira (2007) identify how a "spread maximization" approach can be considered within a social network represented as a graph, and the need to identify the most connected (or influential) individuals that could be introduced to a new technology, in order to maximize the expected number of individuals in the network, later in time, that adopt the new technology. Their model primarily is based on each individual voting like their neighbor (randomly chosen) and using a diffusion process to model how a community of individuals adopt a particular opinion.

In cases where a single social media publisher cannot deliver enough volume to interest brands on their own, or do not have the resources to build up a direct sales force, there are a number of intermediate adverting representatives who can aggregate publishers and manage the sales efforts for them. These include companies like Federated Media, Appsavvy and Alloy Media Marketing.

- **Virtual Currency**: Facebook implements a Credits scheme which acts as a virtual currency within Facebook – with credits mapping to various other physical currencies (currently over 15 international currencies are represented). In this approach users can purchase or earn virtual credits within their applications and then redeem them for virtual gifts or goods.

- **Virtual Gifts**: As the name implies, a virtual gift involves purchasing an icon (representing a gift) from a gift store and sending this to friends. Interestingly, virtual gifts may not always map on to real, physical gifts – yet there is still significant interest in purchasing such gifts within social networks and interactive games. In Facebook a Virtual Marketplace has been established enabling external developers to build such gifts. Purchasing of virtual gifts is now also linked to Facebook Credits – which can be used to purchase real gifts also.

- **Affiliate Fees**: If an application is related to products that users are already accustomed to paying for (books, DVDs, movie tickets, music, or clothing, to name a few) then a developer may be able to successfully charge a fee for helping users locate those goods. For example, book applications like Visual Bookshelf help users identify books they may want to purchase (by exposing social information such as what their friends have read, reviewed, and recommended), and then receive an affiliate fee from Amazon.com (for instance) for books referred through that application. Travel applications can likewise accept affiliate fees.

- **Reciprocation**: Although not a business model in the traditional sense of generating revenue, the aim of reciprocation is to barter resources between individuals involved in a social network. This approach enables participants within a group to share storage or computational capacity with others based on some pre-defined quotas. Often capacity is made available to others on a "best effort" basis – i.e. no guarantees are provided on the overall quality of service offered when these resources are accessed.

4 SOCIAL CLOUDS

In (Chard et al., 2010) the notion of a Social Cloud has been defined and implemented as a Facebook application, to make use of this widely used platform and development environment. In a Social Cloud, services can be mapped to particular users through Facebook identification, allowing for the definition of unique policies regarding the interactions between users. For example, a user could limit trading with close friends only, users in the same country/network/group, all friends, or even friends of friends. A specialized banking component manages the transfer of credits between users while also storing information relating to current reservations. A high level architecture of a Social Cloud is shown in Figure 1.

In a Social Cloud users are able to trade their excess data storage and computer capacity with their friends, when they are not using this capacity themselves. Such an approach is primarily intended for outsourcing storage or computation to resources owned by a friend or colleague. An example includes a user off loading photos from their digital camera to the hard disk of another member in the social network, for instance.

4.1 Business Models

Revenue generation within a Social Cloud is supported through a credit-based business model (as described in Section 3.1. Currently, a "posted price" and a "reverse auction" is supported. In a posted price model providers advertise offers relating to particular service levels for a predefined price or following a linear pricing function (i.e. the price increases linearly with the amount of resource, of a particular kind, used – for instance 10 monetary units for access to a single processor for one hour). Creating such a market requires coordination between a number of the Social Cloud components to: discover Cloud services, create agreements, and transfer credits. In an auction-based market trades are established through a competitive bidding process between users or services. Like the posted price market, a list of friends is discovered and passed to a specialized auctioneer to create and run the auction. The auctioneer uses the list of friends to locate a group of suitable Cloud services; these are termed the bidders in the auction. Each provider requires an agent to act on its behalf to value resource requests,

Figure 1. Social Cloud Architecture. Users register Cloud services and friends are then able to provision and use these resources through the Social Cloud Facebook application. Allocation is conducted by the underlying market infrastructure(s). "MDS" represents a directory service that allows providers to publish properties of their resources.

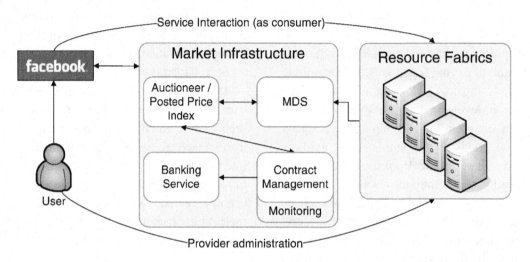

determine a bid based on locally defined policies, and follow the auction protocol (Table 1).

5 CHALLENGES AND OPPORTUNITIES

A number of challenges arise when we combine the service-based approach identified through social networks and Cloud computing. Here we highlight some of the most significant ones:

- **Privacy and secure access:** privacy concerns were highlighted through the Facebook "Beacons" project, part of the advertisement system used by this social networking site that sent data from external websites to Facebook, ostensibly for the purpose of allowing targeted advertisements and allowing users to share their activities with their friends. Over 44 web sites were involved in this project – ranging from media organizations (such as CBS Interactive, Sony Online) to travel services (such as TripAdvisor and STA Travel). When a user made a purchase on one of the 44 web sites involved in the Beacon project, their purchase could be highlighted through the Newsfeed of the individual. Although users could switch-off this feature – i.e. not allow such information to be displayed in their newsfeed, such data was still available to Facebook. It is now possible to turn off this feature – which was recognized by many to be a privacy concern. A good coverage of breaches and consideration for various stakeholders can be found in (Gurses et al., 2008).

- **Data confidentiality:** outsourcing computing (analysis capability) and data storage to a third party implies making data available outside organizational boundaries. Although encryption techniques could be employed prior to transfer, there remain legal and ethical limitations on the types of data that can be remotely stored or analysed.

Table 1. Mapping social cloud to business model from section 4.1

Business Model Criteria	Feature in Social Cloud
Social environment	This would involve privacy considerations, data sharing and confidentiality concerns. Facebook provides a variety of setting to limit how much personal data is made available to others. Identifying who should be made aware of available data storage resources and the current state of the resources should be restricted.
Features of medium	User authentication is supported in Facebook, which is used to identify a user and their associated "friends" network. Quotas should be set on what is being made available to external users.
Potential customer	Social clouds primarily target individual users.
Component Value Chain	In this context, participants are friends of a particular user. The service provider could be any individual in the friend's network. We assume that each individual is able to provide capacity via local resources (such as a portion of a hard disk). Currently we do not envision the existence of aggregators or "brokers".
Features of product	The product primarily focuses on sharing storage.
Financial flow	Primarily supported through a credits transfer system.
Flow of good & services	Two primary services are supported: (i) transfer of data to a remote resource; (ii) access to properties of a storage resource.

- **Trust:** by adding an individual to one's "friends" implies that a user has some degree of trust in the individual being added. Such connectivity between individuals can be used to infer trust relationships between them, as outlined in (AlShabib et al., 2006), and often the basis for product suggestions in social networking sites. However, often such connectivity between individuals does not fully take into account the differing degrees of trust depending on the context of the relationship between the individuals. For instance in Facebook a "friend" can be a member of the family, a colleague at work, a college affiliate, etc. Distinguishing between these different types of relationships could lead to the formation of different types of trust relationships. Facebook has recently recognised the need for the creation of such groups and allows users to create specialised groups to differentiate between, for example, close friends and colleagues. In the context of a Social Cloud scenario, this immediately provides the basis for defining who should be interacted with if these groups are correctly harnessed by the infrastructure.

According to (Zlotogorski, 2010), there will be 4.275 billion mobile phone subscribers worldwide, out of which 1.228 billion will be mobile Internet users and 803 million will be participating in social networks via their mobile phones, which represents one out of every five mobile phone subscribers. The global mobile social networking user population could rise to as much as 873.1 million or 22% of the total mobile subscriber base.

It is also interesting to see the significant growth in Facebook usage (Burcher, 2010) (from March 2010) in emerging economies. For instance, a 1027% growth in the Phillipines, 793% in Indonesia, and 400% increase in India over a 12 month period. In a study conducted by (Korzenny, 2009) on the use of social networks in the US, involving over 2,500 participants, it was discovered that ethnic minorities are more likely to leverage social networks to communicate with groups of family and friends who are geographically dispersed, being drawn to collectivistic values and often looking to one another to help guide decisions and opinions. He found that social media facilitated such collective sharing of information and communication. In addition, social networks provided a platform for enabling such communities to generate and share their own content. He concludes by the observation that "... we now have an unprecedented ability to reach and interact with ethnic minorities; and companies that deliver value to this segment today will be rewarded with the long term loyalty of this market."

In addition, Facebook played a crucial role during the Haiti crisis in helping family members receive and deliver news all around the world. This system was implemented as a Facebook application and was based upon a Cloud infrastructure using multiple service mashups and resources from IBM. The Facebook application platform provided the means for obtaining news when phone lines to particular individuals were un-operational and other means of communication disrupted; clearly demonstrating the societal value of infrastructure such as a Social Cloud, or socially derived cloud infrastructures.

The interaction between users who participate in social networks imply the creation of a "value network" (Allee, 2003) – where the relationships that form between individuals can lead to the creation of both tangible and intangible value. All exchanges of goods, services or revenue, including all transactions involving contracts, invoices, return receipt of orders, request for proposals, confirmations and payment are considered to be tangible value (Allee, 2003). Products or services that generate revenue or are expected as part of a service are also included in the tangible value flow of goods, services, and revenue. Intangible value can include knowledge (such as strategic information, planning knowledge, process knowledge, technical know-how, etc) and benefits (such as seeking volunteers or expertise in a particular context). Although considered in the context of e-commerce, it is useful to note that content generation within communities supported through social networks can provide "social" and "intellectual" value. A business model in this context

would involve identifying how such intellectual value can be converted into financial revenue. Value generation is dependent on the connectivity of the social network community and the number of participants involved. Hence, the larger the network, the greater the overall social value and the greater the possible economic value. Better understanding the relationship between social value derived by a community using the network and the associated business model that would provide economic benefit is an important consideration. In the same context, (Sangwan et al., 2009) emphasise the importance of extending the communications theory of a "sense of community" into a virtual context – an emotionally positive effect which creates an intrinsically rewarding reason to continue participating in an on-line community. They identify how the organizers of a virtual social network can use such theory to increase participation by and satisfaction of their members.

6 CONCLUSION

Virtual social networks enable the formation of virtual communities that share common social interests and generate social "value" for their members. Identifying how business models can be associated with such social value has been a dominant focus of many social networking sites. We describe the notion of a Social Cloud – where computational resources (in addition to simple exchange of content – such as messages, photos, etc) can be exchanged between members. Whereas content is passive – i.e. it is published and accessed via an on-line portal – computational resources are not. A user participating in a Social Cloud must enable access to their hard disk for data storage, and must therefore trust the other individual. We discuss how the friend relationships in social networks can be used as a basis for defining such relationships. A survey of the associated business models is also provided. We believe this is a first step towards better understanding how social networks can be used to support more active resource sharing on the Internet.

REFERENCES

Afuah, A., & Tucci, C. (2001). *Internet Business Models and Strategies*. New York: McGraw Hill.

Allee, V. (2003). *The Future of Knowledge: Increasing Prosperity through Value Networks*. Oxford, UK: Butterworth-Heinemann.

AlShabib, H., Rana, O., & Shaikh Ali, A. (2006). Deriving ratings through social network structures. In *Proceedings of International Conference on Availability, Reliability and Security (ARES'06)*, Vienna, Austria. Washington, DC: IEEE Computer Society Press.

Andrade, N., Brasileiro, F., Mowbray, M., & Cirne, W. (2010). A reciprocation-based Economy for multiple services in a Computational Grid. In Buyya, R., & Bubendorder, K. (Eds.), *Market-Oriented Grid and Utility Computing* (pp. 357–370). New York: John Wiley & Sons.

Black, S., Harrison, R., & Baldwin, M. (2010, May 2-8). A Survey of Social Media Use in Software Systems Development. In *Proceedings of Web2SE workshop*, Cape Town, South Africa.

Black, S., & Jacobs, J. (2010, May 2-8). Using Web 2.0 to Improve Software Quality. In *Proceedings of Web2SE workshop (ICSE 2010)*, Cape Town, South Africa.

Burcher, N. (2010). *Facebook Usage Statistics Based on Country*. Retrieved April 15, 2010, from http://www.nickburcher.com/2010/03/facebook-usage-statistics-march-2010.html

Chard, K., Caton, S., Rana, O., & Bubendorfer, K. (2010, July). Cloud Computing in Social Networks. In *Proceedings of IEEE "Cloud 2010" conference*. Miami, FL: Social Cloud.

Even-Dar, E., & Shapira, A. (2007). A note on maximizing the spread of influence in social networks. In *Proceedings of the Third International Conference On Internet and Network Economics*, San Diego, CA (LNCS 4858, pp. 281-286).

Ghose, A., & Yang, S. (2009). *An Empirical Analysis of Search Engine Advertising: Sponsored Search in Electronic Markets*. Retrieved from http://opimweb.wharton.upenn.edu/documents/seminars/paidsearch.pdf

Gurses, S., Rizk, R., & Gunther, O. (2008). Privacy Design in Online Social Networks: Learning from Privacy Breaches and Community Feedback. In *Proceedings of ICIS, Association for Information Systems Conference*.

Keahey, K., Foster, I., Freeman, T., & Zhang, X. (2005). Virtual workspaces: Achieving quality of service and quality of life in the grid. *Scientific Programming Journal*, *13*(4), 265–276.

Korzenny, F. (2009). *Marketing Trends in a new Multi-Cultural Society*. Retrieved April 10, 2010, from http://felipekorzenny.blogspot.com/2009/02/multicultural-world-of-social-media.html

Leskovec, J., Adamic, L., & Huberman, B. (2007). The dynamics of viral marketing. *ACM Transactions on the Web*, *1*(1).

Nurmi, D., Wolski, R., Grzegorczyk, C., Obertelli, G., Soman, S., Youseff, L., et al. (2009). The Eucalyptus open-source Cloud-computing System. In *Proceedings of 9th IEEE International Symposium on Cluster Computing and the Grid (CCGrid 09)*, Shanghai, China.

Ofcom. (2008). *Social Networking: A quantitative and qualitative research report into attitudes, behaviours and use*. Retrieved from http://www.ofcom.org.uk

Osterwalder, A. (2004). *The Business Model Ontology*. Unpublished doctoral dissertation, HEC, Lusanne, Switzerland.

Sangwan, S., Guan, C., & Siguaw, J. (2009). Virtual Social Networks: Toward A Research Agenda. *International Journal of Virtual Communities and Social Networking, 1*(1).

Shang, R.-A., Chen, Y.-C., & Liao, H.-J. (2006). The value of participation in virtual consumer communities on brand loyalty. *Internet Research, 16*(4), 398–418. doi:10.1108/10662240610690025

Stanoevska-Slabeva, K., Parrilli, D., & Thanos, G. (2008). BEinGRID: Development of Business Models for the Grid Industry. In *Proceedings of GECON 2008 workshop* (LNCS 5206, pp. 140-151).

Szmigin, I., Canning, L., & Reppel, A. (2006). Online community: enchancing the relationship marketing concept through customer bonding. *International Journal of Service Industry Management, 16*(5).

Taylor, S., & McKee, P. (2010). Grid Business Models, Evaluation, and Principles. In Buyya, R., & Bubendorder, K. (Eds.), *Market-Oriented Grid and Utility Computing*. New York: John Wiley & Sons.

Timmers, T. (1998). Business Models for Electronic Markets. *Electronic Markets, 8*(2), 3-8. Retrieved April 15, 2010, from http://www.electronicmarkets.org/issues/volume-8/volume-8-issue-2/businessmodels0.pdf

Yubo, C., & Jinhong, X. (2008). Online Consumer Review: Word-of-Mouth as a new element of Markeing Communication Mix. *Management Science, 54*(3), 477–491. doi:10.1287/mnsc.1070.0810

Zlotogorski, M. (2010). *Becoming More Socially Networked in Emerging Markets*. Retrieved May 1, 2010, from http://www.tmforum.org/community/blogs/leadership_blog/archive/2010/04/19/becoming-more-socially-networked-in-emerging-markets.aspx

This work was previously published in the International Journal of Virtual Communities and Social Networking, Volume 2, Issue 3, edited by Subhasish Dasgupta, pp. 31-41, copyright 2010 by IGI Publishing (an imprint of IGI Global).

Chapter 12
Occupational Networking as a Form of Professional Identification:
The Case of Highly–Skilled IT Contractors

Katerina Voutsina
London School of Economics and Political Science, UK

ABSTRACT

The impact of virtual networks on economic activity and organizational affairs has long occupied the Information Systems (IS) academic community. Yet what has been paid less attention is the impact of networks on the way contemporary workers perceive themselves at work. Taking into account this gap in the literature, the paper aspires to bring forward issues referring to the implication of virtual networks in the construction of occupational identity of highly-skilled Information Technology (IT) contractors. Drawing upon data from interviews with thirty highly-skilled IT contractors, the paper suggests that the virtual networks among IT contractors and individuals who share the same occupational interests become for the contractors the locus of social interaction, the hub of knowledge generation, the source of occupational control and thus the primary object of professional identification.

INTRODUCTION

The networks within which organizational actors are embedded are proved to have important consequences on their working lives and organizational affairs in general. Over the last decade, from Castell's (1996) seminal study of network society till Benkler's (2006) work on social modes of production, and even long time before that

(Granovetter's, 1983) study on social ties), we have learnt a great deal about the various desirable outcomes which stem out of the proliferation of network-like forms of organizing and networks in general.

A long-standing literature analyses the significance of networks among individual organizational actors and refers to the study of *virtual teams, communities of practice* (Brown & Duguid,

DOI: 10.4018/978-1-4666-1553-3.ch012

1991; Lave & Wenger, 1991; Wenger, 1998) and *social networks* (Benkler, 2006). Individuals with common interests come together and collaborate gaining advantage from the associated economies of experience and specialization inherent in collective action (Kallinikos, 2006; McLure Wasko & Faraj, 2005; Nardi, Whittaker, & Schwarz, 2002; Sassen, 2001; Sinha & Van de Ven, 2005). Through their participation in these open and fluid patterns of interaction and collaboration, individuals manage their *knowledge capital* (Barley & Kunda, 2004; Osnowitz, 2006; Zammuto, Griffith, Majchrzak, Dougherty, & Faraj, 2007), seek for *job referrals and job opportunities* (Granovetter, 1983; Laubacher & Malone, 1997; Nardi et al., 2002) and become the producers of information based goods and services (Benkler, 2006; Von Hippel & Von Krogh, 2006).

Common to these studies is that are mainly concerned with the perceived benefits for individuals and organizations as a result of their participation in these networks. Focus of the above research is how the mode of production has been revolutionized as a consequence of the networks' impact on the organization of the resources in the economy. Yet, today we still have much to learn about how networks impact on the way contemporary workers perceive themselves at work. In other words, little is known about the way networks are implicated in the individuals' attempt to make sense of their professional identity and the roles ascribed to it.

Such a research scope is well-timed, since contemporary workers seem to have been left all alone without a strong institutional setting providing guidance and meaning to their work-related actions. In the absence of a "lifetime employment", an "organizational tenure", a stable" career ladder", the individual move from the one organization to the other or enter the contingent workforce according to the fluctuations of the labor market and the conditions governing the corresponding business sector. In a workplace, where an individualized work ethic dominates and the only constant is change, the individual's

struggle to find a source of professional identification is stronger than ever before. This paper seeks to reveal where highly-skilled Information Technology (IT) contractors draw upon in order to construct their professional identities. In particular, it portrays how virtual networks are implicated in the attempt of IT contractors to construct a meaningful and coherent professional identity.

Assuming that the notion of professional identity is very much related to the roles that the individual is expected to fulfill, we investigate the way highly-skilled IT contractors perceive the roles they are called to play in today's turbulent environment. We show how three roles that contractors perceive as being core ones to their professional image (Barley & Kunda, 2004) are influenced by the contractors' participation in virtual networks. We show how the IT contractors' attempt to a) build meaningful careers in their own eyes, b) prove their competency in performing the assigned task in the eyes of the managers and permanent employees, and c) embrace the values of reciprocity and trust in the eyes of the virtual and informal networks, is supported and partly shaped by their participation in virtual networks with other IT contractors/IT peers.

The empirical data indicates that virtual networks among IT contractors and individuals who share the same occupational interests become for the contractors the locus of social interaction, the hub of knowledge generation, the source of occupational control and thus the primary object of professional identification. Although these networks do not have the formal power of traditional occupational communities, they are still powerful social formations. Virtual networks are found to implicitly or explicitly invoke particular patterns of behavior and rules of conduct and be strongly implicated in the construction of IT contractors' professional identity.

The paper is organized as follows: The next section outlines the theoretical underpinnings of the professional identity and a brief literature of IS profession. The third section presents the empirical study. The forth section presents and discusses the finding results and last section concludes the paper.

THEORETICAL UNDERPINNINGS OF PROFESSIONAL IDENTITY AND IS PROFESSIONALS

Identity –the self and the presentation of the self- has long been viewed as emerging and being constructed through a person' s interaction with other people who share and coexist within the same context (Goffman, 1971; Mead, 1934). Social identity refers to a common identification of the person with a collectivity, a social group or a social category (Tajfel, 1982); «a strong identity involves deep connections with others through shared histories and experiences, reciprocity, affection and mutual commitment (Wenger, 2000, p. 239). Social identities support individuals in making sense of who they are, how they relate to other people around them and how they should act in social situations (Kramer, 2006). In practice, identity is often considered synonymous to the internalization of diverse roles; it is composed by the distinctive meanings the person attaches/ inscribes to the multiple roles she is expected to play under various kinds of circumstances and contingencies (Stryker & Burke, 2000). The way a person behaves is the enactment of a spectrum of roles which jointly constitute the amalgam of her identity.

Professional identity - a particular category of social identity- refers to the way individuals perceive and describe themselves and the roles they are expected to fulfill under particular organizational settings; it is the very way individuals perceive and construe themselves in relation to their work and the work of others who jointly participate in the same circuit of production process (Walsham, 1998). It is well known that employees who practice the same profession tend to band together into occupational communities and draw their identities out of the values and norms shared in these communities (Ramachandran & Rao, 2006, p. 198). The members of these communities «claim a distinctive and valued social identity, share a common perspective toward the mission and practices of the occupation and take part in a sort of interactive fellowship that transcends the workplace» (Van Maanen & Barley, 1984). The discourse developed in these communities is considered to be central in the process of identification (Ezzamel & Willmott, 1998).

Research on professional identity testimonies that the latter is related to both moral and work values, such as dignity, altruism, intellectual and personal stimulation (Fagermoen, 1997). Professional identity enables individuals to locate themselves and effectively navigate within the sphere of a globalized and volatile workspace. In other words, the professional identity (Kramer, 2006, p. 29): a) provides guidance, indicating the legitimate and appropriate courses of action, b) ensures consistency and continuity in the worker's behavior over time, and c) defines the degree and nature of distinctiveness of the person in relation to other groups (Karreman & Alvesson, 2001), by reinforcing the reasons that justify particular types of behavior for the members of a specific occupational community.

As far as the Information Systems (IS) community is concerned, there are divergent opinions about whether it should be considered a professional community or not. Generally speaking, the problems associated with the establishment of a professional identity are not new in the literature (Beker, 2001). "The first American programmers were recruited largely on the basis of their enthusiasm, not their credentials" (Kraft & Dubnoff, 1986). Sixty-five years after the emergence of software jobs as distinct occupations, there have been made numerous efforts to delineate the "border lines" of a computer science curriculum and the job content related to it (Leitheiser, 1992; Noll & Wlikins, 2002; Todd & McKeen, 1995).

Scarbrough (1999) claims that IT specialists could be regarded as water-down version of "professionals", as "semi-professionals", members of an occupation that has some but not all the characteristics of a formal profession. He argues that although these IT groups lack the formal power of classic professions, -in the sense that their organizational bodies are weak or non-existent and that they exercise much less control over their work supply conditions/ entry accessibility-, they do display certain attributes of the professional model. Denning (2001) commenting on the extend to which IT craft meets certain criteria for being considered a profession, concludes: a) IT has a significant contribution in today's world, b) IT has established a body of principles which is represented through the conceptual knowledge codified in the curricula of IS degrees, c)there are some global professional associations (mainly ACM and IEEE) which have articulated some codes of ethics, but they are not really in position to enforce them, and d) there is no a licensing organization that certifies the body of practices and technical competence displayed by IT people.

For the purposes of this paper, the notion of professional identity will be treated as being synonymous to the general notion of occupational identity which in turn will be reduced to specific roles that highly-skilled contractors are expected to fulfill as members of the IS occupational community. Let us be more specific.

IT contractors are considered to epitomize the construction of occupational identities for both contingent workers and full-time IT employees who display a great rate of turnover and move frequently from the one employing organization to the other. Highly-skilled IT contractors are always on the move, develop ephemeral types of relationships with heterogeneous groups of people and are continuously called to perform their job in dissimilar organizational settings. A large part of the communication and interaction with their client-firms may take place in a virtual mode, while the actual performance of the task can be done remotely or in-house according to the special needs of the project. By disassociating the notion of the self from the immediate context of

practice and the traditional view of employment, IT contractors are faced with the challenge to develop «a coherent identity that could account for their experience and guide their actions» (Barley & Kunda, 2004, p. 216). In the absence of a powerful corporation or professional association, entitled to enforce a code of ethics and certify the body of legitimized practices, the issue of identity construction for contingent IT workers becomes more crucial than ever before.

The paper reels off the tangle of professional identity by analyzing the multiple roles that IT contractors are called to play. It draws upon the assumption that highly-skilled IT contractors construct their professional identity by ascribing a purposeful meaning to three basic roles inherent in their occupation (Barley & Kunda, 2004): a) In their own eyes, they have to build meaningful careers by pursuing challenging tasks, b) in the eyes of the managers and permanent employees, they have to prove their dexterity, honesty and competency in performing the assigned task, and c) in the eyes of the virtual and informal networks, they have to embrace the values of reciprocity and trust. In each case the expectations to be met vary and the definition of the most appropriate behavior is open to multiple interpretations. Yet all these roles jointly construct the identity of highly-skilled IT contractors.

Placed in this context, the paper suggests that the IT contractors' attempt to fulfill the aforementioned roles and build a coherent professional identity cannot be fully understood without taking into account the possibilities of action and social interaction enabled by virtual networks.

METHODOLOGY

The empirical data of the research stemmed from qualitative interviews (Evans, Kunda, & Barley, 2004; Kunda, Barley, & Evans, 2002; Patton, 1980) which were conducted with thirty IT professionals working as independent contractors in Greece. This group of informants has been deliberately selected as their working practices epitomize the controversial and elusive character of current professional identities. The interviews aspired to delineate the respondents' perceptions about their occupational identity and check the involvement –if any- of ICTs in it. Therefore, the respondents were asked about how they perform their work in a daily basis, the knowledge items they draw upon to do their work, the roles they perceive as mandatory for them to fulfill, where they find their customers, the challenges they face as contractors, etc.

Given that there is no an established classification of IT individuals who work as freelancers, the selection of informants was not a straightforward process (Evans et al., 2004). Informants were selected both from a list of the members of the Federation of Greek IS personnel as well as from the lists of alumni of the two most highly regarded universities in Greece. The selection of the informants followed the logic of a snowball sampling, i.e., respondents were asked to provide details of others whose working profile matched the unit of analysis for the current study (Evans et al., 2004; Faugier & Sargeant, 1997). The choice of three unrelated sources aimed at enhancing objectivity in the selection process of the informants. Nevertheless, the respondents cannot be considered as representative of the relevant population in Greece and the research results of the study did not aim at adhering to the principle of statistical generalization.

The research approach is classified under the realm of the interpretive epistemological paradigm (Kaplan & Maxwell, 1994; Orlikowski & Baroudi, 1991; Walsham, 1993). It displays an exploratory and explanatory orientation and relies upon the analysis of multiple case-studies (Yin, 2003). Each respondent constitutes a case-study. In-depth qualitative interviews (Patton, 1980) were conducted, falling under the logic of replication and being destined to support an analytic generalization of the results (Yin, 2003). By juxtaposing

multiple perspectives and viewpoints stemming from the investigated cases, the study intended to reduce the possibility of significant divergence in the stories recounted and build a well-sustained interpretation of the phenomenon under study.

Eight out of the thirty interviewees were general IT consultants and managers. Five of the interviewees had highly specialized skills in a very particular technology or commercial off-the-shelf software packages such as those manufactured by SAP (www.sap.com). The remaining 17 interviewees specialized in a wider range of technologies. All the interviewees had university degrees in computer science or related subjects, and they all had at least five years work experience. Interviews were conducted at the participants' work places in Athens, Greece, between September 2005 and April 2007. Each interview lasted between 90 and 120 minutes and was recorded for subsequent transcription. In some cases, the initial interview was supplemented by a shorter follow-up interview aimed at clarifying ambivalent issues raised during transcription. In total 38 interviews were conducted totaling 58 hours of recorded interviews with the thirty respondents.

IT-ENABLED PROFESSIONAL NETWORKS AS A SOURCE OF PROFESSIONAL IDENTIFICATION

The Attempt to Form Meaningful Careers and the Need for Knowledge Update

In their own eyes, highly-skilled contractors had to form meaningful careers by pursuing challenging tasks. To them contracting was the opportunity to escape from the irrationalities and boredom related to the negative sides of corporate life. As contractors, they believed that they could regain control over their work and time. Their work activities were no longer dictated by short-sighted managers. They could choose the projects that would allow them to maximize their potential as workers and advance their skills and career. Yet, they were soon faced with a new challenge: in order to be able to assert challenging projects and be sought-after in an open market where competition was strong, they had to keep themselves technically up-to-date and be aware of the latest technological trends in their field. According to their own understanding, their possibility to pursue challenging projects was positively related to their ability to maintain and constantly update the repository of their knowledge. Such an endeavor was not such a straightforward process for IT individual contractors for two main reasons.

Firstly, they all noticed that the rate by which information is recycled/updated and knowledge is renewed in the IS field is so quick that often they can hardly keep track of it. One contractor mentioned that by the time a book is released to press, it is already considered to be obsolete. Secondly, there are too many similar new technologies and suggested approaches that are promoted as solutions to the very same technical problem and very little time to actually try out and compare the various alternatives. Due to information overload, the respondents often felt quite frustrated about what technology/approach to choose and where to invest their resources in order to enhance their career prospects. These kinds of concerns related to the professional development of IT workers were traditionally held by the employing organization and were relatively eased through the social interaction among the corporate employees. Yet, in the case of IT contractors, there was no more a single, «stable» employing organization which would be held responsible for the professional training and career planning of its employees (Barley & Kunda, 2004; Kunda & Van Maanen, 1999) nor a space where individuals could interact and share their occupational concerns.

To fulfill the need of professional development, IT experts formed networks of relationships with ex-peers with whom they shared the same professional interests, as well as with other contractors

whom they had met through their joint participation in projects (Barley & Kunda, 2004). Through these informal networks, IT contractors exchange technical information about problems they encounter on the job, they get informed about new technologies, they get aware of existing opportunities of training seminars, etc. Both the formation and the sustainability of these networks has almost solely relied upon the use of e-mail and instant messaging technologies which enable the easy and cost-effective communication among agents across the globe (Castells, 2000). Additionally to their membership into informal professional networks, the IT contractors frequently participated in internet based bulletin boards, users' groups, etc. It is worth noticing that in these web spaces, the contractors acquire accurate and detailed information not only about the launch and the general use of state-of-the art technologies, but also about how to tackle specific problems and particularities related to that technology.

To put it in other words, the above electronically-enabled networks among peers constituted the virtual places where IT contractors with common interests and concerns gather regularly to "trade stories and share advice" (Laubacher & Malone, 1997, p. 5) about technical problems they were puzzled about. Through dialogue and the juxtaposition of various opinions on the very same subject, the contractors were able to filter the information that they gather in the web and form a more substantiated view of the issues they were interested in.

In the same respect, through dialogue they could access more amount of information in less time. And most importantly this information was judged, evaluated and contextualized since it was usually embedded within the experiential perception of the individual. In addition, due to the personalization of the interaction (the majority of bulletin boards and Usenet groups, etc. required from the participants to register and have a nickname) the reliability of the opinion or the answer articulated was weighed by the participant's reputation in the network. Each member's reputation was formed out of her previous streams of interaction with the members of the network.

It is worth noticing that apart from the accessibility to rich and timely information, these virtual networks constituted hubs of knowledge generation. Professional knowledge has always been dependent upon the on-going interaction of individuals of the same profession. Barley and Kunda (2001) draw the attention to the fact that "technical knowledge is encoded in and transferred through the narratives that technicians recount for themselves and each other". "Intermingling" with peers and sharing a repertoire of commonly accepted norms and resources, such as "language, routines, sensibilities, artifacts, tools, stories, styles, etc." (Wenger, 2000, p. 229) is the process through which competence is tested and built in practice. Learning, understanding and interpreting, being able to distinguish which is the most appropriate decision to make according to the emergent work contingencies – constructing one's own professional identity-, is something which is not easily articulated in words nor embedded in abstract theoretical axioms of knowledge (Brown & Duguid, 1991); it is rather something developed within a communal context and framed through active participation (Brown & Duguid, 1991; Lave, 1988; Wenger, 1998).

For IT contractors, this kind of communal technical knowledge which was previously residing in the verbal narratives of collocated employees is now encapsulated in the electronic threads of dialogue occurring among members of the network dispersed across the globe. In other words, these virtual assemblages offered the respondents accessibility to the accumulated experience and consolidated knowledge of a whole expert community which was considered critical in their attempt to build a meaningful career as contractors.

In conclusion, it could be argued that the electronic networks among ex-peers, friends and people who share the same professional interests are proved to replace the traditional fellowships among co-workers operating under the very same roof. Through their participation in this kind of social assemblages, the IT contractors updated their technical knowledge, built new knowledge and increase their possibility in being able to pursue challenging projects.

THE TESTIMONY OF DEXTERITY, HONESTY AND COMPETENCY

In their attempt to fulfill the role of a good and reliable IT contractor, the respondents had to prove to both managers and permanent employees their dexterity, honesty and competency in performing the assigned task. They could perform their work remotely (from their home or personal office) or within the client's premises according to the special requirements of the project.

Working From Distance and the Importance of Reputation

In cases where they worked from home or their personal office, interaction with the firm's employees was completely absent; IT contractors had regular meetings only with the project manager to whom they were accountable for the progress of their work. Usually the manager was not able to check upon the process by which the highly-skilled contractor performing the assigned task, but aimed at assessing the outcome of the delivered work packages. Commenting on the manager's inability to directly supervise and assess their work, the respondents mentioned that often their dexterity, honesty and competency in performing the prospective project was tested and assessed even before the signing of the contract. They noted that the new digitalized world of work has made them visible to their future client-firms in new ways: their personal web-pages, their membership and active participation to virtual networks, forums, blogs and bulletin boards have rendered their trajectories in the business field more traceable than ever before. And they pursued to be that visible and traceable.

They emphasized that they deliberately pursued the on-line exposure of their past and present contribution to the IS and business community. They actively participated to the on-line forums and Usenet groups, they had built their professional web-page and blog and they were regularly leaving comments on other professional blogs. Through their on-line presence in virtual communities and public virtual spaces, they were demonstrating the practical application of their expertise and their professional ethos and subsequently increased their possibilities to attract new clients. The reputation that the IT contractors build is manifested in the discourse of the virtual community and widely spread across the market. The majority of their client-firms had already formed an idea about their reputation in the market even before meeting them for the signing of the contract.

In this sense, the overall professional conduct and occupational trajectory of individuals became more visible and traceable than ever before. The possibilities of connectivity among geographically dispersed agents and the cost- and time-efficient pace of circulation of the information, enabled by the extended use of Information and Communication Technologies, created 'panopticon-like' structures of surveillance and control (Zuboff, 1988). Recognition of the effect unreliable conduct may have on reputation (Fombrum & Shanley, 1990; Sharma, 1997) and the potential of future employability make contractors think twice before displaying an unreliable kind of behavior. Reputation effects are believed to extend beyond a single agent-principal exchange and the value of human capital is presumed to degrade if word spreads that a particular agent has not previously served principals in good faith (Sharma, 1997, p. 778).

At the absence of an institutionally established professional body or occupational community, the contractors' quality of participation and the degree of socialization in a particular network seemed to reflect of their dexterities and competencies

in being efficient workers. Interestingly enough, these virtual professional assemblages, apart from implicitly certifying the body of scientific principles and practices of their members, they also provided the credentials about their professional ethos and prospective reliable behavior.

Working at the Client's Premises and the Need for Collegiality

In cases where the respondents worked at the client's premises the interaction between the IT contractor and the firm's employees was kept at an elementary level of communication. The highly-skilled IT contractor was hired by the firm to do what the permanent employees could not do and she was often paid double the salary rate of a permanent employee. Hostile reactions and anti-social behavior by the permanent staff were not rare (Barley & Kunda, 2004). After all, the highly-skilled contractor was expected to display superior performance at the client's premises, and not learn-by-doing. The respondents noted that working at the client-firm's premises is like having to take exams every single day. There was no room for wrong estimations or for seeking advice from permanent employees.

Nevertheless, quite often the respondents, no matter how much gifted they were at their craft, were faced with dilemma about how to proceed in order to deliver the assigned task within the agreed time frames and they expressed the necessity of listening a second opinion, or asking for some piece of advice. Under these circumstances, they addressed their concerns and sought assistance from the virtual networks of IT people. IT contractors substituted face-to-face communication among co-located colleagues with virtual communication among IT experts dispersed all around the globe.

The virtual networks the IT contractors were leaning on to ask help and advice may be possibly parallelized with the *intentional networks*, social network of people who collaborate in order to get work done (Nardi et al., 2002). An IT virtual network is consisted by IT experts who come from all over the world and display a significant interest in IS related topics. Although these people do not participate in the very same activity, they all share a general collective motive, namely the evolution of IS artifacts and IS discipline respectively. The notion of an IT virtual network could be considered to include both the idea of cooperation and collaboration, as defined by Lewis (1997, p. 213): "Cooperation depends upon a supportive community of actors who agree to help one another in activities aimed at attaining the goals of each person involved. Collaboration depends upon the establishment of a common meaning and language in the task which leads to the community setting a common goal". Although the members of the virtual networks are not directly involved into the project undertaken by the individual IT contractor, they contribute substantially in the way tasks are being performed by the supply of crucial information that the IT expert could not otherwise acquire.

Embracing the Values of Reciprocity and Trust as Members of the Virtual Network

Members of these networks tend to have the characteristics of the members of clans (Ouchi, 1980). The members are tied together through bonds of reciprocity and trust, share mutually defined goals and have internalized the same norms and values. Through social interaction, contract professionals constitute a culture with informal expectations for participation and standards for occupational practice. Adherence to cultural codes and norms marks practitioners as occupational members in good standing (Osnowitz, 2006). A highly-skilled contractor may choose to behave in generous and collegial way, because such a behavior is consistent with his/her identity as a "good colleague", "real professional", and such a behavior is applauded by the members of the community.

Yet, as already stated in the previous sections, this kind of virtual groups among peers, operated as a repositories of knowledge and indirect triggers of job placement in the market (through the management of members' reputation). Conformance to the values and norms of groups (the tendency to embrace the values of reciprocity and trust) seems to be a necessary prerequisite of a successful contracting career and life; a prerequisite which could not easily overlooked.

As noted above although these virtual networks were not consisted by individuals who knew each other in person, they allowed, at least to some extent, the personalization of the interactions. Quite often, many popular users' groups and bulletin boards require the new member to get registered before having access to their databases. As a result, members of these virtual communities are rendered 'recognizable' through their nicknames. Similarly, every single move a member does is recorded *and* stored in the website, i.e., how many times one has asked for help and how many times she has provided help. In particular, it is easy to detect if a member is strictly self-interested or cares for the welfare of the community. For instance, when a member does not search in the database about a potential answer to her problem and prefers to directly pose a question to the community, if the question has already been answered, this member is considered to waste the resources of the community. And such a behavior is not well viewed by the community. In addition, the quality of the member's answer/contribution is indirectly assessed and appreciated: prompt and substantial contribution to the group allows the member to achieve recognition and fame among the members of the group. And such fame and recognition can be translated in various ways, i.e., job offers, collegial support.

Bearing in mind the above, it could be argued that the values of reciprocity and trust were not solely enforced by the internalization of norms and codes of ethics supported by the occupational culture (Kunda, 1992), but also originated in the realization of the fact that a good reputation among peers has been the only relative 'guarantee' for contractors to stay technically updated, marketable and employable.

DISCUSSION AND CONCLUSION

This paper brings forward issues referring to the implication of virtual networks in the construction of the occupational identity of highly-skilled IT contractors. IT contractors are considered to epitomize the construction of occupational identities in current globalized work place, where time and space become disembedded from the notion of social activity and work becomes fragmented or modular, project-based or network-centered.

In the absence of an institutionally established professional association or a dominant employing organization as the main sources of professional identification and moral attachment (Barley & Kunda, 2004), highly-skilled IT contractors are faced with the challenge to redefine their occupational identity: they need to find another social group or collectivity which would provide some guidance for their actions and ascribe meaning to the various roles that they are called to play (Stryker & Burke, 2000) in current work setting.

Findings of the study suggest that IT contractors' attempt to form a coherent occupational identity is mediated by their participation in electronic occupational networks. These networks among peers constitute the virtual places where IT contractors with common interests and concerns gather regularly to «trade stories and share advice» (Laubacher & Malone, 1997, p. 5). As members of these networks, IT contractors are given the chance to 'intermingle' with peers, share communal problems and occupational interests, and thus construe an image about themselves in relation to their work and the work of their fellows (Walsham, 1998).

In particular, through their participation in these interactive fellowships, they enact three roles which are perceived as vital in the construction of their occupational identity (Barley & Kunda, 2004). Firstly, they are able to pursue challenging tasks and build meaningful careers by updating their knowledge and acquiring new knowledge. Secondly, they are able to prove their competence to the clients and get their skills 'certified' by drawing upon the resources of the network. And thirdly, they can account for collegial and professional behavior by supporting the members of the virtual network and displaying their devotion to their craft. In total, the virtual networks become for IT contractors the locus of social interaction, the hub of knowledge generation, the source of occupational control and thus the primary object of professional identification (Laubacher & Malone, 1997).

It is worth noticing that the importance of the networks in activities, such as knowledge acquisition (Brown & Duguid, 1991), reputation management (Jones, Hesterly, & Borgatti, 1997), work performance (Nardi et al., 2002), collegiality and normative control approaches (Osnowitz, 2006) is not something new in the literature. Yet, the pervasiveness and centrality of the virtual networks in every single occupational practice performed by the highly-skilled IT contractors have given to these networks a new significance whose impact remains still largely unexplored.

The breach and immediacy of connections, the digitization of all interactions and the dissipation of time and space (Castells, 1996) gave these virtual networks a distinctive formative power on the highly-skilled IT contractors' behavior. IT professionals' knowledge, performance, and code of ethics have always accrued and tested in practice and through interaction with peers in real time settings and physical spaces. Yet, the on-line communication and interaction among peers raise new challenges regarding the very constitution of these occupational practices. For instance, several studies have highlighted the fact that the breadth of potential receptors and the bi-directional communication capabilities brought about by the Internet have challenged our understanding of the reputational effects on the individual's prospective employability and access to knowledge (Castells, 1996; Dellarocas, 2003). IT contractors are empowered since they can draw upon the technological capabilities in order to seek advice and get customers from all over the world, while at the same time they become more vulnerable since everything they do is transparent and potentially subject to any kind of criticism. It could be argued that the possibilities of increased transparency and the perceived degree of relative democratization of internet raise concerns of self-discipline, power and control. In addition, the absence of contextual cues and lack of direct observation may potentially blur the boundary between information and interpretation of information challenging the inscription of meaning to actions and roles. Further research should be carried out in order to shed light to the above concerns and provide a fine-grained analysis of the challenges introduced by the electronically constructed occupational identities.

In conclusion, we argue that the role of electronic networks among peers and people who share the same occupational interests becomes more and more prevalent in constitution of occupational practices and subsequently of occupational identities. These networks, although being deprived of formally institutionalized power, are found to implicitly or explicitly invoke particular patterns of behavior and rules of conduct in contemporary work place. Their distinctive impact on the constitution of occupational edifice, -particularly in opposition to the traditional word-of-mouth networks and locally-based occupational associations- needs to be further illuminated and explored.

REFERENCES

Barley, S. R., & Kunda, G. (2001). Bringing Work Back In. *Organization Science, 12*(1), 76–95. doi:10.1287/orsc.12.1.76.10122

Barley, S. R., & Kunda, G. (2004). *Gurus, Hired Guns, and Warm Bodies: Itinerant Experts in a Knowledge Economy*. Princeton, NJ: Princeton University Press.

Beker, J. (2001). Development of professional identity for the child care worker. *Child and Youth Care Forum, 30*(6), 345–354. doi:10.1023/A:1015360917095

Benkler, Y. (2006). *The Wealth of Networks: How Social Production Transforms Markets and Freedom*. New Haven, CT: Yale University Press.

Brown, S. J., & Duguid, P. (1991). Organizational Learning and Communities-of-Practice: Toward a Unified View of Working, Learning and Innovation. *Organization Science, 1*, 40–57. doi:10.1287/orsc.2.1.40

Castells, M. (1996). *The rise of the network society*. Oxford, UK: Blackwell.

Castells, M. (2000). *The rise of the network society* (2nd ed.). Oxford, UK: Blackwell.

Dellarocas, C. (2003). The Digitization of Word of Mouth: Promise and Challenges of Online Feedback Mechanisms. *Management Science, 49*(10), 1407–1424. doi:10.1287/mnsc.49.10.1407.17308

Denning, J. P. (2001). The profession of IT: Who Are We? *Communications of the ACM, 44*(2), 15–19. doi:10.1145/359205.359239

Evans, J. A., Kunda, G., & Barley, S. R. (2004). Beach time, bridge and billable time hours: The temporal structure of technical contracting. *Administrative Science Quarterly, 49*(1), 1–38.

Ezzamel, M., & Willmott, H. (1998). Accounting for teamwork: A critical study of group-based systems of organizational control. *Administrative Science Quarterly, 43*(2), 358–396. doi:10.2307/2393856

Fagermoen, M. S. (1997). Professional identity: values embedded in meaningful nursing practice. *Journal of Advanced Nursing, 25*(3), 434–441. doi:10.1046/j.1365-2648.1997.1997025434.x

Faugier, J., & Sargeant, M. (1997). Sampling hard to reach populations. *Journal of Advanced Nursing, 26*, 790–797. doi:10.1046/j.1365-2648.1997.00371.x

Fombrum, C., & Shanley, M. (1990). What is the name? Reputation building and corporate strategy. *Academy of Management Journal, 33*(2), 233–258. doi:10.2307/256324

Goffman, E. (1971). *The presentation of self in everyday life*. New York: Penguin.

Granovetter, M. (1983). The Strength of Weak Ties: A Network Theory Revisited. *Sociological Theory, 1*, 201–233. doi:10.2307/202051

Jones, C., Hesterly, W. S., & Borgatti, S. P. (1997). A general theory of network governance: Exchange conditions and social mechanisms. *Academy of Management Review, 22*(4), 911–945. doi:10.2307/259249

Kallinikos, J. (2006). *The consequences of information: Institutional implications of technical change*. Cheltenham, UK: Edward Elgar.

Kaplan, B., & Maxwell, J. A. (1994). Qualitative Research Methods for Evaluating Computer Information Systems. In Anderson, G. J., Aydin, E. C., & Jay, J. S. (Eds.), *Evaluating Health Care Information Systems: Methods and Applications* (pp. 45–68). Thousand Oaks, CA: Sage.

Karreman, D., & Alvesson, M. (2001). Making Newsmakers: Conversational Identity at Work. *Organization Studies, 22*(1), 59–89. doi:10.1177/017084060102200103

Kraft, P., & Dubnoff, S. (1986). Job Content, Fragmentation and Control in Computer Software Work. *Industrial Relations, 25*(2), 184–196. doi:10.1111/j.1468-232X.1986.tb00679.x

Kramer, M. R. (2006). Social Identity and Social Capital: The Collective Self at Work. *International Public Management Journal, 9*(1), 25–45. doi:10.1080/10967490600625316

Kunda, G. (1992). *Engineering culture: control and commitment in a high-tech corporation*. Philadelphia: Temple University Press.

Kunda, G., Barley, S. R., & Evans, J. (2002). Why do contractors contract? The experience of highly skilled technical professionals in a contingent labor market. *Industrial & Labor Relations Review, 55*(2), 234–261. doi:10.2307/2696207

Kunda, G., & Van Maanen, J. (1999). *Changing Scripts at Work: Managers and Professionals*. Paper presented at the ANNALS, AAPSS (p. 561).

Laubacher, R. J., & Malone, T. W. (1997). *Flexible work arrangements and the 21st century workers' guilds*. Cambridge, MA: MIT.

Lave, J. (1988). *Cognition in Practice: Mind, Mathematics and Culture in Everyday Life*. New York: Cambridge University Press. doi:10.1017/CBO9780511609268

Lave, J., & Wenger, E. (1991). *Situated Learning: Legitimate Peripheral Participation*. Cambridge, UK: Cambridge University Press.

Leitheiser, L. R. (1992). MIS Skills for the 1990s: A Survey of MIS Managers's Perceptions. *Journal of Management Information Systems, 9*(1), 69–91.

Lewis, R. (1997). An Activity Theory framework to explore distributed communities. *Journal of Computer Assisted Learning*, *13*, 210–218. doi:10.1046/j.1365-2729.1997.00023.x

McLure Wasko, M., & Faraj, S. (2005). Why Should I Share? Examining Social Capital And Knowledge Contribution in Electronic Networks Of Practice. *Management Information Systems Quarterly*, *29*(1), 35–57.

Mead, H. G. (1934). *Mind, self, and society: from the standpoint of a behaviorist*. Chicago: The University of Chicago Press.

Nardi, A. B., Whittaker, S., & Schwarz, H. (2002). NetWORKers and their activity in Intentional Networks. *Activity Theory and the Practice of Design*, *11*(1-2), 205–242.

Noll, L. C., & Wlikins, M. (2002). Critical Skills for IS Professionals: A model for a Curriculum Development. *Journal of Information Technology Education*, *1*(3), 145–154.

Orlikowski, J. W., & Baroudi, J. J. (1991). Studying Information Technology in Organizations: research approaches and assumptions. *Information Systems Research*, *2*(1), 1–28. doi:10.1287/isre.2.1.1

Osnowitz, D. (2006). Occupational Networking as Normative Control: Collegial Exchange Among Contract Professionals. *Work and Occupations*, *33*(1), 12–41. doi:10.1177/0730888405280160

Ouchi, G. W. (1980). Markets, Bureaucracies and Clans. *Administrative Science Quarterly*, *25*, 129–141. doi:10.2307/2392231

Patton, M. D. (1980). *Qualitative Research Methods*. Thousand Oaks, CA: Sage Publications.

Ramachandran, S., & Rao, V. S. (2006, April 13-15). *An Effort Towards Identifying Occupational Culture among Information Systems Professionals*. Paper presented at the SIGMIS-CPR'06, Claremond, CA.

Sassen, S. (2001). *The Global City*. Princeton, NJ: Princeton University Press.

Scarbrough, H. (1999). The Management of Knowledge Workers. In Currie, L. W., & Galliers, B. (Eds.), *Rethinking management information systems* (pp. 475–495). Oxford, UK: Oxford University Press.

Sharma, A. (1997). Professional as Agent: Knowledge Asymmetry in Agency Exchange. *Academy of Management Review*, *22*(3), 758–798. doi:10.2307/259412

Sinha, K. K., & Van de Ven, A. H. (2005). Designing Work Within and Between Organizations. *Organization Science*, *16*(4), 389–408. doi:10.1287/orsc.1050.0130

Stryker, S., & Burke, J. P. (2000). The Past, Present and Future of an Identity Theory. *Social Psychology Quarterly*, *63*(4), 284–297. doi:10.2307/2695840

Tajfel, H. (1982). *Social Identity and Intergroup Relations*. Cambridge, UK: Cambridge University Press.

Todd, A. P., & McKeen, D. J. (1995). The Evolution of IS Job Skills: A Content Analysis of IS Job Advertisements From 1970 to 1990. *Management Information Systems Quarterly*, *19*(1), 1–27. doi:10.2307/249709

Van Maanen, J., & Barley, R. S. (1984). Occupational Communities: Culture and Control in Organizations. In Staw, B., & Cummings, L. L. (Eds.), *Research in Organizational Behaviour* (*Vol. 6*, pp. 287–365). Greenwich, CT: JAI Press.

Von Hippel, E., & Von Krogh, G. (2006). Free revealing and the private-collective model for innovation incentives. *R & D Management*, *36*(3), 295–306. doi:10.1111/j.1467-9310.2006.00435.x

Walsham, G. (1993). *Interpreting Information Systems in Organizations*. London: John Wiley and Sons.

Walsham, G. (1998). IT and Changing Professional Identity: Micro-Studies and Macro-Theory. *Journal of the American Society for Information Science American Society for Information Science*, *49*(12), 1081–1089. doi:10.1002/(SICI)1097-4571(1998)49:12<1081::AID-ASI4>3.0.CO;2-R

Wenger, E. (1998). *Communities of Practice: Learning, Meaning and Identity*. New York: Cambridge University Press.

Wenger, E. (2000). Communities of Practice and Social Learning Systems. *Organization*, *7*(2), 225–246. doi:10.1177/135050840072002

Yin, K. R. (2003). *Case Study Research: Design and Methods*. Thousand Oaks, CA: Sage Publications, Inc.

Zammuto, R. F., Griffith, T. L., Majchrzak, A., Dougherty, D. J., & Faraj, S. (2007). Information Technology and the Changing Fabric of Organization. *Organization Science*, *18*(5), 749–762. doi:10.1287/orsc.1070.0307

Zuboff, S. (1988). *In the age of the smart machine*. New York: Basic Books.

This work was previously published in the International Journal of Virtual Communities and Social Networking, Volume 2, Issue 3, edited by Subhasish Dasgupta, pp. 42-54, copyright 2010 by IGI Publishing (an imprint of IGI Global).

Section 3
Cross Cultural and International Studies

Chapter 13
Tracing Community Life across Virtual Settlements

Demosthenes Akoumianakis
Technological Education Institution of Crete, Greece

ABSTRACT

Recent scholarship has demonstrated that virtual communities can be traced in the online 'tells' retained by popular virtual settlements like Facebook and Twitter. In this article, the authors push this line of research toward an analysis of pre-requisites and constrains of virtual settlements that determine the understanding of community life across settlements. The approach followed is grounded on a 'practice lens' that views virtual communities as enacted cyber-structures revealed through cultural artifacts facilitated by affordances inscribed into virtual settlements. The presence or absence of key affordances determines not only what is retained as online 'tells' in a virtual settlement but also the type and range of cultural artifacts, as well as how these artifacts are used across virtual settlements.

1 INTRODUCTION

For most people daily life is conceived of as activities situated across multiple community settings. Such communities are formed by territorial boundaries (e.g., neighborhoods), affiliation (e.g., organizational or professional settings), spiritual commitments (e.g., religion), etc. Each community maintains its own set of policies (formal or informal), rules of engagement and body of knowledge. Accordingly, members become engaged in different material practices, develop skills to appropriate different kinds of knowledge

and experience the community through designated norms. It is evident therefore that at any time, what is known of anybody is what can be traced of his/her participation and history of engagement across community boundaries in different physical, virtual or spiritual settlements.

Early community settlements were confined to certain places or landmarks and assumed the members' proximity. Crossing community boundaries was typically achieved by arrangements that ensured the member's physical presence and/or co-engagement in each separate settlement. In due time, space-oriented settlements emerged to allow

DOI: 10.4018/978-1-4666-1553-3.ch013

communities where physical presence of members is not a pre-requisite or a sufficient indicator of togetherness. For instance, in communities formed around professional fields of expertise, the key to participation is not so much the physical proximity of members as it is what members actually do, the practice they become engaged in and the capacity to communicate using a shared language. Then, boundary crossing is framed and analyzed in relation to certain configurations of people, artifacts and social relations as they are enacted in practice.

Although such boundary crossing is beyond any doubt, there are very few studies explaining how it is materialized in virtual settings. Phrased differently, it is still difficult to analyze virtual community boundaries and what enables or constrains boundary spanning and cross-settlement community life in virtual space. The problem can be attributed to a number of challenges confronting researchers of social networks. Firstly, it is not always easy or straight forward to establish the appropriate settlements for investigation. This is especially difficult for virtual settlements whose boundaries are not easily defined (Efimova & Hendrick, 2005). Secondly, there is a compelling need for methods allowing the collection of rich and targeted data of appropriate scale to provide insights to how communities and social networks are established, obtain structure and change over time (Ricken et al., 2010). Again, in virtual settings this challenge is more demanding and complex as virtual settlements are not designed to collect the type of user data desired (Gilbert et al., 2008). Finally, another challenge appears to be the lack of consensus on what kind of data constitute virtual 'tells' of community life and how they are traced and processed across settlements so as to provide informative accounts of established and emerging communities (Jones & Rafaeli, 2000). Recent research has emphasized the value of social interaction traces such as listserv postings, user logs, web site structures, messages posted or retwitted and links. However, it is unlikely that

these alone can provide the explanatory insight required to understand cyber-structures at both micro and macro levels. The primary limitations of these online 'tells' is that they represent historical records of online activities decoupled from what collaborators' do and the practices they become engaged in. In response to this shortcoming, the turn into practice (Schatzki, 2001) promises to provide a research strand capable of alleviating obstacles while offering a more epistemic basis for analyzing virtual communities as enacted structures.

This article seeks to shed light into some of the issues that determine human boundary spanning capacity in virtual settings. The challenge is approached through a practice lens intended to frame boundary spanning in relation to the practices appropriated and enacted by human agents as they collaborate with peers in different virtual settlements. To this end, the next section motivates the problem at hand by reviewing relevant works within or closely attached to the practice turn. Then, the following section outlines a proposition for tracing virtual communities across settlements based on both material and immaterial aspects of practice. Finally, the present work is concluded by a brief discussion of implications and areas of future research.

2 THEORETICAL MOTIVATION

With the advent of the Internet and more recently the Web 2.0, virtual communities form one outcome which is increasingly and profoundly 'sensed' in cyberspace (Blanchard & Markus, 2004). Scholars have used a variety of terms to qualify the resulting enacted artificial structures, such as imagined communities (Anderson, 1983), online or virtual communities (Rheingold, 2000), knowledge communities (Lindkvist, 2005), distributed communities (Gochenour, 2006), blogosphere (Efimova & Hendrick, 2005), to name a few. Although, there is substantial debate as to what type of structure these terms imply and the necessary and sufficient conditions for qualifying them as communities, there seems to be agreement on the fact that they constitute emergent structures, enacted in practice and through different technology genres. Nevertheless, very few studies have investigated the prerequisites for these cyber-structures from the perspective of what inscriptions in technology enable or constrain their enactment in virtual settings. More importantly, there is a genuine lack of research on tracing community life across different computer-mediated spaces.

2.1 Virtual Settlements

One perspective to address this question is offered by the theory of virtual settlements introduced by Jones (1997). Jones uses the term 'virtual settlement' to qualify a type of computer-mediated space that under certain conditions may provide the host of virtual communities. The concept is further qualified using four conditions for analyzing virtual settlements, namely interactivity, presence of more than two communicators, common public place where members can meet and interact and sustained membership over time. By this account, Jones separates the virtual settlements from virtual communities and considers the former as a pre-requisite for the latter. In subsequent efforts, Jones and Rafaeli (2000) examine the explanatory power of virtual settlements and investigate how cyber-material provides a basis for a hierarchy of social explanation for cyber-society. In their analysis, the term 'virtual tells' refers to data retained within virtual settlements and provide evidence for the four criteria for qualifying virtual settlements. However, the theory falls short from identifying pre-requisites for virtual tells. In other words, there is no account of intrinsic properties of virtual settlements (or settlement inscribed structures) that enable or constrain what virtual tells are retained.

Recent research confirms and extends Jones' theory by offering empirical evidence on the pre-requisites for considering a virtual settlement as host for virtual communities (Blanchard & Markus, 2004; Efimova & Hendrick, 2005; Gruzd, Wellman, & Takhteyev, 2011). Furthermore, the notion of virtual settlement has inspired works on automatic discovery of virtual communities using a variety of tools such as graph-based techniques and special purpose algorithms (Lin et al., 2006; Zhou & Davis, 2007). In this context some researchers focus on virtual communities emerging in a single virtual settlement such as Twitter (Gruzd, Wellman, & Takhteyev, 2011) or Facebook (Hewitt & Forte, 2006; Zhao, Grasmuch, & Martin, 2008; Zhang, Jiang, & Carroll, 2010). Others explore spaces of interrelated virtual settlements such as blogs (Blanchard, 2004; Chin & Chignell, 2006), blogospheres (Efimova & Hendrick, 2005) or blogspaces (Zhou & Davis, 2007). The latter works bring to the forefront the notion of virtual settlement boundaries. Noticeably, the four conditions of Jones (1997) do not indicate clearly how to define a settlement's boundaries (Liu, 1999; Efimova & Hendrick, 2005). This may not be a problem when studying online communities formed around a shared space e.g., a group communication technology or a social networking site, but it is definitely a challenge for researchers seeking community traces across virtual settlements. Another shortcoming of the theory of virtual settlements is that none of the criteria reveal properties of a technology that enable or constrain a particular type of virtual community.

2.2 The Practice-Based Theories

An alternative approach to cross-settlement community life may be grounded on established theoretical traditions such as structurational models of technology (Giddens, 1984) and practice-based studies (Orlikowski, 2002). At core, these theories imply (as in the case of structuration theory) or posit (as in the case of practice lens) a distinction between 'appropriation' and 'enactment' of technology structures. Appropriation refers to how users make use of the structures inscribed in whatever technology is at hand. Enactment, on the other hand, is used to coin primarily unintended configurations of people, artifacts and social relations (i.e., virtual communities) that result from the use of technology in practice. Orlikowski (2002) offered a contextual assessment of technology constituting structures in relation to properties inscribed in technologies. Using an example, she argued that functional components of Google search, such as handling of directories, databases and indexes, page ranking algorithms, etc., alone do not convey Google engine's material capacity of connectivity which allows it to make use of multiple servers. In other words, it is claimed that, although functionality embodied in technological artifacts is clearly important, it is not likely to be the critical technological inscription facilitating what Orlikowski coins as 'variety of technologies-in-practice' when referring to emergent social practices of a technology. Instead, there is an implied suggestion that it is non-functional attributes that enable or constrain these emergent social practices and determine their boundary spanning manifestation. However, to the best of our knowledge, there are no detailed studies of what non-functional attributes need to be considered and what role they have in boundary spanning.

The practice turn is the term used to coin a wider movement towards an analysis of practice as epistemology useful for the study of work and the kind of practical and 'hidden' knowledge that supports it (Gherardi, 2009). Although such a movement is rather polysemic and non-homogeneous – comprising insights by social scientists (Giddens, 1984; Brown & Duguid, 2001; Suchman, 2007), organization and management scholars (Gherardi, 2001; Orlikowski, 2002; Nicolini, Gherardi, & Yanow, 2003) – it has nevertheless accumulated a critical body of knowledge, which forms the common bond for many practice-based studies

(Schatzki, 2001). In information systems research the practice turn is progressively gaining in momentum with an increasing number of researchers focusing on how information systems of various genders reshape, define or establish new social practices. Such works concentrate on the limitation of traditional community management theory to provide sufficient ground for explaining how certain practices are reconstructed, enriched or augmented in virtual space. Evidence for this may be found in the plethora of new patterns observed in the way people socialize or use language and the resulting communications acts (i.e., phrases such as 'I googled the term XYZ'), but also the way business is (or is not) conducted. Arguably, these new patterns cannot be fully understood by mere analysis of pre-existing community structures. Instead, it is reasonable to suggest that it is the activities themselves and the practices these activities constitute that generate community by forming the 'glue' that holds together a configuration of people, artifacts and social relations (Gherardi, 2009, p. 121).

2.3 Research Focus

In this paper, the intention is to combine concepts from the theory of virtual settlements and practice-based analysis to establish a practice lens for analyzing cross-settlement community life. The term 'practice lens' is borrowed from (Orlikowski, 2000) where it is used as a conceptual metaphor for studying technology in organizations. In this effort, the present work retains the commitment to the analytic distinction between virtual settlements and virtual communities and expands it in the light of practice theory that distinguishes between technology as artifact and technology use in practice. The result is a conceptual model that frames boundary spanning virtual communities in relation to cultural artifacts and affordances inscribed in virtual settlements.

3 TRACING VIRTUAL COMMUNITIES ACROSS VIRTUAL SETTLEMENTS

Recently, we claimed that computer-mediation is as much about reconstructing practices as it is about improvising and defining new practice elements (Akoumianakis, 2009). For instance, in traditional settings the social practice of 'presence' entails making oneself physically available at a specific place for a specific purpose (i.e., socializing with co-present peers) and for a specific time interval. The social character of this practice can be derived when one considers the individual's situational engagement with others. Typically, it entails social awareness (i.e., paying attention to what is happening, searching for people/artifacts), verbal communication (i.e., meeting and addressing colleagues, passing on and exchanging information), non-verbal communication and civil inattention (i.e., communicative patterns implying awareness of a social event, which for some reason is not temporarily worth of being addressed) as well as coordinative acts (i.e., knowing when and how to intervene to an event). Considering how presence is enacted in virtual settings using social media, it becomes apparent that it can hardly be seen as mere reconstruction of the conventional practice. For example, in online discussions there are no such things as civic inattention – one is made known when he/she declares his presence – or being physically co-located with participants. Similar remarks can be made for a wide variety of social practices conducted in virtual space.

In light of the above, it stands to argue that social media foster new linguistic domains by supporting recurrent communicative patterns arising from the cyclical reconstruction of certain practices (Akoumianakis, 2009). This is depicted in Figure 1 in an effort to conceptualize the emergent features of practice when enacted in virtual settings. On this ground, virtual settlements can be conceived as computer-mediated collaborative spaces where members of a virtual ensemble engage in one or more linguistic domains. Then, virtual communities can be traced in the history of co-engagement in linguistic domains. Moreover, when considering alternative virtual settlements, it is interesting to note that cyclical reconstruction of practice takes place not only in the micro-context of a designated virtual settlement where actions are highly situational and localized but also in macro-contexts that establish broad

Figure 1. The concept of a linguistic domain

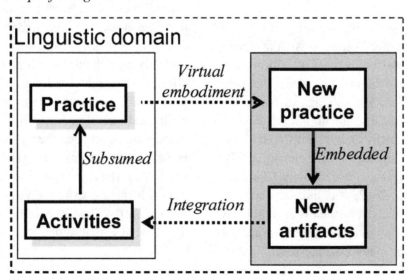

commonalities of action (see Figure 2). Considering as macro-context the prominent technological trajectory at any given time (i.e., the WWW, Web 2.0, Social Semantic Web, etc), it is now possible to analyze virtual settlements under each technological regime in terms of two key dimensions, namely cultural artifacts of practice and affordances or non-functional qualities. Cultural artifacts designate what people actually do in a virtual settlement while affordances detail what is retained by the micro-context of a virtual settlement in the form of virtual tells as well the interoperability across settlements.

3.1 Cultural Artifacts

Archaeologists consider as cultural artifacts any kind of material remains of culture, aiming 'not so much to reconstruct what once was, but to make sense of the past from a viewpoint of today' (Fahlander & Oestigaard, 2004). Such cultural remains are seen as bi-products of culture, but not culture itself. Analysis of artifacts in situ and in relation to other artifacts evokes particular understandings of the culture that they exist within. Using archaeology as a metaphor, it can be argued that virtual communities, as enacted structures of

Internet culture, should be studied in relation to the artifacts that reveal their purpose and existence through material remains of practice. In popular virtual settlements, such material remains of practice are effectively the means through which users engage in designated linguistic domains. In Twitter this is done by messages posted or retweeted, private messages and links (Gruzd, Wellman, & Takhteyev, 2011). In weblogs cultural artifacts include meme paths, weblog reading patterns, weblog conversations, indicators of events, blogrolls and RSS subscriptions (Efimova & Hendrick, 2005). However, there are other types of cultural artifacts being increasingly negotiated in virtual settlements, such as music scores (Sterne, 2006; Patel, 2007; Akoumianakis & Alexandraki, 2010), vacation arrangements (Costa & Ferrone, 1995; Osti, Turner, & King, 2009; Akoumianakis, Vidakis, Akrivos, Milolidakis, Kotsalis, & Vellis, 2011) and virtual tours in museums (Müller, 2010) or cities (Harrison, 2009).

Consequently, material remains of a community's practice in virtual settings are revealed by cultural artifacts unfolding individual or collective activity that takes place within a virtual settlement. Such cultural artifacts can be broadly classified in three categories. The first includes artifacts

Figure 2. Macro- and micro-contexts of practice

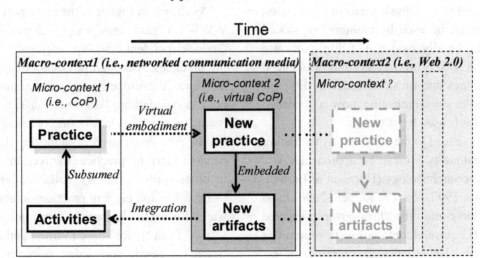

internal to the virtual ensemble that reveal how a designated practice is constructed, negotiated and re-constructed by the members. The second category entails artifacts of collective performance. These are typically decoupled from the member's individual practices and can be shared with others outside the community. The third category, which is rarely recognized, refers to third-party artifacts that reveal how the collective product of a community is used by others in different settings across virtual settlements. For instance, in a recent study of DIAMOUSES – a virtual settlement for collective music performance – the author and colleagues (Akoumianakis & Alexandraki, 2010; Alexandraki & Akoumianakis, 2010) presented an analysis of collaborative networked music performance in terms of a range of cultural artifacts created by the virtual ensemble prior to, in the course of or after an online music performance. Specifically, the music score and its history of collaborative manipulation turned out to be a cultural artifact internal to the virtual ensemble that can be used to reveal how music performance is constructed and negotiated through individual contributions of the collaborators. Another prominent artifact was the recorded collective outcome of the group (i.e., mixed recording or mp3). This is an example of an artifact presenting a historical record of the group's performance at a point in time. It is decoupled from the members' situational practices during the networked music performance session and can either be used by members or shared with others. Finally, evidence of third-party use of a DIAMOUSES mixed recording was traced in wikis, blogs and music samples in different virtual settlements indicating how a recorded performance is used by others.

The above lead to the conclusion that tracing virtual community life can be approached as a type of cyber-archaeology (Harrison & Barthel, 2009; Jones, 1997, Jones & Rafaeli, 2000) in so far as it fosters commitment to discovering enacted structures (i.e., virtual communities) through their cultural 'tells'. Nevertheless in contrast to the tra-

ditional archaeological paradigm, cultural 'tells' of virtual communities are bits of program code and data, which can only be made sense of using dedicated software. Thus, cultural artefacts of a virtual community are inextricably linked with the software toolkits through which such artefacts are instantiated in practice as well as the affordances that allow cultural artefacts to cross community and/or virtual settlement boundaries.

3.2 Affordances, Boundary Spanning and Practices Occupying Multiple Contexts

One approach to understand cross-settlement community life is to consider what boundaries are alleviated, crossed or established and through what technological inscriptions. This will ultimately determine not only what is to be excavated in a virtual settlement but also the 'hidden' knowledge that qualifies a particular community setting. To provide the required insight, it is worthwhile reviewing the transitions in technology leading to the paradigm shift from the early period of the WWW to the Web 2.0 and the notion of the Social Semantic Web. In doing so, we will make an effort to understand each transition in relation to the corresponding enacted communities, their practices and some of the critical qualities characterizing the macro- and micro-context of practice.

As shown in Figure 3, the early period of the WWW (or 'read-write' web) is characterized by device-dependent mark-up scripting and authoring practices. Although physical boundaries are alleviated, the respective online communities still have a 'place-based' orientation (i.e., virtual rooms, electronic classrooms, online neighborhoods, etc). Progressively, authoring device-dependent mark-up practices evolved into posting in blogs (online diaries), collaborative editing using wikis and tagging practices in social software. Respectively, online communities transformed from 'place'-based virtual gatherings to 'space'-oriented, knowledge communities and

Figure 3. Technological trajectories and social practices

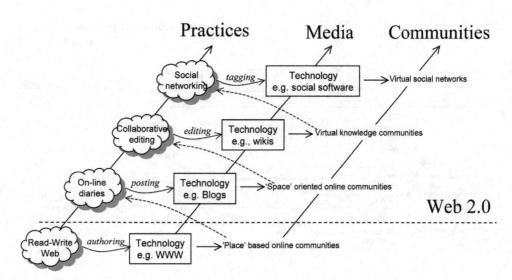

virtual social networks. Through these transitions, the respective boundaries are arguably conceived in relation to practice rather than physical constructs. In fact, it is recurrent co-engagement in interrelated practices that determine participation in communities, irrespective of location or proximity. Moreover, as these communities are formed around different social media, the material aspects of boundary crossing are increasingly confined to non-functional qualities (or affordances) such as sharing, information connectivity, API interoperability, awareness and plasticity. Figure 4 attempts to convey this concept by highlighting the evolving focus on non-functional qualities across technological regimes and digital cultures.

The prominent qualities in the early WWW period were reuse and portability, both inherited from the earlier GUI regime. Information connectivity facilitated sharing of information and recurrent interaction of people with whatever technology is at hand. In this account, it may be considered as a pre-requisite for virtual settlements and a necessary condition for cross-settlement community life. Inherent properties of information connectivity, but potentially more powerful concepts as the number, thematic focus and range

of virtual settlements increase, are the notions of abstraction and interoperability. The presence or absence of these qualities, by and large, determines boundaries of fields and how they are to be spanned. In this sense they are considered as pre-requisites for more advanced and complicated affordances such as social connectivity (i.e., sharing social values rather than mere information) and plasticity (making use of artifacts that withstand changes across fields while preserving usability) which are likely to proliferate in the transition to the social semantic web.

4 IMPLICATIONS

In light of the above, we can now summarize the basic assumption of our research proposition and assess some of its implications. Specifically, it is argued that boundary crossing is a kind of enacted connectivity across boundaries which is enabled or constrained by a particular set of symbols (i.e., cultural artifacts) and the affordances (i.e., non-functional quality attributes) embedded into virtual settlements. Cross-settlement virtual communities emerge when this type of

Figure 4. Digital practices, technological trajectories and technology inscribed quality attributes

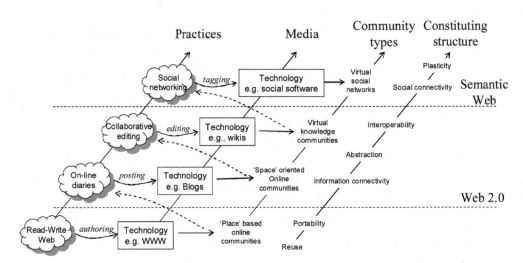

connectivity becomes instantiated in practice through inscriptions in technology. Consequently, connectivity becomes a design quality of virtual settlements determining not only material aspects of the enacted cyber-structures but also what is retained within a single settlement and the means through which these remains are to be excavated. As briefly discussed below, this has implications on the design of virtual settlements.

4.1 Designing for Connectivity

Connectivity is a multifaceted concept which can be subject to many different interpretations. In broad terms, it can be conceived as a property characterizing nodes and edges of a single network or even interconnections between entire networks. In case these networks rely on physical infra-structures such as airports or cities, connectivity obtains tangible and material substance that makes it easier to measure. For networks built on digital media connectivity is intertwined with technical configurations and arrangements which make it much more complex and hard to trace and/or measure. This is partly attributed to the lack of data due to security or privacy policies.

For the purposes of the current analysis connectivity is conceived as a quality feature of virtual settlements which enables or constrains certain uses. As such, it can be designed so as to provide insights on facilitators and/or impediments to social interaction, information sharing and net-working. This is easier to attain in single virtual settlements as they make provisions for assessing polices inscribed in technology (i.e., registration, role attainment, access rights, recurrent engage-ment in practice, etc) and tracking collaborators and their contributions. As a result, it is made possible to trace informational aspects of the collaborating agents (i.e., identity management, commitment to networking, perspective towards peers, etc) by retaining their contributions, as well as the social values shared by a virtual ensemble (i.e., commitment to equal access rights, demo-cratic participation, majority voting, etc). On this account, it stands to argue that virtual settlements should be designed to support connectivity of both persistent and codified information (information connectivity) and social or cultural values (social connectivity).

The design implications of connectivity are slightly different when the focus shifts away from what is being shared (i.e., information or social value) to the settlement boundaries set and/or crossed. Again, it implies design inscriptions which facilitate or impede electronic traces within a virtual settlement to cross boundaries and become accountable in another virtual settlement. It is important to note that such connectivity is more than portability, platform independence or replication which are well-defied non-functional requirements in software engineering. Specifically, in contrast to artefacts that are, portable across different platforms or platform independent or even capable of being replicated across sites while preserving their functional properties, connectivity implicates alternate action, thus differences in use as a result of crossing virtual settlement boundaries. Today, this type of connectivity is only partially addressed through dedicated structures inscribed in technologies such as sharing widgets and RSS feeds which rely on abstraction, device-independent mark-up languages and scripting. Nevertheless, as shown in Figure 4, these qualities are still distant apart from the more demanding technology constituting structures of interoperability, social connectivity and plasticity.

4.2 Excavating Cross-Settlement Communities and the Role of Boundaries

With respect to excavating in virtual settlements our analysis so far suggests that cultural artifacts of practice can provide informative accounts of how members engage in a designated practice as well as how this practice is re-shaped, extended and enriched. Nevertheless, such excavation implies tracing online 'tells' within and across virtual settlements. In both cases excavation is implicitly related to (i.e., enabled or constrained by) boundaries. There are two possible conceptions of boundary in virtual space, namely boundaries imposed by the virtual settlement's non-functional inscriptions and boundaries implicated by the artifacts of the settlement, their information processing properties, and most importantly, their affordances.

An example of a boundary imposed by inscriptions in technology is the application programming interface (API) of a virtual settlement which determines what is retained within the settlement and thus the possibilities of a virtual excavation. Gruzd, Wellman and Takhteyev (2011) in their recent study of Twitter report how they used its application programming interface (API, http://apiwiki.twitter.com) to automatically retrieve a variety of data about inter-tweep connectivity, such as who is connected to whom, who replies to whom, are the relationships mutual, which tweets are passed on, etc. Consequently, Twitter as virtual settlement creates an implicit boundary by retaining only certain data (or traffic). All other network data which is not retained is outside the boundary.

Boundaries implicated by the artifacts of the settlement, their material and information processing properties or their affordances are different in character and related primarily to what collaborators do and the practice they engage in a single or across virtual settlements. Phrased differently, such boundaries are not pre-existent in the sense of an API that confines what is retained within a virtual settlement, but enacted in practice, malleable due to their situational nature, and thus, unstable. Our own work on collaborative vacation package assembly (Akoumianakis, 2010; Akoumianakis, Vidakis, Vellis, Kotsalis, Milolidakis, Plemenos, & Akrivos, 2011) and network music performance (Akoumianakis & Alexandraki, 2010; Alexandraki & Akoumianakis, 2010) provides some useful insights into how these boundaries are established and crossed. In the case of vacation package assembly such enacted boundaries are established at the moment a vacation package is released and made available to customers for negotiating ultimate vacation arrangements. It turns out that customer choices determine what service providers are ultimately engaged in the vacation package, while recurrent choice of certain service providers leads to the establishment of cliques with various implications for all parties concerned (Akoumianakis, Vidakis, Akrivos, et al., 2011). In another study of networked music performance (Akoumianakis & Alexandraki, 2010), it was revealed that a critical boundary is between the online setting and the offline material context of a music performer. Specifically, during experiments it became evident that an interactive music score is not sufficient to guide musicians towards enactment of the appropriate sequence of actions on a musical instrument. Thus, occasionally the recorded audio outcome resulted from wrong notes or erroneous rhythmic patterns which could not be easily revealed unless the music score is augmented so as to afford 'score to audio' alignment (Akoumianakis & Alexandraki, 2010).

There are two conclusions from these studies which are central to the current discussion. The first is that social behaviour in community settings cannot be fully appreciated without crossing boundaries, either virtual or physical. This is because activities tend to occupy multiple online and offline contexts. Phrased differently, an online trace may be stimulated by offline incidents and vice versa. One way to assess such boundary setting and crossing from the perspective of practice is to excavate the intertwining between what is being subject to negotiation online, what is being done offline and the implications these may have on each other.

Secondly, boundaries from the perspective of practice may be assigned two different connotations. *Virtual boundaries* result from inscriptions in technology and suggest a conception of boundary crossing as information sharing that can be facilitated by RSS subscriptions, sharing widgets API extensions and interoperability – all leading to enhancing information connectivity. *Enacted boundaries* are implicated through practice and by account of what takes place online, the offline activities of members and the way these are intertwined. Enacted boundaries are not stable and

thus they do not invite analysis of how they are to be crossed. Instead, they represent the collaborators' joint fields of expertise or agendas as they emerge through their history of co-engagement and as a result, their excavation relies primarily on studying how practice is constructed, negotiated and reconstructed in online and offline settings.

5 CONCLUSION

This paper has been concerned with the study of virtual communities within a single or across virtual settlements. Our proposition rests on and elaborates the assumption that virtual communities are enacted phenomena of the cyberspace that emerge through the history of recurrent co-engagement in a designated practice. Traces of these communities can be (partly) unfolded by focusing on the community's cultural artifacts. Nevertheless, these alone may not be sufficient to reveal boundary spanning behavior, as this assumes certain affordance-based inscriptions in technology. It is these inscriptions that determine boundary spanning in virtual settings and frame it in relation to a complex of intertwining cultural practices that occupy multiple locations, both virtual and physical. The presence or absence of these inscriptions determines not only what is retained as online 'tells' in a virtual settlement, but also the type and material properties of boundary crossing.

ACKNOWLEDGMENT

The present work is grounded on collaborative research and development funded by (a) The General Secretariat for Research and Technology of the Greek Ministry of Development in the context of projects eKoNES (KP-5) and DIAMOUSES (KP-24) of the Regional Operational Programme of Crete, Line 1.2 (Research and Development consortia in Strategic Priority Areas) and (b) The European Commission FP 7 Science in Society program. Special thanks are due to members of the istLab (http://www.istl.teiher.gr/) of the Department of Applied Information Technology & Multimedia, Technological Education Institution of Crete for their contributions in these projects.

REFERENCES

Akoumianakis, D. (2009). Designing practice-oriented toolkits: A retrospective analysis of communities, new media and social practice. *International Journal of Virtual Communities and Social Networking, 1*(4), 50–72. doi:10.4018/jvcsn.2009092204

Akoumianakis, D. (2010). Electronic Community Factories: The model and its application in the tourism sector. *Electronic Commerce Research, 10*(1), 43–81. doi:10.1007/s10660-010-9045-1

Akoumianakis, D., & Alexandraki, C. (2010, November 24-26). Understanding Networked Music Communities through a practice-lens: Virtual 'tells' and cultural artifacts. In *Proceedings of the 2nd International Conference on Intelligent Networking and Collaborative Systems (INCoS 2010),* Thessaloniki, Greece (pp. 62-69). Washington, DC: IEEE Computer Society.

Akoumianakis, D., Vidakis, N., Akrivos, A., Milolidakis, G., Kotsalis, D., & Vellis, G. (2011). Building 'Flexible' vacation packages using collaborative assembly toolkits and dynamic packaging: The Case Study of the eKoNES. *Journal of Vacation Marketing, 17*(1), 17–30. doi:10.1177/1356766710391132

Akoumianakis, D., Vidakis, N., Vellis, G., Kotsalis, D., Milolidakis, G., Plemenos, A., & Akrivos, A. (2011). Transformable boundary artifacts for knowledge-based work in cross-organization virtual community spaces. *Intelligent Decisions Technologies, 14*(1), 65–82.

Alexandraki, C., & Akoumianakis, D. (2010). Exploring New Perspectives in Network Music Performance: The DIAMOUSES Framework. *Computer Music Journal, 34,* 66–83. doi:10.1162/comj.2010.34.2.66

Anderson, B. (1983). *Imagined Communities: Reflections on the Origin and Spread of Nationalism.* London, UK: Verso.

Blanchard, A. (2004). *Blogs as Virtual Communities: Identifying a Sense of Community in the Julie/Julia Project.* Retrieved from http://blog.lib.umn.edu/blogosphere/blogs_as_virtual.html

Blanchard, A. L., & Markus, L. M. (2004). The Experienced "Sense" of a Virtual Community: Characteristics and Processes. *The Data Base for Advances in Information Systems, 35*(1), 65–79.

Brown, S. J., & Duguid, P. (2001). Knowledge and Organization: A Social-Practice Perspective. *Organization Science, 12*(2), 198–213. doi:10.1287/orsc.12.2.198.10116

Chin, A., & Chignell, M. (2006, February 26-28). Finding Evidence of Community from Blogging Co-citations: A Social Network Analytic Approach. In *Proceedings of the 3rd IADIS International Conference Web Based Communities 2006 (WBC06),* San Sebastian, Spain (pp. 191-200).

Costa, J., & Ferrone, L. (1995). Sociocultural perspectives on tourism planning and development. *International Journal of Contemporary Hospitality Management, 7*(7), 27–35. doi:10.1108/09596119510101903

Efimova, L., & Hendrick, S. (2005). In Search for a Virtual Settlement: An Exploration of Weblog Community Boundaries. In *Proceedings of the Communities & Technologies 2005 Conference.* Retrieved from http://doc.telin.nl/dscgi/ds.py/Get/File-46041/weblog_community_boundaries.pdf

Fahlander, F., & Oestigaard, T. (2004). *Material Culture and Other Things, Post-disciplinary Studies in the 21st Century*. Retrieved from http://folk.uib.no/gsuto/ArtiklerWeb/Material_Culture/Oestigaard.pdf

Gherardi, S. (2001). Practice-based Theorizing on Learning and Knowing in Organizations: An Introduction. *Organization, 7*(2), 211–223. doi:10.1177/135050840072001

Gherardi, S. (2009). Introduction: The Critical Power of the 'Practice Lens'. *Management Learning, 40*(2), 115–128. doi:10.1177/1350507608101225

Giddens, A. (1984). *The constitution of society – Outline of the theory of structuration*. Cambridge, UK: Polity Press.

Gilbert, E., Karahalios, K., & Sandvig, C. (2008). The Network in the Garden: An Empirical Analysis of Social Media in Rural Life. In *Proceedings of the CHI 2008 Conference*. New York, NY: ACM Press.

Gochenour, H. P. (2006). Distributed communities and nodal subjects. *New Media & Society, 8*(1), 33–51. doi:10.1177/1461444806059867

Gruzd, A., Wellman, B., & Takhteyev, Y. (2011). Imagining Twitter as an Imagined Community. American Behavioral Scientist. Retrieved from: http://homes.chass.utoronto.ca/~wellman/publications/imagining_twitter/Imagining%20Twitter_AG_Sep1_2010_final.pdf

Harrison, R. (2009). Excavating Second Life - Cyber-Archaeologies, Heritage and Virtual Communities. *Journal of Material Culture, 14*(1), 75–106. doi:10.1177/1359183508100009

Harrison, T. M., & Barthel, B. (2009). Wielding new media in Web 2.0: exploring the history of engagement with the collaborative construction of media products. *New Media & Society, 11*(1-2), 155–178. doi:10.1177/1461444808099580

Hewitt, A., & Forte, A. (2006). Crossing Boundaries: Identity Management and Student/Faculty Relationships on the Facebook. In *Proceedings of the CSCW 2006 Conference*. New York, NY: ACM Press.

Jones, Q. (1997). Virtual-Communities, Virtual Settlements & Cyber-Archaeology: A Theoretical Outline. *Journal of Computer-Mediated Communication, 3*(3).

Jones, Q., & Rafaeli, S. (2000). What do virtual 'Tells' tell? Placing cybersociety research into a hierarchy of social explanation. In *Proceedings of the 33rd Hawaii International Conference on System Sciences*. Washington, DC: IEEE Computer Society.

Lin, Y., Sundaram, H., Chi, Y., Tatemura, J., & Tseng, B. (2006, May 23). Discovery of Blog communities based on Mutual Awareness. In *Proceedings of the 3rd Annual Workshop on the Weblogging Ecosystems: Aggregation, Analysis and Dynamics, WWW2006*, Edinburgh, UK.

Lindkvist, L. (2005). Knowledge Communities and Knowledge Collectivities: A Typology of Knowledge Work in Groups. *Journal of Management Studies, 42*(6), 1189–1210. doi:10.1111/j.1467-6486.2005.00538.x

Liu, G. Z. (1999). Virtual Community Presence in Internet Relay Chatting. *Computer Supported Cooperative Work, 5*(1). Retrieved from http://jcmc.indiana.edu/vol5/issue1/liu.html.

Müller, K. (2010). Museums and Virtuality, Museums and Virtuality. *Curator: The Museum Journal, 45*, 21–33.

Nicolini, D., Gherardi, S., & Yanow, D. (2003). Introduction. In Nicolini, D., Gherardi, S., & Yanow, D. (Eds.), *Organizational Knowledge as Practice* (pp. 3–31). Armonk, NY: ME Sharpe.

Orlikowski, J. W. (2000). Using Technology and Constituting Structures: A Practice Lens for Studying Technology in Organizations. *Organization Science*, *11*(4), 404–428. doi:10.1287/orsc.11.4.404.14600

Orlikowski, J. W. (2002). Knowing in Practice: Enacting a Collective Capability in Distributed Organizing. *Organization Science*, *13*, 249–273. doi:10.1287/orsc.13.3.249.2776

Osti, L., Turner, W. L., & King, B. (2009). Cultural differences in travel guidebooks information search. *Journal of Vacation Marketing*, *15*(1), 63–78. doi:10.1177/1356766708098172

Patel, A. D. (2007). *Music, Language, and the Brain*. Oxford, UK: Oxford University Press.

Rheinghold, H. (2000). *The virtual community: Homesteading on the electronic frontier*. Reading, MA: Addison-Wesley.

Ricken, T. S., Schuler, P. R., Grandhi, A. S., & Jones, Q. (2010). TellUsWho: Guided Social Network Data Collection. In *Proceedings of the 43rd Hawaii International Conference on System Sciences*. Washington, DC: IEEE Computer Society.

Schatzki, R. T. (2001). Introduction. Practice Theory. In Schatzki, T. R., Knorr-Cetina, K., & von Savigny, E. (Eds.), *The Practice Turn in Contemporary Theory* (pp. 1–14). New York, NY: Routledge.

Sterne, J. (2006). The mp3 as cultural artefact. *New Media & Society*, *8*(5), 825–842. doi:10.1177/1461444806067737

Suchman, L. (2007). *Human–Machine Reconfigurations: Plans and Situated Actions*. Cambridge, UK: Cambridge University Press.

Zhang, Jiang, & Carroll (2010). Social Identity in Facebook Community Life. *JVCSN 2*(4) (pp. 65-77)

Zhao, S., Grasmuch, S., & Martin, J. (2008). Identity Construction on Facebook: Digital empowerment in Anchored relationships. *Computers in Human Behavior*, *24*(5), 1816–1836. doi:10.1016/j.chb.2008.02.012

Zhou, Y., & Davis, J. (2007). Discovering Web Communities in the Blogspace. In *Proceedings of the 40th Hawaii International Conference on System Sciences*. Washington, DC: IEEE Computer Society.

This work was previously published in the International Journal of Virtual Communities and Social Networking, Volume 2, Issue 4, edited by Subhasish Dasgupta, pp. 51-63, copyright 2010 by IGI Publishing (an imprint of IGI Global).

Chapter 14
The Impact of Social Networking Websites on the Education of Youth

Sunitha Kuppuswamy
Anna University Chennai, Chennai, India

P. B. Shankar Narayan
Pondicherry University, Puducherry, India

ABSTRACT

Social networking websites like Orkut, Facebook, Myspace and Youtube are becoming more and more popular and has become part of daily life for an increasing number of people. Because of their features, young people are attracted to social networking sites. In this paper, the authors explore the impact of social networking sites on the education of youth. The study argues that these social networking websites distract students from their studies, but these websites can be useful for education based on sound pedagogical principles and proper supervision by the teachers. Moreover, the research concludes that social networking websites have both positive as well as negative impact on the education of youth, depending on one's interest to use it in a positive manner for his or her education and vice versa.

INTRODUCTION

Internet medium is developing with the increased usage and understanding of how to use email, could shop online, and search the web for recipes or the long- lost instruction manual for a piece of equipment in the garage, etc. Now, internet is more about blogs, podcasts, Facebook, Myspace, and Orkut. These are some of the tools and technology associated with a recent phenomenon called social networking and is present everywhere.

Social networking has become part of the daily life experiences for an increasing number of people. The rapid adoption of social network sites by teenagers in the United States and in many other countries around the world raises some important questions. Why do teenagers flock to these sites? What are they expressing on them? How

DOI: 10.4018/978-1-4666-1553-3.ch014

do these sites fit into their lives? What are they learning from their participation? Are these online activities like face-to-face friendships, or are they different, or complementary? (Danah Boyd, 2007). Penuel and Riel define social networking as "a set of people and the relationships between them". That definition is found today in the social networking services that promote the development of online communities of people. Social networking such as Facebook, Orkut, Myspace, Flickr and Youtube are sites where users apply for membership and maintain their personal profile information in a centrally organized database. Each network member controls access to their profile by accepting or declining requests from other network members to be "friends". By expanding and developing their network of friends, social networking members are able to maintain online relationships for work, study, special- interests or leisure- related purposes.

Social networking services utilize the participation technology and software tools to facilitate communication and interaction between members. Social software communication tools include blogs, wikis, instant messaging, chat rooms, message boards and social bookmarking. Members use these tools to share online ideas, documents, photos, videos, and favorite websites actually almost anything. As more people participate in social networking, the question becomes is it merely a social activity or are they involved in learning and development?

And social networking websites is very popular among the youth so that they contribute the majority percentage of the users of these sites. So, the researcher wanted to study the impact of these social networking sites on their education.

LITERATURE REVIEW

Jeff Cain (2008), in the research paper "Online Social Networking Issues Within Academia and Pharmacy Education" has discussed that Facebook is a tool that aids students in developing their identities and finding their "fit" within a college community. Helping students connect, establish a network and stay in contact with old and new friends is the centre of attraction and significant benefits of Facebook. Making connections on campus which help them feel that they belong may be an important factor in student retention. These capabilities along with the many facets of communicating with their friends make social networking sites very appealing. Although extremely popular, especially among younger generations, social networking sites are not without their issues. Controversy surrounds the use of these sites, specifically in terms of privacy, addiction, safety, responsibility and attitudes toward revealing personal information to the world. Most of the press concerning these sites has been negative in focus. Newspapers and magazines related to higher education are replete with cases of college students who experienced negative repercussions from questionable activities that were made public online.9,15-26 The list of incidences are long and revolve around a myriad of issues related to photos, posts, and/or personal profiles.

Social networking sites such as Facebook provide individuals with a way of maintaining and strengthening social ties, which can be beneficial in both social and academic settings. These same sites, however, also pose a danger to students' privacy, safety, health and professional reputations if proper precautions are not taken. Colleges and schools of pharmacy would be advised to consider how these issues might affect their students. At a minimum, schools should take appropriate steps to educate students about these matters. Research is needed on professional students' usage and attitudes toward online social networking sites. Monitoring and usage of these sites by institutions venture into legal grey areas concerning the Fourth Amendment, the right to privacy, and duty of care, and should be approached with caution. Discussion is warranted on how, if at all, material found on student social networking sites should be used in colleges of pharmacy admissions decisions and/or matters of a disciplinary nature. Further research is needed on how best to address the issues surrounding online social networking.

Ana M. Martinez Aleman, Katherine Lynk Wartman and M. Aleman Ana (2009) in their book *Online Social Networking on Campus* said that teenager's online social needs are similar to those of college students. High school students want to stay up to date with their friend's status; they plan activities online; they are "social searchers" who investigate other users with whom they have a real- life connection, and also like college students, they perceive their Facebook community to correspond to their existing real-life social relationships at school or other institutional affiliations (sports teams, music groups, etc.). Though perhaps not a user community that engages in "social browsing" to connect with other users offline, the high school user seems less alien and disparate to Facebook's traditional and original niche user than the older adult user.

Henk Huijser (2007) explores potential educational applications of Web 2.0 technologies, and cuts through some of the hype generated around these technologies, as well as around characteristics of Generation Y, and their implications for learning and teaching. Web 2.0 technologies both reflect and drive a blurring of the lines between students and university educators, which has a potentially profound impact on learning and teaching in higher education. This paper argues that Web 2.0 technologies, and Social Network Sites in particular, offer exciting opportunities but that educational applications of these technologies should be based on sound pedagogical principles and driven by empirical research and careful evaluation, if they are to effect meaningful learning experiences for all students.

Vincent Miller (2008) in his research paper "New Media, Networking and Phatic Culture" has discussed that This article will demonstrate how the notion of 'phatic communion' has become an increasingly significant part of digital media

culture alongside the rise of online networking practices. Through a consideration of the new media objects of blogs, social networking profiles and microblogs, along with their associated practices, I will argue, that the social contexts of 'individualization' and 'network sociality', alongside the technological developments associated with pervasive communication and 'connected presence' has led to an online media culture increasingly dominated by phatic communications. That is, communications which have purely social (networking) and not informational or dialogic intents. I conclude with a discussion of the potential nihilistic consequences of such a culture.

Doris de Almeida Soares and Escola Naval (2008) in their resarch paper "Understanding class blogs as a tool for language development" it has been said that Web 2.0 has allowed for the development of cyber spaces where any computer user can create their own public pages to share knowledge, feelings and thoughts inviting linguistic interactions with people around the globe. This innovation has caught the attention of language practitioners who wish to experiment with blogging to enhance the teaching and learning experience. In 2007 I set up a class blog with my nine pre-intermediate EFL students in a language school in Brazil. This experience gave rise to two central questions: a) did my students see our blog as a learning tool? and b) what was blogging like in other language teaching contexts? To answer the first question I carried out some Exploratory Practice for three months. As for the second question, I designed an online survey which was answered by 16 members of a community of practice called the Webheads. Ultimately I learned that my students saw our blog as a learning tool and that blogs are being used in different ways around the world. This article presents the rationale behind using blogs in language classes, describes my research process and discusses the understanding my students and I have gained from exploring our own practices.

R. Cachia, R. Compano and O. Da Costa (2005) in their research paper "Students Actually

Use the Internet for Education" says that New research released by the National School Boards Association reveals data showing we all might need to reevaluate our assumptions: It turns out kids are actually using the Internet for educational purposes. In fact, according to the study, "Creating & Connecting: Research and Guidelines on Online Social--and Educational--Networking," the percentage of children specifically discussing schoolwork online outpaces the percentage that spend time downloading music.

For the survey, the NSBA teamed up with Grunwald Associates to poll 1,277 9 to 17 year olds, 1,039 parents, and 250 school district leaders who make decisions on Internet policy. It found that a full 50 percent of students who are online spend time discussing schoolwork, and 59 percent spend time talking about education-related topics, including college or college planning; learning outside of school; news; careers or jobs; politics, ideas, religion, or morals; and schoolwork.

Further, these students are spending almost as much time on the Internet visiting websites and social networking services (nine hours per week for teens) as they spend watching television (10 hours).

A full 96 percent of students surveyed responded that they use the Internet for social networking purposes, including Facebook, MySpace, Webkins, and Nick.com chat. Seventy-one percent said they use these services at least on a weekly basis.

Yet, the study asserts, the vast majority of school districts have stringent rules against nearly all forms of social networking during the school day--even though students and parents report few problem behaviors online. Indeed, both district leaders and parents believe that social networking could play a positive role in students' lives and they recognize opportunities for using it in education--at a time when teachers now routinely assign homework that requires Internet use to complete. In light of the study findings, school districts may want to consider reexamining their policies and practices and explore ways in which

they could use social networking for educational purposes.

Jeff Cain (2008) in "Online Social Networking Issues Within Academia and Pharmacy Education" it has been said that Facebook is a tool that aids students in developing their identities and finding their "fit" within a college community. Helping students connect and stay in contact with old and new friends is touted as one of the significant benefits of Facebook. Making connections on campus which help them feel that they belong may be an important factor in student retention. These capabilities along with the many facets of communicating with their friends make social networking sites very appealing. Although extremely popular, especially among younger generations, social networking sites are not without their issues. Controversy surrounds the use of these sites, specifically in terms of privacy, safety, and attitudes toward revealing personal information to the world. Most of the press concerning these sites has been negative in focus. Newspapers and magazines related to higher education are replete with cases of college students who experienced negative repercussions from questionable activities that were made public online.9,15-26 The list of incidences are long and revolve around a myriad of issues related to photos, posts, and/or personal profiles.

Social networking sites such as Facebook provide individuals with a way of maintaining and strengthening social ties, which can be beneficial in both social and academic settings. These same sites, however, also pose a danger to students' privacy, safety, and professional reputations if proper precautions are not taken. Colleges and schools of pharmacy would be advised to consider how these issues might affect their students. At a minimum, schools should take appropriate steps to educate students about these matters. Research is needed on professional students' usage and attitudes toward online social networking sites. Monitoring and usage of these sites by institutions venture into legal grey areas concerning the Fourth Amendment, the right to privacy, and duty of care, and should be approached with caution. Discussion is warranted on how, if at all, material found on student social networking sites should be used in colleges of pharmacy admissions decisions and/or matters of a disciplinary nature. Further research is needed on how best to address the issues surrounding online social networking.

Danah M. Boyd and N.B. Ellison (2007) in their research paper "Social network sites: Definition, history, and scholarship" it has been said that Social network sites (SNSs) are increasingly attracting the attention of academic and industry researchers intrigued by their affordances and reach. This special theme section of the *Journal of Computer-Mediated Communication* brings together scholarship on these emergent phenomena. In this introductory article, the authors describe features of SNSs and propose a comprehensive definition. They then present one perspective on the history of such sites, discussing key changes and developments. After briefly summarizing existing scholarship concerning SNSs, they discuss the articles in this special section and conclude with considerations for future research.

The work described above and included in this special theme section contributes to an on-going dialogue about the importance of social network sites, both for practitioners and researchers. Vast, uncharted waters still remain to be explored. Methodologically, SNS researchers' ability to make causal claims is limited by a lack of experimental or longitudinal studies. Although the situation is rapidly changing, scholars still have a limited understanding of who is and who is not using these sites, why, and for what purposes, especially outside the U.S. Such questions will require large-scale quantitative and qualitative research. Richer, ethnographic research on populations more difficult to access (including non-users) would further aid scholars' ability to understand the long-term implications of these tools. They hope that the work described here and included in this collection will help build a foundation for

future investigations of these and other important issues surrounding social network sites.

M. Brendesha Tynes (2007), in "Internet Safety Gone Wild? Sacrificing the Educational and Psychosocial Benefits of Online Social Environments" it has been said that Many Internet safety and parenting experts suggest that parents prohibit their teens from social networking sites and other online spaces where predators may lurk. But we may do adolescents a disservice when we curtail their participation in these spaces, because the educational and psychosocial benefits of this type of communication can far outweigh the potential dangers. These benefits include developing cognitive skills that are consistent with those required in educational settings and perspective-taking skills that are necessary for citizenship in an increasingly multiracial society. Alternative strategies for keeping adolescents safe online should build on the increasing technological awareness and sophistication of teens themselves.

Danah Boyd (2007) in her research paper "Why Youth Social Network Sites: The Role of Networked Publics in Teenage Social Life" has said that Although news media give the impression that all online teens in the United States are on MySpace, this is not the case. For this reason, I want to take a moment to discuss who is not participating. In 2004, PEW found that 87 percent of teenagers aged twelve to seventeen have some level of Internet access.5 In a study conducted in late 2006, they found that 55 percent of online teens aged twelve to seventeen have created profiles on social network sites with 64 percent of teens aged fifteen to seventeen.6 While these numbers are most likely low,7 it is very clear that not all high school students participate in online communities that require public content creation like social network sites.

Gender also appears to influence participation on social network sites. Younger boys are more likely to participate than younger girls (46 percent vs. 44 percent) but older girls are far more likely to participate than older boys (70 percent vs. 57 percent). Older boys are twice as likely to use the sites to flirt and slightly more likely to use the sites to meet new people than girls of their age. Older girls are far more likely to use these sites to communicate with friends they see in person than younger people or boys of their age.10 While gender differences do exist and should not be ignored, most of what I discuss in this article concerns practices that are common to both boys and girls.

The research paper "Exploring the Educational Potential of Social Networking Sites: The Fine Line between Exploiting Opportunities and Unwelcome Imposition" by Henk Huijser (2007) University of Southern Queensland explores potential educational applications of Web 2.0 technologies, and cuts through some of the hype generated around these technologies, as well as around characteristics of Generation Y, and their implications for learning and teaching. Web 2.0 technologies both reflect and drive a blurring of the lines between students and university educators, which has a potentially profound impact on learning and teaching in higher education. This paper argues that Web 2.0 technologies, and Social Network Sites in particular, offer exciting opportunities but that educational applications of these technologies should be based on sound pedagogical principles and driven by empirical research and careful evaluation, if they are to effect meaningful learning experiences for all students.

In the research paper Social networking sites within Higher Education – threat or opportunity? by Neville Palmer, Jomo Batola, Margaret Jones and Sheila Baron (2007) it has been said that a Southampton Solent University, students predominantly use Facebook to advertise social and sporting events, make new friends, or chat among existing friends. There are currently over 6,200 members of the "official" Southampton Solent network, which represents around 40% of all students at the University, though there may be more in other groups. Currently there seem to be at least 150 different groups representing areas

of interest under the umbrella of the University, ranging from the bizarre to sports clubs, social activities and academic related interests. Most of these groups have a small membership. There are also alumni groups, and some specific course related groups. These seem to have been formed, not by staff, but by students. For example there is a group for journalism students and another for business studies. There is a mixture of social chitchat, but also course related self help discussion. The journalism students are also giving each other leads on where they can get work experience.

Forums are a form of Social Software that can be a useful tool in education. Forums are also related to Blogs, though a blog is centered on an individual, whereas a forum is centered more on an area of interest (Holzsclag 2005). There are many blogs on the Internet posted by individuals to discuss subjects ranging from their personal lives to World events. However some students are using blogs to post and discuss their work and ideas so that others can comment and advice on it (Polly 2007). A forum can be useful when a particular topic or area of interest requires discussion on the Web. This concept is being used at Southampton Solent University.

In the research paper "Youth Impact" it has been said that A combination of the words "iPod" and "broadcast," podcasts are digital media files distributed over the Internet and listened to on a portable media player. A related term is "vodcast," which describes podcasts that incorporate video. Podcasts were originally conceived as a way for people to create their own radio shows without needing a recording studio or transmission network. They evolved into a means of recording and distributing speeches, classes and training sessions, and public safety messages. They are especially popular in K–12 schools and colleges: Teachers and professors use them to record lessons, debates, and guest speakers for absent students or later use, and students use them to record their presentations, projects, and experiments

Podcasters and vodcasters record their audio and video sessions, edit them, and upload them to a feed. Listeners and viewers use a "podcatcher" service such as iTunes to search for and subscribe to one or more feeds. When a new podcast or vodcast is released on the feed, the audio or video file will download automatically to the subscribers' iPod, computer, or other device so that they can listen to or view it at their leisure.

The review of literature gave a clear idea on the use of social networking websites and the aim of the study was formulated to find the Impact of Social Networking Websites on the education of Youth and the objective is to find the trends in the Internet use by youth and to study the impact of social networking websites on the education of youth.

METHODOLOGY

For conducting the research, the researcher has chosen the following two methodologies: Survey and In-depth Interview. The researcher adopted the Stratified Random Sampling technique. Stratified random sampling is done when the universe is heterogeneous i.e. if the people are of different kinds. So the universe is sub-divided into many homogeneous groups or strata. And the random sampling is done in each stratum and the sample size from each stratum is taken proportionally. The total number of samples taken were 500 i.e., 125 in each stratum. The researcher has sub- divided the universe as following strata

- Stratum 1- +1 & +2 students
- Stratum 2- Engineering students
- Stratum 3- medical students
- Stratum 4- Arts & Science and others

Also, the researcher has interviewed experts from the field to know their perspectives of the impact of the Internet on education and to know the impact of social networking sites and how far it complements the students' education.

ANALYSIS

Survey: Statistical Analysis

Survey has been done among five hundred respondents, one hundred and twenty five students from each stratum. Among the five hundred respondents 295 were male and 205 were female. 100 students accessing Internet for more than five years, 140 students for 3-5 years, highest of all- 205 students for 1-3 years and the lowest of all- 55 students for less than a year.

210 students access Internet several times in a week, 125- once in a week, 70- once in a day, 45- several times in a day and 50- rarely. When asked about the number of years the students are using social networking sites (SNS), majority of the students from all stratum have selected the option 1-3 years. Majority of the students sit in the social networking sites several times in a week. Next highest is the option once in a week. The lowest is several times a day.

Maximum number of respondents uses social networking sites more than one hour and exactly only 185 students sit for less than hour. Maximum respondents said the SNS is rarely useful for their education and 140 students said it is useful only during the exams. 65 said it is useful for the education at all times and 85 said it is never useful for the education.

310 students said SNS is time consuming, 195 said they use SNS for education and 135 said they chat regarding academics in SNS. 190 students have not agreed that social networking is time consuming. But out of 190 students, 150 of them sit in SNS more than hour. 75 of them sit for 2-4 hours and 5 sit for more than four once they access the social networking sites.

260 students said their academic performance didn't change because of using SNS and only 15 students said that it has decreased. Others said it has improved.

455 students have an account in Orkut and some of them have account in Facebook, Hi-5 etc. But next to Orkut many are familiar with the

Youtube website and the next is Facebook. SNS is highly used by the students as a messenger, then it is used for sharing photos and videos and then it is used to find new friends.

Only 140 students have joined in the communities regarding academics, out of which 110 had said that those communities were helpful for the education. And only 40 students have said that the social networking sites distract them from the studies.

Thus, from the percentage analysis of the survey data, it is found that 41% of the students are accessing Internet for 1-3 years and 28% for 3-5 years. 42% access Internet several times in a week and 25% once in a week. Apart from social networking many students use the Internet for sending e-mails and chatting. Apart from social networking 51% of the respondents use Internet for downloading music/videos, 76% for sending e-mails/chatting and 60% for educational purposes. Maximum percentage of the students accessing social networking sites for 1-3 years (Figure 1).

33% of the students access SNS several times in a week, 28% once in a week, 18% rarely, 14% once in a day and 7% several times in a day. More percentage of the students sits in SNS more than an hour when accessed (Figure 2).

13% said that SNS is useful in education at all times, 28% said it is useful only during exams, 42% said it is rarely useful and 17% said it is never used for education (Figure 3).

62% had accepted that SNSs are time consuming, 39% agreed that they use SNS for education, 27% chat regarding academic subjects in SNS (Figure 4).

52% of the students said that their academic performance didn't change because of using SNS and only 3% said that it has decreased. 39% said it has improved and 9% said it has improved a lot (Figure 5).

Interview with Prof. V. Sundareswaran

Dr. V. Sundareswaran, the Professor & Head, Department of Media Sciences, Anna University Chennai has thirty one years of experience in the teaching field. When asked about the difference between knowledge level of students ten years back and the students at present he said that

Figure 1. Number of years students accessing SNS

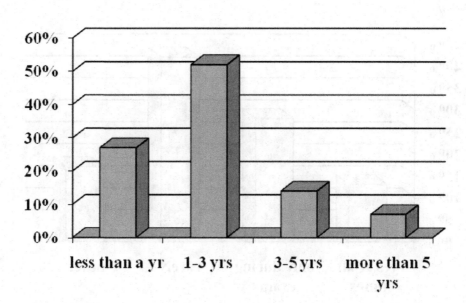

Figure 2. Time spent in SNS

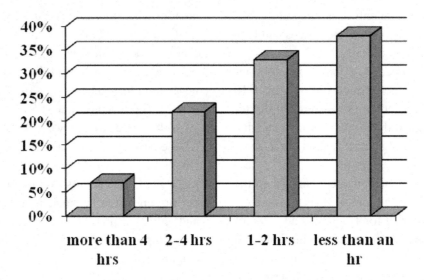

retrieval or gathering of information was very difficult in those days. It took a lot of time to reach the source materials which are in libraries. But nowadays students gather lot of information very quickly and easily using Internet. And said because of the Internet the students at present are more knowledgeable than the students in the past. And also added at times students know more than the teachers also.

He said no one knows about how students are using the Internet. When a student is at home, teachers doesn't know how and for what he/she is using the Internet and when the students are at the institution, parents doesn't know what he/she is doing.

When asked about students- teachers' interaction via Internet he said that it is a good and easy way for a student to reach the teacher and clear

Figure 3. SNS in education

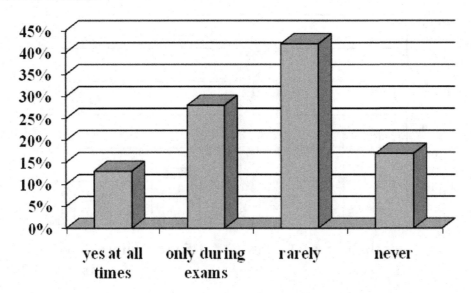

Figure 4. SNS is time consuming

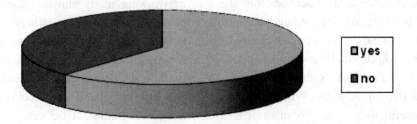

some doubts or gets some guidance at any time. But nothing is equivalent to the conventional class room. He always prefers the traditional classroom teaching method and specifically chalk and board teaching. He doesn't prefer to use the Over Head Projectors and Powerpoint slides also. But he agrees that certain subjects need to be taught using such technology for practical demonstration and easy understanding.

When asked whether he thinks the information is better conveyed through the interactions with the teachers by the students in the Internet, he said he don't know as he doesn't use Internet much. He rarely uses Internet only to guide his research students.

When asked about websites like Orkut and Facebook, he said he don't know about those sites and remembered me his point that at times students know more than their teachers in terms of technology applications.

Interview with Mr. Kiruba Shankar

Mr. Kiruba Shankar, CEO of f5ive technologies, a web based company is also a social media enthusiast.

Figure 5. Academic performance

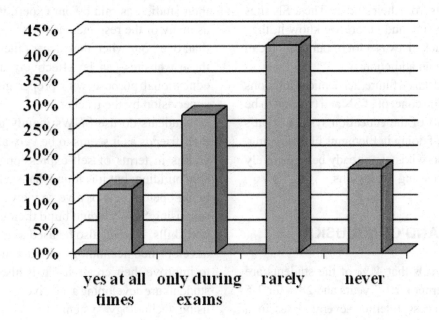

When asked about his opinion about the social networking sites like Orkut and Facebook they are wonderful tools to expand one's contact beyond the first circle of friends. It's a wonderful way to keep one's friends updated about what's happening in his/her life. That said, Social Networking sites are like a two edged knife. While they can be extremely useful, they can also be misused and become a time sink.

He doesn't think social networking sites help improve student's education. But what they do well is improve connections which can be quite useful in the real life. In corporate life, connections and contacts are everything. He believes that SN sites in colleges helps prepare for the real world.

He said most students are using SN sites for the following:

1. To maintain friendship connection with existing friends
2. Reaching out to friends of friends who they would like to be in touch with
3. To improve the brand image of the person in the community
4. Reach out to the opposite sex.

He says that these websites definitely distracting the students from their studies. These SN sites are a big time sink and before we know it, they would have sucked away a lot of our time. It can easily become an addiction.

He also said that in future, academic institutions will embrace the concept of SN and tweak it to be an integral part of the education system. That's the right way of doing it. Elements like blogging, podcasting and wikis are already being actively used in documenting the lessons.

FINDINGS AND CONCLUSION

The study reveals that 41% of the students are accessing Internet for 1-3 years and 28% for 3-5 years. 42% access Internet several times in a

week and 25% once in a week. Apart from social networking many students use the Internet for sending e-mails and chatting. Apart from social networking 51% of the respondents use Internet for downloading music/videos, 76% for sending e-mails/chatting and 60% for educational purposes. More percentage of the students accessing social networking sites for 1-3 years.

33% of the students access SNS several times in a week, 28% once in a week, 18% rarely, 14% once in a day and 7% several times in a day. More percentage of the students sits in SNS more than an hour when accessed. 13% said that SNS is useful in education at all times, 28% said it is useful only during exams, 42% said it is rarely useful and 17% said it is never used for education. 62% had accepted that SNSs are time consuming, 39% agreed that they use SNS for education, 27% chat regarding academic subjects in SNS. 52% of the students said that their academic performance didn't change because of using SNS and only 3% said that it has decreased. 39% said it has improved and 9% said it has improved a lot.

Though students don't accept that SNS distracts them from their studies, it is clear that SNS is time consuming which is found from the survey. So these SNSs clearly distract the students from their studies, as said by our expert, in some way as many of the respondents use these sites more than one hour when they access these sites. But these websites can be effectively used for the educational purpose with proper guidance and supervision by the teachers.

Students do use SNWs mainly to chat with their friends as it seems to be very attractive for youths in terms of self-expression and friendship building; but it is found that such SNWs are being open to new or diverse views. In the long run, using SNWs would build their communication skills. It could also be used as a vital tool to develop their technology skills and a platform to improve their creativity. It is also found that students are developing a positive attitude towards using technology systems that is inclusive of creative use of audio and video, colour, pictures, editing, mixing and customizing content. Students were also found to think about the online design and layout which might give them an idea about graphic / web designing. Such ideas might place them in multimedia jobs in the near future. Thus SNWs are found to be very useful in selecting their career path.

It is found that very few students use SNWs for the purpose of their education as they were unaware of the academic and professional networking opportunities that the Web sites provide. Hence it is time for the teachers to create awareness about the advantages of using SNWs for their education. They're also found to share creative works like power point presentations, poetry, songs and videos and practicing safe and responsible use of information and technology. Thus the web sites do offer tremendous educational potential, but the message has to be taken to the students by the teachers and need to help realize the benefits for improving their academic excellence.

Focusing on the other end, a good percentage of students are found to be addicted to SNWs. Spending abnormal amount of time online for entertainment may affect their academics to a greater extent. Also, wide use of SNWs consequently increases youth's vulnerability to sexual victimization. Though such sexual victimization associated with SNWs is found to be very minimal, prevention efforts that focus on providing psycho-social support may have a greater impact on this least percentage of youth. Some students are engaged in unsafe activities because of lack of understanding of the concept that what they post in those communities is open to public, and are accessible by anyone in the world. Thus there are chances to get mis-leaded because of unsafe disclosure of personal information.

Using these social networking sites is found to be based on the individual's interest, as some of the respondents said that they use these sites for the education purpose. Thus this research proves the Social Network theory which views social rela-

tionships in terms of nodes and ties. Nodes are the individual actors within the networks, and ties are the relationships between the actors. There can be many kinds of ties between the nodes. In its most simple form, a social network is a map of all of the relevant ties between the nodes being studied. The network can also be used to determine the social capital of individual actors. These concepts are often displayed in a social network diagram, where nodes are the points and ties are the lines.

The power of social network theory stems from its difference from traditional sociological studies, which assume that it is the attributes of individual actors -- whether they are friendly or unfriendly, smart or dumb, etc. Here it depends upon the target group's interest, willingness, educational background, environment, etc. Social network theory produces an alternate view, where the attributes of individuals are less important than their relationships and ties with other actors within the network. This approach has turned out to be useful for explaining many real-world phenomena, but leaves less room for individual agency, the ability for individuals to influence their success; so much of it rests within the structure of their network. It is also believed that in future, educational institutions will embrace these SNSs and take it as the integral part of the education system.

SUGGESTIONS

The students cannot be restricted to access these sites, as they find some or the other way to crack into these social networking sites and it is not that good to ban these sites in the educational institutions. Instead by some pedagogic approach, they can be used for learning process and can find a way to give access only to the education related communities and denying access to other communities regarding entertainment like the way many of the institutions do keep firewall for many websites when the students access internet in their institution.

ACKNOWLEDGMENT

We would like to thank Mr. Aravind Karthik, final year student of Department of Media Sciences in Anna University Chennai for assisting the authors with the field data collection.

REFERENCES

Boyd, D. (2007). *Why Youth loves Social Network Sites: The Role of Networked Publics in Teenage Social Life*. Berkeley, CA: University of California-Berkeley.

Boyd, D. (2008). *Taken Out of Context: American Teen Sociality in Networked Publics*. Berkeley, CA: University of California-Berkeley.

Boyd, D., & Ellison, N. B. (2007). Social network sites: Definition, history, and scholarship. *Journal of Computer-Mediated Communication, 13*(1).

Cachia, R., Compano, R., & Da Costa, O. (2005). Grasping the potential of online social networks for foresight. *Technological Forecasting and Social Change, 74*(8), 1179–1203. doi:10.1016/j.techfore.2007.05.006

Cain, J. (2008). Online Social Networking Issues within Academia and Pharmacy Education. *American Journal of Pharmaceutical Education, 72*(1).

de Almeida Soares, D., & Naval, E. (2008). Understanding class blogs as a tool for language development. *Language Teaching Research, 12*(4), 517–533. doi:10.1177/1362168808097165

Huijser, H. (2007). *Exploring the Educational Potential of Social Networking Sites*. Toowoomba, Queensland, Australia: University of Southern Queensland.

Martinez Aleman, M. A., Lynk Wartman, K., & Ana, M. A. (2009). *Online Social Networking on Campus: Understanding What Matters in Student Culture*. London: Taylor & Francis.

Miller, V. (2008). New Media, Networking and Phatic Culture. *Convergence: The International Journal of Research into New Media Technologies, 14*(4), 387–400. doi:10.1177/1354856508094659

Palmer, N., Batola, J., Jones, M., & Baron, S. (2007). *Social networking sites within Higher Education – threat or opportunity?* Southampton, UK: Southampton Solent University.

Tynes, M. B. (2007). Internet Safety Gone Wild? Sacrificing the Educational and Psychosocial Benefits of Online Social Environments. *Journal of Adolescent Research, 22*(6), 575–584. doi:10.1177/0743558407303979

This work was previously published in the International Journal of Virtual Communities and Social Networking, Volume 2, Issue 1, edited by Subhasish Dasgupta, pp. 67-79, copyright 2010 by IGI Publishing (an imprint of IGI Global).

Chapter 15
A Cross–Cultural Examination of Student Attitudes and Gender Differences in Facebook Profile Content

Katherine Karl
University of Tennessee Chattanooga, USA

Joy Peluchette
University of Southern Indiana, USA

Christopher Schlagel
Otto-von-Guericke-University Magdeburg, Germany

ABSTRACT

This paper examines cultural and gender differences in student reports of the likelihood that they would post various types of information on their Facebook profiles and their attitudes regarding non-students accessing their profiles. Significant gender and country differences were found. In general, U.S. students were more likely than German students to report they would post extreme information. Males in both countries (U.S. and Germany) were more likely than females to self-promote and be extreme in the information they would post and less concerned if employers viewed their profiles. Both U.S. and German students reported several items they would likely post on their profiles, but did not want employers to see. Implications of these results and recommendations for future research are also discussed.

INTRODUCTION

Over the past few years, online social networking has exploded in popularity as a means for people to post profiles of their personal information and to communicate with one another ("Social Networking Explodes Worldwide," 2008). Facebook

had 400 million active users and over 150 million new members added in 2009 alone, making it the world's largest social networking site (Facebook Press Room, 2010; Sarno, 2009). Although Facebook originated in 2004 as an internet forum for college students, access was extended to the general public in 2006 to generate additional rev-

DOI: 10.4018/978-1-4666-1553-3.ch015

enue for the company. The age group originally targeted by Facebook (18 to 24 year-olds) now makes up only 35% of all members and the fastest growing group--those who are 35 years old and older—make up 30% of all members (Eldon, 2009; Smith 2009). Global expansion has been another key source of growth for Facebook and its introduction of natural language interfaces in several markets has helped propel the site to 153% growth from June 2007 to June 2008 ("Social Networking Explodes Worldwide," 2008). According to recent user statistics, over 70% of Facebook members are outside the United States and more than 70 translations are available on the site (Facebook Press Room, 2010). Membership gains have been particularly strong in Europe, increasing by ten million in 2009 and comprising about one third of Facebook's active monthly users (Eldon, 2009). The growing global popularity of Facebook is also evidenced in recent statistics showing that the growth rate in the North American region (38%) is far less than other regions. For example, Europe had thirty-five million visitors in June 2008, a 303% increase over the same time in 2007 ("Social Networking Explodes Worldwide," 2008). Other worldwide regions have seen even more dramatic growth: Latin America (up 1055%), Middle East-Africa (up 403%), and Asia Pacific (up 458%).

Although Facebook has prompts for different kinds of personal information (e.g. activities, interests, relationship status, political affiliation, favorite music, etc.), users have considerable freedom to post any information or pictures of their choice (Ellison, Steinfield, & Lampe, 2007). The result is profile content ranging from very 'tame' such as pictures of one's pets to very 'extreme' information (such as pictures and comments about one's sexual activities, use of alcohol and/ or drugs). For instance, according to one study of the Facebook network at Indiana University, a user can find more than 500 groups and over 500 events that contain the search term 'sex' using a basic Facebook search (Brandenburg, 2008).

Similar results occur when using search terms like 'drugs', 'porn', and 'alcohol'.

Despite the increasing popularity of Facebook among the general population, it is still used most frequently by college students and recent graduates (Smith, 2009). Employers who hire graduating students have discovered that social networking sites allow them to learn more than they ever could from reading an applicant's resume and cover letter. Additionally, many employers believe it is important that new hires possess good judgment, discretion, and a sense of propriety, given that employees may have access to a wide range of sensitive materials and information via the rise of the information economy and flattened workplace structures (Brandenburg, 2008). So, how many employers are actually using profile information to screen job applicants? According to the SHRM study entitled *Online Technologies and Their Impact on Recruitment Strategies—Using Social Networking Web Sites to Attract Talent* (2008), 50% of the HR managers surveyed indicated that they spent two or more hours a week screening applicants on social networking sites. Most (88%) of the HR managers used social networking for screening applicants early in the hiring process, either prior to contacting the applicant or prior to offering an interview. At least half of the respondents indicated that social networking was useful in screening applicants because it took little time and reaped large amounts of information beyond what was found through traditional methods.

Similarly, a study by CareerBuilder.com revealed that 26% of 1,150 hiring managers surveyed said that they used Internet search engines in their candidate screening process and 12% said that they used social networking sites. Of this 12%, 63% indicated that they did not hire the person based on what they found (Sullivan, 2006).

It should also be noted that this practice is not limited to the United States. For example, according to a survey of 300 HR managers in German HR consulting companies, 28% use social networks to screen job candidates (job skills as well as leisure time behavior), and 26% reported they found content that resulted in the elimination of job applicants from further consideration in the application process (Beeger, 2007). Likewise, Nesbitt and Marriott (2007) indicated that one in five employers in the United Kingdom use social networking sites as part of their employment screening process.

These actions have prompted questions about student use of social networking, in particular the privacy and appropriateness of information posted. For example, what kinds of information are students likely to post on their profile? Are male and female students different in how they present themselves on their profile? Are some students more likely to post extreme information than others? In other words, are there gender differences in who commits these Facebook *faux pas*? Do students care if other non-students access their profile information? Is there information that they would or would not want employers to see? These questions provide the basis for this study. Given that Facebook now has a significant global presence, it is also important to examine whether the answers to these questions may differ depending on the country or culture being examined. In reviewing the literature, we found only one study which examined cross-cultural differences in social networking communication, where the authors examined the role that Korean and American cultures play in deceptive behavior (Lewis & George, 2008). For this study, we chose to compare students in the United States and Germany with regard to the likelihood that they would post various types of information on their Facebook profiles and their attitudes regarding other non-students accessing their profiles. With the rising popularity of Facebook in Germany and the cultural differences between the United States and Germany on uncertainty avoidance and individualism, it is likely that differences exist.

SELF-PRESENTATION IN SOCIAL NETWORKING PROFILES

Research suggests that, just as with face-to-face communication, users of personal homepages or websites engage in self-presentation behaviors to influence the impressions others form of them (Dominick, 1999; Papacharissi, 2002; Trammell & Keshelashvili, 2005; Walker, 2000). According to Goffman's (1959) theory of self-presentation, we are all actors who stage daily performances in an attempt to manage the impressions of our audience. As actors, we have the ability to choose our stage, props, and costume to suit the situation and our main goal is to maintain coherence from one situation to another. For most people, being onstage is different from being backstage. Most people are onstage when they interact with others in public or professional settings. In contrast, the backstage is a place where actors can loosen some of their self-imposed restrictions, relax, and be themselves. Additionally, access to the backstage is usually limited to a very select and small group. It is a "place where the performer can reliably expect that no member of the audience will intrude" (Goffman, 1959, p. 114). This separation helps actors maintain their onstage personas or facades. Similarly, Leary (1996, p. 109) suggested that "by keeping different targets away from one another, people can avoid the awkwardness of trying to present disparate images of themselves to two or more targets simultaneously."

For many, the people one knows in a classroom setting are different and separate from one's close personal friends who are different and separate from one's family members. According to Donath and boyd (2004, p. 78), we use time and space "in the physical world" to separate the incompatible aspects of our lives and we may even carefully organize our activities to prevent overlap. However, in the virtual world, all one's social network 'friends' are in one virtual space. As a result, 'friends' now means a hodgepodge of real friends, former friends, friends of friends, coworkers or colleagues, relatives of all ages, and perhaps even a boss or professor. Lampinen, Taminen and Oulasvirta (2009) refer to this as the co-presence of multiple groups or having "all my people right here, right now". Facebook users can now classify people into specific groups such as friends, co-workers, or relatives, and grant each category a different level of access to various items. However, Facebook's default setting is 'share' and, according to Facebook's chief privacy officer, only about 20% of users change their privacy settings (Stross, 2009).

Personal websites allow users with a high level of control over the kinds of information they post about themselves, providing an opportunity for strategic self-presentation (Papacharissi, 2002; Vazire & Gosling, 2004). Social networking is somewhat different from other forms of online communication (e.g. chat rooms, web pages) in that there is more of a bridge between online and offline social connections between users. Particularly with Facebook, relationships are generally 'anchored' to reality by such things as a person's legal name, institutions, and/or mutual friends (Zhao, Grasmuck, & Martin, 2008). Thus, it has been argued that, while users would likely present themselves in socially desirable ways, it is unlikely that these additions or omissions would be so exaggerated that they would be discernable in brief offline encounters.

To date, there have been a few studies examining social networking profile content. Some have focused on the frequency with which prompted information is posted (e.g. book, movie, and music preferences) (Stutzman, 2006; Tufekci, 2008), while others have examined how identity is structured through profile content. For example, Zhao, Grasmuck, and Martin (2008) found that Facebook users are more inclined to 'show' their identity through photos rather than narrative descriptions and to stress group identities. Other studies have examined the relationship between personality and profile content (Marcus, Machilek, & Schutz, 2006). For example, in their study of personal website content, Vazire and Gosling (2004) found strong evidence of impression management by those who were extraverts. Likewise, using a sample of German users of the social network site StudiVZ, Kramer and Winter (2008) found that extroverts were more likely to chose less conservative pictures of themselves. These same authors found that those most likely to present themselves in less conservative ways were those who scored high in self-efficacy with regard to self-presentation. While these studies provide some insight into profile content used by individuals in creating their social networking identity, none have examined the more extreme or negative information found on some profiles, such as comments and/or photos about sexual activities, alcohol, and drug use. This study addresses this issue by examining gender differences in who is likely to post such information and commit these social networking *faux pas*.

Existing research on self-presentation and impression management suggests that men and women are likely to present themselves differently to their audience. For example, Guadagno and Cialdini (2007) found that men are more likely to self-promote, take responsibility or credit for positive outcomes, and do favors for others with expectation of reciprocity in their efforts to directly impact the impressions formed by others. Conversely, they found women to be more modest, likely to praise others, and conforming when expressing their opinion. Research on gender differences in self-presentation of one's identity online appears to be consistent with this. For example, Magnuson and Dundes (2008) found females were twice as likely as men to mention their significant other on their profile, indicating women's tendency to see themselves as an extension of their significant other and the need to turn to others for validation. Similarly, Fogel and Nehmad (2009) and Tufekci (2008) found that males were more likely to self-promote on their profile by disclosing personal information about themselves, such as their phone number or address. Raacke and Bonds-Raacke (2008) found that men logged on to their profile more frequently, reported more friends linked to their account, and used their social networking sites for dating and finding out about events more than women. Since these studies indicate that males are more cavalier about the content of their profile, we predict:

Hypothesis 1: Men will be more likely than women to post 'extreme' profile information, such as comments and/or photos about alcohol and drug use, profanity, or sexual activities.

CONCERN FOR AUDIENCE AND DISCLOSURE OF PROFILE CONTENT

Growing awareness that Facebook is being accessed by parties other than students has led to criticism by unhappy students. For example, students at Stanford University were quoted as saying, "I see Facebook as a personal domain, and one that should not be used by employers to judge a student's qualifications" and "I think it's stupid. How would an employer know a good candidate based on their Facebook profile? It's a bunch of random stuff you put for your friends" (Fuller, 2006). Yet, it is not clear how widespread this awareness is since it does not appear to be prompting students to change the content or visibility of their profile. Researchers on several college campuses were able to download about 70% of their campus Facebook networks, indicating that only about 30% of the users (or less) were using privacy settings (Lewis, Kaufman, & Christakis, 2008; Stutzman, 2006). When examining the downloaded information, these researchers were astonished at the amount of personal information (e.g. cell phone number, relationship status, political views) posted on students' profiles, even when students indicated a concern about privacy.

Thus, it appears that not all students want to hide information about their personal life since the internet lets them express themselves and find like-minded friends (St. John, 2006). Still others have found that many Facebook users intentionally misrepresent themselves or join groups that do not accurately depict who they are for the sake of humor or social approval (Mitrano, 2008). For example, in one study, 8% of students said they exaggerated their alcohol or drug use in Facebook posts (Brock, 2007). It has also been suggested that some members of today's younger generation find it empowering to post provocative photos online: "When we see other teens getting attention from their silly (and often confessional) YouTube videos, we learn that keeping one's life an open book is a ticket to fame" (Funk, 2007). According to O'Brien (2007), the Facebook group called "30 Reasons Girls Should Call it a Night," consists of photos of drunken women making fools of themselves and is evidence that "drunken tomfoolery" has become a point of pride for many.

It appears that today's college-aged students have a different comfort level about what is private and what is not, having grown up in a world where any information is 'no more than six clicks away' (Cummins, 2006). If concerned about unwanted audiences, Tufekci (2008) found that students adjusted the visibility of their profile (using privacy settings) as opposed to changing their profile content. However, men were less likely to do this than women. In addition, students expressed little concern when asked about the perceived likelihood of their profile being found by future employers, although women were slightly more concerned than men. Similarly, in their study of social networking, Fogel and Nehamd (2009) found that women had significantly higher ratings on privacy concern and more concern about identity information disclosure than men. Given these findings, we predict:

Hypothesis 2: Men will be less concerned than women about others (employers, family, strangers) viewing their profile.

CULTURAL DIFFERENCES IN PROFILE CONTENT

As noted earlier, one purpose of this study is to examine differences between U.S. and German students in the types of information included in their social network profiles. One of the most popular frameworks for studying international culture has been that of Geerte Hofstede who identified the following dimensions of culture: individualism, uncertainty avoidance, masculinity, power distance and long-term orientation (Hofstede, 1980; Hofstede & Bond, 1984). While these cross-cultural dimensions have received limited attention with regard to social networking (Lewis & George, 2008), there has been some examination of differences with regard to web usage and on-line communication (Cakir & Cagiltay, 2002; Pfeil, Zaphiris, Ang, 2006;). Given these findings, we would expect cultural differences in social networking communication. Two of Hofstede's dimensions, individualism and uncertainty avoidance, would appear to be relevant to social network profiles.

Individualism is the degree to which group members expect that individuals orient their actions for their own benefit rather than for the benefit of the group or collective. Countries with high individualism emphasize the 'I' versus the 'we' and self-actualization and freedom are important. In relationships, honesty and a strong private opinion are valued (Hofstede, 1991). Of the fifty-three countries in Hofstede's (1980) original data, the United States ranked first in individualism with a raw score of 91 and Germany ranked fifteenth with a score of 67. With regard to social networking, it would be expected that those from countries with high individualism scores would be less concerned about the content of the infor-

mation on their profile or with censoring their thoughts and actions.

Uncertainty avoidance is the degree to which members of a group are uncomfortable with and avoid change, ambiguity and uncertainty. In countries with high uncertainty avoidance, people tend to be risk averse, resistant to change, and intolerant of rule-breaking. These countries typically employ rules, conventions, and rituals that are intended to minimize unpredictability (Hofstede, 1991). With regard to uncertainty avoidance, Germany ranked twenty-ninth with a score of 65, while the United States ranked forty-third with a score of 46 (Hofstede, 1980). As such, it would be expected that German students would be more likely than U.S. students to be concerned about their profile content and who has access to their profiles. Therefore, we predict that:

Hypothesis 3: U.S. students will be more likely than German students to post 'extreme' profile information, such as comments and/or photos about alcohol and drug use, profanity, or sexual activities.

Hypothesis 4: U.S. students will be less concerned than German students about others (employers, family, strangers) viewing their profile.

METHOD

Sample

This study utilized a sample of undergraduate students enrolled in management and economics courses at medium-sized universities located in the Midwestern part of the United States and the eastern part of Germany. Participation was voluntary for both groups although the U.S. participants were given some minimal course credit for doing so. Because undergraduate students are the primary users of social networking sites, we intentionally recruited undergraduate students to complete our survey. Of the 480 surveys distributed in the U.S.,

433 were returned for a response rate of 89%. About 59% of the respondents were male (N=256) and the mean age was 21.2 years. Approximately 51% (N=222) indicated they were business majors, while the remaining 49% indicated some other non-business major. The average hours worked per week was 16.89, although 30% reported that they did not work at all and almost 9% reported they worked forty or more hours per week. Of the 350 surveys distributed in Germany, 304 were returned for a response rate of 87%. About 45% of the respondents were male (N=135) and the mean age was 21.5 years. All students indicated they were business or economics majors. The average hours worked per week was 11.62, although 43% reported that they did not work at all and 11.51% reported they worked forty or more hours per week.

Survey Instrument

Both the U.S. and German survey instrument consisted of six sections: (1) demographic items including gender, age, academic major, and hours worked per week; (2) social network usage; (3) beliefs regarding who should be able to access one's social network profile; (4) type of information believed appropriate for one's social network profile; (5) employer's use of students' social network profiles, and (6) items students would not want employers to see.

- **Social network usage**: Four questions were included in this section to assess whether respondents participated in a social network site, which social network sites they participate in, how long they had been participating in social network sites, and how often they logged onto their social network.

- **Others' access to one's social network profile:** This section consisted of five questions adapted from Stutzman (2006). Respondents were asked the following question about five different groups (friends, family, classmates, prospective or current employers, and strang-

ers), "I am OK with _____ accessing my social network profile." All items were rated on a five-point scale (*1=Strongly Disagree, 5=Strongly Agree*).

- **Type of information believed appropriate for one's social network profile:** This scale measured beliefs regarding the appropriateness of including various types of information on one's social network profile. Respondents were asked how likely they would be to include 36 different items in their personal profile if they were to join a social network site or if they already participated in a social network site. The 36 items included various demographic information, photos, and beliefs. All items were rated on a five-point scale (*1=Very Unlikely, 5=Very Likely*).

- **Employer's use of social network profiles:** This scale measured beliefs regarding the appropriateness of including various types of information on one's social network profile if access to such information were available to current or prospective employers. More specifically, respondents were asked their level of agreement that they would "be OK with prospective or current employers" having various types of information about them. This scale included the same thirty-six items mentioned above. All items were rated on a five-point scale (*1=Strongly Disagree, 5=Strongly Agree*).

- **Items students would not want employers to see:** This was an open-ended question in which respondents were asked "Are there any photos or comments on your social network site that you would NOT want current or prospective employers to see?" This was followed by a "Yes" or "No" response scale and "If yes, please list them in the space below."

RESULTS

With regard to usage, 80% of our U.S. respondents (N=346) and all of our German respondents reported using social network sites. The most frequently used social network site for our sample was Facebook comprising 71% of the U.S. sample and 91% of the German sample. Two other sites used by many students included MySpace (used by 48% of the U.S. sample) and studiVZ (a German Facebook clone used by 41% of the German sample). The majority of our respondents reported that they had been participating in a social network site for one to two years (37% of the U.S. sample, N=162; and 43% of the German sample, N=90) and logged on to their social network site either one or two times per day (47% of the U.S. sample, N=163 and 51% of the German sample, N=149).

Table 1 shows the items for which there were significant differences between males and females in their self-reported likelihood of including this information in their personal profile if they had a social network site. Because the use of multiple univariate tests leads to a greatly inflated overall type I error rate (Stevens, 1986), a MANOVA was conducted in order to examine gender differences in students' ratings of the thirty-six items. The results of the multivariate test revealed a significant effect for gender [$F (36, 682) = 7.98$, $p <.000$], country [$F (36, 682) = 29.08$, $p <.000$] and the interaction between gender and country [$F (36, 682) = 2.52$, $p <.000$]. An examination of the univariate tests revealed that males were more likely than U.S. females to report posting eighteen of the items, many of which were either self photos of various types (e.g., sexy, semi-nude, with alcohol, with firearms), comments (e.g. sexual activities, use of alcohol, use of drugs), or personal information (e.g., email address, home address, phone number, hometown). Females, on the other hand, were more likely than males to report they would include items of a 'mushy' or 'cutesy' nature (e.g., photos of pets, family,

or romantic partners and favorite books or TV shows). Thus, hypothesis 1 was supported.

An examination of the cross-country results showed significant differences between U.S. and German students on 27 of the 36 items, showing support for hypothesis 3. U.S. respondents were more likely than German respondents to report they would post 25 of the items. The only two items in which German respondents reported they would be more likely than U.S. respondents to post was their academic status (M=3.88, SD=.96 versus M= 3.64, SD= 1.20) and their hometown (M=4.21, SD=.82 versus M=4.04, SD=1.18). In addition to the main effects for gender and country, there were nine significant interactions between gender and country. For three of the items, comments regarding sexual activities or preferences [$F (1, 717) = 7.71$, $p <.01$], self-photo with firearms [$F (1, 717) = 5.51$, $p <.05$], and phone number [$F (1, 717) = 7.27$, $p <.01$], both German and U.S. males were more likely to report posting these items, but the differences between males and females were much greater in the U.S. than Germany. For three of the items, birth date, self-photo goofy, and comments regarding personal beliefs and values, the interaction was crossed such that U.S. males were more likely to report posting these items than U.S. females; however, in Germany, females were more likely to report posting these items than males. U.S. males and females were equally likely to say they would post photos of friends; however, German females were more likely than German males to say they would post these photos. Finally, U.S. males and females were equally likely to report posting their religious beliefs, but in Germany, females were more likely to do so than males.

Table 2 shows a comparison of males and females in whether they would be comfortable with others accessing their Facebook profile information. In general, both males and females were not concerned with either friends or classmates accessing their Facebook profile (means ranged between 4.17 and 4.64) and there were

Table 1. A comparison of means by gender and country in the likelihood that respondents would include items in their personal profile if they had a social network site

Informational Item	Male		Female		Gender Comparison	Germany		US		Cross-Country Comparison	Total Sample	
	Mean	SD	Mean	SD	F (1, 717)	Mean	SD	Mean	SD	F (1, 717)	Mean	SD
1. Interests	4.30	.85	**4.31**	.78	**2.86**	4.00	.84	4.51	.73	**75.55*****	4.30	.82
2. Major	4.20	.88	**4.36**	.72	**8.43****	4.25	.72	4.29	.87	**1.40**	4.27	.81
3. Favorite Music	4.17	1.01	**4.16**	.95	**2.14**	3.78	1.07	4.43	.82	**86.38*****	4.17	.98
4. Favorite Movies	4.09	1.07	**4.17**	.98	**6.57***	3.78	1.10	4.37	.90	**66.34*****	4.13	1.03
5. Hometown	4.22	.96	**3.99**	1.14	**7.45****	4.21	.82	4.04	1.18	**6.80****	4.11	1.05
6. Photo of friends	3.96	1.18	**4.04**	1.12	**6.30***	3.63	1.16	4.26	1.08	**60.24*****	4.00	1.15
7. Birthdate	4.03	1.13	**3.91**	1.21	**.43**	3.91	1.07	4.01	1.23	**.80**	3.97	1.67
8. Job/Occupation	4.00	1.07	**3.93**	1.07	**.17**	3.63	1.03	4.21	1.03	**54.42*****	3.97	1.07
9. Favorite TV Shows	3.90	1.19	**3.99**	1.13	**7.31****	3.44	1.23	4.29	.97	**114.87*****	3.94	1.17
10. Self photo (humorous or goofy)	3.98	1.13	**3.88**	1.16	**.08**	3.82	1.07	4.01	1.19	**4.40***	3.93	1.14
11. Favorite Books	3.77	1.29	**4.04**	1.09	**11.26*****	3.73	1.11	4.01	1.26	**13.27*****	3.90	1.20
12. Relationship Status	3.94	1.16	**3.81**	1.25	**.15**	3.29	1.24	4.29	1.00	**140.33*****	3.88	1.21
13. Group Affiliations	3.89	1.03	**3.75**	1.07	**1.18**	3.56	1.02	4.01	1.03	**31.18*****	3.82	1.05
14. Self Photo (traditional)	3.91	1.28	**3.73**	1.38	**.00**	3.22	1.41	4.25	1.09	**119.80*****	3.82	1.33
15. Academic Status	3.66	1.18	3.83	1.02	**2.27**	3.88	.96	3.64	1.20	**6.19***	3.74	1.11
16. Sexual Orientation	3.91	1.31	3.32	1.53	**15.61*****	2.62	1.42	4.34	.95	**354.86*****	3.63	1.45
17. Photo of family members	3.14	1.45	3.39	1.39	**16.03*****	2.71	1.31	3.65	1.38	**16.03*****	3.26	1.43
18. Email Address	3.44	1.44	3.02	1.43	**6.75****	2.57	1.39	3.72	1.29	**119.45*****	3.24	1.45
19. Self-photo (athletic)	3.45	1.43	2.86	1.43	**19.31*****	2.78	1.32	3.45	1.49	**30.35*****	3.17	1.46
20. Photo of Romantic Partner	3.05	1.39	3.31	1.40	**8.15****	2.96	1.29	3.33	1.46	**15.85*****	3.17	1.40
21. Photo of pets	2.98	1.48	3.39	1.41	**23.54*****	2.79	1.38	3.44	1.46	**23.54*****	3.17	1.46
22. Religious Beliefs	3.01	1.44	2.84	1.46	**.54**	2.41	1.25	3.30	1.47	**69.97*****	2.93	1.45
23. Comments regarding your personal beliefs and values	2.96	1.31	2.87	1.34	**.12**	2.55	1.16	3.17	1.37	**.12**	2.92	1.33
24. Political Affiliation	3.04	1.37	2.75	1.36	**5.54***	2.60	1.25	3.12	1.41	**22.19*****	2.90	1.37
25. Self photo drinking alcohol	2.80	1.54	2.33	1.36	**14.10*****	2.49	1.34	2.64	1.56	**.55**	2.58	1.48
26. Self photo (sexy or provocative)	2.51	1.45	2.16	1.28	**11.56*****	2.35	1.25	2.35	1.47	**.27**	2.35	1.38
27. Comments regarding your personal use of alcohol	1.89	1.17	1.26	.67	**14.17*****	1.25	.59	1.84	1.17	**14.17*****	2.14	1.32
28. Phone Number	2.12	1.34	2.12	1.34	**42.21*****	1.52	.87	2.01	1.34	**21.96*****	1.81	1.20
29. Comments regarding your sexual activities or sexual preferences	2.37	1.37	1.88	1.21	**51.84*****	1.67	1.00	2.46	1.42	**51.84*****	1.59	1.02
30. Comments regarding your participation in activities which are in violation of University Policy	1.74	1.12	1.34	.76	**18.30*****	1.24	.62	1.77	1.13	**18.30*****	1.55	.99

continued on following page

Table 1. Continued

Informational Item	Male		Female		Gender Comparison	Germany		US		Cross-Country Comparison	Total Sample	
	Mean	SD	Mean	SD	F (1, 717)	Mean	SD	Mean	SD	F (1, 717)	Mean	SD
31. Self photo semi-nude	1.78	1.17	1.26	.65	45.47***	1.46	.84	1.58	1.08	.33	1.53	.99
32. Home Address	1.67	1.05	1.32	.73	23.95***	1.48	.86	1.52	.98	.09	1.50	.93
33. Comments regarding your use of illegal drugs	1.54	1.04	1.29	.82	6.60**	1.20	.61	1.58	1.10	6.60**	1.42	.95
34. Self photo with firearms	1.77	1.29	1.11	.48	63.37***	1.27	.78	1.60	1.18	9.33**	1.27	.78
35. Self photo in the nude	1.36	.88	1.07	.35	29.23***	1.17	.55	1.26	.78	.85	1.23	.70
36. Self photo with sexual props	1.38	.97	1.06	.36	26.45**	1.14	.58	1.29	.87	3.14	1.23	.76

* p <.05, **, p <.01, *** p <.001

no significant differences between males and females on these items. Likewise, there were no significant differences between males and females in whether they would be 'ok' with employers accessing their Facebook profile, and in general, respondents were somewhat neutral on this item (means ranged between 2.90 and 2.91). However, females were significantly more likely to be 'ok' with family viewing their Facebook profile (M=4.20, SD=1.08) than males (M=3.76, SD=1.28). In contrast, males were significantly more likely to be 'ok' with strangers viewing their Facebook profile (M=3.15, SD=1.42) than females (M=2.67, SD=1.37). Hypothesis 2 was therefore only partially supported.

Table 2 also shows a cross-country comparison of whether respondents would be comfortable with others accessing their Facebook profile information. These results show that U.S. respondents were more comfortable than Germans with classmates and employers seeing their profile, whereas German respondents were more comfortable than the U.S. students with family viewing their profile information. This provides partial support for hypothesis 4. In addition to the main effects, there was one significant interaction between country and gender such that both German

and U.S. males (M=3.33, SD=1.41 and M=2.86, SD=1.38, respectively) were more likely than German or U.S. females (M=2.71, SD=1.29 and M=2.63, SD= 1.45, respectively) to be comfortable with strangers viewing their profile but the difference between males and females was much greater in the U.S. than Germany.

Additional gender and country comparison analyses were performed regarding respondents attitudes about employers' use of their social network profiles. Once again, the results of the MANOVA revealed a significant effect for gender [F (36, 677) = 2.94, p <.000], country [F (36, 677) = 23.13, p <.000], and the interaction between gender and country [F (36, 677) = 1.78, p <.01]. Similar to the results reported above, an examination of the univariate tests revealed that both U.S. and German males were more 'ok' than females with employers having photos of various types (e.g. sexy, semi-nude, with firearms) or comments (e.g. use of alcohol, use of drugs, participation in activities which violate university policy). However, it should be noted that the means for many of the items were very low (less than 2). Thus, both males and females were generally in low agreement that they would be comfortable with employers having this information.

Table 2. A comparison by gender and by country in whether respondents would be ok with others accessing their Facebook profile information

Person	Total Sample		Male		Female		Gender Comparison	Germany		U.S.		Cross-country Comparison
	Mean	SD	Mean	SD	Mean	SD	F (1, 627)	Mean	SD	Mean	SD	F (1, 627)
Friends	4.62	.78	4.59	0.76	4.64	.80	0.74	4.61	0.83	4.62	.73	.05
Classmates	4.21	1.01	4.25	1.01	4.17	1.02	0.09	4.03	1.03	4.36	.98	15.15***
Family	3.97	1.21	3.76	1.28	4.20	1.08	16.73***	4.19	1.06	3.78	1.30	12.33***
Strangers	2.93	1.41	3.15	1.42	2.67	1.37	14.20***	2.77	1.33	3.06	1.47	3.07
Employer	2.90	1.43	2.90	1.44	2.91	1.41	1.65	2.46	1.30	3.27	1.42	56.95***

* p <.05, **, p <.01, *** p <.001

The cross-country comparison shows that U.S. respondents, compared to German respondents, are more comfortable with employers having access to 29 of the 36 items. In fact, there were no items for which German respondents reported they were more 'ok' with employers viewing than U.S. respondents. In addition to the main effects for gender and country, there were two significant interactions. Both German and U.S. males (M=1.11, SD=.36 and M=1.41, SD=.82, respectively) were more likely than females from either country (M=1.06, SD=.26 and M=1.09, SD =.39, respectively) to be ok with employers having comments regarding sexual activities or preferences but the difference between males and females was much greater in the U.S. than Germany. The same type of interaction was found for the self-photo with firearms item (means for German and U.S. males were M=1.13, SD=.54 and M=1.36, SD=.82, respectively, whereas the means for German and U.S. females were M=1.04, SD=.20 and M=1.08, SD =.38, respectively).

Using ANOVA with repeated measures, we also examined whether there were significant differences in students' responses regarding the likelihood they would include a particular item in their personal profile if they had a social network site and whether they would be comfortable with employers having the information. Significant within-subjects effects were found for all 36

items. There were nine items for which students approve of employers having access to but that they would not be likely to include on their social network profile (e.g. email address, home address, phone number, academic status, major, hometown, birthdate, job/occupation, and a traditional self photo). However, for the remaining 27 items, students' ratings regarding the likelihood of including the item on their social network profile were significantly higher than their ratings regarding whether they were comfortable with employers having the information.

Finally, we examined the results of the open-ended question in which respondents were asked "Are there any photos or comments on your social network site that you would NOT want current or prospective employers to see?" Sixty-nine (19.9%) of the U.S. respondents and 94 of the German respondents (30.9%) indicated that there were items on their current profile that they would not want current or prospective employers to see. The most commonly listed item (N=39, 56.5%) that U.S. students did not want employers to see was drinking or alcohol-related photos or comments. Several also listed party photos or comments (N=8, 11.6%). Some (N=10, 14.5%) mentioned other non-alcohol related comments (e.g., comments left by friends, comments about work, inappropriate humor, etc.). Others (N=10, 14.5%) listed other non-alcohol or party-related photos (e.g., acting crazy, silly or nonprofessional, social life, me in a bathing suit). Marijuana was listed by three respondents. Two respondents reported "All of them" and one respondent reported "Most of them." Three respondents stated they didn't care if employers saw their profile. For example, their responses included "If I cared, I wouldn't put them on there," 'I keep my networking site "G-rated,"' and "I am who I am and proud of it!" One gave a mixed response, "Well maybe the drinking ones, but if they saw it, that would be just too bad."

Similar results were found in the German sample. The most commonly listed item (N=50, 53.2%) that German students did not want employers to see was party photos. Several students also listed drinking or alcohol-related photos or comments (N = 22, 23.4%). Others listed their group affiliations (N=13, 13.8%) and photos in general (N=7, 7.4%). Four respondents reported that their sport activities might be perceived as dangerous by employers. Drugs were listed by two respondents. Two respondents stated that employers should concentrate on the job interview rather than looking at the social networking sites. One respondent stated that most of his/her profile was just for fun and does not represent his/her personality.

Given that our survey solicited students' self-reported use of social networking, we gathered additional data to gauge students' actual use of such sites. To get a sense of how concerned students were about privacy, we randomly sampled 100 U.S. students' Facebook profiles (students at the same U.S. institution as those we surveyed) and found that only 25% utilized the privacy option which limits access to personal information. We then selected a sample of 200 profiles that had no privacy option selected and examined the information posted. While most students who completed our survey indicated that they would be unlikely to include comments about alcohol or sexual activities, we found that 42% of the profiles examined had comments regarding alcohol, 53% had photos involving alcohol use, 20% had com-

ments regarding sexual activities, and 25% had semi-nude or sexy photos. Although we did not survey students about this issue, at least 50% of the profiles included profanity. We also examined wall comments which are 'public' messages that individuals post on each others' profiles. We found that about 50% of the wall comments involved issues of partying, 40% incivility (negative comments about other people), 25% derogatory comments about employers, 18% sexual activities, and 10% negative racial comments.

DISCUSSION

Overall, our findings show that college students in both the U.S. and Germany are relatively heavy users of social networking sites. This was not surprising given the popularity of these forums as a means of communication among young people and their friends worldwide. When asked about information that they would post on their social networking site, we found significant differences based on gender and nationality. Both U.S. and German males were more likely to post 'extreme' profile information, such as self-photos of various types or comments about drugs, sex, or alcohol. Females, from both countries, reported a greater likelihood to include less offensive or more 'cute' information about themselves, their family, or partner. These findings are consistent with previous studies of gender differences in the use of the electronic communications (Harper, 2002).

When comparing U.S. and German responses regarding the likelihood of posting various types of information, U.S. students were significantly more likely to report they would post more of the 36 items included in our survey and they were also more likely to post those items that were 'extreme' in nature. Given differences in how the two countries rate on uncertainty avoidance and individualism, this was not surprising. With higher ratings on individualism and lower ratings on uncertainty avoidance, we expected U.S. students to post more information about themselves and be more cavalier in the kind of information they post on their profiles. Although we found significant interactions between country and gender for several of the items, it was interesting to find that, while U.S. women were generally more cautious than U.S. males about their likelihood to post certain items, German women appeared to be much bolder about expressing themselves when compared to German males. For example, German females indicated they would be more inclined to post their religious beliefs, comments about personal beliefs and values, a goofy self-photo, their birth date, and photos of friends.

When examining what our respondents would be comfortable with others having access to, both males and females indicated they were comfortable with friends or classmates viewing their profile. This was give that their peers are most likely to be the anticipated audience on social networking sites. However, U.S. students expressed greater comfort with classmates accessing their profile than their German counterparts, indicating more openness and honesty which is consistent with individualism. With regard to family accessing their profile, females expressed greater comfort with this than males, presumably because they are less likely to post what would be considered extreme material. When examining this by country, it was interesting to find that German respondents were more comfortable than their U.S. counterparts with family members viewing their profile. One explanation for this may be because of differences in the type of information one is likely to post to their profile, with U.S. students indicating a greater likelihood to post more 'extreme' kinds of information---photos and/or comments that they may be ashamed for their family to see. Mixed results were also found when respondents were asked about whether they would mind having strangers access their profile. Males from both countries were significantly more comfortable than females with strangers viewing their profile, although the gender difference was much greater

with the U.S. than German respondents. Females generally have a greater concern for their personal safety and identity information, as found in a recent study of social networking by Fogel and Nehmad (2009). This concern may be even more acute in the U.S., due to the size of the country and the prevalence of Internet security issues.

Given the human resource management implications, we were most interested in how our respondents felt about employers having access to their profile. While there was no significant gender difference on this issue, U.S. respondents were more comfortable with employers accessing their Facebook profile than their German counterparts and, when examined by item, this involved a majority of the profile items in question. Again, we attributed this to the differences between the two nations on uncertainty avoidance and individualism, with U.S. students having a greater sense of freedom of expression and honesty (high individualism) and greater risk taking (low uncertainty avoidance) in the kinds of information they are willing to post on their profile. There were significant interactions by gender and country on two items with males from both countries indicating a greater likelihood than females from either country to post comments about sexual activities or preferences and a self-photo with firearms. So, regardless of country, males clearly demonstrated a tendency towards riskier behavior.

Although it was fairly limited, there was some personal information that students seemed to be comfortable with employers having access to but that they did not necessarily have on their profile, such as address, birth date, or phone number. It is possible that such information was not on the students' sites due to more general concerns that they had about security or identity theft. However, there were quite a number of items that students indicated that they would place on their site but were less comfortable with employers having access to. For both U.S. and German respondents, these were primarily drinking, alcohol-related or party photos or comments. These findings show that students are somewhat naïve about the potential negative consequences concerning the access and use of such information. It is ironic that, while they were less likely to want employers to have access to certain kinds of information, many respondents still indicated the likelihood to post such information on their profile.

Our results certainly have implications for colleges and universities. Students should be advised of the possible consequences of their website postings during orientation sessions and through student codes of conduct and information technology policies. One example of a university that has taken initiative with this is Cornell. Their IT Policy Office has a "Thoughts on Facebook" document on their web site (http://www.cit.cornell.edu/oit/) which advises students to think about their social networking behavior. For instance, the first section of the document, labeled "invincibility", advises students to "think about not only your marketability today as a cool guy or girl in your college social circle, but who you might want to be in five or ten years when posting an 'identity' on the Internet." Although career services centers on college campuses can be proactive about advising students in general about how they are using their social network sites, it may be important to direct attention to particular groups of students. Our findings suggest that male students show more naiveté in how information from social networking sites can be accessed and the potential consequences of how it might be used so greater attention to this demographic would be important.

There are also some implications for employers. Given that some of our respondents were so cavalier with sharing information about themselves via the Internet, it raises questions about whether, once employed, they would be similarly inclined to share what would be considered private or confidential workplace information. Students' fascination with and usage of social networking sites also presents potential problems for employers in whether such sites would be accessed during work. A recent study of employees in four countries (U.S., Germany, United Kingdom, and Japan) found that 'risky' online behavior at work (such as visiting social networking sites, making online purchases, and browsing websites unrelated to work) was more likely to take places in small businesses and put these businesses at a greater risk of virus attacks and security breaches ("Risky Online Behavior More Likely to Happen in Small Businesses," 2008). While some organizations have put mechanisms in place to restrict internet access, employers should be diligent in providing guidance to employees through policy statements and orientation or training programs on issues of confidentiality and Internet/cell phone use at work.

Concerns are also typically raised about how such online behavior impacts productivity in the workplace. While this has generally been viewed negatively, a recent study of 2500 employees in five European countries (France, Great Britain, Germany, Belgium, and the Netherlands) shows that some employers may be changing their stance on this. Sixty-five percent of those surveyed indicated that their company had adopted social networking as part of their working culture, with employees seeing benefits in increased knowledge, problem solving, information sharing with internal and external stakeholders, and collaboration ('Social Networking in the Workplace Increases Efficiency," 2008). An increasing number of U.S. employers including Ernst & Young, Sodexho, Unilever, Accenture and the Georgia Army National Guard are also establishing their own Facebook pages (Zeidner, 2008). In addition, a New York-based recruitment advertising firm, TMP Worldwide is marketing a new application, the "Work with Me" widget, which allows companies to encourage their employees to post job listings voluntarily on their personal Facebook pages. In return, they would be paid a finder's fee for hires made as a direct result of the posting (Zeidner, 2008).

CONCLUSION

This study is not without limitations. For example, our survey was limited in that we could have included several additional profile items such as favorite quotes, what they are 'looking for' in a relationship, or whether they are 'interested in' men or women, or use of profanity. It may also have been useful to gather information on the number of 'friends' or 'groups' one belongs to, or the type of 'wall' comments posted by the students' friends. In addition, because we used self-reports, we believed that students might be under-reporting the likelihood that they would include certain behaviors such as alcohol or drug use or sexual behavior. In our follow-up random sample of 200 profiles, we did indeed find a greater number of comments or photos of such behavior than we would have expected, based on our survey results.

Currently, there is no research demonstrating that the content of one's social networking profile is predictive of on-the-job behavior. In other words, do students leave their wild and uninhibited behavior from college days behind when they enter the workforce? One of our respondents made such a comment on his survey, stating there were some drinking activities that he would rather not have employers see because they would not be appropriate for work, "'but have nothing to do with how I would behave on the job." Other respondents commented that some "drinking" was expected in college and that, although it might make a bad first impression on employers, "they probably participated in the same things when they were in college." So, is all the concern about students posting their drinking or sexual-related exploits just much ado about nothing? Or, are students who post inappropriate information more likely to have related performance problems in the workplace such as carelessness, lack of integrity, poor attendance, or inappropriate use of the Internet or email?

Earlier, we suggested that students may bring their Internet behavior with them into the workplace by stealing company time to keep in touch with 'friends' on their social networking sites. To date, there appears to be no empirical evidence of this. It would therefore be important to investigate this, with particular attention given to determining how much work time these employees spend monitoring their sites. Finally, we recommend that future researchers examine possible positive outcomes of social networking sites. For example, are social network users more connected to others and, thus, have greater social capital? Furthermore, are these individuals able to take advantage of these connections in the workplace by having access to more information? So, for those organizations making social networking part of their workplace culture, what are the benefits to the business? While there is evidence that employers are using social networking sites to weed out candidates who post inappropriate information, could or should employers use social network sites as a means of proactively searching and identifying candidates with desirable experience and qualifications who may not be actively searching for jobs themselves?

Given the limited number of empirical studies of social networking use, this study was an effort to tap students' usage and perceptions regarding the inclusion of various types of information on their site. In addition, we were interested in comparing U.S. and German student responses regarding their use of social networking. We hope that our findings will provide a foundation for further investigations of this issue, particularly how it might impact human resource concerns in employment and workplace behavior.

REFERENCES

Beeger, B. (2007). *Soziale netzwerke: Karrierekiller im Internet*. Retrieved from http://www.stern.de/computer-technik/internet/:Soziale-Netzwerke-Karrierekiller-Internet/596742.html

Brandenburg, C. (2008). The newest way to screen job applicants: A social networker's nightmare. *Federal Communications Law Journal, 60*(3), 597–626.

Brock, R. (2007). Online. *The Chronicle of Higher Education, 53*(19), A31.

Cakir, H., & Cagiltay, K. (2002). Effects of cultural differences on e-mail communication in multicultural environments. In F. Sudweeks & C. Ess (Eds.), *Proceedings of the Third International Conference on Cultural Attitudes towards Technology and Communication* (pp. 29-50). Montreal, Canada: School of Information Technology, Murdoch University.

Comscore. (2008). *Social networking explodes worldwide as sites increase their focus on cultural relevance.* Retrieved from http://www.comscore.com/press/release.asp?press=2396

Cummins, H. (2006). *Bosses peek in on Facebook to screen job applicants.* Retrieved June 12, 2010, from http://seattlepi.nwsource.com/business/265153_facebook03.html

Dominick, J. (1999). Who do you think you are? Personal home pages and self-presentation on the World Wide Web. *Journalism & Mass Communication Quarterly, 79*(3), 643–660.

Donath, J., & Boyd, D. (2004). Public displays of connection. *BT Technology Journal, 22*(4), 71–82. doi:10.1023/B:BTTJ.0000047585.06264.cc

Eldon, E. (2009). *Europe grew by 10 million new Facebook users last month, Here's the top 20 gainers.* Retrieved January 6, 2010, from http://www.insidefacebook.com/2009/11/06/europe-grew-by-10-million-new-facebook-users-last-month-heres-the-top-20-gainers/

Ellison, N., Steinfeld, C., & Lampe, C. (2007). The benefits of Facebook "friends": Social capital and college students' use of online social network sites. *Journal of Computer-Mediated Communication, 12*(4), 143–1168. doi:10.1111/j.1083-6101.2007.00367.x

Facebook Press Room. (2010). *Company statistics.* Retrieved January 6, 2010, from http://www.facebook.com/press/info.php?statistics

Fogel, J., & Nehmad, E. (2009). Internet social network communities: Risk taking, trust, and privacy concerns. *Computers in Human Behavior, 25*(1), 153–160. doi:10.1016/j.chb.2008.08.006

Fuller, A. (2006). *Employers snoop on Facebook.* Retrieved June 12, 2010 from http://daily.stanford.edu/article/2006/1/20/employersSnoopOnFacebook

Funk, L. (2007, September 19). Women on Facebook think provocative is empowering. *USA Today,* 11a.

Goffman, E. (1959). *The Presentation of Self in Everyday Life.* Garden City, NY: Double Day Anchor.

Guadagno, R., & Cialdini, R. (2007). Gender differences in impression management in organizations: A qualitative review. *Sex Roles, 56*(7-8), 483–494. doi:10.1007/s11199-007-9187-3

Harper, V. (2002). Sex differences in perceived outcomes of electronic mail interactions. *Psychological Reports, 90*(2), 701–702.

Hofstede, G. (1980). *Culture's Consequences: International Differences in Work-Related Values.* Thousand Oaks, CA: Sage Publications.

Hofstede, G. (1991). *Cultures and Organizations—Software of the Mind.* London: McGraw-Hill.

Hofstede, G., & Bond, M. (1984). Hofstede's culture dimensions: An independent validation using Rokeach's Value Survey. *Journal of Cross-Cultural Psychology*, *15*(4), 417–433. doi:10.1177/0022002184015004003

Krämer, N. C., & Winter, S. (2008). Impression management 2.0: The relationship of self-esteem, extraversion, self-efficacy, and self-presentation within social networking sites. *Journal of Media Psychology: Theories, Methods, and Applications*, *20*(3), 106–116. doi:10.1027/1864-1105.20.3.106

Lampe, C., Ellison, N., & Steinfeld, C. (2007). A familiar Face(book): Profile elements as signals in an online social network. In *Proceedings of the Conference on Human Factors in Computing System* (pp. 435-444). New York: ACM Press.

Lampinen, A., Tamminen, S., & Oulasvirta, A. (2009). "All my people right here, right now": Management of group co-presence on a social networking site. In *Proceedings of GROUP, 2009*, 281–290.

Leary, M. R. (1996). *Self Presentation – Impression Management and Interpersonal Behavior*. Boulder, CO: Westview.

Lewis, C., & George, J. (2008). Cross-cultural deception in social networking sites and face-to-face communication. *Computers in Human Behavior*, *24*(6), 2945–2964. doi:10.1016/j.chb.2008.05.002

Lewis, K., Kaufman, J., & Christakis, N. (2008). The taste of privacy: An analysis of college student privacy settings in an online social network. *Journal of Computer-Mediated Communication*, *14*(1), 79–100. doi:10.1111/j.1083-6101.2008.01432.x

Magnuson, M., & Dundes, L. (2008). Gender differences in "social portraits" reflected in MySpace profile. *Cyberpsychology & Behavior*, *11*(2), 239–241. doi:10.1089/cpb.2007.0089

Marcus, B., Machilek, F., & Schutz, A. (2006). Personality in cyberspace: Personal web sites as media for personality and impressions. *Journal of Personality and Social Psychology*, *90*(6), 1014–1031. doi:10.1037/0022-3514.90.6.1014

Mitrano, T. (2008). Facebook 2.0. *EDUCAUSE Review*, *43*(2). Retrieved from http://connect.educause.edu/Library/EDUCAUSE+Review/Facebook20/46324.

Nesbitt, S., & Marriott, C. (2007, October 29). 'Caught in the net'. *The Lawyer*, 30-33.

O'Brien, T. (2007). *Females flock to Facebook to post pictures of their drunken antics*. Retrieved from http://www.switched.com/2007/11/06/females-flock-to-facebook-to-post-pictures-of-their-drunken-antics/

Papacharissi, Z. (2002). The presentation of self in virtual life: Characteristics of personal home pages. *Journalism & Mass Communication Quarterly*, *79*(3), 643–660.

Pfeil, U., Zaphiris, P., & Ang, C. S. (2006). Cultural differences in collaborative authoring of Wikipedia. *Journal of Computer-Mediated Communication*, *12*(1), 88–113. doi:10.1111/j.1083-6101.2006.00316.x

Raacke, J., & Bonds-Raacke, J. (2008). MySpace and Facebook: Applying the uses and gratifications theory to exploring friend-networking sites. *Cyberpsychology & Behavior*, *11*(2), 169–174. doi:10.1089/cpb.2007.0056

Risky online behavior more likely to happen in small businesses. (2008, June 2). *PR Newswire*, 1.

Sarno, D. (2009). Facebook reports milestones in cash flow, users. *Los Angeles Times*, B 4.

Smith, J. (2009). Number of US Facebook users over 35 nearly doubles in last 60 days. *Inside Facebook*. Retrieved January 6, 2010, from http://www.insidefacebook.com/2009/03/25/number-of-us-facebook-users-over-35-nearly-doubles-in-last-60-days/

Social networking in the workplace increases efficiency. (2008, November 11). *PR Newswire*, 2.

Society for Human Resource Management. (2008) *Online Technologies and Their Impact on Recruitment Strategies—Using Social Networking Web Sites to Attract Talent*. Retrieved January 18, 2010, from http://www.shrm.org/Research/SurveyFindings/Articles/Pages/OnlineTechnologiesandTheirImpactonRecruitmentStrategiesUsingSocialNetworkingWebsitesToAttractTalent.aspx

St. John, W. (2006, September 10). When information becomes T.M.I. *The New York Times, 155*(53698), 8.

Stevens, J. (1986). *Applied Multivariate Statistics for the Social Sciences*. Hillsdale, NJ: Lawrence Erlbaum Associates.

Stross, R. (2009). When everyone's a friend, is anything private? *The New York Times*. Retrieved from http://www.nytimes.com/2009/03/08/business/08digi.html?_r=2&pagewanted=print

Stutzman, F. (2006). *An evaluation of identity-sharing behavior in social network communities*. Paper presented at the 2006 iDMAa and IMS Code Conference, Oxford, Ohio.

Sullivan, S. (2006). *One-in-four hiring managers have used internet search engines to screen job candidates; One-in-ten have used social networking sites, CareerBuilder.com survey finds*. Retrieved from http://www.careerbuilder.com/share/aboutus/pressreleasesdetail.aspx?id=pr331&ed=12%2F31%2F2006&sd=10%2F26%2F2006&cbRecursionCnt=1&cbsid=a5015667d80f4b599c46d2b08f406b67-241548812-RI-4&ns_siteid=ns_us_g_One%2din%2dFour_Hirin_

Trammell, K., & Keshelashvili, A. (2005). Examining the new influencers: A self-presentation study of A-list blogs. *Journalism & Mass Communication Quarterly, 82*(4), 968–982.

Tufekci, Z. (2008). Can you see me now? Audience and disclosure regulation in online social network sites. *Bulletin of Science, Technology & Society, 28*(1), 20–36. doi:10.1177/0270467607311484

Vazire, S., & Gosling, S. (2004). E-Perceptions: Personality impressions based on personal websites. *Journal of Personality and Social Psychology, 87*(1), 123–132. doi:10.1037/0022-3514.87.1.123

Walker, K. (2000). It's difficult to hide it: The presentation of self on internet home pages. *Qualitative Sociology, 23*(1), 99–120. doi:10.1023/A:1005407717409

Zeidner, R. (2008). *Employers give Facebook a poke*. Retrieved from http://www.shrm.org/hrtx/library_published/nonIC/CMS_024693.asp

Zhao, S., Grasmuck, S., & Martin, J. (2008). Identity construction on Facebook: Digital empowerment in anchored relationships. *Computers in Human Behavior, 24*(5), 1816–1836. doi:10.1016/j.chb.2008.02.012

This work was previously published in the International Journal of Virtual Communities and Social Networking, Volume 2, Issue 2, edited by Subhasish Dasgupta, pp. 11-31, copyright 2010 by IGI Publishing (an imprint of IGI Global).

Chapter 16
Networking Identities:
Geographies of Interaction and Computer Mediated Communication[1]

Lhoussain Simour
Sidi Mohamed Ben Abdellah University, Morocco

ABSTRACT

Electronic connections allow the individual to be at various global sites while sitting in front of his or her computer. By being electronically connected, one's participation in virtual worlds raises important questions about the nature of our communities and problematizes our identities. This paper examines how experiences in virtual interactions affect people's real lives and what impact computer mediated communication has on the formation of a virtual community and its relation to individuals' identities. Virtual communities stimulate experiences that redefine the basic concepts and contexts that have characterized the essence of human societies. They offer new contexts for rethinking the concept of identity and provide a new space for exploring the extent to which participation in computer mediated interaction modifies the subject in terms of identity, leading to a reconstruction and a reconstitution of self.

INTRODUCTION

Globalization refers to the ways in which previously isolated parts of the world have become connected in a historically unprecedented manner, in such a way that developments in one part of the world are now able to rapidly produce effects on geographically distant localities. This has in fact made it possible to think of the world as a single global space, or 'global village', thanks to the drastic growth of the New Communication

Technologies. In the present environment, one cannot consider identity without reference to the technological innovations that have changed the background against which identity is constructed; they have reshaped and redefined the "generalized elsewheres" (Meyrowitz 1989) from which the self takes its different configurations. So as the human society enters the twenty first century, a new era of change continues to unfold; there is an apparent openness of change among countries and cultures and a free flow of information, goods and ideas. Information and technology, or what Arjun

DOI: 10.4018/978-1-4666-1553-3.ch016

Appadurai calls "media scapes" (1996) are at the centre of this shift and have led to the emergence of a largely mysterious world of virtual reality.

Increasingly, people's interactions with the world around them are mediated by computer technology and the contact with machines is becoming more frequent to the extent that everyday activities have almost become machinated. Those who use the Internet, mailing lists, IRC (Internet Relay Chat), MUDs (Multi User domains), e-mail services, know quite well what it means to live the experience of participating in a virtual community. The interconnection of these existing virtual networks which use computer mediated technology to link people all over the world is informally known as "the net".

The central argument of this article is that the net is a leading force which creates and simulates experiences that redefine the basic concepts that have characterized the essence of human societies. Social space, interaction norms and identity are being altered in computer mediated communication. I explore the notion of community and its relation to identity in the context of computer mediated communication. I argue that virtual communities are offering a new context for rethinking the concept of identity and are providing a new space for exploring the extent to which participation in computer mediated interaction modifies the subject's identity leading to a reconstruction and a reconstitution of the self. In fact, the new technologized ways of communicating "have freed interaction from the requirements of physical co-presence; these technologies have expanded the array of generalized others contributing to the construction of the self" (Cerulo 1997, p. 386).

Electronic connections allow the individual to be at various global sites while sitting in front of the computer; and by being electronically connected, one's participation in virtual worlds raises important questions about the status in quo of communities and problematizes paradigmatic structures of identities. So my major concern is to investigate how experiences in virtual interactions affect people's real lives and what impact computer mediated communication has on the formation of a virtual community and its relation to individuals' identities.

Joshua Meyrowitz was one of the pioneers to explore the relationships between the New Communication Technologies and identity construction. His works on *No Sense of Place* (1985), *The generalized Elsewhere* (1989) and *Shifting worlds of strangers: medium theory and changes in "them" versus "us"* (1997) reconsider the ways in which electronic interactions reconfigure social interaction terrains. They remodify the self to locate it in new arenas of hybridized subjectivities. He gives the example of television as a new invention that has sanctioned the "disabled and the disenfranchised" by allowing them to have access to social information despite being physically dislocated or disabled. The notion of place within NCTs paradigm has reconfigured the borders and has allowed the complexity of identity to emerge.

In his *An Ecology of Communication: Cultural Formats of Control* (1995), David Altheide has also attempted to theorize different positions on NCTs and the configurations of the self. He argues that NCTs give new possibilities of being and becoming through communication interactions. They are important mediums that allow for the emergence of new modes of selecting, organizing, and presenting information. These new possibilities redefine social interaction and remodify current practices to give new ways of being.

Beniger (1987) has also talked extensively on the impact of New Communication Technologies on community construction and on collective identity. He suggests very specific directions in which communities constructed through media interactions provide new configurations of "pseudo" selves.

It is clear, then, that computer mediated communication largely affects people's experiences of virtual community and identity. My main focus is to explore the relationship between a virtual community and identity and how participants in computer mediated connections negotiate this relationship.

METHOD OF INVESTIGATION

The methodology adopted in my research includes both a virtual participation on the net and a face-to-face interview with those who communicate and interact online. Virtual participation has allowed me to investigate patterns of interaction among net users, and observe participants' interests especially in "Pal talk"[2], a well structured IRC channel which has a public access and which includes chat rooms administered by Moroccans. I have also conducted a number of interviews; specifically with students from the Higher School of Technology in Casablanca where I am teaching English as a Foreign Language to students majoring in computer studies. The choice of this school is twofold: Firstly because of time constraints I have chosen to conduct my research where I work given the already established contact with students. I believe that my study should have included different cyber spaces and, therefore, a whole range of net users from different social categories; but, this would have demanded a lot of time which could be extended over two or four months' investigation. Even, the sample taken for my research is not indeed claimed to be representative of the majority of Moroccan population engaged with computer mediated connections. Secondly, I have conducted my research at this same school because it is equipped with computer facilities and has a cyberspace for both personnel and students.

All these elements – the online observation and face-to- face interviews with those who use computers daily – converge to inform my understanding of electronic connections and their impact on perceptions of community and identity. I have also thought of conducting online interviews, but it is certainly evident that in so doing I would be collecting virtual information, which would ultimately lead to a virtual research, leaving out real people themselves. I also believe that, by conducting online interviews, I would get a number of individuals from various diasporic identities; but, I won't be totally convinced that they are truly Moroccans. In face to face interviews, I am better positioned to explore the interviewees' history and to understand the role technology has played in their lives. With face to face interviews, I am also able to obtain the consent of every individual interviewed; a procedure that will undoubtedly be impossible to carry out online.

Participation and observation are used to investigate the patterns of interaction among net users. This technique has allowed me to acquire the preliminary knowledge about people's virtual interaction, their activities online, and the structure of the social world in cyberspace. Virtual participant observation has been conducted specifically at Pal talk, as stated before. This network has public access and anybody can lurk[3] in on any discussion. As a lurker, my identity has remained anonymous. I have created a pseudo name to log online. I have gone online on different occasions to observe participants' interests and patterns of interaction, as well as to gain insights about the content available.

However, the main body of the data comes from direct interviews with students who communicate and interact through the computer. In total I have met with twenty young people aged between eighteen and twenty two. I have chosen to rely on interviews so that I can understand on the one hand what participants in computer mediated communication believe a virtual community is from their own perspective and experience; and on the other hand be aware of the impetus behind choosing to interact on the net. In a nutshell, my aim is to understand what participants believe their electronic connections are in terms of virtual community and how participation in online activities affects the construction of their identities. Participants' beliefs on community and identity arise from the individuals' experiences resulting from socially shaped ideas and assumptions. Some of the ideas and assumptions that influence participants' views on electronic communities and virtual identities include attitudes towards their physical communities and individualistic tendencies of each participant.

I have constructed an interview guide and I have structured the interview along two different aspects: what participants believe their electronic connections are in terms of community and how their identities are deconstructed, constructed and reconstructed in computer mediated communication. Participants have extremely been eager to talk about their experiences online, and almost all areas of inquiry I have conceptualized are covered; but, the most fascinating thing is that some areas of great interest I have not considered came up consistently during the interviews.

The section entitled, "Multiplicity and instability: The Net and the postmodern society" is an attempt to explore how virtual identities offer an experience of multiplicity and instability of meaning that is characteristically postmodern. I will explore the postmodern theoretical framework in order to understand the reconfiguration of the self and of the formation of communities in computer mediated interactions.

"Postmodern identity and Community" is meant to demonstrate how computer mediated communication and interaction allows for the emergence of communities based on similar interests and shared ideas; and how electronic networks are not fostering a sense of community, but are mainly highlighting individualistic tendencies.

"Net interaction and the virtual self" is an investigation into the configuration and reconfigurations identities take in a computer mediated interaction. Since communities are made up of identities and selves, I deem it relevant to discuss how a virtually separated identity is shaped and grounded. I will examine the notion of how a virtual self maintains existence within electronic connections.

MULTIPLICITY AND INSTABILITY: THE NET AND THE POSTMODERN SOCIETY

In this section, I take note of Sherry Turkle's statement that society is moving from a "modernist culture of calculation to a postmodern culture of simulation" (Turkle, 1995, p. 10). Turkle conceives of the culture of simulation as the new cultural context defined by "eroding boundaries between the real and the virtual, the animate and the inanimate, the unitary and the multiple self" (p.10). So, according to her, computer mediated experiences develop models that are postmodern: they admit multiplicity and flexibility. They also promote the constructed nature of reality, self and other.

Thus, the net is another cultural element that suggests the value of approaching one's narrative in several ways. Fluid, decentralized, emergent and flexible identities and communities are what characterize the net. Computer mediated communication and interaction describes a trend consistent with the post modern idea that identity and community are not fixed objective entities, but fluid social constructs; narratives that may be subject to revision.

Turkle argues also that computers carry with them new ways of knowing, heightening and making concrete the postmodern theory. Virtual identities offer an experience of multiplicity and instability of meaning that is characteristically postmodern. The electronic experience of multiple selves, Turkle claims, allows the possibility of changing their ways of thinking about the self and others, situating them in the postmodern deconstruction of human subjectivity:

When people explore simulation games and fantasy worlds or log on to a community where they have virtual friends and lovers, they are thinking of the computer as an analytical engine, but as an intimate machine (p. 306)

Computer mediated narratives radically decentre the human body, the sacred icon of the essential modern self. Turkle argues that this deconstruction provides new forms of social liberation especially for women.

While Turkle is optimistic about the liberating postmodern potential of computer mediated interaction, Kroker and Weinstein's theory of postmodernism, elaborated in their *Data Trash: the Theory of the Virtual Class* (1994), assume that modernism and postmodernism are great ideological phases of "recline". Fundamentally contrasting Turkle's culture of simulation, culture of recline is not characterized by liberating multiplicity but by the wish to be replaced. The notion of a "disappearing body" is what characterizes Kroker and Weinstein's theory of recline.

Contrary to Turkle and in agreement with Kroker and Weinstein, most interviewees in this paper do not perceive any connection between computers mediated communication and the community at large. The connections participants are making are essentially instrumental. Even though computer mediated interaction illustrate ideas associated with postmodernism, it is not leading to thinking about contemporary social issues; rather it represents a wish to be replaced. Most interviewees observe that, by being online, individuals are being replaced by the computer interface allowing them to avoid others, select people to whom they want to talk and hear what they want to hear. So my point is that Participating in computer mediated connection does not lead to thinking about real life issues, it leads rather to a network of "lonely crowds" who are not fostering a sense of real community, but whose main wish is to be replaced; a replacement of body and mind. In this section, I will explore the postmodern theoretical framework in order to understand the reconfiguration of the self and of the formation of communities in computer mediated interactions.

Computer mediated connections are mostly concerned with simulation, navigation and interaction. Participants interact in networks, navigating the web, surfing its links that instantaneously take them from site to site. The emerging culture of simulation has affected the understanding of bodies and minds at many levels. Sherry Turkle assumes that:

Now in post-modern times, multiple identities are no longer so much at the margins of things. Many more people experience identity as a set of roles that can be mixed and matched, whose diverse demands need to be negotiated. A wide range of social and psychological theorists have tried to capture the new experience of identity. Robert Jay Lifton has called it protean. Kenneth Gergen describes its multiplication of masks as saturated self. Emily Martin talks of the flexible self as a contemporary virtue of organisms, persons and organizations (p. 180).

It is clear, then, that postmodern concepts of multiple selves as played out are more visible and tangible in the medium of the Internet. The Internet reflects and creates postmodern ideas by enabling diversity. Simultaneously, this medium offers a space in which different forms of homogeneity and a connected global culture is experienced. However, global online culture is different from global "onground" culture, in that the contexts and parameters in which culture is constructed are different. Although other media, such as newspapers, TV and Radio have also had effects on blurring boundaries of culture, they have rendered the receiver into a more passive role. Interactivity, speed, shifts of space and time allow for a larger presence and action of individuals online. I consider these the key factors in enabling the impact of the internet on personal experiences to be felt on a larger scale.

What in fact emerges in the realm of computer mediated communication is a world without origins, as theorists of postmodernism like Leyotard and Baudrillard have assumed. In computer mediated interaction, the line between things and their representation breaks down; what remains are just copies that have no originals. Virtual communities and virtual characters on computer networks function as copies of objects that have no originals. During my face-to-face interviews, it becomes apparent that most participants' handles or characters within electronic networks are not a representation of their real life selves, or their life communities. One of my informants explains that he doesn't desire to meet face-to-face those he communicates with online; "you build an image of the individual you interact with on the net, the person has often a personality on the net; but, you don't want to discover that they are different when you meet him or her in real life".

So, pretending to be the opposite sex, or pretending whatever one wishes is to represent a self that has no origins. The notion of communities and identities without origins is clearly illustrated in a computer mediated world. Everything is superficial and instrumental; there is no level of depth and the absence of physical interaction doesn't lead to real life bonds and ties. As captured in the set of interviews I have conducted, real physical interactions are a prerequisite to know each other as individuals. Computer mediated interaction is an efficient and convenient means that allows to say things one would not dare to say face to face.

Additionally, people are not also building virtual communities as images of real physical communities. There are no ties or bonding communities, no shared values; rather people hear what they want to hear without having to put up with things that they find bothersome. The search for meaning can only occur through exploring the surfaces, and the only objects that can represent this world of surface are computer mediated interactions.

Virtual communities and virtual identities are postmodern to the extent that they represent nothing but themselves. Virtual identities are not representing the real person but the personae or characters played by that person. Invented or false, virtual identities are not representations of real life identities. Virtual actions are the personae's actions, not the person's own actions. Hence, computer mediated connections offer the possibility of inventing models of reality which contest the distinction between the real and the virtual..

Kroker and Weinstein believe that the virtual communities of electronic networking have a charismatic appeal, that is individuals are drawn to them, because "we are re-entering the burning atmosphere of the lonely crowd" (Kroker & Weinstein, 1994, p. 39). This crowd is logged on screens, willing to become part of a virtual network, while alone with the computer interface. The technologically generated communication exists as a simulated world for hiding loneliness. So, the appeal of electronic networking operates in inverse relation to the disconnectedness of people from each other and from their own bodies. As Kroker and Weinstein assume, the ideological perspective of a computer mediated culture is electronic mediation at the top and physical disconnection from below (p. 39). In individuals' search for connection they find in computer mediated interaction a substitute and simulation: a virtual community and a virtual identity.

Kroker and Weinstein see the 1990s as an era of cultural recline; "a time for cynical romanticism and cold love, where the body disappears into a virtual imaging system" (p. 2). Recline is, therefore, about surrendering to technologically mediated virtual identities and virtual individualism, and it is "expressed in the will to be incorporated by technologically produced environments" (p. 46). Moreover, reclining is not about seeking for solutions to social inequalities, but coping with these inequalities in a technological compromise that provides safety and convenience as Kroker and Weinstein believe. Computer mediated is really about "the disappearing of reality into a virtual world of technological automata and no-space" (p. 49).

This illusion of reality is, in fact, what characterizes the Computer mediated communication.

At the surface level, this means that instead of talking with real people, participants converse through the computer interface; Instead of real life distraction, people choose online distractions. In short, contacts with humans are replaced by the machine. Also, instead of real sex, there is cybersex, and instead of being one's own self and one's own gender, various characters can be played, some of which allow the ability to become a different virtual sex.

POSTMODERN IDENTITY AND COMMUNITY

Computer mediated communication and interaction clearly illustrates both postmodern theory specifically with regards to the construction and reconstruction of identity, and provides virtual places where the self is multiple and constructed by language. As Sherry Turkle argues, the essence of the self and its identities are no longer unitary and stable:

What most characterizes the model of a flexible self is that the lines of communication between its various aspects are open. The open communication encourages an attitude of respect for the many within us and the many within others (Turkle, 1995, p. 267).

In postmodern virtual reality, participants self-create themselves, and in this sense computer mediated connections allow experiences of postmodern selves. Their context is postmodern with its parallel narratives in chat rooms, where participants are displaced and distributed. As Turkle suggests, traditional ideas about identity are bound by a notion of authenticity that virtual experiences actively subvert. Participants in chat lines can use handles to create virtual personae, and individuals can have their identities distributed in the net. The self is not only decentred but multiple without limitations. One can easily retire

or destroy their character and simply start a new life with another. Hence, virtual personae are never used up; they can be recreated, reassigned and reconstructed with a number of different names and different user accounts. People don't have to be who they are in real life; age, sex, gender and sexual preferences, and everything one claims, can be true or invented: "cultural identities are played out, and sometimes exaggerated, in online communication" (Graouid, 2005, p. 65).

Virtual communities in chat rooms, forums and emails illustrate postmodernism because they are not bound by physical time and space. They also offer the experience of multiplicity since any participant can subscribe to a variety of these communities. Individuals can access their virtual communities at any time without having to physically dislocate themselves. Additionally, these virtual communities offer a virtual environment where social and physical expressions are not present. In the participants' self descriptions, in the roles they play, in the handles they create and their choice of networks, what emerges in fact are communities based on similar interests and shared ideas but with no commitment to a shared past or future. What computer mediated communication creates, instead, is lifestyles base on people's own interests whereby browsing or surfing can hardly be considered activities that fall within a community. There are only individual activities based on individual desires and needs. Through chat lines, emails and forums, individuals are able to connect with exactly those who give them the most satisfaction; with whom they share interests, opinions, projects, sexual preferences and for whom they have a need.

So, electronic networks are not fostering a sense of community, but they are mainly highlighting individualistic tendencies. People can choose with whom to communicate and to communities to subscribe to. What holds these communities together is not a common vision or values, but an individual need or desire for information and communication. Once this need is satisfied, there is no further commitment to the interaction.

NET INTERACTIONS AND VIRTUAL SELVES

What can be seen along the development of different forms of virtual systems is the increasing split between the bodies of the members of virtual communities and their locus of agency. Computer users can be members of a virtual community sitting in front of their computers, while their sphere of social intercourse is elsewhere. In fact, the drastic revolution in communication technologies has been central in creating a sense of proximity between societies and has enabled us to enter "into an altogether new condition of neighborliness, even with those most distant from ourselves" (Appadurai, 1996, p. 271). Global networks allow people to interact in virtual communities while they remain unaware of how geographically dispersed their co-members may be, or which borders their interactions cross.

The de-territorialized virtual world of computer networks is conceived of as a space for the recreation of cultural identity. Sherry Turkle argues that the playful environments constituted by MUDs[4] reveal new forms of thinking of human identity and the relation between people and machines. Individuals spend several hours in front of their machines creating spaces whereby "reconstituted instrumental identities" (Poster 1995) are invented and played with.

So, computer mediated communication offers a new means for the process of self constitution and new possibilities for playing with identities. In virtual worlds, people engage in anonymous social interaction and play roles as close to or as far from their real life self as they choose. They build up masks, construct personae and interactively engage in creating environments, building characters and then live within this virtual situation. Life on the screen allows participants to express

unexplored parts of their lives and project themselves into scenarios where they become actors with faked roles. Individuals may shift identities for personal satisfaction. Identities appear and disappear but can be false created and deceptive. Adil, a twenty four-year old student confirms how his girlfriend, Amal, turned virtually into Yassmine one day just to destroy their relationship which lasted virtually for long.

Sherry Turkle analyses how the computer profoundly shapes individuals' way of thinking and feeling, how ideas carried by computer technology are reshaped by people for their own purposes, how computers are not just changing lives but changing selves as well; and how Virtual communities "offer permission to play, to try things out, facilitating the development of self and identity" (Turkle, 1995, p. 205).

Turkle's own metaphor of windows serves well to introduce how she sees life on the screen:

Windows have become a powerful metaphor for thinking about the self as multiple, distributed system [...] the self is no longer playing different roles in different setting at different times. The whole practice is that of a de-centered self that exists in many worlds, that plays many roles at the same time (pp. 13-14).

Turkle also argues that "life on the screen makes it very easy to present oneself as other than one is in real life. And although some people think that representing oneself as other than one is, is always a deception, many people turn to online life with the intention of playing it precisely this way. They insist that a certain amount of shape shifting is part of the online game" (p. 228). Shape shifting refers to the process by which participants can become whatever they want: the physical body can go virtual and then can turn back into its initial status.

Shape shifting, being part of the online game, shows to what extent individuals negotiate between their online masks and their real identities.

The relationship between the user's real life and virtual life can lead to what Turkle calls "slippage". She argues that slippage is a characteristic feature of identity play in computer mediated interaction. Slippages are spaces "where personae and self merge, places where the multiple personae join to comprise what the individual thinks of his or her authentic self" (p. 186). Hence, slippages in this respect, are about processes of self-creation and self-discovery in the relationship between a constructed personae and a real-life self. The process of slipping, then, occurs when the virtual personae and the real life selves merge. It is best captured in the words of an eighteen-year old student: "I spend 8 hours a day chatting. I always forget my real world. In fact internet has become my second world".

In dealing with the logics of identity, Stuart Hall assumes that: "collective social identities [...] can't any longer be thought in the same homogeneous form. We are [...] attentive to their inner differences, their inner contradictions, their segmentations and their fragmentations" (Hall, 1991, p. 45). So, beyond the rigidities and restraints of fixed and unitary identities, computer mediated interaction allows the emergence of multiple identities that subvert the traditional ideas about the self. Online participants can create many characters and can use an infinite variety of pseudo names and handles to create virtual personae. The self becomes multiple; characters are invented and destroyed easily to start a new life with another handle and so on. Hence, virtual personae are never used up, as mentioned earlier; they are recreated to suit new situations. We can, definitely, talk about an identity in crisis.

The computer's culture, therefore, allows us to think concretely about identity in crisis. The signifier no longer points clearly to the thing that is signified in virtual spaces. The computer, likewise, expands to include many other selves. New, faked, multiple, emergent and reinvented identities simultaneously exist within unknown boundaries in all kinds of electronic networks whereby virtual identities are not representing the real person, but the personae or the character played by that person. Invented or false, virtual identities can't be representations of real life identities.

ROLE PLAYING: CHARACTERS AND HANDLES

In the Internet, people may learn to accept multiplicity of roles and ways of being. Individuals play with aspects of themselves and create virtual personae. Role-playing in general, whether pretending to be of the opposite sex, or pretending to be a faked friend, can be used to reveal new aspects of identity and to permit greater complexity of relationships. In the net, the self becomes free of absolute values or rigid moral obligations and can alter its behavior to adapt to others and to various social roles. It can play all of them as a game, playing with particular social identities, yet never changing its own basic identity, because that identity depends only on discovering and pursuing its own impulses and desires. For some, virtual identities are merely an opportunity to express different or repressed aspects of their selves; thereby, functioning as a replacement, or representing the wish to be replaced.

Role playing and creating handles are a common way of constructing a virtual identity. Handles are used instead of the participants' real life names, and are used to play with identity. For some, handles and the characters they play allow them to express aspects of themselves or their lifestyle. Imane frequently uses "Mchicha" (a Kitty) as handle and believes that a virtual identity should be an expression of aspects of one's self. She uses Mchicha not to conceal her real identity because if anybody asks she will tell him or her. The character she uses has to do most of all with her family background where everybody calls her Mchicha. Furthermore, she believes that the net in general makes her more beautiful: "I am virtually much more beautiful than the real".

When most of my interviewees initially log on chat rooms, they assume that they experience a side of themselves. I take the example of Mchicha because I find it revealing. The virtual identity has allowed her to express repressed parts of herself. During a chat session, she turns into a lesbian in front of her cam to satisfy the needs of a young male on the other side of the computer. She has played the role with a friend of hers who happens to be in her room at that moment. It is within this interaction that she really discovers part of herself and the online experience has made her feel more like her real self.

So, whether role playing to learn aspects of themselves or to experience different fantasies, online interaction allows participants to develop a virtual identity. Sherry Turkle believes that the anonymity of most MUDs provides ample room for individuals to express unexplored parts of themselves (Turkle, 1995, p. 183). Yet, it seems to me that anonymity is not an important consideration to those I have interviewed. Most of them don't feel particularly anonymous in their chat lines or interactive games interaction. Anonymity is not maintained by all of them during a computer mediated interaction. Since they seem to divulge some of their real life identity, such as phone numbers for example, their anonymity is only partial.

As Turkle argues, MUD games and other electronic networks are laboratories for constructing identity where "you can play roles as close to or as far from your real self as you choose" (p.183). Participants in online interaction can learn and express aspects of themselves by playing as many roles as they wish. A common role playing characteristic of computer mediated interaction is gender swapping in MUDs and chat lines. People seem to be curious about turning into the opposite sex. This curiosity is no way new, but in online interactions it becomes easier to be of the opposite sex or of no sex at all.

CONCLUSION

In this study I have tried to understand how experiences in virtual interactions affect participants' real lives. The central point of my research is that the Net is able to create and simulate experiences and, in the process, to redefine the basic concepts that have characterized the essence of human societies. Social space, interaction norms and the self are being altered in computer mediated interactions and connections. In addition, I have also attempted to analyze electronic communities and identities in terms of postmodern theory. The analysis of information technology within a postmodern condition includes the works of Sherry Turkle and Kroker and Weinstein. The main issue in the relationship between the net and the postmodern thought concerns the extent to which electronically mediated lifestyles and identities reflect the fragmentation of today's reality.

Beyond the restraints of fixed identities, computer mediated interaction allows the emergence of multiple identities that subvert the traditional ideas about the self. New images of multiplicity, flexibility and fragmentation are dominating the current thinking about individuals' identities. The internet is another element of the computer culture that has contributed to thinking about identity as multiple, diverse and complex. Participating in computer mediated connections does not lead to thinking about real life issues, and does not foster a sense of real community. Individualistic tendencies within virtual communities emerge through multifarious constructions of the self. These processes are what I term "shifting selves".

The shifting selves fluctuate between real identities and imagined ones as defined by the shifting notions of time and space in virtual interactions. This leads to the decomposition and recomposition of a hybrid self that comes into formation through the intricacies of virtual spaces and contexts. The emergence of hybrid identity formation also demonstrates how culture and nation become instable narratives that keep shifting through the negotiations of identity construction in internet experiences as shown in the different cases introduced in this essay. These negotiations are hierarchically constituted and are, concurrently, enframed within what Homi Bhabha calls "third space of enunciations" whereby identity witnesses slippages of authority and exists not as an ontological reality, but as a linguistic construct where hybrid formations are reconfigured and where the dominant articulations normalize ways of being and ways of becoming.

REFERENCES

Altheide, D. L. (1995). *An Ecology of Communication: Cultural Formats of Control*. Hawthorne, NY: Aldine de Gruyter.

Appadurai, A. (1996). *Modernity at large: Cultural Dimensions of Globalization, Public Worlds* (*Vol. 1*). Minneapolis, MN: University of Minnesota Press.

Beniger, J. R. (1987). The personalization of mass media and the growth of pseudo-community. *Communication Research, 14*(3), 352–371. doi:10.1177/009365087014003005

Bhabha, K. H. (1994). *The Location of Culture*. London: Routledge.

Cerulo, K. A. (1997). Identity Construction: New Issues, New Directions. *Annual Review of Sociology, 23*, 385–409. doi:10.1146/annurev.soc.23.1.385

Graouid, S. (2005). *Social Exile and Virtual H'rig*. Rabat, Morocco: Mohamed V University Press.

Hall, S. (1991). Old and New Identities, Old and New Ethnicities. In King, A. D. (Ed.), *Culture, Globalization and the world-system: Current debates in Art History 3*. Binghamton, NY: State University of New York.

Kroker, A. (1994). *Data Trash: The Theory of the Virtual Class*. Montreal, Quebec, Canada: New World Perspectives.

Meyrowitz, J. (1985). *No Sense of Place*. New York: Oxford University Press.

Meyrowitz, J. (1989). The Generalized Elsewhere. *Critical Studies in Mass Communication, 6*(3), 323–334.

Meyrowitz, J. (1997). Shifting Worlds of Strangers: Medium Theory and Changes in "them" versus "us". *Sociological Inquiry, 67*(1), 59–71. doi:10.1111/j.1475-682X.1997.tb00429.x

Poster, M. (1995). *Cyber democracy, Internet and the Public Sphere*. Retrieved from www.hnet.uci.edu/mposter/writings/democ.htlm

Turkle, S. (1995). *Life on the Screen: Identity in the Age of the Internet*. New York: Simon and Schuster.

Wilson, S. M., et al. (2002). *The Anthropology of Online Communities: the Annual Review of Anthropology*. Retrieved from http://www.anthro.annualreviews.org

ENDNOTES

1. This work has been conducted as part of a project for the fulfilment of the requirements of MA degree in Cultural studies: culture and identity in Morocco. I would like to thank Professor Abdellatif Khayati for his insightful remarks during the discussion of my paper. Maria José Ferreira's work on *Information Technology and the Postmodern Community* has been an important source of inspiration to me. I would also like to thank Professor Zoual Mansouri for proof-reading and correcting this essay. The peer reviewers of the *International Journal of Virtual Com-*

munities and Social Networking provided me with perceptive comments, I would like to thank them as well. The merits of my article are derived from the excellent advice that I have received; its shortcomings are entirely my responsibility.

2. This IRC channel can be downloaded at http://www.paltalk.com.

3. To lurk in refers to reading information or observing online interaction without actively contributing to it.

4. MUDs are real time spaces on the Internet where participants interact through written texts.

This work was previously published in the International Journal of Virtual Communities and Social Networking, Volume 2, Issue 2, edited by Subhasish Dasgupta, pp. 32-42, copyright 2010 by IGI Publishing (an imprint of IGI Global).

Chapter 17
Computational Trust in SocialWeb:
Concepts, Elements, and Implications

Kiyana Zolfaghar
K.N.Toosi University of Technology, Iran

Abdollah Aghaie
K.N.Toosi University of Technology, Iran

ABSTRACT

Trust as a major part of human interactions plays an important role in addressing information overload and helping users collect reliable information in SocialWeb applications. This paper examines the current situation and future trends of computational trust for these systems. Achieving this, the authors present an overview of existing social trust mechanisms and identify their strengths and weaknesses through discussion and analysis. In this paper, the authors also provide a comprehensive framework of social trust-inducing factors that contribute to the trust formation process and discuss key research issues and challenges to find future research trends in computing trust in the SocialWeb context.

INTRODUCTION

The Web is providing an ever-growing set of applications and environments where users interact with one another. In this regard, the SocialWeb is introduced as an ecosystem of participation, where value is created by the aggregation of many individual user contributions in generating web content (Gruber, 2008). Web-based social net-works, online social media sites, and large-scale information sharing communities are prominent examples of social web applications which rely heavily on the opinions, contributions or actions of communities of online users. In these applications, users are both producers and consumers of information (Lytras, 2009). To be assured of the reliability of these user generated contents, users need to know if the source of this information is

DOI: 10.4018/978-1-4666-1553-3.ch017

trustworthy or not. In other words, the trustworthiness of the user providing the information is as important as the reliability of information they provide. In this case, trust is often not an issue of security or reliability, but a matter of opinion and perspective (O'Donovan, 2009; Golbeck, 2009). So the more trust users have earned, the more weight will be given to their opinions. With so much user-interaction and user-generated content, the needs for establishing trust mechanisms online become apparent. If trust can be estimated accurately, the user can then use this trust estimation to make decisions on the information. But, trust in social web is a complex concept influenced by many factors which online systems cannot yet model it completely. It may be affected by history of interactions, similarity in preferences, similarity in background and demographics, information from third parties about the reputation of one another, and each individual's separate life experiences which may impact users' propensity to trust.

In recent years, there has been a lot of research attention towards issues of trust and reputation on the SocialWeb. Many computational models proposed to asses and predict users' trustworthy in their online social communication. These models come in many flavors and can be classified in several ways. They consider different aspects in computing trust values. Some of them focus on user's reputation and behavior in the system while some others just relies on qualitative assessments based on connections and relationships found in social networks and online communities. They are also different in the sources of information which use as a basis for trust calculation. Most of the work on trust computation just rely on explicit trust information indicated by users and do not pay attention to implicit information such as rating, similarity features and profile information which can be exploited to infer trust value indirectly (kim et al., 2008).

The objective of this paper is finding out the current situation and future trends of social trust in computational sense. It also aims at looking for common necessary compositional elements that can be exploited to infer trust value between pair of users in SocialWeb and summarizing their common weaknesses through comparison, discussion and analysis. The rest of the paper is organized as follows. First, a general overview of trust is provided to illustrate the nature and concept of trust. Based on this overview, characteristics of social trust, various information sources used by trust models and different architecture of these models are elaborated. Following this, we try to identify factors that are pertinent to formation of trust in SocialWeb applications through reviewing relevant studies. Based on existing literature, a framework of trust-inducing factors is proposed to enhance social trust computation. We go through some of the most popular models and algorithms that are proposed for social trust computation and summarizing their weaknesses through comparison. Major challenges to computing with social trust are also discussed. And finally, the paper concludes with limitations and suggestions for further research on social trust to help the community to promote the research of computational trust on the SocialWeb.

THE NATURE AND CONCEPT OF SOCIAL TRUST

Social ecosystems are growing across the web and consistently trust is becoming an important factor for many systems that seek to use social factors to improve functionality and performance. In a virtual environment where participants are usually anonymous and do not engage in direct face-to-face communication, trust can be a significant issue. In this regard, trust is a prerequisite of social behavior, especially on the subject of important decisions. Social trust has been defined in several different ways depending on the research area and the context of the computation. Fukuyama (1995) describes social trust as "the expectations that arise within a community of regular, honest cooperative behavior, based on commonly shared norms, on the part of the members of the community". While according to Mui et al. (2002), trust is a subjective expectation that a partner has about another's future behavior based on the history of their encounters. In this paper we accept Golbeck (2005) definition in the context of SocialWeb as where "A trusts B if she commits to an action based on a belief that B's future actions will lead to a good outcome".

Characteristics of Trust

To facilitate a better understanding of the nature of trust in SocialWeb context, trust characteristics should be identified in the first step. According to mentioned definitions, trust is subjective and inherently a personal opinion in a particular context. So, it can be affected by individual differences and situational factors. Another primary property of trust is transitivity which means that if A trusts B, and B trusts C, then A can be inferred to trust C to some degree. Although there is conflict concerning trust transitivity in the literature, this property is considered as a base for trust calculation in many trust models especially in the social networks (Golbeck, 2005; Lesani & Bagheri, 2006; Taherian et al., 2008). However, trust is not perfectly transitive and degrades along a chain of acquaintances. Trust is dynamic and usually non-monotonically changed with time. This characteristic of trust is more salient in online social contexts since everyday new relationships are formed and old ones weaken gradually. The forth property is trust asymmetry which says that the levels of trust that two partners place on each other may not be necessarily the same. Most of the computational models for social trust assessment reflect this characteristic by representing trust as an oriented relationship between the trustor and the trustee in a directed graph. In the following sections, we will see that how these characteristics are taken into account in construction of social trust models.

Trust Information Sources

As mentioned before, social trust derived from the opinions about a target user so can be classified based on the origin of these opinions. The study of Casare et al. (2005) emphasizes that beliefs can be obtained from several sources, such as *direct experiences*, *received information* and *social prejudice*. According to Sabater et al. (2005), *direct experiences* and *witness information* are the traditional information sources used by current computational trust and reputation models. It is more reliable to take account of both *direct experiences* and *witness information*; but it will make computation models more complex. However, according to what Levien (2002) said the primary information source to social trust computation is a representation of the social graph, the nodes of which are users, and the edges of which are relationships between these users. In General, the information sources that a trust model has to deal with in a typical SocialWeb environment is of three types:

- Direct information is information that the user obtains directly from the target node in social web application as a result of direct interactions without intermediaries. This is the most relevant and reliable information source for computing social trust.
- Third-party information which is also called word-of-mouth or indirect information is the information that comes from other users of the system or community (Sabater & Paolucci, 2007). The receiver cannot safely assume that this information is always true and accurate because third-party information is prone to distortion and therefore it needs to be evaluated carefully before it can be incorporated as part of the user beliefs and used to make decisions. Although this type of information is abundant compared with direct information, but it is complex for models to use.

- Social graph which refers to the information associated to the social relations among members of the society is the third type of information source for trust models (Levien, 2002). This information is considered as the basis of trust computation in most recent models in SocialWeb domain. To analyze this information, techniques like social network analysis may be used to study the social relationships between individuals and social structure of the society. A clear example is the information associated to structural attributes of each user in social network such as degree, centrality (measured by average shortest path length), and clustering coefficient. The use of these methods, therefore, depends on the availability of relational data in the target system (Scott, 2002).

Architecture

In addition to information sources, social trust models differ in the place where trust relationships are evaluated. Ziegler (2005) defines two main types of trust computation approaches according to the network architecture called centralized and distributed. Local or centralized approaches perform all computations in one single machine and hence need to be granted full access to relevant trust information. The trust data itself may be distributed over the network. Most of the trust models in the online social context count among the class of centralized approaches in which they assume the presence of a centralized trust manager whose job is to compute trust ratings for users in the network and to communicate these trust ratings to users when needed. A centralized trust approach is helpful in fostering trust among strangers. In the second approach, distributed metrics for the computation of trust and reputation equally deploy the load of computation on every trust node in the network. So, the entire process of trust computation is necessarily asynchronous and its convergence depends on the eagerness or laziness of nodes to propagate information. Though the individual computation load is decreased with respect to centralized computation approaches, nodes need to store trust information about any other node in the system.

FACTORS INFLUENCING SOCIAL TRUST

Without attempting to identify the elements that are pertinent to the formation of trust, it is difficult to derive effective and reliable design principles or implications on enhancing users trust in social web applications. As trust is a complex and abstract concept, it is difficult to identify the elements that construct it. To identify factors influencing trust value between online users in these applications, one of the best ways may be a quick reference to proposed conceptual trust models which aim to find out the complicated relationships among trust and other multiple factors as its antecedents. As a result of reviewing relevant studies on this subject, the following factors are usually considered important in the social trust formation mechanism on the web (Figure 1). Many of the computational trust models exploit different combination of these factors to asses trust value.

Knowledge-Based Trust

Knowledge-based trust refers to the trust building mechanism where individuals get to know each other through interactions and then predict others' behaviors based on the information they obtain from this interactive process (Lu et al., 2009). This factor can also be applied to social trust, as people are usually prone to trust others that they are familiar with through repeated interactions, as one needs time to accumulate trust-relevant knowledge resulting from experience with other parties (Gefen et al., 2003). This factor can be derived from the first type of trust information

Figure 1. A framework of social trust-inducing factors

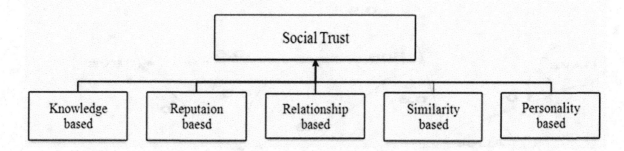

which is existed in the SocialWeb domain. However, considering the scale and dynamism of such social web application and the number of users interacting through these systems, there is a lack of data available as the basis for knowledge-based trust due to the fact that most users do not interact directly with others, and the fact that these interactions are generally very limited.

Relationship-Based Trust

Relationship-based trust is another dimension of online trust relies on qualitative assessments based on connections found in social networks and online communities (Kwan & Ramachandran, 2009). Although online trust is not perfectly transitive, viewing information about a person's extended relationships is useful when making inferences about other people's trustworthiness. Communities naturally exploit the relationship dimension of online trust since it is an extension of people's need to interact. A graph structure is usually used to model trust relationships of people in social web applications in order to determine how much one person in the trust network should trust another one who is not directly connected to him. In this graph, called web of trust (or trust network), each node represents a person and each edge represents the trust relationship (Figure 2). A label is assigned to each edge to indicate the trust value of the relationship. In order to cover the asymmetric characteristic of trust, trust network usually is shown as a directed graph. Till now, many researches on trust prediction strongly rely on a web of trust, which is directly collected from users. However, the web of trust is not always available in online social applications and, even when it is available, it is often too sparse to accurately predict the trust value between two unacquainted people since most people are reticent to express trust values. In fact, the distribution of such user-specified trust relationships can often be modeled by a power law function with a small proportion of users specifying many trust relationships while the large majority specifying very few or none trust relationships (Ma et al., 2009). So, if trust is being used to support decisions, it is important to have an accurate estimate of trust when it is not directly available. To overcome the sparseness problem of a web of trust, other factors should be also considered in trust models to estimate trust value more accurately.

Reputation-Based Trust

Reputation-based trust refers to the trust building mechanism in which past interactions or performance for an entity are combined to assess its future behavior. It depends on feedback about an interacting party's behavior given by other users in the system and it affects the interacting party's future payoffs (Dellarocas, 2003). In other words, Reputation is a social notion of trust (Golbeck, 2005) since it is based upon collective belief of the

Figure 2. Trust network in which nodes are users and edges are trust statements

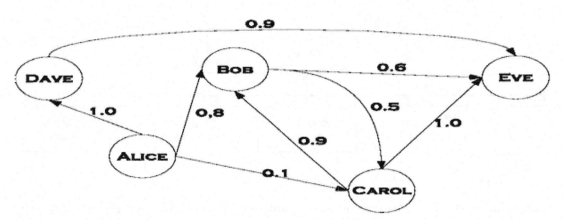

society towards the stand point of a single person within the context of that society. In the context of SocialWeb, reputation is also one of the most important factors which can be used to derive trust connectivity and the degree of trust value between users. This factor usually known as global trust measure since it has a universal value for each user over the whole system by considering the trustor behavior in the system to compute the amount of his trustworthiness. Rating systems are the most common method for establishing reputation on the SocialWeb in which rating data provided by users of online communities such as Epinions and YouTube (Kwan, 2009). This rating data is easily collected and is much more frequently expressed by users than trust so it can be considered as a solution to address the problem of data sparseness in web of trust. A properly estimated reputation creates incentives for users to behave honestly and reputably. Therefore, it is important to build algorithms and measure feedbacks quantitatively to promote positive behavior in the system (Zheng, 2009). However, reputation mechanisms can be manipulated through collusion by groups of friends or the creation of false identities. One approach to this problem may be use of the reputation beside relationship-based trust mechanisms which become so popular by growing availability of online social networks.

Similarity-Based Trust

Similarity-based trust refers to a trust building mechanism which implies that trust is established based on social similarities (Zucker, 1986). Similarity can involve several aspects such as common characteristics the trustor perceives of the trustee including interests, values, and demographic traits which can lead to establish a new trust relationship between two sufficiently similar users. There exists significant evidence described in social science literature that confirms the propagation of trust based on similarity. Montaner (2002) claims that trust should be derived from user similarity, implying that friends are exactly those people that resemble our very nature. However, Montaner's model only extends to the agent world and does not reflect evidence acquired from real-world social studies concerning the formation of trust. A more recent study by Ziegler et al. (2007) experimentally proves that there exists a significant correlation between the trust expressed by the users and their similarity based on the recommendations they made in the system. Consistently, Golbeck (2009) describes that the similarity of profile attributes (such as ratings of movies) induces trust among people. Analyzing data from FilmTrust, she found that several profile features beyond overall similarity affect the degree to which subjects trust other users. Although the positive impact of similarity factor on the social trust behavior is proven, most of the studies on this subject just investigate the correlation of these two constructs or exploit them in parallel to improve filtering mechanism and recommender system performance (O'Donovan, 2009). While in order to estimate social trust more accurately, one should suppose trust to reflect user similarity to some extent and this similarity should support computational trust directly. Similarity-based trust can be more valuable for the ones who are new users of the system and have not yet established their own trust relations that can be the basis of their trust value because similarity-based trust usually uses item rating data that is available on most of web-based social systems and is much denser than direct trust data. But on the other hand, it should be clear that similarity-base trust propagation needs to be well defined and studied before it is applied directly to trust computation in practice.

Personality-Based Trust

Personality-based trust refers to users' individual traits that lead to expectations about the one's trustworthiness (Zucker, 1986). Many studies treat trust as a situational construct, neglecting the role of individual differences while in reality users have different developmental experiences, personality types, and cultural backgrounds so they differ in their inherent inclination toward trust. This trustor-specific antecedent of trust has been referred to by other scholars as *dispositional trust* (Kramer, 1999), *generalized trust* (Stack, 1978), and *trust propensity* (Mayer et al., 1995; Jason, 2007). Trust propensity reflects one's tendency to believe or not to believe in others (Gefen et al., 2003). This tendency is based not upon experience with or knowledge of a specific trusted party, but instead it is a general willingness based on extended socialization and life experience to depend on others (Ridings et al., 2002). In fact, trust

propensity known as a factor of trustor that determines how easy a trustor trusts others (Figure 3). Personality-based trust has been shown to relate to trust especially when the trustor is still unfamiliar with the trustee (Mayer et al., 1995). If an online user has a high tendency to trust others in general, this disposition is likely to positively affect his or her trust in a specific trust party, whereas a user with a low tendency to trust others in general is likely to develop a relatively lower trust in other party (Kim et al., 2008).Since there is usually no established scales or direct data from online social applications to measure trust propensity, most of the models don't not take account this factor in their computations. However, according to Marsh(1994), this factor can be calculated from all the experiences accumulated by the user in a way that good experiences lead to a greater disposition to trust, and vice versa.

SOCIAL TRUST MODELS

A plethora of computational trust and reputation models have been appeared in the last few years, each one with its own characteristics and using different technical solutions. In this section, we go through some of the most popular models and algorithms that are proposed to asses trust value between users in social web applications. We discuss the benefits and drawbacks of these models in the context of SocialWeb.

Marsh Model

The trust model proposed by Marsh (1994) is considered the first prominent, comprehensive, formal, computational model of trust. His work is founded in the social sciences, from which he extracts real world parameters for evaluating trust from properties inherent in social networks. Marsh thought that knowledge, utility, importance, risk, and perceived competence are important aspects related to trust. He defined three types of trust:

Figure 3. Classification of factors influencing online social trust

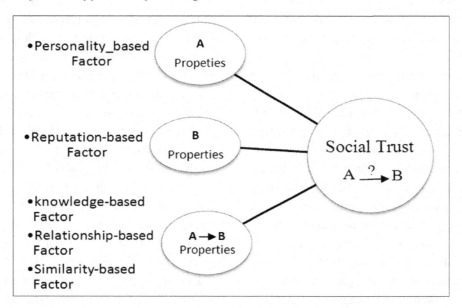

- •Personality_based Factor
- •Reputation-based Factor
- •knowledge-based Factor
- •Relationship-based Factor
- •Similarity-based Factor

basic trust, general trust and situational trust. Basic trust, similar to personality-based factor of social trust, just models the general trustor disposition independently of who is the trustee that is in front. General trust is the trust that one agent has on another without taking into account any specific situation. Finally, situational trust is the amount of trust that one agent has in another taking into account a specific context. Marsh model only takes into account direct interaction without referencing to the recommendations from other users. His model is complex and based on social and psychological factors. Although this work is widely cited, the model is highly theoretical and often considered too difficult to practically implement.

TidalTrust Model

TidalTrust, proposed by Golbeck (2005), is one of the most famous and highly cited algorithms for inferring trust in social web. With an assumption that a web of trust is available in online communities, TidalTrust propagates an explicit trust rating through the social networks in order to infer trust value between any random two users. This model performs a modified breadth first search in the trust network to make a prediction. Basically, it finds all raters with the shortest path distance from the source user and aggregates their ratings weighted by the trust between the source user and these raters. Studying the structure of real world social networks and their properties, Golbeck applied two restrictions on her algorithm. First, she showed that trust values inferred through shorter paths may be more accurate, so she only considered shortest paths from source to sink in her inference algorithm. Second, she extracted from her analysis that the most trustworthy information usually comes from highest trusted neighbors. In a nutshell, highly trusted neighbors and closer neighbors are more accurate in predicting a user's trust value in golbeck opinion. Perhaps, the most important preference of Golbeck's model with respect to other ones is its simplicity and its low time complexity (O (V + E)). Despite of popularity of the TidalTrust algorithm, it has some drawbacks. This model is considering path length more attention than trust value. By Golbeck's restriction on the length of inference paths, some useful information from users a little further apart in the network may be missed. Moreover, TidalTrust model is only applicable to a social network with continuous trust values which are not usually available in practice. Finally, the performance of TidalTrust algorithm is strongly affected by the density of a web of trust. If a web of trust is too sparse, it is hard to find trustworthy paths from a service user to the target service provider.

Advogato Model

Raph Levin's Advogato (2002) is a reputation-based trust model which calculates a global reputation for individuals in the network, but from the perspective of designated seeds (authoritative nodes). The Advogato calculates trust by using a network flow model in order to discover which users are trusted by members of an online community. The input for Advogato is given by an integer number n (the number of members to trust). The model composes 3 levels of certification between members to determine the trust level of a person, and thus their membership within a group. The Advogato metric is quite attack resistant. By identifying individual nodes as "bad" and finding any nodes that certify the "bad" nodes, the metric cuts out an unreliable portion of the network. Subsequent calculations are based primarily on the good nodes, so the network as a whole remains secure. However, to assign capacities to the edges of the network, they need to transform the network, so it needs to know the whole structure of the network. Moreover, it only computes the nodes to trust and does not compute different degrees of trust. So the number of users to trust is independent of users and items and there is no distinction between the trusted users.

MoleTrust Model

Massa and Avesani (2005) introduced MoleTrust as a depth-first graph walking algorithm with a tunable trust propagation horizon that allows to control the distance to which trust is propagated. MoleTrust predicts the trust score of source user on target user by walking the social network starting from the source user and by propagating trust along trust edges. Intuitively the trust score of a user depends on the trust statements of other users on her and their trust scores. Since the ideas used in MoleTrust and TidalTrust are similar, MoleTrust has the same drawbacks of TidalTrust algorithm. But MoleTrust considers all raters up to a maximum-depth given as an input. It also tries to reduce the trust prediction error for a significant portion of users called controversial users whom are trusted and distrusted by many people.

Appleseed Model

Ziegler and Lausen (2005) proposed the Appleseed trust model to compute trust for local groups by borrowing ideas from spreading activation models in neuropsychology. Instead of using maximum flow as Advogato does, it employs spreading activation strategies to produce a trust ranking of individuals in the network. Source node u is activated through an injection of energy e, which is then fully propagated to other nodes along edges proportional to the weight of the edge. This mechanism is also attack resistant but requires performing normalization on trust values which means a person who has made many high trust ratings will have lower value than if only one or two people had been rated. Jamali and Ester (2009) claims that, Appleseed considers the trust to be additive. It means that if there are many weakly trusted paths between two users, this pair of users will obtain a high trust value, which is not intuitive. Another weakness of Appleseed algorithm is that it requires exponentially higher computation with increasing number of users, thus not scalable due to this complexity.

Fuzzy Trust Model

Bharadwaj and Al-Shamri (2009) propose a fuzzy computational model for both trust and reputation concepts in open environments such as social networking, e-commerce, and recommender systems. In this work, trust and reputation systems are rating systems where each individual is asked to give his opinion after completion of each encounter in the form of ratings. Reciprocity and experience are used for trust modeling. To model the reciprocity property of trust, they try to find the agreement and disagreement between two partners by defining two fuzzy subsets on each partner's ratings namely satisfied and unsatisfied, while experience factor are computed based on the number of encounters the partner has made in the past and the confidence which the trustor have on that experience (knowledge-based trust). They regard the past history as the basis for trust but in the lack of personal experience, they rely on reputation as an alternative (reputation-based trust). So they also proposed a reputation mechanism which is a fuzzy extension of beta reputation model (Jøsang, 2002). Rather than considering reputation as a trust element, they assume it as a separate concept which can reinforce trust value. Since the main focus of this work is to incorporate trust and reputation concepts into movie RS, sparsity and scalability problems have not been considered while incorporating reputation feature into trust mechanisms with efficient way can overcome the sparsity and scalability problems.

Random-Walk Trust Model

Random walk is a PageRank-style trust measure, in which a random walker surfs the social network much like the random surfer in the popular PageRank approach for web ranking (Page, 1998). In the long run, the random walker will visit high-quality users more often than low-quality ones. More recently, similar random walk models have been applied to online social network application and studied more closely in the context of expertise networks (yahia, 2007; Jamali & Ester, 2009). In all of these models, a link (or relationship) from one node to another is a crude quality indicator of the target node. While a single link may not confer great confidence in the quality (or trust) of a user, in the aggregate, it might be expected the many links to a user (and recursively, the many links to user's who link to a target user) to provide a signal about a target user's trustworthiness. However, random walk trust is based solely on network topology and is divorced from the underlying behavior of the users in the network.

Social Trust Model

SocialTrust, proposed by Caverlee et al. (2010), is a reputation-based trust aggregation framework for supporting tamper-resilient trust establishment in social networks. SocialTrust augments the relationship-based trust in the social network with a personalized feedback mechanism so that a user's trust rating can reflect his behavior as well as the user's position in the social network. SocialTrust updates trust value through dynamic revision of trust ratings according to the three components includes the current rating, the history, and the adaptation to change. So unlike most of the proposed models, SocialTrust consider the dynamism characteristic of trust and trust assessments are dynamically updated as the social network evolves and as the quality of each user changes over time. Another distinguishing feature of this mechanism is making distinction between user relationship quality and trust so it differentiates between users who consistently engage in high-quality relationships with other users versus users who tend to engage in lower quality relationships. Initial experiment results show that SocialTrust is more robust against malicious users where its accuracy of trust inference remains relatively unchanged as percentage of malicious users increases due to its link quality and feedback ratings mechanism. However, SocialTrust model is just compared with Trust models like PopTrust (Monastersky, 2005) and random-walk Trust which are based solely on network topology.

Trust Models Comparison

In this section we show a table (see Table 1) that makes a summary of the models analyzed in this review from the point of view of the classification dimensions. We have considered a set of classification aspects that allow a comparison between social trust models. However, due to the diversity of such models, the classification aspects do not always fit exactly with the characteristics of the models. These models approach the problem of computing social trust from different perspectives. From dimension perspective, most models are basis on two dimensions: relationship and reputation. While these factors are not the only dimensions that can be used to deduce trust. Algorithms such as TidalTrust, Mole Trust, Advogato, Appleseed and random walk just focus on relationship-based trust and make the assumption that trust value between users can be inferred solely based on trust network topology and calculation of parameters such as the node centrality and the strongest or shortest paths between users. However, the effectiveness of these models in general depends on the connectivity of the known web of trust and can be quite poor when the connectivity is very sparse which is often the case in practice. The more recent models such as SocialTrust or Fuzzy trust pay more attention to other factors which can be exploited to infer trust value. In this regard, some additional information available in the systems except the trust information itself can be used to improve the quality of the trust assessments. Consistently, knowledge and reputation factors are included in Fuzzy trust model. SocialTrust proposes a reputation-based trust model on the basis of how well each user in the network behaves which derived from user feedbacks. One of the distinguishing features of SocialTrust is that trust assessments dynamically updates as the social network evolves while most of approaches compute trust assuming time is static. Table1 shows the comparison of different computational models for social trust. In Information source section, DI, WI and SG in sequence refer to Direct, Witness and Social graph information.

SOCIAL TRUST ISSUES, CONTROVERSIES AND PROBLEMS

The purpose of this work has been to describe and analyze the state of the art in social trust models and algorithms. Despite technological advancements, the SocialWeb is still very much in its infancy when it comes to accurately modeling human trust mechanisms. This section details the major challenges for modeling trust on the SocialWeb that were encountered during reviewing the models mentioned earlier.

Integration of Trust Dimensions

As mentioned in previous sections, the main factor of computation used by the social trust models is explicit trust relationships. There are very few models that take into account other aspects to calculate trust values. Trust models based on relationship factor are very much dependent on trust connectivity among users. So, they may not work well when such connectivity is sparse.

Table 1. Comparison of different computational models for social trust

Model	Computational principle	Info. Source	Architecture	Dimension	weakness
Marsh	$T_x(y,a) = U_x(a) * I_x(a) * T_x(a)$	DI	Distributed	Knowledge-based, Personality-based	Highly theoretical and difficult to implement adopt in the real world since much of the information.
Tidal Trust	$t_{is} = \dfrac{\sum_{j \in adj(i), t_{ij} > max} t_{ij} t_{js}}{\sum_{j \in adj(i), t_{ij} > max} t_{ij}}$	SG	Centralized	Relationship-based	it excluded information that may be useful from nodes of longer paths
Mole Trust	$\dfrac{\sum_{i=pred(u)} trust(i) * edge(i,u)}{\sum_{i=pred(u)} trust(i)}$	SG	Centralized	Relationship-based	Restriction on the length of inference paths
Advogato	Based on network flow assigns a "capacity" cx to each node x as a non increasing function of the distance from the seed.	SG	Centralized	Relationship-based	Only computes the nodes to trust and not degrees of trust. /vulnerable to malicious attacks in theoretic scenario.
Appleseed	Uses spreading activation strategies to compute trust.	SG	Centralized	Relationship-based	Not scalable due to complexity and requires exponentially higher computation with increasing number of users.
Random walk	$RwTrust(i) = \lambda \sum_{j \in rel(i)} \dfrac{RwTrust(j)}{|rel(j)|} + (1-\lambda)\dfrac{1}{n}$	SG	Centralized	Relationship-based	based solely on network topology and is divorced from the underlying behavior of the users in the network
Social Trust	$st(i,t) = áTr(i,t) + á\dfrac{1}{t}\int_0^t St(i,x)\,dx + ã\dot{Tr}(i,t)$	WI SG	Centralized	Reputation-based, Relationship-based	Not pay attention to trust subjectivity enough and more focus on trust dynamic
Fuzzy Trust	$trust_{ai}(a_j) = \dfrac{2.Exper_{aj}(a_j) \times recip(a_i, a_j)}{Exper_{aj}(a_j) + recip(a_i, a_j)}$	DI WI	Centralized	Knowledge-based, Reputation-based	Sparsity and scalability problems have not been considered in the model

To overcome this problem, recent models try to taking account other effective dimensions of social trust by using contextual information such as user behavior instead of explicit trust relationships to improve trust prediction. Coming back again to Table 1, we see that few models propose methods to combine different dimensions of trust. These methods are too much dependent on the characteristics of the environment so they are far from being a general solution. A solution for this problem could be the use of non static methods, that is, adaptive methods that can modify how to combine the different factors of trust according to the environment, which is not an easy task. We believe an integrated solution that combines all trust factors is very promising and need to be studied with a great detail. Through reviewing the literature, the study proposes that a complete computational social trust model should at least have five fundamental elements, however, very few models propose links between these factors to build trust model. One of the main reason is that considering all of these factors together may increase the complexity of computational models and, moreover, they have to be used in an environment where usually it is not possible to exploit their capabilities due to lack of data because most users do not interact directly with other and their interactions are generally very limited. Consistently, this lack of data means that frequently researches on trust models and inference algorithms are published with very little empirical analysis.

Social Trust Applications

Trust derived from simple or complex models becomes important when used in applications. There are lots of domains on the SocialWeb which could benefit from use of trust models. The main merits of such trust models in SocialWeb applications can be summarized in detecting malicious users in the system, helping users in decision making, judging the quality of user-generated content, selecting the best user from a number of candidates to enter into a transaction with, and improving quality of services through applying trust mechanism. But it is still an open question as to which applications see the best improvement for the user from computing social trust values and where trust is not as reliable as it needs to be to add significant value. This understanding can only come from further development and evaluation of a wide range of applications in SocialWeb domain. Moreover, different applications have their own situation, events, or information and depending on the context, trust should be indicated in different ways. There is no single solution that will be suitable in all contexts and applications so how to best match trust algorithms with the requirements of a specific application is a problem that has received very little attention.

Social Trust Evaluation Methods

Evaluation is very difficult when working with modeling social trust. Different models are evaluated from different perspectives. Some of them just focus on improving the accuracy and precision of trust inference value calculation and ignoring

other important aspects such as model complexity or scalability while over millions of members in social web applications may prove prohibitive for complex mechanisms. In some of trust models such as SocialTrust, evaluating the robustness of inference mechanism in the presence of large-scale manipulation by malicious users, clique formation, and dishonest feedback is considered as the main criteria of comparison. These models supports tamper-resilient trust establishment since accuracy of trust inference remains relatively unchanged as percentage of malicious users increases. Another aspect we have observed is that it is not usual to provide reliability measures of the calculated trust values, something that could be very important. Computing trust accurately, avoiding attacks by untrustworthy users, and understanding the differences between trust models, all are important research problems that must be addressed if these values are to be useful. Analyzing the models presented in this article, we found that there is a complete absence of test-beds and frameworks to evaluate and compare the models under a set of representative and common conditions. This situation is quite confusing, especially for the possible users of these trust models. It is thus urgent to define a set of test-beds and evaluation criteria that allow the research community to judge the quality and soundness of trust computation and establish comparisons between alternative models in a similar way.

CONCLUSION

With the rising of Web 2.0 technology, more and more people have been using online social applications in order to share knowledge, experiences and user generated contents for many different purposes. The reliability of this information is a function of the trustworthiness of the producers of that content. Research into trust and reputation of the producers of information in the SocialWeb is still very much in its infancy. To better predict trust value between pair of users, it is necessary to identify factors that influence trust formation process and perhaps reconsider the construct of trust in the context of SocialWeb environments. In this regard, Trust formation is a societal process that takes place in social environment and therefore is influenced by social factors. Plenty of interests have been attracted to the construction of computational trust from various research communities. Through reviewing these studies, this paper proposed that a complete computational trust model should at least have five major elements consist of relationship, reputation, knowledge, similarity and personality-based trust that all participate in trust formation process and therefore can be used to facilitate prediction of trust between a trustor and a trustee in the web-based social applications. Analyzing and comparing of trust models showed that none of them exploit all of these factors together in trust value prediction since they usually limit the source of the trust values to direct trust relations between users in the trust networks while it is possible to extract trust relation from other relations and contextual information which is available in the system. Social trust evaluation methods and integrating trust mechanisms into SocialWeb applications are other controversial subjects that are all under researched areas. There are some limitations in this work. The first limitation is the lack of data and general criteria to assess the effectiveness of computational trust models, practically. Empirical experiments can provide us the opportunity to evaluate the trust models based on practical criteria such as time complexity and resource consumption. Although, the recent proliferation of social networking applications produces a rich data resource, but some of these models have considered some particular assumptions which caused some difficulty in implementing them practically. Secondly, although this research attempted to identify the trust-inducing factors that contribute in trust formation process, but it did not involve in qualitative measurement of these factors. As the future work, we focus on mapping each qualitative factor in the proposed framework into some corresponding measurable feature values that can be used to build quantitative trust model for inferring or predicting trusts among users in online social applications.

REFERENCES

Bharadwaj, K., & Al-Shamri, H. (2009). Fuzzy computational models for trust and reputation systems. *Electronic Commerce Research and Applications*, *8*(1), 37–47. doi:10.1016/j.elerap.2008.08.001

Casare, S., & Sichman, J. (2005). Towards a Functional Ontology of Reputation. In *Proceedings of the Fourth International Joint Conference on Autonomous Agents and Multiagent Systems* (pp. 505-511). New York: ACM.

Caverlee, J., Liu, L., & Webb, S. (2010). The SocialTrust framework for trusted social information management: Architecture and algorithms. *Information Sciences*, *180*(1), 95–112. doi:10.1016/j.ins.2009.06.027

Dellarocas, C. (2003). The Digitization of Word-of-Mouth: Promise and Challenges of Online Reputation Systems. *Management Science*, *49*(10), 1407–1424. doi:10.1287/mnsc.49.10.1407.17308

Fukuyama, F. (1995). *Trust: The Social Virtues and the Creation of Prosperity*. New York: Free Press.

Gefen, D., Karahanna, E., & Straub, D. W. (2003). Trust and TAM in online shopping: an integrated model. *Management Information Systems Quarterly*, *27*(1), 51–90.

Golbeck, J. (2005). *Computing and Applying Trust in Web-based Social Networks*. Unpublished doctoral dissertation, University of Maryland, College Park.

Golbeck, J. (2009). Trust and nuanced profile similarity in online social networks. *ACM Transactions on the Web, 3*(4), 1–30. doi:10.1145/1594173.1594174

Gruber, T. (2008). Collective knowledge systems: Where the Social Web meets the Semantic Web. *Journal of Web Semantics, 6*(1), 4–13.

Jamali, M., & Ester, M. (2009). TrustWalker: A Random Walk Model for Combining Trust-based and Item-based Recommendation. In *Proceedings of the 15th ACM SIGKDD International Conference on Knowledge Discovery and Data Mining,* Paris (pp. 397-406).

Jason, A., Scott, A., & LePine, A. (2007). Trust, trustworthiness, and trust propensity: A meta-analytic test of their unique relationships with risk taking and job performance. *The Journal of Applied Psychology, 92*(4), 909–927. doi:10.1037/0021-9010.92.4.909

Jøsang, A., & Ismail, R. (2002). The beta reputation system. In *Proceedings of the 15th Bled Electronic Commerce Conference,* Bled, Slovenia (pp. 1-14).

Kim, D. J., Ferrin, D. L., & Rao, H. R. (2008). A trust-based consumer decision-making model in electronic commerce: The role of trust, perceived risk,and their antecedents. *Decision Support Systems, 44*(2), 544–564. doi:10.1016/j.dss.2007.07.001

Kim, Y., Le, M. T., Lauw, H. W., Lim, E. P., Liu, H., & Srivastava, J. (2008). Building a Web of Trust without Explicit Trust Ratings. In *Proceedings of the 2008 IEEE 24th International Conference on Data Engineering Workshop,* Cancun, Mexico (pp. 531 - 536).

Kramer, R. M. (1999). Trust and distrust in organizations: Emerging perspectives, enduring questions. *Annual Review of Psychology, 50*(1), 569–598. doi:10.1146/annurev.psych.50.1.569

Kwan, M., & Ramachandran, D. (2009). Trust and Online Reputation Systemse. In J. Golbeck (Ed.), *Computing with Social Trust* (pp. 287-311). London: Spring.

Lesani, M., & Bagheri, S. (2006). Applying and Inferring Fuzzy Trust in Semantic Web Social Networks. In *Canadian Semantic Web* (pp. 23–43). New York: Springer. doi:10.1007/978-0-387-34347-1_3

Levien, L. (2002). *Attack resistant trust metrics.* Unpublished PhD thesis, Department of Computer Science, University of California, Berkeley.

Lu, Y., Zhao, L., & Wang, B. (2009). From virtual community members to C2Ce-commerce buyers: Trust in virtual communities and its effect on consumers' purchase intention. *Electronic Commerce Research and Applications.* doi:10.1016/j.elerap.2009.07.003

Lytras, M. D. (2009). *Web 2.0 The Business Model.* New York: Springer.

Ma, N. L. (2009). Trust Relationship Prediction Using Online Product Review Data. In *Proceedings of the 1st ACM International Workshop on Complex Networks Meet Information & Knowledge Management,* Hong Kong, China (pp. 47-54).

Marsh, S. (1994). *Formalising Trust as a Computational Concept.* Unpublished PhD thesis, University of Stirling, California.

Massa, P., & Avesani, P. (2005). Controversial users demand local trust metrics: An experimental study on epinions.com community. In *Proceedings of the 20th National Conference on Artificial Intelligence,* (pp. 121-126). AAAI Press

Mayer, R. C., Davis, J. H., & Schoorman, F. D. (1995). An integration model of organizational trust. *Academy of Management Review, 20*(1), 709–734. doi:10.2307/258792

Monastersky, R. (2005). *The number that's devouring science.* The Chronicle of Higher Education.

Montaner, M. L. (2002). Opinion-based filtering through trust. In *Proceedings of the Sixth International Workshop on Cooperative Information Agents,* Madrid, Spain (pp. 164-178). Berlin: Springer-Verlag.

Mui, L., Mohtashemi, M., & Halberstadt, A. (2002). A computational model of trust and reputation. In *Proceedings of the 35th International Conference on System Science* (pp. 280-287). Washington, DC: IEEE Computer Society.

O'Donovan, J. A. (2009). Using Trust in Social Web Applications. In Golbeck, J. (Ed.), *In Computing with Social Trust* (pp. 213–257). London: Springer. doi:10.1007/978-1-84800-356-9_9

Page, L., Brin, S., Motwani, R., & Winograd, T. (1998). *The PageRank citation ranking: bringing order to the Web*. Palo Alto, CA: Stanford University.

Ridings, C. M., Gefen, D., & Arinze, B. (2002). Some antecedents and effects of trust in virtual communities. *The Journal of Strategic Information Systems, 11*(3), 271–295. doi:10.1016/S0963-8687(02)00021-5

Sabater, J., & Paolucci, M. (2007). On representation and aggregation of social evaluations in computationaltrust and reputation models. *International Journal of Approximate Reasoning, 4*(3), 458–483. doi:10.1016/j.ijar.2006.12.013

Sabater, J., & Sierra, C. (2005). Review on computing trust and reputation models. *Artificial Intelligence Review, 24*(1), 33–60. doi:10.1007/s10462-004-0041-5

Scott, J. (2002). *Social networks: Critical concepts in sociology*. New York: Routledge.

Stack, L. C. (1978). Trust. In London, H., & Exner, J. E. Jr., (Eds.), *Dimensionality of personality* (pp. 561–599). New York: Wiley.

Taherian, M., Amini, M., & Jalili, R. (2008) Trust Inference in Web-Based Social Networks Using Resistive Networks. In *Proceedings of the Third International Conference on Internet and Web Applications and Services,* Athens, Greece (pp. 233-238).

Yahia, S. A., Benedikt, M., & Bohannon, P. (2007). Challenges in searching online communities. *A Quarterly Bulletin of the Computer Society of the IEEE Technical Committee on Data Engineering, 30*(2), 23–31.

Zheng, W. (2009). Online Reputation Systems in Web 2.0 Era. In Nelson, M. (Ed.), *Value Creation in e-Business Management* (pp. 296–306). New York: Springer. doi:10.1007/978-3-642-03132-8_24

Ziegler, N., & Lausen, G. (2005). Propagation Models for Trust and Distrust in Social Networks. In *Information Systems Frontiers* (pp. 337–358). New York: Springer.

Zucker, L. G. (1996). Production of trust: Institutional sources of economic structure. In *Research in Organizational Behavior* (pp. 53–111). Greenwich, CT: JAI Press.

This work was previously published in the International Journal of Virtual Communities and Social Networking, Volume 2, Issue 2, edited by Subhasish Dasgupta, pp. 60-74, copyright 2010 by IGI Publishing (an imprint of IGI Global).

Chapter 18
Impact of Social Networking on College Students:
A Comparative Study in India and the Netherlands

Rajalakshmi Kanagavel
Anna University, India

Chandrasekharan Velayutham
Anna University, India

ABSTRACT

In today's world where Internet has experienced tremendous growth, social networking sites have become highly significant in peoples' lives. This comparative study between India and the Netherlands will concentrate on youngsters more precisely college going students in Chennai and Maastricht. The research explores how college students create identity for themselves in the virtual world and how they relate to others online. It will analyze the cultural differences from the youth perspective in both the countries and discuss whether social networking sites isolate youngsters from the society or help them to build relationships; the participation in these sites is also explored. Survey technique, interview, and online observation were the research methods used. Findings show that Indian students spend more time in these sites than Dutch students and Dutch students participate more actively than Indian students. It was also found that virtual interaction taking place in these sites is just a supplement to real life interaction.

INTRODUCTION

We are living in a world primarily characterized by objects in motion. Appadurai (2001) states that, "These objects include ideas and ideologies, people and goods, images and messages, technologies and techniques" (p. 5). Media has always played a crucial role in the stepping up of globalization

and Internet can be considered as a breakthrough in the globalization era. The Internet has provided an opportunity to build a global communication base that would link people around the world together. It allows groups of computers to interact simultaneously. This technical consideration signifies that the Internet can support and mediate new forms of communication, thus bettering the social relationship between individuals.

DOI: 10.4018/978-1-4666-1553-3.ch018

Miller and Slater (2000) argue that most discussions of the Internet have accentuated both the abolition of distance and a following detaching of relationships from particular place. In their research they showed this conclusion to be deceptive. They state that, "the Internet media are very capable of bringing dispersed things into immediate, virtually face-to-face, contact: prices and commodities, families, music, cultures, religious and ethnic diasporas" (Miller & Slater, 2000, p. 1). They found that in Trinidad, online relationships were treated similarly to offline relationships and therefore they emphasize that Internet is not a virtual or a disembodied world set off from the real but connected to the everyday lives of the people. This theory is tested by comparing the role of Internet in the students' lives in India and the Netherlands as they also emphasize that Internet may be different in different places.

With Web 2.0 technologies, the Internet has become a communication platform on which virtual communities are formed and it provides scope for interactivity, collaborative learning, social networking and participation (Flew, 2007). So, there are tremendous advancements taking place and most importantly youngsters form the majority of the consumers.

In order to examine the Internet in a more precise and measurable way, this study focuses on social networking sites. Social networking sites (SNSs) are now among the fastest growing Internet resources. The chances for the young people to form and maintain relationships on the Internet have increased in the last few years. SNSs have become the choice for the youngsters, who reach out to others on the web, receiving and distributing information on a real-time basis. Today almost each and every youngsters has a profile and is part of the virtual world. There are different types of SNSs depending on the relationships they focus. In this study only generic friend SNSs like Facebook are concentrated.

The key point to examine is not only what is happening on these sites but also why it is happening since human beings relate to people both in the virtual world as well as real world. Nowadays, young people seek to have more interactive communication and have become producers of content rather than consumers. This paper primarily focuses on college going students in both the countries since youth or young people cannot be defined to a specific age group. The effectiveness of virtual communities and the impact the SNSs have created among young people in the two countries, India, a country in South Asia and Netherlands, a North European country are examined in this article. Media consumption habits and preferences show a discrepancy significantly across the countries, where one is a developing and the other is a developed country.

It is assumed that the consumption of social media where Internet plays a vital role generally ascends with socio-economic status. Hence a significant need to figure out how far the change has influenced both the countries makes it essential to survey and explore as to why youngsters prefer and interact with the social media. The objectives of the study are as follows: To find out how social networking websites help in building relationships among the college going students; To study the level of participation of the young people while at these sites; To analyse whether these sites are isolating youngsters from society or vice versa; and to find out whether there are differences between India and Dutch students in these respects.

The current situation of the engagement of the students from India and the Netherlands in social networking sites will be discussed to provide a base for speculations on the future potential. And yet in the world of swiftly developing and up-and-coming technologies, the current circumstance does not hang around for a long period to be studied entirely. So this article will make some speculations for future research but every assumption will be based on the current status. The aim of this study is to map the current status of college going students' exposure, access, use and impact of social networking sites in both the countries and to establish cross-national similarities and differences.

Flew (2002) stated that as a result of the evolution of new media technologies, globalization occurs. So we will have a look at few terms which brings implication to the study as a whole. It is interesting to find social networking sites as a widespread aspect of culture since it is consumed by people all over the world.

LITERATURE REVIEW

Globalization

Globalization is the tendency of integration for a global reach and culture is a broad term which cannot be defined or confined to a particular sphere. And cultural globalization is the dissemination of cultural ideas across borders. With the emergence of new media and technological developments, everybody participates in this. Today globalization, technology and people build the culture and media plays a pivotal role in distinguishing how these three have an effect on the society on a large-scale.

Cultural globalization refers to "the intensification and expansion of cultural flows across the globe" (Steger, 2003, p. 69). American culture is dominant as global culture in case of social media. The discourse of cultural imperialism can be considered as one of the most outstanding viewpoints that have been adopted towards the globalization of culture (Tomlinson, 1999). Schiller (1976) gives description about Cultural Imperialism Theory that the media is dominated by the western nations around the globe which in return has an influential effect on third world cultures by striking them western views and therefore destroying their native cultures.

Even though many theorists do not agree with this cultural imperialism thesis, they recognize its significance. It is very difficult to find whether globalization makes people across the world alike or different. Nederveen-Pieterse (2004) supposes that a common thesis in media and cultural studies is global cultural homogenization and he thinks that globalization leads to hybridization. Globalization is diverse in itself and there are discrepancies in its basic understanding. Media has larger effect when it comes to globalization. The rate of this effect varies country from country according to its audiences and their media consumption.

New Media

The advent of Web 2.0 and the emergence of new digital technologies in the 20th century constitute new media. New media has the ability to bond people worldwide. Apparently, this has driven people to be part of digital culture which came into sight with the development of networked computers.

Communication in the social media sites occurs by the sharing of information through blogs, wikis, comments and feedbacks. The content in these sites are mostly produced by the users. Both producers and consumers of the content are involved in the communication and this leads to participatory culture. In 1984, Rice defined the new media as communication technologies that enable or facilitate user-to-user interactivity and interactivity between user and information. Social media is interactive media and since it engages Internet and web based technologies it can be said to be a subset of new media. The explosion in SNSs is widely regarded as an exciting opportunity, especially for youth and there is no doubt that digital culture is exerting a massive influence over young people in various ways.

Social Networking Sites

Social media has become a huge part of the lives of millions of people worldwide. Social network analysis views social relationships in terms of nodes (individual actors within the networks) and ties (relationships between the actors) (Wasserman & Faust, 1994). A new tie is created between the nodes when an user engages himself/herself in any activity. So there is building up of social relationship for every single act. A good example to quote here is the game, Mafia wars where the user adds persons to increase their family strength to fight their enemy.

According to comscore.com, Orkut is the most popular social networking site in India, which is powered by Google, and Hyves is famous among youngsters in the Netherlands. So the students from the Netherlands and India are more likely to use Hyves and Orkut respectively. Even though India has developed its own SNSs like Fropper and Bigadda, students are attracted more towards global sites like Facebook.

These SNSs allow content creation and the opportunity to exhibit content created elsewhere into one mutual place. Indeed, the very act of creating a profile on a social network site leads to content creation. This trend towards engagement has led to the development of new term, "participatory media."

Participatory Culture

The framework of mass broadcast persistently kept the means of production in the possession of a selected few but with the emergence of Web 2.0, the consumer has control and can participate in the production of both entertainment and culture.

As Mark Deuze (2006) emphasizes, participation is an important and principle component of a digital culture. The users engage themselves in a way that their participation contributes lot to the content. Communication between users takes place through a wide range of forms apart from e-mail: posts, comments, reviews, ratings, gestures and tokens, votes, links, badges, photo and video (Manovich, 2008).

Henry Jenkins (2006) notes that, along with the rise in popularity of participatory media applications, there has also been a concurrent development of "participatory cultures" that serve to encourage all of this user-contributed content. According to him, "the term participatory culture contrasts with the older notions of passive media spectatorship. Rather than talking about media consumers and producers occupying separate roles we might now see them as participants who interact with each other"(Jenkins, 2006). But not all participants are producers of content.

It is interesting to explore about participation and find how many have participated or participating in one or more among a wide range of content-creating activities on the Internet from blogging to social networking to other creation of digital material. Participation varies according to the individuals, region and the environment. This study will explore how the students get involved in this by using SNSs in which they are active and investigate whether they share or upload photos or videos created by them and post comments on their friends' web pages and blogs. It is apparent that some will be inactive by not participating at all. Time is another factor to be considered. The users who use these sites for long hours are more likely to participate actively. The results of the survey will be examined to enhance the strength of these deductions. And some are not able to participate because Internet is not available and it is not accessed by all.

Digital Divide

The digital divide differs in every country and can be based on the gender, income and the economic status of the people. It is the gap between people having access to the technology and the people who have limited or no access. This is different from global digital divide. Norris proposes "'global divide' as the differential Internet access between nations based on access to networked ICT infrastructures, computers, information transmission capacity, local website hosts, etc,"(Flew, 2005, p. 26).

According to Pippa Norris (2001), the global divide refers to the difference of internet access between developed and developing societies and the democratic divide signifies the differences between those who do, and do not, use the range of digital resources to engage, mobilize and participate in public life.

Following rapid growth in Internet usage in the late 1990's there was widespread diffusion in the year 2001 in many European countries including the Netherlands and there were very few Internet users found in Asia including India. The present scenario is completely different where in Asia out of 3,808,070,503 (2009 Est.)People, 704,213,930 use Internet and in Europe out of 803,850,858 (2009 Est.), 402,380,474 people use Internet. Nearly half of the European population use Internet. In India out of 1,156,897,766, 5,000,000 people used Internet in the year 2000 and lately 81,000,000 people use Internet and in the Netherlands out of 16,715,999 people, 14,272,700 uses Internet. India accounts for 11.6% users in Asia and Netherlands accounts for 3.5% users in Europe (www.internetworldstats.com).

At present world's internet using population is becoming more diverse and of the estimated Internet users in December 2006, the majority are from Asia and Europe. Since our study majorly concentrates on cities, it can be supposed that this study is not affected by this digital divide.

Urban Youth Culture

The Urban focus provides a way of exploring the broader issues associated with the globalization process. The city is where we see the consequences of global change in their full intensity. So this research focuses on two cities namely Maastricht in the Netherlands and Chennai in India, both of which are not capital cities to their respective countries. It is interesting to find the differences of two different city cultures of two different countries which belong to two different continents.

Chennai, which has been endowed with rich heritage of art and culture, is famous for its various college cultural events among youngsters, presenting the performing arts such as dance, music and drama at its best. It is notable that cinema is considered to be pulse of Chennai youngsters whereas Maastricht city's love for culture culminates in numerous parties, festivals, fairs and performances throughout the year and the youngsters actively participate in these activities and most importantly they are independent.

Western culture imposes a considerable amount of influence upon Indian youth therefore they are exposed to whatever global audiences are exposed to. Social networking is at the crux of its popularity, dominating the social culture of urban young people worldwide. Youth is a generalised term and doesn't adhere to a particular group of people. Since adolescents or teen-agers enjoy limelight often, let us focus on college going students in both the countries. The features of Dutch youth culture are by nature international, but in the sense of western culture. This is a contrast to Indian culture where not all youngsters are westernized in a conventional society.

Social class, gender and ethnicity can be important in relation to youth subcultures (Wikipedia, 2009). The power that adults hold over youth explains more than just complications in identity development. It can be said that it is the root of why students are on SNSs primarily.

After analysing terms and studying the cultural differences, it is interesting to observe the reason behind college students going to these sites. It has given rise to questions like what do the Indian and Dutch students gain from the SNSs? What are they expressing on them? How do these sites fit into their lives? How do they relate themselves to others in the virtual world? Are these online activities like face-to-face relationships or are they different? Are there differences between Dutch and Indian students in these aspects? This study deals with these questions, and explores their significances for creating identities for the youth in both the countries.

METHODS

The research methodologies used are survey and online observation. Survey method included distribution of questionnaire both online and offline. Online observation included analysis of profiles in Hyves and Orkut, most popular sites in the Netherlands and India respectively. Sampling considered is non-probability sampling since only students who are active in SNSs and those who use them regularly. So here people are not chosen randomly but intentionally, so that the sample represents particular group of people. Chennai is a hub of many educational institutes and colleges. So the collection of data is distributed among students belonging to different colleges. Whereas in Maastricht since there are few universities, the responses were collected from Maastricht University and Zuyd University of Applied Sciences.

Online Observation

Online observation was done to study the extent of Dutch and Indian students' usage of social networking sites. The statements made here are based on ethnographic data collected on Dutch and Indian youth engagement with Hyves and Orkut respectively. It constitutes of observing the participants in the virtual medium, documenting and talking to students about their uses.

A total of 160 random profiles of students those who are basically from Maastricht and Chennai and active users of SNSs were analysed, of which 39 were females and 47 were males in Orkut and 33 females and 41 males in Hyves. The profiles were studied from October 24th 2009 to November 3rd 2009.

Survey

A Sample of 140 students who use SNSs regularly was surveyed using simple purposive sampling. In Maastricht, 71 students were surveyed out of which girls form the majority with 42 in number and the remaining 29 students are boys. In Chennai, the survey was conducted among 69 students with 36 girls and 33 boys. Questionnaires were distributed among Dutch students in Maastricht in the University library and the faculties but the majority of the responses were collected by uploading an online questionnaire. And the responses from the Chennai students were collected by sending the questionnaire via mail and uploading the questionnaire in forums of SNSs.

RESULTS

Online Observation

In Hyves, background and text can be formatted by the user and any design, pattern or picture can be incorporated. In Orkut, default themes are available which can be applied to the profile page. While observing many profiles, Roadies (popular show of MTV) theme was very popular among Chennai boys. While interviewing two Dutch people, it was found out that most of the students in the Netherlands are members of the Hyves site to stay in touch with their Dutch peers. But slowly Facebook is taking over Hyves and some Dutch students in Maastricht spent more time in Facebook than in Hyves since their friends' circle is growing with other international students. So obviously, students are rarely part of just one social networking site.

Boys and girls have different perspectives while filling in details in their profiles and they exhibit different characters when it comes to privacy settings. The default profile is publicly accessible to anyone, but most SNSs have privacy feature that allow participants to restrict who can see what (Boyd, 2005). In Hyves there is a feature which displays, from when a particular user is active. Very few profiles of both boys and girls were made private and the profiles were not accessible. In Orkut all profiles were visible but only certain information was made private by different users. Almost all boys had their profile accessible to everyone including their photo albums, videos and scrapbook (similar to wall in Facebook). Even though contact details along with the profile were visible to others, out of 39 profiles viewed, about 28 girls had locked their photo albums and scrapbook in Orkut. And boys mostly had made their scrapbook private and not their photos. But in Hyves out of 41 profiles, 14 boys and out of 33 profiles only 16 girls had made their profile pages private. A fact which is to be well noted in Orkut is that opposite gender associates are very less when compared to Hyves.

In Orkut, nearly half of the girls' profiles analyzed did not have a personal photograph but other pictures like photos of film stars and some had uploaded pictures of babies, dogs, hearts and teddies. Even 2% of the boys profiles analyzed had movie star as their display picture. It can be clearly seen that many students idolize film stars in Chennai. Almost all girls had locked their photo and video albums. The minimum number of friends a college student has in her/his friends list is 120 and maximum is 550 in Hyves whereas in Orkut the former is 50 and the latter is 320.

So, the ways in which youth incorporate their identity in their profiles and interaction of the youth in a particular social networking site most importantly in a particular country is profoundly different from another.

Survey

As we discuss about young people and their engagement with these sites, it is very clear that their participation is a social activity. SNSs allow its users both to maintain existing social ties and to form new connections. First and foremost it is evident that connecting through SNSs is a differ-

ent way of bonding when compared to real life interaction. It was interesting to find that part of the attractiveness among college students towards SNSs was the chance to learn more about their friends and acquaintances through profiles and status updates.

Now we will look through our survey results in terms of cultural perspectives and analyse the findings. An important point to discuss here is the age of the college going students in Maastricht and Chennai. As discussed earlier, Dutch students are very independent. So there are chances of them joining university one or two years later after their high school. And moreover the Dutch education system is structured in such a way that students attend school till the age of 18. Whereas in India almost all the students join college as soon as they complete their high school at the age of 17. So age differences were expected to occur before surveying Indian and Dutch students. And the result proves this where the majority of the respondents from Chennai fall under the age group of 17-21 and 20-24 in Maastricht.

It is surprising to see that in both the cities majority of the students use two SNSs (52% in Maastricht and 48% in Chennai). Orkut, which is powered by Google, is the most popular site used among college going students in Chennai whereas in Maastricht, Hyves, which was developed in the same country, is famous among Dutch students but an interesting point to make a note of is that nearly same amount of respondents use Facebook regularly. In both the countries Facebook is very popular among youngsters because of the latest and appealing features available when compared to other sites. Facebook which was developed in America reached 350 million users around the world on December 2nd 2009. Though it has global reach, it attains local levels to a great extent with its applications and most essentially there is no language barrier. Since Hyves, which was developed mainly for Dutch, is available only in Dutch language and is not very famous outside the Netherlands. One of the reasons why Orkut and Facebook is popular in India is because of the lack of technological developments since there is no social networking site developed yet inside the country with features on par with these globally famous sites.

Internet has become indispensible that almost every day there is a small dose of it in students' lives. Considering the time spent on SNSs while using Internet, it is found that students in Chennai spend more time when compared to Maastricht students (Figure 1).

Usually those who spend more time online using SNSs are supposed to show greater use of it, have more friends and participate in more groups. They are more likely to change their profiles and most of their personal details. But the survey proved otherwise conveying that the level of participation of Chennai youngsters is comparatively less to Maastricht youngsters (Figure 2). The interface of the using social networking site can be one of the constraints for participation since some features like chat, poke, applications, themes or games are unique to a site

which makes a user active. So the participation within a community differs a lot when compared to any other region.

Many students from Chennai have a maximum of 200 friends but in Maastricht majority of the students have more than 200 friends. This is probably because of the college lifestyle. In Maastricht youngsters are exposed to different activities like attending parties, going to pubs and get-togethers. So they come across many new people every day. Not necessarily they make friends out of everyone but they are acquainted and meet often. Since the city is small there are probabilities of meeting someone anywhere, be it university or at a party. But the scenario is different in Chennai since there are fewer chances for students meeting new people often other than their friends and classmates. They do hang out and mingle with people from other places but it is comparatively less when seen with Maastricht students. This can be the reason why Dutch students have more real life friends in their friends list when compared to Indian students. 36% of the students in Chennai

Figure 1. Time spent on SNSs

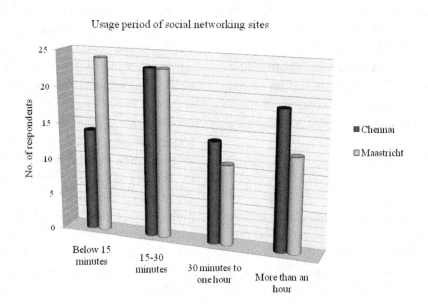

Figure 2. Level of participation

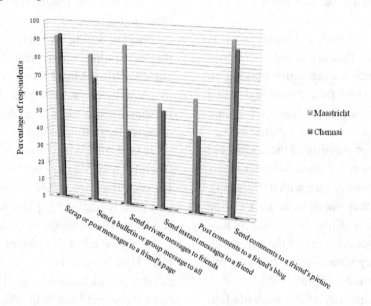

and 49% in Maastricht have 80 percent of their real life friends in their friends list.

Nearly 30% of the students from Chennai send friend invitations to anonymous persons whereas very few about 8% in students from Maastricht send invites to anonymous persons. This shows the urge among Chennai students to make new friends. None of the students in Chennai and Maastricht totally agree with the statement that they have closer relationships with friends who are on these sites than with friends who aren't.

Figure 3. Feeling less lonely on these sites

You feel less lonely in these sites

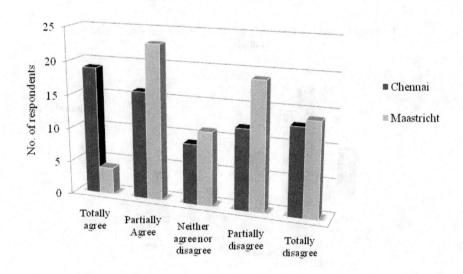

So this clearly confirms that real life interaction cannot be replaced.

It is found that both Dutch and Indian students feel less lonely when they are at the SNSs. Students mostly do multi-tasking while working on systems so they share their thoughts through status messages and chat with their friends for leisure while they are stressed and work for their assignments and exams. But majority of the students in Chennai totally agree and majority of the students from Maastricht partially agree with it (Figure 3).

This is because they spend more time online with their friends than offline. In Maastricht requisite doesn't arise because most of them live with their friends and they have chances of going out frequently than Chennai people.

In Chennai the majority of the students find online communication easier than offline communication (Figure 4). There can be many reasons for students to flock themselves to SNSs like peer pressure, loneliness and sometimes even to find a date and socialize in that medium. More people converse here than in real life due to lack of time and social constraints like boys and girls not allowed to interact in college. Many of the engineering colleges in Tamil Nadu (state in India in which Chennai is the capital city) in order to

maintain the discipline have imposed rule where boys and girls aren't allowed to interact among themselves during the class hours and even when they are in the campus. But this is in contrast of students' life in Maastricht where they are allowed to interact with one and other. It can be one of the reasons for the users from Maastricht to totally disagree for finding online communication easier.

It is significant to find that students in both Chennai and Maastricht don't concur with the fact that they are at SNSs so that they can be a completely different person. Thus it can be rightly said that youngsters do not want themselves to be portrayed in the virtual world as someone else. They want to be seen as their true self as in the real world. So SNSs don't detach youngsters from the society but helps the students to bridge or build relationships.

It is found that the majority of the respondents in Chennai and Maastricht are using SNSs to keep in contact with their recent and old friends. It also helps in finding friends with identical thoughts and ideas. And many people revealed that it is the medium where they can convey information to many people through a single status message. A substantial amount of students use them for finding and sharing information and some use

Figure 4. Online communication easier than offline communication

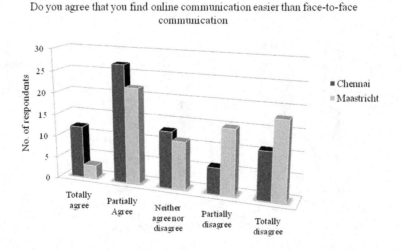

Figure 5. Why SNSs are used?

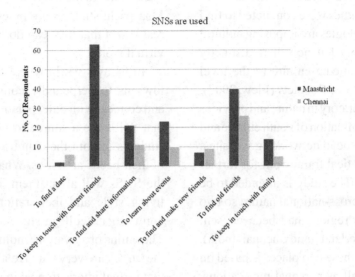

to learn about various events happening in their particular communities (Figure 5).

Firstly as it has been discussed beforehand, students experiencing problems with face-to-face communication are less likely to find communicating online easier or more relaxing than communicating face-to-face, it is also to be expected that they would not report that joining SNSs had led to an improvement in their social skills. Instead, this finding seems to affirm that for those, online communication is easy that it has also helped them to benefit their social skills. The majority of the Maastricht students partially agree with the fact that SNSs helps them to socialize. In Chennai, 62% of the respondents agreed that SNSs have helped them to socialize in the real world. The major differentiation here is that 66% of the girls in Chennai and 26% of the girls in Maastricht agreed. This can be explained with the fact that most of the Chennai girls exposed to a more conventional society tend to be reserved compared to the more gregarious students from Maastricht.

When the respondents were asked to envision a situation with SNSs not existing and whether they would be concerned, 65% of Dutch students and 33% of the Indian students state that they

wouldn't be bothered at all. It is interesting to find that students from Chennai were more interested to be part of the virtual world. Nearly 3 out of 4 students, 75% of the respondents in Maastricht and 68% of the respondents in Chennai declare that they wouldn't mind if they were not able to access SNSs for some time with 41% and 32% of the students absolutely in accord. Regarding respondents' reported importance of these sites' usage, significant difference existed in relation to the report that respondents would not mind if unable to use these sites for some time. So, it can be seen vividly that even though SNSs play an imperative role in youngsters' life, they are not very much obsessed with it.

CONCLUSION AND FUTURE RESEARCH

This article emphasizes that the digital media have become dominant in the consumption of youth as Internet has set up a position for itself as frequently used media and communication. In particular the development of social media and web 2.0 technologies has produced trends towards the users of digital media who are producers of the content. Many studies were conducted to find whether these technologies are imposing cultural changes in the society but now it is distinctly embedded in global media culture to the level that we live in a 'always on' society (Flew, 2007).

This study is exploratory in nature and provides an outline for the examination of youth culture and their engagement in social networking websites. It provides a hypothetical framework for further research in the field. The study is intended to be of comparative and cross-national nature so two countries as well as regions had been chosen: Maastricht (The Netherlands) and Chennai (India). And the decision for these two places is based on study-oriented as well as personal motivations. On one hand, the choice for the Netherlands comes from the fact that it is a highly developed country where new technologies are used by most of the people and Maastricht is chosen because it is the place where the research study was done. And on the other hand, choice for India comes from the fact that it is a developing country and technological innovations are beginning to take root and has decent reach among youngsters in cities and also from the personal reason since it is the place where the researcher lives and study. However, the main limitation of this comparative study is the confinement to just these two cities and the small sample size. Examining only about hundred people makes it challenging to generalize the findings. A further study will require analysis of a much broader sample including samples from other important cities in both countries to get an overall divergence between Indian and Dutch students.

The findings confirm that many college students use SNSs to maintain relationship with their school friends and to create new friends in college. According to the results, it can be said that SNSs are embedded in Chennai youngsters' lives to some extent even though they do not actively participate as Maastricht students since it

does matter to them if SNSs did not exist whereas Maastricht students are much content with their real world that they can do without being in the virtual world.

In today's world where the environment allows us to perpetually communicate, interfere and connect with other person's life, it can be said that SNSs are a source to young college going students in both the countries for keeping track of their peers' activities. Whatever way they use, the SNSs will affect them, especially –culture, living style and their rational thinking. SNSs don't isolate college students from the society. The online observation findings and the results of the survey are very much related. So it can be said that virtual interaction taking place in these sites is just a supplement to real life interaction. And the conclusions deduced account to the cultural differences in both the countries in various ways.

Interaction between people who share interests and explore interests has led to building of online communities. Users benefit by interacting with a likeminded community and finding a channel for their energy and giving. But then does it make one more or less social? It is not really because it might be an icebreaker, something one might have in common with someone else to make a remark about, but generally it's too diminutive and kind of embarrassing that one would spend time on it that it doesn't really act as a social catalyst. Thus SNSs has an impact on college students in Chennai and Maastricht and its usage and participation differs according to the place.

Finally, in terms of suggestions for future research, the same cross-cultural approach to the study will be helpful. Moreover even in-depth behavioral studies to find the motive behind the usage of social networking sites can be done with this research serving as a basis.

The comprehension of how cultural factors account for discrepancy in individuals' behavior and involvement will strengthen the generalization and substantiation of such research.

REFERENCES

Appadurai, A. (2003). *Globalization-Grassroots Globalization and the Research Imagination*. Durham, NC: Duke University Press.

Boyd, D. (2007). Why Youth (Heart) Social Network Sites: The Role of Networked Publics in Teenage Social Life . In Buckingham, D. (Ed.), *MacArthur Foundation Series on Digital Learning - Youth, Identity, and Digital Media Volume*. Cambridge, MA: MIT Press.

Boyd, D., & Ellison, N. B. (2007). Social Network Sites: Definition, History, and Scholarship. *Journal of Computer-Mediated Communication, 13*(1).

Deuze, M. (2006). Participation, Remediation, Bricolage: Considering Principal Components of a Digital Culture. *The Information Society, 22*(1), 63–75. doi:10.1080/01972240600567170

Flew, T. (2007). *New media: an Introduction* (3rd ed.). South Melbourne, Australia: Oxford University Press.

Internet world statistics. (2009). Retrieved November 14, 2009, from http://www.internetworldstats.com/stats.htm

Ito, M., Horst, A. H., Bittanti, M., Boyd, D., Herr-Stephenson, B., & Lange, G. P. (n.d.). *Living and Learning with New Media: Summary of Findings from the Digital Youth Project*. The John D. and Catherine T. *MacArthur Foundation Reports on Digital Media and Learning*.

Jenkins, H. (2006a). *Convergence Culture: Where Old and New Media Collide*. New York: New York University Press.

Manovich, L. (2008). The Practice of Everyday (Media) Life . In Lovink, G., & Sabine, N. (Eds.), *Video Vortex Reader: Responses to YouTube* (pp. 33–44). Amsterdam, The Netherlands: Institute of Network Cultures.

Miller, D., & Slater, D. (2000). *The Internet- an Ethnographic Approach*. Oxford, UK: Berg Publishers.

Nederveen-Pieterse, J. (2004). *Globalization and Culture: Global Melange*. MD: Rowman and Littlefield Publishers.

New Media. (n.d.). In *Wikipedia*. Retrieved November 24, 2009, from http://en.wikipedia.org/wiki/New_media

Norris, P. (2001). *Digital Divide*. Cambridge, UK: Cambridge University Press.

Robertson, R. (1992). *Globalization- Social Theory and Global Culture*. London: Sage Publications.

Schiller, H. J. (1973). *Communication and Cultural Domination*. White Plains, NY: International Arts and Sciences Press.

Steger, B. (2003). *Globalization: A Very Short Introduction*. Oxford, UK: Oxford University Press.

Tomlinson, J. (1999). *Globalization and Culture*. Cambridge, UK: Blackwell Publishers.

Wasserman, S., & Faust, K. (1994). *Social Networks Analysis: Methods and Applications*. Cambridge, UK: Cambridge University Press.

This work was previously published in the International Journal of Virtual Communities and Social Networking, Volume 2, Issue 3, edited by Subhasish Dasgupta, pp. 55-67, copyright 2010 by IGI Publishing (an imprint of IGI Global).

Chapter 19
Managing Collaborative Research Networks:
The Dual Life of a Virtual Community of Practice

Dimitrina Dimitrova
York University, Canada

Emmanuel Koku
Drexel University, USA

ABSTRACT

This paper explores how management practices shape the way dispersed communities of practice (CoPs) function. The analysis is a case study of a dispersed community engaged in conducting and managing collaborative research. The analysis uses data from a social network survey and semi-structured interviews to capture the management practices in the community and demonstrate how they are linked to the patterns of information flows and communication.

This analysis is a test case for the broader issue of how distributed communities function. It shows that even highly distributed CoPs may have a dual life: they exist both online and offline, in both face-to-face meetings and email exchanges of their participants. The study examines a dispersed community engaged in conducting and managing collaborative research. The analysis uses data from a social network survey and interviews to examine its managerial practices, information exchanges and communication practices.

INTRODUCTION

The last few decades have seen scientific research become more collaborative, more dispersed, and more reliant on technology. The emergence of large collaborative research networks is but just one of the manifestations of this trend. While researchers have always collaborated informally in "invisible colleges", their networks are now more formally designed and more tightly coordinated organizational structures (Crane, 1972). Research today is carried out in large and diverse networks that often operate on national or even global levels, across disciplines and across sectors. Such networks

DOI: 10.4018/978-1-4666-1553-3.ch019

require significant technological infrastructures for the participants to work collaboratively and to communicate.

Within the broad trend of networked research and technologically sophisticated cyber science, collaborative research networks come in a variety of organizational forms, tasks, and technological infrastructure (Bos, 2008). One organizational form that has caught the attention of the practitioners, but has yet to receive a serious treatment by academics, is research consortia. The purpose of research consortia is to conduct research which meets the needs of users and enable them to act. As a rule, research consortia involve multiple funders and focus on complex problems requiring extensive collaboration. It is not surprising that such consortia create large distributed research networks that can sometimes span national boundaries. What is distinctive about consortia is the strong partnership between practitioners and academics. Other organizational forms of collaborative research may also involve cross-sectoral partnerships. Research consortia, however, require that practitioners from the funding organizations and academics reach a shared understanding of its research goals and of the means to achieve them. In addition to the knowledge creation taking place in the research projects, research consortia involve learning processes on the level of all participants. They generate a shared view of the significant research issues in an area, mutual understanding of the need of diverse stakeholders, and more accurate mutual expectations. In other words, research consortia serve double duty as coordinating mechanisms of large collaborative research networks and as distributed CoPs. Managing research consortia is as much about coordinating research projects as it is about enabling exchange of ideas and learning. However, despite a growing body of literature on the design and management of virtual communities (VC) and dispersed CoPs, their management practices are not well understood.

This study sets out to explore how the management of CoPs affects the way such communities function. The analysis examines a research consortia program run by a Canadian Network of Centres of Excellence (NCE) referred to as the Water Agency. The NCE was created by the Canadian federal government to foster research and innovation in the area of water. All NCEs are responsible for encouraging multidisciplinary and nation-wide research conducted in partnerships with industrial and government participants. They adopt a network structure in order to avoid the "functional silos", rigidity, and delays common for traditional bureaucracies. In essence, NCEs create collaborative research networks of academics and practitioners whose participants are dispersed across the country.

The NCE under investigation runs two programs: a General program with traditional mechanisms of research funding and a Consortia program following a research consortia model[1]. This discussion focuses on the network of professionals involved in the Consortia program. Among them are academics from diverse disciplines and a wide range of research areas whose work contribute to the understanding water issues such as: watershed and ecosystems research, water infrastructure, threats to water supplies, or water treatment. In turn, the practitioners in the network include employees at different levels of government, industry partners, conservation authorities and non-governmental organizations (NGOs). Some of them fund or contribute in-kind to the research conducted through the consortia. Others are stakeholders who have a vested interest in the research results even though they do not contribute directly to them.

At the moment, the Consortia program has a network of about 140 members. Current members are affiliated with two fully operational consortia and a few new consortia still in their design stages. Members have an email list, which the Consortia program staff uses to send updates of the program activities, summary documents of consortia decisions or research progress, and invitations for meetings such as consultation and scoping workshops, committees or sub-committees meetings, projects workshops, or scholarly conferences which the Agency has co-sponsored. The boundaries of the consortia network are not rigidly defined: researchers may flow in and out of the network depending on whether they have a project funded through the program; industry and government partners change jobs and drop out of the membership lists. Program events often target the broader professional community in the area of water, especially if the Consortia program co-sponsors events. Nonetheless, the membership list of the program is a reasonable approximation of the network participants.

The Consortia program has developed distinctive ways to manage its research process, which inevitably affect the connections among the participants as well as their collaboration and communication practices. The central concern of this analysis is how the management of the program shapes the structure and functioning of the consortia network, and how the use of various communication media is implicated in and influenced by management practices. The arguments are informed by an earlier research of the General program (Dimitrova & Koku, 2009) but they focus on the network created by the Consortia program.

LITERATURE REVIEW AND RESEARCH QUESTIONS

Research consortia issues lie at intersection of several bodies of literature: studies on scientific research, literature on learning and knowledge processes, and social network analysis. Each of these can inform the current study and help develop the research questions for the analysis.

Today, large collaborative research networks are a given in science. It is widely assumed that they can bring significant gains to society, advance science, and benefit scientists themselves (Olson et al., 2008) although the indicators for measuring their success are not well developed. While it is easy to measure the number of published papers written by the researchers in a network, it is not so easy to capture scientific breakthroughs or their societal impact (Bielak et al., 2009). Further, regardless of how their impact is measured, collaborative research networks are not always successful. A lot of their characteristics go against the grain of the way scientists have traditionally done research. For instance, the complexity of current research problems requires the contributions of multiple researchers from different disciplines. However, researchers from different disciplines do not have a shared understanding of the issues and lack the common methodologies and practices, created by disciplinary training and by interaction at scientific forums (Caruso & Rhoten, 2001; Rhoten, 2003; Cummings & Kiesler, 2005; Shrum et al., 2001). To collaborate, researchers need to establish a shared understanding of issues and common practices as well as overcome the lack of social bonding. That is why Cummings and Kiesler (2005) suggested that multi-disciplinary teams require management of both tasks and relationships. Our own research (Dimitrova & Koku, 2009) and the research of others (Rhoten, 2003; Moore, 1989; Pellmar & Eisenberg, 2000) show that most universities do not usually recognize nor appropriately reward scientists engaged in such large-scale collaborative research. Put differently, the difficulties of multi-disciplinary collaboration are compounded by the lack of institutional rewards. In turn, multi-institutional collaboration brings the benefits of pooling of research expertise, coordination of research activities on a broader scope, and more efficient use of infrastructure but it is hindered by competition for funding or efforts to guard intellectual property (Bos et al., 2008). Some studies link complex collaboration to negative effects. For instance, Rhoten (2003) found a negative correlation between the success of collaborative research networks and the number of participating institutions.

Two findings on the challenges of large collaborative research networks and the potential solutions are particularly relevant for the current study. First, the difficulties, created by diverse disciplinary and institutional background, are heightened by distance and mediated communication. Mediated communication increases the opportunity for misunderstanding, slows down communication, decreases the incentive of participants to adapt, and makes the development of trust difficult (Olsons & Olson, 2003; Jarvenpaa & Leidner, 1999; Bos et al., 2001). Perhaps that is why researchers, who need to communicate novel and complex knowledge, have a strong preference for face-to-face rather than mediated communication (Bos, 2008; Dimitrova & Koku, 2009; Rhoten, 2003). This preference for face-to-face communication looms even larger in applied user-oriented research which requires the interactions of researchers and users. Engaging users in the planning of programs and projects and communicating findings is best done face-to-face (Bielak et al., 2009). While some have argued that big science today has become e-Science or cyber-science, this preference for face-to-face communication suggests that dispersed collaborative networks can be expected to rely on a mix of online and offline practices, specifically, of mediated technology and face-to-face communication (Hey & Trefethen, 2008).

A second, somewhat surprising, result in existing research is that such networks do not necessarily encourage learning. Researchers organize their collaborative work in a way that minimizes interdependence and decreases the need for coordination and communication across distance (Olson et al., 2008; Dimitrova & Koku, 2007). Haythornwhaite and her colleagues found that researchers often organize their collaboration like a jigsaw puzzle where pieces just fit together (Haythornwhaite et al., 2003). Such type of collaboration, however, with its well-defined pre-determined roles, goals, and schedules, does not encourage learning. It is only integrative projects without pre-determined goals and results that enable learning (Haythornwhaite et al., 2003). In a similar vein, Rhoten (2003) suggested that researchers' ties across disciplines tend to be collegial information sharing rather than close knowledge creating ties. Paradoxically, complex collaborative networks might be at odds with learning among researchers.

Such a claim must be placed in the context of what we know about learning and knowledge processes in general. The newly emerging social learning theory emphasizes the social and relational nature of human learning (Wenger, 2010). In other words, knowledge is collectively created and embedded in social practices. The key to understanding how learning occurs and knowledge is created and transmitted is the concept of Communities of Practice (CoPs), defined as "groups of people informally bound together by shared expertise and passion for a joint enterprise" (Wenger & Snyder, 2000). Such informal groups may share discipline, problem, or situation (Wenger, 2004). Whatever the case may be, it is these shared concerns that spur them into action and maintain their commitment and norms of reciprocity. Important aspects of the groups are relations of mutuality, strong engagement and identification with the group (Wenger, 2000).

Since its introduction in the 1980s, the concept of informal self-selected and self-organizing communities of learners have been applied to a range of domains, from companies to government to inter-organizational professional communities; it has been inevitably developed and refined to encompass the broad reality to which it is now being applied (Lesser & Prusak, 1999; Brown & Duguid, 1991; Snyder & Wenger, 2003). Wenger and Lave initially envisioned CoPs as tightly bound groups with local practices. In contrast, later work builds on the concept of CoPs but turned to larger groups in which learning unfolds within inter-related entities. Constellations of interdependent

CoPs co-exist in social learning systems, form Networks of Communities of Practice or are scattered in a landscape of other practices (Wenger, 2000, 2010; Brown & Duguid, 2000). Especially relevant for this study is the idea that CoPs form learning loops with cross-functional projects so that CoPs develop capacity and new knowledge, which is then brought by CoPs members to their project teams and applied (Wenger, 2000, p. 237).

Next, while the definition of CoPs highlights properties such as self-selection and self-organization, later interest in fostering CoPs led to the understanding that their facilitation is not only possible but necessary (Wenger, 2000; Wenger & Snyder, 2000). In the words of Wenger (2004), knowledge management is a doughnut where management practices occupy the empty space at the centre. Strong intervention and outside management are detrimental but CoPs can be cultivated by providing infrastructure and recognition (Wenger, 2004; Wenger & Snyder, 2000). This understanding is related to numerous studies on the factors that facilitate the emergence of CoPs. Designed virtual communities provided a fertile test ground for such studies.

A particularly fruitful extension of the concept of CoP resulted from its marriage with technology. CoPs involving numerous dispersed participants have morphed into Virtual Communities of Practice (VCoPs) – defined as loosely bound groups of professionals with common expertise who exchange information and ideas or problem-solve online (Boss et al., 2007; Daniel et al., 2003). Such communities can include hundreds of participants, include globally dispersed employees of multinational organizations, or stretch across companies (Restler & Woolis, 2007; Chiu et al., 2006). Such large dispersed communities can still function as CoPs if they have intellectual and social leadership (Wenger & Snyder, 2000). VCoPs seem especially malleable and suitable to deliberate design. The factors that help them succeed have attracted considerable attention. Research links the strength of VCoPs with reciprocity, identity, and trust – community properties that do not easily develop in dispersed communities (Chiu, 2006; Wellman & Gulia, 1998; Daniel et al., 2007; Bos et al., 2007). In turn, the strong emphasis on relational properties has led to explicit links between social capital and VCoPs (Lesser & Prusak, 1999; Daniel et al., 2007; Wenger & Snyder, 2000, p. 230). The concept of social capital, however, is usually used as a metaphor. Although researchers recognize the structural dimension of social capital, few studies actually explore it (Lesser & Prusak, 1999; Daniel et al., 2007). That is, the structure of VCoPs is not yet systematically studied and not well understood.

To summarize, studies shows that research projects do not exist in a vacuum and may be linked through learning loops with CoPs or VCoP, by definition the building blocks of learning and knowledge creation. Applied to the community under investigation, these concepts highlight the double duty of research consortia: directing and coordinating collaborative research while fostering the collective development of research agenda, mutual understanding, and trust. Next, like all large collaborative research networks, research consortia face significant challenges compounded by distance and mediated communication. Frequent solutions to the problems of coordination and communication across boundaries are organizing research into chunks of independent work – a solution that decreases the opportunities for learning, and providing communication and collaboration technology – a solution that does not always fit with the preferences for face-to-face communication of researchers and users alike. In dispersed research networks, therefore, communication is shaped by opposite forces: distance encourages mediated communication and online collaboration while participants' preferences, diverse background, and the nature tasks foster face-to-face interaction. The pull to face-to-face communication may be especially strong in research communities involving users, where there is sectoral diversity.

In view of the above, the current study seeks to answer the following questions:

- What is the structure of the VCoP involved in the consortia network?
- How does the consortia network function? How do managerial practices and work demands shape the functioning of the network?
- In what ways do these managerial practices influence the structure of information exchange relationships within the network?
- To what extent is the use of online and offline media implicated in and influenced by network structure? For example, do core members of the network communicate with each other differently than the less active members in the periphery? How do clique members communicate with each other? Do communication patterns differ among cliques?

Methods and Data

- **Data:** This analysis draws mainly on qualitative (semi-structured interviews) and quantitative (network survey) data collected from Consortia program participants in 2010. The network survey targeted participants in the two fully operational research consortia as well as members of several consortia which are still in their design stage. The survey collected information about who consortia participants knew in the program, and, among the people they knew, whom they worked, exchanged advice, or networked with. In addition, the survey questions covered overall communication and media use patterns as well as some socio-demographic characteristics such as position, professional affiliation, education, and gender. Out of 140 participants, 59 members of the consortia completed and provided usable data. By

contrast, the semi-structured interviews solicited respondents' views on the benefits and values of the program, feedback on the procedures used to set up and run the consortia, as well as the their recommendations for changes. The interviews also covered the reasons for, and the extent of, respondents' involvement in the Consortia program. Our analysis focuses on two main outcome measures:

- **Advice Exchanges:** These are measured as a binary variable indicating (a) whether respondent *i* reported giving advice to respondent *j*, and (b) whether respondent *i* reported receiving advice from respondent *j*. The cells of each matrix take the value of 1 if the specified tie/relation exists and 0, if otherwise.
- **Communication and Media Use:** The study elicited information on the frequency of communication between any pair of respondents, and what percentage of the total communication is conveyed via email, phone and face-to-face media. These variables yielded four relations/matrices capturing respondents' reported frequency of contact and media use (via email, phone and face-to-face contact).
- **Analytical Strategy:** Given our interest in examining the impact of managerial practices on information exchanges and media use, all the relational data collected were processed as binary and/or valued matrices and analyzed by UCINET, a specialized software for analyzing social network structures (Borgatti, Everett, & Freeman, 2002). We used UCINET to compute a number of indicators such as density, cliques, core and periphery partitions as well as centrality scores, all of which allowed us to characterize the structure of the network as well as the role/position of the respondents in it. We then imported these indices into SPSS (SPSS Inc.,

2009) for further processing and analysis. The qualitative data was also entered into and analyzed by NVivo software (QSR International, 2010) for emergent themes. Where appropriate, this analysis is informed by the results of a 2007 study of participants in the General program conducted by the authors (Dimitrova & Koku, 2009).

MANAGEMENT OF THE GENERAL AND CONSORTIA NETWORKS

The Launch of the Consortia Program

The Water Agency is a small organization that operates at arms' length from the government. The few members of its permanent staff manage research funding, organizes events, provide advice, and network on behalf of its members. The mandate of the Water Agency is to bring together expertise from across the country, to serve as a catalyst for socially relevant research, and to foster innovation that will improve the life of Canadians and assist the Canadian economy. Knowledge and technology transfer are always the ultimate goals of its research activities. By design, then, the Water Agency funds a particular type of research: nation-wide and cross-disciplinary research that is oriented to the needs of partners from the public and private sector.

Since its inception in 2001, the Agency has operated a traditional General program. While projects in the program have government and industry partners and aim at knowledge and technology transfer, the General program is driven by academics and funded by the federal government. In 2006, the Water Agency initiated a second research program based on a consortia model where research is user driven, user managed, and user funded. The first research consortium was launched in 2007 and has completed a full cycle

of research projects; a second consortium started in 2008 and has just approved its first projects. Several consortia are still in their consultation stages.

The Consortia program was initiated to achieve two quite different goals. First, the research consortia are expected to better achieve the mandate of the Water Agency to encourage innovation. The program, as the long-term members of the Water Agency see it, is a natural development of the Networks' "desire to have impact" (a practitioner). A user described the approach of the General program to the adoption of research results as "You toss it over the fence and hope somebody is there to catch it" (a practitioner). By contrast, the Consortia program creates different conditions for innovation due to the active involvement of users. However, because of their greater influence on the research outcomes and early involvement in the research process, users in the Consortia programs are expected to be better prepared and more willing to adopt research outcomes.

The second goal of the Consortia program is creating a "legacy entity" for the Water Agency. NCEs such as the Water Agency have a "sunset" clause: they are only funded by the government for a specific period of time. In contrast, the Consortia program solicits funding directly from users, independent from federal government sources. Such funding can ensure the survival and viability of the research activities in the network. While the Water Agency as a distinct organization will inevitably disappear after its final year of government funding, its research activities will continue in the form of research consortia.

Hence, compared to the General program, the Consortia program of the Water Agency is guided by a fundamentally different logic. It has developed distinct procedures to achieve its research goals. The most salient differences lie in the governing structures of the program and in its approach to the main steps of the research funding process: setting the research agenda, selecting research proposals, and enabling knowledge transfer.

Governing Structure and Procedures

In the General program, the research agenda is set by academics. The central governing body in the General program is the General Management Committee (GMC) – a small group of less than a dozen people. The committee members are – with a couple of exceptions – academics. It is the responsibility of the GMC to set the research agenda in the General program, monitor projects, provide annual feedback to the researchers, and evaluate the projects after their completion. All the members are volunteers and their committee work comes on top of multiple commitments and heavy workloads. They meet a couple of times a year to discuss in person how the progress of the projects, rethink research agendas, and consider administrative issues. Usually, such meetings are organized around larger events attended by members such as annual retreats or annual conferences.

The research consortia projects start out differently. Before even setting up a governance structure, consortia require a lengthy period of preparation. The initial steps of the Consortia staff are to identify potential participants and to help them find their shared research priorities. This may vary depending on circumstances. In one of the consortia, a partner organization set things into motion by bringing its research needs to the Water Agency. In another consortium, the Water Agency took the initiative and conducted a series of workshops with users, which outlined the research agenda of the future consortium. Regardless of these variations, in all consortia the research agenda is defined by users.

The governing bodies of consortia, created after consortia become operational, are comprised entirely by practitioners. The members of the Consortia Management Committees (CMC) meet more often, at least 3 – 4 times annually. Although there have been a couple of teleconferences and a web conference, most meetings are in person: they involve complex discussions and negotiations that cannot be done over mediated channels. In addition to CMCs, the consortia have subcommittees targeting specific issues and involving fewer people.

The research consortia handle the research process differently. A noticeable difference is their much more specific and targeted calls for proposals. Further, the staff of the Water Agency coordinates research and monitors projects in the Consortia program in a much more deliberate fashion than the General program. The CMCs do not manage projects – this is considered the responsibility of the researchers. However, consortia funded projects have several mandatory workshops at the consortia level. For instance, during a 2 ½ year-long project undertaken by a consortia, its researchers and users met three times: at a kick-off workshop before the projects start, in mid-stream for a progress report, and for a wrap-up after completion. These workshops included funders and users from the consortium as well as the academics from all the projects currently funded by the consortium. Their goal was to enable active discussion and feedback on each project by diverse parties. By the participants' accounts, this improved both individual projects and the overall coordination of the research effort in the consortia.

They [the Consortia funded projects] had conference calls, they had workshops, they had annual reports that were reviewed by committees... It was a much more accelerated, or, focused attention [compared to] the four-year projects [in the General program] ... Partially, that was because of they [the program staff] had a deliverable that they needed to provide to the government [funder] on a specific topic... So they had a responsibility, and we [the academics] were their workers in a sense (Academic).

The preparation of consortia, the coordination of research and the monitoring of projects result in numerous interactions among consortia participants. They involve complex discussions, negotiations, and integration of diverse perspectives. In essence, they enable intense learning processes, in which both practitioners and researchers learn from each other. The management practices of consortia and the processes they support inevitably affect the network of consortia participants.

THE CONSORTIA NETWORK

Participants and Their Connections

The Consortia participants come from different sectors and institutions but they all are mature established professionals with years of experience in their fields. The program recruits specifically among senior government officials, or the people "who hold the purse strings" (a Practitioner). Practitioners are more numerous than the academics and a lot of them are in decision-making positions (Table 1).

Most of consortia participants know ten or more people in the program – which a substantial number of ties in the type of network examined here (Table 2). The size of respondents' networks is reflective of the number of meetings the program involves as well as of the seniority of its participants. Literature on organizational networks often links formal status and social capital. In other words, researchers find that organizational members with high status know more people, more high status people like themselves, and often people outside their own units (Tichy et al., 1979). When such well-connected professionals join consortia, they bring their prior ties with them, hence the size of the reported networks.

In addition, the results suggest that at least some of the ties in the consortia network have been created through the program. This is evident from the fact that most consortia participants have known others in the network for a short time – the duration of ties roughly coincides with the existence of the program – and the people they

Table 1. Sector and position

Variables	2010 N=59 Freq	%
A. Sector		
Academic / Researcher	29	49.2
Fed Government & CWN	13	22.0
Provincial Government	8	13.6
Local & Regional Government	7	11.9
Industry	1	1.7
Other	1	1.7
Total	59	100
B. Position		
Professional: Coordinator / Specialist / Epidemiologist	6	10.5
Professor / Researcher	28	49.1
Manager / Supervisor / Advisor	6	10.5
Senior decision maker in Academia or Research Institute	7	12.3
Senior decision maker in government, industry, NGO (Head of Department, General Manager, Director, Minister)	9	15.8
Other	1	1.7

Table 2. Tie level summaries of selected relational variables

Variable	N=59 Freq	%
A. Mean Number of Ties in Respondent's Network	**59**	**100%**
Less than 10 Ties	7	11.9
10 to 20 Ties	26	44.1
More than 20 Ties	26	44.1
B. Average Friendship Category (Mode)	**45**	**100%**
Friend / close friend	6	13.3
Acquaintance	39	86.7
Missing	14	

know are acquaintances rather than friends (Table 3). Hence, the participants have both old ties that they bring into the consortia network and new ties they created through involvement in the program.

These characteristics of the consortia participants and their connections have several implications for the learning processes in the network. The diversity of sectors and institutions means that participants bring to the consortia different opportunities, constraints, views and cultures. Further, the consortia network involves, in addition to old ties, more recent ties that may not have been able to build trust. In short, while the Consortia program requires its participants to engage in intense learning processes, the diversity of participants and the short duration of some of the ties among them do not make this easy. Are consortia participants able to cope with this challenge and learn from each other? This issue is the focus of the next sections.

The Ways the Consortia Community Functions

To understand how a learning community such as the consortia network functions, the analysis examines advice exchanges in it. Specifically, we focus on giving advice and seeking advice. At a first glance, it may seem redundant to examine separately giving advice and seeking advice. However, advice exchanges are inherently asym-

metrical and often status related. For instance, an expert may be actively giving advice to junior colleagues without seeking advice from them. Alternatively, an expert may be seeking advice from colleagues in other fields without giving advice to anyone. In a community, members may be engaged to a different degree in giving and seeking advice and, typically, members giving advice may not necessarily be the ones seeking advice. For these reasons, it is best to treat giving and seeking advice as distinct processes.

Mentors vs. Learners (Centrality)

Indeed, giving and seeking advice have distinct patterns. Participants in the consortia network are more active in seeking advice than in giving advice. This may come as a surprise: seniority and reputation are typically associated with advice giving and most of the participants in the consortia networks are experienced professionals in senior positions. Despite their experience and

Table 3. Years Respondent Has Known Tie

	46	100%
Known Less than 5 Yrs	30	65.2
Known 5 to 10 Yrs	9	19.6
Known 10 Yrs or more	7	15.2
Missing	13	

seniority, they are more active in seeking advice than giving advice. This process is not unexpected in an interdisciplinary group where members may need to learn different skill sets and disciplinary norms from each other.

To some extent, this emphasis on seeking advice is also related to the way advice exchanges occur in the network. Advice giving is not always a conscious or deliberate activity. Instead, it is intertwined with other activities. For instance, people named by others as giving advice often do not see themselves as advice givers. Because many advice givers are not aware of their role, fewer people appear active in giving advice (mentors) but many more recognize and acknowledge the advice they received (learners).

Leaders in Mentoring and Learning

An important aspect of advice exchanges is whether – within the overall consortia network – there are particularly active or passive sub-groups. Typically, not all members of a network participate in its exchanges to the same extent: some are closely involved in network exchanges, while others take a more passive role. Core-periphery analysis captures precisely the uneven participation of network members and identifies the members of the network core. By definition, core members are most closely connected with each other and, in addition, are also a magnet for the less connected network members in the periphery. Periphery members, on their part, are more connected to the core than among themselves.

A core-periphery analysis of the advice exchanges in the consortia network reveals strikingly different results between giving and receiving advice. In advice giving, the analysis uncovers a core of 9 network members who actively give advice; the density values follow neatly the requirements for identifying a core (Table 4A). In contrast, a total of 30 network members – more than half the sample – are at the core of the advice receiving network; the density values further sug-

gest that interpreting such a large group as "core" is unwarranted (Table 4B).

Giving and seeking advice in the consortia network therefore unfolds quite differently. Advice giving, which is relatively infrequent activity, is dominated by a small group of "idea people" or "thought leaders" and experts, who consult each other actively and, in addition, are consulted by those in the periphery for advice. This group of advice givers include senior members of the Consortia program staff, practitioners from industry and municipal government, and academics. Notably, the nine core members come from four provinces and seven cities. Core members, therefore, bring distinct regional and institutional perspectives to their discussions. At the same time, their geographic dispersal means that very few of them are co-located and can easily meet in person.

Seeking advice, on the other hand, is more evenly distributed across the network. So many people are involved that it is hard to distinguish a core. The majority of the 30 especially active advice seekers are mostly practitioners who come from just about any corner of the country.

In short, in advice exchanges, participants in the consortia networks are more actively seeking advice than giving advice. However, leaders emerge only in domain of giving advice where fewer people engage in the activity. Further, practitioners outnumber academics among the leaders of the advice exchanges. This is true for giving and especially for seeking advice. Last but not least, the consortia network – through the dispersed nature of its core members – has enabled advice exchanges on a national level.

Who Mentors Whom? Who Seeks Advice from Whom?

The analysis above has identified the leaders of advice exchanges in the consortia networks but it does not reveal who directly mentors whom and who learns from whom. Such patterns are captured through clique analysis: a technique that identifies

Table 4. Density matrix of core – periphery relations

A. Giving Advice in Consortia Network		
	Core	Periphery
Core	0.667	0.129
Periphery	0.129	0.047
B. Seeking Advice		
	Core	Periphery
Core	0.159	0.034
Periphery	0.034	0.029

subgroups of network members who are closely and directly connected among themselves. In a sense, cliques show where "the action" is and who is involved in it. Their number, composition, and membership overlap provide a fine-grained understanding of how the "action" is carried out. For instance, the diversity of the participants in the network would contribute little to accessing new ideas or to understanding of different perspectives if the members of each clique are similar to each other. Because of their connectivity, the members of a clique inevitably have common interests and concerns – this is what makes them a clique in the first place. However, cliques comprised of people with similar socio-demographic characteristics suggest different processes compared to cliques with diverse members. For instance, if a clique includes only academics, this means that academics are not really working with and are not learning from practitioners. The benefits of the network for exchanging different ideas and understanding different perspectives will be diminished.

The analysis finds three cliques of people who give advice to each other. Each clique includes five participants but most of them participate in several cliques and the memberships of the cliques substantially overlap. As a result, a total of seven people are involved in giving advice. These patterns suggest that each of the seven clique members provides advice to several other people and does this in slightly different configurations.

Remarkably, the people giving advice to each other are mostly practitioners: only one clique includes an academic. By comparison, there are more cliques and participants in advice seeking relations. More importantly, of the larger group of 14 clique participants, 5 clique members are academics. These results confirm that seeking advice is the more active process in the consortia network.

Despite this difference, the give and seek advice relationships have some similar clique patterns. For instance, each member participates in more than one clique. In other words, people seek advice from several groups with slightly different configurations. Advice exchanges are targeted, specific and selective activities: people can work or discuss their ideas with many but pertinent advice comes from only a few members in their network. As a result, network members direct their advice or seek advice on specific issues from different subgroups. This suggests that clique members do not isolate themselves in a single group of people with whom they are most familiar or most comfortable. Instead, they have a chance to exchange ideas and see the perspectives of different people. In turn, the membership overlap across the cliques means that the consortia network is not fragmented in several insulated cliques; the cliques are connected to each other. Such links strengthen the integration of the consortia network as a whole.

In both give and seek advice relationships, cliques members in the consortia network are dominated by practitioners. Out of 7 clique members involved in giving advice, 2 are academics; out of 14 members involved in seeking advice, 5 are academics. In other words, more practitioners than academics have cliques of trusted confidants in the consortia network to whom they give advice or from whom they seek advice.

The crucial test for access to new ideas, however, is the composition of each individual clique. Such access is predicated on clique membership that includes both academics and practitioners.

Results show that over half of the cliques (6 out of 10 cliques for give and seek advice relationships) are mixed: they include both practitioners and academics. Mixed cliques are more common for seeking advice: five out of seven cliques in the seek advice relationship include both practitioners and academics. Academics and practitioners are therefore especially active in seeking advice and learning from each other.

By comparison, in giving advice, only one of the three cliques has such a mixed composition and only one of the five members in this clique is academic; giving advice and mentoring therefore takes place mostly among practitioners. One possible reason for this is that the role of academics in the consortia network is fairly specific and once the research questions are specified by practitioners, academics conduct independently their research. This is consistent with a "hands-off approach" to the research process emphasised by practitioners and the Water Agency staff. They argue that—once the research questions are identified - they "cannot babysit the researcher" and "will not tell the researchers how to do the work" (Participants).

Further, clique members as a whole and the members of each individual clique are dispersed in terms of geographic area. Clique participants come from four provinces and nine cities in Canada; two members come from different countries. With one exception, the members of each clique are located in two or three provinces and in different cities. In their advice exchanges, which are rather specialized and selective relationships, clique members in the consortia network have access to diverse views. Such patterns also suggest that distance has not been a problem in building trust: clique members have confidants scattered across the country.

In short, there is no doubt that consortia participants are overcoming the challenges of diversity and distance and actively exchanging advice with each other. There are pockets of ac-

tive advice exchanges in the consortia network, in which members mentor and learn from each other. More practitioners than academics have such cliques of trusted people with whom they exchange advice; a finding that confirms the active engagement of practitioners. In more than half of the cliques, practitioners and academics seek advice and learn from each other and, to a lesser degree, give advice to each other suggesting a true partnership across sectors. Finally, with the exception of one clique, cliques are geographically dispersed. Interview data suggest that the opportunity to get information on national and international level is much appreciated. Of course, this begs the question how these dispersed consortia participants overcome distance to mentor and learn from each other. The analysis now turns to the question how exactly consortia participants communicate with each other.

Communication and Media Use

As the analysis above shows, consortia participants exchange advice in dispersed groups and contact distant colleagues. How they manage to overcome distance is doubly more important given their diverse institutional backgrounds and the sectoral boundaries between academics and practitioners – two factors that are known to weaken social bonds and make the development of trust difficult. While distance among participants pulls their communication choices towards mediated communication, diversity and the need to develop trust folds it back into face-to-face interaction. Finding a solution to this ongoing tension in dispersed communities has important implications for the creation, management, and study of research consortia and VCoPs in general. For instance, findings emphasizing mediated communication and online collaboration mean that the management of such communities should include appropriate technologies; in turn, their research can rely on online traces left by their communication or collaboration such as phone call records, emails, online shared documents or activity logs. In contrast, findings emphasizing face-to-face communication demands different infrastructure and suggests different ways of studying such communities.

To capture the patterns of communication in the consortia network, the analysis examines the average use of three different media: email, phone and face-to-face communication. Because there are significant differences in the number of contacts conducted via each media by participants, the analysis draws on median rather than the mean. The main concerns are with the overall balance of different media and with the ways in which the structure of the network affects communication. In other words, do core members of active mentors and learners communicate with each other differently than the less active members of the periphery? How do clique members stay in touch with each other? Does choice of communication media differ across cliques?

Overall Communication Patterns

As Table 5 shows, in the network as a whole, the participants rely equally on email and face-to-face contacts (each of which account for 25% of their total communication choices); phone use is far behind, accounting for merely 3.7% of total communication. This pattern is surprising in a group that is so widely dispersed. The high reliance on face-to-face communication, however, can be explained by the number of meetings organized for consortia participants by the Water Agency staff. Several large face-to-face workshops with practitioners were conducted in order to identify potential funders and to set research priorities. After the consortia were launched, a series of committees were set up to finalize the scope of their work and to govern their activities. Later, committee work and workshops with researchers continued to provide opportunities for face-to-face contact. With a few exceptions, these meetings and workshops were conducted in person. The

complexity of the issues as well as the need to integrate different viewpoints and to reach a common understanding of the work ahead all required face-to-face discussions. The Water Agency went to great lengths to provide the opportunities for such discussions. Notably, most meetings included only practitioners. It is only after the projects had been approved that researchers and practitioners started discussing issues of mutual interest. Again, the Water Agency took the lead in organizing the meetings.

In turn, the distance among consortia participants inevitably requires the use of media and results in the high use of email. The popularity of email is likely due to its ease of use, non-intrusiveness, low cost, and the opportunity to leave an electronic trail. By comparison, phone is perceived as intrusive and its use is limited.

Core: Periphery Communication Patterns

Within these general patterns, there are marked differences between the communication patterns of active participants (core members) and the less active participants (peripheral members) in the network. As Figure 1 shows, core members communicate with each other above all through face-to-face contacts.

Core members are the most committed and the most active among the program participants. They are expected to attend large meetings or workshops regularly. In addition, many of them have joined various committees; quite a few of the core participants are members of several committees. Their committee work provides additional opportunities to meet other core members in person. Of course, these opportunities for face-to-face meetings have to be there to begin with; it is the Water Agency that organizes and facilitates in person meetings. But the active engagement of the core members in the program translates into attending many meetings and, hence increased opportunities for face-to-face communication

Table 5. Core - Periphery Media Use

A. Give Advice			
	Proportion of Total Communication by Email	Proportion of Total Communication by Phone	Proportion of Total Communication by face-to-face
Core	20	3.47	30
Periphery	25	4.95	25
Total	25	3.7	25
B. Seek Advice			
	Proportion of Total Communication by Email	Proportion of Total Communication by Phone	Proportion of Total Communication by face-to-face
Core	20	4.44	30
Periphery	40	4.54	12.5
Total	25	3.7	25

among them. These patterns hold for both giving advice and seeking advice: regardless of whether core members give to or seek advice from each other, they do this most often in person.

By contrast, periphery members rely on face-to-face communication to a much lesser degree.

For giving advice, periphery members use email and face-to-face to the same degree; for seeking advice, email dominates their communication (Figure 2). Such less active and less committed members may not be attending all face-to-face meetings and workshops organized by the Water Agency; in addition, they do not participate

Figure 1. Face-to-Face contact by Gave Advice Position by Sector

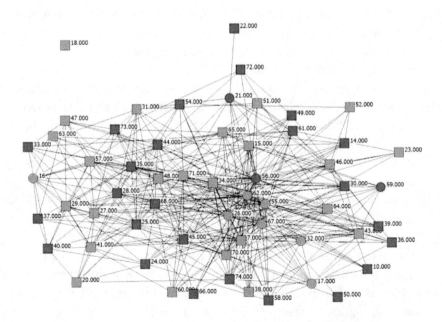

Figure 1: Face-to-Face Contact by Gave Advice Position by Sector

(Position: Core=Circle, Periphery=Square.   Sector: Academics = Blue, Practitioners = Pink)

Figure 2. Email contact by Gave Advice Position by Sector

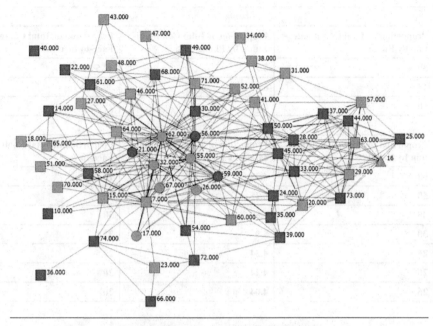

Figure 2: Email Contact by Gave Advice Position by Sector

(Position: Core=Circle, Periphery=Square.   Sector: Academics = Blue, Practitioners = Pink)

in committees and thus have fewer opportunities to meet face-to-face. It is also possible that they do not utilize meetings fully: if their ties are weaker, proximity to other experts during a meeting may not translate into advice exchanges. In such a situation, periphery members compensate for the fewer face-to-face contacts by using email. Notably, the communication patterns in giving advice and seeking advice for periphery members differ: while they give advice to a similar degree by email and in person, seeking advice is decidedly done by email.

Cliques Communication Patterns

The communication patterns within the cliques offer further insights into how advice exchanges in a distributed network take place. Unlike core-periphery communication differences that differentiate highly active from less active participants, clique communication patterns show how the con-

sortia participants contact their closest confidantes and mentors in regular day-to-day exchanges and with specific issues in mind.

Both the balance of different media use and the level of communication across cliques vary significantly. Multiple reasons account for the differences, including the specific concerns which brought the clique members together, including the stage of research projects; the background of participants; the existence of prior ties; or the opportunities to travel. Several patterns emerge in the analysis.

First, in the daily exchanges among clique members, the use of email increases. This is especially true for the cliques whose members seek advice from each other. A stronger use of email by the members of the advice seeking cliques is consistent with the preponderance of email among the periphery members seeking advice. These results hint that the medium of email may be especially compatible with such behaviour; it

Table 6. Median proportion of media use in Cliques

A. Give Advice			
	Proportion of Total Communication by Email	Proportion of Total Communication by Phone	Proportion of Total Communication by Face-to-face
Clique 1	30	5.9	32.5
Clique 2	45	6.86	30
Clique 3	50	6.25	25
B. Seek Advice			
	Proportion of Total Communication by Email	Proportion of Total Communication by Phone	Proportion of Total Communication by Face-to-face
Clique 1	50	4.28	15
Clique 2	50	6.25	25
Clique 3	45	6.86	30
Clique 4	30	5.9	32.5
Clique 5	25	4.34	22.5
Clique 6	20	4.24	20
Clique 7	25	4.04	20

enables the seeker of advice to compose carefully their request while not intruding on the potential giver of advice.

Next, the presence of academics decreases face-to-face contacts in a clique and pulls the balance of media in favour of email. For giving advice, the single clique with an academic member - clique #3 – predominantly uses email compared to face-to-face contact: over half of their overall communication is via email compared to a quarter of face-to-face contact (Table 6). For seeking advice, the cliques with academics (cliques #2, #5, #6, and especially #1 and #7) also have fewer face-to-face contacts – from 15% to 25% (Table 6). By comparison, the cliques including only practitioners (clique # 3 and #4) have more face-to-face contacts and, in the case of clique #4, email use falls below face-to-face contacts. Partly, this pattern is a result of the fewer opportunities of the academics to meet other consortia members in person: academics are not part of the governance structure of the consortia and can meet with other consortia participants mostly at project workshops. Partly, this pattern is a result of choosing email

for its expediency and for the autonomy it affords. Historically, academics have been the early users of email and the medium is still widely used in academic communities.

In some cases, email use is linked to the relatively straightforward nature of the communication content. When clique members know each other well, they have less negotiation to do - they have already established shared understanding of how work should be done. Clique #1, for instance, includes several academics, who are long term members of the Water Agency. They have known each other for a long time and have worked together before. They meet rarely but contact each other extensively by email. In contrast, clique #7 includes the same number of academics but its members have only recently joined the Water Agency and have known each other for a short time. Their contacts are fewer. Nonetheless, email use is more common for these academics than face-to-face contacts.

Further, cliques differ in how actively their members communicate with each other. The overall number of contact in some cliques (cliques

#1 through #4) is significantly higher compared to the rest of the cliques (cliques #5 through #7). How exactly cliques with more extensive communication achieve this higher communication depends to a great extent on their composition. Where practitioners dominate more active cliques, members start with a strong use of face-to-face meetings and add email as needed (cliques #4 and #5). Where academics dominate the clique, as in clique #1, members have few opportunities to meet in person and they compensate by extensive use of email. In less active cliques, members use face-to-face and email contacts to a similar extent; they go to fewer meetings to begin with and add fewer email contacts to them. The differences in the communication, associated with the presence of academics and practitioners in such cliques, are less pronounced.

To summarize, the results suggests that despite the distributed nature of the consortia network, communication takes place as much online and as it does offline. The high reliance on face-to-face meetings is required by the complex discussions taking place in the network; they are made possible by the Water Agency whose staff takes the role of an organizer and facilitator. The management of the network thus has a direct impact on the communication practices of the participants and the context in which its collaboration takes place.

What makes this community virtual is the use of email – the least intrusive medium. This analysis suggests that email might be particularly suitable for seeking advice. In the consortia network, seeking advice is a more extensive exchange than giving advice; this may further promote the use of email among its members.

The balance of face-to-face meetings and email contacts varies across structural groupings and types of participants. Compared to academics, all practitioners have more opportunities to meet in person. The more active members of the consortia network have more opportunities to meet in person and more fully utilize them. Academics, who attend fewer meetings, compensate for

this by higher email use, especially if they know each other well. In cliques, a variety of factors shape media use and lead to a variation of the communication patterns across cliques. In addition to clique composition and the nature of ties, factors probably include unique circumstances on the level of the clique. It is safe to assume that the members of each clique develop their own communication practices to meet their needs and to make use of the opportunities available to them.

By all means, the analysis suggests that the online traces of the collaborative and advice exchanges can capture only part of the activities of virtual communities. Even in highly dispersed communities such as the consortia network under investigation here, some crucial exchanges take place in person and these do not leave online tells.

DISCUSSION AND CONCLUSION

The analysis provides interesting insights into the learning processes in research networks and the communication patterns in virtual communities.

The consortia network examined in this study acts as a large, 140-member strong, distributed CoP. The active advice exchanges among the participants in the network suggest the existence of consultation and mentoring processes and, ultimately, the existence of learning processes. Qualitative data, representing the voice of the participants themselves, also clearly demonstrate the learning benefits of the network. Many participants recall the initial steps of the consortia as a learning process for everyone involved. At the workshops, practitioners learn to appreciate the viewpoints of different stakeholders and to collectively develop a shared understanding of research issues and their importance. They learn, as well, how a research consortium works and what their role in it is. On their part, the Agency staff learns to play a facilitating and organizing role. The project workshops with researchers were similarly intense learning experiences. One funder admitted:

Actually, to be honest, I didn't know a lot what I was getting into or what it was for... (Practitioner).

It was only at a later kick-off workshop that the novelty of the consortia approach crystallized:

We had more discussion between us on what the regulators need and what the researches were doing. I think the researchers got a lot out of that meeting hearing different viewpoints from the regulators. To be honest I learned more at that meeting than I had in all the earlier meetings: everything sort of found its place... that meeting ... really cemented the things in my head about what we were doing (Practitioner).

An interesting twist in the learning processes in the consortia network is the role of practitioners. Practitioners are just as active, if not more active, than academics in the advice exchanges. They certainly outnumber academics in the leading positions in the network and this holds true for both mentoring and learning processes. There is no doubt that, in many cliques, practitioners and academics consult and mentor each other. Again, the patterns of practitioners immersed in solving problems and actively creating new knowledge together with academics is consistent with the concept of CoPs. However, it is not an image common for the studies of collaborative research networks.

The advice exchanges between practitioners and academics are reminiscent of the idea of learning loops which Wenger has discussed in his work (Wenger, 2000). In his initial interpretation, CoPs of professionals with similar expertise create new ideas and build knowledge capacity, which members of the CoPs later bring to their functionally diverse projects teams. In the consortia network, knowledge is created on the level of the consortia by members who differ in their disciplinary and institutional background. Their shared understanding and agreed upon goals are later brought by academics to their disciplinary and institutionally diverse project teams.

Learning processes in the consortia network are captured through advice exchanges and specifically, through the relationships of giving and seeking advice. Somewhat unexpectedly, the process of seeking advice is much more active than giving advice in the community. Advice exchanges are inherently asymmetrical and status based. The consortia network involves mature professionals in senior positions who would be expected to take the role of advice givers. However, the seeking advice in the network is a much more intense activity. Such advice seeking behaviour is an indirect indication of the learning processes in the consortia network: giving advice may bring fame and professional reputation but it does not usually provide opportunities for learning new things. Confronted by different perspectives, local viewpoints from across the country, and new ideas, consortia participants are more apt to engage in learning and advice seeking than in advice giving.

Further, the analysis draws the attention to the importance of the organization and facilitation activities in distributed CoPs as well as to the governance of large distributed collaborative networks. The Water Agency has been instrumental in launching the consortia and in providing the conditions for their management. The content of their facilitation certainly involves identifying domains and practitioners and providing the infrastructure for their work as envisioned by CoP theorists. While they do not make any of the decisions on the scope of work or project approval, without their support the processes in the consortia network will be very different. The staff organizes events and meetings, facilitates the discussion in them, writes up calls for proposals on behalf of the consortia participants, networks with external experts who evaluate proposals and projects, and prepares documents summarizing decisions or projects results. They extensively consult individual members and network on their behalf. For instance, the face-to-face interactions, which are so important for the learning processes in the consortia community, would be much fewer without the efforts of the program staff. This level of facilitation activity also suggests that designed VCoPs with intense learning processes might need more extensive organizational support than VCoPs based on information exchanges.

The communication patterns emerging in the analysis shed further light into how this distributed community functions. The strongest finding is the importance of face-to-face interactions. The dispersal of clique members is evidence for active advice exchange across distance. Yet half of the exchanges among distant members take place face-to-face. The importance of in-person interaction can be linked to several factors. The diverse background of the participants and the short duration of some of their ties mean that they need to create trust and build relationships. Further, the complex issues they discuss require negotiation and integration of diverse viewpoints. Such complex communication and trust building are best done in person. Despite distance, participants travel to meet in person. Next, academics and practitioners in the consortia network unanimously link learning to face-to-face meetings – a positive feedback consistent with the preferences for in-person interaction found in previous research (Bos et al., 2008; Bielak et al., 2009). For instance, project workshops are conducted face-to-face, with discussions at the level of the consortia and in smaller break-off groups. Participants describe them as learning processes and an opportunity to build trust, especially in the relationships between practitioners and academics:

I found that going to those meetings actually helped me better understand what we needed to tell the researchers that needed to be done. And to hear the problems that they were aware of in the [this research area] helped us better understand the type of questions that we needed to ask (Practitioner).

The difficulties of building trust and shared understanding from a distance have often been discussed with respect to the demands of research and project teams in organizations (Olsons & Olson, 2003; Jarvenpaa & Leidner, 1999; Bos et al., 2001). Trust has been acknowledged as problematic in VCoPs and some researchers have recommended initial face-to-face meetings for building trust (Daniel et al., 2003; Zheng et al., 2002). This issue is not extensively explored because learning processes in CoPs are seen as local while learning processes in VCoPs are assumed to take place via mediated communication. The question of trust then becomes one of adequate technological support. By comparison, this analysis shows that the solution to trust may involve organizational practices rather than technology. In addition, it also demonstrates that management choices in designed communities powerfully affect communication: the staff of the Water Agency designed the planning and management of the consortia research as face-to-face meetings and workshops and shaped the communication of its participants. This is evident in the more extensive face-to-face communication of practitioners. While both academics and practitioners need to build trust and shared understanding and prefer in-person communication, it is the practitioners, who participate in the planning and management of research, that have more face-to-face communication.

The analysis implies that the nature of the participants, the task at hand, and the management of dispersed communities all affect the extent of online tells in a community. In the case of the community under study, the need for complex discussions and the diversity of the participants demand face-to-face contacts among community members; the management practices are designed to respond to that need. These observations do not imply that online contacts are not important – the use of email in advice seeking confirms their significance; rather, it cautions against ignoring offline contacts. In this sense, the analysis becomes a test case for the broader issue of the online tells of collaboration and communication in dispersed communities. It shows that even highly distributed CoPs may have a dual life: they exist both online and offline, in both face-to-face meetings and mediated exchanges of their participants, and their traces, or tells, are not only limited to online exchanges. Email and phone records, online documents and logs, or other traces of communication and collaboration have to be complemented by knowledge of the offline activities of the members of the community. As Koku and Wellman have long ago argued, communication patterns can only be understood by jointly examining media use and in person practices (Koku et al., 2001; Wellman & Gulia, 1998).

REFERENCES

Bielak, A. T., Holmes, J., Savgard, J., & Schaefer, K. (2009). *A comparison of European and North American approaches to the management and communication of environmental research* (Tech. Rep. No. 5958). Stockholm, Sweden: Swedish Environmental Protection Agency.

Borgatti, S. P., Everett, M. G., & Freeman, L. C. (2002). *UCINET for Windows: Software for Social Network Analysis*. Cambridge, MA: Analytic Technologies.

Bos, N., Gergle, D., Olson, J., & Olson, G. (2001). Being there versus seeing there: Trust via video. In *Proceedings of the CHI Conference*. Retrieved September 12, 2007, from http://www.crew.umich.edu/publications.html

Bos, N., Zimmerman, A., Olson, J., Yew, J., Yerkie, J., Dahl, E., & Olson, G. (2008). From shared databases to Communities of Practice: A taxonomy of collaboratories. *Journal of Computer-Mediated Communication, 12*(2), 318–338.

Bresnen, M., Edelmanb, L., Newellb, S., Scarbrough, H., & Swana, J. (2003). Social practices and the management of knowledge in project environments. *International Journal of Project Management, 21*(3), 157–166. doi:10.1016/S0263-7863(02)00090-X

Brown, J. S., & Duguid, P. (1991). Organizational learning and Communities-of-Practice: toward a unified view of working, learning, and innovation. *Organization Science, 2*(1), 40–57. doi:10.1287/orsc.2.1.40

Caruso, D., & Rhoten, D. (2001). *Lead, follow, get out of the way: Sidestepping the barriers to effective practice of interdisciplinarity*. Retrieved from http://www.hybridvigor.net/publications.pl?s=interdis&d=2001.04.30# Crane, D. (1972). *Invisible colleges: diffusion of knowledge in scientific communities*. Chicago, IL: University of Chicago Press.

Chiu, C., Hsu, M., & Wang, E. (2006). Understanding knowledge sharing in virtual communities: An integration of social capital and social cognitive theories. *Decision Support Systems, 42*(3), 1872–1888. doi:10.1016/j.dss.2006.04.001

Cross, R., Borgatti, S. P., & Parker, A. (2002). *Making invisible work visible: Using social network analysis to support strategic collaboration*. Retrieved September 5, 2008, from https://webapp.comm.virginia.edu/SnaPortal/portals%5C0%5Cmaking_invisible_work_visible.pdf

Cummings, J., & Kiesler, S. (2005). Collaborative research across disciplinary and organizational boundaries. *Social Studies of Science, 35*(5), 703–722. doi:10.1177/0306312705055535

Daniel, B., Schwier, R. A., & McCalla, G. (2003). Social capital in virtual learning communities and Distributed Communities of Practice. *Canadian Journal of Learning and Technology, 29*(3), 113–139.

Dimitrova, D., & Koku, E. (2009). Research communities in context: Trust, independence and technology in professional communities. In Akoumianakis, D. (Ed.), *Virtual community practices and social interactive media: Technology lifecycle and workflow analysis* (pp. 352–377). Hershey, PA: IGI Global. doi:10.4018/978-1-60566-340-1.ch018

Haythornthwaite, C., et al. (2003). *Challenges in the practice and study of distributed, interdisciplinary collaboration* (Tech. Rep. No. UIUCLIS--2004/1+DKRC). Retrieved from http://www.lis.uiuc.edu/~haythorn/hay_challenges.html

Hey, T., & Trefethen, A. (2008). E-science, cyberinfrastructure, and scholarly communication. In Olson, G., Zimmerman, A., & Bos, N. (Eds.), *Scientific Collaboration on the Internet* (pp. 15–33). Cambridge, MA: MIT Press.

International, Q. S. R. (2010). *NVivo qualitative data analysis software*. Doncaster, VIC, Australia: Author.

Jarvenpaa, S., & Leidner, D. (1999). Communication and trust in global virtual teams. *Organization Science, 10*(6), 791–815. doi:10.1287/orsc.10.6.791

Koku, E., Nazer, N., & Wellman, B. (2001). Netting scholars: online and offline. *The American Behavioral Scientist, 44*(10), 1752–1774. doi:10.1177/00027640121958023

Lesser, E., & Prusak, L. (1999). Communities of Practice, social capital and organizational knowledge. *Information Systems Research, 1*(1), 3–9.

Moore, M. N. (1989). Tenure and the university reward structure. *Nursing Research, 38*(2), 111–116. doi:10.1097/00006199-198903000-00015

Olson, G., & Olson, J. (2003). Mitigating the effects of distance on collaborative intellectual work. *Economics of Innovation and New Technology, 12*(1), 27–42. doi:10.1080/10438590303117

Olson, J., Hofer, E., Bos, N., Zimmerman, A., Olson, G. D., Cooney, G., & Faniel, I. (2008). A theory of remote scientific collaboration. In Olson, G., Zimmerman, A., & Bos, N. (Eds.), *Scientific Collaboration on the Internet* (pp. 73–99). Cambridge, MA: MIT Press.

Pellmar, T., & Eisenberg, L. (2000). *Bridging disciplines in the brain, behavioral, and clinical sciences*. Washington, DC: National Academy Press.

Restler, S., & Woolis, D. (2007). Actors and Factors: Virtual Communities for Social Innovation. *Electronic Journal of Knowledge Management, 5*(1), 89–96.

Rhoten, D. (2003). *A multi-method analysis of the social and technical conditions for interdisciplinary collaboration*. Retrieved from http://hybridvigor.net/interdis/pubs/hv_pub_interdis-2003.09.29.pdf

Shrum, W., Chompalov, I., & Genuth, J. (2001). Trust, conflict and performance in scientific collaborations. *Social Studies of Science, 31*(5), 681–730. doi:10.1177/030631201031005002

Snyder, W., Wenger, E., & Briggs, X. (2004). Communities of practice in government: Leveraging knowledge for performance. *Public Management, 32*(4), 17–21.

SPSS Inc. (2009). *PASW Statistics - Release Version 18*. Chicago, IL: Author.

Tichy, N., Tushman, M., & Fombrun, C. (1979). Social network analysis for organizations. *Academy of Management Review, 4*(4), 507–519. doi:10.2307/257851

Walsh, J., & Bayama, T. (1996). Computer networks and scientific work. *Social Studies of Science, 26*(3), 385–405. doi:10.1177/030631296026003006

Wellman, B., & Gulia, M. (1998). Net surfers don't ride alone: Virtual communities as communities. In Smith, M. A., & Kollock, P. (Eds.), *Communities in Cyberspace* (pp. 163–190). Berkley, CA: University of California Press.

Wenger, E. (2004). Knowledge management as a doughnut: Shaping your knowledge strategy through Communities of Practice. *Ivey Business Journal Online, 3*(1), 1–8.

Wenger, E. (2010). Communities of Practices and Social Learning Systems: the Career of a Concept. In Blackmore, C. (Ed.), *Social learning systems and Communities of Practice* (pp. 179–198). London, UK: Springer. doi:10.1007/978-1-84996-133-2_11

Wenger, E. C. (2000). Communities of Practice and Social Learning Systems. *Organization, 7*(2), 225–246. doi:10.1177/135050840072002

Wenger, E. C., & Snyder, W. M. (2000). Communities of Practice: The organizational frontier. *Harvard Business Review, 78*(1), 139–145.

Zheng, J., Veinott, E., Bos, N., Olson, J., & Olson, G. (2002). Trust without touch: Jumpstarting long-distance trust with initial social activities. In *Proceedings of the CHI Conference.* Retrieved from http://www.crew.umich.edu/publications.html

ENDNOTE

[1]   For a detailed analysis of the General program, see Dimitrova and Koku (2009).

This work was previously published in the International Journal of Virtual Communities and Social Networking, Volume 2, Issue 4, edited by Subhasish Dasgupta, pp. 1-22, copyright 2010 by IGI Publishing (an imprint of IGI Global).

Chapter 20
Some Research Challenges for Studies of Virtual Communities Using On–Line Tells

Chris Kimble
Euromed Management, Université Montpellier II, France

ABSTRACT

This article reports on a study of learning and the coordination of activities in a geographically distributed community (a research consortium) using survey / Social Network Analysis methods combined with interviews. This article comments on and expands some of the important issues that were raised. After outlining the wider context, it highlights two broad themes related to research in the area of Virtual Communities: the nature of the communities themselves and the way in which they are studied. Following this, four areas for future research are outlined: the continuing role of face-to-face communication in Virtual Communities; the significance of the dual nature of such groups; the importance (or otherwise) of the structure of such communities; and the role played by exogenous factors. The article concludes with some comments on where this field relates to the debate among social theorists about the role of agency and structure in human activities.

1 INTRODUCTION

The article reports on a study of learning and the coordination of activities within a geographically distributed community (the research consortium) that is involved in conducting and managing collaborative research. The consortium was created by the Canadian federal government to encourage multidisciplinary research and innovation in the area of water related issues such as watershed and ecosystems research, water infrastructure, threats to water supplies and water treatment. It consists of around 140 academics and practitioners dispersed across the country. The academics are drawn from a wide range of disciplines and cover many different research areas; the practitioners include employees from various levels of government, industrial partners, conservation bodies and members of Non-Governmental Organizations. The membership of the community changes over

DOI: 10.4018/978-1-4666-1553-3.ch020

time and with projects and, although a number of the groups engage in face-to-face meetings of various sorts, the group as a whole is described as a Virtual Community of Practice.

Although the research consortium has a number of unique features, it is also an example of the wider phenomenon of virtual (i.e. geographically distributed) groups that work together and are described variously as Virtual Teams, Task or Project Groups; Virtual or Electronic Communities of Practice and Knowledge Networks or Networks of Practice (Dubé, Bourhis, & Jacob, 2005; Jarvenpaa & Leidner, 1999; Vaast, 2004; Wasko & Faraj, 2000). The principal objective of this article is to take some of the themes highlighted by Dimitrova and Koku and place them in a wider research context. We will begin by examining two fundamental questions that any research into this area must face.

2 TWO BROAD RESEARCH QUESTIONS RELATING TO VIRTUAL COMMUNITIES

Before looking at the issues raised by Dimitrova and Koku's article, it is perhaps worthwhile to step back and look at some of the more general problems faced by research into Virtual Communities. Exactly what do we mean by Virtual Communities and what are the most appropriate ways to study them? Although the questions might seem banal, pausing for a moment to reflect on these issues will help to highlight some of the key difficulties that are faced in attempting to examine the themes for future research that are contained in the following section.

2.1 What is the Nature of Such Groups?

People working together as geographically distributed groups is not a new phenomenon as such, however the explosive growth of digital technologies, and the communications revolution that followed (Cairncross, 1997; McLuhan & Powers, 1989), opened the door to the myriad of "new organisational forms" that can be found in the current literature. Although the term "Virtual Community" only came into popular use about a decade ago following the publication of Howard Rheingold's book (Rheingold, 1993), this new concept has been quickly accepted and has become part of everyday life (Sayago & Blat, 2010). The notion of "Virtual" working has become commonplace.

Although the notion of Virtual Communities may be commonplace, this does not mean that it is fully understood. While co-located, face-to-face groups have been the topic of study and conjecture for many years, their similarities to, and differences from, "Virtual" groups is far from clear. For example, although many of the early studies of Virtual Communities focused on the issue of identity (Bruckman, 1993; Turkle, 1995), understanding how the sense of identity that characterizes the "esprit de corps" of co-located groups (who share the same experiences in the physical world) translates to the virtual world (where the nature of the shared experience is much less tenuous) remains vague.

2.2 How Do We Study Them?

If the way these groups function is not well understood, how then should we study them to improve our knowledge? Geographically distributed groups that rely on technologically mediated forms of communication and computer based communication in particular, offer opportunities to collect data that do not exist in "natural" groups. Because interaction takes place via some form of technology, the traces of that interaction are easily accessible and available in a form that facilitates processing and analysis. However, although messages and patterns of interaction between individuals can be captured in volume and analysed in detail, as with the groups themselves, the limitations of this approach is not always well understood. The lure of quantity and the illusion of accuracy to three decimal places produced by Social Network Analysis (SNA) can sometimes cloud the true value of such data.

The data contained in on-line tells is a by-product of on-line communication, the residue that remains after an activity has taken place, they are not the activity itself and do not tell the whole story. Measuring the frequency of communicative acts may show something is happening but does not tell us much about the nature of that activity and the meaning it holds for the participants. Uncovering these meanings can be problematical both from the point of view of privacy and from the point of view of convenience. Even if members of a group are willing and able to share this information with others, few will be prepared to spend the time it takes to be interviewed or to fill in a questionnaire and although more traditional social science methods, such as ethnographic studies, can provide some of the missing detail, they are costly and time consuming (Clark, Ting, Kimble, Wright, & Kudenko, 2006).

3 FOUR POTENTIAL RESEARCH THEMES FOR FUTURE WORK ON VIRTUAL COMMUNITIES

Having looked at the broader issues, we now turn to the specific themes for future research that appear in this article.

3.1 The Continuing Importance of Face to Face Meetings

As we have noted, the whole notion of Virtual Communities is relatively new, nevertheless, a recurring theme in the literature on virtual groups is the continuing importance of face-to-face meetings (Akkerman, Petter, & de Laat, 2008; Coakes, Coakes, & Rosenberg, 2008; Jarvenpaa & Leidner, 1999; Kimble & Hildreth, 2005; Kimble, Li, &

Barlow, 2000). Why are face-to-face meetings important? One way to find an answer is to look at what happens inside such virtual groups and to contrast the need for coordination between members (the factual exchange of information) with what is required for learning (the sharing of ideas and co-construction of common knowledge).

Carlile (2002) argues that different forms of coordination are found in collaborative working. When a situation is familiar and routine, a simple sign, perhaps only a single word, is all that is needed for a group to coordinate its activities. This type of syntactic coordination can be supported by even the simplest form of electronic communication. As the complexity of the situation increases, the members of the group are faced with the need to establish a common understanding of what is happening. There is a need for greater informational richness in communication, which may require the use of more sophisticated forms of communication. Finally, in situations that involve change, negotiation and compromise, coordination between actors becomes difficult to achieve, as change can prove costly.

In order to learn, most people need time to reflect and a safe environment in which to experiment. By working together over a period of time the members of a group are able develop a sense of trust and shared identity that increases their ability to share and learn from each other. Once a group develops a sense of trust and mutual respect, then people feel able to share their thinking, the reasons behind their conclusions, and even the doubts that they have about their conclusions. Together they can build on each other's ideas, create new ideas, and develop new insights (Kimble, 2011). Consequently, most "Virtual" communities tend to operate in multiple modes: sometimes face to face, sometimes via electronic communication, sometimes interacting with each other directly and at other times working as individuals. As Dimitrova and Koku observe, the most intense learning experiences tend to be restricted to face-to-face meetings and workshops.

3.2 The Importance of Structure in Virtual Communities of Practice

Looking at learning leads us to consider the role played by Communities of Practice in this article. The term Communities of Practice was first coined in the *book Situated Learning: Legitimate Peripheral Participation* (Lave & Wenger, 1991). The book was not really about Communities of Practice as such but about how unstructured and informal learning took place around shared activities in small co-located groups. The relationships in the groups they studied were essentially Master - Apprentice relationships. Lave and Wenger used the term Legitimate Peripheral Participation (LPP) to describe the dynamic of the movement from apprentice to master; "Community of Practice" was used simply as a convenient shorthand to describe the groups in which LPP took place.

Since then, as Dimitrova and Koku note, the term Community of Practice has now been "*developed and refined to encompass the broad reality to which it is now being applied*". Brown and Duguid (1991) took Communities of Practice from their original small, informal setting and placed them within the context of large commercial organizations. Wenger's later works (1998, 2002) focused increasingly on the structure of the group rather than on how the learning within it took place. New terms such as Constellations of Practice (Wenger, 1998), Networks of Practice (Brown & Duguid, 2000) and Electronic Communities of Practice (Wasko & Faraj, 2000) began to appear. Communities of Practice themselves became CoPs as others struggled to classify the structure of the different types of groups they found. Progressively, new terms such as Virtual Communities of Practice (Dubé et al., 2005), Electronic Networks of Practice (Wasko & Faraj, 2005) and Collectivities of Practice (Lindkvist, 2005) were added to the CoP lexicon.

While there is undoubtedly value in looking at structures, patterns of communications and functional relationships, the question might be asked, "Is there too much focus on the structure of the group rather than on what is happening within it"? For example, what is the qualitative difference between the interactions of the core members and those of the distributed periphery in Dimitrova and Koku's study? What is the nature of the practice of the community at these different levels?

3.3 The Apparent Dual Nature of "Virtual" Groups

While it is important not to lose sight of the raison d'être for the group, one of the advantages of focusing on its structure as revealed in on-line tells is that it helps to highlight what might otherwise be hidden patterns of interaction within the group, such as the "dual" nature of Virtual Communities of Practice in Dimitrova and Koku's study. This is not the first time that this type of distinction has been noted, but thanks to the use of SNA based techniques, the scale and scope of the duality can now be put into sharper relief. However, while it has shown that a "Virtual" Community of Practice exists in more than one dimension, it does not address the issue of why this duality exists.

Much of the early work on Virtual Communities focused on the issue of individual identity in virtual environments and the problems this posed for establishing trust relationships (Donath, 1999). From the point of view of the group, identity helps to establish shared meanings through providing a common perspective, without which it becomes difficult to share knowledge effectively as, unless shared meanings can be established, even "common sense" words and terms become open to different interpretations (Duguid, 2005). From theory, we can argue that the dual nature of the groups in this study result from what they are trying to achieve, building the trust and mutual understanding needed to learn as part of a community or simply coordinating a series of events across geographically distributed groups. Validating this theory through empirical observations however poses different problems.

We noted above that different methodological approaches produce different types of data and that focusing on the residue of an activity rather than the activity itself will not tell the whole story. While quantitative techniques such as SNA can provide data about the scale and scope of a phenomenon, we need to turn to qualitative techniques to uncover more detail about what is happening. Ribeiro et al.(2010) used Grounded Theory to show that what appeared on the surface to be a stable Community of Practice actually consisted of several "Quantum" Communities of Practice that repeatedly came into, and disappeared from, view. Such communities could remain quiescent for months at a time and would be difficult to observe and interpret using only techniques such as SNA.

3.4 The Importance of Local (Non-Structural) Factors

The discussion above paints a picture of Virtual Communities in general, and Virtual Communities of Practice in particular, as complex entities where simple epithets such as "Virtual" or "Community" do not do justice to the range of phenomena to which they are applied. While some have sought to address this by attempting to develop ever more refined distinctions between different types of community, this commentary has argued that we should not lose sight of what happens within the community in the struggle to identify its structural characteristics. This final section seeks to argue that even focusing on what happens within the community may not be sufficient to describe its behaviour adequately.

A persistent criticism of the literature on Communities of Practice is that it ignores or underplays the role of exogenous factors such as externally imposed power relationships and presents a neutral and idealised view of the way such groups function. The distinction made between the funders and the funded in Dimitrova and Koku's study is a clear example of this. Geographically distributed communities such as the research consortium in the study do not exist in a vacuum and the explanation for what happens does not lie solely within the group.

The majority of the literature in this area tends towards what Tsoukas (1996) describes as a taxonomic approach: seeking to discover global, or at least generic, solutions. He claims however that this approach is fundamentally flawed (Tsoukas & Chia, 2002); quoting Boden (1994) he argues that the structures that shape how knowledge is shared are always and inevitably influenced by *"immediate circumstances and local agendas"* (Boden, 1994, p. 18). He argues that where categories and taxonomies exist, *"The stability of their meanings is precariously maintained"* (Tsoukas & Chia, 2002, p. 573).

Several studies exist that illustrate this. Teigland and Wasko (2003) note that, for political and professional reasons, groups of professionals will readily share knowledge related to their profession within their own network but will not share this knowledge with outsiders. Swan, Scarbrough and Robertson (2002) and Hislop (2003) observe that Communities of Practice set up to share knowledge can become "silos" where the knowledge they contain never crosses the boundaries of the group. Similarly, Kimble et al (2010) combine two independent studies to show the same dynamic of political interplay between, on one hand, what is acceptable within the group and, on the other, the interests of powerful institutions, groups or individuals outside.

4 CONCLUSION

The goal of this article was to take some of the themes highlighted by Dimitrova and Koku in their article and place them in a wider research context, that of Virtual Communities in general. There is however, another level at which this could be considered. The editorial for this special issue asks the question:

Is it communities as pre-existent social structures that define the activities members engage in, or is it the activities themselves that generate a community by forming the "glue" that holds together a configuration of people, artefacts and social relations?

In many ways the arguments that were put forward above could be recast as another instance of the long running structure-agency debate among social theorists such as Giddens and Archer (Archer, 2000; Giddens, 1979): to what extent can human behaviour be explained by external factors such as social or organizational structures and to what extent are humans "free agents" capable of independent thought and autonomous action?

The concepts of structure and agency are theoretically useful but methodologically clumsy. Few would argue that, whatever the structures that surround them, individuals do not retain a certain level of agency, i.e. of the ability to choose a different path to that dictated by the structures they face. Similarly, few would argue that an individual is able to transcend the social and emotional conditioning imposed on them by their surroundings and make truly autonomous decisions. In practice, it is the interplay between agency and structure that is of interest rather than the crude concepts themselves, and it is here that the methodological challenge lies.

By using survey / SNA methods combined with interviews, Dimitrova and Koku placed the emphasis on the structural dimension rather than on the thoughts and motivations of the actors involved. This approach has value in that it has highlighted the size and scope of dual nature of such communities. Although this has been noted in previous qualitative studies, the use of survey and SNA methods provides more tangible evidence of its scale and scope. However as Clark et al (2006) have demonstrated, quantitative and qualitative data-gathering methods can be used together to enhance our understanding of what is happening in virtual settings; the challenge for future re-

search in this area is find ways to combine these two approaches and throw light on the interplay between the thoughts and motivations of the actors in virtual environments and the constraints and opportunities of the structures that surround them.

REFERENCES

Akkerman, S., Petter, C., & de Laat, M. (2008). Organising communities-of-practice: facilitating emergence. *Journal of Workplace Learning, 20*(6), 383–399. doi:10.1108/13665620810892067

Archer, M. S. (2000). *Being Human: The Problem of Agency*. Cambridge, UK: Cambridge University Press. doi:10.1017/CBO9780511488733

Boden, D. (1994). *The Business of Talk*. Boston, MA: Polity.

Brown, J. S., & Duguid, P. (1991). Organizational Learning and Communities of Practice: Toward a Unified View of Working, Learning, and Innovation. *Organization Science, 2*(1), 40–57. doi:10.1287/orsc.2.1.40

Brown, J. S., & Duguid, P. (2000). *The Social Life of Information*. Boston, MA: Harvard Business School Press.

Bruckman, A. S. (1993, August). *Gender Swapping on the Internet*. Paper presented at the International Networking Conference (INET'93), San Francisco, CA.

Cairncross, F. (1997). *The Death of Distance: How the Communications Revolution Will Change Our Lives*. Boston, MA: Harvard Business School Press.

Carlile, P. R. (2002). A Pragmatic View of Knowledge and Boundaries: Boundary Objects in New Product Development. *Organization Science, 13*(4), 442–455. doi:10.1287/orsc.13.4.442.2953

Clark, L., Ting, I.-H., Kimble, C., Wright, P., & Kudenko, D. (2006). Combining Ethnographic and Clickstream Data to Identify User Web Browsing Strategies. *Information Research, 11*(2).

Coakes, E. W., Coakes, J. M., & Rosenberg, D. (2008). Co-operative work practices and knowledge sharing issues: A comparison of viewpoints. *International Journal of Information Management, 28*(1), 12–25. doi:10.1016/j.ijinfomgt.2007.10.004

Donath, J. S. (1999). Identity and Deception in the Virtual Community. In Smith, M., & Kollock, P. (Eds.), *Communities in Cyberspace* (pp. 27–58). London, UK: Routledge.

Dubé, L., Bourhis, A., & Jacob, R. (2005). The impact of structuring characteristics on the launching of virtual communities of practice. *Journal of Organizational Change Management, 18*(2), 145–166. doi:10.1108/09534810510589570

Duguid, P. (2005). The Art of Knowing: Social and Tacit Dimensions of Knowledge and the Limits of the Community of Practice. *The Information Society: An International Journal, 21*(2), 109–118.

Giddens, A. (1979). *Central Problems in Social Theory: Action, Structure Contradictions in Social Analysis*. Berkley, CA: University of California Press.

Hislop, D. (2003). The Complex Relations between Communities of Practice and the Implementation of Technological Innovations. *International Journal of Innovation Management, 7*(2), 163–188. doi:10.1142/S1363919603000775

Jarvenpaa, S. L., & Leidner, D. E. (1999). Communication and Trust in Global Virtual Teams. *Organization Science, 10*(6), 791–815. doi:10.1287/orsc.10.6.791

Kimble, C. (2011). Building effective virtual teams: How to overcome the problems of trust and identity in virtual teams. *Global Business and Organizational Excellence, 30*(2), 6–15. doi:10.1002/joe.20364

Kimble, C., Grenier, C., & Goglio-Primard, K. (2010). Innovation and knowledge sharing across professional boundaries: Political interplay between boundary objects and brokers. *International Journal of Information Management, 30*(5), 437–444. doi:10.1016/j.ijinfomgt.2010.02.002

Kimble, C., & Hildreth, P. (2005). Dualities, distributed communities of practice and knowledge management. *Journal of Knowledge Management, 9*(4), 102–113. doi:10.1108/13673270510610369

Kimble, C., Li, F., & Barlow, A. (2000). *Effective Virtual Teams through Communities of Practice*. Glasgow, UK: University of Strathclyde.

Lave, J., & Wenger, E. (1991). *Situated Learning: Legitimate Peripheral Participation*. Cambridge, UK: Cambridge University Press.

Lindkvist, L. (2005). Knowledge Communities and Knowledge Collectivities: A Typology of Knowledge Work in Groups. *Journal of Management Studies, 42*(6), 1189–1210. doi:10.1111/j.1467-6486.2005.00538.x

McLuhan, M., & Powers, B. R. (1989). *The Global Village: Transformations in World Life and Media in the 21st Century*. New York, NY: Oxford University Press.

Rheingold, H. (1993). *The Virtual Community: Homesteading on the Electronic Frontier*. Reading, MA: Addison-Wesley.

Ribeiro, R., Kimble, C., & Cairns, P. (2010). Quantum phenomena in Communities of Practice. *International Journal of Information Management, 30*(1), 21–27. doi:10.1016/j.ijinfomgt.2009.11.003

Sayago, S., & Blat, J. (2010). Telling the story of older people e-mailing: An ethnographical study. *International Journal of Human-Computer Studies, 68*(1-2), 105–120. doi:10.1016/j.ijhcs.2009.10.004

Swan, J., Scarbrough, H., & Robertson, M. (2002). The construction of 'communities of practice' in the management of innovation. *Management Learning, 33*(4), 477–496. doi:10.1177/1350507602334005

Teigland, R., & Wasko, M. M. (2003). Integrating knowledge through information trading: Examining the relationship between boundary spanning communication and individual performance. *Decision Sciences, 34*(2), 261–286. doi:10.1111/1540-5915.02341

Tsoukas, H. (1996). The firm as a distributed knowledge system: A constructionist approach. *Strategic Management Journal, 17*, 11–25.

Tsoukas, H., & Chia, R. (2002). On organizational becoming: Rethinking organizational change. *Organization Science, 13*(5), 567–582. doi:10.1287/orsc.13.5.567.7810

Turkle, S. (1995). *Life on the Screen: Identity in the Age of the Internet*. New York, NY: Simon & Schuster.

Vaast, E. (2004). O Brother, Where are Thou? From Communities to Networks of Practice Through Intranet Use. *Management Communication Quarterly, 18*(1), 5–44. doi:10.1177/0893318904265125

Wasko, M. M., & Faraj, S. (2000). "It is what one does": why people participate and help others in electronic communities of practice. *The Journal of Strategic Information Systems, 9*(2-3), 155–173. doi:10.1016/S0963-8687(00)00045-7

Wasko, M. M., & Faraj, S. (2005). Why should I share? Examining social capital and knowledge contribution in electronic networks of practice. *Management Information Systems Quarterly, 29*(1), 35–57.

Wenger, E. (1998). *Communities of Practice: Learning, Meaning, and Identity*. New York, NY: Cambridge University Press.

Wenger, E., McDermott, R. A., & Snyder, W. M. (2002). *Cultivating communities of practice: a guide to managing knowledge*. Boston, MA: Harvard Business School Press.

This work was previously published in the International Journal of Virtual Communities and Social Networking, Volume 2, Issue 4, edited by Subhasish Dasgupta, pp. 23-30, copyright 2010 by IGI Publishing (an imprint of IGI Global).

Compilation of References

Adjei, M., Noble, S., & Noble, C. (2007). Online Customer-to-Customer Communications as Drivers of Relationship Quality and Purchase Behavior. In *Proceedings of the AMA Winter Educators' Conference* (Vol. 16, pp. 166).

Afuah, A., & Tucci, C. (2001). *Internet Business Models and Strategies*. New York: McGraw Hill.

Ajzen, I. (1985). From intentions to actions: A theory of planned behaviour. In Kuhi, J., & Beckman, J. (Eds.), *Action-control: From Cognition to Behavior* (pp. 11–39). Berlin: Springer.

Ajzen, I. (1991). The Theory of Planned Behavior. *Organizational Behavior and Human Decision Processes, 50*, 179–211. doi:10.1016/0749-5978(91)90020-T

Ajzen, I., & Fishbein, M. (1973). Attitudinal and normative variables as predictors of specific behaviors. *Journal of Personality and Social Psychology, 27*, 41–57. doi:10.1037/h0034440

Ajzen, I., & Fishbein, M. (1977). Attitude-Behavior Relations: A Theoretical Analysis and Review of Empirical Research. *Psychological Bulletin, 84*(5), 888–918. doi:10.1037/0033-2909.84.5.888

Ajzen, I., & Fishbein, M. (1980). *Understanding attitudes and predicting social behavior*. Englewood Cliffs, NJ: Prentice-Hall.

Akkerman, S., Petter, C., & de Laat, M. (2008). Organising communities-of-practice: facilitating emergence. *Journal of Workplace Learning, 20*(6), 383–399. doi:10.1108/13665620810892067

Akoumianakis, D., & Alexandraki, C. (2010, November 24-26). Understanding Networked Music Communities through a practice-lens: Virtual 'tells' and cultural artifacts. In *Proceedings of the 2nd International Conference on Intelligent Networking and Collaborative Systems (INCoS 2010)*, Thessaloniki, Greece (pp. 62-69). Washington, DC: IEEE Computer Society.

Akoumianakis, D. (2009). Designing practice-oriented toolkits: A retrospective analysis of communities, new media and social practice. *International Journal of Virtual Communities and Social Networking, 1*(4), 50–72. doi:10.4018/jvcsn.2009092204

Akoumianakis, D. (2010). Electronic Community Factories: The model and its application in the tourism sector. *Electronic Commerce Research, 10*(1), 43–81. doi:10.1007/s10660-010-9045-1

Akoumianakis, D., Vidakis, N., Akrivos, A., Milolidakis, G., Kotsalis, D., & Vellis, G. (2011). Building 'Flexible' vacation packages using collaborative assembly toolkits and dynamic packaging: The Case Study of the eKoNES. *Journal of Vacation Marketing, 17*(1), 17–30. doi:10.1177/1356766710391132

Akoumianakis, D., Vidakis, N., Vellis, G., Kotsalis, D., Milolidakis, G., Plemenos, A., & Akrivos, A. (2011). Transformable boundary artifacts for knowledge-based work in cross-organization virtual community spaces. *Intelligent Decisions Technologies, 14*(1), 65–82.

Alexa. (n.d.). Retrieved March 8, 2008, from http://www Alexa.com

Alexandraki, C., & Akoumianakis, D. (2010). Exploring New Perspectives in Network Music Performance: The DIAMOUSES Framework. *Computer Music Journal, 34*, 66–83. doi:10.1162/comj.2010.34.2.66

Al-Gahtani, S. S., & King, M. (1999). Attitudes, satisfaction and usage: factors contributing to each in the acceptance of information technology. *Behaviour & Information Technology, 18*(4), 277–297. doi:10.1080/014492999119020

Allee, V. (2003). *The Future of Knowledge: Increasing Prosperity through Value Networks.* Oxford, UK: Butterworth-Heinemann.

AlShabib, H., Rana, O., & Shaikh Ali, A. (2006). Deriving ratings through social network structures. In *Proceedings of International Conference on Availability, Reliability and Security (ARES'06)*, Vienna, Austria. Washington, DC: IEEE Computer Society Press.

Altheide, D. L. (1995). *An Ecology of Communication: Cultural Formats of Control.* Hawthorne, NY: Aldine de Gruyter.

Anderson, B. (1983). *Imagined Communities: Reflections on the Origin and Spread of Nationalism.* London, UK: Verso.

Anderson, E. W., Fornell, C., & Rust, R. T. (1997). Customer satisfaction, productivity, and profitability: Differences between goods and services. *Marketing Science, 16*(2), 129–145. doi:10.1287/mksc.16.2.129

Andrade, N., Brasileiro, F., Mowbray, M., & Cirne, W. (2010). A reciprocation-based Economy for multiple services in a Computational Grid. In Buyya, R., & Bubendorder, K. (Eds.), *Market-Oriented Grid and Utility Computing* (pp. 357–370). New York: John Wiley & Sons.

Andrews, D. (2002). Audience-specific online community design. *Communications of the ACM, 45*(4), 64–68. doi:10.1145/505248.505275

Androutsellis-Theotokis, S., & Spinellis, D. (2004). A survey of peer-to-peer content distribution technologies. [CSUR]. *ACM Computing Surveys, 36*(4), 335–371. doi:10.1145/1041680.1041681

Ansari, A., & Mela, C. (2002). E-Customization. *JMR, Journal of Marketing Research, 40*(2), 131–145. doi:10.1509/jmkr.40.2.131.19224

Appadurai, A. (1996). *Modernity at large: Cultural Dimensions of Globalization, Public Worlds (Vol. 1).* Minneapolis, MN: University of Minnesota Press.

Appadurai, A. (2003). *Globalization-Grassroots Globalization and the Research Imagination.* Durham, NC: Duke University Press.

Archer, M. S. (2000). *Being Human: The Problem of Agency.* Cambridge, UK: Cambridge University Press. doi:10.1017/CBO9780511488733

Armitage, C. J., & Conner, M. (2001). Efficacy of the Theory of Planned Behaviour: A meta-analytic review. *The British Journal of Social Psychology, 40*, 471–499. doi:10.1348/014466601164939

Armstrong, A., & Hagel, J. (1996). The Real Value of On-Line Communities. *Harvard Business Review, 74*(3), 134–141.

Arnold, J. (2009, December). Twittering and Facebooking while they work. *HRMagazine*, 53–55.

Arrington, M. (2006). Facebook goes beyond college, high school markets. *TechCrunch*. Retrieved March 29, 2009, from http://www.techcrunch.com/2006/04/26/facebook-goes-beyond-college-high-school-markets/

Ashforth, B. E., & Mael, E. (1989). Social identity theory and the organization. *Academy of Management Review, 14*, 20–39. doi:10.2307/258189

Atkinson, J., Johnson, C., & Phippen, A. D. (2007). Improving protection mechanisms by understanding online risk. *Information Management & Computer Security, 15*(5), 382–393. doi:10.1108/09685220710831125

Auchard, E. (2006, August 22). *Friendster looks to recover lost glory.* Retrieved August 22, 2006, from http://news.yahoo.com/s/nm/20060822/tc_nm/friendster_dc_4&printer=1

Auld, G. (2007). Ndjebbana talking books: A technological transformation to fit Kunibidji social practice. In Dyson, L. E., Hendriks, M., & Grant, S. (Eds.), *Information technology and indigenous people* (pp. 197–199). Hershey, PA: Idea Group Publishing.

Babbie, E. R. (1973). *Survey research methods.* Belmont, CA: Wadsworth.

Baker-Eveleth, L. J., Eveleth, D. M., & O'Neill, M. (2010). Developing a community of practice through classroom climate, leader support and leader interaction. In *Proceedings of the American Society of Business and Behavioral Sciences Conference*, Las Vegas, NV.

Baker-Eveleth, L. J., Sarker, S., & Eveleth, D. M. (2005). Formation of an online community of practice: An inductive study unearthing key elements. In *Proceedings of the Hawaii International Conference on System Sciences*, Big Island, Hawaii.

Balabanis, G., Reynolds, N., & Simintiras, A. (2006). Bases of E-Store Loyalty: Perceived Switching Barriers and Satisfaction. *Journal of Business Research*, 59(2), 214–224. doi:10.1016/j.jbusres.2005.06.001

Balasubramanian, S., & Mahajan, V. (2001). The Economic Leverage of the Virtual Community. *International Journal of Electronic Commerce*, 5(3), 103–138.

Bani Ali, A. (2004). *Project Management Software Effectiveness Study*. Unpublished doctoral dissertation, George Washington University, Washington, DC.

Barley, S. R., & Kunda, G. (2001). Bringing Work Back In. *Organization Science*, 12(1), 76–95. doi:10.1287/orsc.12.1.76.10122

Barley, S. R., & Kunda, G. (2004). *Gurus, Hired Guns, and Warm Bodies: Itinerant Experts in a Knowledge Economy*. Princeton, NJ: Princeton University Press.

Baron, R. M., & Kenny, D. A. (1986). The moderator-mediator variable distinction in social psychological research: Conceptual, strategic, and statistical considerations. *Journal of Personality and Social Psychology*, 51(6), 1173–1182. doi:10.1037/0022-3514.51.6.1173

Basso, K. (1997). *Wisdom sits in places*. Albuquerque, NM: University of New Mexico Press.

Bauer, H., & Grether, M. (2005). Virtual Community Its Contribution to Customer Relationships by Providing Social Capital. *Journal of Relationship Marketing*, 4(1-2), 91–109. doi:10.1300/J366v04n01_07

Baym, N. K. (1995). The emergence of community in computer-mediated communication. In Jones, S. (Ed.), *CyberSociety* (pp. 138–163). Newbury Park, CA: Sage.

Baym, N. K. (2007). The new shape of online community: The example of Swedish independent music fandom. *First Monday*, 12(8). Retrieved from http://firstmonday.org/issues/issue12_8/baym/index.html.

Baym, N. K. (2009). A call for grounding in the face of blurred boundaries. *Journal of Computer-Mediated Communication*, 14(3), 720–723. doi:10.1111/j.1083-6101.2009.01461.x

Beeger, B. (2007). *Soziale netzwerke: Karrierekiller im Internet*. Retrieved from http://www.stern.de/computer-technik/internet/:Soziale-Netzwerke-Karrierekiller-Internet/596742.html

Beker, J. (2001). Development of professional identity for the child care worker. *Child and Youth Care Forum*, 30(6), 345–354. doi:10.1023/A:1015360917095

Beniger, J. R. (1987). The personalization of mass media and the growth of pseudo-community. *Communication Research*, 14(3), 352–371. doi:10.1177/009365087014003005

Benkler, Y. (2002). Coase's Penguin, or, Linux and the Nature of the Firm. *The Yale Law Journal*, 112(3), 369–436. doi:10.2307/1562247

Benkler, Y. (2006). *The Wealth of Networks: How Social Production Transforms Markets and Freedom*. New Haven, CT: Yale University Press.

Bentler, P. M. (1989). *EQS Structural Equations Program Manual*. Los Angeles, CA: BMDP Statistical Software.

Betts, J. D. (2007). Community computing and literacy in Pascua Yaqui Pueblo. In Dyson, L. E., Hendriks, M., & Grant, S. (Eds.), *Information technology and indigenous people* (pp. 305–309). Hershey, PA: Idea Group Publishing.

Bhabha, K. H. (1994). *The Location of Culture*. London: Routledge.

Bharadwaj, K., & Al-Shamri, H. (2009). Fuzzy computational models for trust and reputation systems. *Electronic Commerce Research and Applications*, 8(1), 37–47. doi:10.1016/j.elerap.2008.08.001

Bhattacherjee, A. (2001). Understanding Information Systems Continuance: An Exptectation-Confirmation Model. *Management Information Systems Quarterly, 25*(3), 351–370. doi:10.2307/3250921

Bielak, A. T., Holmes, J., Savgard, J., & Schaefer, K. (2009). *A comparison of European and North American approaches to the management and communication of environmental research* (Tech. Rep. No. 5958). Stockholm, Sweden: Swedish Environmental Protection Agency.

Black, S., & Jacobs, J. (2010, May 2-8). Using Web 2.0 to Improve Software Quality. In *Proceedings of Web2SE workshop (ICSE 2010),* Cape Town, South Africa.

Black, S., Harrison, R., & Baldwin, M. (2010, May 2-8). A Survey of Social Media Use in Software Systems Development. In *Proceedings of Web2SE workshop*, Cape Town, South Africa.

Blanchard, A. (2004). *Blogs as Virtual Communities: Identifying a Sense of Community in the Julie/Julia Project.* Retrieved from http://blog.lib.umn.edu/blogosphere/blogs_as_virtual.html

Blanchard, A. L., & Markus, L. M. (2004). The Experienced "Sense" of a Virtual Community: Characteristics and Processes. *The Data Base for Advances in Information Systems, 35*(1), 65–79.

Blanchard, A., & Horan, T. (2000). Virtual communities and social capital. In Lesser, E. (Ed.), *Knowledge and social capital* (pp. 159–178). Boston, MA: Butterworth Heinemann. doi:10.1016/B978-0-7506-7222-1.50010-6

Blume, L., & Durlauf, S. N. (2003). Equilibrium Concepts for Social Interaction Models. *International Game Theory Review, 5*(3), 193–209. doi:10.1142/S021919890300101X

Boden, D. (1994). *The Business of Talk*. Boston, MA: Polity.

Borgatti, E., & Freeman, L. C. (2002). *UCINet 6 Network analysis software. Analytic technologies*. Retrieved from http://www.analytictech.com/downloaduc6.htm

Borgatti, S. P. (2005). Centrality and network flow. *Social Networks, 27*(1), 55–71. doi:10.1016/j.socnet.2004.11.008

Borgatti, S. P., & Everett, M. G. (1999). Models of Core/Periphery Structures. *Social Networks, 21*, 375–395. doi:10.1016/S0378-8733(99)00019-2

Borgatti, S. P., & Everett, M. G. (2006). A Graph-Theoretic Perspective on Centrality. *Social Networks, 28*(4), 466–484. doi:10.1016/j.socnet.2005.11.005

Borgatti, S. P., Everett, M. G., & Freeman, L. C. (2002). *UCINET for Windows: Software for Social Network Analysis*. Cambridge, MA: Analytic Technologies.

Bos, N., Gergle, D., Olson, J., & Olson, G. (2001). Being there versus seeing there: Trust via video. In *Proceedings of the CHI Conference.* Retrieved September 12, 2007, from http://www.crew.umich.edu/publications.html

Bos, N., Zimmerman, A., Olson, J., Yew, J., Yerkie, J., Dahl, E., & Olson, G. (2008). From shared databases to Communities of Practice: A taxonomy of collaboratories. *Journal of Computer-Mediated Communication, 12*(2), 318–338.

Bosses Unpopular as Facebook friends. (2009, April 29). *The Globe and Mail*, B20.

Bourgeois, M. J., & Perkins, J. (2003). A test of evolutionary and sociocultural explanations of reactions to sexual harassment. *Sex Roles, 49*(7/8), 343–351. doi:10.1023/A:1025160120455

Boyd, D. (2006). A Blogger's Blog: Exploring the Definition of a Medium. *Reconstruction: Studies in Contemporary Culture, 6*(4). Retrieved from http://reconstruction.eserver.org/064/boyd.shtml

Boyd, D. (2007). *Why Youth loves Social Network Sites: The Role of Networked Publics in Teenage Social Life*. Berkeley, CA: University of California-Berkeley.

Boyd, D. (2008). *Taken Out of Context: American Teen Sociality in Networked Publics*. Berkeley, CA: University of California-Berkeley.

Boyd, D., & Ellison, N. B. (2007). Social network sites: Definition, history, and scholarship. *Journal of Computer-Mediated Communication, 13*(1).

Boyd, J. T., Peters, C. O., & Tolson, H. (2007). An exploratory investigation of the virtual community MySpace.com. *Journal of Fashion Marketing and Management, 11*(4), 587–603. doi:10.1108/13612020710824625

Brandenburg, C. (2008). The newest way to screen job applicants: A social networker's nightmare. *Federal Communications Law Journal, 60*(3), 597–626.

Bresnen, M., Edelmanb, L., Newellb, S., Scarbrough, H., & Swana, J. (2003). Social practices and the management of knowledge in project environments. *International Journal of Project Management, 21*(3), 157–166. doi:10.1016/S0263-7863(02)00090-X

Brewer, M. B. (1991). The Social Self: On Being the Same and Different at the Same Time. *Personality and Social Psychology Bulletin, 17*(5), 475–482. doi:10.1177/0146167291175001

Brey, P. (2003). Theorizing modernity and technology. In Misa, T. J., Brey, P., & Feenberg, A. (Eds.), *Modernity and Technology*. Cambridge, MA: MIT Press.

Brock, R. (2007). Online. *The Chronicle of Higher Education, 53*(19), A31.

Brooks, K. (2008). Networking the pros and cons of trolling the internet for sources sites. *Quill, January/February*, 25-26.

Browne, K. R. (2006). Sex, power, and dominance: The evolutionary psychology of sexual harassment. *Managerial and Decision Economics, 27*, 145–158. doi:10.1002/mde.1289

Browne, M. W., & Cudeck, R. (1993). Alternative ways of assessing model fit. In Bollen, K. A., & Long, J. S. (Eds.), *Testing structural equation models* (pp. 136–162). Mewbury Park, CA: Sage.

Brown, J. S., & Duguid, P. (1991). Organizational learning and Communities-of-Practice: toward a unified view of working, learning, and innovation. *Organization Science, 2*(1), 40–57. doi:10.1287/orsc.2.1.40

Brown, J. S., & Duguid, P. (2000). *The Social Life of Information*. Boston, MA: Harvard Business School Press.

Brown, S. A., Massey, A. P., Montoya-Weiss, M. M., & Burkman, J. R. (2002). *European Journal of Information Systems, 11*, 283–295. doi:10.1057/palgrave.ejis.3000438

Brown, S. J., & Duguid, P. (2001). Knowledge and Organization: A Social-Practice Perspective. *Organization Science, 12*(2), 198–213. doi:10.1287/orsc.12.2.198.10116

Bruckman, A. S. (1993, August). *Gender Swapping on the Internet*. Paper presented at the International Networking Conference (INET'93), San Francisco, CA.

Budd, R. J. (1986). Predicting cigarette use: The need to incorporate measures of salience in the theory of reasoned action. *Journal of Applied Social Psychology, 16*, 663–685. doi:10.1111/j.1559-1816.1986.tb01752.x

Bump, J. (1990). Radical changes in class discussion using networked computers. *Computers and the Humanities, 24*, 44–65. doi:10.1007/BF00115028

Burcher, N. (2010). *Facebook Usage Statistics Based on Country*. Retrieved April 15, 2010, from http://www.nickburcher.com/2010/03/facebook-usage-statistics-march-2010.html

Burt, R. S. (1992). *Structural Holes*. Cambridge, MA: Harvard University Press.

Butler, B. (2001). Membership size, communication activity, and sustainability: The internal dynamics of networked social structures. *Information Systems Research, 12*(4), 346–362. doi:10.1287/isre.12.4.346.9703

Cachia, R., Compano, R., & Da Costa, O. (2005). Grasping the potential of online social networks for foresight. *Technological Forecasting and Social Change, 74*(8), 1179–1203. doi:10.1016/j.techfore.2007.05.006

Cain, J. (2008). Online Social Networking Issues within Academia and Pharmacy Education. *American Journal of Pharmaceutical Education, 72*(1).

Cairncross, F. (1997). *The Death of Distance: How the Communications Revolution Will Change Our Lives*. Boston, MA: Harvard Business School Press.

Cakir, H., & Cagiltay, K. (2002). Effects of cultural differences on e-mail communication in multicultural environments. In F. Sudweeks & C. Ess (Eds.), *Proceedings of the Third International Conference on Cultural Attitudes towards Technology and Communication* (pp. 29-50). Montreal, Canada: School of Information Technology, Murdoch University.

Cao, J., Wang, J., Law, K., Zhang, S., & Li, M. (2006). An Interactive Service Customization Model. *Information and Software Technology, 48*(4), 280–296. doi:10.1016/j.infsof.2005.04.007

Carlile, P. R. (2002). A Pragmatic View of Knowledge and Boundaries: Boundary Objects in New Product Development. *Organization Science*, *13*(4), 442–455. doi:10.1287/orsc.13.4.442.2953

Carroll, J. M. (2011). *The Neighborhood and the Internet: Design Research Projects in Community Informatics*. London, UK: Routledge.

Caruso, D., & Rhoten, D. (2001). *Lead, follow, get out of the way: Sidestepping the barriers to effective practice of interdisciplinarity*. Retrieved from http://www.hybridvigor.net/publications.pl?s=interdis&d=2001.04.30# Crane, D. (1972). *Invisible colleges: diffusion of knowledge in scientific communities*. Chicago, IL: University of Chicago Press.

Casare, S., & Sichman, J. (2005). Towards a Functional Ontology of Reputation. In *Proceedings of the Fourth International Joint Conference on Autonomous Agents and Multiagent Systems* (pp. 505-511). New York: ACM.

Castells, M. (1999). *Information technology, globalization and social development* (UNRISD Discussion Paper No. 114). Geneva, Switzerland: United Nations Research Institute for Social Development.

Castells, M. (1996). *The rise of the network society*. Oxford, UK: Blackwell.

Castells, M. (2000). *The rise of the network society* (2nd ed.). Oxford, UK: Blackwell.

Castronova, E. (2008). *A test of the law of demand in a virtual world: Exploring the petri dish approach to social science* (CESifo Working Paper Series No. 2355). Retrieved May 1, 2009, from http://ssrn.com/abstract=1173642

Castronova, E. (2005). *Synthetic Worlds: The Business and Culture of Online Games*. Chicago: The University of Chicago Press.

Caverlee, J., Liu, L., & Webb, S. (2010). The SocialTrust framework for trusted social information management: Architecture and algorithms. *Information Sciences*, *180*(1), 95–112. doi:10.1016/j.ins.2009.06.027

Cerulo, K. A. (1997). Identity Construction: New Issues, New Directions. *Annual Review of Sociology*, *23*, 385–409. doi:10.1146/annurev.soc.23.1.385

Chafkin, M. (2007, June 1). How to kill agGreat idea! *Inc.com*, Retrieved March 2, 2010, from http://www.inc.com/magazine/20070601/features-how-tokill-a-great-idea.html

Chapin, M., Lamb, Z., & Threlkeld, B. (2005). Mapping indigenous lands. *Annual Review of Anthropology*, *34*, 619–638. doi:10.1146/annurev.anthro.34.081804.120429

Chard, K., Caton, S., Rana, O., & Bubendorfer, K. (2010, July). Cloud Computing in Social Networks. In *Proceedings of IEEE "Cloud 2010" conference*. Miami, FL: Social Cloud.

Chatman, J. A., & Flynn, F. J. (2001). The influence of demographic heterogeneity on the emergence and consequences of cooperative norms in work teams. *Academy of Management Journal*, *44*(5), 956–974. doi:10.2307/3069440

Chaudhuri, A., & Holbrook, M. B. (2001). The chain of effects from brand trust and brand affect to brand performance: The role of brand loyalty. *Journal of Marketing*, *65*(2), 81–93. doi:10.1509/jmkg.65.2.81.18255

Chau, M., & Xu, J. (2007). Mining Communities and Their Relationships in Blogs: A Study of Online Hate Groups. *International Journal of Human-Computer Studies*, *65*(1), 57–70. doi:10.1016/j.ijhcs.2006.08.009

Chewar, C., McCrickard, D. S., & Carroll, J. M. (2005). Analyzing the social capital value chain in community network interfaces. *Internet Research*, *15*(3), 262–280.

Chidambaram, L. (1996). Relational development in computer-supported groups. *Management Information Systems Quarterly*, *20*(2), 143–163. doi:10.2307/249476

Chin, A., & Chignell, M. (2006). *A Social Hypertext Model for Finding Community in Blogs*. Paper presented at the ACM Conference on Hypertext and Hypermedia, New York.

Chin, A., & Chignell, M. (2006, February 26-28). Finding Evidence of Community from Blogging Co-citations: A Social Network Analytic Approach. In *Proceedings of the 3rd IADIS International Conference Web Based Communities 2006 (WBC06)*, San Sebastian, Spain (pp. 191-200).

Chiu, C., Hsu, M., & Wang, E. (2006). Understanding knowledge sharing in virtual communities: An integration of social capital and social cognitive theories. *Decision Support Systems*, *42*(3), 1872–1888. doi:10.1016/j.dss.2006.04.001

Clark, L., Ting, I.-H., Kimble, C., Wright, P., & Kudenko, D. (2006). Combining Ethnographic and Clickstream Data to Identify User Web Browsing Strategies. *Information Research, 11*(2).

Clayfield, M. (2007). A Certain Tendency in Videoblogging and Rethinking the Rebirth of the Author. *Post Identity, 5*(1). Retrieved from http://hdl.handle.net/2027/spo.pid9999.0005.2106.

Clegg, C. W. (1983). Psychology of employee lateness, absence, and turnover: A methodological critique and an empirical study. *The Journal of Applied Psychology*, *68*, 88–101. doi:10.1037/0021-9010.68.1.88

Coakes, E. W., Coakes, J. M., & Rosenberg, D. (2008). Co-operative work practices and knowledge sharing issues: A comparison of viewpoints. *International Journal of Information Management*, *28*(1), 12–25. doi:10.1016/j.ijinfomgt.2007.10.004

Coleman, J. S. (1988). Social capital in the creation of human capital. *American Journal of Sociology*, *94*, 95–120. doi:10.1086/228943

Collier, J. E., & Bienstock, C. C. (2006). Measuring Service Quality in E-Retailing. *Journal of Service Research*, *8*(3), 260–275. doi:10.1177/1094670505278867

Collison, G., Elbaum, B., Haavind, S., & Tinker, R. (2000). *Facilitating online learning: Effective strategies for moderators*. Madison, WI: Atwood.

Compeau, D. R., & Higgins, C. A. (1995, June). Computer self-efficacy: Development of a measure and initial test. *Management Information Systems Quarterly*, *19*(2), 189–211. doi:10.2307/249688

Comscore. (2008). *Social networking explodes worldwide as sites increase their focus on cultural relevance*. Retrieved from http://www.comscore.com/press/release.asp?press=2396

Cooper, D. R., & Emory, C. W. (1995). *Business Research Methods* (5th ed.). Scarborough, ON, Canada: Thomson Nelson.

Costa, J., & Ferrone, L. (1995). Sociocultural perspectives on tourism planning and development. *International Journal of Contemporary Hospitality Management*, *7*(7), 27–35. doi:10.1108/09596119510101903

Cothrel, J., & Williams, R. (1999). On-Line Communities. *Knowledge Management Review*, *1*(6), 20–25.

Cotton, J. L., & Tuttle, J. M. (1986). Employee turnover: A meta-analysis and review with implications for research. *Academy of Management Review*, *11*, 55–70. doi:10.2307/258331

Cross, R., Borgatti, S. P., & Parker, A. (2002). *Making invisible work visible: Using social network analysis to support strategic collaboration*. Retrieved September 5, 2008, from https://webapp.comm.virginia.edu/SnaPortal/portals%5C0%5Cmaking_invisible_work_visible.pdf

Cummings, J., & Kiesler, S. (2005). Collaborative research across disciplinary and organizational boundaries. *Social Studies of Science*, *35*(5), 703–722. doi:10.1177/0306312705055535

Cummins, H. (2006). *Bosses peek in on Facebook to screen job applicants*. Retrieved June 12, 2010, from http://seattlepi.nwsource.com/business/265153_facebook03.html

Curry, M. (1995). Rethinking rights and responsibilities in geographic information systems. *Cartography and Geographic Information Systems*, *22*, 58–69. doi:10.1559/152304095782540573

Curry, M. (1998). *Digital place: Living with geographic information technologies*. New York: Routledge Press.

Daft, R. L., & Lengel, R. H. (1986). Organizational information requirements, media richness and structural design. *Management Science*, *32*(5), 554–571. doi:10.1287/mnsc.32.5.554

Daly, A. (2007). The diffusion of new technologies: Community online access centres in indigenous communities in Australia. In Dyson, L. E., Hendriks, M., & Grant, S. (Eds.), *Information technology and indigenous people* (pp. 272–285). Hershey, PA: Idea Group Publishing.

Daniel, B. K., & Poon, N. (2006, July). Social Network Techniques and Content Analysis of Interactions in a Video-Mediated Virtual Community. In *Proceedings of the 6th IEEE International Conference on Advanced Learning Technologies*, Kerkrade, The Netherlands.

Daniel, B. K., Schwier, R. A., & Ross, H. (2005, October 24-28). Intentional and Incidental Discourse Variables in a Virtual Learning Community. In *Proceedings of E-Learn 2005: World Conference on E-Learning in Corporate, Government, Healthcare, and Higher Education,* Vancouver, BC, Canada. De Laat, M. F. (2002, March). *Network and content analysis in an online community discourse.* Paper presented at the Networked Learning Conference, Sheffield, UK.

Daniel, B., Schwier, R. A., & McCalla, G. (2003). Social capital in virtual learning communities and Distributed Communities of Practice. *Canadian Journal of Learning and Technology, 29*(3), 113–139.

Davis, F. D. (1986). *A Technology Acceptance Model for Empirically Testing New End-User Information: Theory and Results, Doctoral Dissertation.* Unpublished doctoral dissertation, MIT Sloan School of Management, Cambridge, MA.

Davis, F. (1989). Perceived Usefulness, Perceived Ease of Use, and User Acceptance of Information Technology. *Management Information Systems Quarterly, 13*(3), 319–340. doi:10.2307/249008

Davis, F. D. (1989). Perceived Usefulness, Perceived Ease of Use, and User Acceptance of Information Technology. *Management Information Systems Quarterly, 13*(3), 319–340. doi:10.2307/249008

Davis, F. D., Bagozzi, R. P., & Warshaw, P. R. (1989). User acceptance of computer technology: a comparison of two theoretical models. *Management Science, 35*(8), 982–1003. doi:10.1287/mnsc.35.8.982

Davis, F. D., Bagozzi, R. P., & Warshaw, P. R. (1992). Extrinsic and intrinsic motivation to use computers in the workplace. *Journal of Applied Social Psychology, 24*(14), 1111–1132. doi:10.1111/j.1559-1816.1992.tb00945.x

de Almeida Soares, D., & Naval, E. (2008). Understanding class blogs as a tool for language development. *Language Teaching Research, 12*(4), 517–533. doi:10.1177/1362168808097165

Dellarocas, C. (2003). The Digitization of Word-of-Mouth: Promise and Challenges of Online Reputation Systems. *Management Science, 49*(10), 1407–1424. doi:10.1287/mnsc.49.10.1407.17308

DeLone, W. H., & McLean, E. R. (2003). The DeLone and McLean Model of Information Systems Success: A ten-Year Update. *Journal of Management Information Systems, 19*(4), 9–30.

Denning, J. P. (2001). The profession of IT: Who Are We? *Communications of the ACM, 44*(2), 15–19. doi:10.1145/359205.359239

Deuze, M. (2006). Participation, Remediation, Bricolage: Considering Principal Components of a Digital Culture. *The Information Society, 22*(1), 63–75. doi:10.1080/01972240600567170

Diaz, J. (2008). Facebook's squirmy chapter. Site's evolution blurs line between boss and employee. *The Boston Globe.* Retrieved March 29, 2009, from http://www.boston.com/lifestyle/articles/2008/04/16/facebooks_squirmy_chapter/

DiMicco, J. M., & Millen, D. R. (2007). Identity management: multiple presentations of self in facebook. In [New York: ACM Press.]. *Proceedings of GROUP, 2007,* 383–386.

Dimitrova, D., & Koku, E. (2009). Research communities in context: Trust, independence and technology in professional communities. In Akoumianakis, D. (Ed.), *Virtual community practices and social interactive media: Technology lifecycle and workflow analysis* (pp. 352–377). Hershey, PA: IGI Global. doi:10.4018/978-1-60566-340-1.ch018

Dishaw, M. T., Strong, D. M., & Bandy, D. B. (2002, August 9-12). Extending the Task-Technology Fit Model with Self-Efficacy Constructs. In *Proceedings of the Eighth Americas Conference on Information Systems,* Dallas, TX.

Dishaw, M. T., & Strong, D. M. (1999). Extending the technology acceptance model with task-technology fit constructs. *Information & Management, 36*(1), 9–21. doi:10.1016/S0378-7206(98)00101-3

Dominick, J. (1999). Who do you think you are? Personal home pages and self-presentation on the World Wide Web. *Journalism & Mass Communication Quarterly, 79*(3), 643–660.

Donath, J. S. (1999). Identity and Deception in the Virtual Community. In Smith, M., & Kollock, P. (Eds.), *Communities in Cyberspace* (pp. 27–58). London, UK: Routledge.

Donath, J., & Boyd, D. (2004). Public displays of connection. *BT Technology Journal, 22*(4), 71–82. doi:10.1023/B:BTTJ.0000047585.06264.cc

Doney, P. M., & Cannon, J. P. (1997). An examination of the nature of trust in buyer-seller relationships. *Journal of Marketing, 61*(2), 35–51. doi:10.2307/1251829

Donovan, M. (2007). Can information communication technology tools be used to suit Aboriginal learning pedagogies? In Dyson, L. E., Hendriks, M., & Grant, S. (Eds.), *Information technology and indigenous people* (pp. 93–104). Hershey, PA: Idea Group Publishing.

Doran, L. I., Stone, V. K., Brief, A. P., & George, J. M. (1991). Behavioral intentions as predictors of job attitudes: The role of economic choice. *The Journal of Applied Psychology, 76*, 40–45. doi:10.1037/0021-9010.76.1.40

Dubé, L., Bourhis, A., & Jacob, R. (2005). The impact of structuring characteristics on the launching of virtual communities of practice. *Journal of Organizational Change Management, 18*(2), 145–166. doi:10.1108/09534810510589570

Duerden, F. (1992). GIS and land selection for native claims. *The Operational Geographer, 10*(4), 11–14.

Duerden, F., & Kuhn, R. G. (1996). The application of geographic information systems by First Nations and government in northern Canada. *Cartographica, 33*(2), 49–62.

Duguid, P. (2005). The Art of Knowing: Social and Tacit Dimensions of Knowledge and the Limits of the Community of Practice. *The Information Society: An International Journal, 21*(2), 109–118.

Dutton, J. E., Dukerich, J. M., & Harquil, V. V. (1994). Organisational images and member identification. *Administrative Science Quarterly, 39*(2), 239–263. doi:10.2307/2393235

Dyson, L. E., Hendriks, M., & Grant, S. (2007). *Information technology and indigenous people*. Hershey, PA: Idea Group Publishing.

Earley, P. C., & Lituchy, T. R. (1991). Delineating goal and efficacy effects: A test of three models. *The Journal of Applied Psychology, 76*, 81–98. doi:10.1037/0021-9010.76.1.81

Ebel, H., Lutz-Ingo Mielsch, & Bornholdt, S. (2002). Scale Free Topology of E-Mail Networks. *Physical Review E: Statistical, Nonlinear, and Soft Matter Physics, 66*(3), 1–4. doi:10.1103/PhysRevE.66.035103

Efimova, L., & Hendrick, S. (2005). In Search for a Virtual Settlement: An Exploration of Weblog Community Boundaries. In *Proceedings of the Communities & Technologies 2005 Conference*. Retrieved from http://doc.telin.nl/dscgi/ds.py/Get/File-46041/weblog_community_boundaries.pdf

Eglash, R. (2007). Ethnocomputing with Native American design. In Dyson, L. E., Hendriks, M., & Grant, S. (Eds.), *Information technology and indigenous people* (pp. 210–219). Hershey, PA: Idea Group Publishing.

Eichmann, D. (1994). The RBSE Spider: Balancing Effective Search against Web Load. In *Proceedings of the First World Wide Web Conference*, Geneva, Switzerland.

Eldon, E. (2009). *Europe grew by 10 million new Facebook users last month, Here's the top 20 gainers*. Retrieved January, 6, 2010, from http://www.insidefacebook.com/2009/11/06/europe-grew-by-10-million-new-facebook-users-last-month-heres-the-top-20-gainers/

Ellison, N., Steinfeld, C., & Lampe, C. (2007). The benefits of Facebook "friends": Social capital and college students' use of online social network sites. *Journal of Computer-Mediated Communication, 12*(4), 143–1168. doi:10.1111/j.1083-6101.2007.00367.x

Epitropaki, O., & Martin, R. (2005). From ideal to real: A longitudinal study of implicit leadership theories, leader-member exchanges and employee outcomes. *The Journal of Applied Psychology, 90*, 659–676. doi:10.1037/0021-9010.90.4.659

Evans, J. A., Kunda, G., & Barley, S. R. (2004). Beach time, bridge and billable time hours: The temporal structure of technical contracting. *Administrative Science Quarterly, 49*(1), 1–38.

Evans, M., O'Malley, L., & Patterson, M. (2001). Bridging the Direct Marketing-Direct Consumer Gap: Some Solutions from Qualitative Research. *Qualitative Market Research: An International Journal, 4*(1), 17–24. doi:10.1108/13522750110364532

Even-Dar, E., & Shapira, A. (2007). A note on maximizing the spread of influence in social networks. In *Proceedings of the Third International Conference On Internet and Network Economics*, San Diego, CA (LNCS 4858, pp. 281-286).

Ezzamel, M., & Willmott, H. (1998). Accounting for teamwork: A critical study of group-based systems of organizational control. *Administrative Science Quarterly*, *43*(2), 358–396. doi:10.2307/2393856

Facebook Press Room. (2010). *Company statistics*. Retrieved January 6, 2010, from http://www.facebook.com/press/info.php?statistics

Facebook, Press Room. (2010). *Company Statistics*. Retrieved January 6, 2010, from http://www.facebook.com/press/info.php?statistics

Facebook, T. LinkedIn and Compliance: What are companies doing? (2009). *Society of Corporate Compliance and Ethics*. Retrieved June 22, 2010, from http://www.corporatecompliance.org/AM/Template.cfm?Section=Surveys&CONTENTID=4741&TEMPLATE=/CM/ContentDisplay.cfm

Facebook. (2009). *Home*. Retrieved from http://www.facebook.com

Fagan, M. H., Wooldridge, B. R., & Neill, S. (2008). Exploring the intention to use computers: An empirical investigation of the role of intrinsic motivation, extrinsic motivation, and perceived ease of use. *Journal of Computer Information Systems*, 31–37.

Fagermoen, M. S. (1997). Professional identity: values embedded in meaningful nursing practice. *Journal of Advanced Nursing*, *25*(3), 434–441. doi:10.1046/j.1365-2648.1997.1997025434.x

Fahlander, F., & Oestigaard, T. (2004). *Material Culture and Other Things, Post-disciplinary Studies in the 21st Century*. Retrieved from http://folk.uib.no/gsuto/Artikler-Web/Material_Culture/Oestigaard.pdf

Faugier, J., & Sargeant, M. (1997). Sampling hard to reach populations. *Journal of Advanced Nursing*, *26*, 790–797. doi:10.1046/j.1365-2648.1997.00371.x

Finholt, T., & Sproull, L. (1990). Electronic groups at work. *Organization Science*, *1*, 41–64. doi:10.1287/orsc.1.1.41

Fishbein, M., & Ajzen, I. (1975). *Belief, attitudes, intentions, and behavior: An introduction to theory and research*. Reading, MA: Addison-Wesley.

Flanagin, A. J., Park, H. S., & Seibold, D. R. (2004). Group performance and collaborative technology: A longitudinal and multilevel analysis of information quality, contribution equity, and members' satisfaction in computer-mediated groups. *Communication Monographs*, *71*(3), 352–372. doi:10.1080/0363452042000299902

Flew, T. (2007). *New media: an Introduction* (3rd ed.). South Melbourne, Australia: Oxford University Press.

Fogel, J., & Nehmad, E. (2009). Internet social network communities: Risk taking, trust, and privacy concerns. *Computers in Human Behavior*, *25*(1), 153–160. doi:10.1016/j.chb.2008.08.006

Fombrum, C., & Shanley, M. (1990). What is the name? Reputation building and corporate strategy. *Academy of Management Journal*, *33*(2), 233–258. doi:10.2307/256324

Fornell, C., & Larcker, D. F. (1981). Evaluating structural equation models with unobservable and measurement error. *Journal of Marketing Research*, *18*, 39–50. doi:10.2307/3151312

Freeman, L. C. (1977). A Set of Measures of Centrality Based on Betweenness. *Sociometry*, *40*, 35–41. doi:10.2307/3033543

Freeman, L. C. (2004). *The development of social network analysis: A study in the sociology of science*. Vancouver, BC, Canada: Empirical Press.

Fried, C. (1970). *An anatomy of values: Problems of personal and social choice*. Cambridge, MA: Harvard University Press.

Fukuyama, F. (1995). *Trust: The Social Virtues and the Creation of Prosperity*. New York: Free Press.

Fuller, A. (2006). *Employers snoop on Facebook*. Retrieved June 12, 2010 from http://daily.stanford.edu/article/2006/1/20/employersSnoopOnFacebook

Funk, L. (2007, September 19). Women on Facebook think provocative is empowering. *USA Today*, 11a.

Gaertner, S. L., Dovidio, J. F., Bachman, B. A., & Rust, M. C. (1993). The common ingroup identity model: Recategorization and the reduction of intergroup bias. *European Review of Social Psychology*, *4*, 1–26. doi:10.1080/14792779343000004

Galbraith, J. (1973). *Designing Complex Organizations.* Reading, MA: Addison-Wesley Publishing Co.

Garton, L., Haythornthwaite, C., & Wellman, B. (1999). Studying online social networks. In Jones, S. (Ed.), *Doing internet research* (pp. 75–105). Thousand Oaks, CA: Sage.

Gefen, D., Karahanna, E., & Straub, D. W. (2003). Trust and TAM in online shopping: an integrated model. *Management Information Systems Quarterly*, *27*(1), 51–90.

Gefen, D., & Straub, D. W. (2005). A practical guide to factorial validity using PLS-graph: Tutorial and annotated example. *Communications of the AIS*, *16*(5), 91–109.

Gerbing, D. W., & Anderson, J. C. (1988). An Updated Paradigm for Scale Development Incorporating Unidimensionality and its Assessment. *JMR, Journal of Marketing Research*, *XXV*, 186–192. doi:10.2307/3172650

Gerhard, M., Moore, D., & Hobbs, D. (2004). Embodiment and copresence in collaborative interfaces. *International Journal of Human-Computer Studies*, *61*(4), 453–480. doi:10.1016/j.ijhcs.2003.12.014

Gerstner, C. R., & Day, D. V. (1997). Meta-analytic review of leader-member exchange theory: Correlates and construct issues. *The Journal of Applied Psychology*, *82*, 827–844. doi:10.1037/0021-9010.82.6.827

Gharajedaghi, J. (2006). *Systems Thinking: Managing Chaos and Complexity: a platform for designing business architecture.* Burlington, MA: Elsevier.

Gherardi, S. (2001). Practice-based Theorizing on Learning and Knowing in Organizations: An Introduction. *Organization*, *7*(2), 211–223. doi:10.1177/135050840072001

Gherardi, S. (2009). Introduction: The Critical Power of the 'Practice Lens'. *Management Learning*, *40*(2), 115–128. doi:10.1177/1350507608101225

Ghose, A., & Yang, S. (2009). *An Empirical Analysis of Search Engine Advertising: Sponsored Search in Electronic Markets.* Retrieved from http://opimweb.wharton. upenn.edu/documents/seminars/paidsearch.pdf

Giddens, A. (1979). *Central Problems in Social Theory: Action, Structure Contradictions in Social Analysis.* Berkley, CA: University of California Press.

Giddens, A. (1984). *The constitution of society – Outline of the theory of structuration.* Cambridge, UK: Polity Press.

Gilbert, E., Karahalios, K., & Sandvig, C. (2008). The Network in the Garden: An Empirical Analysis of Social Media in Rural Life. In *Proceedings of the CHI 2008 Conference.* New York, NY: ACM Press.

Ginsburg, F. (1997). 'From little things, big things grow': Indigenous media and cultural activism. In Fox, R. G., & Starn, O. (Eds.), *Between Resistance and Revolution: Cultural Politics and Social Protest* (pp. 118–144). New Brunswick, NJ: Rutgers University Press.

Gochenour, H. P. (2006). Distributed communities and nodal subjects. *New Media & Society*, *8*(1), 33–51. doi:10.1177/1461444806059867

Godwin, M. (1994). Nine principles for making virtual communities work. *Wired 2.06*, 72–73.

Goffman, E. (1959). *The presentation of self in everyday life.* Garden City, NY: Double Day Anchor.

Golbeck, J. (2005). *Computing and Applying Trust in Web-based Social Networks.* Unpublished doctoral dissertation, University of Maryland, College Park.

Golbeck, J. (2009). Trust and nuanced profile similarity in online social networks. *ACM Transactions on the Web*, *3*(4), 1–30. doi:10.1145/1594173.1594174

Golle, P., Leyton-Brown, K., Mironov, I., & Lillibridge, M. (2001). Incentives for Sharing in Peer-to-Peer Networks. In *Electronic Commerce* (LNCS 2232, pp. 75-87).

Goodhue, D. L. (1995, December). Understanding User Evaluations of Information Systems. *Management Science*, *41*(12), 1827–1844. doi:10.1287/mnsc.41.12.1827

Goodhue, D. L. (1998). Development and measurement validity of a task-technology fit instrument for user evaluations of information systems. *Decision Sciences*, *29*(1), 105–138. doi:10.1111/j.1540-5915.1998.tb01346.x

Goodhue, D. L., & Thompson, T. L. (1995, June). Task-technology fit and individual performance. *Management Information Systems Quarterly, 19*(2), 213–236. doi:10.2307/249689

Goodwin-Gomez, G. (2007). Computer technology and native literacy in the Amazon rain forest. In Dyson, L. E., Hendriks, M., & Grant, S. (Eds.), *Information technology and indigenous people* (pp. 117–119). Hershey, PA: Idea Group Publishing.

Gordon, S. (2006). Rise of the Blog (Journal-Based Website). *IEE Review, 52*(3), 32–35. doi:10.1049/ir:20060301

Grace-Farfaglia, P., Dekkers, A., Sundararajan, B., Peters, L., & Park, S. (2006). Multinational Web Uses and Gratifications: Measuring the Social Impact of Online Community Participation across National Boundaries. *Electronic Commerce Research, 6*(1), 75–101. doi:10.1007/s10660-006-5989-6

Graen, G. B., & Uhl-Bien, M. (1995). Relationship-based approach to leadership: Development of leader-member exchange LMX theory. *The Leadership Quarterly, 6*, 219–247. doi:10.1016/1048-9843(95)90036-5

Graen, G., Novak, M., & Sommerkamp, P. (1982). The effects of leader-member exchange and job design on productivity and job satisfaction: Testing a dual attachment model. *Organizational Behavior and Human Performance, 30*, 109–131. doi:10.1016/0030-5073(82)90236-7

Granovetter, M. (1978). Threshold Models of Collective Behavior. *American Journal of Sociology, 83*(6), 1420–1443. doi:10.1086/226707

Granovetter, M. (1983). The Strength of Weak Ties: A Network Theory Revisited. *Sociological Theory, 1*, 201–233. doi:10.2307/202051

Graouid, S. (2005). *Social Exile and Virtual H'rig*. Rabat, Morocco: Mohamed V University Press.

Graves, L. N. (1992). Cooperative learning communities: Context for a new vision of education and society. *Journal of Education, 174*(2), 57–79.

Gray, K. (2009). *Social networking policies vary by job, company*. Retrieved September 2, 2009, from http://moss07.shrm.org/hrdisciplines/employeerelations/articles/Pages/SocialNetworkingPolicies.aspx

Gruber, T. (2008). Collective knowledge systems: Where the Social Web meets the Semantic Web. *Journal of Web Semantics, 6*(1), 4–13.

Gruzd, A., Wellman, B., & Takhteyev, Y. (2011). Imagining Twitter as an Imagined Community. *American Behavioral Scientist*. Retrieved from: http://homes.chass.utoronto.ca/~wellman/publications/imagining_twitter/Imagining%20Twitter_AG_Sep1_2010_final.pdf

Guadagno, R., & Cialdini, R. (2007). Gender differences in impression management in organizations: A qualitative review. *Sex Roles, 56*(7-8), 483–494. doi:10.1007/s11199-007-9187-3

Gummerus, J., Liljander, V., Pura, M., & van Riel, A. (2004). Customer Loyalty to Content-Based Web Sites: The Case of an Online Health-Care Service. *Journal of Services Marketing, 18*(3), 175. doi:10.1108/08876040410536486

Guriting, P., & Ndubisi, N. O. (2006). Borneo online banking: evaluating customer perceptions and behavioural intention. *Management Research News, 29*(1-2), 6–15. doi:10.1108/01409170610645402

Gurses, S., Rizk, R., & Gunther, O. (2008). Privacy Design in Online Social Networks: Learning from Privacy Breaches and Community Feedback. In *Proceedings of ICIS, Association for Information Systems Conference*.

Gutek, B. A. (1985). *Sex and the Workplace: The Impact of Sexual Behaviour and Harassment on Women, Men and the Organization*. San Francisco, CA: Jossey-Bass.

Hagel, J. III, & Armstrong, A. (1997). *Net Gain: Expanding Markets through Virtual Communities*. Boston: Harvard Business School Press.

Hair, J. F. Jr, Anderson, R. E., Tatham, R. L., & Black, W. C. (1998). *Multivariate data analysis* (5th ed.). Upper Saddle River, NJ: Prentice Hall.

Hair, J. F. Jr, Black, W. C., Babin, B. J., Anderson, R. E., & Tatham, R. L. (2006). *Multivariate data analysis* (6th ed.). Upper Saddle River, NJ: Pearson Prentice Hall.

Hall, H., & Graham, D. (2004). Creation and Recreation: Motivating Collaboration to Generate Knowledge Capital in Online Communities. *International Journal of Information Management, 24*(3), 235–246. doi:10.1016/j.ijinfomgt.2004.02.004

Hall, S. (1991). Old and New Identities, Old and New Ethnicities. In King, A. D. (Ed.), *Culture, Globalization and the world-system: Current debates in Art History 3.* Binghamton, NY: State University of New York.

Hanneman, R. A., & Riddle, M. (2005). *Introduction to social network methods.* Riverside, CA: University of California, Riverside. Retrieved from http://faculty.ucr.edu/~hanneman/

Harper, V. (2002). Sex differences in perceived outcomes of electronic mail interactions. *Psychological Reports, 90*(2), 701–702.

Harrison, R. (2009). Excavating Second Life - Cyber-Archaeologies, Heritage and Virtual Communities. *Journal of Material Culture, 14*(1), 75–106. doi:10.1177/1359183508100009

Harrison, T. M., & Barthel, B. (2009). Wielding new media in Web 2.0: exploring the history of engagement with the collaborative construction of media products. *New Media & Society, 11*(1-2), 155–178. doi:10.1177/1461444808099580

Harrison-Walker, L. J. (2001). The measurement of word-of-mouth communication and an investigation of service quality and customer commitment as potential antecedents. *Journal of Service Research, 4,* 60–75. doi:10.1177/109467050141006

Harvey, F. (2002). Developing GI infrastructure for local government: The role of trust. In D. Turlloch, E. Epstein, D. Moyer, S. Ventura, B. Niemann, & R. Chenoweth (Eds.) *Proceedings of the Geographic information science & technology in a changing society: A research definition workshop,* Columbus, Ohio.

Harvey, F., & Chrisman, N. R. (1998). Boundary objects and the social construction of GIS technology. *Environment & Planning A, 30,* 1683–1694. doi:10.1068/a301683

Ha, S., & Stoel, L. (2009). Consumer e-shopping acceptance: Antecedents in a technology acceptance model. *Journal of Business Research, 62,* 565–571. doi:10.1016/j.jbusres.2008.06.016

Haveman, H. A. (1993). Organizational size and change: Diversification in the savings and loan industry after deregulation. *Administrative Science Quarterly, 38,* 20–50. doi:10.2307/2393253

Haythornthwaite, C., et al. (2003). *Challenges in the practice and study of distributed, interdisciplinary collaboration* (Tech. Rep. No. UIUCLIS--2004/1+DKRC). Retrieved from http://www.lis.uiuc.edu/~haythorn/hay_challenges.html

Hennig-Thurau, T., Gwinner, K. P., Walsh, G., & Gremler, D. D. (2004). Electronic Word-of-Mouth Via Consumer-Opinion Platforms: What Motivates Consumers to Articulate Themselves on the Internet? *Journal of Interactive Marketing, 18*(1), 38–52. doi:10.1002/dir.10073

Herring, S., & Scheidt, L. (2004). Bridging the Gap: A Genre Analysis of Weblogs. In *Proceedings of the Hawaii International Conference on System Science,* Waikoloa, HI.

Hersberger, J. A., Murray, A. L., & Rioux, K. S. (2007). Examining information exchange and virtual communities: an emergent framework. *Online Information Review, 31,* 2. doi:10.1108/14684520710747194

Heuer, B. P., & King, K. P. (2004). Leading the band: The role of the instructor in online learning for educators. *The Journal of Interactive Online Learning, 3*(1), 1–11.

Hewitt, A., & Forte, A. (2006). Crossing Boundaries: Identity Management and Student/Faculty Relationships on the Facebook. In *Proceedings of the CSCW 2006 Conference.* New York, NY: ACM Press.

Hey, T., & Trefethen, A. (2008). E-science, cyber-infrastructure, and scholarly communication. In Olson, G., Zimmerman, A., & Bos, N. (Eds.), *Scientific Collaboration on the Internet* (pp. 15–33). Cambridge, MA: MIT Press.

Hill, R. A., & Dunbar, R. I. M. (2003). Social Network Size in Humans. *Human Nature (Hawthorne, N.Y.), 14*(1), 53–72. doi:10.1007/s12110-003-1016-y

Hiltz, S. R. (1984). *Online communities: A case study of the office of the future.* Norwood, NJ: Ablex.

Hislop, D. (2003). The Complex Relations between Communities of Practice and the Implementation of Technological Innovations. *International Journal of Innovation Management, 7*(2), 163–188. doi:10.1142/S1363919603000775

Hofacker, C. F., Goldsmith, R. E., Bridges, E., & Swilley, E. (2006). E-Services: A Synthesis and Research Agenda. *Journal of Value Chain Management, 1*(1), 13–44.

Hoffman, D. L., Novak, T. P., & Peralta, M. A. (1999). Building Consumer Trust Online. *Communications of the ACM, 42*(4), 80–85. doi:10.1145/299157.299175

Hofstede, G. (1980). *Culture's Consequences: International Differences in Work-Related Values.* Thousand Oaks, CA: Sage.

Hofstede, G. (1991). *Cultures and Organizations—Software of the Mind.* London: McGraw-Hill.

Hofstede, G., & Bond, M. (1984). Hofstede's culture dimensions: An independent validation using Rokeach's Value Survey. *Journal of Cross-Cultural Psychology, 15*(4), 417–433. doi:10.1177/0022002184015004003

Hogg, M. A., & Terry, D. J. (2000). Social identity and self-categorization processes in organizational contexts. *Academy of Management Review, 25*(1), 121–140. doi:10.2307/259266

Hogg, M., Terry, D., & White, K. (1995). A tale of two theories: A critical comparison of identity theory with social identity theory. *Social Psychology Quarterly, 58,* 255–269. doi:10.2307/2787127

Holahan, C. (2006). Q&A with Amanda Congdon. *BusinessWeek.* Retrieved from http://www.businessweek.com/technology/content/nov2006/tc20061114_907330.htm

Hollenbeck, J. R., & Klein, H. J. (1987). Goal commitment and the goal-setting process: Problems, prospects, and proposals for future research. *The Journal of Applied Psychology, 72,* 212–220. doi:10.1037/0021-9010.72.2.212

Holton, G., Berez, A., & Williams, S. (2007). Building the Dena'ina language Alaska archive. In Dyson, L. E., Hendriks, M., & Grant, S. (Eds.), *Information technology and indigenous people* (pp. 205–208). Hershey, PA: Idea Group Publishing.

Hornsey, M. J., & Hogg, M. A. (2000). Assimilation and diversity: An integrative model of subgroup relations. *Personality and Social Psychology Review, 4,* 143–156. doi:10.1207/S15327957PSPR0402_03

Horowitz, E. (2008). Befriending your boss on Facebook. *The Age.* Retrieved March 28, 2009, from http://thebigchair.com.au/news/career-couch/befriending-your-boss-on-facebook

Hsu, M. K., Wang, S. W., & Chiu, K. K. (2009). Computer attitude, statistics anxiety and self-efficacy on statistical software adoption behavior: An empirical study of on-line MBA learners. *Computers in Human Behavior, 25,* 412–420. doi:10.1016/j.chb.2008.10.003

Huang, C. Y., Shen, Y. Z., Lin, H. X., & Chang, S. S. (2007). Bloggers' Motivations and Behaviors: A Model. *Journal of Advertising Research, 47*(4), 472–484. doi:10.2501/S0021849907070493

Huang, E. (2008). Use and gratification in e-consumers. *Internet Research, 18*(4), 405–426. doi:10.1108/10662240810897817

Huijser, H. (2007). *Exploring the Educational Potential of Social Networking Sites.* Toowoomba, Queensland, Australia: University of Southern Queensland.

Hu, L. T., & Bentler, P. M. (1999). Cut-off criteria for fit indexes in covariance structure analysis: conventional criteria versus new alternatives. *Structural Equation Modeling, 6,* 1–55. doi:10.1080/10705519909540118

Igbaria, M., Parasuraman, S., & Baroudi, J. (1996). A motivational model of microcomputer usage. *Journal of Management Information Systems, 13*(1), 127–143.

Indik, B. P. (1965). Organization size and member participation. *Human Relations, 18,* 339–350. doi:10.1177/001872676501800403

International, Q. S. R. (2010). *NVivo qualitative data analysis software.* Doncaster, VIC, Australia: Author.

Internet world statistics. (2009). Retrieved November 14, 2009, from http://www.internetworldstats.com/stats.htm

Ishii, K., & Morihiro, O. (2007). Links between Real and Virtual Networks: A Comparative Study of Online Communities in Japan and Korea. *Cyberpsychology & Behavior, 10*(2), 252–257. doi:10.1089/cpb.2006.9961

Ito, M., Horst, A. H., Bittanti, M., Boyd, D., Herr-Stephenson, B., & Lange, G. P. (n.d.). *Living and Learning with New Media: Summary of Findings from the Digital Youth Project.* The John D. and Catherine T. *MacArthur Foundation Reports on Digital Media and Learning.*

Jamali, M., & Ester, M. (2009). TrustWalker: A Random Walk Model for Combining Trust-based and Item-based Recommendation. In *Proceedings of the 15th ACM SIG-KDD International Conference on Knowledge Discovery and Data Mining,* Paris (pp. 397-406).

Jarvenpa, L., & Leidner, D. E. (1999). Communication and trust in global virtual teams. *Organization Science, 10,* 791–815. doi:10.1287/orsc.10.6.791

Jason, A., Scott, A., & LePine, A. (2007). Trust, trustworthiness, and trust propensity: A meta-analytic test of their unique relationships with risk taking and job performance. *The Journal of Applied Psychology, 92*(4), 909–927. doi:10.1037/0021-9010.92.4.909

Jawecki, G., Fueller, J., & Verona, G. (2008). Innovative Consumer Behavior in Online Communities. In *Advances in Consumer Research - European Conference Proceedings* (Vol. 8, pp: 513-518).

Jenkins, H. (2006a). *Convergence Culture: Where Old and New Media Collide.* New York: New York University Press.

Jian, G., & Jeffres, L. W. (2006). Understanding employees' willingness to contribute to shared electronic databases: A three-dimensional framework. *Communication Research, 33,* 242–261. doi:10.1177/0093650206289149

Jones, Q., & Rafaeli, S. (2000). What do virtual 'Tells' tell? Placing cybersociety research into a hierarchy of social explanation. In *Proceedings of the 33rd Hawaii International Conference on System Sciences.* Washington, DC: IEEE Computer Society.

Jones, C., Hesterly, W. S., & Borgatti, S. P. (1997). A general theory of network governance: Exchange conditions and social mechanisms. *Academy of Management Review, 22*(4), 911–945. doi:10.2307/259249

Jones, Q. (1997). Virtual-Communities, Virtual Settlements & Cyber-Archaeology: A Theoretical Outline. *Journal of Computer-Mediated Communication, 3*(3).

Jordan, K., Hauser, J., & Foster, S. (2003). The Augmented Social Network: Building identity and trust into the next-generation Internet. *First Monday, 8*(8).

Jøsang, A., & Ismail, R. (2002). The beta reputation system. In *Proceedings of the 15th Bled Electronic Commerce Conference,* Bled, Slovenia (pp. 1-14).

Josefsson, U. (2005). Coping with Illness Online: The Case of Patients Online Communities. *The Information Society, 21*(2), 143–153. doi:10.1080/01972240590925357

Josefsson, U., & Ranerup, A. (2003). Consumerism Revisited: The Emergent Roles of New Electronic Intermediaries between Citizens and the Public Sector. *Information Polity: The International Journal of Government & Democracy in the Information Age, 8*(3/4), 167–180.

Kacmar, K. M., Witt, L. A., Zivnuska, S., & Gully, S. M. (2003). The interactive effect of leader-member exchange and communication frequency on performance ratings. *The Journal of Applied Psychology, 88,* 764–772. doi:10.1037/0021-9010.88.4.764

Kallinikos, J. (2006). *The consequences of information: Institutional implications of technical change.* Cheltenham, UK: Edward Elgar.

Kaplan, B., & Maxwell, J. A. (1994). Qualitative Research Methods for Evaluating Computer Information Systems. In Anderson, G. J., Aydin, E. C., & Jay, J. S. (Eds.), *Evaluating Health Care Information Systems: Methods and Applications* (pp. 45–68). Thousand Oaks, CA: Sage.

Kardaras, D., & Karakostas, B. (in press). *Services Customization Using Web Technologies.* Hershey, PA: IGI Global.

Karl, K., Peluchette, J., & Schlaegel, C. (2010). A cross-cultural examination of student attitudes and gender differences in Facebook profile content. *International Journal of Virtual Communities and Social Networking, 2*(2), 11–31.

Karreman, D., & Alvesson, M. (2001). Making Newsmakers: Conversational Identity at Work. *Organization Studies, 22*(1), 59–89. doi:10.1177/017084060102200103

Keahey, K., Foster, I., Freeman, T., & Zhang, X. (2005). Virtual workspaces: Achieving quality of service and quality of life in the grid. *Scientific Programming Journal, 13*(4), 265–276.

Keating, B., Rugimband, R., & Quzai, A. (2003). Differentiating between Service Quality and Relationship Quality in Cyberspace. *Managing Service Quality, 13*(3), 217–232. doi:10.1108/09604520310476481

Keegan, T. T., Cunningham, S. J., & Apperley, M. (2007). Indigenous language usage in a bilingual interface: Transaction log analysis of the Niupepa web site. In Dyson, L. E., Hendriks, M., & Grant, S. (Eds.), *Information technology and indigenous people* (pp. 175–188). Hershey, PA: Idea Group Publishing.

Kelly, C. (2009, August 15). Fired on Facebook: Don't rip boss when he's your 'friend'; Woman let go after rant: 'I guess you forgot about adding me on here?' *The Toronto Star*, A03.

Kiesler, S. (1986). The Hidden Messages in Computer Networks. *Harvard Business Review, 64*, 46–60.

Kim, Y., Le, M. T., Lauw, H. W., Lim, E. P., Liu, H., & Srivastava, J. (2008). Building a Web of Trust without Explicit Trust Ratings. In *Proceedings of the 2008 IEEE 24th International Conference on Data Engineering Workshop,* Cancun, Mexico (pp. 531 - 536).

Kim, A. (2000). *Community Building on the Web*. Berkeley, CA: Peachpit Press.

Kimble, C. (2011). Building effective virtual teams: How to overcome the problems of trust and identity in virtual teams. *Global Business and Organizational Excellence, 30*(2), 6–15. doi:10.1002/joe.20364

Kimble, C., Grenier, C., & Goglio-Primard, K. (2010). Innovation and knowledge sharing across professional boundaries: Political interplay between boundary objects and brokers. *International Journal of Information Management, 30*(5), 437–444. doi:10.1016/j.ijinfomgt.2010.02.002

Kimble, C., & Hildreth, P. (2005). Dualities, distributed communities of practice and knowledge management. *Journal of Knowledge Management, 9*(4), 102–113. doi:10.1108/13673270510610369

Kimble, C., Li, F., & Barlow, A. (2000). *Effective Virtual Teams through Communities of Practice*. Glasgow, UK: University of Strathclyde.

Kim, D. J., Ferrin, D. L., & Rao, H. R. (2008). A trust-based consumer decision-making model in electronic commerce: The role of trust, perceived risk, and their antecedents. *Decision Support Systems, 44*(2), 544–564. doi:10.1016/j.dss.2007.07.001

Kim, G. S., Oh, J., & Park, S. B. (2008). An examination of factors influencing consumer adoption of short message service (SMS). *Psychology and Marketing, 25*(8), 769–786. doi:10.1002/mar.20238

Kirkman, B., Rosen, B., Tesluk, P. E., & Gibson, C. B. (2004). The impact of team empowerment on virtual team performance: The moderating role of face-to-face interaction. *Academy of Management Journal, 47*, 175–192.

Kleinman, G., Palmon, D., & Lee, P. (2003). The effects of personal and group level factors on the outcomes of simulated auditor and client teams. *Group Decision and Negotiation, 12*, 57–84. doi:10.1023/A:1022256730300

Ko, H., Cho, C., & Roberts, M. S. (2005). Internet Uses and Gratifications: A Structural Equation Model of Interactive Advertising. *Journal of Advertising, 34*(2), 57–71.

Koh, J., Kim, Y., Butler, B., & Bock, G. (2007). Encouraging Participation in Virtual Communities. *Communications of the ACM, 50*(2), 69–73. doi:10.1145/1216016.1216023

Koku, E., Nazer, N., & Wellman, B. (2001). Netting scholars: online and offline. *The American Behavioral Scientist, 44*(10), 1752–1774. doi:10.1177/00027640121958023

Kollock, P., & Smith, M. (1999). *Communities in cyberspace*. London, UK: Routledge.

Kopytoff, V. (2004, February 9). Clicking for Connections. *San Francisco Chronicle*, E-1. Retrieved October 13, 2004, from http://sfgate.com/cgi-bin/article.cgi?file=/c/a/2004/02/09/BUGMD4RAMALDTL

Korzenny, F. (2009). *Marketing Trends in a new Multi-Cultural Society*. Retrieved April 10, 2010, from http://felipekorzenny.blogspot.com/2009/02/multicultural-world-of-social-media.html

Kotha, S. (1995). Mass Customization: Implementing the Emerging Paradigm for Competitive Advantage. *Strategic Management Journal, 16*, 21–42. doi:10.1002/smj.4250160916

Kow, M.P.M. (2009). *Feasibility study on sourcing of passive candidates via social networking sites.*

Kraft, P., & Dubnoff, S. (1986). Job Content, Fragmentation and Control in Computer Software Work. *Industrial Relations, 25*(2), 184–196. doi:10.1111/j.1468-232X.1986.tb00679.x

Kramer, M. R. (2006). Social Identity and Social Capital: The Collective Self at Work. *International Public Management Journal, 9*(1), 25–45. doi:10.1080/10967490600625316

Krämer, N. C., & Winter, S. (2008). Impression management 2.0: The relationship of self-esteem, extraversion, self-efficacy, and self-presentation within social networking sites. *Journal of Media Psychology: Theories, Methods, and Applications, 20*(3), 106–116. doi:10.1027/1864-1105.20.3.106

Kramer, R. M. (1999). Trust and distrust in organizations: Emerging perspectives, enduring questions. *Annual Review of Psychology, 50*(1), 569–598. doi:10.1146/annurev.psych.50.1.569

Kratochvil, M., & Carson, C. (2005). *Growing Modular: Mass Customization of Complex Products, Services and Software*. Berlin: Springer.

Krebs, V., & Holley, J. (2002). *Building Smart Communities Through Network Weaving*. Retrieved from http://www.orgnet.com/BuildingNetworks.pdf

Kroker, A. (1994). *Data Trash: The Theory of the Virtual Class*. Montreal, Quebec, Canada: New World Perspectives.

Kumar, R., Novak, J., Raghaven, P., & Tomkins, A. (2004). Structure and Evolution of Blogspace. *Communications of the ACM, 47*(12), 35–39. doi:10.1145/1035134.1035162

Kunda, G., & Van Maanen, J. (1999). *Changing Scripts at Work: Managers and Professionals*. Paper presented at the ANNALS, AAPSS (p. 561).

Kunda, G. (1992). *Engineering culture: control and commitment in a high-tech corporation*. Philadelphia: Temple University Press.

Kunda, G., Barley, S. R., & Evans, J. (2002). Why do contractors contract? The experience of highly skilled technical professionals in a contingent labor market. *Industrial & Labor Relations Review, 55*(2), 234–261. doi:10.2307/2696207

Kwan, M., & Ramachandran, D. (2009). Trust and Online Reputation Systemse. In J. Golbeck (Ed.), *Computing with Social Trust* (pp. 287-311). London: Spring.

Lampe, C., Ellison, N., & Steinfeld, C. (2007). A familiar Face(book): Profile elements as signals in an online social network. In *Proceedings of the Conference on Human Factors in Computing System* (pp. 435-444). New York: ACM Press.

Lampe, C., Ellison, N., & Steinfield, C. (2006). A Face(book) in the crowd: Social searching vs. social browsing. In *Proceedings of the 2006 20th Anniversary Conference on Computer Supported Cooperative Work* (pp. 167-170). New York: ACM Press.

Lampinen, A., Tamminen, S., & Oulasvirta, A. (2009). "All my people right here, right now": Management of group co-presence on a social networking site. In [New York: ACM Press.]. *Proceedings of GROUP, 2009*, 81–290.

Lanseng, E., & Andreassen, T. (2007). Electronic Healthcare: A Study of People's Readiness and Aattitude toward Performing Self-Diagnosis. *International Journal of Service Industry Management, 18*(4), 394–417. doi:10.1108/09564230710778155

Latour, B. (1987). *Science in action: How to follow scientists and engineers through society*. Cambridge, MA: Harvard University Press.

Latour, B. (2005). *Reassembling the social: An introduction to actor-network-theory*. Oxford, UK: Oxford University Press.

Laubacher, R. J., & Malone, T. W. (1997). *Flexible work arrangements and the 21st century workers' guilds*. Cambridge, MA: MIT.

Lave, J. (1988). *Cognition in Practice: Mind, Mathematics and Culture in Everyday Life*. New York: Cambridge University Press. doi:10.1017/CBO9780511609268

Lave, J., & Wenger, E. (1991). *Situated Learning: Legitimate Peripheral Participation*. Cambridge, UK: Cambridge University Press.

Law, J., & Mol, A. (2002). *Complexities: Social Studies of Knowledge Practices*. Durham, NC: Duke University Press.

Lea, M., O'Shea, T., Fung, P., & Spears, R. (1992). 'Flaming☐ in computer-mediated communication: Observations, explanations, implications. In Lea, M. (Ed.), *Contexts of computer-mediated communication* (pp. 89–112). London, UK: Harvester-Wheatsheaf.

Leary, M. R. (1996). *Self Presentation – Impression Management and Interpersonal Behavior*. Boulder, CO: Westview.

Leavy, B. (2007). Digital songlines: Digitising the arts, culture and heritage landscape of aboriginal Australia. In Dyson, L. E., Hendriks, M., & Grant, S. (Eds.), *Information technology and indigenous people* (pp. 159–169). Hershey, PA: Idea Group Publishing.

Lechner, U., & Hummel, J. (2002). Business Models and System Architectures of Virtual Communities: From a Sociological Phenomenon to Peer-to-Peer Architectures. *International Journal of Electronic Commerce, 6*(3), 41–53.

Leclair, C., & Warren, S. (2007). Portals and potlatch. In Dyson, L. E., Hendriks, M., & Grant, S. (Eds.), *Information technology and indigenous people* (pp. 1–13). Hershey, PA: Idea Group Publishing.

Lee, M. K. O., Cheung, C. M. K., & Chen, Z. H. (2007). Understanding user acceptance of multimedia messaging services: An empirical study. *Journal of the American Society for Information Science and Technology, 58*(13), 2066–2077. doi:10.1002/asi.20670

Leimeister, J., Ebner, W., & Krcmar, H. (2005). Design, Implementation, and Evaluation of Trust-Supporting Components in Virtual Communities for Patients. *Journal of Management Information Systems, 21*(4), 101–135.

Leitheiser, L. R. (1992). MIS Skills for the 1990s: A Survey of MIS Managers's Perceptions. *Journal of Management Information Systems, 9*(1), 69–91.

Leonard, A. (2004, June 15). You are who you know. *Salon.com Technology.* Retrieved October 13, 2004, from http://www.salon.com/tech/feature/2004/06/15/social_soctware_one/

Lesani, M., & Bagheri, S. (2006). Applying and Inferring Fuzzy Trust in Semantic Web Social Networks. In *Canadian Semantic Web* (pp. 23–43). New York: Springer. doi:10.1007/978-0-387-34347-1_3

Leskovec, J., Adamic, L., & Huberman, B. (2007). The dynamics of viral marketing. *ACM Transactions on the Web, 1*(1).

Lesser, E. L., & Storck, J. (2001). Communities of practice and organisational performance. *IBM Systems Journal, 40*(4), 831–841.

Lesser, E., & Prusak, L. (1999). Communities of Practice, social capital and organizational knowledge. *Information Systems Research, 1*(1), 3–9.

Levien, L. (2002). *Attack resistant trust metrics.* Unpublished PhD thesis, Department of Computer Science, University of California, Berkeley.

Lewis, C., & George, J. (2008). Cross-cultural deception in social networking sites and face-to-face communication. *Computers in Human Behavior, 24*(6), 2945–2964. doi:10.1016/j.chb.2008.05.002

Lewis, K., Kaufman, J., & Christakis, N. (2008). The taste of privacy: An analysis of college student privacy settings in an online social network. *Journal of Computer-Mediated Communication, 14*(1), 79–100. doi:10.1111/j.1083-6101.2008.01432.x

Lewis, R. (1997). An Activity Theory framework to explore distributed communities. *Journal of Computer Assisted Learning, 13,* 210–218. doi:10.1046/j.1365-2729.1997.00023.x

Liao, C. H., Tsou, C. W., & Huang, M. F. (2007). Factors influencing the usage of 3G mobile services in Taiwan. *Online Information Review, 31*(6), 759–774. doi:10.1108/14684520710841757

Liebermann, Y., & Stashevsky, S. (2002). Perceived risks as barriers to Internet and ecommerce usage. *Qualitative Market Research: An International Journal, 5*(4), 291–300. doi:10.1108/13522750210443245

Lin, Y., Sundaram, H., Chi, Y., Tatemura, J., & Tseng, B. (2006, May 23). Discovery of Blog communities based on Mutual Awareness. In *Proceedings of the 3rd Annual Workshop on the Weblogging Ecosystems: Aggregation, Analysis and Dynamics, WWW2006*, Edinburgh, UK.

Lin, C., Hu, P. J., & Chen, H. (2004). Technology Implementation Management in Law Enforcement. *Social Science Computer Review, 22*(1), 24–36. doi:10.1177/0894439303259881

Lindkvist, L. (2005). Knowledge Communities and Knowledge Collectivities: A Typology of Knowledge Work in Groups. *Journal of Management Studies*, *42*(6), 1189–1210. doi:10.1111/j.1467-6486.2005.00538.x

Lin, H.-F. (2007). The role of online and offline features in sustaining virtual communities: an empirical study. *Internet Research*, *17*(2). doi:10.1108/10662240710736997

Lin, H., & Lee, G. (2006). Determinants of Success for Online Communities: An Empirical Study. *Behaviour & Information Technology*, *25*(6), 479–488. doi:10.1080/01449290500330422

Liu, G. Z. (1999). Virtual Community Presence in Internet Relay Chatting. *Computer Supported Cooperative Work*, *5*(1). Retrieved from http://jcmc.indiana.edu/vol5/issue1/liu.html.

Locke, E. A. (1969). What is job satisfaction? *Organizational Behavior and Human Performance*, *4*(4), 309–336. doi:10.1016/0030-5073(69)90013-0

Locke, E. A., & Latham, G. P. (1990). *A theory of goal setting and task performance*. Englewood Cliffs, NJ: Prentice-Hall.

Lock, J. V. (2002). Laying the groundwork for the development of learning communities with online courses. *Quarterly Review of Distance Education*, *3*, 395–408.

Long, Y., & Siau, K. (2006). Social Network Dynamics for Open Source Software Projects. In *Proceedings of the Americas Conference on Information Systems*, Acapulco, Mexico.

Lu, H., & Ali, A. (2004). Prevent Online Identity Theft – Using Network Smart Cards for Secure Online Transactions. In *Information Security* (LNCS 3225, pp. 342-353).

Lu, Y., Zhao, L., & Wang, B. (2009). From virtual community members to C2C e-commerce buyers: Trust in virtual communities and its effect on consumers' purchase intention. *Electronic Commerce Research and Applications*. doi:10.1016 /j.elerap.2009.07.003

Luers, W. (2007). Cinema Without Show Business: A Poetics of Vlogging. *Post Identity*, *5*(1). Retrieved from http://hdl.handle.net/2027/spo.pid9999.0005.2105.

Lytras, M. D. (2009). *Web 2.0 The Business Model*. New York: Springer.

Ma, N. L. (2009). Trust Relationship Prediction Using Online Product Review Data. In *Proceedings of the 1st ACM International Workshop on Complex Networks Meet Information & Knowledge Management*, Hong Kong, China (pp. 47-54).

Macaulay, L., Keeling, K., McGoldrick, P., Dafoulas, G., Kalaitzakis, E., & Keeling, D. (2007). Coevolving E-tail and On-Line Communities: Conceptual Framework. *International Journal of Electronic Commerce*, *11*(4), 53–77. doi:10.2753/JEC1086-4415110402

Madden, M., Fox, S., & Smith, A. (2007). *Digital footprints: Online identity management and search in the age of transparency*. Washington, DC: Pew Internet and American Life Project. Retrieved October 31, 2010, from http://www.pewinternet.org/PPF/r/229/report_display.asp

Madrigal, R. (2001). Social identity effects in a belief-attitude-intentions hierarchy: Implications for corporate sponsorship. *Psychology and Marketing*, *18*, 145–165. doi:10.1002/1520-6793(200102)18:2<145::AID-MAR1003>3.0.CO;2-T

Mael, F., & Tetrick, L. (1992). Identifying organizational identification. *Educational and Psychological Measurement*, *54*, 813–824. doi:10.1177/0013164492052004002

Magnuson, M., & Dundes, L. (2008). Gender differences in "social portraits" reflected in MySpace profile. *Cyberpsychology & Behavior*, *11*(2), 239–241. doi:10.1089/cpb.2007.0089

Malhotra, Y., & Galletta, D. F. (1999, January 4-7). Extending the Technology Acceptance Model to Account for Social Influence: Theoretical Bases and Empirical Validation. In *Proceedings of the 32nd Hawaii International Conference on System Sciences (HICSS-32)*. Washington, DC: IEEE Computer Society.

Ma, M., & Agarwal, R. (2007). Through a Glass Darkly: Information Technology Design, Identity Verification, and Knowledge Contribution in Online Communities. *Information Systems Research*, *18*(1), 42–67. doi:10.1287/isre.1070.0113

Manovich, L. (2008). The Practice of Everyday (Media) Life. In Lovink, G., & Sabine, N. (Eds.), *Video Vortex Reader: Responses to YouTube* (pp. 33–44). Amsterdam, The Netherlands: Institute of Network Cultures.

Marchand, M. E., & Winchell, R. (1992). Tribal implementation of GIS: a case study of planning applications with the Colville Confederated Tribes. *American Indian Culture and Research Journal, 16*(4), 175–183.

Marcus, B., Machilek, F., & Schutz, A. (2006). Personality in cyberspace: Personal web sites as media for personality and impressions. *Journal of Personality and Social Psychology, 90*(6), 1014–1031. doi:10.1037/0022-3514.90.6.1014

Marsh, S. (1994). *Formalising Trust as a Computational Concept.* Unpublished PhD thesis, University of Stirling, California.

Martinez Aleman, M. A., Lynk Wartman, K., & Ana, M. A. (2009). *Online Social Networking on Campus: Understanding What Matters in Student Culture.* London: Taylor & Francis.

Massa, P., & Avesani, P. (2005). Controversial users demand local trust metrics: An experimental study on epinions.com community. In *Proceedings of the 20th National Conference on Artificial Intelligence,*(pp.121-126). AAAI Press

Mathieu, J. E., & Zajac, D. M. (1990). A review and meta-analysis of the antecedents, correlates, and consequences of organizational commitment. *Psychological Bulletin, 108*, 171–194. doi:10.1037/0033-2909.108.2.171

Mayer, R. C., Davis, J. H., & Schoorman, F. D. (1995). An integration model of organizational trust. *Academy of Management Review, 20*(1), 709–734. doi:10.2307/258792

McAfee, A., & Oliveau, F.X. (2002). Confronting the limits of networks. *MIT Sloan Management Review, Summer*, 85-87.

McCalla, G. (2000). The fragmentation of culture, learning, teaching and technology: Implications for artificial intelligence in education research. *International Journal of Artificial Intelligence, 11*(2), 177–196.

McCarthy, C. (2009, February 10). Whee! New numbers on social network usage. *CNET News, The Social.* Retrieved February 25, 2009, from http://news.cnet.com/8301-13577_3-10160850-36.html

McDonald, B., Noakes, N., Stuckey, B., & Nyrop, S. (2005). *Breaking down learner isolation: How social network analysis informs design and facilitation for online learning.* Retrieved February 4, 2011, from http://cpsquare.org/wp-content/uploads/2008/07/stuckey-etal-aera-sna.pdf

McLuhan, M., & Powers, B. R. (1989). *The Global Village: Transformations in World Life and Media in the 21st Century.* New York, NY: Oxford University Press.

McLure Wasko, M., & Faraj, S. (2005). Why Should I Share? Examining Social Capital And Knowledge Contribution in Electronic Networks Of Practice. *Management Information Systems Quarterly, 29*(1), 35–57.

McMillan, D. W., & Chavis, D. M. (1986). Sense of community: A definition and theory. *American Journal of Community Psychology, 14*(1), 6–23. doi:10.1002/1520-6629(198601)14:1<6::AID-JCOP2290140103>3.0.CO;2-I

Mead, H. G. (1934). *Mind, self, and society: from the standpoint of a behaviorist.* Chicago: The University of Chicago Press.

Metzger, M. J., & Docter, S. (2003). Public opinion and policy initiatives for online privacy protection. *Journal of Broadcasting & Electronic Media, 47*(3), 350–374. doi:10.1207/s15506878jobem4703_3

Meuter, M. L., Bitner, M. J., Ostrom, A. L., & Brown, S. W. (2005). Choosing among Alternative Service Delivery Modes: An Investigation of Customer Trial of Self-Service Technologies. *Journal of Marketing, 69*(2), 61–83. doi:10.1509/jmkg.69.2.61.60759

Meyrowitz, J. (1985). *No Sense of Place.* New York: Oxford University Press.

Meyrowitz, J. (1989). The Generalized Elsewhere. *Critical Studies in Mass Communication, 6*(3), 323–334.

Meyrowitz, J. (1997). Shifting Worlds of Strangers: Medium Theory and Changes in "them" versus "us". *Sociological Inquiry, 67*(1), 59–71. doi:10.1111/j.1475-682X.1997.tb00429.x

Miles, A. (2007). New Media Studies and the New Internet Cinema. *Post Identity, 5*(1). Retrieved from http://hdl.handle.net/2027/spo.pid9999.0005.2102

Miles, A. (2003). Softvideography. In Eskelinen, M., & Koskimaa, R. (Eds.), *Cybertext Yearbook 2002-2003* (pp. 218–236). Saarijarvi, Finland: University of Jyvaskyla.

Miles, A. (2006). A Vision for Genuine Rich Media Blogging. In Bruns, A., & Jacobs, J. (Eds.), *Uses of Blogs* (pp. 213–222). New York: Peter Lang.

Miller, C. J. (1998). The social impacts of televised media among the Yucatec Maya. *Human Organization, 57*(3), 307–314.

Miller, D., & Slater, D. (2000). *The Internet- an Ethnographic Approach*. Oxford, UK: Berg Publishers.

Miller, V. (2008). New Media, Networking and Phatic Culture. *Convergence: The International Journal of Research into New Media Technologies, 14*(4), 387–400. doi:10.1177/1354856508094659

Mitrano, T. (2008). Facebook 2.0. *EDUCAUSE Review, 43*(2). Retrieved from http://connect.educause.edu/Library/EDUCAUSE+Review/Facebook20/46324.

Monastersky, R. (2005). *The number that's devouring science*. The Chronicle of Higher Education.

Monmonier, M. (1996). *How to Lie with Maps*. Chicago: University of Chicago Press.

Montaner, M. L. (2002). Opinion-based filtering through trust. In *Proceedings of the Sixth International Workshop on Cooperative Information Agents,* Madrid, Spain (pp. 164-178). Berlin: Springer-Verlag.

Moon, J., & Kim, Y. (2001). Extending the TAM for a World-Wide-Web Context. *Information & Management, 38*(4), 217–230. doi:10.1016/S0378-7206(00)00061-6

Moore, M. N. (1989). Tenure and the university reward structure. *Nursing Research, 38*(2), 111–116. doi:10.1097/00006199-198903000-00015

Moorman, C., Deshpande, R., & Zaltman, G. (1993). Factors affecting trust in market research relationships. *Journal of Marketing, 57*, 81–102. doi:10.2307/1252059

Morgan, T. (2009, February 27). Fired for saying my job was boring on Facebook. *The Express, 43*.

Mowday, R. T., Porter, L. W., & Steers, R. M. (1982). *Employee-organization linkages: The psychology of commitment, absenteeism, and turnover*. New York: Academic Press.

Mui, L., Mohtashemi, M., & Halberstadt, A. (2002). A computational model of trust and reputation. In *Proceedings of the 35th International Conference on System Science* (pp. 280-287). Washington, DC: IEEE Computer Society.

Müller, K. (2010). Museums and Virtuality, Museums and Virtuality. *Curator: The Museum Journal, 45*, 21–33.

Murdoch, J. (2006). *Post-structuralist geography: A guide to relational space*. London: Sage.

Murray, K. E., & Waller, R. (2007). Social networking goes abroad. *International Educator, 16*(3), 56–59.

Nardi, A. B., Whittaker, S., & Schwarz, H. (2002). NetWORKers and their activity in Intentional Networks. *Activity Theory and the Practice of Design, 11*(1-2), 205–242.

Nardi, B. A., Schiano, D. J., Gumbrecht, M., & Swartz, L. (2004). Why We Blog. *Communications of the ACM, 47*(12), 41–46. doi:10.1145/1035134.1035163

Nederveen-Pieterse, J. (2004). *Globalization and Culture: Global Melange*. MD: Rowman and Littlefield Publishers.

Nelson, R., Todd, P., & Wixom, B. (2005). Antecedents of Information and System Quality: An Empirical Examination within the Context of Data Warehousing. *Journal of Management Information Systems, 21*(4), 199–235.

Nesbitt, S., & Marriott, C. (2007, October 29). 'Caught in the net'. *The Lawyer*, 30-33.

New Media. (n.d.). In *Wikipedia*. Retrieved November 24, 2009, from http://en.wikipedia.org/wiki/New_media

Newman, A. C., & Thomas, J. G. (2009). *Enterprise 2.0 Implementation*. New York: McGraw-Hill.

Nicolini, D., Gherardi, S., & Yanow, D. (2003). Introduction. In Nicolini, D., Gherardi, S., & Yanow, D. (Eds.), *Organizational Knowledge as Practice* (pp. 3–31). Armonk, NY: ME Sharpe.

Noll, L. C., & Wlikins, M. (2002). Critical Skills for IS Professionals: A model for a Curriculum Development. *Journal of Information Technology Education, 1*(3), 145–154.

Norazah, M. S., Ramayah, T., & Norbayah, M. S. (2008). Internet shopping acceptance: examining the influence of intrinsic versus extrinsic motivations. *Direct Marketing: An International Journal, 2*(2), 97–110. doi:10.1108/17505930810881752

Norman, D. A. (1996). Cognitive engineering. In Norman, D. A., & Draper, S. W. (Eds.), *User centered systems design-new persepectives on human-computer interaction* (pp. 31–61). Hillsdal, NJ: Lawrence Erlbaum.

Norris, P. (2001). *Digital Divide*. Cambridge, UK: Cambridge University Press.

Nurmi, D., Wolski, R., Grzegorczyk, C., Obertelli, G., Soman, S., Youseff, L., et al. (2009). The Eucalyptus open-source Cloud-computing System. In *Proceedings of 9th IEEE International Symposium on Cluster Computing and the Grid (CCGrid 09)*, Shanghai, China.

O'Brien, T. (2007). *Females flock to Facebook to post pictures of their drunken antics*. Retrieved from http://www.switched.com/2007/11/06/females-flock-to-facebook-to-post-pictures-of their-drunken-antics/

O'Donovan, J. A. (2009). Using Trust in Social Web Applications. In Golbeck, J. (Ed.), *In Computing with Social Trust* (pp. 213–257). London: Springer. doi:10.1007/978-1-84800-356-9_9

Ofcom. (2008). *Social Networking: A quantitative and qualitative research report into attitudes, behaviours and use*. Retrieved from http://www.ofcom.org.uk

Ogata, H., & Yano, Y. (2000). Combining knowledge awareness and information filtering in an open-ended collaborative learning environment. *International Journal of Artificial Intelligence in Education, 11*, 33–46.

Oh, S., Ahn, J., & Kim, B. (2003). Adoption of broadband Internet in Korea: The role of experience in building attitudes. *Journal of Information Technology, 18*, 267–280. doi:10.1080/0268396032000150807

Olson, G., & Olson, J. (2003). Mitigating the effects of distance on collaborative intellectual work. *Economics of Innovation and New Technology, 12*(1), 27–42. doi:10.1080/10438590303117

Olson, J., Hofer, E., Bos, N., Zimmerman, A., Olson, G. D., Cooney, G., & Faniel, I. (2008). A theory of remote scientific collaboration. In Olson, G., Zimmerman, A., & Bos, N. (Eds.), *Scientific Collaboration on the Internet* (pp. 73–99). Cambridge, MA: MIT Press.

Organ, D. W. (1988). *Organizational Behavior*. Lexington, MA: Lexington Books.

Orlikowski, J. W. (2000). Using Technology and Constituting Structures: A Practice Lens for Studying Technology in Organizations. *Organization Science, 11*(4), 404–428. doi:10.1287/orsc.11.4.404.14600

Orlikowski, J. W. (2002). Knowing in Practice: Enacting a Collective Capability in Distributed Organizing. *Organization Science, 13*, 249–273. doi:10.1287/orsc.13.3.249.2776

Orlikowski, J. W., & Baroudi, J. J. (1991). Studying Information Technology in Organizations: research approaches and assumptions. *Information Systems Research, 2*(1), 1–28. doi:10.1287/isre.2.1.1

Osnowitz, D. (2006). Occupational Networking as Normative Control: Collegial Exchange Among Contract Professionals. *Work and Occupations, 33*(1), 12–41. doi:10.1177/0730888405280160

Osterwalder, A. (2004). *The Business Model Ontology*. Unpublished doctoral dissertation, HEC, Lusanne, Switzerland.

Osti, L., Turner, W. L., & King, B. (2009). Cultural differences in travel guidebooks information search. *Journal of Vacation Marketing, 15*(1), 63–78. doi:10.1177/1356766708098172

Ouchi, G. W. (1980). Markets, Bureaucracies and Clans. *Administrative Science Quarterly, 25*, 129–141. doi:10.2307/2392231

Page, L., Brin, S., Motwani, R., & Winograd, T. (1998). *The PageRank citation ranking: bringing order to the Web*. Palo Alto, CA: Stanford University.

Palmer, M. (2007). Cut from the same cloth: The United States Bureau of Indian Affairs, geographic information systems, and cultural assimilation. In Dyson, L. E., Hendriks, M., & Grant, S. (Eds.), *Information technology and indigenous people* (pp. 220–231). Hershey, PA: Idea Group Publishing.

Palmer, M. (2009). Engaging with Indigital geographic information networks. *Futures*, *41*, 33–40. doi:10.1016/j.futures.2008.07.006

Palmer, N., Batola, J., Jones, M., & Baron, S. (2007). *Social networking sites within Higher Education – threat or opportunity?* Southampton, UK: Southampton Solent University.

Papacharissi, Z. (2002). The presentation of self in virtual life: Characteristics of personal home pages. *Journalism & Mass Communication Quarterly*, *79*(3), 643–660.

Papacharissi, Z., & Rubin, A. (2000). Predictors of internet use. *Journal of Broadcasting & Electronic Media*, *44*(2), 175–196. doi:10.1207/s15506878jobem4402_2

Papathanassiou, E. (2004). Mass Customisation: Management Approaches and Internet Opportunities in the Financial Sector in the UK. *International Journal of Information Management*, *24*(5), 387–399. doi:10.1016/j.ijinfomgt.2004.06.003

Parasuraman, A., Zeithaml, V. A., & Malhotra, A. (2005). E-S-Qual: A Multiple-Item Scale for Assessing Electronic Service Quality. *Journal of Service Research*, *7*(3), 213–233. doi:10.1177/1094670504271156

Parker, C., & Pfeiffer, S. (2005). Video Blogging: Content to the Max. *IEEE MultiMedia*, *12*(2), 4–8. doi:10.1109/MMUL.2005.41

Patel, A. D. (2007). *Music, Language, and the Brain*. Oxford, UK: Oxford University Press.

Patton, M. D. (1980). *Qualitative Research Methods*. Thousand Oaks, CA: Sage Publications.

Patton, M. Q. (2002). *Qualitative research and evaluation methods* (3rd ed.). Thousand Oaks, CA: Sage.

Payne, A., & Frow, P. (2005). A Strategic Framework for Customer Relationship Management. *Journal of Marketing*, *69*(4), 167–176. doi:10.1509/jmkg.2005.69.4.167

Pellmar, T., & Eisenberg, L. (2000). *Bridging disciplines in the brain, behavioral, and clinical sciences*. Washington, DC: National Academy Press.

Pentina, I., Prybutok, V., & Zhang, X. (2008). The Role of Virtual Communities as Shopping Reference Groups. *Journal of Electronic Commerce Research*, *9*(2).

Perkowitz, M., & Etzioni, O. (1999). Towards Adaptive Web Sites: Conceptual Framework and Effectiveness. *Computer Networks*, *3*(11), 1245–1258. doi:10.1016/S1389-1286(99)00017-1

Perrier, F. (2007). *Facebook cost US $ 3.4 billion to the corporate world in lost productivity*. Retrieved December 27, 2008, from http://www.franckperrier.com/2007/11/14/facebooks-productivity-cost-to-the-corporate-world-us-34-billion/

Peters, L., & Saidin, H. (2000). IT and the Mass Customization of Services: The Challenge of Implementation. *International Journal of Information Management*, *4*(2), 103–119. doi:10.1016/S0268-4012(99)00059-6

Pfeil, U., Zaphiris, P., & Ang, C. S. (2006). Cultural differences in collaborative authoring of Wikipedia. *Journal of Computer-Mediated Communication*, *12*(1), 88–113. doi:10.1111/j.1083-6101.2006.00316.x

Phillips, J. M., Douthitt, E., & Hyland, M. A. M. (2001). The role of justice in team member satisfaction with the leader and attachment to the team. *The Journal of Applied Psychology*, *86*(2), 316–325. doi:10.1037/0021-9010.86.2.316

Pickles, J. (1995). *Ground truth: The social implications of geographic information systems*. New York: Guilford Press.

Porter, L. W., & Lawler, E. E. (1968). *Managerial attitudes and performance*. Homewood, IL: Irwin.

Poster, M. (1995). *Cyber democracy, Internet and the Public Sphere*. Retrieved from www.hnet.uci.edu/mposter/writings/democ.htlm

Preece, J. (1999). Empathetic communities: Balancing emotional and factual communication. *Interacting with Computers*, *12*(1), 63–77. doi:10.1016/S0953-5438(98)00056-3

Preece, J. (2000). *Online communities: Designing usability and supporting sociability*. Hoboken, NJ: Wiley.

Prestholdt, P. H., Lane, I. M., & Mathews, R. C. (1987). Nurse turnover as reasoned action: Development of a process model. *The Journal of Applied Psychology, 72*, 221–227. doi:10.1037/0021-9010.72.2.221

Putnam, R. D. (1993). *Making democracy work: Civic traditions in modern Italy*. Princeton, NJ: Princeton University Press.

Raacke, J., & Bonds-Raacke, J. (2008). MySpace and Facebook: Applying the uses and gratifications theory to exploring friend-networking sites. *Cyberpsychology & Behavior, 11*(2), 169–174. doi:10.1089/cpb.2007.0056

Rafaeli, S., Ravid, G., & Soroka, V. (2004, January). *De-lurking in virtual communities: A social communication network approach to measuring the effects of social capital*. Paper presented at the Hawaii International Conference on System Sciences.

Ramachandran, S., & Rao, V. S. (2006, April 13-15). *An Effort Towards Identifying Occupational Culture among Information Systems Professionals*. Paper presented at the SIGMIS-CPR'06, Claremond, CA.

Ramayah, T., Ignatius, J., & Aafaqi, B. (2004). PC usage among students in a private institution of higher learning: The moderating role of prior experience. *Journal of Business Strategy*.

Ramayah, T., Muhamad, J., & Noraini, I. (2003, May 13-15). *Impact of intrinsic and extrinsic motivation on Internet usage in Malaysia*. Paper presented at the 12th International Conference on Management of Technology, Nancy, France.

Ramayah, T., & Bushra, A. (2004). Role of self-efficacy in e-library usage among students of a public university in Malaysia. *Malaysian Journal of Library & Information Science, 9*(1), 39–57.

Ramayah, T., Chin, Y. L., Norazah, M. S., & Amlus, I. (2005). Determinants of intention to use an online bill payment system among MBA students. *E-Business, 9*, 80–91.

Ramayah, T., & Ignatius, J. (2005). Impact of perceived usefulness, perceived ease of use and perceived enjoyment on intention to shop online. *ICFAI Journal of Systems Management, 3*(3), 36–51.

Raynes-Goldie, K. (2010). Aliases, creeping, and wall cleaning: Understanding privacy in the age of Facebook. *First Monday, 15*(1-4).

Reed, D. P. (2001). The Law of the Pack. *Harvard Business Review*, (February): 23–24.

Regan, P. M. (2002). Privacy as a common good in the digital world. *Information Communication and Society, 7*(1), 92–114.

Reibstein, D. J. (2008). A Broader Perspective of Network Effects. *JMR, Journal of Marketing Research, XLVI*, 154–156.

Ren, Y., Kraut, R., & Kiesler, S. (2007). Applying Common Identity and Bond Theory to Design of Online Communities. *Organization Studies, 28*(3), 377–408. doi:10.1177/0170840607076007

Restler, S., & Woolis, D. (2007). Actors and Factors: Virtual Communities for Social Innovation. *Electronic Journal of Knowledge Management, 5*(1), 89–96.

Rheingold, H. (1993). *The virtual community: Homesteading on the virtual frontier*. New York, NY: Addison-Wesley.

Rheingold, H. (2003). *Smart mobs*. New York, NY: Basic Books.

Rhoten, D. (2003). *A multi-method analysis of the social and technical conditions for interdisciplinary collaboration*. Retrieved from http://hybridvigor.net/interdis/pubs/hv_pub_interdis-2003.09.29.pdf

Ribeiro, R., Kimble, C., & Cairns, P. (2010). Quantum phenomena in Communities of Practice. *International Journal of Information Management, 30*(1), 21–27. doi:10.1016/j.ijinfomgt.2009.11.003

Ricken, T. S., Schuler, P. R., Grandhi, A. S., & Jones, Q. (2010). TellUsWho: Guided Social Network Data Collection. In *Proceedings of the 43rd Hawaii International Conference on System Sciences*. Washington, DC: IEEE Computer Society.

Ridings, C. M., Gefen, D., & Arinze, B. (2002). Some antecedents and effects of trust in virtual communities. *The Journal of Strategic Information Systems, 11*(3), 271–295. doi:10.1016/S0963-8687(02)00021-5

Risky online behavior more likely to happen in small businesses. (2008, June 2). *PR Newswire*, 1.

Ritter, C., & Polnick, B. (2008). Connections: An essential element of online learning communities. *International Journal of Educational Leadership Preparation*, *3*(3). Retrieved from http://ijelp.expressacademic.org.

Roberts, B. (2008). Social networking at the office. *HR-Magazine*, *53*(3), 81–83.

Robertson, R. (1992). *Globalization- Social Theory and Global Culture*. London: Sage Publications.

Robinson, D. F., & Foulds, L. R. (1980). *Digraphs: Theory and techniques*. New York, NY: Gordon and Breach.

Robinson, T. G. (2006). Not so private lives. *CED*, *32*(9), 45–46.

Roccas, S., & Brewer, M. B. (2002). Social identity complexity. *Personality and Social Psychology Review*, *6*, 88–106. doi:10.1207/S15327957PSPR0602_01

Roffe, L., & Foster, C. (2008). *Macmillan Online Discussion Study: Exploring Macmillan's Share Discussion Forum*. Southampton, UK: Macmillan Cancer Support and University of Southampton School of Nursing and Midwifery.

Rosenbloom, A. (2004). Into the Blogosphere: Introduction. *Communications of the ACM*, *47*(12), 30–33. doi:10.1145/1035134.1035161

Rosenheck, D. (2003, August 4). Will you be my Friendster? *New Statesman*. Retrieved October 13, 2004, from http://www.newstatesman.com/200308040005

Rothaermel, F., & Sugiyama, S. (2001). Virtual Internet communities and commercial success: Individual and community-level theory grounded in the atypical case of TimeZone.com. *Journal of Management*, *27*(3), 297–312. doi:10.1016/S0149-2063(01)00093-9

Rotundo, N., Nguyen, D., & Sackett, P. R. (2001). A meta-analytic review of gender differences in perceptions of sexual harassment. *The Journal of Applied Psychology*, *86*(5), 914–922. doi:10.1037/0021-9010.86.5.914

Rouibah, K. (2008). Social usage of instant messaging by individuals outside the workplace in Kuwait. *Information Technology & People*, *21*(1), 34–68. doi:10.1108/09593840810860324

Rovai, A. P. (2002). *Building sense of community at a distance*. Retrieved from http://www.whateverproductions.net/Rovai-2.pdf

Ruettimann, L. (2009). *How to avoid your boss on Facebook*. Retrieved March 29, 2009, from http://www.lemondrop.com/2009/02/12/facebook-friend-your-boss/

Ruiz-Mafé, C., Sanz-Blas, S., & Aldas-Manzano, J. (2009). Drivers and barriers to online airline ticket purchasing. *Journal of Air Transport Management*.

Rundstrom, R. A. (1995). GIS, Indigenous peoples, and epistemological diversity. *Cartography and Geographic Information Systems*, *22*, 45–57. doi:10.1559/152304095782540564

Rust, R. T., Ambler, T., Carpenter, G. S., Kumar, V., & Srivastava, R. K. (2004). Measuring marketing productivity: Current knowledge and future directions. *Journal of Marketing*, *68*(4), 76–89. doi:10.1509/jmkg.68.4.76.42721

Rust, R., & Kannan, P. (2002). *E-Service: New Directions in Theory and Practice*. Armonk, NY: M.E. Sharpe.

Rust, R., & Kannan, P. (2003). E-Service: A New Paradigm for Business in the Electronic Environment. *Communications of the ACM*, *46*(6), 36–42. doi:10.1145/777313.777336

Rutledge, P. (2008). *The truth about profiting from social networking*. Upper Saddle River, NJ: Pearson Education, FT Press.

Sabater, J., & Paolucci, M. (2007). On representation and aggregation of social evaluations in computational trust and reputation models. *International Journal of Approximate Reasoning*, *4*(3), 458–483. doi:10.1016/j.ijar.2006.12.013

Sabater, J., & Sierra, C. (2005). Review on computing trust and reputation models. *Artificial Intelligence Review*, *24*(1), 33–60. doi:10.1007/s10462-004-0041-5

Salazar, J. F. (2007). Indigenous peoples and the cultural construction of information and communication technology (ICT) in Latin America. In Dyson, L. E., Hendriks, M., & Grant, S. (Eds.), *Information technology and indigenous people* (pp. 14–26). Hershey, PA: Idea Group Publishing.

Sanders, I. T. (1958). *The Community: An Introduction to a Social System*. New York, NY: Ronald Press Company.

Sangwan, S., Guan, C., & Siguaw, J. (2009). Virtual Social Networks: Toward A Research Agenda. *International Journal of Virtual Communities and Social Networking, 1*(1).

Santos, J. (2003). E-Service Quality: A Model of Virtual Service Quality Dimensions. *Managing Service Quality, 13*(3), 233–246. doi:10.1108/09604520310476490

Sarason, S. B. (1986). Commentary: The emergence of a conceptual center. *Journal of Community Psychology, 14*, 405–407. doi:10.1002/1520-6629(198610)14:4<405::AID-JCOP2290140409>3.0.CO;2-8

Sarno, D. (2009). Facebook reports milestones in cash flow, users. *Los Angeles Times*, B 4.

Sassen, S. (2001). *The Global City*. Princeton, NJ: Princeton University Press.

Sayago, S., & Blat, J. (2010). Telling the story of older people e-mailing: An ethnographical study. *International Journal of Human-Computer Studies, 68*(1-2), 105–120. doi:10.1016/j.ijhcs.2009.10.004

Scandura, T. A., & Schriesheim, C. A. (1994). Leader-member exchange and supervisor career mentoring as complementary constructs in leadership research. *Academy of Management Journal, 37*(6), 1588–1602. doi:10.2307/256800

Scarbrough, H. (1999). The Management of Knowledge Workers. In Currie, L. W., & Galliers, B. (Eds.), *Rethinking management information systems* (pp. 475–495). Oxford, UK: Oxford University Press.

Schatzki, R. T. (2001). Introduction. Practice Theory. In Schatzki, T. R., Knorr-Cetina, K., & von Savigny, E. (Eds.), *The Practice Turn in Contemporary Theory* (pp. 1–14). New York, NY: Routledge.

Schau, H. J., & Gilly, M. C. (2003). We Are What We Post? Self-Presentation in Personal Web Space. *The Journal of Consumer Research, 30*(3), 385–405. doi:10.1086/378616

Schiano, D. J., Nardi, B. A., Gumbrecht, M., & Swartz, L. (2004). Blogging by the Rest of Us. In *Proceedings of the ACM Conference on Computer Human Interaction*, Vienna, Austria.

Schiller, H. J. (1973). *Communication and Cultural Domination*. White Plains, NY: International Arts and Sciences Press.

Schlager, M., & Fusco, J. (2003). Teacher Professional Development, Technology, and Communities of Practice: Are We Putting the Cart Before the Horse? *The Information Society, 19*(3), 203–220. doi:10.1080/01972240309464

Schoder, D., & Fischbach, K. (2005). Core Concepts in Peer-to-Peer (P2P) Networking. In R. Subramanian & B. Goodman (Eds.), *P2P Computing: The Evolution of a Disruptive Technology*. Hershey, PA: Idea Group Inc.

Schwier, R. A. (2001). Catalysts, emphases, and elements of virtual learning communities. Implication for research. *The Quarterly Review of Distance Education, 2*(1), 5–18.

Schwier, R. A., & Daniel, B. K. (2008). Implications of Virtual Learning Communities for Designing Online Communities of Practice in Higher Education. In Kimbel, C., & Hildreth, P. (Eds.), *Communities of Practice: Creating Learning Environments for Educators*. Greenwich, CT: Information Age Publishing.

Scott, J. (2000). *Social network analysis: A handbook* (2nd ed.). London, UK: Sage.

Scott, J. (2002). *Social networks: Critical concepts in sociology*. New York: Routledge.

Scott, J. C. (1998). *Seeing like a State: How Certain Schemes to Improve the Human Condition have Failed*. New Haven, CT: Yale University Press.

Seyal, A. H., & Rahman, N. A. (2007). The influence of external variables on the executives' use of the Internet. *Business Process Management Journal, 13*(2), 263–278. doi:10.1108/14637150710740491

Shamir, B. (1990). Calculations, values, and identities: The sources of collectivistic work motivation. *Human Relations, 43*, 313–332. doi:10.1177/001872679004300402

Shang, R.-A., Chen, Y.-C., & Liao, H.-J. (2006). The value of participation in virtual consumer communities on brand loyalty. *Internet Research*, *16*(4), 398–418. doi:10.1108/10662240610690025

Sharma, A. (1997). Professional as Agent: Knowledge Asymmetry in Agency Exchange. *Academy of Management Review*, *22*(3), 758–798. doi:10.2307/259412

Sheppard, B. H., Hardwick, J., & Warshaw, P. R. (1988, December). The Theory of Reasoned Action: A Meta-Analysis of Past Research with Recommendations for Modifications and Future Research. *The Journal of Consumer Research*, *15*(3), 325–343. doi:10.1086/209170

Sheppard, E. (1995). GIS and society: towards a research agenda. *Cartography and Geographic Information Systems*, *22*(1), 5–16. doi:10.1559/152304095782540555

Shin, D.-H., & Kim, W. Y. (2008). Applying the Technology Acceptance Model and Flow. *Cyberpsychology & Behavior*, *11*(3), 378–382. doi:10.1089/cpb.2007.0117

Shrum, W., Chompalov, I., & Genuth, J. (2001). Trust, conflict and performance in scientific collaborations. *Social Studies of Science*, *31*(5), 681–730. doi:10.1177/030631201031005002

Sieber, R. E. (2000). Conforming (to) the opposition: the social construction of geographic information in social movements. *International Journal of Geographical Information Science*, *14*(8), 775–793. doi:10.1080/136588100750022787

Simon, B. (2004). *Identity in Modern Society: A Social Psychological Perspective*. London, UK: Blackwell.

Sinha, K. K., & Van de Ven, A. H. (2005). Designing Work Within and Between Organizations. *Organization Science*, *16*(4), 389–408. doi:10.1287/orsc.1050.0130

Skeels, M. M., & Grudin, J. (2009). When social networks cross boundaries: A case study of workplace use of Facebook and LinkedIn. In [New York: ACM Press.]. *Proceedings of the GROUP*, *2009*, 95–104.

Skinner, R. (2003). The Value of Information Technology in Healthcare. *Frontiers of Health Services Management*, *19*(3), 3–15.

Smith, J. (2009). Number of US Facebook users over 35 nearly doubles in last 60 days. *Inside Facebook*. Retrieved January 6, 2010, from http://www.insidefacebook.com/2009/03/25/number-of-us-facebook-users-over-35-nearly-doubles-in-last-60-days/

Smith, L. C. (2005). *Meditating Indigenous Identity: Video, Advocacy, and Knowledge in Oaxaca, Mexico*. Unpublished doctoral dissertation, University of Kentucky.

Smith, H. J., Milberg, S. J., & Burke, S. J. (1996). Information Privacy: Measuring Individuals' Concerns About Organizational Practices. *Management Information Systems Quarterly*, *20*(2), 167–196. doi:10.2307/249477

Smith, L. (2008). Indigenous geography, GIS, and land-use planning on the Bois Forte Reservation. *American Indian Culture and Research Journal*, *32*(3), 139–151.

Smith, L. C. (2006). Mobilizing indigenous video: The Mexican Case. *The Journal of Latin American Geography*, *5*(1), 113–128. doi:10.1353/lag.2006.0012

Snyder, W., Wenger, E., & Briggs, X. (2004). Communities of practice in government: Leveraging knowledge for performance. *Public Management*, *32*(4), 17–21.

Social networking explodes worldwide as sites increase their focus on cultural relevance. (2008, August 12). Retrieved December 30, 2008, from http://www.comscore.com/press/release.asp?press=2396

Social networking in the workplace increases efficiency. (2008, November 11). *PR Newswire*, 2.

Society for Human Resource Management. (2008) *Online Technologies and Their Impact on Recruitment Strategies—Using Social Networking Web Sites to Attract Talent*. Retrieved January 18, 2010, from http://www.shrm.org/Research/SurveyFindings/Articles/Pages/OnlineTechnologiesandTheirImpactonRecruitmentStrategiesUsingSocialNetworkingWebsitesToAttractTalent.aspx

Solis, B. (2009, January 19). Social Networks Grow Up: More Adults Connecting Online. *PR 2.0*. Retrieved March 4, 2009, from http://www.briansolis.com/2009/01/social-networks-grow-up-more-adults.html/

Sousa, R., Yeung, A., & Cheng, T. (2008). Customer Heterogeneity in Operational E-Service Design Attributes: An Empirical Investigation of Service Quality. *International Journal of Operations & Production Management, 28*(7), 592–614. doi:10.1108/01443570810881776

Sparke, M. (1998). A Map that Roared and an Original Atlas: Canada, Cartography, and the Narration of a Nation. *Annals of the Association of American Geographers. Association of American Geographers, 88*(3), 463–495. doi:10.1111/0004-5608.00109

SPSS Inc. (2009). *PASW Statistics - Release Version 18.* Chicago, IL: Author.

Srinivasan, R., Lilien, G. L., & Rangaswamy, A. (2004). First in, First Out? The Effects of Network Externalities on Pioneer Survival. *Journal of Marketing, 68*(1), 41–58. doi:10.1509/jmkg.68.1.41.24026

St. John, W. (2006, September 10). When information becomes T.M.I. *The New York Times, 155*(53698), 8.

Stack, L. C. (1978). Trust. In London, H., & Exner, J. E. Jr., (Eds.), *Dimensionality of personality* (pp. 561–599). New York: Wiley.

Stanoevska-Slabeva, K., Parrilli, D., & Thanos, G. (2008). BEinGRID: Development of Business Models for the Grid Industry. In *Proceedings of GECON 2008 workshop* (LNCS 5206, pp. 140-151).

Steger, B. (2003). *Globalization: A Very Short Introduction.* Oxford, UK: Oxford University Press.

Steinfield, C., DiMicco, J. M., Ellison, N. B., & Lampe, C. (2009). Bowling online: Social networking and social capital within the organization. In *Proceedings of the fourth international conference on communities and technologies 2009* (pp. 245-254).

Sterne, J. (2006). The mp3 as cultural artefact. *New Media & Society, 8*(5), 825–842. doi:10.1177/1461444806067737

Stevens, J. (1986). *Applied Multivariate Statistics for the Social Sciences.* Hillsdale, NJ: Lawrence Erlbaum Associates.

Strauss, A., & Corbin, J. (1998). *Basics of Qualitative Research: Techniques and Procedures for Developing Grounded Theory.* London: Sage.

Stross, R. (2009). When everyone's a friend, is anything private? *The New York Times.* Retrieved March 29, 2009, from http://www.nytimes.com/2009/03/08/business/08digi.html?_r=2&pagewanted=print

Stryker, S. (1968). Identity Salience and Role Performance: The Relevance of Symbolic Interaction Theory for Family Research. *Journal of Marriage and the Family, 30*(4), 558–564. doi:10.2307/349494

Stryker, S., & Burke, P. J. (2000). The Past, Present, and Future of an Identity Theory. *Social Psychology Quarterly, 63*(4), 284–297. doi:10.2307/2695840

Stutzman, F. (2006). *An evaluation of identity-sharing behavior in social network communities.* Paper presented at the 2006 iDMAa and IMS Code Conference, Oxford, Ohio.

Suchman, L. (2007). *Human–Machine Reconfigurations: Plans and Situated Actions.* Cambridge, UK: Cambridge University Press.

Sullivan, S. (2006). *One-in-four hiring managers have used internet search engines to screen job candidates; One-in-ten have used social networking sites, CareerBuilder.com survey finds.* Retrieved from http://www.careerbuilder.com/share/aboutus/pressreleasesdetail.aspx?id=pr331&ed=12%2F31%2F2006&sd=10%2F26%2F2006&cbRecursionCnt=1&cbsid=a5015667d80f4b599c46d2b08f406b67-241548812-RI-4&ns_siteid=ns_us_g_One%2din%2dFour_Hirin_

Swan, J., Scarbrough, H., & Robertson, M. (2002). The construction of 'communities of practice' in the management of innovation. *Management Learning, 33*(4), 477–496. doi:10.1177/1350507602334005

Szmigin, I., Canning, L., & Reppel, A. (2006). Online community: enchancing the relationship marketing concept through customer bonding. *International Journal of Service Industry Management, 16*(5).

Taherian, M., Amini, M., & Jalili, R. (2008) Trust Inference in Web-Based Social Networks Using Resistive Networks. In *Proceedings of the Third International Conference on Internet and Web Applications and Services,* Athens, Greece (pp. 233-238).

Tajfel, H. (1981). Social stereotypes and social groups. In Turner, J. C., & Giles, H. (Eds.), *Intergroup Behavior* (pp. 144–167). Oxford, UK: Basil Blackwell.

Tajfel, H. (1982). *Social Identity and Intergroup Relations*. Cambridge, UK: Cambridge University Press.

Tajfel, H., & Turner, J. C. (1979). An Integrative Theory of Intergroup Conflict. In Austin, W. G., & Worchel, S. (Eds.), *The Social Psychology of Intergroup Relations* (pp. 33–47).

Takatalo, J., Hakkinen, J., Komulainen, J., Sarkela, H., & Nyman, G. (2006). Involvement and presence in digital gaming. In *Proceedings of the 4th Nordic Conference on Human-Computer Interaction* (Vol. 189, pp. 393-396).

Taylor, S., & McKee, P. (2010). Grid Business Models, Evaluation, and Principles. In Buyya, R., & Bubendorder, K. (Eds.), *Market-Oriented Grid and Utility Computing*. New York: John Wiley & Sons.

Teigland, R., & Wasko, M. M. (2003). Integrating knowledge through information trading: Examining the relationship between boundary spanning communication and individual performance. *Decision Sciences, 34*(2), 261–286. doi:10.1111/1540-5915.02341

Teo, H., Chan, H., Wei, K., & Zhang, Z. (2003). Evaluating Information Accessibility and Community Adaptivity Features for Sustaining Virtual Learning Communities. *International Journal of Human-Computer Studies, 59*(5), 671–697. doi:10.1016/S1071-5819(03)00087-9

Teo, T. S. H., Lim, V. K. G., & Lai, R. Y. C. (1999). Intrinsic and extrinsic motivation in Internet usage. *Omega, 27*(32), 25–37. doi:10.1016/S0305-0483(98)00028-0

Terry, D. J., & Hogg, M. A. (1996). Group norms and the attitude-behavior relationship: A role for group identification. *Personality and Social Psychology Bulletin, 22*(8), 776–793. doi:10.1177/0146167296228002

Tichy, N., Tushman, M., & Fombrun, C. (1979). Social network analysis for organizations. *Academy of Management Review, 4*(4), 507–519. doi:10.2307/257851

Timmers, T. (1998). Business Models for Electronic Markets. *Electronic Markets, 8*(2), 3-8. Retrieved April 15, 2010, from http://www.electronicmarkets.org/issues/volume-8/volume-8-issue-2/businessmodels0.pdf

Todd, A. P., & McKeen, D. J. (1995). The Evolution of IS Job Skills: A Content Analysis of IS Job Advertisements From 1970 to 1990. *Management Information Systems Quarterly, 19*(1), 1–27. doi:10.2307/249709

Tomlinson, J. (1999). *Globalization and Culture*. Cambridge, UK: Blackwell Publishers.

Tong, D. Y. K. (2009). A study of e–recruitment technology adoption in Malaysia. *Industrial Management & Data Systems, 109*(2), 281–300. doi:10.1108/02635570910930145

Tönnies, F. (1887). *Community and Civil Society*. Cambridge, MA: Cambridge University Press.

Trammell, K., & Keshelashvili, A. (2005). Examining the new influencers: A self-presentation study of A-list blogs. *Journalism & Mass Communication Quarterly, 82*(4), 968–982.

Trochim, W. M. K. (2005). *Probability and non-probability sampling*. Retrieved from http://socialresearchmethods.net/kb/sampprob.htm

Tsoukas, H. (1996). The firm as a distributed knowledge system: A constructionist approach. *Strategic Management Journal, 17*, 11–25.

Tsoukas, H., & Chia, R. (2002). On organizational becoming: Rethinking organizational change. *Organization Science, 13*(5), 567–582. doi:10.1287/orsc.13.5.567.7810

Tufekci, Z. (2008). Can you see me now? Audience and disclosure regulation in online social network sites. *Bulletin of Science, Technology & Society, 28*(1), 20–36. doi:10.1177/0270467607311484

Turk, A. (2007). Representations of tribal boundaries of Australian Indigenous peoples and the implications of geographic information systems. In Dyson, L. E., Hendriks, M., & Grant, S. (Eds.), *Information technology and indigenous people* (pp. 232–244). Hershey, PA: Idea Group Publishing.

Turkle, S. (1995). *Life on the Screen: Identity in the Age of the Internet*. New York: Simon and Schuster.

Turner, J. C. (1982). Towards a cognitive redefinition of the social group. In Tajfel, H. (Ed.), *Social identity and intergroup relations* (pp. 66–101). Cambridge, UK: Cambridge University Press.

Turner, J. C. (1985). Social categorization and the self-concept: A social cognitive theory of group behavior. In Lawler, E. J. (Ed.), *Advances in group processes: Theory and research* (Vol. 2, pp. 77–122).

Tynes, M. B. (2007). Internet Safety Gone Wild? Sacrificing the Educational and Psychosocial Benefits of Online Social Environments. *Journal of Adolescent Research, 22*(6), 575–584. doi:10.1177/0743558407303979

U.S. Bureau of Indian Affairs (U.S. BIA). (1988). *Issue paper: Indian integrated resource information program.* Lakewood, CO: Department of the Interior.

Vaast, E. (2004). O Brother, Where are Thou? From Communities to Networks of Practice Through Intranet Use. *Management Communication Quarterly, 18*(1), 5–44. doi:10.1177/0893318904265125

Van der Heijden, H. (2000). *Using the Technology Acceptance Model to Predict Website Usage: Extensions and Empirical Test.* Amsterdam, The Netherlands: Vrije Universiteit.

Van der Heijden, H. (2004). User acceptance of hedonic information systems. *Management Information Systems Quarterly, 28*(4), 695–704.

van Knippenberg, D., & van Schie, E. C. M. (2000). Foci and correlates of organizational identification. *Journal of Occupational and Organizational Psychology, 73*(2), 137–147. doi:10.1348/096317900166949

Van Maanen, J., & Barley, R. S. (1984). Occupational Communities: Culture and Control in Organizations. In Staw, B., & Cummings, L. L. (Eds.), *Research in Organizational Behaviour* (*Vol. 6*, pp. 287–365). Greenwich, CT: JAI Press.

Vazire, S., & Gosling, S. (2004). E-Perceptions: Personality impressions based on personal websites. *Journal of Personality and Social Psychology, 87*(1), 123–132. doi:10.1037/0022-3514.87.1.123

Venkatesh, V., & Davis, F. D. (2000). A theoretical extension of the technology acceptance model: four longitudinal field studies. *Management Science, 46*(2), 186–204. doi:10.1287/mnsc.46.2.186.11926

Venkatesh, V., Morris, M. G., Davis, G. B., & Davis, F. D. (2003). User acceptance of information technology: toward a unified view. *Management Information Systems Quarterly, 27*(3), 425–478.

Venkatesh, V., Speier, C., & Morris, M. G. (2002). User acceptance enablers in individual decision making about technology: Toward an integrated model. *Decision Sciences, 33*(2), 297–316. doi:10.1111/j.1540-5915.2002.tb01646.x

Von Hippel, E., & Von Krogh, G. (2006). Free revealing and the private-collective model for innovation incentives. *R & D Management, 36*(3), 295–306. doi:10.1111/j.1467-9310.2006.00435.x

Vroom, V. H. (1964). *Work and motivation.* New York: Wiley.

Walker, K. (2000). It's difficult to hide it: The presentation of self on internet home pages. *Qualitative Sociology, 23*(1), 99–120. doi:10.1023/A:1005407717409

Walker, R. H., & Johnson, L. W. (2006). Why consumers use and do not use technology-enabled services. *Journal of Services Marketing, 20*(2), 125–135. doi:10.1108/08876040610657057

Wallace, A. R., & Boylan, C. R. (2001, December). *Interaction patterns in the extended classroom via satellite technology in the Australian outback.* Paper presented at the Annual Meeting of the New Zealand Association for Educational Research, Christchurch, NZ.

Waller, M. (2007). Bank's fairy demonstrates magic of the net. *Times (London, England)*, 56.

Walsham, G. (1993). *Interpreting Information Systems in Organizations.* London: John Wiley and Sons.

Walsham, G. (1998). IT and Changing Professional Identity: Micro-Studies and Macro-Theory. *Journal of the American Society for Information Science American Society for Information Science, 49*(12), 1081–1089. doi:10.1002/(SICI)1097-4571(1998)49:12<1081::AID-ASI4>3.0.CO;2-R

Walsh, J., & Bayama, T. (1996). Computer networks and scientific work. *Social Studies of Science, 26*(3), 385–405. doi:10.1177/030631296026003006

Walther, J. B. (1996). Computer-mediated communication: Impersonal, inter-personal and hyperpersonal interaction. *Human Communication Research, 23*(1), 3–43.

Wang, H., Deng, Y., & Chiu, S. (2005). Beyond Photoblogging: New Directions of Mobile Communication. In *Proceedings of the Conference on Human Computer Interaction with Mobile Devices and Services*, Salzburg, Austria.

Wang, J., & Chen, C. (2004). An Automated Tool for Managing Interactions in Virtual Communities - Using Social Netwrok Analysis Approach. *Journal of Organizational Computing and Electronic Commerce, 14*(1), 1–26. doi:10.1207/s15327744joce1401_1

Wang, S. S., Moon, S.-I., Kwon, K. H., Evans, C. A., & Stefanone, M. A. (2010). Face off: Implications of visual cues on initiating friendship on Facebook. *Computers in Human Behavior, 26*(2), 226–234. doi:10.1016/j.chb.2009.10.001

Warr, W. A. (2008). Social software: fun and games, or business tools? *Journal of Information Science, 34*(4), 591–604. doi:10.1177/0165551508092259

Warshaw, P. R., & Davis, F. D. (1985). Disentangling behavioral intention and behavioral expectation. *Journal of Experimental Social Psychology, 21*, 213–228. doi:10.1016/0022-1031(85)90017-4

Wasko, M. M., & Faraj, S. (2000). "It is what one does": why people participate and help others in electronic communities of practice. *The Journal of Strategic Information Systems, 9*(2-3), 155–173. doi:10.1016/S0963-8687(00)00045-7

Wasko, M. M., & Faraj, S. (2005). Why should I share? Examining social capital and knowledge contribution in electronic networks of practice. *Management Information Systems Quarterly, 29*(1), 35–57.

Wasserman, S., & Faust, K. (1994). *Social network analysis: Methods and applications*. Cambridge, UK: Cambridge University Press.

Wayne, S. J., Shore, L. M., & Liden, R. C. (1997). Perceived organizational support and leader-member exchange: A social exchange perspective. *Academy of Management Journal, 40*, 82–111. doi:10.2307/257021

Weber, L. (2007). *Marketing to the Social Web*. Hoboken, NJ: John Wiley & Sons.

Weijters, B., Devarajan Rangarajan, D., Falk, T., & Schillewaert, N. (2007). Determinants and Outcomes of Customers' Use of Self-Service Technolog in a Retail Setting. *Journal of Service Research, 10*(1), 3–21. doi:10.1177/1094670507302990

Weisband, S., & Atwater, L. (1999). Evaluating self and others in electronic and face-to-face groups. *The Journal of Applied Psychology, 84*, 632–639. doi:10.1037/0021-9010.84.4.632

Wellman, B. (1999). The network community: An introduction. In Wellman, B. (Ed.), *Networks in the global village* (pp. 1–48). Boulder, CO: Westview Press.

Wellman, B., & Gulia, M. (1998). Net surfers don't ride alone: Virtual communities as communities. In Smith, M. A., & Kollock, P. (Eds.), *Communities in Cyberspace* (pp. 163–190). Berkley, CA: University of California Press.

Wenger, E. (2000). Communities of Practice and Social Learning Systems. *Organization, 7*(2), 225–246. doi:10.1177/135050840072002

Wenger, E. (2004). Knowledge management as a doughnut: Shaping your knowledge strategy through Communities of Practice. *Ivey Business Journal Online, 3*(1), 1–8.

Wenger, E. (2010). Communities of Practices and Social Learning Systems: the Career of a Concept. In Blackmore, C. (Ed.), *Social learning systems and Communities of Practice* (pp. 179–198). London, UK: Springer. doi:10.1007/978-1-84996-133-2_11

Wenger, E. C. (2000). Communities of Practice and Social Learning Systems. *Organization, 7*(2), 225–246. doi:10.1177/135050840072002

Wenger, E. C., & Snyder, W. M. (2000). Communities of Practice: The organizational frontier. *Harvard Business Review, 78*(1), 139–145.

Wenger, E., McDermott, R. A., & Snyder, W. M. (2002). *Cultivating communities of practice: a guide to managing knowledge*. Boston, MA: Harvard Business School Press.

Westheimer, J., & Kahne, J. (1993). Building school communities: An experience-based model. *Phi Delta Kappan, 75*(4), 324–328.

Westin, A. F. (1967). *Privacy and Freedom*. New York: Atheneum.

Wikipedia. (2006a). *Theory of reasoned action.* Retrieved October 25, 2006, from http://en.wikipedia.org/wiki/Theory_of_reasoned_action

Wikipedia. (2006b). *Friendster.* Retrieved October 25, 2006, from http://en.wikipedia.org/wiki/Friendster

Wildbit. (2005). *Social Networks Research Report.* Retrieved February 8, 2006, from http://tidbit.wildbit.com

Wilkins, L., Swatman, P., & Castleman, T. (2002). Mustering Consent: Government-Sponsored Virtual Communities and the Incentives for Buy-in. *International Journal of Electronic Commerce, 7*(1), 121–134.

Williams, R. L., & Cothrel, J. (2000). Four Smart Ways to Run Online Communities. *Sloan Management Review, 41*(4), 81–91.

Wilson, S. M., et al. (2002). *The Anthropology of Online Communities: the Annual Review of Anthropology.* Retrieved from http://www.anthro.annualreviews.org

Wilson, E. V. (2006). *The Case for E-Health in the Information Systems Curriculum.* Madison, WI: University of Wisconsin.

Wilson, J. M., Straus, S. G., & McEvily, B. (2006). All in due time: The development of trust in computer-mediated and face-to-face teams. *Organizational Behavior and Human Decision Processes, 99,* 16–33. doi:10.1016/j.obhdp.2005.08.001

Wilson, P., & Stewart, M. (2008). *Global Indigenous Media: Cultures, Practices, and Politics.* Durham, NC: Duke University Press.

Wixom, B. H., & Todd, P. A. (2005, March). A Theoretical Integration of User Satisfaction and Technology Acceptance. *Information Systems Research, 16*(1), 85–102. doi:10.1287/isre.1050.0042

Wolfinbarger, M., & Gilly, M. C. (2003). Etailq: Dimensionalizing, Measuring and Predicting Etail Quality. *Journal of Retailing, 79*(3), 183–198. doi:10.1016/S0022-4359(03)00034-4

Wood, D. (1992). *The power of maps.* New York: Guildford Press.

Wu, J. H., & Wang, S. C. (2005). What Drives Mobile Commerce? An Empirical Evaluation of the Revised Technology Acceptance Model. *Information & Management, 42,* 719–729. doi:10.1016/j.im.2004.07.001

Xie, E., Teo, H., & Wan, W. (2004). Volunteering Personal Information on the Internet: Effects of Reputation, Privacy Notices, and Rewards on Online Consumer Behaviour. *Research, 18*(4), 336–355.

Yager, T. (2002). Sense of Community. *InfoWorld, 24*(38), 32.

Yahia, S. A., Benedikt, M., & Bohannon, P. (2007). Challenges in searching online communities. *A Quarterly Bulletin of the Computer Society of the IEEE Technical Committee on Data Engineering, 30*(2), 23–31.

Yang, B., & Garcia-Molina, H. (2002). *Designing a super-peer network.* Palo Alto, CA: Stanford University. Retrieved from http://dbpubs.stanford.edu/pub/2002-13

Yang, Z., & Jun, M. (2002). Consumer Perception of E-Service Quality: From Internet Purchaser and Non-Purchaser Perspectives. *The Journal of Business Strategy, 19*(1), 19–41.

Yee, N. (2006). Motivations for play in online games. *Cyberpsychology & Behavior, 9*(6), 772–775. doi:10.1089/cpb.2006.9.772

Yi, M., & Hwang, Y. (2003). System self-efficacy, enjoyment, learning goal orientation, and the technology acceptance model. *International Journal of Human-Computer Studies, 59,* 439–449. doi:10.1016/S1071-5819(03)00114-9

Yin, K. R. (2003). *Case Study Research: Design and Methods.* Thousand Oaks, CA: Sage Publications, Inc.

Yoo, B., & Donthu, N. (2001). Developing a Scale to Measure the Perceived Quality of an Internet Shopping Site (Sitequal). *Quarterly Journal of Electronic Commerce, 2*(1), 31–46.

Yoo, W., Suh, K., & Lee, M. (2002). Exploring the Factors Enhancing Member Participation in Online Communities. *Journal of Global Information Management, 10*(3), 55–71.

Your Boss Doesn't Want to be Your Facebook friend. (2009, August 21). *The Globe and Mail,* B12.

Yuan, L., & Buckman, R. (2006). Social networking goes mobile; MySpace, Facebook strike deals with cell companies; A new set of safety concerns. *Wall Street Journal,* D1.

Yubo, C., & Jinhong, X. (2008). Online Consumer Review: Word-of-Mouth as a new element of Markeing Communication Mix. *Management Science, 54*(3), 477–491. doi:10.1287/mnsc.1070.0810

Yu, C., & Young, M. (2008). The virtual group identification process: A virtual educational community case. *Cyberpsychology & Behavior, 11*(1), 87–90. doi:10.1089/cpb.2007.9929

Zammuto, R. F., Griffith, T. L., Majchrzak, A., Dougherty, D. J., & Faraj, S. (2007). Information Technology and the Changing Fabric of Organization. *Organization Science, 18*(5), 749–762. doi:10.1287/orsc.1070.0307

Zeidner, R. (2008). *Employers give Facebook a poke.* Retrieved from http://www.shrm.org/hrtx/library_published/nonIC/CMS_024693.asp

Zeithaml, V., Parasuraman, A., & Malhotra, A. (2000). *A Conceptual Framework for Understanding e-Service Quality: Implications for Future Research and Managerial Practice.* Marketing Science Institute.

Zhang, Jiang, & Carroll (2010). Social Identity in Facebook Community Life. *JVCSN 2*(4) (pp. 65-77)

Zhao, S., Grasmuck, S., & Martin, J. (2008). Identity construction on Facebook: Digital empowerment in anchored relationships. *Computers in Human Behavior, 24*(5), 1816–1836. doi:10.1016/j.chb.2008.02.012

Zheng, J., Veinott, E., Bos, N., Olson, J., & Olson, G. (2002). Trust without touch: Jumpstarting long-distance trust with initial social activities. In *Proceedings of the CHI Conference.* Retrieved from http://www.crew.umich.edu/publications.html

Zheng, W. (2009). Online Reputation Systems in Web 2.0 Era. In Nelson, M. (Ed.), *Value Creation in e-Business Management* (pp. 296–306). New York: Springer. doi:10.1007/978-3-642-03132-8_24

Zhou, Y., & Davis, J. (2007). Discovering Web Communities in the Blogspace. In *Proceedings of the 40th Hawaii International Conference on System Sciences.* Washington, DC: IEEE Computer Society.

Ziegler, N., & Lausen, G. (2005). Propagation Models for Trust and Distrust in Social Networks. In *Information Systems Frontiers* (pp. 337–358). New York: Springer.

Zigurs, I., & Buckland, B. K. (1998, September). A Theory of Task/Technology Fit and Group Support Systems Effectiveness. *Management Information Systems Quarterly, 22*(3), 313–334. doi:10.2307/249668

Zlotogorski, M. (2010). *Becoming More Socially Networked in Emerging Markets.* Retrieved May 1, 2010, from http://www.tmforum.org/community/blogs/leadership_blog/archive/2010/04/19/becoming-more-socially-networked-in-emerging-markets.aspx

Zuboff, S. (1988). *In the age of the smart machine.* New York: Basic Books.

Zucker, L. G. (1996). Production of trust: Institutional sources of economic structure. In *Research in Organizational Behavior* (pp. 53–111). Greenwich, CT: JAI Press.

About the Contributors

Subhasish Dasgupta is an associate professor of information systems in the School of Business, George Washington University. Dasgupta received his PhD from Baruch College, The City University of New York (CUNY). He received both his MBA and BS from the University of Calcutta (India). He has published his research in refereed journals such as *Decision Support Systems*, the *European Journal of Information System*, the *Journal of Global Information Management*, the *Electronic Markets Journal* and the *Simulation and Gaming Journal*. Dasgupta has published two edited books, *Internet and Intranet Technologies in Organizations* and *Encyclopedia of Virtual Communities and Technologies*. He has also presented his research in major regional, national and international conferences.

* * *

Abdollah Aghaie is an associate professor in the department of Industrial Engineering at K.N. Toosi University of Technology in Tehran, Iran. He received his BSc from Sharif University of Technology in Tehran, MSc from New South Wales University in Sydney and PhD from Loughborough University in U.K. His main research interests are in Modeling and Simulation, Semantic Web, Social Networks and Trust, Statistical Process Control, Total Quality Management, Knowledge Management, Internet Marketing and Ergonomics.

Demosthenes Akoumianakis is Professor at the Department of Applied Information Technology & Multimedia, Technological Education Institution of Crete and founder and director of the interactive Software and Systems Engineering Laboratory (iSTLab, http://www.istl.teiher.gr/). He received a BA (Hons) in Computing in Business from The University of Huddersfield (1990) and MSc and PhD degrees in Human Computer Interaction from the University of Kent at Canterbury, UK in 1995 and 1999 respectively. His current work concentrates on on-line communities, scenario-based requirements engineering, multiple user interfaces and the development of collaborative technologies and toolkits.

Jinwei Cao is an Assistant Professor of Management Information Systems at the University of Delaware. She received her PhD in Management Information Systems from the University of Arizona. Her research interests include human computer interaction, social computing, and technology supported learning. She has published in Journal of Management Information Systems, MIS Quarterly Executive, DATA BASE for Advances in Information Systems, Journal of the American Society for Information Science and Technology and many other prestigious journals and conferences.

John M. Carroll is Edward M. Frymoyer Chair Professor of Information Sciences and Technology at Penn State. He was a Research Staff Member at the IBM T.J. Watson Research Center, and founding manager of the IBM User Interface Institute (1976-1994). He was Professor of Computer Science, and Head of Department, at Virginia Tech (1994-2003). Recent books include Making Use (MIT Press, 2000) and HCI in the New Millennium (Addison-Wesley, 2001). Carroll serves on several editorial and advisory boards, and is Editor-in-Chief of the ACM Transactions on Computer-Human Interactions. He received the ACM CHI Lifetime Achievement Award.

Simon Caton is a Senior Research Associate at the Karlsruhe Services Research Institute and Research Division Leader for Cloud and Corporate Services at the Institute for Information Systems and Management, both at the Karlsruhe Institute of Technology. His research topics include: the adoption of autonomic computing for market systems, social cloud computing, service value networks and service level agreements. He received his PhD in 2010 from Cardiff University with a focus on the autonomic management of volunteered resources (Campus Grids) in the application domain of parallel and distributed image processing. He completed his undergraduate degree also at Cardiff University in the UK.

Ben K. Daniel, PhD is a Research and Innovation Analyst, with the Joint Office of Health Research and Innovation at the University of Saskatchewan and Saskatoon Health Region—Saskatchewan, Canada. He is also a Lecturer of Research Methods and Applied Statistics, with the Department of Language and Linguistics, College of Arts and Sciences, and a Community Clinical Faculty Member at the Graduate School of Public Health—University of Saskatchewan. Ben is a member of the Virtual Learning Communities Lab since it was founded. His research work focused on development of computational approaches for modeling complex social and learning issues in virtual learning communities and distributed communities of practice. Currently, he is interested in e-health, measurement and evaluation of health programs and systems, and broadly in the development of methods, techniques, and processes for studying virtual communities.

Dimitrina (Dima) Dimitrova received her Ph.D. from the University of Toronto. She teaches organizational studies at York University and has a research and consulting business. Her primary research interests include work, social networks, and new technologies. She has almost 20 years of experience in the research of remote collaboration, workplace and research networks, and virtual communities. Her current projects examine on large research networks. She applies social network analysis and focuses on the way network structure is linked to collaborative and management practices. Her findings have been published in edited collections and journals in the US, Austria, Britain, Norway, Italy, Russia, and Bulgaria. She is affiliated with NetLab, a social network group at the University of Toronto; GRAND, a Centre of Excellence for the study of new media and information technologies; and CERIS, a Centre of Excellence for research on immigration and settlement.

Alex B. Eveleth, Western Washington University, is a senior Computer Science and Music student at Western Washington University, Bellingham, Washington. His computer science interests include biocomputing, humanitarian software, sustainable energy development and open source software development.

Daniel M. Eveleth, PhD Washington State University, is an associate professor of management and human resources at the University of Idaho, Moscow, Idaho. His current research interests include expertise development, knowledge management, analogical reasoning, and using technology to enhance pedagogy. He has published in a variety of journals, including EduCause Quarterly, Journal of Service Research, Journal of Information System Education, Journal of Education for Business, Journal of Ethics and Behavior, and Journal of Interactive Marketing.

Richard Hall is a Professor of Information Science and Technology and Director of the Center for Technology Enhanced Learning at Missouri University of Science and Technology. He has published over 90 peer reviewed articles, and served as an investigator on more than 12 million dollars in external grant funding for research covering humans interacting with technology, with a particular focus on learning technologies. He teaches classes in digital media, web studies, and human-computer interaction evaluation techniques.

Jack Hanney graduated with a Masters degree in geography from the University of Missouri-Columbia, Department of Geography in 2010. His thesis research focused on discourses embedded in media produced by the Chickasaw Nation in Oklahoma, USA.

Charles F. Hofacker has a Ph. D. in Mathematical Psychology from the University of California, Los Angeles, and is Professor of Marketing at Florida State University. He was Visiting Professor at Università Bocconi in Milan, Italy in 2001 and 2007. His current research interests are at the intersection of marketing and information technology. His work in that and other areas has appeared in the Journal of Marketing Research, Journal of the Academy of Marketing Science, Psychometrika, Management Science, and other outlets. Along with Edward Malthouse, he is co-editor of the Journal of Interactive Marketing. Dr. Hofacker currently serves as Webmaster for the American Marketing Association's Academic Resource Center (ARC) and is also the moderator of ELMAR, an electronic newsletter and community platform for academic marketing with over 6,300 subscribers.

Hao Jiang is a Ph.D student in Human-Computer Interaction Center in Pennsylvania State University, USA. He is interested in design research, computer-supported collaborative work (CSCW), and community informatics. Since 2005, he has participated in CSCW research and system development in computer-supported collaboration and learning (CSCL) lab in Pennsylvania State University. He has developed strong interest in area of social computing.

Rajalakshmi Kanagavel is a media student currently pursuing her final year, Master of Sciences in Electronic Media at the Department of Media Sciences, Anna University, Chennai, India. She has successfully completed her research internship project for a period of three months at the Faculty of Arts and Social Sciences, Maastricht University, the Netherlands under the student exchange programme. She has also presented the same paper at the 19th Asian Media Information and Communication Centre (AMIC) Annual Conference. She has always been passionate to learn about new media and is very active in social networking sites too. She is enthused in meeting new people and it can be said that it interests her more than anything else. Her areas of research interests are web 2.0 and social media.

Bill Karakostas is a senior lecturer with the Centre for HCI Design in the School of Informatics, City University, London. He holds Masters and PhD degrees in Computer Science from University of Manchester, UK. He has a twenty year research track record in software systems with over a million euros research income. He has authored over 100 publications including two books on systems requirements engineering and service engineering.

Dimitris Kardaras is an Assistant Professor in Information Management with the Business Informatics Lab, in the department of Business Administration, at the Athens University of Economics and Business (AUEB), Athens, Greece. He holds a BSc (Hons) in Informatics and a BSc (Hons) in Management both from AUEB, an MSc and a PhD in Information Systems both from UMIST, Manchester, UK. Dr. Kardaras has participated to many research projects in IS/IT since 1990 and he has published in the areas of IS planning, Fuzzy Cognitive Maps, IS modelling and e-commerce.

Katherine A. Karl is an Associate Professor in the College of Business at the University of Tennessee Chattanooga. Her research publications have focused on the topics of job values, performance feedback, the use of videotaped feedback in management education and development, social networking websites, and human resource policies and practices regarding employment terminations, workplace attire, workplace romance, and workplace fun.

Chris Kimble is an associate professor at Euromed Management, Marseille, France. Previously he worked in the UK as a lecturer in Information Systems and Management at the University of York, in Information Technology at the University of Newcastle, and as a researcher with the Business School and Department of Informatics at the University of Northumbria. His broad research interests are how to manage the fit between technology and the social world. He is best known for his work on Communities of Practice and Knowledge Management although he has also published articles on Information Systems, Strategy and technological support for geographically distributed work. He has over 20 years of experience as an academic in France and the UK and he has published more than 80 articles in books and journals. He is the Senior Academic editor for Global Business and Organizational Excellence, and serves on the editorial boards of the journals Information Research and e-Minds.

Emmanuel Koku is Assistant Professor of Sociology in the Department of Culture and Communication at Drexel University, Philadelphia, USA. He is a graduate of the University of Ghana (Legon), Queens University (Canada), and the University of Toronto (Canada). His research interests include social network analysis, virtual communities, sociology of health, research methods and social statistics. His current research examines socio-demographic determinants of HIV risk in Africa, the lived-experiences of persons living with HIV in Africa and US, as well as professional and informal networks of academic researchers and policy makers in Canada and USA.

Michelle Kow Pei Ming graduated with a Masters of Business Administration from the School of Management, Unviersiti Sains Malaysia. Her research focused on the acceptance of users towards social networking sites as a job search tool. Currently she is attached to a multinatinational company in the Bayan Lepas Free Trade Zone in Penang.

Sunitha Kuppuswamy is a Lecturer of Media Sciences in Anna University Chennai. She has guided more than 25 post graduation projects. She has been serving as a Consultant for the United Nations Development Programme (UNDP). Her areas of academic interest include Science & Technology Communication, ICT for Development, Community Based Disaster Risk Management, Development Communication, Environmental Communication, and Media & Disaster Management. She has published two books *Tally* (TNCDW 2006), *This is how we communicate: ICT initiatives by NGOs in tsunami affected areas of Tamilnadu* (TNTRC 2007). She has contributed chapters on child rights, gender, ICT and disaster management, ICT and women empowerment, etc for several books. She has published research papers and articles in peer reviewed national and international journals such as International Journal of Innovation and Sustainable Development. She has presented papers at several national and international conferences. She has been on academic visits to Taiwan, Malaysia, etc. She is a member of the Indian Broadcasting Society & Indian Science Congress Association.

Lionel Mew, Ph.D., has worked as an applications developer, database specialist, systems analyst, project manager and program manager for information system development projects. He has also worked as a consultant on such diverse projects as application development, systems analysis and design, disaster recovery, program and project management, information systems development and deployment, organizational behavior and business process reengineering. Dr. Mew's current research interests include online social networking, online collaboration, business process reengineering, and project management. He teaches as an adjunct at George Washington University and American University. He holds the Ph.D. from George Washington University in Information Systems and Technology Management (2008), an MS in Information Systems also from George Washington University (1999), and a BS in Physical Science from the US Naval Academy (1980). He is a retired US Naval and US Coast Guard Flight Officer, where he flew the E-2C Hawkeye airborne early warning and control aircraft, with numerous operational and staff assignments in electronic warfare, air defense and marine safety.

William H. Money, Ph.D, Associate Professor Associate Professor of Information Systems, School of Business, The George Washington University September 1, 1992 - present. He previously acquired over 12 years of direct line management experience in the design, development, installation, and support of management information systems (1980-92). His academic publications and research focus on collaboration solutions, business process engineering, information system development tools and methodologies, and Agile development. His consulting experience include: strategic planning, program and project management; CPIC analysis & reporting; requirements analysis; software integration planning, and information systems development. Dr. Money's academic training includes the Ph.D., Organizational Behavior, 1977, Northwestern University, Graduate School of Management (with course work in systems analysis and design); the M.B.A., Management, 1969, Indiana University; and a B.A., Political Science, 1968, University of Richmond. His previous teaching background (1976-80) includes one year at the Purdue University, Graduate School of Industrial Administration, four years at the Kent State University, Graduate School of Business, and 1 year 1986 – 987; in the information systems program, American University.

Margherita Pagani is Assistant Professor of Management at Bocconi University (Milan), Affiliate at Massachusetts Institute of Technology and Executive Faculty Member at Lorange Institute of Business (Zurich). She was Visiting Scientist at MIT's Sloan School of Management in 2008 and 2003 and Visiting Professor at Redlands University (California) in 2004. She serves as Associate Editor for the Journal of Information Science and Technology. His current research interests are at the intersection of consumer behavior and information technology. Her work in that and other areas has appeared in Information&Management, Journal of Business Research, Journal of Interactive Marketing, Technology Analysis and Strategic Management, Technological Forecasting and Social Change and a variety of other outlets. For her research activity and publications in the mobile marketing field, she won the 2009 Mobile Marketing Association Global Award *"Academic of the Year"*.

Mark H. Palmer is an assistant professor of geography in the College of Arts and Sciences at the University of Missouri-Columbia in Columbia, Missouri. His research interests are in critical-GIS and society, actor-network theory (ANT), counter-mapping/GIS and Indigenous geographies. His early research focused upon the social aspects of geographic information systems including the uneven development of geographic information networks within government agencies and their connections/disconnections within indigenous communities in North America. Currently, he is working with Indigenous people in Oklahoma, USA on a community-integrated conservation GIS. Dr. Palmer teaches courses in geographic information systems, resources and Indigenous peoples, Native American geographies, and critical-GIS and society.

T. Ramayah has an MBA from Universiti Sains Malaysia (USM). Currently he is an Associate Professor at the School of Management in USM. He teaches mainly courses in Research Methodology and Business Statistics. Apart from teaching, he is an avid researcher, especially in the areas of technology management and adoption in business and education. His publications have appeared in Computers in Human Behavior, Resources, Conservation and Recycling, Turkish Online Journal of Education Technology, Journal of Research in Interactive Marketing, Information Development, Journal of Project Management (JoPM), IJITDM, International Journal of Services and Operations Management (IJSOM), Engineering, Construction and Architectural Management (ECAM) and North American Journal of Psychology. He is constantly invited to serve on the editorial boards and program committees of many international journals and conferences of repute. His full profile can be accessed from http://www.ramayah.com

Omer Rana is Professor of Performance Engineering in the School of Computer Science & Informatics at Cardiff University, with interests spanning three areas of Computing; (1) Problem Solving Environments (PSEs) for computational science and commercial computing, (2) Data analysis and management for large scale computing, and (3) scalability in high performance agent systems. Underpinning these three areas are the core concepts of "scalability" and "performance management". He holds a PhD in "Neural Networks and Parallel Computing" from Imperial College, London University. Prior to joining Cardiff University, he worked as a software developer for London-based Marshall BioTechnology Limited, working on scientific data analysis.

P.B. Shankar is serving as an Assistant Professor in the Department of Social Work of Pondicherry University in India. He has also conducted more than 50 training programmes of RTI Act - 2005 for various stake holders and developed HR policy for the trust. He has been the SEO of Help Age India in Chennai, involving himself in the fund raising with Schools, Individuals, Donors, and Corporate sectors. He has also been the Team Leader for Tsunami Relief & Rehabilitation Programme and organized workshops for social work trainees on NGO management. Mr. Shankar has guided more than 10 M.Phil. and post graduation research projects. He has presented/published research papers at several National/International Conferences/Journals. He has associated himself with community development, women empowerment, transgender issues, etc. He has undertaken various field studies on ICT for development, women empowerment, human rights issues, transgender, HIV AIDS, and disaster management. He is a life member of the Indian Society for Professional Social Work in India and Youth Hostel Association of India.

Christopher Schlaegel is an Assistant Professor at the Otto-von-Guericke-University, Magdeburg, Germany. He has completed his academic education in the field of International Management in Magdeburg. His current research focuses on electronic commerce, entrepreneurship, and human resource management, with particular emphasis on cross-country comparisons.

Richard. A. Schwier is a Professor of Educational Technology and Design at the University of Saskatchewan, where he teaches graduate courses in learning theory and instructional design. He is the principal investigator in the Virtual Learning Communities Research Laboratory, which is currently studying the characteristics of non-formal and informal online learning communities. Dr. Schwier's other research interests include instructional design, authentic learning design and social change agency.

Hong Sheng is an Assistant Professor of Information Science and Technology (IST) at the Department of Business and Information Technology in the Missouri University of Science and Technology (Missouri S&T) (formerly University of Missouri-Rolla). She is also co-directing the Laboratory of Information Technology Evaluation (LITE lab) at Missouri S&T. Her research interests include mobile commerce and ubiquitous commerce, trust and privacy issues in information systems, use of IT to support teaching and learning, and Human-Computer Interaction. She has published research papers in journals such as Journal of Associations for Information Systems, Information Systems Journal, Journal of Strategic Information Systems, Communications of the ACM, IEEE Transaction on Education, and Journal of Database Management.

Lhoussain Simour is a Ph.D. candidate affiliated to the Moroccan Cultural Studies Centre, Sidi Mohamed Ben Abdellah University (Fez), Morocco. His primary academic interest centers on cultural studies, colonial discourse, postcolonial theory and media studies. He is currently working on the image of America in Moroccan narratives and writing a dissertation entitled, *The Native Travels: America through Moroccan Eyes*. His research interests also include Moroccan cinema, cultural festivals and cultural tourism.

Norazah Mohd Suki is currently an Associate Professor at the Labuan School of International Business & Finance, Universiti Malaysia Sabah, Labuan International Campus. She has supervised several postgraduate students at MBA and PhD level. Her research interests include Electronic Marketing, E-Commerce, M-Commerce, Consumer Behaviour, Mobile Learning and areas related to Marketing. She actively publishes articles in international journals. She is the editor-in-chief to Labuan e-Journal of Muamalat & Society, a member in the International Advisory Board for GLOBUS An International Journal of Management, and reviewer to many international journals. She has sound experiences as speaker to public and private universities, government bodies on courses related to Structural Equation Modelling (SEM), Statistical Package for Social Sciences (SPSS), Research Methodology. She can be contacted at azahsuki@yahoo.com.

Joy Van Eck Peluchette is a Professor of Management in the College of Business at the University of Southern Indiana. She teaches primarily in the areas of organizational behavior and leadership. Her research publications are in the areas of workplace fun, impression management, workplace attire, social networking, leadership behavior, and student incivility.

Katerina Voutsina is a Research Officer at the London School of Economics and Political Science, UK. She received her Ph.D. in 2009 from the same institution. Her research interests include the study of emerging forms of work, virtual networks and communities of practice, the cognitive organization of IT professional knowledge and the construction of professional identities. Her research has been presented in various conferences worldwide, such ICIS, ECIS, AMCIS, EGOS, IREC, etc. and has been recently under review in several Information Systems and Organization Studies journals. She has also served as a reviewer to scholarly peer-reviewed journals and international conferences.

Chandrasekharan Velayutham holds an M.Phil. in Communication from the University of Madras. He was awarded the British Chevening Scholarship in Broadcast Journalism by Cardiff University, Wales, United Kingdom in 2003. He has eight years of professional experience in Television Journalism. He worked with Sun Network, a leading Tamil television channel, as a Special Correspondent and feature producer from 1998 to 2005 during which period he had taken up many national and international assignments. He has been on official visits to Sri Lanka, Mauritius, Japan, the UK and Europe. He was with BBC, Wales and ITV, Nottingham on a work-attachment in 2004 during the Training Programme conducted by Thompson Foundation, United Kingdom. He is also an accredited media trainer at the Radio Nederland Training Centre, Hilversum, the Netherlands. In May 2006, he was offered the Royal Dutch Government fellowship to be a part of Training the Trainers Programme - an International Media Course in the Netherlands. His areas of research interests are Conflicts Studies and Development Communication.

John Warmbrodt graduated from the Master program in Information Science and Technology (IST) at the Missouri University of Science and Technology (Missouri S&T) in summer 2007. Since graduating, he has been working in the areas of software systems development and implementation.

Shaoke Zhang is a Ph.D. student in the Human-Computer Interaction Center at Pennsylvania State University. His research interests lie at social computing and online community, with publications on issues such as social identity, social tie, social tagging, collective sensemaking, online source credibility, and activity centered computing. Prior to his PhD study, he graduated from Dept. of Psychology at Peking University, and worked as a HCI researcher at IBM China Research Lab during 2003-2007.

Kiyana Zolfaghar earned a bachelor's degree in information technology from Amirkabir University of Technology, Tehran-IRAN. She is now working on her thesis in order to earn a master's degree in information technology from K.N. Toosi University of Technology, Tehran-IRAN. Her research has focused on trust and reputation systems in social web applications .She is also interested in the fields of marketing communication, consumer behavior in electronic commerce, e-readiness and IT adoption. She may be reached at kzolfaghar@sina.kntu.ac.ir .

Index